P9-CIU-116

THE RESOURCEFUL EARTH

THE RESOURCEFUL EARTH

A Response to Global 2000

Edited by
JULIAN L. SIMON and
HERMAN KAHN

Basil Blackwell

© Julian L. Simon and Herman Kahn 1984

First published 1984
Basil Blackwell Publisher Limited
108 Cowley Road, Oxford OX4 1JF, England

Basil Blackwell Inc.
432 Park Avenue South, Suite 1505
New York, NY 10016, USA

British Library Cataloguing in Publication Data
The Resourceful earth.
1. Economic history, 1971–00
I. Simon, Julian L.   II. Kahn, Herman
330.9   HC59
ISBN 0-631-13467-0

Typesetting by Oxford Verbatim Limited
Printed in the United States of America

Contents

Preface

This volume is dedicated to Herman Kahn who died on 7 July, 1983. This is not the place to write about Herman, but it needs saying that many of the authors expressed great personal loss, even those knowing him only slightly. And so it is with me. Though we had only a couple of days and a dozen long phone calls together, I miss him.

The project will miss Herman, too. Though he was a moving force at the organizational meeting, and though his spirit pervaded the project, his main contribution was to have come later; he died before there was time. Regrettably, I take responsibility for the Introduction – Herman only had a chance to skim the first draft – and for the Editors' Notes. Nevertheless, I write as "we" because Herman and I saw eye to eye on the matters addressed here.

We are very grateful to those of our authors who, out of passion for truth and outrage at bad science, have given their time and effort to prepare chapters. All have had the opportunity to read the Introduction, to check the sections in their chapters for accuracy, and to dissent about any of the rest of it; their comments on the Introduction were most helpful in revision. Absence of written dissent should not be understood as agreement with, or approval of, the entire Introduction; the Introduction is the editors' interpretation of the material in the chapters plus whatever else seems relevant.

The chapters by William Baumol and Wallace Oates, Richard Peto, Roger Revelle, and Gilbert White were written for other publications rather than being commissioned by us, and those authors, therefore, have no responsibility for, and are not necessarily in sympathy with, the volume as a whole. We do, however, thank them and their publishers for permission to use their work.

Statements made in the Introduction without respect to the published literature refer to the findings presented in the chapters of this volume.

We are also grateful to Heritage Foundation's Burton Yale Pines, who – without ado – decided that Heritage should support this work, and to

Herb Berkowitz, Edwin J. Feulner, Jr., Richard N. Holwill and Phil N. Truluck, who helped the project with advice and good offices. We appreciate wise counsel by Max Singer and first-rate organizational editing by David Asman and Philip Lawler. And we admire René Olivieri's enterprise as a publisher that led to our happy connection with Basil Blackwell.

Julian L. Simon
Chevy Chase, Maryland
Thanksgiving, 1983

Acknowledgements

The publishers and editors acknowledge with gratitude permission to reprint the following texts:

Roger Revelle "The World Supply of Agricultural Land," in Just Faaland (ed.) *Population and the World Economy in the 21st Century*, pp. 50–69, © The Norwegian Nobel Institute, 1982; Gilbert F. White "Water Source Adequacy: Illusion and Reality," *Natural Resource Forum*, January 1983, pp. 11–21, © United Nations, New York; William J. Baumol and Wallace E. Oates, "Long-Run Trends in Environmental Quality," *Economics, Environmental Policy and the Quality of Life*, pp. 9–42, © 1979 Prentice-Hall, Inc. Englewood Cliffs, N.J; "The World Environment, 1972–82," pp. 31, 35–8, 135–47, © The United Nations Environment Programme and Tycooly International Publishing Ltd, Dublin 1982; Richard Peto "Why Cancer?" *Times Health Supplement*, 6 November 1981.

Introduction

JULIAN L. SIMON AND HERMAN KAHN

EXECUTIVE SUMMARY

The original 1980 *Global 2000 Report to the President* (*Global 2000* hereafter) is frightening. It received extraordinarily wide circulation, and it has influenced crucial governmental policies. But it is dead wrong. Now *The Resourceful Earth*, a response to Global 2000, presents the relevant reliable trend evidence which mainly reassures rather than frightens.

Two paragraphs summarize the "Major Findings and Conclusions" of *Global 2000* on its page 1:

> If present trends continue, the world in 2000 will be more crowded, more polluted, less stable ecologically, and more vulnerable to disruption than the world we live in now. Serious stresses involving population, resources, and environment are clearly visible ahead. Despite greater material output, the world's people will be poorer in many ways than they are today.

> For hundreds of millions of the desperately poor, the outlook for food and other necessities of life will be no better. For many it will be worse. Barring revolutionary advances in technology, life for most people on earth will be more precarious in 2000 than it is now – unless the nations of the world act decisively to alter current trends.

To highlight our differences as vividly as possible, we restate the above summary with our substitutions in italics:

> If present trends continue, the world in 2000 will be *less crowded* (though more populated), *less polluted, more stable ecologically,* and *less vulnerable to resource-supply disruption* than the world we live in now. Stresses involving population, resources, and environ-

ment *will be less in the future than now* . . . The world's people will be *richer* in most ways than they are today . . . The outlook for food and other necessities of life will be *better* . . . life for most people on earth will be *less precarious* economically than it is now.

The high points of our findings are as follows:

(1)   Life expectancy has been rising rapidly throughout the world, a sign of demographic, scientific, and economic success. This fact – at least as dramatic and heartening as any other in human history – must be fundamental in any informed discussion of pollution and nutrition.

(2)   The birth rate in less developed countries has been falling substantially during the past two decades, from 2.2 percent yearly in 1964–5 to 1.75 percent in 1982–3, probably a result of modernization and of decreasing child mortality, and a sign of increased control by people over their family lives.

(3)   Many people are still hungry, but the food supply has been improving since at least World War II, as measured by grain prices, production per consumer, and the famine death rate.

(4)   Trends in world forests are not worrying, though in some places deforestation is troubling.

(5)   There is no statistical evidence for rapid loss of species in the next two decades. An increased rate of extinction cannot be ruled out if tropical deforestation is severe, but no evidence about linkage has yet been demonstrated.

(6)   The fish catch, after a pause, has resumed its long upward trend.

(7)   Land availability will not increasingly constrain world agriculture in coming decades.

(8)   In the U.S., the trend is toward higher-quality cropland, suffering less from erosion than in the past.

(9)   The widely-published report of increasingly rapid urbanization of U.S. farmland was based on faulty data.

(10) Water does not pose a problem of physical scarcity or disappearance, although the world and U.S. situations do call for better institutional management through more rational systems of property rights.

(11) The climate does not show signs of unusual and threatening changes.

(12) Mineral resources are becoming less scarce rather than more scarce, affront to common sense though that may be.

(13) There is no persuasive reason to believe that the world oil price will rise in coming decades. The price may fall well below what it has been.

(14) Compared to coal, nuclear power is no more expensive, and is probably much cheaper, under most circumstances. It is also much cheaper than oil.

(15) Nuclear power gives every evidence of costing fewer lives per unit of energy produced than does coal or oil.

(16) Solar energy sources (including wind and wave power) are too dilute to compete economically for much of humankind's energy needs, though for specialized uses and certain climates they can make a valuable contribution.

(17) Threats of air and water pollution have been vastly overblown; these processes were not well analyzed in *Global 2000*.

We do not say that all is well everywhere, and we do not predict that all will be rosy in the future. Children are hungry and sick; people live out lives of physical or intellectual poverty, and lack of opportunity; war or some new pollution may do us in. *The Resourceful Earth does* show that for most relevant matters we have examined, aggregate global and U.S. *trends* are improving rather than deteriorating.

In addition we do not say that a better future happens *automatically* or *without effort*. It will happen because men and women – sometimes as individuals, sometimes as enterprises working for profit, sometimes as voluntary non-profit making groups, and sometimes as governmental agencies – will address problems with muscle and mind, and will *probably* overcome, as has been usual throughout history.

We are confident that the nature of the physical world permits continued improvement in humankind's economic lot in the long run, indefinitely. Of course there are always newly arising local problems, shortages and pollutions, due to climate or to increased population and income. Sometimes temporary large-scale problems arise. But the nature of the world's physical conditions and the resilience in a well-functioning economic and social system enable us to overcome such problems, and the solutions usually leave us better off than if the problem had never arisen; that is the great lesson to be learned from human history.

We are less optimistic, however, about the constraints currently imposed upon material progress by political and institutional forces, in conjunction with popularly-held beliefs and attitudes about natural resources and the environment, such as those urged upon as by *Global 2000*. These constraints include the view that resource and environmental trends point towards deterioration rather than towards improvement, that there are physical limits that will increasingly act as a brake upon progress, and that nuclear energy is more dangerous than energy from other sources. These views lead to calls for subsidies and price controls, as well as government ownership and management of resource production, and government allocation of the resources that are produced. To a considerable extent the U.S. and the rest of the world already suffer from such policies (for example, on agriculture in Africa), and continuation and intensification could seriously damage resource production and choke economic progress. In particular, refusal to use nuclear power could hamper the U.S. in its economic competition with other nations, as well as cause unnecessary deaths in coal mining and other types of conventional energy production. We wish that there were grounds to believe that a shift in thinking will take place on these matters, but we do not find basis for firm hope. So in this respect we are hardly optimistic.

We also wish to emphasize that though the global situation may be reasonably satisfactory or improving in some given respect, there are likely to be areas in which there are severe difficulties which may be on the increase. Such local problems may be due to local mismanagement, or they may be due to natural catastrophe which the larger community may not yet have been able to help mitigate. Such local problems should not be glossed over in any global assessment.

Background

More than one million copies of the original *Global 2000 Report to the President of the United States* have been distributed. It has been translated into five major languages. Other countries such as Germany have commissioned studies imitating *Global 2000*.

Global 2000 also underlies important U.S. policy pronouncements. For example, the following paragraphs, and the rest of the full speech at the Alpbach European Forum in 1980, which was an official "American perspective on the world economy in the 1980s," were founded squarely on *Global 2000*:

Defying the generally buoyant mood, Richard Cooper, U.S. under secretary of state for economic affairs, delivered a grim message. If present trends continue, he said, the world population will swell to five billion by 1990 from four billion at present, leading to "open conflict, greater terrorism and possibly localized anarchy," as well as "congestion, famine, deforestation."

The decade's population growth would equal "nearly half the total world population when I was born," he said. Even then, he added ominously, "some political leaders were calling for more lebensraum" (or living space). (*The Wall Street Journal*, 15 September, 1980, p. 32)

Before *Global 2000* was even completed, President Carter had discussed its conclusions with other world leaders at an economic summit held in Italy. Immediately upon receiving the Report, the President established a task force to ensure that *Global 2000* received priority attention. The task force included the Secretary of State, the director of the Office of Management and Budget, the President's Assistant for Domestic Affairs, and the director of the Office of Science and Technology Policy. Secretary of State Edmund Muskie used *Global 2000* as the centrepiece for an address to the UN General Assembly. The Joint Economic Committee of Congress launched a series of hearings on the Report. The President instructed the State Department to arrange an international meeting of environmental and economic experts to discuss population, natural resources, environment, and economic development, the subjects of *Global 2000*. Finally, in his farewell address to the nation, President Carter referred to the subject of *Global 2000* as one of the three most important problems facing the American people (the other two being arms control and human rights). And *Global 2000*'s effect did not disappear with the change of administration. It continues to be cited as support for a wide variety of forecasts by governmental agencies.[1]

The press received *Global 2000* with great respect and enormous attention. *Time* and *Newsweek* ran full-page stories, and *Global 2000* made front-page newspaper headlines across the country as an "official" government study forecasting global disaster. Though the Report included some qualifications, it was interpreted by all as a prediction of gloom-and-doom. For example, *Science's* story title was: "Global 2000 Report: Vision of a Gloomy World."[2] *Time's* title was "Toward a Troubled 21st Century: a presidential panel finds the global outlook extremely bleak."[3] *Newsweek's* title was "A Grim Year 2000."[4] The typical local paper in central Illinois had this banner across the top of the front page: "U.S. Report Says World Faces Ecological Disaster."[5] And its story began:

Mass poverty, malnutrition and deterioration of the planet's water and atmosphere resources – that's a bleak government prediction that says civilization has perhaps 20 years to act to head off such a world-wide disaster.

A full-page advertisement for the volume in *The New York Review of Books* was headed:

Government Report as follows: Poisoned seas, acid rain, water running out, atmosphere dying.

However – and seldom can there have been a bigger "however" in the history of such reports – the original *Global 2000* is totally wrong in its specific assertions and its general conclusion. It is replete with major factual errors, not just minor blemishes.[6] Its language is vague at key points, and features many loaded terms. Many of its arguments are illogical or misleading. It paints an overall picture of global trends that is fundamentally wrong, partly because it relies on non-facts and partly because it misinterprets the facts it does present. (In partial defense of the writers who prepared the *Global 2000* work, the summary Volume I – which was the main basis for the news stories – egregiously mis-stated, for reasons which we can only surmise,[7] many analyses and conclusions in the working-paper Volume II, thereby turning optimistic projections into pessimistic ones.)

Our statements about the future in *The Resourceful Earth* are intended as unconditional predictions in the absence of an unforeseeable catastrophe such as nuclear war or total social breakdown. We feel no need to qualify these predictions upon the continuation of current policies, as *Global 2000* claimed to do, and in fact we believe that such a qualification is not meaningful. Throughout history, individuals and communities have responded to actual and expected shortages of raw materials in such fashion that eventually the materials have become more readily available than if the shortages had never arisen. These responses are embodied in the observed long-run trends in supply and cost, and therefore extrapolation of such trends (together with appropriate theoretical attention) takes into account the likely future responses.

Aside from this Introduction and one section in most of the chapters, *The Resourceful Earth* is not primarily an evaluation or criticism of *Global 2000*. (For evaluation and criticism see Clawson, 1981; Dubos, 1981; Kahn and Schneider, 1981; Simon, 1981.) It is a compendium of careful, authoritative, independent studies of many of the topics dealt with by *Global 2000* plus some others, by writers selected by the editors because their claim to the label "expert" is as strong as any such claim can be. Taken together, the chapters are intended to be a fair assessment of the trends together with an analysis of what the trends portend for the future. We hope that *The Resourceful Earth* will also serve as a reference volume of first resort for persons seeking knowledge on these topics. This introduction summarizes the findings of the technical chapters. It also offers some general observations about *Global 2000*, global modeling, and policy recommendations. The findings express the views of the authors of the individual chapters. The editors are responsible for the general observations, though the individual chapter authors have commented upon these general observations. We have also included a section at the end of the volume where individual authors may express their disagreements with any of these general views.

The Resourceful Earth chapters were produced without a penny's added cost to the public. The chapters are presented here exactly as written, with the authors having final authority over their chapters without bureaucratic tampering. This process is in contrast to the largely staff-written and politically edited *Global 2000*; more details are given below about the process of financing, writing, and editing *Global 2000* and *The Resourceful Earth*.

The Specific Conclusions

We now briefly summarize the main issues raised by *Global 2000* as covered by our topical chapters. For convenience, the order will be the same as in the *Global 2000* summary quoted above for the topics mentioned there, followed by the other central issues raised in their summary volume.

"More crowded"

There surely will be more people on earth in the year 2000 than there are now, barring a calamity. But a growing population does not imply that human living on the globe will be more "crowded" in any meaningful fashion. As the world's people have increasingly higher incomes, they purchase better housing and mobility. The homes of the world's people progressively have more floorspace, which means people dwell in less-crowded space with more privacy. The United States, for which data are readily available, illustrates the trends in developed countries. In 1940, fully 20.2 percent of households had 1.01 or more persons per room, whereas in 1974 only 4.5 percent were that crowded (U.S. Department of Commerce, 1977, p. 90). (Also relevant: in 1940 44.6 percent of housing units lacked some or all plumbing facilities; but in 1974 only 3.2 percent were lacking. In 1940, 55.4 percent had all plumbing facilities, whereas in 1974, 96.8 percent had all plumbing; U.S. Department of Commerce, 1977, p. 91). The world's people are getting better roads and more vehicles; therefore they can move around more freely, and have the benefits of a wider span of area. In the U.S., paved highways have increased from zero to over 3 million miles since the turn of the century. Natural park areas have been expanding (figure 1). And trips to parks have increased to an extraordinary degree (figure 2). These trends mean that people increasingly have much more space available and accessible

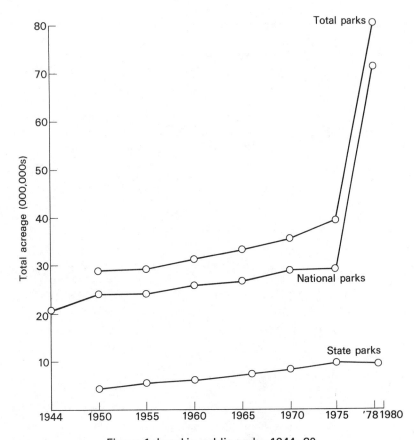

Figure 1 Land in public parks, 1944–80.
Sources: *Statistical Abstract of the U.S.*, 1973, p. 202, 1980, p. 242 for 1950–79; *Information Related to the National Park System*, United States Department of the Interior, National Park Service, 30 June 1944, p. 35 for 1944.

for their use, despite the increase in total population, even in the poorer countries. All this suggests to us that the world is getting less crowded by reasonable tests relevant to human life.

"More polluted"

Global 2000 asserts that the world is getting more polluted. But it cites no systematic data for the world or even for regions. It is certainly reasonable to *assume* that man-made industrial pollutions increase as the most backward countries begin to modernize, get somewhat less poor, and purchase pollution-creating industrial plants. The same is true of con-

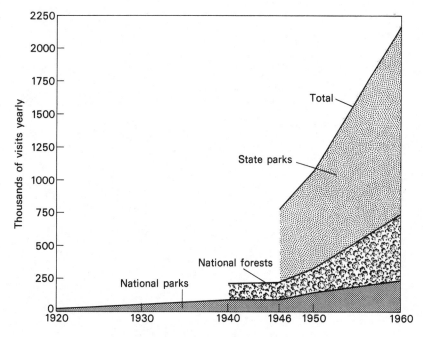

Figure 2 Visits to public parks, 1920–60.
Source: see Simon, 1981, Figure 16-5.

sumer pollution – junked cars, plastic bags, and pop tops of beverage cans. But it is misleading to suggest that there are *data* showing that such pollution is a major problem.

In the early stages of industrialization, countries and people are not yet ready to pay for clean-up operations. But further increases in income almost as surely will bring about pollution abatement. (At the same time, biological disease pollution has been declining, even in the poor countries, at a rate far outweighing any hazardous effect of man-made pollution, as seen in increased life-expectancy.)

In the richer countries there is solid evidence that hazardous air pollution has been declining. Figure 3 shows the Council on Environmental Quality's new Pollutant Standard Index for the U.S., and figure 4 shows one key measure of air quality for which data are available since 1960; the benign trend has been under way for quite a while, and does not stem only from the onset of the environmental movement around 1970.

Water quality too, has improved in the richer countries. Figure 5 shows the improvements in drinkability of water in the U.S. since 1961. Such alarms of the 1960s and 1970s as the impending "death" of the Great

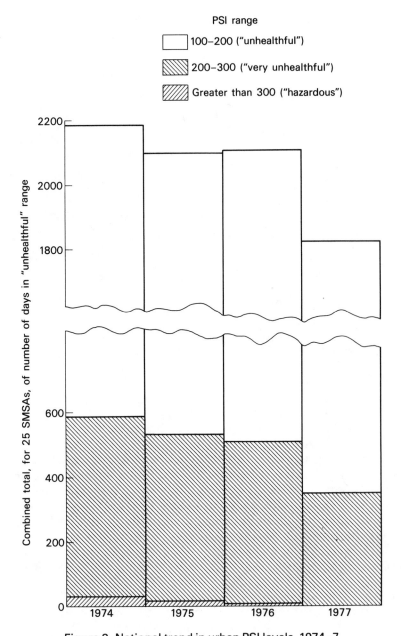

Figure 3 National trend in urban PSI levels, 1974–7.
Source: Based on U.S. Environmental Protection Ageny data, reproduced from the tenth annual
report of the Council on Environmental Quality, 1979, p. 39.

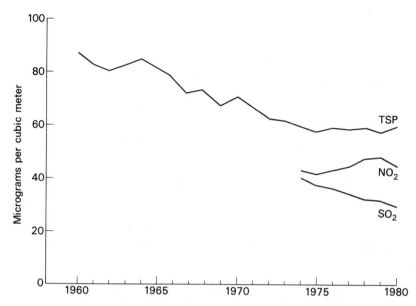

Figure 4 National ambient concentrations of total suspended particulates, nitrogen dioxide, and sulfur dioxide, 1960–80. Data may not be strictly comparable, see figure 16.22 below.
Source: U.S. Environmental Protection Agency.

Lakes have turned out totally in error; fishing and swimming conditions there are now excellent. (Ironically, the "death" that was warned of is really a condition of too much organic "life", and is therefore self-curing as soon as people stop adding so much nutrient to the water.) In the developing countries the proportion of the urban population served by a safe water supply rose modestly in the 1970s, and rose markedly among the rural population (but from 14 percent to only 29 percent; Holdgate *et al.*, 1982, p. 135).

The long-run historical record, to the extent that there are data, offers examples upon which one may seize to argue almost any shade of opinion about pollution. But many of the oft-cited series that purportedly show "deterioration" prove, upon inspection, to be the result of forces other than recent human activities.

"Less stable ecologically, and more vulnerable to disruption"

These concepts are so diffuse that we have no idea how one would measure them directly. *Global 2000* gives no relevant trend data.

Perhaps *Global 2000* had in mind that there is more danger of disruption as humankind's capacity to alter the ecosystem increases. In itself,

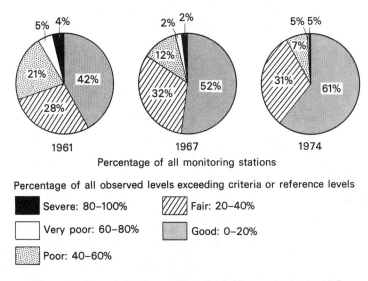

1961   1967   1974

Percentage of all monitoring stations

Percentage of all observed levels exceeding criteria or reference levels

■ Severe: 80–100%   ▨ Fair: 20–40%

□ Very poor: 60–80%   ▦ Good: 0–20%

▧ Poor: 40–60%

Figure 5 Trends in the quality of drinking water in the U.S.
Source: U.S. Council on Environmental Quality, Annual Report, 1975, p. 352.

this must be true. But at the same time, humankind's ability to restore imbalances in the ecosystem also increases. And the trend data on pollution, food (discussed below), and life expectancy suggest that the life-supporting capacities have been increasing faster than the malign disturbances. Of course some unprecedented catastrophe such as the Black Death may occur, but we can only look into the future as best we can, and conclude that no such catastrophe is in view. The one crucial exception is war, which is outside our scope here, and which is not a matter of the natural resource constraints that depend upon the nature of the physical world.

"Serious stresses involving population, resources, and environment . . ."

This *Global 2000* phrase sounds ominous, but like many other *Global 2000* warnings it is hard to pin down. If it means that people will have a poorer chance of survival in the year 2000 than now, due to the greater number of people, the trends in life expectancy suggest the contrary. Declining mortality and improving health have accompanied unprecedented population growth in the world (as well as in the U.S., of course). Figure 6 shows the long-run trend of life expectancy in the more-developed world, a pattern toward which the less-developed countries are converging. For example, life expectancy in less-developed regions rose from 43 years in 1950/55 to 53 years in 1970/75 (the rise in

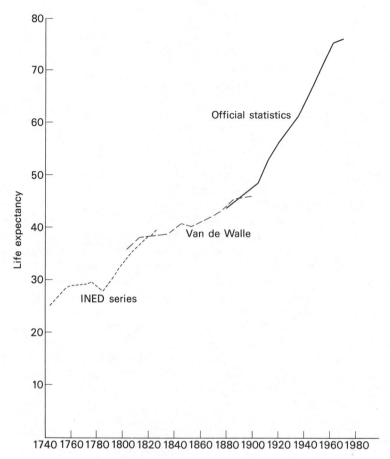

Figure 6 Female expectation of life at birth, France.

Asia being even greater), a much bigger jump than the rise from 65 years to 71 years in the more-developed regions (Gwatkin, 1980).

If the phrase "serious stresses" implies that along with more people in the year 2000 will come more costly resources and a deteriorated environment, the trends suggest the opposite, as noted above for the environment, and as discussed next for resources. If the phrase means that life expectancy, resource availability, and the quality of the environment could be even better in the year 2000 with fewer people than are expected, *Global 2000* has not even attempted to demonstrate such a complex causal correction. The existing research on the subject does not suggest to us that such would be the case.

". . . resources . . ."

Global 2000 projected a 5 percent yearly increase in the real price of non-fuel minerals until the year 2000. There has always been "serious stress" in the sense that people have to pay a price to get the resources they want. But the relevant economic measures of "stress" – costs and prices – show that the long-run trend is toward less scarcity and lower prices rather than more scarcity and higher prices, hard as that may be for many people to believe. The cost trends of almost every natural resource have been downward over the course of recorded history.

An hour's work in the United States has bought increasingly more of copper, wheat, and oil (which are representative and important raw materials) from 1800 to the present (see, for example, figure 7). The trend is less dramatic in the poorest countries, but the direction of the trend is unmistakable there, too, because per person income has been rising in poor countries as well as rich ones. The same trend has held throughout human history for such minerals as copper and iron (Clark, 1957, Appendix). Calculations of expenditures for raw materials as a falling proportion of total family budgets make the same point even more strongly.

These trends mean that raw materials have been getting increasingly available and less scarce relative to the most important and most fundamental element of economic life, human work-time. The prices of raw materials have even been falling relative to consumer goods and the Consumer Price Index. All the items in the Consumer Price Index have been produced with increasingly efficient use of labor and capital over the years, but the decrease in cost of raw materials has been even greater than that of other goods. This is a very strong demonstration of progressively decreasing scarcity and increasing availability of raw materials. The trend of raw material prices relative to consumer goods, however, has much less meaning for human welfare than does the trend of resource prices relative to the price of human time – a trend which is decidedly benign, as we have seen. Even if raw materials were rising in price relative to consumer goods, there would be no cause for alarm as long as it takes progressively less effort, and a smaller proportion of our incomes, to obtain the service from raw materials that we need and want.

Moreover, the observed fall in the prices of raw materials understates the positive trend, because as consumers we are interested in the services we get from the raw materials rather than the raw materials themselves. We have learned to use less of given raw materials for given purposes, as well as to substitute cheaper materials to get the same services. Consider a copper pot used long ago for cooking. The consumer is interested in a container that can be put over heat. After iron and aluminium were discovered, quite satisfactory cooking pots – with advantages as well as

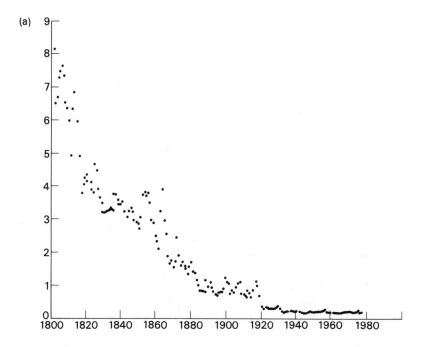

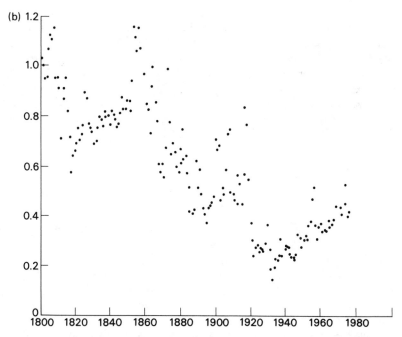

Figure 7 The scarcity of copper (a) as measured by its price relative to wages and (b) as measured by its price relative to the consumer index. The diagrams are typical of the pattern for each of the metals (see Simon, 1981, Appendix).

disadvantages compared with pots of copper – could be made of those materials. The cost that interests us is the cost of providing the cooking service, rather than the cost of the copper.

A single communications satellite in space provides intercontinental telephone connections that would otherwise require thousands of tons of copper. Satellite and microwave transmission and the use of glass fibers in communications are dramatic examples of how a substitute process can supply a service much more cheaply than copper.

"The world's people will be poorer in many ways . . ."

The Global 2000 qualifying phrase "in many ways" could imply that a decrease in the number of elephants, or the deaths of some elderly beloved persons, are ways in which the world's people will be poorer in the future than now; if so, the statement is logically correct. But if we consider more general and economically meaningful measures, the world's people have been getting richer rather than poorer, and may be expected to be richer in the future. Measured in conventional terms, average income for the world's population has been rising. Particularly noteworthy, and contrary to common belief, income in the poorer countries has been rising at a percentage rate as great or greater than in the richer countries since World War II (Morawetz, 1978). Another vivid proof of the rise in income in poorer countries is the decline in the proportion of the labor force devoted to agriculture – from 68 percent to 58 percent between 1965 and 1981 in the developing countries, consistent with the trend in developed countries where the agricultural labor force has plummeted to, for example, well below 3 percent in the U.S. The rising average income in poorer countries combined with the rough stability of their internal income-distribution shares suggests that the poorer classes of representative countries have been participating in this income rise along with the richer classes.

"The outlook for food . . . will be no better"

Consumption of food per person in the world is up over the last 30 years (figure 8). And data do not show that the bottom of the income scale is faring worse, or even has failed to share in the general improvement, as the average has improved. Africa's food production per capita is down, but no one thinks that has anything to do with physical conditions; it clearly stems from governmental and other social conditions. Famine deaths have decreased in the past century even in absolute terms, let alone relative to population. World food prices have been trending lower for decades and centuries (figure 9), and there is strong reason to believe that this trend will continue. This evidence runs exactly counter to *Global*

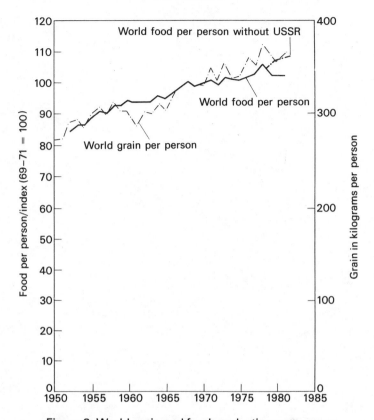

Figure 8 World grain and food production per person.

Source: USDA, FAS FG-8-82 (3-15-82); USDA WASDE-133 (5-11-82); Brown, *Building A Sustainable Society* (Norton, 1981), p. 81 (with authors' extrapolation of 1981 and 1982 population). The Food index includes all food commodities – including grain, pulses, oil-seeds, vegetables, and fruit; it excludes the PRC. Source of index USDA ERS, Statistical Bulletin No. 669, July 1981; USDA, Personal Communication, Dr Patrick M. O'Brien (1980, 1981 index).

2000's conclusion that "real prices for food are expected to double." If a problem exists for the U.S., it is a problem caused by abundance. Food production in the U.S. is now so great that farmers are suffering economically. Food stocks in the world are so high that they are causing major problems (figure 10). Agricultural yields per hectare have continued to rise in such countries as China, France, and the U.S. These gains in production have been accomplished with a decreasing proportion of the labor force – the key input for and constraint upon the economic system.

Careful study of the quantities of actual and potential agricultural land in various countries, plus possibilities for irrigation and multicropping

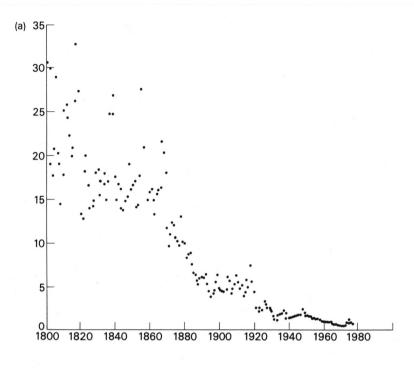

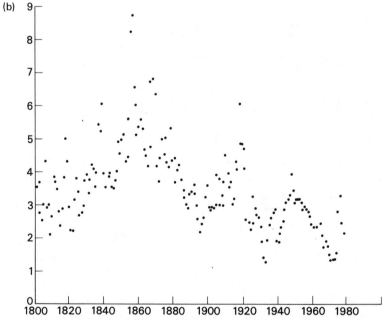

Figure 9   The price of wheat in the U.S. (a) relative to wages and (b) relative to the consumer price index.

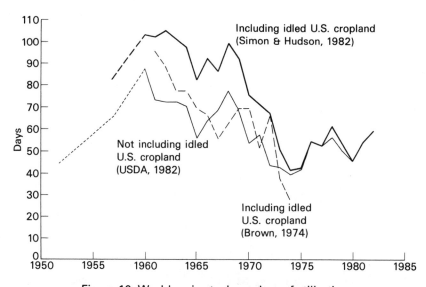

Figure 10 World grain stocks as days of utilization.
Sources: (1) USDA, FAS, FG 8-82 (3-15-82); USDA WASDE-133 (5-11-81); (2) Brown, *By Bread Alone* (Praeger, 1974), p. 60; Brown, *Building a Sustainable Society*, p. 96; authors' estimates for 1981, 1982. Data for 1952 and 1957 from D. Gale Johnson, *World Food Problems and Prospects*; USDA, ERS 479, *U.S. Corn Industry*, February 1982, Table 46.

together with yields already routinely reached in the developed countries, suggests that agricultural land will not be a bottleneck in the foreseeable future, even without new technological breakthroughs. And the supply of water for agriculture (which is by far the largest use of water) poses even fewer problems arising from purely physical conditions. Physical measurements of water withdrawal in the world as a whole provide no relevant information. The possibility of the world as a whole running out of water is zero. The supply of water is always a local or regional issue within a country (or occasionally at the border of two countries). The key constraints upon the supply of water arise from institutional and political conditions, and especially the structure of property rights to water and the price structure for water, rather than mere physical availability.

The issue of a well-constituted system of property rights – the absence of which often leads to "the tragedy of the commons" – arises sharply with respect to water rights; but appropriate rules for private property are also of fundamental importance in many other natural resource and environmental situations. Drilling rights in oil basins, rights to pollute the air and water, and hunting rights for wild animals, are but three dramatic examples. A sound set of social rules with respect to property can go far to ensure a satisfactory supply of resources and an acceptably clean environ-

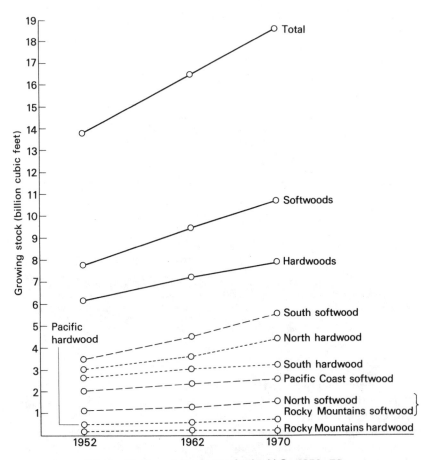

Figure 11   Forest resources in the U.S., 1952–70.
Source: *Perspectives on Prime Lands*, U.S. Department of Agriculture (1975).

ment. On this there is ever-growing agreement among naturalists, economists, geologists, and others concerned with these matters.

> *"Significant losses of world forests will continue over the next 20 years"*

According to *Global 2000*, "by 2000 some 40 percent of the remaining forest cover in LDCs will be gone." If nonsense is a statement utterly without factual support, this is nonsense. Forests are not declining at all in the temperate regions. In the U.S., for example, the total quantity of trees has been increasing, and wood production has been increasing rapidly (figure 11). The rate of deforestation in tropical areas has been far slower than suggested by *Global 2000*. The prospects for world wood production to meet demand without grave deforestation are excellent, especially because plantations which require only small land areas have just begun to make the major contribution to total world production of which they are capable.

"Arable land will increase only 4 percent by 2000. . . . Serious deterioration of agricultural soils will occur worldwide, due to erosion"

Arable land has been increasing at a rate very much faster in recent decades than the rate *Global 2000* projected for coming decades – an increase which we can approximate at fully 16 percent over the 20-year period from 1950 to 1975 for which there are good data (table 1). There is no apparent reason why in the next decades the increase should fall anywhere nearly as low as the 4 percent *Global 2000* suggests. A comprehensive assessment of the earth's land resources for agriculture by an authoritative President's Science Advisory Committee suggested that arable land will not be a key constraint upon food production in the world, and our findings agree. Rather, social and economic conditions are the key constraints on the amount of land brought into production.

In the United States, the conversion of farmland to urbanized land is proceeding at about the same rate as in recent decades, rather than at three times that rate, as was widely reported recently by a now-discredited agency of the U.S. Department of Agriculture (the National Agricultural Lands Study), the source of the *Global 2000* statement on the subject. Furthermore, each year more (and better) new land is being brought into cultivation by irrigation and drainage than is being urbanized and built upon.

Concern about the "loss" of cropland to new housing, and the resulting governmental regulations that have constrained housing starts and raised the price of new homes, especially in California, does not square with contemporary federal policies for reducing planted acreage to meet the problem of "overproduction" of grain. In 1983 perhaps 39 percent of U.S. crop acreage was kept idle by federal subsidy programs, at an unprecedented high cost to U.S. taxpayers of $18.3 billion (compared to an original estimate of $1.8 billion for the year; *New York Times*, 31 January 1983, p. 5). The argument is sometimes made that governments must act to save cropland for future generations, but this argument lacks support from either economic analysis or technological considerations. The driving motive behind urging government action to "preserve" farmland seems to be more aesthetics than economics.

Soil erosion is not occurring at a dangerous pace in most parts of the United States, contrary to much recent publicity. In most areas top soil is

22 Julian L. Simon and Herman Kahn

TABLE 1(a) CHANGES IN LAND USE, 1950–60

	Arable land as a percentage of total area		Percentage of arable land that is cultivated		Cultivated land as a percentage of total land (1 × 3) and (2 × 4)		Agricultural land (arable and pasture) as a percentage of total area	
	(1) 1950	(2) 1960	(3) 1950	(4) 1960	1950	1960	1950	1960
Africa	14.27	15.30	36.21	42.72	5.2	6.5	46.50	49.02
Middle East	12.87	13.91	52.11	57.88	6.7	8.1	13.06	17.34
Asia	19.03	20.78	82.06	86.17	15.6	17.9	46.35	49.60
North and South America, U.S.S.R., Australia, New Zealand	6.88	7.75	82.75	82.96	5.7	6.4	34.27	38.59
Europe	30.79	30.98	89.02	90.06	27.4	27.9	45.63	46.10
All regions	10.73	11.73	82.74	83.99	8.9	9.9	37.35	41.07

Source: Kumar, 1973, p. 107.

TABLE 1(b) CHANGES IN LAND USE, 1961–5 TO 1975

	Arable land as a percentage of total area				Agricultural land (arable and pasture) as a percentage of total area			
	1961–65	1966	1970	1975	1961–65	1966	1970	1975
Africa	6.28	6.50	6.76	6.96	32.88	32.96	33.13	33.29
Middle East	6.25	6.38	6.54	6.79	21.91	22.12	22.32	22.62
Far East	28.87	29.37	29.88	30.73	33.08	33.62	33.80	34.56
North America	11.50	11.43	12.17	13.08	26.10	25.85	25.88	25.50
U.S.S.R.	10.24	10.24	10.39	10.37	26.83	27.34	27.09	26.97
Latin America	5.64	5.97	6.43	6.82	29.56	30.29	31.29	32.41
Western Europe	27.21	26.55	25.97	25.04	46.35	45.08	44.83	43.72
All regions	10.41	10.58	10.93	11.25	33.13	33.38	33.71	33.99

Source: UN, Food and Agriculture Organization, 1976.

not being lost at a rate that makes broad changes in farming practices economical from either the private or public standpoint, though recent advances in tillage may change the picture somewhat. Regulating or subsidizing particular tillage practices portends greater social cost than benefit in the long run. The largest social cost of soil erosion is not the loss of top soil, but rather the silting-up of drainage ditches in some places, with consequent maintenance expenses. In the aggregate, just the opposite of land ruination has been taking place, as the soil of American farms has been improving rather than deteriorating, and as fewer rather than more crop acres suffer from severe erosion over the decades since the 1930s. The continuing advance in agricultural productivity per acre is consistent with the improvement in the quality of farmland.

"Extinctions of plant and animal species will increase dramatically. Hundreds of thousands of species – perhaps as many as 20 percent of all species on earth – will be irretrievably lost as their habitats vanish, especially in tropical forests"

This assertion by *Global 2000* is remarkably unsupported by statistical evidence. The only scientific observations cited in support of a numerical estimate of future species extinction are (a) between 1600 and 1900 perhaps one species every 4 years was extinguished, and (b) between 1900 and 1980 perhaps one species every year was extinguished. The leap to *Global 2000*'s estimate of 40,000 species extinguished each year by the year 2000 is based on pure guesswork by the *Global 2000* writers and the source upon which they draw (Myers, 1979). We do not neglect the die-off of the passenger pigeon and other species that may be valuable to us. But we note that extinction of species – billions of them, according to Mayr (1982) – has been a biological fact of life throughout the ages, just as has been the development of new species, some or many of which may be more valuable to humans than extinguished species whose niches they fill.

"Atmospheric concentrations of carbon dioxide and ozone-depleting chemicals are expected to increase at rates that could alter the world's climate and upper atmosphere significantly by 2050"

The longest available records of climatic variations reveal very wide temperature swings, much or all of which may be thought of as random. In that context, recent changes in temperature may reasonably be viewed as normal oscillation rather than as a structural change induced by man's activity, including changes in CO_2.

The CO_2 question is subject to major controversy and uncertainty – about the extent of the buildup, about its causes, and especially about its effects. It would not seem prudent to undertake expensive policy alterations at this time because of this lack of knowledge, and because problems that changes in CO_2 concentration might cause would occur far in the future (well beyond the year 2000). Changes in the CO_2 situation may reasonably be seen, however, as an argument for increased use of nuclear power rather than fossil fuel. Continued research and monitoring of the CO_2 situation certainly is called for.

If it is considered desirable to reduce the amount of CO_2 released into the atmosphere by human activity, on the grounds that atmospheric change with unknown effects carries undesired risks, only two possibilities are feasible: reduce total energy consumption, or increase energy production from nuclear power plants. Reduction in total world energy consumption below the level determined by prices reflecting the production cost of energy is clearly unacceptable to most nations of the world because of the negative effects on economic growth, nutrition and health, and consumer satisfaction. This implies an inverse tradeoff relationship between CO_2 and non-fossil (especially nuclear) power.

"Acid rain ..."

There is trend evidence that the pollution of acid rain has been getting more intense, and that it has some ill effects on fresh water lakes and their fish, upon perhaps forests, and hence upon people's ability to enjoy nature. Emissions from combustion of fossil fuels are undoubtedly a partial cause, although natural sources also contribute. There is some evidence of limited local ecological damage, but no proven threat to agriculture or human life. The trend deserves careful monitoring. The consensus of recent official committee reports (with which we agree) questions the use of high-sulfur coal for power production. This squares with our general advocacy of nuclear electricity generation. Whether any tighter pollution controls are warranted, economically or otherwise, has not been established. Fighting acid-rain effects on fish by liming lakes does not generally seem economically feasible. The acid-rain issue increases the comparative advantage of nuclear power plants relative to coal-burning plants. As with CO_2, then, there is an inverse tradeoff relationship between nuclear power and acid rain.

"Regional water shortages will become more severe"

In the previous decade or so, water experts have concluded that the "likelihood of the world running out of water is zero." The recent UN Report of the World Environment, for example, tells us not to focus upon the ratio between physical water supply and use, as *Global 2000* does nevertheless, and emphasizes making appropriate social and economic as well as technological choices. From this flows "cautious hope from improved methods of management." That is, an appropriate structure of property rights, institutions, and pricing systems, together with some modicum of wisdom in choosing among the technological options open to us, can provide water for our growing needs at reasonable cost indefinitely.

Moreover, *Global 2000*'s statements about the world's future water situation are completely inconsistent with – in fact, are completely opposed to – *Global 2000*'s own analysis of what can reasonably be said about the world's water resources. It develops a sound analysis that finds that no reasonable or useful forecasts can be made about the world's water supply, but then proceeds to offer frightening forecasts totally inconsistent with its analysis. This inconsistency should be more than sufficient grounds to reject *Global 2000*'s gloomy conclusions out of hand.

"Energy . . ."

The prospect of running out of energy is purely a bogeyman. The availability of energy has been increasing, and the meaningful cost has been decreasing, over the entire span of humankind's history. We expect this benign trend to continue at least until our sun ceases to shine in perhaps 7 billion years, and until exhaustion of the supply of elemental inputs for fission (and perhaps for fusion).

Barring extraordinary political problems, we expect the price of oil to go down. Even with respect to oil, there is no basis to conclude that the price will rise until the year 2000 and beyond, or that humankind will ever face a greater shortage of oil in economic terms than it does now; rather, decreasing shortage is the more likely, in our view. For the next decade or two, politics – especially the fortunes of the OPEC cartel, and the prevalence of war instability – are likely to be the largest element in influencing oil prices. But no matter what the conditions, the market for oil substitutes probably constitutes a middle-run ceiling price for oil not much above what it is now; there could be a short-run panic run-up, but the world is better protected from that now than in the 1970s. And if free competition prevails, the price will be far below its present level.

Electrical power from nuclear fission plants is available at costs as low or much lower than from coal, depending upon the location, and at lower costs than from oil or gas. Even in the U.S., where the price of coal is unusually low, existing nuclear plants produce power more cheaply than from coal. Nuclear energy is available in unlimited quantity beyond any conceivable meaningful human horizon. And nuclear power gives every evidence of costing fewer lives per unit of energy produced than does coal or oil. The main constraints are various political interests, public misinformation, and cost-raising counter-productive systems of safety regulation. Nuclear waste disposal with remarkably high levels of safeguards presents no scientific difficulties.

Energy from sources other than fossil fuel and nuclear power, aside from hydropower where it is available, do not hold much promise for supplying the bulk of human energy elements, though solar power can be the cheapest source of power for heating buildings and water in certain geographic locations. The key defect of solar power, as well as with its relatives such as power from waves, is that it is too dilute, requiring very large areas and much capital to collect the energy.

"Rapid growth in world population will hardly have altered
by 2000 . . . The rate of growth will slow only marginally from
1.8 percent a year to 1.7 percent"

Population forecasting involving fertility is notoriously unreliable. The birth rate can go down very rapidly, as numerous countries have demonstrated in the past few decades, including a country as large as China. (The rate can also go up rapidly, as the baby boom in the U.S. following World War II demonstrated.) Therefore, confidence in any such forecast for a matter of decades would be misplaced. The passage of only a handful of years already seems to have knocked the props out from under *Global 2000*'s forecast quoted above. The world's annual growth rate, which was 2.2 percent less than two decades ago in 1964–5, is down to 1.75 percent (U.S. Department of Commerce News, 31 August 1983), a broad decline over the bulk of all the poorer and faster-growth nations. Though the growth rate may have stabilized in the last few years, these data alone seem inconsistent with the *Global 2000* forecast. The author of that forecast acknowledges that we have already moved from their "medium" forecast to their "low" forecast.

Even the apparently sure-fire *Global 2000* forecast that "in terms of sheer numbers, population will be growing faster in 2000 than it is today" might very well turn out to be wrong. Because the total population will be larger in 2000 than now, the fertility rate would have to be considerably smaller than it is now to falsify that forecast. But the drop would have to be only of the magnitude of the drop during the past two decades for that to come about, which would not seem beyond possibility.

More generally, the *Global 2000* forecasts of a larger population are written in language that conveys apprehension. But viewing the long sweep of human history, larger population size has been a clear-cut sign of economic success and has accompanied improvement in the human lot. The growth in numbers over the millennia, from a few thousands or millions living at subsistence to billions living well above subsistence, is proof positive that the problem of sustenance has eased rather than intensified. And the increase in life expectancy, which is the main cause of the increase in population size, is not only a sign of success in agriculture and public health, but also is the fundamental human good.

In the long run, human beings are the only possible source of human progress. Therefore, we consider *Global 2000*'s choice of language to describe population developments to be inappropriate and misleading.

Our positive statements about the recession of the physical constraints upon human progress are based primarily upon presently known progress, not taking into account possible or even likely advancements in technology. If we were to take into account such possibilities as the resources available to us in space and other such advances – even those possibilities which are already solidly worked out scientifically – our assessment would be much more "optimistic" than it is.

Why the Extraordinary Differences Between *Global 2000* and *The Resourceful Earth*?

The stark differences between *Global 2000* and *The Resourceful Earth* cry out for explanation. There are several causes:

(1)   *The Resourceful Earth* relies heavily on trend data, which we present in abundance. *Global 2000* said that trend data are the proper basis for such an analysis, but nevertheless presented few such data. (It is ironic that we follow this recommendation of *Global 2000*, whereas the original did not follow its own advice.) Our projections of agriculture and natural resource availability exemplify the fundamental role of such trend data.

(2)   Even in the rare cases in which *Global 2000* did present trend series, it heavily weighted a few recent observations, rather than looking at the long-run trends. The fish catch may serve as an example. *Global 2000* presented a data series ending in 1975, and it extrapolated continued stagnation from the last few years' data leading up to 1975. Data for the years since 1975, which we show, indicate that in spite of the extraordinary rise and fall of the Peruvian anchovy fishery in the 1960s and 1970s, the long-run trend toward a larger catch has resumed, as we would have expected based on the overall trend in the series (see figure 12), though the rate of increase may have been decreasing.

(3)   *Global 2000* drew far-reaching conclusions about many issues in the almost total absence of data. The rate of deforestation, and of species loss, are two examples. Reinspection of the skimpy data used to "demonstrate" species loss reveals that *Global 2000*'s extrapolation from those scraps of evidence is quite unsupported by the evidence. Our further investigation of deforestation time-series provides much firmer ground for our unworried assessments than the one-time survey data provide for *Global 2000*'s alarming projections.

(4)   *Global 2000* relied on inappropriate assumptions for its projections. For example, it projected that food prices would double, in large part because it assumed that energy prices would go up. This assumption about energy prices was unsound in several demonstrable ways. First, there was no sound reason simply to assume without evidence that energy prices would rise, especially in the

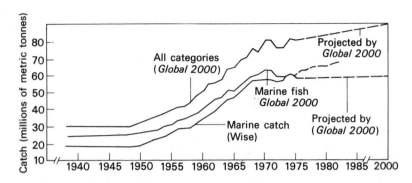

Figure 12 Annual marine yield as shown and projected by *Global 2000*, and
as tabulated by Wise in this volume, Table 3.1, column *d*.
Source: Global 2000, p. 106 and this volume, p. 114.

face of the long-run trend of falling energy prices. Second, *Global
2000* focused on the price of energy rather than the price of
fertilizer, the production of which accounts for much of the use of
petroleum in agriculture. The price of fertilizer has been falling in
the 1970s, due to technological improvements, even despite
energy price rises. Perhaps most important, *Global 2000*
implicitly assumed that private farmers do not respond to
economic incentives to produce more food, which is as wrong as
any assumption possibly could be.

(5)   There are glaring inconsistencies between *Global 2000*'s statements about particular matters in its various chapters.[8] The very
pessimistic assertions in the summary (Volume I) conflict sharply
with statements in the working papers (Volume II).

The Forecasting Capacity of Government

The Resourceful Earth is not "the U.S. Government's projections,"
as *Global 2000* said about itself, or the projections of any other organization. Rather, *The Resourceful Earth* is a compendium of work by independent U.S. scientists who are employed outside the government,
and who are considered authorities by their scientific peers. The work has
not passed through any bureaucratic editing. Other authorities probably
would disagree with some of our emphases and evaluations, but few (if
any) would disagree with the trend facts adduced here.

The fact that the writers of *The Resourceful Earth* are outside government is crucial, in our view, because we believe that government agencies are not well-equipped to produce sound assessments of long-run future trends concerning resources. Too often the agency making the assessment has an axe to grind that derives from its perceived mission and which biases its forecasts. Furthermore, staff-produced government reports must pass through reviews at various stages up the chain of command, and the final conclusions of the staff report, therefore, are likely to emphasize conventional views and to reduce the range of opinion expressed. The resulting work cannot then be attributed to individuals, and no individuals need take full responsibility. In contrast, individuals take full responsibility in *The Resourceful Earth*, and our reputations hang on the quality of the work. Our aim here is not to denigrate the efforts of capable, hard-working, and dedicated civil servants, or to suggest that all (or even most) bureaucratic review is bad. Rather our aim is to point out that internally prepared assessments can and do suffer scientifically because of the organizational forces that prevail in government no matter what the administration. (If all this sounds a bit holier-than-thou, please forgive us. We admit we are proud of *The Resourceful Earth*'s independence as well as convinced of the importance of this fact.)

By its own admission, *Global 2000* did indeed present the public with views distorted by such bureaucratic procedures. Gerald Barney, director of *Global 2000*, has written, for example, that much "misunderstanding" was caused by the first four words on page 1 of Volume I in the "Major Findings and Conclusions" section, "If present trends continue." He notes that

the statement "If present trends continue . . ." was that of an editor at CEQ, and although I objected to the statement as incorrect, it was not possible to have it corrected. (Barney, 1982, p. 9)

If bureaucratic editing can have that much effect, little in such an "official" report as *Global 2000* can be considered scientifically reliable.

Still another disability of internal "government" analyses is that they are often a hodge-podge of elements of unknown origin and nature. Barney says that *Global 2000* suffered from this disability, too. "The technological assumptions were left entirely to the professionals in the government's agencies," (Barney, 1982, p. 9), and were not necessarily the assumptions that the director or staff would have chosen. Independent outside studies of the sort that underlie *The Resourceful Earth* are less vulnerable to this danger. Again, the individual authors of *The Resourceful Earth* take full responsibility for the assumptions they make.

After completion of *Global 2000*, Barney made clear how troublesome these institutional circumstances are for carrying out a study such as that one:

As they have evolved, the Government's agencies now have a hidden layer of decision makers – computer programmers and modelers. These decision makers are, by and large, very skilled professionals, but they are often working in institutional circumstances which prevent them taking into account all the factors they know should be taken into account. Furthermore, the assumptions that they make have a profound influence on the range of policy options considered by senior government officials, and their assumptions are not well documented, are not understood by senior government officials, and are not available for peer review and comment. (Barney, 1982, p. 3)

The inability of government agencies to predict resource trends, and the ill effects of such "official" but badly-made forecasts, would be amusing if not so sad. After a sharp price rise in the late 1970s, timber prices in 1983 fell about three-quarters, causing agony for lumber companies that contracted for government timber at the high prices.

Industry trade groups argue that the government owes the industry help because its policies led to the bidding disaster. In the late 1970s, [an industry spokesman] says, government economists predicted timber shortages and helped to fan the bidding. (*Wall Street Journal*, 1 April 1983, p. 13)

The Department of Energy caused havoc for airplane manufacturers, airlines, for a host of other industries, and for foreign governments by its forecasts that the price of oil would continue to rise after 1979. And that was the forecast in *Global 2000*, in contrast to the editors of this volume and of the authors of the chapters on oil, who are all on record as predicting that the price would *not* continue to rise. The same story describes the recent histories of the other raw materials, too. (Being right does not endear one to others, or make one's opinions more sought, as a rule.) Does this history constitute the basis for increasing the role of government in these matters, or of decreasing it?

We suggest that it would be sensible to compare systematically the record of long-run government forecasts against the record of a reasonable sample of forecasts made outside the government, before making any decision in favor of further centralization. The only available data, those of Ascher (1978) suggest no advantage to government forecasts over private forecasts. To proceed without evidence of a governmental advantage in the activity would not seem responsible legislation.

We know of no body of scientific evidence assessing the effects of ill-founded pessimistic forecasts about resources and the environment upon public morale, innovation, and economic progress. We are agreed, however, that we adjudge the effects, past and future, to be severe and costly.

Political Fruits of *Global 2000*

Enter now the Global Tomorrow Coalition, an umbrella organization consisting (as of October 1982) of 49 environmentalist and population organizations[9] with total membership of 5 million persons; it represents the Global 2000 movement that has evolved since the publication of *Global 2000*. In response to the circumstances mentioned in the quotation from Gerald Barney above, Barney and the Global Tomorrow Coalition are calling for more government computer modeling in the form of a "government global model," and for more centralized control of that modeling. "[I]ncreased coordination of models development and documentation (sic) is needed by the Executive Office of the President" (Barney, 1982, p. 3). Barney sees the matter as follows:

Some of the problems of using computer-based models are illustrated by the difficulties encountered in using the government's models to conduct the *Global 2000* study. The *Global 2000* analysis was initiated with an eight-page memorandum listing all of the projections which would be needed for the study. This memorandum was circulated to the participating agencies along with an indication of which of the projections the agencies would be responsible for. The agencies were all visited and the most professional personnel, the best models, most current and complete data were located. The professionals were then asked to produce a first draft within six weeks.

At the time the first drafts were due, a weekend-long retreat was held at the Belmont House in Maryland. The primary discovery at that meeting was that none of the professionals directly responsible for the long-term global analysis in each of the participating agencies had ever met. They were total strangers. The energy expert had never met the water expert. The food expert had never met the population expert, etc. As a result, our first priority was to make acquaintance and begin the process of seeing that the assumptions being used by the various departments were as internally consistent as we could make them.

At that time we also began the analysis of the content of the models. We knew in advance that the Government does not have what is normally thought of as a "global model," i.e., a single model containing separate interacting sectors dealing with the population, resources and environment. We discovered, however, the Government does have a "global model". In the Government's global model, the population sector is located in a computer at the Bureau of the Census. The energy sector is located in a different computer at the Department of Energy. The food sector is located in a different computer at the Department of Agriculture, etc.

In analyzing these sectoral models, we discovered that they are in fact an interacting set of global sectoral models that collectively constitute the Government's global model. Each of the sectors needs information from the others. The energy sector for example, needs economic and demographic and water projections for input. The population projections require information on the social and economic conditions that influence fertility and mortality rates as inputs. The food model needs information on fertilizer and energy prices, on water availability, economic conditions, and demographic trends.

In analyzing these models, we found that information was flowing from one sectoral model to another even though the persons responsible for the models did not know each other. The medium of communication was the Government Printing Office. Studies were prepared with one sector of the Government's global model, sent off to the Government Printing Office, printed, purchased by another government agency, and the results entered into another sector of the Government's global model. In the process of conducting the *Global 2000* study, we introduced all the Government's professionals to each other, expediting interaction among the models by a factor of perhaps as much as a million simply by bypassing the normal mode of communication through the Government Printing Office. (Barney, 1982, pp. 16–18)

At the behest of the Global Tomorrow Coalition and its member organizations, legislation concerning "foresight capability" with respect to population and resource is now (August 1983) before the Congress. Integrating the various models used in government into a single grand "global model" is one of the objectives of these bills. Another aim is to establish an "Office of Research and Policy Analysis on Global Population, Resources, Energy and the Environment" (Willson memo, 17 September 1982, p. iii).

We do not share the belief that such integration of models will advance "global foresight capability." One of the outcomes of our preparation of *The Resourceful Earth* is that we believe even more strongly than ever that creating one big "government global model" by hooking up the various sectoral models used by various government agencies will *not* improve long-run predictions concerning the topics to which *Global 2000* is addressed. We have great respect for some computer models; almost all of the authors of *The Resourceful Earth* are heavy users of such models in our own work. But we are wary of the call for a governmental "global model" of the sort envisaged by the Global 2000 movement for these reasons:

(1) Models that are developed for one purpose often are fatally flawed for other purposes; using them for such other purposes is likely to produce fallacious results. For example, a model intended to estimate the price and usage of oil in the U.S. in the short run of, say, the next month or year, will probably give worse results than no model at all for predicting price and usage in the long run of 5 or 10 years. Some of the key factors that operate in the long run – such as the substitution of other fuels in response to increased prices of oil – are not likely to be included in the short run model.

(2) We do not agree that data on all (or even on most, or some) of the various elements discussed in *Global 2000* are crucial inputs for predicting the other elements. For example, the future price of energy is not a key input for estimating the future price and quality of food; actions by governments concerning agricultural price controls and subsidies, and the amount of agricultural research done, among other forces, are likely to be far more important in the long run of 20 and more years. Population growth may even not be a central variable if viewed in the conventional fashion of more people implying a higher price of food; in the long run the effect may be the opposite, as greater population density leads to better farm-to-market transportation, and to a host of institutional and technological developments, as has been the history of humanity until now. Ignoring most or all of the interdependencies among the sectors touched on by *Global 2000* may not be disastrous, as *Global 2000* suggests it is and necessarily will be. It may even be a prudent scientific strategy to ignore them. (This assertion may seem preposterous until you examine the track records of predictions about resources and environment made without extensive consideration of such interdependencies, and compare them with predictions of the global modelers who insist – at least in principle – on including such interdependencies in models.)

(3) The strength of computer simulation models for prediction is dealing with the following type of problem: (a) each of the relevant interacting forces is understood rather well, and (b) there is relatively little uncertainty about the underlying conditions, but

(c) there are too many such forces for an analyst to be able to sort them out with paper and pencil alone. Properly programmed for the behavior of each of the forces, and for their interactions and feedbacks, the great calculating power of the computer can work through the large number of necessary computations to arrive at a better answer than can an analyst without the aid of such computing power.

The analytic problems confronted by *Global 2000* have quite different characteristics, however, not only because the interaction of the individual elements is not well understood as yet – a drawback that has properly been emphasized by *Global 2000* and by its director after the completion of the Report – but even more because the key assumptions cannot be made with confidence. In the illustrative case of energy again, *Global 2000* believed it necessary to feed energy price forecasts into the agricultural and the resource models. But what forecast of energy prices should be used? That forecast must depend on such factors as whether OPEC will collapse, the state of future public opinion toward nuclear power from fission, and whether nuclear fusion will become economical (which would affect the present price of oil even if fusion were not commercially available for decades). These are the kinds of considerations for which simple paper-and-pencil analyses are likely to prove best (perhaps with the help of the computer for parts of the analysis). The sort of "scenario" analysis offered in our chapter on the demand for oil exemplifies such analyses.

A major advantage of paper-and-pencil analyses is that they clearly reveal the extent of the uncertainties, and thereby reduce the likelihood of carrying faulty partial analyses from one part of an overall global assessment to another. The writers of *Global 2000* and the Global Tomorrow Coalition believe that more intensive and more integrated modeling is the answer; we believe that such reliance on complex modeling was responsible for the misleading statement made by *Global 2000* about the future course of energy prices, and also was responsible for the confusion caused in *Global 2000*'s agricultural analysis by the introduction into that analysis of the computer-generated forecast of energy prices.

Nobel prizewinner Gunnar Myrdal commented as follows on complex modeling, in the context of the Club of Rome's "Report," *The Limit to Growth*, of which *Global 2000* is a direct lineal descent both in its personnel and its approach to modeling:

[T]he use of mathematical equations and a huge computer, which registers the alternatives of abstractly conceived policies by a "world simulation model," may impress the innocent general public but has little, if any, scientific validity. That this "sort of model is actually a new tool for mankind" is unfortunately not true. It represents quasi-learnedness of a type that we have, for a long time, had too much of, not least in economics, when we try to deal with problems simply in "economic terms."

In the end, those conclusions from the [*Limits to Growth*] Report's analysis that are at all sensible are not different and definitely not more certain than could have been reached without the elaborate apparatus by what Alfred Marshall called "hard simple thinking aware of the limitations of what we know." (Myrdal, 1975, pp. 204–5)

Great difficulties were caused for *Global 2000* by reliance upon the outputs of various computer models, which were inconsistent with each other and with judgments derived from other sources. This is starkly revealed in the section called "Closing the Loops," which deals with the environmental consequences of various projections of population and resources given elsewhere in *Global 2000*. As a reviewer noted:

Whereas the report up to this point has emphasized the environmental impacts of the projections, now the direction of the analysis is reversed and the authors explore the effect of environmental considerations on the realism of the projections. This is a commendable undertaking for it reveals inconsistencies among the projections. But it is virtually a total repudiation of the projections made by the agencies and as modified by the *Global 2000* staff. Time and time again, the earlier projections are characterized as inadequate, incomplete, inconsistent, or inaccurate. Originally, the federal agencies' assistance had been sought because of their expertise, but here the study staff substitutes its judgments for those of the agencies.

Why was such a curious and circuitous process followed? Once the projections were considered unreliable, why were they then published, only to be refuted? One is left to guess at the reasons, but whatever they may be, their effect is confusing at best. At worst, the abrupt turnabout raises questions about the credibility of the entire project. (Clawson, 1981, p. 20)

(4) Another perspective on the matter of "centralized foresight": a larger place for government activity in this field implies a smaller

place for outside assessments – that is, fewer assessments such as we are now offering in *The Resourceful Earth*. More reliance upon a "government global computer model" implies less reliance on assessments built upon the entire armamentarium of scientific tools, including wide-ranging experience and historical perspective, such as is the approach of *The Resourceful Earth*. In considering the desirability of our approach compared with "centralized foresight" and a "government global model," it would seem prudent to compare track records. Many of the authors represented in *The Resourceful Earth* are on record with forecasts made more than a decade ago which ran exactly counter to the forecasts of the gloom-and-doom modelers in *The Limits to Growth* tradition, in the middle of which squarely stands *Global 2000*. And *The Resourceful Earth* authors were correct – especially on such topics as nutrition and famine; climate; pollution in the U.S.; and prices and supplies of agricultural products, mineral resources, and oil. In contrast, the global modelers were dead wrong. Such a comparison does not build confidence or lend support for placing more rather than less reliance upon global modelers in *The Limits-to-Growth-cum-Global 2000* tradition. Comparison of predictive success would seem to recommend more reliance upon wide-ranging and independent outside studies such as we offer here, and less reliance upon global computer-simulation modeling in the vein of *The Limits to Growth* and *Global 2000*.

(5)   Staff-performed government studies such as *Global 2000* have a built-in tendency toward self-perpetuating error in their chosen method of modeling by compilation of other government studies. (Barney said that *Global 2000* "should be thought of as an image of the future as seen by government agencies, rather than as an independent study of the subject." This is in stark contrast with *The Resourceful Earth*, which stands on its own, and can duck no responsibility for error by pinning the blame upon other studies which served as our base.) The self-perpetuating nature of the process may already be seen in the many government reports since *Global 2000* that base *their* conclusions upon *Global 2000* as a source of authoritative information.

(6)   Studies performed inside government are more subject to manipulation by political pressure groups than are studies by independent scholars. For example, governments usually do not like to say that a report which they urged upon the world was out-and-out wrong. Diplomats worry about "credibility." Such a disavowal seems "unstatesmanlike," especially when a report is

labeled "the U.S. government projection" as is *Global 2000*. Therefore, governments usually try to do an about-face without showing the movement – now you see it, now you don't. *The Resourceful Earth* was originally conceived out of an initiative by the Environmental Protection Agency to the editors. When the environmental movement learned of this, our views about *Global 2000* and our analyses of resources and environment being on record, there began a campaign to prevent the project from being funded. The campaign included such public ventures as a leaked story in the *New York Times*, protest letters from congressmen to EPA, and a press release from Stanford University; the private politicking cannot be so well documented, but was widespread; and EPA never came through with funding.

The reader may wonder whether this account is sour grapes. We think not. We initiated the project in May 1982, before it was clear that EPA would not fund it, because we found low-budget backup support from Heritage and because we were too impatient to wait for the EPA funding battle to come to an end. Along the way we offered to sell the product to any major government agency or responsible individual for just one dollar ($1). Our aim in making that offer was to obtain an "official" label for the volume. We adjudged that it was its "official" label that obtained such wide circulation for *Global 2000*. The fact that *The Resourceful Earth* received considerable attention early on was a pleasant surprise to us, but if a tenth or even a twentieth of the number of copies of *The Resourceful Earth* are sold as of *Global 2000*, one of us will eat a copy of this introduction – with an appropriate sauce, of course.

(7) Once a model is entrenched inside a government agency, it is likely to remain in use long after it is no longer credible, due to lack of channels for independent criticism. A frightening example of this tendency has recently surfaced right smack in the middle of the context of Club of Rome *Limits to Growth* models (as are also *Global 2000* and the Global 2000 movement's recommendation for further work). The Department of Defense – or more specifically, the Strategic Plans and Policy Branch of the Military Studies and Analysis Division of the Command and Control Technical Center (CCTC/C313) – uses as its "major analytic tool" what it calls the "World Integrated Model" ("WIM"), which is an outgrowth of the Mesarovic–Pestel model, which in turn was the Club of Rome's first successor to its *Limits to Growth* model. This DOD adaptation dates from 1974, and continues on

its merry way regardless of the fact that the Mesarovic–Pestel and *Limits to Growth* models have been damned as foolishness or fraud by every serious economic critic; for example, Myrdal's assessment. No scientific support or even scientific publication – where criticism is possible – is cited for DOD's WIM model, and though its operators talk about comparing the output with actual data from 1975 to 1980, apparently no such comparison has been made. Its operators refer to it as "the finest global forecasting model available today" (Hamilton memo, p. 6). But the only basis given for belief in its usefulness is the following laudatory remark from an "Executive Office of the President memorandum":

> Basically the Mesarovic–Pestel (WIM) is in a class to itself. There appear to be no detailed dynamic feedback models of similar quality that take a world perspective. The model incorporates a great deal of knowledge and has a strong systems perspective. (Hamilton memo, p. 5)

The WIM is run at great cost to the taxpayer; 2–3 person-years are required just to *update* the WIM model every 2 years; far more than the cost of the entire *The Resourceful Earth* enterprise. Worse, the WIM output is used for "strategic" purposes, on the assumption that there is a connection between impending violence, and the WIM model's forecasts about raw material and population forecasts.

In brief, WIM is a model using an economic framework and publicly available economic data, built and operated without roots in the community of professional economists and without publication for examination in the economic literature (none is cited in its list of references), and using a basic model (*Limits to Growth* type) universally condemned by economists who have looked into it. Yet so seductive is this kind of work that it continues to help shape the nation's fortunes.

In short, we must not be seduced by the magic that computer modeling promises but cannot deliver. Centralization of such modeling, as is called for by the Global Tomorrow Coalition, is particularly dangerous because it reduces the opportunity for independent checks upon erroneous programming and inappropriate assumptions. Difficult and unpleasant as it is for many people to accept, it is crucial to understand that governments are not repositories of wisdom, and can be as mistaken on crucial matters – including scientific issues – as the least-educated layman. Such understanding is especially important because of the Global Tomorrow Coalition's current push toward "centralized foresight."

Recommendations

The Resourceful Earth aims to provide sound and balanced assessments of key issues concerning resources and the environment, and thereby to correct false, gloomy impressions left by *Global 2000*. Policy recommendations are not our mission, and practically no recommendations are contained in the chapters. However, we do have a few views about possible policies which we mention briefly in passing. (We have already expressed our views about a policy of centralizing the government's "foresight capability.")

The recommendations that flow from *Global 2000*, and which are at the core of the Global 2000 movement and the Global Tomorrow Coalition, are contained in *Global Future: Time to Act* (called *Global Future* hereafter). In the words of that document:

> *The Global 2000 Report* to the President identified the problems; it did not attempt to find solutions. The President then directed agencies of the government to undertake the next step – to look at present government programs related to these long-term global issues, assess their effectiveness, and recommend improvements. One of us, Gus Speth, Chairman of the Council on Environmental Quality (CEQ), chaired this effort. [The other was Edmund Muskie, Secretary of State.]
>
> The report that follows, prepared by the Council on Environmental Quality and the Department of State, responds to the President's charge. (1981, pp. iii–iv)

Global Future contains approximately 100 recommendations which fall into three general categories: (1) mobilize interest in the general topic among foreign governments and within the U.S. public; (2) increase U.S. spending in Global 2000-related programs; (3) create governmental institutions that will centralize activities concerning resources and the environment and require various governmental agencies to heed the recommendations of these "global oversight" institutions. The specific recommended programs cover so many activities in the U.S. and abroad that we will not even try to characterize them. We wish to focus attention, however, on the last of the ten sets of recommendations, those which *Global Future* classifies as "Institutional Changes: Improving Our National Capacity to Respond." These recommendations are:

Recommendations (quoted from *Global Future*): The United States should:

Establish a government center as coordinator to insure adequate data collection and modeling capability as the basis for policy analysis on long-term global population, resource, and environmental issues.

Improve the quality of data collection and modeling for global issues and promote wider access to data and models.

Establish a Federal Coordinating Unit, preferably in the Executive Office of the President, to develop federal policy and coordinate ongoing federal programs concerning global population, resource, and environmental issues. Activities should include coordinating data and modeling efforts described above; issuing biennial reports; assessing global population, resource, and environment problems; and serving as a focal point for development of policy on long-term global issues.

Adopt action-forcing devices, such as budget review procedures, a Presidential message, creation of a blue-ribbon commission, establishing an office in each federal agency to deal with long-term global issues, or passage of legislation formalizing a mandate to federal agencies to address long-term global issues and creating a federal coordinating unit and hybrid public–private institute.

Create the Global Population, Resources, and Environment Analysis Institute, a hybrid public–private institution, to strengthen and supplement federal government efforts on long-term global analyses.

Improve the budget process to make technical expertise of U.S. agencies more readily available to other countries.

Assure environmental review of major U.S. government actions significantly affecting natural or ecological resources of global importance; designate tropical forests, croplands, and coastal wetland-estuarine and reef ecosystems as globally important resources.

Continue to raise global population, resource, and environment issues in appropriate international forums; work with and support appropriate international organizations and other countries in formulating solutions.

Enlist the business community in formulating responses to long-term global problems.

Increase public awareness of global population, resources, and environment issues. (1981, pp. li–liii)

A closely related recommendation made elsewhere in *Global Future*:

Develop a U.S. national population policy that includes attention to issues such as population stabilization; availability of family planning programs; just, consistent, and workable immigration laws; improved information needs; and institutions to ensure continued attention to domestic population issues. (1981, p. xxx)

The recommended government center deserves special attention. This is the full description:

Recommendation [of *Global Future*]: A single government center should act as coordinator for the federal government to insure availability of an adequate data and modeling capability to carry out policy analysis on long-term global population, resource, and environment issues. To be most effective, this center should be part of the Federal Coordinating Unit for policy, discussed below, or at least closely coordinated with it. The center should:

Identify long-range problems of global significance.

Promote the development of appropriate analytical tools and data required to assess long-term implications of global problems.

Coordinate and insure preparation, at timely intervals, of long-term projections of trends in global population, resources, and environment and carry out other studies related to these problems.

Prepare timely reports that assess the state of global modeling and data collection, evaluate these analytic activities in the federal government, and make recommendation for improvements.

Name lead agencies for each population, resource, and environment subject area to decide what data should be collected, by whom, and with what methodology.

Coordinate modeling activities of government agencies to insure linkage, feedback, and compatibility of data among various models.

Establish and support a nongovernmental center as part of the public–private Global Population, Resources, and Environment Analysis Institute, discussed below, to enhance global modeling and analysis. (1981, pp. 160–1)

We disagree with all of these recommendations by Global Future. Our reasons for disagreeing lie in one or more of these general propositions:

(1)   The public will be best served both in price and availability with respect to natural resources such as copper and oil, which are mainly produced by the private sector and whose environmental externalities can be dealt with by governmental rules in a reasonably routine fashion, if the government takes no actions at all that affect production or distribution, except for building strategic stockpiles. (We do favor continued government funding of research in agriculture and some potential energy sources such as fusion.)

(2)   Scientific research and assessments of these topics should continue to be carried out independently in a variety of locations, rather than becoming more centralized than now. The government's policy tool affecting these activities is funding. We recommend against any funding for new government agencies of the sort envisioned by the Global 2000 movement by way of the Global Tomorrow Coalition or otherwise, unless that agency is able to win funding through competition in the normal research channels with peer-group review.

(3)   We believe that the government should *not* take steps to make the public more "aware" of issues concerning resources, environment, and population. We consider that the public has been badly served by having been scared by a very large volume of unfounded and/or exaggerated warnings about these matters. Many of these scientifically unsupported and injudicious warnings have derived from government agencies. The results have been disastrous from the standpoint of the allocation of social resources – for example, the contracts entered into by airlines for airplane manufacturers to build new fuel-saving airliners, contracts later cancelled by the airlines at high cost to all; the high price of natural gas resulting from long-term contracts to pay-or-take entered into on the assumption that energy prices would continue to rise; the federal regulations on average fuel mileage of automobiles sold by particular makers, leading to vast unnecessary expenditures for redesign, with consequent weakening of U.S. automobile firms; and federal grants to recycling centers that process waste at much higher social cost than ordinary waste disposal; we could fill a book with examples. The results of unfounded public fears about the future of resources and the environment probably have also caused declines in morale and the will to exert effort for continued improvements.

It is a matter of great public importance that we reverse these patterns of the 1960s and 1970s. The U.S. public must come to hear the truth that conditions have been getting better rather than worse, and that enthusiastic and vigorous efforts to do even better even faster will benefit the public as well as the individuals who act economically to bring about this social progress. In our view, the world is ready to turn its back on its pessimism, and is waiting to hear some good news. All the more reason to tell the true good news that there is to tell.

(4) With respect to population growth in the U.S., whose "stabilization" is called for by the Global 2000 movement (as seen, for example, in the recommendation by *Global Future*, p. 11, and in the bills before Congress urged by the Global 2000 movement), we make no recommendation other than that government should not attempt to influence individuals' family-size decisions in any fashion. Even if there were economic advantages to cessation of population growth in the U.S., too many wider issues and values are involved to justify such a far-reaching policy; human population is not simply an economic matter. We also do not consider it our place to discuss whether our government should attempt to stimulate fertility; we see no compelling economic reason for such a policy, and many sound reasons against discussion of the matter. Immigration is an extremely complex topic that is far beyond our purview – and beyond that of *Global 2000*, which implied, however, that immigration has been too great though *Global 2000* did not provide even the hint of a rationale for such a proposition.

Our viewpoint on population growth in the rest of the world is much the same as in the United States. Recommendations to other countries – and even more so, pressure upon them – to institute and carry out policies with respect to their population growth rates are not warranted by any facts about resources and population, and they constitute unjustifiable interference in the activities of other countries, because such policies must necessarily rest upon value judgments. Hence we consider that such recommendations by the Global 2000 movement are unfounded and unacceptable, ignorant and arrogant.

The cost of any policy recommendation should always be reckoned, even if the policy by itself might have positive effects. For example, the recommendation of the Global 2000 movement for government collection of more secondary "global" data seems unobjectionable, on its face. But there is no reason to presume that such collection or analysis of data would be done efficiently or cost-effectively. For example, the cost of

Global 2000 executed by the federal government was roughly 1 million dollars (Barney, 1982). The cost of *The Resourceful Earth*, carried out by independent scholars as an extension of the work they have been doing much of their professional lives, and in some cases which they have already largely completed or published in other contexts, is roughly $30,000, less than a thirtieth of *Global 2000*'s cost. Our contributors were paid out of private funds at the rate of $1000 per paper, truly only an "honorarium" for persons of this caliber and for work this serious; conference travel expenses took most of the rest. (Of course we believe that at *no* price would *Global 2000* have been a purchase of value.) This comparison, which we consider typical, does not build much confidence in the government's ability to spend taxpayers' money well for activities of this sort, and it testifies against internal staff-prepared reports on subjects that are essentially scientific.

As editors, it might be appropriate for us to boast in detail of the qualifications of our contributors. Instead of doing so, we suggest simply that you examine the lists of their writings and the writings themselves, check their professional histories in *Who's Who* and similar reference volumes, and compare those credentials with the credentials of the staff of persons who prepared *Global 2000*, listed in their introductory pages. Then think again about the costs of *Global 2000* and *The Resourceful Earth*, and what the public gets for its money with its expenditures for a staff-performed study such as *Global 2000*.

It does not follow that, because we are not proposing new things for governments to do about resources and the environment, we therefore think that nothing needs to be done. Much is being done spontaneously, by individuals, by non-governmental bodies, and by governments; and much more needs to be done. We believe, however, that it is a mistake to presume that the government usually handles these tasks better than, or even as well as, persons outside of government; sometimes government does better, sometimes worse. The case against government action is especially strong where there are relatively few difficult externalities, as is the case with the production of food, energy, and other natural resources.

Capsule Conclusion

The letter of transmittal of *Global 2000* to the President of the United States said:

Our conclusions, summarized in the pages that follow, are disturbing. They indicate the potential for global problems of alarming proportions by the year 2000. Environmental, resource, and population stresses are intensifying and will increasingly determine the quality of human life on our planet. These stresses are already severe enough to deny many millions of people basic needs for food, shelter, health, and jobs, or any hope for betterment. At the same time, the earth's carrying capacity – the ability of biological systems to provide resources for human needs – is eroding. The trends reflected in the Global 2000 suggest strongly a progressive degradation and impoverishment of the earth's natural resource base.

We radically re-write the statement as follows:

Our conclusions are reassuring, though not grounds for complacency. Global problems due to physical conditions (as distinguished from those caused by institutional and political conditions) are always possible, but are likely to be less pressing in the future than in the past. Environmental, resource, and population stresses are diminishing, and with the passage of time will have less influence than now upon the quality of human life on our planet. These stresses have in the past always caused many people to suffer from lack of food, shelter, health, and jobs, but the trend is toward less rather than more of such suffering. Especially important and noteworthy is the dramatic trend toward longer and healthier life throughout all the world. Because of increases in knowledge, the earth's "carrying capacity" has been increasing throughout the decades and centuries and millenia to such an extent that the term "carrying capacity" has by now no useful meaning. These trends strongly suggest a progressive improvement and enrichment of the earth's natural resource base, and of mankind's lot on earth.

AFTER NOTE

Editors' Note on Economic Growth
to the Year 2000 and Beyond

Underlying this volume's general point of view is the following implicit assumption about future economic growth in the world as a whole, and in the less-developed countries (LDCs) considered as a sector. We expect that in the long run – both before, and also subsequent to, the year 2000 – economic growth will continue at a rate at least as fast as in the decades since World War II. The words "as fast as" are purposely vague with respect to absolute or percentage growth, because a similar rate of proportional growth in the long-run future, as in the past, would imply much faster (and ever-increasing) absolute growth that would soon have income at levels higher than ever seen before; the world's lack of economic experience with such high rates and income levels suggests we should be cautious about the possibility that such could be the case. Our intention is simply to imply that there is no reason to expect stagnation or a lower percentage rate of growth for the LDCs in the future compared to the past; this expectation is quite unlike the expectation stated by *Global 2000*.

Our main reason for making this assumption is that the history of mankind has shown economic growth generally proceeding at an increasing rather than a decreasing pace. This is true over the very long sweep of history as well as over the past century. And there is no persuasive structural reason – certainly not a shortage of raw materials, as we establish here – to expect that we are at a turning point now in that respect. Of course the world and the LDCs can find ways to do ourselves in, by such policies as pushing up the price of energy by foreswearing power from nuclear fission and from coal, or so structuring economic systems that incentives for individuals are reduced and the power of markets is choked off by government control. But we believe that if such disastrous policies are put in place, their effects will eventually teach nations to follow more productive policies – though perhaps only after economic growth has declined for a while.

Upon close inspection, the gloomy *Global 2000* projection of declining growth in per person income until the year 2000 is seen to arise directly and solely from the underlying assumption that the rate of increase in per person productivity will be declining. All the rest of their "modeling" depends entirely upon this key assumption. No justification is given for this key assumption, however. And the likely course of productivity change until the year 2000 is in sharp dispute by reasonable persons. A pessimist may cite the slowdown since 1973, which could be part of a cyclical downturn in the long upward trend. An optimist, on the other hand, may cite the fast world growth since 1950, and the observed rate of growth in the LDCs which is as high or higher than in the MDCs over that period (Morawetz, 1978); from the latter evidence an optimist may judge (as we do) that the recent downturn is not a reasonable basis for projecting a continued low rate of growth in coming decades. Additionally, international politics involving resource cartels such as OPEC, as well as domestic politics involving fiscal and monetary and welfare policies, can affect growth until 2000. And no-one can build politics into an economic forecasting model with any confidence. So there obviously is much reason for lack of agreement about expectations for economic growth until the year 2000, and a confident forecast for that date itself would be foolish.

For the purposes of assessing and forecasting the state of *resources and environment* until the year 2000, however, it does not matter much whether the economic forecasts of even the extreme pessimists or the extreme optimists will prove to be the case; the availability of most resources and the cleanliness of the environment over only the next 17 years are not likely to be sensitive to such differences in income. Therefore we need not enter into detailed discussion of the matter; it would only obscure our main aim here. (It is not part of *The Resourceful Earth*'s mission to develop our own economic forecast, just as it was not part of *Global 2000*'s assignment.)

For the longer run, with some confidence we can say that future rates of economic growth no worse than those in the past will have many salutary effects upon the environment, as higher income permits countries and individuals to pay for cleaner, more attractive, and healthier living space. Similarly, higher income in the long run will probably lead to greater availability and lower prices of resources rather than greater scarcity and higher prices; such has been the entire course of human history, though in the short run increased income causes increased prices. Perhaps the largest and most threatening uncertainty connected with income growth concerns the climate, if there is continued fossil-fuel use rather than a shift to nuclear power; we assess that issue separately and at length later.

In short: for present purposes, detailed analysis and forecast of income growth until the year 2000 is unnecessary, and might misdirect the reader's attention from topics deserving that attention here. Therefore we shall not pursue the subject further.

Notes

1   Paragraph adapted from Kahn and Schneider (1981). Various other material adapted from Simon (1981).
2   Luther J. Carter, "Global 2000 Report: Vision of a Gloomy World," *Science*, **209**, 1 August 1980, pp. 575–6.

48   *Julian L. Simon and Herman Kahn*

3 *Time*, 4 August 1980, p. 54.
4 *Newsweek*, 4 August 1980, p. 38.
5 Champaign-Urbana *News Gazette*, 24 July 1980, p. 1.
6 For additional material on *Global 2000*'s factual errors and internal inconsistencies, see Simon (1981).
7 Ned Dearborn, one of the three *Global 2000* staff writers, stated in the abstract of a public talk he gave at the 1982 meeting of the American Association for the Advancement of Science:

> By deliberate political choice, only part of the *Global 2000 Report to the President* was featured in the Report's summary volume and press releases – the part containing the Report's projections. The other part, while not suppressed, was barely mentioned in the official material receiving the widest distribution.

8 In addition to the inconsistencies pinpointed in the chapters here, one might consult Simon (1981).
9 Action for World Development. Alan Guttmacher Institute. American Farm Foundation. American Institute for Biological Sciences. American Society for the Prevention of Cruelty to Animals. Audubon Naturalist Society of Central
9 Atlantic States. Bolton Institute for a Sustainable Future. Carrying Capacity. Center for Law & Social Policy. Concern, Inc. Conservation Foundation. Defenders of Wildlife. Environmental Coalition of North America. Environmental Defense Fund. Environmental Fund. Environmental Policy Center. Environmental Policy Institute. Federation for American Immigration Reform. Friends of the Earth. Greater Caribbean Energy & Environment Foundation. International Institute for Environment & Development. Izaak Walton League. League of Women Voters. Monitor International. National Audubon Society. National Family Planning & Reproductive Health Association. National Wildlife Federation. Natural Resources Defense Council. Negative Population Growth. New York Zoological Society. Ohio Conservation Foundation. Overseas Development Council. Planned Parenthood of New York City. Population Crisis Committee. Population Communication. Population Institute. Population Resource Center. Population Services International. Rachel Carson Council. Renewable Natural Resources Foundation. Scenic Shoreline Preservation Conference. Sierra Club. Texas Committee on Natural Resources. Trust for Public Land. U.S. Association for the Club of Rome. U.S. Women's Health Coalition. Wilderness Society. Windstar Foundation. World Population Society. Zero Population Growth.

References

Ascher, William (1978) *Forecasting*, Baltimore: Johns Hopkins Press.
Barney, Gerald O. (1982) "Improving the Government's Capacity to Analyze and Predict Conditions and Trends of Global Population Resources and Environment." Manuscript dated 24 March.
Carter, Luther, J. (1980) "Global 2000 Report: Vision of a Gloomy World." *Science*, **209**, 1 August 575–6.

Champaign-Urbana *News Gazette*, 24 July 1980, p. 1.

Clark, Colin (1957) *Conditions of Economic Progress* (3rd edn) New York: Macmillan.

Clawson, Marion (1981) "Entering the Twenty-First Century – The Global 2000 Report to the President." *Resources*, **66** (Spring), 19.

Council on Environmental Quality, United States Department of State (1981) *Global Future: Time to Act.* January, pp. 1–209.

Dearborn, Ned (1982) Address to American Association for the Advancement of Science, January.

Dubos, Rene (1981) "Half Truths About the Future." *Wall Street Journal*, 8 May, editorial page.

Global 2000 Report to the President, Vols. I, II and III. Washington, D.C.: U.S. Government Printing Office, 1980.

Gwatkin, Davidson R. (1980) "Indications of Change in Developing Country Mortality Trends: The End of an Era?" *Population and Development Review*, **6** (December), 615–44.

Hamilton, C. F. (1982) Memo from Command and Control Technical Center, Defense Communications Agency.

Holdgate, Martin W., Mohammed Kassas and Gilbert F. White (1982) *The World Environment, 1971–1982*, Dublin: Tycooly.

Kahn, Herman and Ernest Schneider (1981) "Globaloney 2000" *Policy Review*, Spring, pp. 129–47.

Kumar, Joginden (1973) *Population and Land in World Agriculture*, Berkeley: University of California Press.

Mayr, Ernst (1982) *The Growth of Biological Thought: Diversity and Inheritance.* Cambridge, Mass.: Belknap Press of Harvard University Press.

Morawetz, David (1978) *Twenty-Five Years of Economic Development 1950–1975*, Baltimore: Johns Hopkins.

Myers, Norman (1979) *The Sinking Ark*, New York: Pergamon.

Myrdal, Gunnar (1975) *Against the Stream – Critical Essays on Economics*, New York: Vintage Books.

New York Times, 31 January 1983, p. 5.

Newsweek, 4 August 1980.

Simon, Julian L. (1981) "Global Confusion, 1980: A Hard Look at the Global 2000 Report." *The Public Interest*, **62** (Winter), 3–21.

Time, 9 August 1980.

U.S. Department of Commerce, Bureau of the Census. *Social Indicators: 1976*, Washington, D.C.: U.S. Government Printing Office, 1977.

U.S. Department of the Interior, National Park Service. *Information Relations to the National Park System*, 30 June 1944.

Wall Street Journal, 15 September 1980, p. 32.

Wall Street Journal, 1 April 1983, p. 13.

Willson, Pete (1982) Memorandum, The Alan Guttmacher Institute, 17 September.

1

The Role of Population Projections
for the Year 2000

MARK PERLMAN

Introduction

From the beginning, let us note that the outstanding demographic fact of
our times is the relatively recent continued expansion of life expectancy
for virtually all age groups. Table 1.1 shows that life expectancy at birth in
rich countries has almost tripled in the past two centuries; and life
expectancy in the poorer countries has risen by more than a decade in the
short span of time since World War II, as is documented in the accom-
panying essay by Johnson (chapter 2). Though these changes bring
problems with them, they are welcome to all who share the standard
values of human civilization. Considering the very long sweep of human
history, our present world population size, several orders of magnitude
larger than in earlier periods, is a clear-cut sign of economic success in
that we now have the know-how and wherewithal to keep many more
people alive as well as provide more goods and leisure to people on
average than in past millennia. And these numbers have also been the
cause of human progress in the long run (there can be no other cause),
though in the short run additional persons inevitably bring with them
additional burdens to others. The weighing of the burdens imposed by the
presence of the additional persons relative to the benefits inescapably
involves the particular value system of the person making the
comparison.

The first "Principal Finding" of *The Global 2000 Report to the
President: Entering the Twenty-first Century* is:

Rapid growth in world population will hardly have altered by 2000.
The world's population will grow from 4 billion in 1975 to 6.35 billion
in 2000, an increase of more than 50 percent. The rate of growth will
slow only marginally from 1.8 percent a year to 1.7 percent. In
terms of sheer numbers, population will be growing faster in 2000
than it is today.

Table 1.1   FEMALE EXPECTATION OF LIFE AT BIRTH, FRANCE

/ (1) INED series Dates	$\overset{0}{e}_0$	(2) van de Walle Dates	$\overset{0}{e}_0$	(3) Official statistics Dates	$\overset{0}{e}_0$
1740–1749	25.7				
1750–1759	28.7				
1760–1769	29.0				
1770–1779	29.6				
1780–1789	28.1				
1790–1799	32.1				
1800–1809	34.9	1801–1810	36.4		
1810–1819	37.5	1811–1820	38.3		
1820–1829	39.3	1821–1830	38.6		
		1831–1840	38.8		
		1841–1850	40.9		
		1851–1860	40.4	1861–1865	40.6
		1861–1870	41.8	1877–1881	43.6
		1871–1880	43.0		
		1881–1890	45.1	1899–1903	48.7
		1891–1900	46.0	1908–1913	52.4
				1920–1923	55.9
				1928–1933	59.0
				1933–1938	61.6
				1946–1949	67.4
				1952–1956	71.2
1960–				1960–1964	74.4
				1966–1970	75.4

Note: $\overset{0}{e}_0$ = life expectancy
Sources: (1) Yves Blayo, "La mortalité en France de 1740 à 1829", in *Démographie Historique*, special issue of *Population*, November 1975, p. 141; (2) Etienne van de Walle, "La mortalité des départements français ruraux au XIXe siècle", in Hommage à Marcel Reinhard, *Sur la population française au XVIIIe et en XIXe siècles*, Société de démographie historique, Paris, 1973, p. 584; (3) Alain Monnier, "La mortalité", in *La population de la France*, special issue of *Population*, June 1974, p. 107. Reproduced with permission from W. R. Lee, *European Demography and Economic Growth*. New York: St. Martins, Press 1979, p. 142.

That "finding" is written in language which immediately arouses apprehension. Its pitch reveals the tenor of *Global 2000* as a whole: Things are not only bad, they are getting much worse, and rapidly too. I shall argue that there are few, if any, real or historical grounds here for this numbing fear. My case is not built on my offering alternative projections, but on examining what the official projections previously offered implied, what accuracy they possessed, and what those projections, put into appropriate historical perspective, really should mean. In this sense, this chapter stands apart from and is unlike the rest of this book. Rather, I argue that the apparently terrifying projections for the year 2000 proffered by *Global 2000* are not meaningful for a variety of reasons, each of which by itself should be enough to cause us to put aside this doomsday finding.

The reasons are: (1) there is already evidence that the projections for the year 2000 are off the mark; (2) even if the past few years had not already shown *Global 2000*'s projections to be awry, there are general reasons to be skeptical of such projections; (3) and most of all, even if the projections were still (unexpectedly) to prove on (or even relatively close to) the mark, the outcome is not very relevant to the main concerns of *Global 2000*.

Projections Already Awry

As is the practice of the U.S. Bureau of the Census, *Global 2000* made three variant projections – "high," "medium," and "low" – based on different sets of assumptions, which are intended to bracket almost all possible outcomes. There is a tendency to put more faith in the "medium" projection, because it seems more "balanced" – in the "broad middle ground," as a diplomat would put it – and such is the case with *Global 2000*'s summary, though there is little objective warrant for doing so.

In 1982 the writer of the *Global 2000* population section, Samuel Baum, reviewed the projections originally made between 1977 and their publication in 1980. In that short span of time, events had already changed sufficiently so that the projections were clearly below the "medium" variant.

This shift to emphasis on the low variant is by itself sufficient reason to call into question the overall *Global 2000* more than 6 billion estimate for the year 2000. In Baum's words:

> On the global level we now [1982] estimate that there were 25 million more people in the world in 1975 than we estimated for the same date 4½ years ago. The largest percentage difference is for Africa. The only region for which the earlier estimates now seem too high is Latin America.

> . . . on a global level we find 28 million more people now [1982] estimated for 1980 than were projected in the medium series of Global 2000.

> . . . [But] putting together these [newer] partial projections we come up with . . . a somewhat lower global population in the year 2000 – 6,217 million, as compared to the 6,350 million in the medium

series of the Global 2000 projections. *However, the latest estimates or projection compilations are well within the bounds of the low series in the Global 2000 study.*" (italics added)

If what Baum writes seems to be only a "minor" discrepancy after so short a time, my italics suggests something significantly more important. Without stressing the point, something which it seems to me that he owes to any reader, he has moved from the originally *prima facie* preferred *medium* series to the *low* series. Little wonder that population projection *users* often fail to perceive the fine changes which the projection *makers* introduce when both groups write papers which are meant on the one hand to be scientific and on the other hand to be policy-useful. This sleight of hand or casuistry has led our leading commentators on the policy uses of social and, specifically, population data, Oskar Morgenstern (Morgenstern, 1950, 1953) and William Ascher (Ascher, 1978), figuratively to throw up their hands in dismay.

The second part of the *Global 2000* forecast also has become doubtful in the few short years since it was made. The rate of growth of the world's population has *already* fallen from its peak of about 1.8 percent a year, a fall which *Global 2000* projected to occur only by 2000. Of course, changes in one direction (down) can be replaced by changes in the other direction (up), but what stands out is that for the moment the change is down, and sooner than expected (cf. Mauldin, 1983).

In short, *Global 2000*'s projections do not engender confidence.

Twenty-year Population Forecasts Dubious

Even if the *Global 2000* forecasts had not already shown themselves to be off the mark, there would be considerable reason to place little confidence in *any* such forecasts. The basis for skepticism is the record of such forecasts in the past. I shall mostly use the example of U.S. forecasts to make an *a fortiori* argument. The U.S. has an unusually long history of censuses and of forecasts based on them. Even with all the technical resources of the Bureau of the Census, these forecasts have not had an enviable record. If forecasting is that unreliable for the U.S., it must be even more tenuous for the world as a whole.

On first thought, making projections about world population for an interval as short as 17–25 years does not seem surpassingly difficult. All one has to do is to start with the data reported to the United Nations about present population levels, combine them with the reported fertility rates and mortality rates, and make some further assumptions about changes in fertility and mortality. That would seem to be enough for the

TABLE 1.2 U.S. POPULATION PROJECTIONS (IN MILLIONS)

	1920	1930	1940	1945	1950	1960	1965	1970	1975	1980	1985	1990	2000	2010	2020	2100
1. Actual	105.7	122.8	131.7		151.3	179.3		203.3		226.5						
2. 1852: Bonynge	120.2		186.8		198.7	290.5				451.8			703.0			
3. 1924: Pearl-Reed		122.4	136.3					167.9		174.9		180.4	184.7		190.3	196.7
4. 1928: Whelpton		123.6	138.3		151.6	162.7		171.5	175.1							
5. 1931: Dublin: High			131.0		139.0	147.0		150.0			154.0		152.0			140.0
Low			131.0		139.0	146.0		148.0			147.0		140.0			87.0
6. 1931: Whelpton			132.5		139.8	143.9		144.6		142.9	Declined thereafter					
7. 1933: Thompson & Whelpton: High			135.1		150.8	167.3		184.2		202.0						
Low			131.9		137.1	137.9		134.9		129.2						
8. 1936: Whelpton: High			132.6		146.1	159.5		172.8		185.8						
Low			131.2		136.2	137.1		134.0		127.6						
9. 1938: National Resources Comm. High			132.0		141.6	149.4		155.0		158.3						
Low			131.3		137.1	139.5		138.5		133.9						
10. 1940: Pearl-Reed: High			136.3		148.7	159.2		167.9		174.9		180.4	184.7	Asymptote 197.3		
Low			132.8		143.8	153.0		160.4		166.3		170.8	174.3			
11. 1943: Thompson & Whelpton: High					145.0	156.5		167.9		179.4		189.4	198.7			
Low					143.0	147.7		148.7		145.8		138.9	129.1			
12. 1947: Whelpton: High					148.0	162.0		177.1	185.1							
Low					144.9	149.8		151.6	151.1							
13. 1950: CPR: P-25, No. 43: High					151.6	179.8										
Low					150.9	161.2										
14. 1958: CPR: P-25, No. 187: High						181.2		219.5		272.6						
Low						179.4		202.5		230.8						
15. 1967: CPR: P-25, No. 381: High								208.6		250.5		300.1				
Low								204.9		227.7		256.0				
16. 1972: CPR: P-25, No. 476: High										236.7		278.6	322.3	381.2	447.0	
Low										227.8		251.4	271.1	290.7	307.4	
17. 1975: CPR: P-25, No. 601: High										225.7		257.7	287.0	322.0	362.3	
Low										220.4		235.6	245.1	250.2	251.9	
18. 1977: CPR: P-25, No. 704: High										224.1		254.7	282.8	315.2	354.1	
Low										220.7		236.3	245.9	250.9	253.0	
19. 1982: CPR: P-25, No. 922: High												254.7	282.3	311.1	341.9	
Low												245.5	255.6	260.7	261.6	

computer to crank out reliable answers for the variously different specified time periods – or so it seems.

I have collected in table 1.2 a variety of United States population predictions made over the past 130 years. Those data provide no basis for confidence in such estimates for a 20-year period.

One might wonder whether the art of forecasting has recently improved to the extent that the lack of accuracy of past forecasts may reasonably be put aside. In a recent article Frank Notestein describes the new ways that forecasts were made in the 1920s and 1930s (Notestein, 1982). But it is Keyfitz's pioneer work in evaluating the newer forecasts which offers some show of improvement (Keyfitz, 1982); this can be inferred from table 1.3, taken from his work. Furthermore, Keyfitz's own conclusions about the amount of such improvement are very guarded:

[T]here are at least three ways of treating the results of the table in application to what is now the future, that is, for forecasts being made in 1981:

Notes:

1. U.S. Bureau of the Census, U.S. Census of Population.
2. Projections of Francis Bonynge, *The Future Wealth of America*, New York, 1852 printed in P. K. Whelpton, "Population of the United States, 1925 to 1975," *The American Journal of Sociology*, 34(2), September 1928.
3. Raymond Pearl, *The Biology of Population Growth*, New York: Alfred Knopf, 1925. p. 219.
4. P. K. Whelpton, "Population of the United States, 1925 to 1975," *American Journal of Sociology*, 34(2), September 1928, 253–270.
5. Louis I. Dublin, "The outlook for the American birth-rate," *Problems of Population*. Report of the Proceedings of the Second General Assembly of the International Union for the Scientific Investigation of Population Problems, 1932, 115–25. (Estimated from a graph presented in the paper.)
6. P. K. Whelpton, "The future growth of the population of the United States," *Problems of Population*. Report of the Proceedings of the Second General Assembly of the International Union for the Scientific Investigation of Population Problems, 1932, 77–86.
7. Warren S. Thompson and P. K. Whelpton, *Population Trends in the United States*. New York: McGraw-Hill, 1933, p. 5.
8. P. K. Whelpton, *Journal of the American Statistical Association*, 31, 1936, 457–73. (High is based on the assumptions of high fertility, low mortality, 200,000 net immigrants annually beginning 1940; low is based on the assumptions of low fertility, high mortality,no net immigration.)
9. National Resources Committee, *The Problems of a Changing Population*, 1938. (High is based on the assumptions of medium fertility, medium mortality and net annual immigration of 100,000; low is based on the assumptions of low fertility, medium mortality and no immigration.)
10. Raymond Pearl, Lowell J. Reed, and Joseph F. Kish, "The logistic curve and the census count of 1940," *Science*, 92 (November 22, 1940), 486–488. (High is logistics curve I and low is logistics curve II.)
11. Warren S. Thompson and P. K. Whelpton, *Estimates of Future Population of the United States 1940–2000 for the National Resources Planning Board, 1943*. Washington, D.C.: GPO, 1943. (High is based on the assumptions of high fertility, low mortality, no net immigration; low is based on the assumptions of low fertility, high mortality, no net immigration.)
12. P. K. Whelpton, *Forecasts of the Population of the United States 1945–1975*, U.S. Department of Commerce, 1947. Washington, D.C.: GPO, 1947. (High is based on the assumptions of high fertility, low mortality, average net annual immigration of 200,000; low is based on the assumptions of low fertility, high mortality, no net immigration.)
13–19. U.S. Department of Commerce, U.S. Bureau of Census, *Current Population Surveys*.

TABLE 1.3 ROOT-MEAN-SQUARE DEPARTURE OF FORECAST
FROM SUBSEQUENT REALIZATION, ESTIMATES PUBLISHED
1939–68, EXPRESSED IN PERCENTAGE

	Date of forecast	Forecasts for years	Number of forecasts	Root-mean-square error
Canada[a]	1939–54	1950–70	14	1.123
United States[b]	–1950	1955–75	15	0.907
	1950+	1955–80	92	0.340
Europe and the Soviet Union[c]	1944	1950–70	96	0.949
Nine countries of Eastern Europe[d]	1965	1965–80	96	0.219
All countries[e] >1,000,000	1958–68	1960–74	810	0.476
All forecasts	1939–68	1950–80	1,123	0.530

Notes: [a] Statistics Canada (1954)   [b] U.S. Bureau of the Census (1975)   [c] Notestein, Frank *et al.*
1944, *The Future Population of Europe and the Soviet Union: Population Projections 1940–
1970*. Geneva: League of Nations   [d] *U.S. Bureau of the Census (1965)*   [e] United Nations (1958,
1966, 1973, 1979)
Source: Reproduced with permission from Nathan Keyfitz, *Population Change and Social Policy.*
Cambridge: Abt Books, 1982, p. 188.

(1) One could argue that the future will be as changeable as the
past, and present demographic methods on the whole are
neither better nor worse than those of the past, and average
over the entire record, with a root-mean-square of about 0.5
percentage points.

(2) One could say that the early work has been improved on, and
the current forecasts would at most be subject to the amount of
error shown in the late 1960s. Corresponding to this view, one
would take the root-mean-square as . . . roughly 0.4 percentage
points.

(3) One could go on to say that errors of the later 1960s are
two-thirds of those of the late 1950s, and hence those of the late
1970s will be two-thirds of those of the 1960s, a root-mean-
square of about 0.24 percentage points. *To count on this narrow
range derived from this consideration would seem imprudent.*
(Italics added.)

The main difficulty in making world forecasts at present is predicting
fertility. To predict with any confidence would require substantive knowledge other than present and past birth rates, because national birth rates
can change rapidly – as a variety of evidence since World War II demon-

strates. Note the fluctuations in table 1.4 not only between countries and, I might add gratuitously within countries and particularly over very brief intervals. Doubtless much of this fluctuation is associated with the propensity of fertility rates to change suddenly and significantly, and their causes remain essentially unknown: Charles Tilly put the matter all too well:

> The problem is that we [economists, demographers, historians and sociologists] have too many explanations [of the interdependence of fertility decline, industrialization, and urbanization] which are individually plausible in general terms, which contradict each other to some degree, and which fail to fit some significant part of the facts. (Tilly, 1978, p. 3)

Social science, as Tilly puts it, does not yet provide us with a well-agreed-upon body of such tested knowledge. We have reason to believe that birth and fertility rates influence and are themselves influenced by the very economic conditions that the *Global 2000* Report assumed (without adequate evidence in my view) those rates would affect. But there is thorough-going disagreement among economic demographers on the direction of these influences, as we see in the disagreement between the Becker and Kuznets theoretical formulations (cf. Perlman, 1981). And with respect to non-economic variables as attitudes and values – which surely are influenced by economic conditions in the long run but which have a life of their own, there is no solid body of evidence to assess the extent of their importance relative to the economic conditions alone. In short, there is no sound body of knowledge to help us project fertility rates, and hence there is a crucial hole in the forecasting apparatus for a world in which national fertility rates change.

Where Does This Leave Us?

No matter what the population that one expects for the year 2000, one may properly ask what are the general and per capita environmental conditions going to be. And even then, so what?

The total number of people in the year 2000 would matter if there were an "us" who are working and supporting a (non-working but consuming) "them" with "our" limited supplies of resources. But the world is not made up of "us" and "them" societies and/or countries. Rather, countries mostly feed (and/or trade in goods and services) to support themselves.

Even if we take the perspective of the world as a whole, the actual population size in 2000, within any conceivable variation, matters little

TABLE 1.4 CRUDE BIRTH RATES 1950–1980 AND CRUDE BIRTH RATE DECLINES 1950–65, 1965–80, AND 1950–80: LDCs

	CBR 1950	CBR 1965	CBR 1980	% decline in CBR 1950–65	% decline in CBR 1965–80	% decline in CBR 1950–80
Africa (Countries arranged by CBR decline, 1965–80)						
1 Reunion	49.4	42.9	25.0	13.2	41.7	49.4
2 Mauritius	46.3	35.7	27.0	22.9	24.4	41.7
3 Tunisia	46.5	43.1	35.0	7.2	18.8	24.7
4 Egypt	43.8	45.4	40.0	-3.7	11.9	8.7
5 Morocco	48.0	48.0	45.0	0.0	6.3	6.3
6 Togo	50.8	49.0	48.0	3.5	2.0	5.5
7 Benin	51.0	50.0	48.7	2.0	2.7	4.6
8 Burundi	48.0	48.0	46.0	0.0	4.2	4.2
9 Sierra Leone	48.0	46.0	46.0	4.2	0.0	4.2
10 Sudan	49.0	47.0	47.0	4.1	0.0	4.1
11 S Africa	39.0	39.0	38.0	0.0	2.6	2.6
12 Chad	46.0	45.0	45.0	2.2	0.0	2.2
13 Guinea	47.0	47.0	46.0	0.0	2.1	2.1
14 Algeria	48.3	50.0	47.5	-3.5	4.9	1.6
15 Senegal	48.0	47.6	47.4	0.8	0.5	1.3
16 Ivory Coast	46.0	46.0	45.5	-0.1	1.3	1.2
17 Niger	52.4	52.3	52.0	0.2	0.6	0.8
18 Mali	50.1	49.6	50.0	1.0	-0.8	0.2
19 Angola	47.0	47.0	47.0	0.0	0.0	0.0
20 Botswana	48.0	48.0	48.0	0.0	0.0	0.0
21 Cen Afr Em	46.0	46.0	46.0	0.0	0.0	0.0
22 Congo	45.0	45.0	45.0	0.0	0.0	0.0
23 Ethiopia	50.0	50.0	50.0	0.0	0.0	0.0
24 Gabon	33.0	33.0	33.0	0.0	0.0	0.0
25 Gambia	50.0	50.0	50.0	0.0	0.0	0.0
26 Ghana	48.0	48.0	48.0	0.0	0.0	0.0
27 Kenya	50.0	50.0	50.0	0.0	0.0	0.0

28	Liberia	50.0	50.0	50.0	0.0	0.0	0.0
29	Libya	48.0	48.0	48.0	0.0	0.0	0.0
30	Madagascar	48.0	48.0	48.0	0.0	0.0	0.0
31	Malawi	51.0	51.0	51.0	0.0	0.0	0.0
32	Mauritania	50.0	50.0	50.0	0.0	0.0	0.0
33	Mozambique	45.0	45.0	45.0	0.0	0.0	0.0
34	Rwanda	49.0	49.0	49.0	0.0	0.0	0.0
35	Zimbabwe	48.7	48.2	48.7	1.1	−1.1	0.0
36	Uganda	45.0	45.0	45.0	0.0	0.0	0.0
37	Cameroon	42.0	42.0	42.0	0.0	0.0	0.0
38	Tanzania	46.0	46.0	46.0	0.0	0.0	0.0
39	Upper Volta	50.0	50.0	50.0	0.0	0.0	0.0
40	Zaire	45.0	45.0	45.0	0.0	0.0	0.0
41	Zambia	49.0	49.0	49.0	0.0	0.0	0.0
42	Nigeria	49.1	49.8	49.3	−1.4	1.1	−0.3
43	Guinea-Big	40.1	40.3	40.4	−0.5	−0.3	−0.8
44	Somalia	47.3	47.7	47.7	−0.7	−0.2	−0.9
45	Namibia	44.4	44.6	45.0	−0.5	−0.9	−1.3
46	Lesotho	38.9	38.1	39.5	2.1	−3.8	−1.7
	Sub-total	46.9	47.1	46.1	−0.2	2.4	2.2
	Americas						
1	Argentina	25.2	22.4	25.0	11.1	−11.6	0.8
2	Bolivia	47.0	46.0	45.0	2.1	2.2	4.3
3	Brazil	45.3	41.5	32.0	8.4	22.9	29.4
4	Chile	35.2	32.8	22.2	6.7	32.3	36.9
5	Colombia	46.6	46.6	30.0	0.0	35.6	35.6
6	Costa Rica	47.6	41.1	31.1	13.6	24.3	34.6
7	Cuba	28.3	34.3	13.9	−21.2	59.5	50.9
8	Domin Rep	50.1	47.3	37.5	5.7	20.6	25.1
9	Ecuador	46.0	45.0	42.0	2.0	6.7	8.6
10	El Salvador	48.1	46.1	41.0	4.2	11.0	14.7
11	Guatemala	48.7	45.1	42.0	7.4	6.8	13.7
12	Guyana	42.9	39.9	28.3	7.0	29.1	34.0
13	Haiti	45.0	44.0	42.0	2.2	4.5	6.7
14	Honduras	50.0	50.0	46.9	0.0	6.2	6.2
15	Jamaica	34.8	38.5	27.0	−10.6	29.8	22.4

TABLE 1.4 (cont.)

	CBR 1950	CBR 1965	CBR 1980	% decline in CBR 1950–65	% decline in CBR 1965–80	% decline in CBR 1950–80
16 Mexico	46.6	43.7	34.0	6.2	22.3	27.1
17 Nicaragua	53.4	19.3	46.0	7.7	6.7	13.8
18 Panama	40.7	39.8	26.8	2.1	32.6	34.1
19 Paraguay	45.5	41.8	36.0	8.1	13.8	20.8
20 Peru	44.2	42.9	38.0	3.0	11.3	14.0
21 Puerto Rico	36.6	29.0	22.8	20.9	21.2	37.7
22 Trin and Tob	37.7	32.8	25.3	13.0	22.9	32.9
23 Uruguay	23.2	22.2	18.6	4.1	16.2	19.7
21 Venezuela	46.5	42.1	36.2	9.4	14.0	22.1
Sub-total	42.2	40.2	32.4	5.8	19.6	24.7
Asia and Pacific						
1 Afghanistan	50.0	50.0	48.5	0.0	3.0	3.0
2 Bangladesh	48.0	48.0	48.0	0.0	0.0	0.0
3 Bhutan	46.3	44.6	43.4	3.6	2.7	6.1
4 Burma	43.6	41.3	39.0	5.2	5.6	10.6
5 China	37.0	34.0	20.0	8.1	11.2	15.9
6 Cyprus	27.4	24.4	18.0	10.9	26.2	31.3
7 East Timor	47.0	45.8	44.2	2.6	3.5	6.0
8 Fiji	44.3	35.7	29.4	19.4	17.7	33.6
9 Hong Kong	33.1	28.3	17.0	14.5	40.0	48.7
10 India	42.3	42.6	36.0	-0.7	15.5	15.0
11 Indonesia	45.0	45.9	35.0	-2.0	23.7	22.2
12 Iran	48.0	45.9	45.0	4.3	2.0	6.2

13 Iraq	49.4	48.0	2.8	0.0	2.8	− 1.5
14 Jordan	45.4	48.0	46.1	−5.7	4.0	16.1
15 Kampuchea	45.4	44.4	38.1	2.2	14.2	11.9
16 Korea, N	37.0	39.1	31.5	−5.8	19.5	38.4
17 Korea, S	37.0	32.2	22.8	13.0	29.2	6.7
18 Kuwait	45.2	46.0	42.2	−1.6	8.2	4.6
19 Lao, PR	44.2	44.5	42.1	−0.7	5.3	26.8
20 Lebanon	41.0	41.0	30.0	0.0	26.8	34.6
21 Malaysia	45.4	42.2	29.7	7.1	29.6	5.5
22 Mongolia	40.0	41.6	37.8	−4.0	9.1	2.4
23 Nepal	46.1	44.7	45.0	3.0	−0.7	11.5
24 Pakistan	47.9	46.8	42.4	2.3	9.4	8.4
25 Papua N.G.	44.1	43.0	40.7	3.2	5.4	24.9
26 Philippines	45.3	44.2	34.0	2.4	23.1	1.7
27 Saudi Arabia	50.8	50.2	50.0	1.2	0.4	61.9
28 Singapore	44.4	29.4	16.9	33.7	42.6	29.4
29 Sri Lanka	38.5	33.1	27.2	14.0	17.8	0.3
30 Syria	46.5	47.6	46.4	−2.3	2.5	49.8
31 Taiwan	45.8	33.0	23.0	27.8	30.4	29.6
32 Thailand	46.9	44.3	33.0	5.5	25.5	42.4
33 Turkey	48.2	41.0	27.8	14.9	32.3	9.3
34 Vietnam, N	41.0	41.5	37.2	−1.2	10.4	—
35 Vietnam, S	41.3	41.5	—	−0.5	—	—
36 Yemen, N	47.0	47.0	47.0	0.0	0.0	0.0
37 Yemen, PDR	50.8	50.2	48.9	1.2	2.5	3.8
Sub-total	40.9	39.4	30.0	4.1	26.2	28.8
Total	41.8	40.5	32.6	3.7	22.3	24.9
World total	—	—	—	—	—	—

Source: Reproduced with permission from W. Parker Mauldin, "Levels, Trends and Prospects of Fertility in Developing Countries", a paper given at the 1983 Annual Meeting, Population Association of America, 14–16 April 1983.

for the questions at hand here. To know the exact population size would be like knowing whether 9 or 10 guests will come for dinner tomorrow. A host or hostess knows that the level of consumption will not be much affected by the difference between 9 and 10 guests. In the case of human populations, the "guests" have, in the recorded historical past, provided most of their own sustenance. In either case, the "host" has time to adjust to the additional numbers.

Additionally, children account for most of the variation among possible population sizes for the year 2000, because it takes almost 20 years to grow an adult. In poor countries, additional children mostly affect only their own families. There is at present no empirical research that can test this point of view with respect to resources only. But if more people were to mean increasingly strained resources, the effects would necessarily appear in studies of the relationship of population growth to changes in the standard of living. Here there is an impressive body of data, which has been summarized recently by Ronald D. Lee in a review commissioned by the International Union for the Scientific Study of Population (Lee, 1983, p. 54):

> [D]ozens of studies, starting with Kuznets' (1967), have found no association between the population growth rate (n) and per capita income growth rate ($\dot{y}/y$), despite the obvious fact that at least since WWII, population growth rates have varied considerably (Chesnais and Sauvy, 1973; Isbister, 1975; Thirlwall, 1972; for example). These studies control for other factors such as trade, aid and investment to varying degrees. Two recent studies add historical depth to this analysis (Bairoch, 1981, and Browning, 1982); even within countries (and thus looking *only* at disequilibrium), over periods as long as a century or as short as 25 years, there is no significant association of n and $\dot{y}/y$, for either DCs or LDCs; put differently, one can't reject the hypothesis that the regression coefficient of $\dot{y}/y$ on n is unity. I know of just two exceptions to this general picture: the studies by Hazeldine and Moreland (1977) and Suits and Mason (1978), both dealing with cross-sections; both find negative effects of population growth of magnitude roughly equal to the share of non-labor inputs in production, as many theories would predict. However, data problems render these results suspect.

The empirical evidence thus indicates no negative correlation between the rate of population growth and the standard of living, and by logical extension, no negative effect upon the state of natural resource availability.

Conclusion

My perspective on the present world's population and its growth in numbers in the next few decades is quite different from that of *Global 2000*. Certainly it is a problem to sustain many billions of people, a problem for each human to sustain himself and his/her own family. But the growth in numbers over the millennia from a few thousands or millions of humans living at low subsistence, to billions living well above subsistence, is a most positive assurance that the problem of sustenance has eased rather than grown more difficult with the years. The trend in population size by itself should suggest cheer rather than gloom.

Even more conclusive are the trends in mortality and life expectancy. After millennia of agonizingly slow increase in length of life, there has come in the now-developed countries within the last century or two, breathtaking tripling of life expectancy at birth; table 1.1 showed this for the case of France; and in the essay by Johnson, chapter 2 in this volume, there are data showing that since World War II, life expectancy in the poorer countries has leaped at a rate that must astound anyone, and must give confidence to those who respect humanity.

In brief, the latest *Global 2000* population forecasts have already been shown to be faulty. But even if they had been sound, they would not be grounds for a hysterical concern regarding the balance between population and the environment.

Note

I appreciate helpful criticisms and suggestions by the editors.

References

Ascher, William. *Forecasting: An Appraisal for Policy-Makers and Planners*, Baltimore: Johns Hopkins Press, 1978.
Baum, Samuel. "Global 2000 population projections reappraised." (Mimeo); a paper presented to the annual meeting of the American Association for the Advancement of Science, 3–8 January 1982, Washington D.C., p. 14.
Council on Environmental Quality and the Department of State. *The Global 2000 Report to the President*. Washington, D.C.: GPO, 1980.
Keyfitz, Nathan. *Population Change and Social Policy*. Cambridge: Abt Books, 1982.
Lee, Ronald. "Economic consequences of population size, structure and growth", [*International Union for the Scientific Study of Population*] Newsletter 17 (January 1983), 43–59.
Lee, W. R. *European Demography and Economic Growth*. New York: St. Martin's Press, 1979.
Mauldin, W. Parker, "Levels, trends and prospects of fertility in developing countries." (Mimeo); a paper delivered to the 1983 Population Association of America.
Morgenstern, Oskar. *On the Accuracy of Economic Observations,* Princeton: Princeton University Press, 1950, 1953.
Notestein, Frank *et al.* *The Future Population of Europe and the Soviet Union: Population Projections 1940–1970*, Geneva: League of Nations, 1944.
Notestein, Frank W. "Demography in the United States: A Partial Account of the Development of the Field," *Pop. Dev. Rev.*, **8** (December 1982), 651–87.
Perlman, Mark. "*Population and Economic Change in Developing Countries*: A review article, *J. Econ. Lit.*, **19** (March 1981), 74–82.
Statistics Canada, memo on the Projection of Population Statistics, Ottawa: Dominion Bureau of Statistics, 1954.
Tilly, Charles (ed.) *Historical Studies of Changing Fertility*. Princeton: Princeton University Press, 1978.
United Nations. *The Future Growth of World Population*, Population Studies No. 28, New York: United Nations Press, 1958.
——, *World Population Prospects as Assessed in 1963*, Population Studies No. 41, New York: United Nations Press, 1966.
——, *World Population Prospects as Assessed in 1968*, Population Studies No. 53, New York: United Nations Press, 1973.

——, *World Population Trends and Policies, 1977 Monitoring Report*, Volume 1, *Population Trends*, Population Studies, No. 62, New York: U.N., 1979.

U.S. Bureau of the Census, *Projections of the Population of the Communist Countries of Eastern Europe, by Age and Sex, 1965–1985*, J. L. Scott. International Population Reports, Series P-91, no. 14, Washington D.C.: Government Printing Office, 1965.

——, *Population Estimates and Projections: Projections of the Population of the United States; 1975 to 2050*, Current Population Reports, Series P-25, no. 601. Washington, D.C.: Government Printing Office, 1975.

EDITORS' APPENDIX

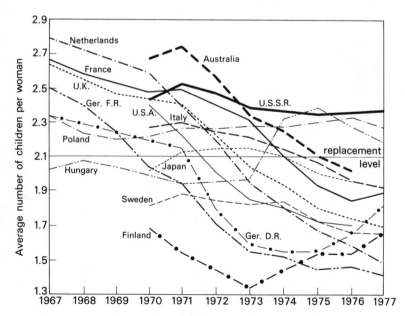

Figure 1.1 Fertility and the replacement level in developed countries.

Mark Perlman

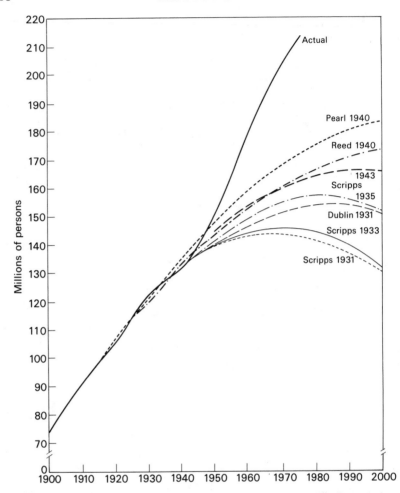

Figure 1.2 U.S. population forecasts made 1931–43, and the actual population.

2

World Food and Agriculture

D. GALE JOHNSON

Prospective developments in world food supply and demand continue to be of great importance in a world in which almost half of the population lives in countries that had less than $420 gross national product per capita in 1980. In these countries most families allocate from 50 to 70 percent of their incomes to the acquisition of food. Most of the world's poor live in rural areas and are directly or indirectly involved in the production of food and other agricultural products.

The access to food by a family has now become primarily dependent upon the family's income and not upon the availability of food to be purchased. This is a major change that has occurred over the past three or four decades. It is a change that needs to be recognized in designing efforts to improve the nutritional levels of the world's poor. In the past three decades a world food system has been created. This system is now capable of making food available to almost every person in the world. This was impossible just a few years ago.

My assignment is to review the major trends in world food production, trade and prices for the past several decades and to indicate how future trends are likely to be related to the past trends. It is, of course, not always easy to discern what trends are actually prevailing. During the past two decades there were two occasions when fears were expressed that world food supplies would be insufficient to prevent wide-scale suffering and loss of life. One such period was the early and mid-1960s; the second came during the early 1970s. One objective of this effort is to explore the major reasons why the production, trade and price developments after 1972 did not result in a deterioration in the world food situation but actually provided for some modest improvement for the world's poor people.

More important than what has happened in the past, however, is the prospective course of events for the future. A number of reasons may be given for anticipating that it is likely to be difficult to increase food production at a rate at least equal to the growth of demand and to do so at reasonable prices. But I hope to show that the reasons that have been given are not weighty enough to result in declining adequacy of the food supply or in rising real prices of food. On the contrary, the prospects for the long run are in the direction of continuing gradual declines in the real prices of the primary sources of calories for poor people.

Some Recent Views

Anyone who is at all observant knows that there is significant disagreement about the current state of the world food system. Estimates of the number of seriously malnourished persons in the world range from a billion or more to a few tens of millions (Poleman, 1982). With such uncertainty existing about the current situation, it is not surprising that there are equal or greater differences in views concerning expected developments for the next decade or the remainder of the century. It is not my intent to review in detail the projections of trends in the demand and supply of food. I shall, however, present a range of views to provide the flavor of the existing state of opinion on these matters.

I have no intention of concealing what I believe; namely that the weight of the evidence supports the following points:

(1)   There has been modest improvement in food supplies per capita in the low-income countries of the world during the past three decades.

(2)   The real prices of the major sources of calories for poor people – the grains – have declined in recent decades rather than increased, and at the present time the real international prices for grains, vegetable oils, and sugar are at or near all-time low levels.

(3)   International trade in grain has grown rapidly during the past decade, but the low-income countries have not been a significant source of the import growth as had been feared at the time of the World Food Conference.

(4)   It is reasonable to expect that the international prices of grains and vegetable oils will remain at historically low, and perhaps declining, levels for the next one or two decades.

(5)   Resources are available that would permit increasing the rate of growth of per capita food production in the developing countries.

(6)   A world food system has evolved over the past three decades that has substantially reduced the risks of food shortages, famine and hunger resulting from natural disasters, and by the end of this century nearly every person in the world could have access to the world food system if that person has adequate income to purchase the food that is available; at present a much larger percentage of

the world's people could be participants in the world food system than is now the case if governments did not intervene in the movement of food.

Patrick O'Brien of the U.S. Department of Agriculture is the primary custodian of the USDA Grain-Oilseed-Livestock (GOL) Model. In an article published in 1981 he summarized the results of his analysis as follows (p. 20):

> Should this prognosis prove correct, the early eighties will bring two fundamental changes in the U.S. agriculture. First, annual increases in foreign and domestic demand due to population and income growth will be greater, on average, than the increases in productive capacity due to resource expansion and productivity gains. The real prices received by farmers – given normal weather – should increase; scenarios generated using several longrun equilibrium simulation models suggest real price increases of 1 to 3 percent per year, compared with declines averaging 1 to 2 percent per year for the postwar period to date. Moreover, if the gains in capacity in the early eighties due to productivity and resource growth are more than offset by the losses in capacity resulting from unit cost increases and increasingly stringent environmental constraints, the real prices associated with the output needed to balance foreign and domestic demand could be substantially higher.

The time period to which the annual real price increases of 1 to 3 percent are to apply is the first half of the 1980s. The tightening of the demand–supply relationship referred to clearly has not occurred by early 1983.

John Mellor, Director of the International Food Policy Research Institute, has accepted the view that real food prices are likely to increase during the 1980s. In November 1981 he stated (IFPRI):

> [I]n commenting on the global food situation, I want to present a somewhat different picture from the standard one of the last few years. Third World countries will increase their food imports in the next few decades by so much that they themselves will bring about tight global supplies and rising real food prices.
>
> This situation is the result of rapidly rising real incomes. I think it is important to keep in mind that this income growth is what will dictate the food problem in the next few decades. Currently, some 700 million people in Third World Countries are experiencing an extraordinary 4 per cent or more growth rate of per capita income. That is more rapid growth than Europe was able to sustain in the post-World War II recovery period. The portion of the population

sharing in this rapid growth could easily double in the next few years.

Demand for food in these countries is growing at 4–6 percent a year. I am talking about effective demand – what people are able and willing to pay – and about rates of growth of demand that are rarely exceeded, even in countries that have good agricultural research systems and are following optimal agricultural development policies.

It is reasonable to conclude that the rapidly growing middle-income developing countries will increase their grain and food imports in the years ahead. As an aside, it is rather interesting that the source of the growth of demand for imports is now said to be the middle-income developing countries and not, as was the case less than a decade ago, low-income countries such as India and Pakistan. But as I will show later, some of the sources of rapid growth of food imports during the 1970s are likely to show much slower growth during the 1980s.

In the latter part of this chapter I shall comment in detail on the food and agriculture projections presented in *Global 2000*. That report paints a very gloomy picture of the future food supply situation for the world, giving emphasis to the view that the real price of food is likely to increase significantly by the end of this century. *Global 2000* states that the world's food situation is likely to deteriorate significantly by the end of this century. My objective is to show that the food situation has improved in recent years and that it will continue to improve in the years ahead if governments of the world follow appropriate policies.

Before presenting my own views, however, I want to call attention to a major report on the prospective food situation for the remainder of this century, a report that was first presented in November 1979 well before *Global 2000* was completed. *Agriculture: Toward 2000* was prepared by the United Nations Food and Agriculture Organization. *Agriculture: Toward 2000* supports the view that the trend in food supplies for the developing countries is a positive one and, furthermore, with appropriate actions that significant improvements are possible by 2000.

Things are improving slowly scenario

I classify the major report of the UN Food and Agriculture Organization *Agriculture: Toward 2000* (1981) as falling in the "Things are Improving Slowly Scenario." This is my classification, not FAO's, and FAO might mildly object. But the report indicates that if recent trends are continued per capita food supplies in the 90 developing countries would increase by almost 9 percent between 1980 and 2000 and that increases of 15–20 percent in per capita food consumption could be achieved. While gross cereal imports of the developing countries are projected to increase from 86 million tons in 1980 to from 146 to 220 million tons, trend agricultural production would be at an annual rate of 2.8 percent compared to a trend projection of demand of 2.9 percent. The difference between 2.8 percent and 2.9 percent is so small that the increase in cereal imports would more than provide for the production shortfall. Net cereal imports have trend values for 2000 of 165 million tons (exports of 61 million tons).

The trend analysis provides this striking conclusion:

A continuation of production and demand trends world-wide implies large global surpluses in some commodities, despite the growing millions of seriously undernourished, and deficits in other, mainly livestock products. Thus the net surplus of cereals of the developed countries would tend to stand at 213 million tons at a time when the developing countries would have a deficit of 165 million tons. Projected net availabilities from the developing countries of such competing products as sugar, citrus fruit and vegetable oils and oilseeds would substantially outstrip import demand in the developed countries, whose continued protectionism would limit severely any expansion in their imports of these products.

All in all, the tendency is for global surpluses worth roughly $20 billion 1975. The developed countries as a group would tend to become a substantial net agricultural exporter, growing exports from their cereals and livestock sectors would not be offset by similar expansions in imports of other commodities, either competing or tropical.

At the same time, the trend is for the developing countries to have production balances sufficient to maintain their position as net agricultural exporters although their overall agricultural trade surplus would continue to decline. But this outcome implies that their net exports to the developed countries of competing and noncompeting tropical products increase sufficiently to offset increases in the imports of cereals and livestock products, and this is contrary to the projected import trends of developed countries. Obviously, therefore, the trend projections of the developed and developing countries are incompatible.

The projected imbalances will not actually materialize; spontaneous or policy-induced adjustments will bring balance. The policy issue is how orderly adjustments can be brought about. They should increase rather than reduce trade – the developing countries should be able to import and consume more of the cereals produced in the developed countries and help to pay for them with increased exports of the commodities they are best suited to produce. Such an evolution would eliminate the irony in the situation of a world afflicted with under-nutrition, but where there is a danger of global surpluses.

The seriousness of the deterioration in the production and import trends of developing countries comes out most strongly in the self-sufficiency ratios (SSRs) for cereals, their major agricultural import. For every region and every income category of developing countries this deterioration holds. In Latin America and the Far East, the decline is only 3 to 4 percent, but with an SSR for 1980 put equal to 100, the year 2000 index is 87 for the Near East and only 74 for Africa. For low-income countries, the index falls to 93, while for the least developed group of countries it is barely 80.

The most optimistic aspect of the FAO report, however, consists of the outlines of feasible alternatives to the trend projections. Either of the major alternatives, if realized, would permit significant further improvement in income growth, agricultural output, per capita food supplies, a reduction in cereal imports and an increase in the net surplus in agricultural trade for the 90 developing countries. The two scenarios that were developed indicate that annual agricultural output growth rates for the low-income developing countries could be increased from the 2.7 percent to 3.1–3.8 percent.[1] For the 41 low-income developing countries the scenario that could result in a 3.1 percent annual growth of agricultural production would provide an increase in calories sufficient to increase per capita consumption from 89 percent of average requirements for 1974–76 to 103 percent in 2000; if agricultural output grew at the trend rate of 2.7 percent there would have been significant nutritional improvements and caloric intake would reach 97 percent of average requirement.

I do not want to imply that *Agriculture: Toward 2000* provides a basis for complacency; it was certainly not so intended by its authors. But the report can, and I believe should, be interpreted as indicating that the resources – physical and human – exist to provide for a significant improvement in the nutritional status for the vast majority of the population of the developing countries. Even with the trend projections of agricultural production and incomes the percentage of the population of the developing countries (excluding China) classified as "seriously undernourished" would decline from 23 percent in 1975 to 17 percent in 2000. However, with the scenario providing for modest improvement over trend the percentage malnourished in 2000 would decline to 11 percent and with the more optimistic scenario the decline would be to 7 percent.

I want to emphasize that those of us who are cautiously optimistic about the continued improvement in the consumption levels of most of the poor people of the world do not believe there is any room for complacency. If circumstances are to improve, it is because efforts are made to make the improvement occur and at least some of the hindrances that exist, such as trade restrictions, low farm prices due to governmental constraints, and inadequate provision of farm inputs, are ameliorated. Thus to say that things are going to get better does not mean that this will be the outcome if nothing is done; what it means is that with the resources devoted to food production, and with the policies that are likely to be followed, improvement is likely to occur. Under more appropriate circumstances, the rate of improvement could be increased. The two alternative scenarios presented in *Agriculture: Toward 2000* indicate what is possible with added effort and modest policy changes.

The recent past

During the 1960s and 1970s the developing countries as a group had a modest improvement in per capita food supplies. However, according to FAO estimates the increase from 1961–65 to 1974–76 was only 3 percent for the period and was unevenly distributed among the developing countries (FAO, 1981). The 41 countries with per capita gross domestic product of less than $300 (1975) had constant per capita supplies of calories while the middle-income developing countries (all others) had an increase of just 7 percent.

For the developing world per capita food production increased by 14 percent between 1951–53 and 1979–81 (USDA, 1981). This represents a quite modest rate of growth of 0.46 percent. However, the growth rate for total food production looks very impressive at 2.89 percent annually. This compares to an output growth rate of food production in the developed market economies of 2.1 percent. Given the subsidies provided for the agricultures of the developed countries the performance of the agricultures of the developing countries looks good, indeed.

The modest growth in food production per capita for the developing world reflects the very poor performance of Africa for three decades and the very slow growth in South Asia during the 1970s. Africa had a constant average level of per capita food production during the 1950s and 1960s and a shocking decline during the 1970s. In 1980 per capita food production in Africa (excluding South Africa) was 15 percent below 1969–71. Total food production increased 10 percent while population grew by about 25 percent, resulting in an unprecedented decline in per capita food production. The decline in per capita food production was not due to a lack of resources but to many factors that were primarily political in nature – the exploitation of farmers through low prices, civil unrest, military conflict and the creation of millions of refugees.

The only slightly better recent performance of South Asia compared to Africa may be a greater source of concern. There are many more people

D. Gale Johnson

in South Asia than in Africa, and there are relatively limited potentials for further land developments in South Asia while Africa has significant potentials for land development. Consequently most of the increased output of food in South Asia must come from higher yields per unit of land. This is not entirely unfortunate since the experience of the last three decades in the industrial countries, as well as in some of the developing countries, has indicated that expanding output through higher yields costs less than bringing new land into cultivation.

But perhaps the best indicator of the improved state of nutrition and health has been the continuing increase in life expectancy among all of the developing regions and at all national income levels. In fact, the data on life expectancy cast some doubts that the improvements in per capita food supplies and nutrition were as modest as the aggregate food data indicate, and may cast even greater doubts on the estimated declines in, and low level of, per capita food consumption in many African countries. Table 2.1 compares changes in life expectancies for groups of countries for the years from 1950 to 1978. Low-income countries had less than $360 per capita gross national product in 1978 and had a population of 1.29 billion; the middle-income developing countries had a population of 873 million.

The largest absolute increase in life expectancy at birth between 1950 and 1978 occurred in the low-income countries. The increase was 14.7 years and in 1978 the life expectancy in these countries was nearly 50 years and at about the same level as the middle-income developing countries were in 1950.

The World Bank has presented estimates of life expectancy for African countries as of mid-1979 for different regions and country income levels. These data, presented in table 2.2 are compared with developing countries generally and with specific developing countries. Life expectancy in Sub-Saharan Africa is somewhat lower than for all low-income developing countries (excluding Centrally Planned Economies); but the difference is not very large – 47 years for all of Sub-Saharan Africa and 50

TABLE 2.1 LIFE EXPECTANCY AT BIRTH, 1950, 1960 AND 1978 (IN YEARS)

	1950	1960	1978	Increase, 1950–78
Industrialized countries	66.0	69.4	73.5	7.5
Middle-income countries	51.9	54.0	61.0	9.1
Low-income countries	35.2	41.9	49.9	14.7
Centrally planned economies[a]	62.3	67.1	69.9	7.6

Note: [a] Excludes China.
Source: World Bank, *World Development Report, 1980,* p. 34.

TABLE 2.2 LIFE EXPECTANCY AT BIRTH, AFRICAN AND OTHER DEVELOPING COUNTRIES, 1960 AND 1979

Country group	Life expectancy			GNP per capita 1979 (U.S. dollars)	Index of per capita food production 1977–9 (1969–71 = 100)	Daily calorie supply per capita, 1977	
	1960	1979	Increase			Calories	Percentage of requirement
Africa[a]							
Low-income	38	46	8	239	91	2,040	91
Low-income, semi-arid	37	43	6	187	88	1,992	89
Low-income, other	39	47	8	247	91	2,086	93
Middle-income oil importers	41	50	9	532	95	2,180	97
Middle-income oil exporters	39	48	9	669	86	1,970	89
Sub-Saharan Africa	–	47	–	411	91	–	–
Selected low-income countries	42	50	8	200	97	2,052	91
India	43	51	8	180	100	2,021	91
Bangladesh	40	47	7	90	90	1,812	78
Developing countries by per capita income							
Less than $390	42	50	8				
$390–1,050	46	55	9				
$1,060–2,000	47	64	7				
$2,040–3,500	65	71	6				

Note: [a] Excludes South Africa.
Source: World Bank publications.

for all low-income developing countries. Higher per capita incomes in Africa do not, as yet, seem to bring as large an increase in life expectancy as the same income differentials do in other regions.

Current estimates of hunger and malnutrition

How much hunger and malnutrition is there in the world? There is no reasonable precise or generally accepted answer to this question. As noted above, the estimates of the seriously malnourished range from more than a billion to a few tens of millions. *Global 2000*, however, refers to only one of the several available estimates, thus apparently implying that the figures presented were a reasonable indication of the current and prospective situation. Robert MacNamara, then President of the World Bank, was quoted as having stated that the number of malnourished persons in the LDCs "could increase from the current figure (400–600 million) to as many as 1,300 million by the year 2000" (p. 275). While quoting this statement, apparently with approval, *Global 2000* does not present its own estimate of the number of malnourished currently or in the future.

In fact, the projections of per capita food consumption in the LDCs presented in *Global 2000* do not support the view that the nutritional situation is likely to deteriorate by the end of the century. The most pessimistic of the scenarios projects that for all LDCs the daily per capita caloric intake in 2000 would be the same as in 1969–71 at an average of 94 percent of FAO standards. Under the most optimistic scenario a significant improvement in per capita caloric food intake is indicated, with the average for all LDCs increasing to 104 percent of the FAO standard by 2000. Each of the major regions was projected to have improved food supplies, except for Africa other than North Africa. But there is not the slightest shred of evidence that the continued poor performance of food and agriculture in most of Africa is in any way related to resource restraints. The issue of political constraints that result in enormous exploitation of agriculture was wholly ignored by *Global 2000*.

Returning to the question of how many people or what percentage of the world's population is malnourished, much, much more work is required before we can have an answer. In recent papers by T. N. Srinivasan (1982) and Thomas T. Poleman (1982) it is argued that there is little analytical or factual basis for the existing estimates of the number of malnourished people. FAO, on the basis of the Fourth World Food Survey (1977) estimates that, in the developing countries (excluding China), 455 million people have an insufficient protein-energy supply; World Bank estimates vary but range from 600 million to more than 1,000 million.

Srinivasan (1982) argued that the estimates of hunger and under-nutrition by the FAO and the World Bank have very little scientific basis. He reaches this conclusion on the basis of the faulty methodology of the estimation, the most serious fault being lack of recognition "that human beings can and do vary their intakes within limits without any deleterious consequences to their health and activity" (p. 35). The other major point is that many individuals deemed malnourished by their energy intake relative to some requirement are often not malnourished by clinical and biomedical assessment. Srinivasan's argument is brought home to me by remembering that during and after World War II the caloric intakes of the Japanese people fell short of FAO's standard at the time.

Poleman takes a different approach. He argues that malnutrition exists primarily among two groups of people – children under 5 years of age and pregnant and lactating mothers. Assuming that 50 percent of all members of these two groups suffered from nutritional deficiency in 1975, for all developing countries (excluding China) the number of individuals affected was about 240 million or approximately one half of the FAO estimate and only a quarter of the higher World Bank estimate. If only 10 percent of the vulnerable groups are malnourished, the number of malnourished in 1975 would have been 62 million.

Earlier I referred to the substantial increase in life expectancy that has occurred in the developing countries during the past three decades. These rapid increases convince me that the percentage of the population of the developing countries that have suffered from hunger or malnutrition has been gradually declining. In addition, the incidence of famine has diminished radically over the past century (Johnson, 1970). Even though the world's population is now almost three times what it was a century ago, the absolute number of famine deaths in the most recent quarter-century was almost certainly less than during the last quarter of the nineteenth century. Most of the famines that have occurred during the past quarter-century have resulted from war, civil strife or refusal of governments to act in time to provide famine relief. Unavailability of food is no longer an important source of famine; the famines that do occur result primarily from man's inhumanity to man, not from a hostile nature.

Post-1972 developments affecting world food

The information brought together in the previous section indicates that for most of the low-income countries of the world food supplies and nutrition improved during the 1970s. Such improvement was contrary to the widely expressed views that developments in food demand, supply, costs and prices opened a new era of scarcity and human suffering, with the latter to be on an unparalleled scale. There was talk of the necessity of triage with respect to access to the world's food supply, and of the overcrowded lifeboat analogy as though the world's capacity to produce food were fixed.

The summary of an article published in *Science* (12 December 1975) stated quite accurately what was the "conventional wisdom" of the day as perceived by most of the media organizations:

> The scarcity of basic resources required to expand food output, the negative ecological trends that are gaining momentum year by year in the poor countries, and the diminishing returns on the use of energy and fertilizer in agriculture in the industrial countries lead me to conclude that a world of cheap, abundant food with surplus stocks and a large reserve of idled cropland may now be history. In the future, scarcity may be more or less persistent, relieved only by sporadic surpluses of a local and short-lived nature. The prospects are that dependence on North America will be likely to continue to increase, the increase probably being limited only by the region's export capacity.

What happened during the last half of the 1970s and the early 1980s that negated, at least up to now, the gloomy prediction just presented? It is to this matter that I now turn. I shall consider first price trends of the 1970s and for earlier periods, in some cases for the years since 1910.

Price trends

In 1972 and 1973 there were numerous predictions or projections that the world was faced with a sharp reversal of the declining trend in the prices of the major food products. Lester Brown, among others, believed that a new price era had emerged: "Food prices are likely to remain considerably higher than they were during the past decade." Such a conclusion as this could be described as the "conventional wisdom"; the dissenters from this view received little notice from either the media or the policy-makers.

It is essential to view trends and patterns of agricultural prices from a number of different perspectives. One perspective is to view prices from the relatively long run; in our case the availability of data on prices received by American farmers permits such a review for somewhat more than a century. Most of the time, except for sugar, the prices of U.S. farm products have been reasonable approximations of international market prices. Following the presentation of the long-run data, data for export prices of major sources of calories are presented, with primary emphasis on the period since 1950 though some data are given for wheat and corn back to 1910. Actual prices are not presented; instead all of the prices have been converted to 1967 dollars by dividing actual prices by the U.S.

wholesale price index with 1967 equal to 100. In this way we have eliminated most of the effects of inflation that distort the impression that one otherwise obtains from viewing price data for long time periods.

The first set of price charts, figures 2.1–2.7, are for crops.[2] All prices are in 1967$. Even when the effects of inflation and deflation are removed, the price charts reveal very wide price variability. Declines of 50 percent or increases of 100 percent occur within 5-year periods. However, our main purpose is not to display price variability but to display long-run trends. The charts for crop prices indicate that prices have declined over the past century. This has certainly been true for wheat, rice, barley, and sugar cane. Both corn and cotton prices appear to have had a slow upward trend from 1870 to about 1945, interrupted by quite low prices during the 1920s and 1930s, but with sharply falling real prices since the mid-1940s. Both corn and cotton prices appear to have returned to their historically low prices.

The second group of price charts, numbers 2.8 through 2.12, are for livestock and poultry products. Again, the charts reflect large short-term price variability. The differences in trends are striking, both with the group and compared to the crop products. The price trend for the century for hogs and cattle is positive – real prices have increased. Hog prices have increased at an annual rate of about 0.55 percent while cattle prices have increased by 0.7 percent. An annual rate of increase of 0.7 percent results in a doubling in a century. Milk prices have also increased during the last seven decades.

The two most striking price charts are for chicken and egg prices (figures 2.11 and 2.12). Their real prices increased from 1870 through 1945 and then started a remarkable and sharp decline. From the mid-

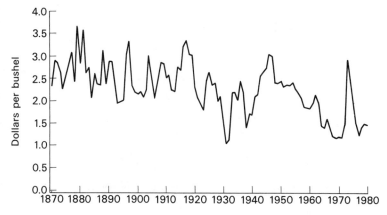

Figure 2.1 Wheat prices received by farmers (deflated by 1967 = 100 W.P.I.)

D. Gale Johnson

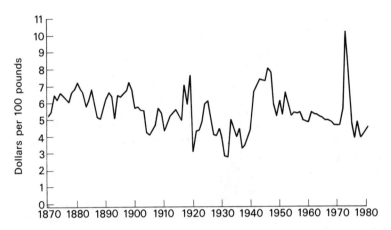

Figure 2.2 Rice prices received by farmers (deflated by 1967 = 100 W.P.I.).

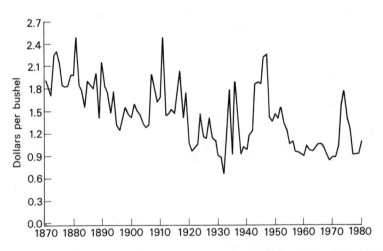

Figure 2.3 Barley prices received by farmers (deflated by 1967 = 100 W.P.I.).

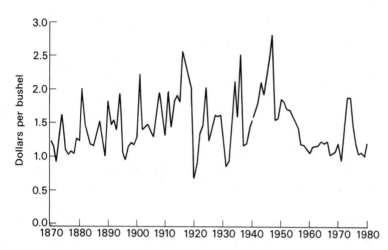

Figure 2.4 Corn prices received by farmers (deflated by 1967 = 100 W.P.I.).

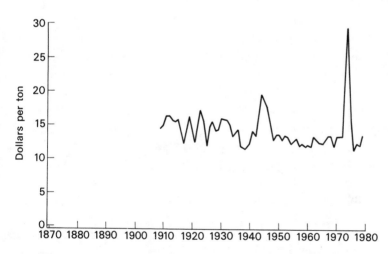

Figure 2.5 Sugar beet prices received by farmers (deflated by
1967 = 100 W.P.I.)

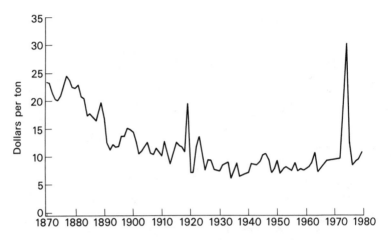

Figure 2.6 Sugar cane prices received by farmers
(deflated by 1967 = W.P.I.)

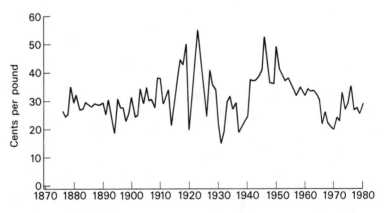

Figure 2.7 Cotton prices received by farmers (deflated by 1967 = 100 W.P.I.)
(series revised 1945).

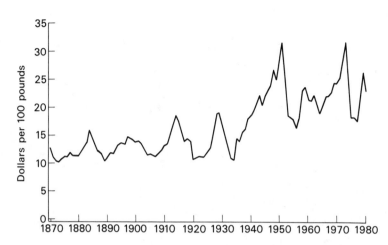

Figure 2.8 Beef cattle prices received by farmers
(deflated by 1967 = 100 W.P.I.)

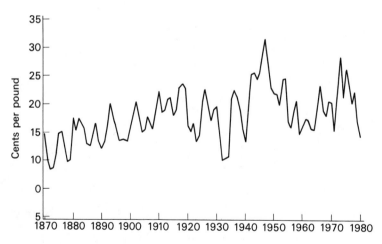

Figure 2.9 Hog prices received by farmers (deflated by 1967 = 100 W.P.I.).

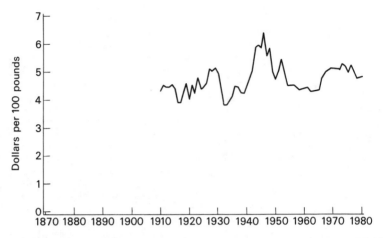

Figure 2.10 Milk prices received by farmers (deflated by 1967 = 100 W.P.I.).

Figure 2.11 Chicken prices received by farmers
(deflated by 1967 = 100 W.P.I.)

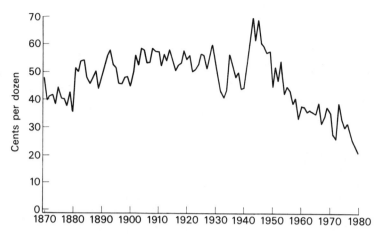

Figure 2.12   Egg prices received by farmers (deflated by 1967 = 100 W.P.I.).

1940s chicken prices fell by almost 90 percent by 1980, while egg prices declined by 70 percent. When I was a boy, chicken was considered the luxury meat to be eaten only on Sunday. Today it is by far the cheapest of the meats. The scientific and management successes that have made it possible so strikingly to reduce the costs of producing poultry and eggs can only be described as remarkable.

Figures 2.13–2.16 present real prices that reflect international market prices for important food commodities. Figures 2.13 and 2.14 give wheat and corn prices, based on U.S. real export unit values, starting with 1910 for selected periods and annually since 1960. Figures 2.15 and 2.16 give the real price for two other important sources of calories, namely soy oil and sugar, since 1950. The soy oil price reflects international prices quite accurately and also reflects quite closely the prices of all important vegetable oils that are used for food. Figure 2.17 includes the deflated export unit values for cotton. In many parts of the world the production of cotton is competitive with the production of cereal crops; in addition, of course, the price and cost of cotton is important as a component of living costs for low-income families in most areas of the world.

The figures show the pattern of prices of numerous farm products compared to the average of all prices in the economy at the wholesale level. As is clear, the prices of the major grains and poultry and egg products have declined relatively to wholesale prices for recent decades. What these comparisons show is how much more (or less) of a farm product can be bought with a dollar of a given base year, such as 1967.

86 *D. Gale Johnson*

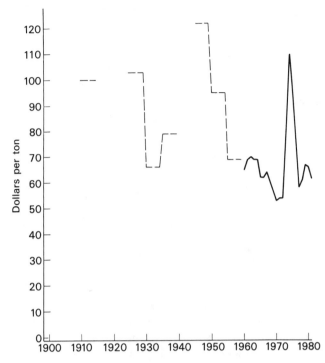

Figure 2.13 U.S. wheat export prices, selected years 1910–81 (deflated by 1967 = 100 W.P.I.).

There is another comparison that shows an even more striking picture of the combined effects of improved productivity in agriculture and rising real wages over time. This comparison is shown in figure 2.18, which shows the price of wheat deflated or divided by the average wage rate in the United States since 1800. Over the past century the quantity of wheat that could be purchased with a day's wages has increased by approximately five times.

The price trends we have presented are for commodities that are traded internationally in significant amounts. The real prices were generally lower or the same at the end of the 1970s and the beginning of the 1980s than at the beginning of the 1970s. One possible explanation of such trends could be that international trade in these products lagged or was actually less at the end of the decade than at the beginning. Such an explanation has no validity – trade in grain nearly doubled, as did the trade in soybeans. In spite of the trade restrictions that limit international trade in sugar, trade increased by a quarter during the decade. World trade in

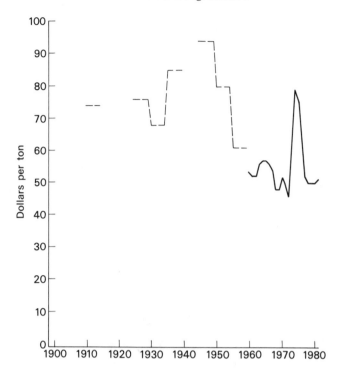

Figure 2.14 U.S. corn export prices, selected years 1910–81 (deflated by 1967 = 100 W.P.I.).

vegetable oils more than doubled, increasing by 148 percent from 1969–70 to 1979–80 (from 4.4 million to 10.9 million tons).

The real prices of four of the five agricultural products reached peak levels for the 1960s and 1970s in 1974; cotton was the exception, reaching its peak real price in 1977. It is worthy of note, though, that even the high prices of 1974, which were up by 70 percent or more from the levels of the early 1970s, were of the same order for wheat and corn as the real prices of the late 1920s and below the 1945–9 prices.

For the four commodities that reached peak prices in 1974, price declines occurred suddenly and dramatically. The real price of wheat fell by almost half in 3 years, corn by more than a third in 4 years, sugar by 80 percent in 4 years, and soy oil by more than half in 2 years. The prices of the mid-1970s that were thought to represent a new and higher level very soon declined to the levels of the early 1970s. Thus the price experience of the late 1970s and the early 1980s has not borne out the expectation that the real costs of food products were going to increase significantly after the mid-1970s.

88   *D. Gale Johnson*

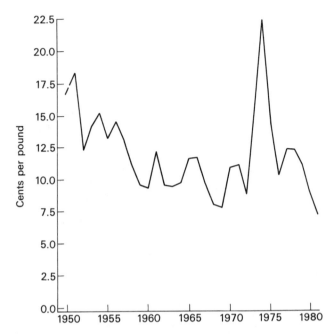

Figure 2.15 Decatur soy oil prices, 1950–81 (deflated by 1967 = 100 W.P.I.).

Cotton prices exhibited greater price stability during the 1970s than did any of the four food products. The peak of real prices was not reached until 1977, the year that was the low point for wheat and nearly so for the other three products; and the 1977 peak was 55 percent over the 1970 low.

It should come as no surprise that cotton prices were the most stable and sugar prices were the most unstable. Of the five commodities cotton was least subject to protection and governmental intervention, and sugar was the most protected and interfered with. According to estimates made by Valdes and Zietz (1980) wheat was the most protected of the remaining three, and corn the least. Wheat prices were significantly more unstable than corn prices, though less unstable than soy oil. With the exception of soy oil, the instability of the prices of the other four products was consistent with expectations derived from the degree of protection and governmental intervention in the markets.

One of the important sources of price instability is governmental intervention. In particular, where governments stabilize domestic prices of food products, they contribute to international price instability. They do so by preventing their own producers and consumers from reacting to

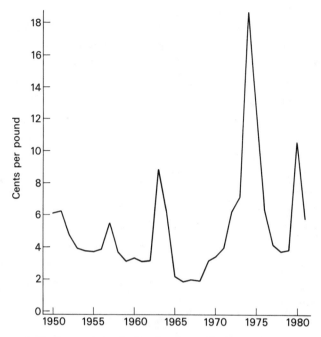

Figure 2.16 Raw sugar wholesale prices, Caribbean ports, 1950–81
(deflated by 1967 = 100 W.P.I.)

changes in world supply and demand conditions and all of the adjustment must be made in that part of the world market where consumers and producers react to the same prices as those prevailing in the world market or prices that vary to some degree with the world prices (Johnson, 1975a).

The translation from current prices to deflated or real dollars has been through the use of the U.S. wholesale price index. Some may question the validity of this index as a measure of the prices confronting the developing countries. The World Bank publishes data on the prices of farm and mineral products as well as of farm inputs such as fertilizer. The World Bank uses the c.i.f. measure of unit values of imports of manufactured products by the developing countries from the developed countries as a deflator. This index increased much more rapidly between 1967 and 1977 than did the U.S. wholesale price index – the World Bank index increased to 243 while the wholesale price index was 193. The use of the World Bank index of manufactured goods prices would have reduced the real prices of U.S. farm products by 20 percent, compared to the use of the U.S. wholesale price index.

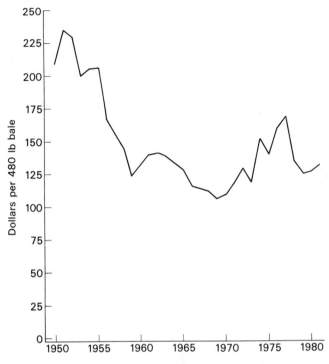

Figure 2.17 U.S. Cotton export prices, 1950–81
(deflated by 1967 = 100 W.P.I.)

In table 2.3 the index of the export unit values of manufactured exports
from the developed market economies is compared with the U.S. wholesale price index. The index, which is the product of the United Nations
Statistical Office, has increased at a somewhat slower rate than the World
Bank index since 1970 but at a rate significantly greater than the U.S.
wholesale price index through 1980. Consequently it can be said that the
use of the wholesale price index to deflate export prices did not exag-
gerate the decline of real prices during the 1970s; in fact, the contrary may
be the case in terms of the alternatives facing the developing countries.

It has been noted that the U.S. wholesale price index has increased at a
significantly slower rate than either of the two indexes of manufactured
product prices. But the developing countries pay for their imports of food
products with their own foreign exchange earnings. If the unit value or
price of the exports of the developing countries have increased at a slower
pace than the U.S. wholesale price index in recent years, these countries

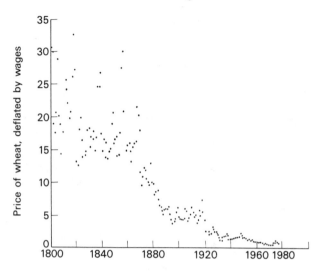

Figure 2.18 Price of wheat (deflated by wages).
Source: see Simon, 1981, p. 75.

would have had to increase the volume of their exports to pay for the same quantity of food imports.

However, the contrary occurred. The export unit value of agricultural exports from the developing countries increased more during the 1970s than did the U.S. wholesale price index according to the data in table 2.4. By the end of the 1970s and the beginning of the 1980s the increase in the relative purchasing power of the developing countries' agricultural exports was substantial. On a base of 1967 = 100, by 1980 the export unit value had increased to an index of 342 while the wholesale price index stood at 269. Thus the export unit value increased by 27 percent compared to the U.S. wholesale price index between 1967 and 1980. As a result, if the export prices of the major cereals were deflated by the export unit values of agricultural products of the developing countries, the relative prices of the cereals in 1980 would be significantly below the levels of the late 1960s and early 1970s.

Another relevant comparison is with the export unit values of North American agricultural products. These data are in column (4) of table 2.4. While these export unit values increased more than the whole-sale price index between 1967 (or 1970) and the mid-1970s, by 1978 the indexes were approximately the same and in 1980 the index of the export unit values for North American agricultural products was below the wholesale price index. Column (5) shows that the export unit values for

TABLE 2.3 INDEXES OF EXPORT UNIT VALUES FOR
MANUFACTURED EXPORTS FROM INDUSTRIAL COUNTRIES
AND U.S. WHOLESALE PRICE INDEX, 1964–81 (1967 = 100)

	Export unit values, manufactured exports[a] (1)	U.S. wholesale price index (2)	Ratio (1)/(2)
1964	96	95	1.01
1965	98	97	1.01
1966	99	100	0.99
1967	100	100	1.00
1968	101	102	0.99
1969	102	106	0.96
1970	111	110	1.01
1971	117	114	1.03
1972	127	119	1.07
1973	148	135	1.10
1974	180	160	1.12
1975	202	175	1.15
1976	203	183	1.11
1977	221	194	1.14
1978	253	209	1.21
1979	290	250	1.16
1980	319	269	1.19
1981	303	293	1.03
1982	295	296	1.00

Note: [a] Exports from industrial countries.
Sources: United Nations Statistical Office, *United Nations Monthly Bulletin of Statistics*, various issues; U.S. Department of Commerce, *Statistical Abstract of the United States* and *Survey of Current Business*, various issues.

agricultural products from the developing countries have risen relative to North American agricultural export prices by about a third.

Finally, it may be noted that between 1970 and 1980 the developing market economies' terms of trade for agricultural products improved and did so to a significant degree. On a 1969–71 base the export unit value of agricultural exports increased to an index of 320; the import unit value index was 288 (*FAO Trade Yearbook*, 1980). The improvement in the terms of trade was 11 percent. Improvement occurred in every region except the Near East where the terms of trade in agricultural products declined by 20 percent; however, Africa's terms of trade in agricultural products increased by 15 percent and Latin America's by 27 percent. It is my impression that these changes in the terms of trade of the developing market economy are different than what "most people" think occurred during the 1970s.

TABLE 2.4 COMPARISON OF EXPORT UNIT VALUES FOR
AGRICULTURAL PRODUCTS OF DEVELOPING COUNTRIES
AND NORTH AMERICA AND U.S. WHOLESALE PRICES,
1964–81 (1967 = 100)

Year	Agricultural export unit values, developing countries (1)	U.S. wholesale price index (2)	Ratio (1)/(2) (3)	Agricultural export unit values, North America (4)	Ratio (1)/(4) (5)
1964	108	95	1.14	96	1.13
1965	103	97	1.06	97	1.06
1966	101	100	1.01	100	1.01
1967	100	100	1.00	100	1.00
1968	102	102	1.00	97	1.05
1969	103	106	0.97	98	1.05
1970	110	110	1.00	99	1.11
1971	111	114	0.97	106	1.05
1972	118	119	0.99	111	1.06
1973	157	135	1.16	166	0.95
1974	232	160	1.45	234	0.99
1975	230	175	1.31	225	1.02
1976	232	183	1.27	208	1.12
1977	301	194	1.55	208	1.45
1978	284	209	1.36	212	1.34
1979	317	250	1.27	241	1.32
1980	340	269	1.26	258	1.32
1981	290	293	0.99	271	1.07

Note: Developing countries exclude centrally planned economies.
Source: FAO, *FAO Trade Yearbook*, 1975 and 1981 and U.S. Department of Commerce, *Statistical Abstract of the United States*, 1980 and *Survey of Current Business*, various issues.

Why Real Food Prices Were Supposed to Have Increased

I shall review the arguments that were made during the early 1970s in support of the projection that real grain and other food prices would be at a new and higher level after the events of 1973 and 1974. Since similar arguments are being made once again, the discussion is not primarily a matter of flogging a dead horse. It remains important to determine if there are significant trends now under way that could cause real food prices to increase in the next decade or two. It is always possible that the adverse effects of a particular factor have not yet occurred but may do so in the near future.

Affluence – feed versus food

During 1973 and 1974 it was commonplace to view with alarm the increased use of grains for livestock feed. It was concluded by some that increasing incomes – affluence – both in the industrial countries and in the rapidly growing middle-income developing countries would increase the feed use of scarce grains at such a rapid rate as to reduce the amount of grain available for food for low-income people.

In a monograph that I wrote in early 1975 I made the argument that the reverse was actually the case – that increasing affluence in the industrial countries increased the supply of grain available to low-income countries because affluence increased supply as well as demand (Johnson, 1975b). Since World War II it has been quite clear that rising productivity, the primary source of increasing affluence or rising per capita incomes, had added more to the supply of grains than to demand in the industrial countries. The proof of this statement was the sharp increase in net exports by the industrial market economies. In 1960–2 the grain exports from the industrial market economies was but 20.3 million tons; in 1969–71 such exports had increased to 31.9 million tons and could have been substantially greater had the demand been greater, since during those years the major exporters were actually engaged in reducing grain production.

In response to the sharp increase in world grain prices, grain exports from the industrial market economies increased to nearly 60 million tons in both 1972/3 and 1973/4; and by the end of the 1970s and the beginning of the 1980s net grain exports from the industrial economies were almost four times as large as at the beginning of the 1970s.

There were several reasons for the sharp increase in grain exports from the industrial market economies, but the primary point to be made here is that there was almost no increase in feed use of grains after 1973/4 in these economies. In fact, the United States has still not regained the level of feed use for 1973/4 while the increase in feed use in the European Community and the rest of Western Europe has been very modest. For all industrial market economies the feed use of grain was 280 million tons in 1979/80 or almost identical to the use of 272 million tons in 1973/4 (USDA, 1980). As a result essentially all of the increased grain production in the industrial market economies was available for export or for increasing stocks after 1973/4. From 1973/4 until the end of the decade grain production increased by 66 million tons and net exports by 61 million tons.

In Eastern Europe and the Soviet Union there was a continued growth in the feed use of grain during the 1970s, continuing after 1973/4. This growth can be attributed to some considerable degree to the food price subsidies that have kept the prices of meat and milk very low and thus has encouraged the consumption of livestock products and the use of grain as feed (Johnson, 1982). Had these countries permitted the consumer prices of meat and milk to reflect the prices paid to the farms, instead of subsidizing consumer prices by as much as half, there would have been significantly slower growth in the use of grain as feed. During the 1960s the feed use of grain in the U.S.S.R. more than doubled (from 43 million tons in 1960/1–1962/3 to 89 million tons in 1969/70–1971/2) while in Eastern Europe the increase was slightly more than 60 percent for the same period (from 29 to 46 million tons). Grain use continued to increase during the 1970s – by 33 million tons or 37 percent in the Soviet Union and by 24 million tons or 50 percent in Eastern Europe. The feed use of grain in Eastern Europe and the U.S.S.R. now exceeds that of the United States by about 60 million tons or by 40 percent (USDA, 1980).

The feed use of grain is increasing in the developing market economies, though most of the growth is occurring in a small number of middle-income developing economies. These include South Korea, Taiwan, Brazil, Mexico, and the Philippines. But feed use in all of Asia, Africa, and Latin America, excepting only Japan, in 1979/80 was just 56 million tons or 4 percent of world grain production. Since the late 1960s the annual growth rate in grain used as feed in these economies has been approximately 7 percent. If this growth rate were to continue through the 1980s, feed use of grain at the end of the decade would be about 110 million tons or less than 6 percent of the trend level of world grain production for 1989. As rapid as the growth of feed use of grain may be in these economies, the continuation of that growth for another decade does not represent a significant threat to the grain availability for people.

Instead of affluence being an enemy of the poor, the rising productivity that has been associated with affluence has added more to the world's supply of food than to its demand. The more rapid growth of supply than of demand has been most evident in the developed market economies over the past three decades, with food supply increasing much more rapidly than domestic demand. Consequently, the rapid growth of exports from the developed market economies during the 1960s and 1970s contradicts the widely held view that affluence affects primarily demand and has little influence over supply.

The world's cultivated land can be increased

The view that there remains very little land to bring under cultivation in the world, and that this places a significant limitation on the expansion of food production, is both factually incorrect and, even if true, largely irrelevant. There is a substantial potential for expanding the amount of cultivable land in South America, Africa, and South-east Asia (World Food Conference). The amount of arable land in the developing market economies increased during the 1970s, from 565 million hectares in 1970 to 598 million hectares in 1980 or by 5.8 percet (FAO, 1980). Revelle's paper in this volume (chapter 6) fully supports the view that much more land can be cultivated than is now in crops.

But the expansion of the cultivated area is probably not the lowest-cost means of increasing food and agricultural production. The United States now has the same arable area that it did in 1950 though it is generally agreed that cropland in the United States could be increased by from 10 to 15 percent. However, farmers have not taken that approach in increasing crop production at an annual rate of about 2 percent over the past two decades. It has been cheaper to increase production by increasing yields per unit of land, instead of increasing the arable area.

The developing countries, while continuing to expand the cultivated area, have also been successful in increasing yields. For 1961–5 to 1978–80 approximately two-thirds of the 3 percent annual growth in cereal production can be attributed to higher yields (CYMMYT, 1981). For that period the growth of grain production in the developing countries was at the same or slightly higher rate than in the developed countries.

The emphasis upon the amount of cultivated land ignores the changes that can be made to improve the productive capacity of that land and to increase significantly the stability of production. One of the most important trends in the developing countries has been the increase in the amount of land irrigated. In India the area of irrigated land has increased from 25.5 million hectares in 1961–5 to 39.1 million hectares in 1979. In China the increase was from 38.5 million to 49.2 million hectares for the same time period. These two countries have a large fraction of the irrigated land in the developing world, where the irrigated area increased from 70.0 million hectares in 1961–5 to 100.0 million hectares in 1979. India alone accounted for almost half of the increase for all developing countries (FAO, 1980).

There has also been a significant though smaller increase in irrigated land in the industrial countries – from 27.2 million hectares in 1961–5 to 31.0 million hectares in 1979.

Depending upon the particular situations, irrigated land yields from two or four times as much as the same land before it was irrigated. Thus irrigating 1 hectare of land is the same as "finding" 1–3 additional hectares of cropland even when the irrigated area had been cultivated before.

By the mid-1970s almost all of the land in the U.S. that had been diverted and idled had returned to cultivation. True, not all 60 million acres (24.3 million hectares) diverted under the farm programs during the early 1970s returned to cultivation, but the acreage of crops harvested increased by approximately 40 million acres (16.1 million hectares) by 1977. Some have argued that return of the idle and diverted land to cultivation implies that there is no surplus productive capacity, and that the prospects are for slower growth of output in the future than in the past. This conclusion assumes that the acreage diversion programs had a major impact upon agricultural output. Some work that I did several years ago indicated that the effect of the acreage reduction and diversion programs reduced total farm output by 2 percent and crop output by about 4 percent (Johnson, 1973). The signifcant increase in purchased inputs since 1970 has been far more important than the return of land to cultivation in increasing farm production. Fred Singer, in chapter 12, develops in detail the errors in the report's analysis of energy shortages and price increases.

Energy prices

After the sharp increase in petroleum prices in 1973 there was a legitimate concern that increased energy prices would have an adverse effect upon the growth of agricultural output in both the industrial and developing economies. Since agriculture in the industrial economies as well as the new yield- and output-increasing technologies being adopted in the developing economies, such as those embodied in the Green Revolution, were energy intensive, higher energy prices might lead to a substantial increase in production costs. *Global 2000* gave major emphasis to the effect of sharp increases in the prices of energy on increases in real food prices. The erroneous nature of their analysis is discussed later.

In particular it was feared that rapidly increasing fertilizer prices would result in slower yield growth. In the United States, as elsewhere, fertilizer prices increased sharply between 1970 and 1975 – by 140 percent in terms of prices paid by farmers. The nominal price fell by a sixth over the next two years. Table 2.5 presents the prices-paid indexes for U.S farmers for all production items and for three production inputs with a large energy component – fertilizer, agricultural chemicals and fuels, and energy. Compared to 1970, fertilizer prices at mid-1982 have increased by less than 10 percent more than all farm production items. The prices of agricultural chemicals increased by only 70 percent as much as all farm production items. True, fuel and energy prices.have increased by more than all production items by about 40 percent.

The U.S. comparisons are affected by the base year chosen. If 1967 were the base year, by mid-1982 the index of fertilizer prices was 12 percent *below* the index of prices for all production items while fuels and energy prices had increased by a little less than a third. It is clear from the table, and from the price comparisons with the 1967 base, that relative shifts in the prices of production items with a high energy component have not been great. In particular, the increases in fertilizer prices were

TABLE 2.5   FARM INPUT PRICES, THE UNITED STATES AND
THE EUROPEAN COMMUNITY (1970 = 100)

	1973	1975	1977	1979	1980	1981	Mid-1982
United States							
All production items	135	169	185	231	256	274	278
Fertilizer	117	250	208	225	279	300	304
Agricultural chemicals	108	165	161	154	165	178	195
Fuels and energy	110	169	192	263	362	410	384
Feed	159	185	185	203	228	248	235
European Community[a]							
Goods and services used							
in agriculture	130	169	211	234	257	291	–
Fertilizer	120	198	211	243	286	332	–
Energy and lubricants	123	194	245	306	376	454	–
Feeding stuffs	134	156	204	215	228	258	—

Note: [a] Data are for the nine members, except that 1981 price indexes were based on differences between 1981 and 1980 prices for the ten members.
Sources: United States: U.S. Department of Agriculture, Agricultural Prices, various issues.
European Community: Commission of the European Communities, The Agricultural Situation in the Community, annual reports for 1976, 1980 and 1981.

modest, indeed, compared to the increase in petroleum prices from about $3 per barrel in 1970 to more than $35 per barrel in 1981.

The pattern of relative price changes for energy-intensive farm inputs in the European Community during the 1970s was similar to what occurred in the United States. The data are presented in the bottom part of table 2.5. Compared to 1970, fertilizer prices in the EC had increased by 14 percent compared to the index of goods and services used in agriculture. The relative index of prices of energy and lubricants increased by 56 percent in EC and by 50 percent in the United States.

It may be argued that fertilizer prices have not yet felt the full brunt of increased energy costs in the United States, since natural gas prices are still under control. Natural gas is the primary energy source for the production of nitrogen fertilizers. When natural gas prices are fully decontrolled, there will be an increase in the cost of producing fertilizer in the United States; but this may not mean that there will be a significant increase in the price of nitrogen fertilizers in the United States. What is more likely is that production of nitrogen fertilizer will decline in the United States and increase in areas where natural gas continues to be flared or where gas prices are lower than in the United States. Fertilizers are freely traded in the world, and U.S. prices cannot depart far from the prices in the international markets.

Prices of energy and energy-intensive products used in agriculture have not increased so dramatically as to impose a major threat to food production. Productivity improvements in fertilizer production have been an important factor in limiting the impact of higher energy prices. In addition, the prices that farmers pay for a particular product reflect many costs other than energy – transportation, marketing services, credit, for example. Thus it was naive to assume that there would be anything approximating a one-to-one relationship between changes in the price of oil and the products farmers use.

In the developing countries there are numerous governmental interventions that affect the prices of fertilizer; and in many countries actual and official prices may differ substantially. However, a review of FAO fertilizer price data for several developing countries give approximately the same pattern of price changes as occurred in the United States or the European Community, though there is considerable diversity from country to country. In many developing countries the ready and assured availability of fertilizer may be of greater concern than prices.

There can be an increase in the growth rate of food production in the developing countries during the remainder of this century, if the numerous countries that exploit agriculture and farm people for the benefit of their urban minorities adopt price policies that are both more efficient and equitable. In all too many developing countries the governments have imposed prices for agricultural products that are significantly below even the recent world prices. The low price policy serves one or both of two ends – to maintain low food prices for urban people even though they generally have significantly higher incomes than farm people, and to extract resources from the rural areas for urban investment or national aggrandizement.

The World Bank's *World Development Report*, 1982 (p. 48) summarizes estimates of the nominal protection for agricultural products in 26 developing countries. In the clear majority of cases the protection was negative, meaning that the prices received by farmers were less than the international market price after adjusting for marketing and transportation costs. Consider a few examples of the situation in the late 1970s. In Egypt, the farm price of rice was 30 percent of the world price and for cotton, about 40 percent; in Yemen, Brazil, Malawi, and Upper Volta the farm price of cotton was just 70 percent of the world price; in India, the Philippines, Bangladesh, Pakistan, and Senegal rice prices were 30 percent below the world price, but Tanzanian farmers would have been overjoyed with such treatment since their rice prices were 70 percent *below* the world price. In several of the developing countries, as in all of the developed market economies, some farm products had positive rates of nominal protection. But the dominant pattern in the developing countries was significant exploitation of farm people through low prices imposed by their governments. If these governments permitted their domestic farm prices to increase to the international market level, the level and rate of growth of farm production would both increase.

The discussion in *Agriculture: Toward 2000* of the low food price policies of many developing countries is worth quoting at some length (pp. 95–6):

> Higher food prices raise farmers' incomes, lead to increases in production, and may thus result in lower food prices in the long term. But if these initially higher prices are passed on directly to the consumer, they may lead, for example, to urban unrest, or to a worsening of rural inequalities between surplus-producing farmers and the landless or near landless who have to buy most of their food. Lower prices, on the other hand, tend to depress production, creating demand pressures that may subsequently result in higher long-term prices or a rapid rise in food imports. Further, low controlled producer prices have often been enforced by compulsory procurement, in some cases backed up by coercion. This leads inevitably to rural discontent and constitute serious discentives to producers.
>
> Most developing countries have tended to resolve this dilemma in favour of urban areas, keeping producer prices low. While this approach may appear politically necessary, it is usually economically mistaken. It has been adopted partly because priority has been given to industrialization, but also because farmers have been less well organized to exert pressure on governments than urban interest groups.
>
> By widening urban/rural income differentials (and the agricultural/ non-agricultural income disparity in favour of the latter is large and growing in most developing countries), the disincentives of low producer prices have encouraged migration from rural areas. At the same time, however, they have often failed to produce the hoped-for effect on economic or industrial growth, because they have restricted the potential rural market for manufactured goods as well as the long-term domestic supply of food to urban markets. In the future, if production targets, especially those of Scenario A, are to be met, farmers will have to be assured of favourable prices for their produce – prices that provide them with a fair return on their investment and inputs and enable them to buy consumer goods in increasing quantities. Prices should also be fairly stable and predictable, providing a climate in which the farmer can invest with confidence in the future. This implies not only national price-stabilization policies but also international action to reduce the price instability of agricultural commodities or to enable governments themselves to offset part of the price swings by national measures.

Agricultural products as an energy source

A potential threat to world food supplies emerged in the late 1970s. In these years there was emphasis upon production of large quantities of ethanol from corn and sugar. The United States announced a program of producing 10 billion gallons of ethanol from farm products, primarily corn, by 1990. This program, if carried out, would have required 100 million tons of corn or perhaps a fourth of total grain production in 1990.[3] *If* such a program had been carried out there is little doubt that there would have been a sharp increase in the real costs of producing grain and of the prices of the major grains. Similarly if the ambitious Brazilian plans for producing a large share of motor fuel from sugar were carried out, sugar prices would move to a higher level.

On the basis of a criterion of economic efficiency neither the U.S. nor the Brazilian alcohol programs made sense. Fortunately the gasohol program in the United States has been greatly reduced and the same appears to be occurring with the Brazilian program. Both programs required large-scale subsidies and in the case of the U.S. program the net gain in energy that could substitute for fossil fuels was modest, indeed. I believe that it can now be assumed that for some time in the future our cars and trucks will not be a major threat to the world price of food.

Prospects for the 1980s

The previous discussion has given important reasons why a sustained increase in the real price of food and other agricultural products did not occur by the late 1970s, as had been feared by many and is unlikely to occur in the current decade. Other factors besides those discussed were, and are, important. In particular, productivity changes continued to be important in providing additional food output while offsetting much if not all of the small increases in the relative prices of energy-intensive farm production inputs. While fear was expressed during the mid-1970s that productivity growth was slowing down in the United States, this fear seems to have been based primarily upon a failure to consider the impact of climate upon agricultural output in the United States. Perhaps the remarkable aspect of agriculture in the United States and Western Europe is that productivity improvements have continued at a rapid rate in contrast to the sharp declines in productivity growth in the non-farm sectors of the economies.

Figure 2.19 is taken from a paper by Earl Swanson (1981). The figure gives the annual yield of corn in the United States for 1930 through 1979. It is presented here for two reasons. The first is that the solid line, which

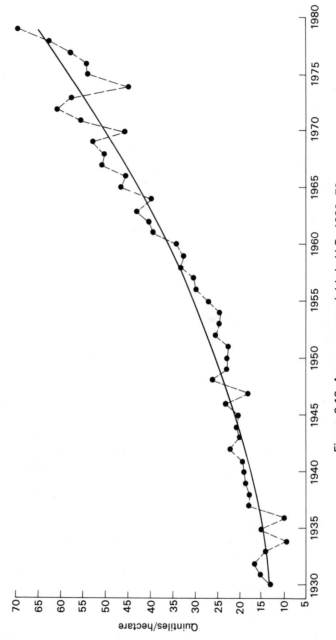

Figure 2.19 Average corn yields in U.S., 1930—79.
Source: Duvick, 1980, reproduced from Swanson, 1981.

are representations of the relationships between yields and time, indicate that corn yields have not been slowing down in recent years. In fact, the solid line indicates that the absolute increase in yields has been increasing during the 1970s. The second is that corn yields were relatively low in 1974, through 1976, but then increased to an all-time high in 1979. These yield variations were associated with climatic factors, but some observers inappropriately attributed the low yields in 1974–6 to long-run factors.

There can be significant improvement in the food situation of the developing countries during the 1980s and the years beyond. To some considerable degree the rate of improvement will depend more upon the rate of economic growth generally than upon changes in the rate of growth of food production in particular countries. Rapid economic growth that is associated with reliance upon international markets for both exports and imports can quickly result in significant improvements in nutrition. But there is much that can be done to improve the perform-ance of agriculture in most developing countries. The potential benefits from eliminating rural exploitation through low farm prices are sub-stantial, both in terms of improving food production and promoting equity within the economy. Further positive measures can be taken, such as allocating a larger percentage of national investment to rural areas, irrigation, roads, marketing facilities, and schools.

Global 2000 Report Projections

There is much in chapter 6 of *Global 2000* with which I am in agreement. In particular, this sentence, italicized in the original: "The world has the capacity, both physical and economic, to produce enough food to meet substantial increases in demand through 2000" (p. 77). The text goes on to note that the projections of *Global 2000* "are compatible in this regard with a number of other studies suggesting a world food potential several times higher than current production levels. The food growth rates implied in this Study's production and consumption projections are com-parable to the record increases reported for the 1950s and the 1960s."

I cannot understand how it was possible for the report's authors to go from a reasonably optimistic projection of future food supply prospects to a strikingly gloomy projection of the world food supply and price situa-tion by the end of this century. Most of the reason for the gloomy outcome for food lies in particular assumptions that were imposed upon the world grain–oilseed–livestock (GOL) model of the United States Department of Agriculture. While further improvements in the GOL model are possible, and I am confident are being made, the primary reason for the unreasonable and shockingly gloomy projections of food supply stringencies and sharp increases in real food prices by the end of the century were the assumptions about how certain relationships would change over time, and not with fundamental shortcomings of the model itself. The GOL model can be, and has been, used to show how changes in some variable, such as the weather, reduction in trade barriers, or an increase in the rate of income growth, will affect production, prices, and trade of agricultural products. But the GOL model does not contain within it any superior knowledge of how the variables that will affect the supply and demand for food will change over the next quarter-century. Changes in variables must be introduced from outside; and the well-known saying about models and computers applies here: "Garbage in; garbage out."

Chapter 6 of *Global 2000* presents several tables of various assumptions made with respect to such variables as population growth rates, per capita income growth rates, and yield variations due to different weather conditions. In the text, rather less explicit assumptions are given concerning technological changes that would affect yield changes for grains: "Growth in yields, ultimately raised or lowered by the producer prices generated under a specific alternative, is projected at rates compatible with the technological advances of the past two decades" (p. 77). But most important, and left largely undocumented in the report, are the assumptions that result in the conclusion that the costs of producing food products will increase sharply, perhaps even double, by 2000. Since it was assumed that technological advances would continue at the same rate as during the past two decades, the sharp increase in the costs and prices of food have to result from either *sharp increases* in the prices of inputs used in agricultural production or to movement outward on a sharply rising supply curve for farm products.

The study emphasizes the costs of energy as a major contributor to rising costs of producing food. It is argued that since modern agriculture is highly energy-intensive, rising prices of energy would have a major impact upon the supply of food. There are two important aspects of the discussion of the impacts of rising energy costs upon the world's food situation that will be considered below. One is that under an alternative in which real energy prices are assumed to be at the 1974–6 level, the world market prices of food are projected to increase by 45 percent over the 1969–71 level by 2000. The 1975 price of oil, in real terms, was actually significantly less than the real price of oil when *Global 2000* was completed. The price of oil in 1980 that would have been the same in real terms as the $15 per barrel East Coast (U.S.) price in 1975 was approximately $22, well below the actual 1980 price.

A second aspect of the modeling of energy prices and food output and prices is the quite remarkable explanation of the reasons for the wide differences in the price projections for 2000 when energy prices are assumed to be the same as in 1973–5 real prices or somewhat more than double the 1973–5 real prices. As noted, with energy prices at the 1973–5 level, international food prices in 2000 were projected to be 45 percent higher than in 1969–71; with somewhat more than a doubling of real energy prices, the increase in food prices was projected to be 95 percent. While other price projections were presented, the two noted are for assumptions that are the same except for the difference in energy prices. But now for the remarkable explanation of the reasons for the wide differences in food price projections attributed to the different energy price assumptions:

> The range (in food prices) reflects not so much uncertainty about petroleum price increases as uncertainty about the effect changing petroleum prices have on agriculture and the ability of farmers to maintain or expand protection while shifting away from energy-intensive inputs (p. 85). (Italicized in original.)

One can perhaps be permitted to marvel at the arrogance of the authors in expressing such confidence in their ability to project energy prices while displaying so little confidence in the capacity, so remarkably demonstrated over recent decades, of farmers to adjust to changing conditions. So far there can be no doubt that it is the farmers who merit our confidence and not the report's authors, who should now be rather more circumspect in their evaluation of their own ability to say something useful about the future.

As is clear from table 2.5, there is no simple relationship between energy prices, as represented by petroleum prices, and the costs of inputs that have a high energy content. This is particularly true for nitrogen fertilizer and fertilizer generally. Fertilizer prices paid by farmers have increased very little compared to 1970, and not at all compared to 1967 if the effects of inflation are eliminated. The sharp differences between the paths of fertilizer prices and petroleum prices were evident by 1978 or 1979, yet no notice appeared to have been taken of this development.

Even more unsubstantiated is the projection that the share of the world's resources devoted to food production will increase significantly by 2000. The conclusion is stated without support or qualification, or any indication of how it was derived. If it were true it would represent a sharp break with the trends of the past two centuries. In fact, it is hard to square an increase in the share of food in total world income with the increasing per capita incomes projected under each of the three alternatives. From 1975 to 2000 the most pessimistic projection of the increase in real per capita income for the world is 25 percent, while the most optimistic is 97 percent. It is highly unlikely that, with an increase in per capita income of just 25 percent, the share of resources devoted to food production would increase. In fact, there is some question of whether there could be an increase in per capita income of 25 percent if the share of the world's income devoted to food production increased. For the share of the world's income devoted to food production to increase, the income elasticity of demand for food would have to be very high. By very high I mean approaching one; this means that a 1 percent increase in per capita income would increase the amount of food demanded at a constant price by about 1 percent. From my review of the documents describing the GOL model, the weighted income elasticities of demand for food fall far short of the level required to induce an increase in the share of world income (and resources) devoted to food.

One measure of the share of the world's resources devoted to food is the percentage of the world's labor force engaged in agriculture. In 1965 the estimated share of the economically active population engaged in agriculture in the world was 54 percent; by 1981 this percentage had declined to 45 (FAO, 1977, 1981). For the same period the decline in the economically active population engaged in agriculture in the developing market economies was from 68 to 58 percent. It is obvious that the projected calamity of the world needing to devote an increased share of its resources to food production has not yet occurred, either for the entire world or for the developing market economies. For the projection to be valid it would require also that the percentage of the world's income spent on food would increase. Quite the contrary has occurred over the past century wherever there has been a significant increase in per capita income.

There appears to be a problem of consistency among the projected outcomes for 2000 for per capita food consumption, per capita income and real food prices. If real prices increase as projected, per capita food consumption and per capita incomes would be lower than projected. Not enough information is given about the model to permit one to say what went wrong; but something surely did go wrong.

Agriculture: Toward 2000 (1979) speaks directly to the issue of the share of the world's income that might be devoted to agriculture in 2000. The study explicitly analyzed the inputs that were likely to be associated with the various patterns of agricultural output growth. For the 90 developing countries it is projected that purchased inputs might increase from 20 percent of the value of gross farm output in 1980 to 26 percent in 2000. The current share in developed countries is 50 percent, plus or minus five percentage points (FAO, 1979, p. 35). What is expected to happen to the share of income of the economies devoted to the production of food? One measure of this trend is the percentage of gross domestic product that is produced in agriculture. In the 90 developing countries it is estimated that in 1975 21 percent of the gross domestic product was produced in agriculture; for 2000 this share falls drastically to 8 percent. For the low-income developing countries the decline in the percentage of gross domestic product originating in agriculture is projected to be from 45 percent in 1975 to 26 percent in 2000 (FAO, 1979, p. 36). *Global 2000* referred to an increase in the share of total resources devoted to agriculture; *Agriculture: Toward 2000* clearly contradicts such a conclusion, as do all long-term trends.

The two most striking and unsubstantiated conclusions of *Global 2000* have been presented – a sharp increase in real food prices of from 35 to 115 percent over 1969–71 by the year 2000, and a significant increase in the share of the world's resources committed to food production (p. 96). Other major conclusions are:

(1) World food production "is projected to increase more rapidly than world population, with average per capita consumption increasing about 15 percent between 1970 and 2000. Per capita consumption in the industrialized countries is projected to increase 21 percent, with increases of "from 40 to more than 50 percent in Japan, Eastern Europe, and the U.S.S.R., and 28 percent in the United States" (p. 17).

(2) "An increase of 9 percent in per capita food consumption is projected for the LDCs as a whole, but with enormous variation among regions and nations" (p. 17). Little improvement is projected for South Asia while per capita consumption in Sub-Saharan African LDCs was projected to decline.

(3) "The food problem in many of the LDCs with the slowest growth appears to be as much a problem of effective market demand as a problem of expanding production" (p. 90).

(4) "The surplus productive capacity of the traditional exporters – particularly Canada, South Africa, and Australia – is projected to decrease beyond 1985 as a result of growth in domestic demand" (p. 95).

(5) "The projections indicate that most of the increase in food production will come from more intensive use of yield-enhancing, energy-intensive inputs and technologies such as fertilizer, pesticides, herbicides, and irrigation – in many cases with diminishing returns. Land under cultivation is projected to increase only 4 percent by 2000 because most good land is already being cultivated. In the early 1970s one hectare of arable land supported an average of 2.6 persons; by 2000 one hectare will have to support 4 persons. Because of this tightening land constraint, food production is not likely to increase fast enough to meet rising demands unless world agriculture becomes significantly more dependent on petroleum and petroleum-related inputs" (p. 16).

I shall not comment in detail concerning each of the five conclusions listed above. However, brief comments on three of the conclusions are appropriate since they have not been specifically discussed before. With respect to the first of the listed conclusions, which was to support a view that there would be great differences in growth of food consumption between poor and rich countries, it may be noted that almost 40 percent of the time between 1970 and 2000 has elapsed. The increases in per capita consumption of food for the industrialized countries as a group, for Japan, and the United States simply have not been occurring at the rate implied by the projections. In the United States per capita food consumption, as measured by the USDA index of per capita food consumption, increased by about 3 percent between 1970 and 1982; this is far short of the rate required to achieve a 28 percent growth by 2000. Total consumption of grain in the United States in 1981/2 was just 10 percent greater than in 1969–71. Over the same period of time the U.S. population increased by slightly more than 11 percent; thus per capita grain use for all purposes (human use, animal feed, industrial use, seed, and waste) actually declined. The projected increase in per capita grain consumption in the United States, given alongside the increase in per capita food consumption, for 1970–2000, was 35 percent. In the European Community grain use has increased less than 10 percent and per capita use has actually declined slightly, as in the United States. Only Japan appears to have increased its grain use at a rate roughly approximating what was projected.

The conclusion (number 4) that the surplus capacity of Canada, South Africa, and Australia would decrease after 1985 "as a result of growth in domestic demand" is quite incredible. It is difficult to understand how two of these countries whose population growth is falling and approaching 1–1.5 percent, and where the income elasticities of demand are so low, can suffer a decline in their export capability. It is true that South Africa continues to have population growth rates of more than 2.5 percent, but South Africa is far less important as an exporter than either Canada or Australia. What is more, under each of the alternative projections of grain trade presented in the report, the absolute volume of grain exports from the three countries is greater in 2000 than in 1985. Apparently whoever drafted this conclusion was misled by table 6-8 where it is projected that exports *per capita* were smaller in 2000 than in 1985. But with a larger population, more grain would be exported if the projections accurately depict what will occur.

The third conclusion (number 3 above) is quite remarkable given the stress elsewhere in the report upon the resource restraints upon output growth: "The food problem in many of the LDCs with the slowest growth appears to be as much a problem of effective market demand as a problem of expanding production." In other words, low-income people with slow or no growth in their incomes have not in the past, and will not in the future, achieve a significant improvement in the nutritional intake. There is now general agreement that poverty is the primary source or cause of inadequate diets. If people have the income, they will generally have adequate diets. I find it somewhat ironic that in all too many places in *Global 2000* there is concern expressed over the consequences of rapidly growing incomes. It seems to me more appropriate to welcome such growth in the developing countries.

At the risk of undue repetition, I want to return briefly to the projections of large increases in the real price of food by the year 2000 and the equally stunning projection that there will be "a substantial increase in the share of the world's resources committed to food production . . ." to meet demand growth by the end of the century. Both projections represent sharp reversals of past trends. I have presented real price trends for a considerable number of food products. It was clear that trends for farm products important in the diets of low-income countries have been either for stable or declining prices for the past several decades and, in some cases, for the past century. The price projections in *Global 2000* refer to the period 1970–2000. Real food prices as of the end of 1982 are at or below the levels of 1970; consequently if real food prices are to increase by 95 percent by 2000 the annual rate of price increase must be a most remarkable 3.8 percent. Even the smallest of the projected price increases (30 percent) would require annual real price changes of 1.7 percent between now and 2000.

It is simply not possible to accept the gloomy projections related to food and agriculture in *Global 2000*. Real food price increases of 30–100 percent are not going to occur, nor will the share of the world's resources devoted to food increase by the end of this century. In the writing of *Global 2000* there seemed to be so much fascination with a large-scale model of world agriculture that little or no attention was given to the accumulation of knowledge and information about food and agriculture that is available from looking back at historical developments. It is quite remarkable that, with a passage of one-third of the 30-year period with which the study dealt by the time the study was completed, no-one bothered to review what had happened already. To have done so could have shown that many of the highly distorted and misleading conclusions had been strikingly contradicted even before the study was completed.

Concluding Comments

I want there to be no misunderstanding. There has been a modest improvement in food and nutrition in the poor countries of the world, with the possible exception of a number of African countries. Further-

D. Gale Johnson

more, I am confident that the rate of improvement can be increased if further feasible efforts are made. The recent rate of improvement has occurred as a result of a number of conscious efforts on the parts of governments and by the application of the enormous talents and initiative of hundreds of millions of farm families. The output growth has resulted from agricultural research, investments in irrigation, development of roads, the expansion of markets, increases in education and literacy of farm people, the availability of extension services, and increased ease of communication. Further expenditures and investments in these areas will yield additional returns.

There is much that can be done to improve the economic setting within which farmers function. Policies that assist farmers to make the appropriate decisions in lieu of policies that put barriers in the way of farmers and other poor people in their efforts to improve their incomes and the satisfactions that they derive from life must receive priority. While there appears to have been some improvement during the past decade, all too many countries still exploit farm people through export taxes and other methods of keeping domestic prices below world market levels.

Notes

This chapter was originally prepared for presentation at a meeting of the American Association for the Advancement of Science, Detroit, Michigan, 29 May 1983.

1   The two scenarios, labeled A and B, are not forecasts: "they are quantified explorations of feasible future developments." Scenario A assumes relatively rapid growth of gross domestic product for 90 developing countries of 7.0 percent, while Scenario B assumes a 5.7 percent annual growth rate in GDP. Each scenario develops growth patterns for food and agricultural production and changes in nutritional status. The factors that might lead to the differences in the rate of growth of agricultural production are outlined in chapter 4 of *Agriculture: Toward 2000*.

2   The data in the figures do not reflect the income payments made under the various farm programs in the United States. Relative to prices received by farmers, the payments were approximately three times higher from 1967 to 1971 than for 1977 to 1981 for corn, wheat, and cotton. There were no payments for soybeans or soy oil. The sugar price in figure 2.16 is an international price and does not reflect prices received by U.S. farmers.

3   If 100 million tons of corn were used to produce ethanol, approximately 30 million tons of a medium-level protein feed would be available. This 30 million tons of feed would replace about 18 million tonnes of soybean meal.

References

Barney, Gerald O., Study Director (1982) *The Global 2000 Report to the President*. A report prepared by the Council on Environmental Policy and the Department of State. New York: Penguin Books.
Brown, Lester R. (1981) "The Worldwide Loss of Cropland." In Richard G. Woods. (ed.) *Future Dimensions of World Food and Population*, Boulder: Westview Press, 1981.
Crosson, Pierre R., (ed.) (1982) *The Cropland Crisis: Myth or Reality?* Washington, D.C: Resources for the Future.
CYMMYT (International Maize and Wheat Improvement Center) (1981) *World Wheat Facts and Trends*. Report One. Mexico: CYMMYT, August.
Food and Agriculture Organization of the United Nations (FAO). *FAO Production Yearbook*. Rome: FAO, annual issues.
——, *FAO Trade Yearbook*. Rome: FAO, annual issues.
——, (1979) *Agriculture: Toward 2000*, C 79/24. Rome: FAO, 1979.
——, (1981) *Agriculture: Toward 2000*. Rome: FAO, 1981.
International Food Policy Research Institute (IFPRI) (1981) *Report 1981*. Washington, D.C.: IFPRI.
Johnson, D. Gale (1970) "Famine," *Encyclopedia Britannica*, 1970 edition, pp. 58–60.
——, (1973) *Farm Commodity Programs: An Opportunity for Change*. Washington, D.C.: American Enterprise Institute for Public Policy Research.
——, (1975a) "World agriculture, commodity policy, and price variability." *American Journal of Agricultural Economics*, **57**, 823–8.
——, (1975b) *World Food Problems and Prospects*. Washington, D.C.: American Enterprise Institute for Public Policy Research.
——, (1980) "Inflation, agricultural output, and productivity." *American Journal of Agricultural Economics*, **62**, 917–23.
——, (1982) "Agriculture in the Centrally Planned Economies." Office of Agricultural Economics Research, University of Chicago, Paper No. 15, 21 July.
O'Brien, Patrick M. (1981) "Global prospects for agriculture." In *Agricultural-Food Policy Review: Perspectives for the 1980s*, AFPR-4, April, pp. 2–26.
Poleman, Thomas T. (1982) "World hunger: extent, causes and cures." Paper prepared for conference on "The Role of Markets in the World Food Economy," Minneapolis, 14–16 October.
Schultz, Theodore W. (1982) "The dynamics of soil erosion in the United States: a critical review." Agricultural Economics Research, the University of Chicago, Paper No. 82:9, 12 March; revised 22 March.
Simon, Julian L. (1981) *The Ultimate Resource*. Princeton: Princeton University Press.
Srinivasan, T. N. (1982) "Hunger: defining it, estimating its global incidence and alleviating it." Paper prepared for conference on "The Role of Markets in the World Food Economy," Minneapolis, 14–16 October.
United States Department of Agriculture (1980) Foreign Agricultural Service. *Utilization of Grain for Livestock Feed*. Foreign Agricultural Circular, Grains, FG-14-80, 1 May.

112   *D. Gale Johnson*

——, (1981) Economic Research Service. *World Indices of Agricultural and Food Production*. Stat. Bul. No. 669, July.

Valdes, Alberto and Joachim Zietz (1980) *Agricultural Protection in OECD Countries: Its Costs to Less-Developed Countries*, Research Report 21. Washington, D.C.: International Food Policy Research Institute.

World Bank. *World Development Report*, annual issues.

3

The Future of Food from the Sea

JOHN P. WISE

There are various methods for predicting what will happen in the future. One is to assume that recent trends will continue. Nearly all of the trends in the world fish catch data through 1981, the latest year for which they are available, are upward (table 3.1). Everything important has been increasing at from 1 to 6 percent per year for the last 10 years, except the Peruvian anchovy.

The Peruvian anchovy made up 20 percent of the total world catch and 25 percent of the marine finfish in 1970. The anchovy catch had dropped nearly 95 percent by 1980. The cause was unfavorable oceanographic conditions aggravated by gross overfishing.

Thus it makes sense to look at the most recent 10 years of statistics two ways, with and without the Peruvian anchovy (table 3.2).

These figures seem to point toward continuing increases in catches, and nearly doubling marine catches by the turn of the century. But there is a limit to how far we can safely go in making predictions based on extrapolations of time series. Projections based on 1960–70, when marine catches were growing at 5 percent annually, led by the Peruvian anchovy at over 10 percent, would have proved wrong. Recent rates of increase are less than the rates of a few years ago. A prediction based on past data is likely to be valid only if the past and the future can reasonably be assumed to belong to the same statistical universe.

There are at least three different universes reflected in recent world fisheries data. The first is the post-war period up to about 1960. It was followed by the explosion of far distant-water fisheries during the 1960s, led by Japan and the U.S.S.R. (table 3.3), and the spectacular increase in Peruvian anchovy catches. Then there were three dramatic events in roughly 5 years – the collapse of the Peruvian anchovy fishery in 1971–2, the oil crisis of 1973–4 with escalation of fuel prices, and the world-wide establishment of 200-mile limits starting around 1977. Japanese catches are increasing again after a setback, but the U.S.S.R.'s catches have decreased considerably (table 3.3). Other effects have yet to run their full course, so the near future constitutes at least one more universe.

TABLE 3.1 WORLD FISHERIES CATCH STATISTICS (MILLION METRIC TONS) 1938–81, TREATED VARIOUS WAYS

Year	a	b	c	d	e	f	g	h	j	k	l
1938	21.0	21.0	2.2	18.8	0.0	18.8	0.6	1.2	19.2	17.0	17.0
1948	19.6	19.6	1.8	17.8	0.0	17.8	0.6	1.3	17.7	15.9	15.9
1950	21.1	21.1	2.4	18.7	0.0	18.7	0.7	1.6	18.8	16.4	16.4
1952	25.1	25.1	2.8	22.3	0.0	22.3	0.7	1.9	22.5	19.7	19.7
1954	27.6	27.6	3.2	24.4	0.0	24.4	0.9	1.9	24.8	21.6	21.6
1956	30.8	30.7	3.5	27.3	0.1	27.2	0.9	1.9	28.0	24.5	24.4
1958	33.3	32.5	4.5	28.8	0.8	28.0	0.9	2.1	30.3	25.8	25.0
1960	40.2	36.7	5.6	34.6	3.5	31.1	1.0	2.6	36.6	31.0	27.5
1962	44.8	37.7	5.8	39.0	7.1	31.9	1.1	2.7	41.0	35.2	28.1
1964	51.9	42.1	6.2	45.7	9.8	35.9	1.2	2.7	48.0	41.8	32.0
1965	53.2	45.5	7.0	46.2	7.7	38.5	1.2	3.0	49.0	42.0	34.3
1966	57.3	47.7	7.3	50.0	9.6	40.4	1.3	3.0	53.0	45.7	36.1
1967	60.4	49.9	7.2	53.2	10.5	42.7	1.4	3.2	55.8	48.6	38.1
1968	63.9	52.6	7.4	56.5	11.3	45.2	1.5	3.5	58.9	51.5	40.2
1969	64.4	54.7	7.6	56.8	9.7	47.1	1.5	3.2	59.7	52.1	42.4
1970	65.6	52.5	8.4	57.2	13.1	44.1	1.6	3.4	60.6	52.2	39.1
1971	66.1	54.9	9.0	57.1	11.2	45.9	1.7	3.4	61.0	52.0	40.8
1972	62.0	57.2	5.7	56.3	4.8	51.5	1.8	3.6	56.6	50.9	46.1
1973	62.7	61.0	5.8	56.9	1.7	55.2	2.3	3.7	56.7	50.9	49.2
1974	66.5	62.5	5.8	60.7	4.0	56.7	2.5	3.7	60.3	54.5	50.5
1975	66.1	62.8	6.0	60.1	3.3	56.8	2.5	4.1	59.5	53.5	50.2
1976	69.6	65.3	5.7	63.9	4.3	59.6	2.5	4.4	62.7	57.0	52.7
1977	68.7	67.9	5.9	62.8	0.8	62.0	2.8	4.6	61.3	55.4	54.6
1978	70.4	69.0	5.8	64.6	1.4	63.2	2.9	4.8	62.7	56.9	55.5
1979	71.3	69.9	5.9	65.4	1.4	64.0	3.1	4.9	63.3	57.4	56.0
1980	72.4	71.6	6.2	66.2	0.8	65.4	3.3	5.2	63.9	57.7	56.9
1981	74.8	73.2	6.6	68.2	1.6	66.6	3.3	5.2	66.3	59.7	58.1

Notes: Includes in recent years some 6 million tons of aquaculture production, about 50 percent freshwater finfish and 20 percent molluscs.
a – Total catch
b – Total catch, excluding Peruvian anchovy (a minus e)
c – Freshwater catch (FAO Groups 11–13)
d – Marine catch (a minus c)
e – Peruvian anchovy catch
f – Marine catch, excluding Peruvian anchovy (d minus e)
g – Crustacean catch (FAO Groups 41–47)
h – Mollusc catch (FAO Groups 51–58)
j – Finfish catch (a minus g minus h)
k – Marine finfish catch (d minus g minus h)
l – Marine finfish catch, excluding Peruvian anchovy (k minus e)

Source: FAO Yearbook of Fishery Statistics, vol. 52 and preceding volumes.

TABLE 3.2   ANNUAL PERCENTAGE RATE OF
INCREASE, 1972–81

Category	With anchovy	Without anchovy
Total catch	2.0	2.6
Marine catch	2.1	2.7
Marine finfish	1.7	2.4
Shellfish	5.2	5.2

Shellfish = crustaceans plus molluscs

There is another way of looking at the future of fisheries, based on what we know of present fisheries and their zoogeography and demography. Let us examine some major components of the catches from these points of view.

Many stocks of marine fish have been heavily exploited or over-exploited in the last few years. As some have become scarce, overall catches have been kept up by turning to formerly less desirable kinds of fish. The Alaska pollock is a good example. Landings were around a million tons per year in the mid-1960s, but in recent years they have risen to 4–5 million tons (table 3.4). In some cases, heavily fished species have been replaced in the ecosystem by other species. This phenomenon shows in a comparison of tables 3.3 and 3.4. Peruvian national catches have not decreased as much as would be expected, and Chilean catches have increased substantially – the sardine has to a large degree replaced the anchovy.

There has been a decrease in Northern Hemisphere finfish production because of overfishing. This decrease has been compounded by imposition of quotas to reduce overfishing and permit rebuilding. As the stocks recover, catches should once again increase. The Food and Agriculture Organization of the United Nations (FAO) has suggested that about 20 million tons of increase could be expected from improved management of depleted species, and has documented in some detail how this could be achieved (FAO Fisheries Circular No. 710, Revision 1, 1979).

An example is the Atlantic cod, which peaked in 1968 at 4 million tons, but which has recently been producing in the order of 2 million tons a year. Effective management, now in force, will permit a gradual rise in landings to something like 3 million tons, but it is unlikely that they will again reach the 1968 level, which was based on overfishing.

The geographic distribution of the fisheries is a critical factor. More than half of the marine catches in 1981 came from the North Atlantic and the North Pacific, although these regions have only about 30 percent of the continental shelf area of the world outside the Arctic and the

TABLE 3.3 WORLD FISHERIES CATCH (MILLION METRIC TONS) BY COUNTRIES, 1938–81

Year	a	b	c	d	e	f	g	h	j	k	l
1938	21.0	3.7	1.5	—	2.3	0.0	0.0	1.1	—	0.8	11.6
1948	19.6	2.5	1.5	—	2.4	0.1	0.1	1.4	—	0.3	11.3
1950	21.1	3.4	1.6	1.0	2.6	0.1	0.1	1.5	0.8	0.2	9.8
1952	25.1	4.8	2.0	1.7	2.4	0.1	0.2	1.8	0.7	0.3	11.1
1954	27.6	4.5	2.3	2.3	2.8	0.1	0.2	2.1	0.8	0.3	12.2
1956	30.8	4.8	2.6	2.8	3.0	0.2	0.7	2.2	1.0	0.3	13.2
1958	33.3	5.5	2.6	4.3	2.7	0.2	1.1	1.4	1.1	0.4	14.0
1960	40.2	6.2	3.1	6.1	2.8	0.3	3.7	1.5	1.2	0.5	14.8
1962	44.8	6.9	3.6	3.8	3.0	0.6	7.2	1.3	1.0	0.5	16.9
1964	51.9	6.4	4.5	5.1	2.6	1.2	9.3	1.6	1.3	0.6	19.3
1965	53.2	6.9	5.1	5.7	2.7	0.7	7.6	2.3	1.3	0.6	20.3
1966	57.3	7.1	5.3	6.1	2.5	1.4	8.8	2.9	1.4	0.7	21.1
1967	60.4	7.9	5.8	5.6	2.4	1.1	10.2	3.3	1.4	0.8	21.9
1968	63.9	8.7	6.1	5.9	2.5	1.4	10.6	2.9	1.5	0.8	23.5
1969	64.4	8.1	6.3	6.1	2.5	1.1	9.2	2.5	1.7	0.9	26.0
1970	65.6	8.8	7.2	3.1	2.8	1.2	12.5	2.9	1.8	0.7	24.6
1971	66.1	9.4	7.3	3.4	2.9	1.5	10.5	3.0	1.9	1.0	25.2
1972	62.0	9.7	7.8	3.7	2.8	0.8	4.7	3.1	1.6	1.2	26.6
1973	62.7	10.1	8.6	3.8	2.8	0.7	2.3	2.9	2.0	1.5	28.0
1974	66.5	10.1	9.3	4.1	2.8	1.1	4.1	2.6	2.3	1.7	28.4
1975	66.1	9.9	10.0	4.2	2.8	0.9	3.4	2.5	2.3	1.9	28.2
1976	69.6	10.0	10.1	4.3	3.1	1.4	4.3	3.4	2.2	2.1	28.7
1977	68.7	10.1	9.4	4.5	3.0	1.3	2.5	3.4	2.3	2.1	30.1
1978	70.4	10.2	8.9	4.4	3.4	1.9	3.5	2.6	2.3	2.1	31.1
1979	71.3	9.9	9.0	4.1	3.5	2.6	3.7	2.7	2.3	2.2	31.3
1980	72.4	10.4	9.5	4.2	3.6	2.8	2.8	2.4	2.4	2.1	32.2
1981	74.8	10.7	9.5	4.6	3.8	3.4	2.8	2.6	2.4	2.4	32.6

Notes: "—" means data not available.
 a – Total catch
 b – Japan
 c – U.S.S.R.
 d – China (major revision of statistics, 1969–70.)
 e – U.S.A.
 f – Chile
 g – Peru
 h – Norway
 j – India
 k – Republic of Korea
 l – All others (over 200, 10 of which caught one million tons or more in 1981.)
Source: as in table 3.1.

TABLE 3.4 WORLD MARINE FISHERIES CATCHES (MILLION METRIC TONS) BY PRINCIPAL KINDS OF FISH, 1938–81, EXCLUDING PERUVIAN ANCHOVY

Year	a	b	c	d	e	f	g	h	j	k	l
1938	18.8	5.3	3.2	0.2	0.6	0.4	0.4	1.1	0.4	1.8	6.0
1948	17.8	4.8	3.5	0.2	0.6	0.3	0.6	1.1	0.4	1.9	4.9
1950	18.7	5.0	3.6	0.2	0.7	0.4	0.7	1.4	0.5	2.3	4.5
1952	22.3	5.8	4.1	0.2	0.9	0.5	1.1	1.6	0.6	2.6	5.6
1954	24.4	6.5	4.4	0.3	0.8	0.5	1.3	1.7	0.7	2.8	6.2
1956	27.2	6.7	5.1	0.3	0.9	0.6	1.4	1.7	0.9	2.8	7.4
1958	28.0	6.5	4.5	0.3	1.0	0.5	1.7	2.0	1.0	3.0	8.0
1960	31.1	7.4	5.0	0.5	1.1	0.6	1.7	2.3	1.0	3.6	8.9
1962	31.9	7.4	5.5	0.6	1.1	0.7	2.1	2.4	1.2	3.8	8.2
1964	35.9	8.6	6.1	0.9	1.2	0.9	2.0	2.6	1.4	3.9	9.7
1965	38.5	9.2	6.8	1.0	1.5	1.1	2.2	3.0	1.4	4.2	10.0
1966	40.4	9.2	7.3	1.2	1.8	1.4	2.1	3.2	1.5	4.3	10.9
1967	42.7	9.2	8.4	1.7	2.5	2.0	2.1	3.3	1.6	4.6	11.0
1968	45.2	9.2	9.6	2.2	2.9	2.3	2.0	3.3	1.6	5.0	11.6
1969	47.1	8.4	9.9	2.6	3.0	2.3	2.0	3.2	1.6	4.7	14.3
1970	44.1	8.5	10.5	3.1	3.1	2.5	4.1	4.0	1.6	5.0	7.3
1971	45.9	8.5	10.7	3.6	3.3	2.5	4.7	4.1	1.8	5.1	7.7
1972	51.5	8.5	11.4	4.2	3.2	2.5	5.0	4.3	2.0	5.4	11.7
1973	55.2	9.8	12.0	4.6	4.1	2.8	5.7	4.6	2.1	6.0	10.9
1974	56.7	10.0	12.7	4.9	4.3	3.0	5.6	5.1	2.2	6.2	10.6
1975	56.8	10.2	11.9	5.0	4.2	3.1	6.1	5.2	2.1	6.6	10.5
1976	59.8	10.7	12.1	5.1	3.8	2.8	7.5	5.1	2.3	6.9	11.4
1977	62.0	11.8	10.6	4.3	4.1	3.0	8.8	5.7	2.3	7.4	11.3
1978	63.2	13.0	10.3	3.9	4.8	3.6	8.1	5.6	2.5	7.7	11.2
1979	64.0	14.3	10.6	3.9	4.4	3.2	7.9	5.3	2.4	8.0	11.1
1980	65.2	15.4	10.7	4.0	4.0	2.7	7.3	5.3	2.6	8.5	11.4
1981	66.6	15.9	10.6	4.2	3.7	2.4	8.0	5.2	2.5	8.5	12.2

Notes:

a – Marine catch, excluding Peruvian anchovy
b – Herring, sardine, anchovy (FAO Group 35) catch, excluding Peruvian anchovy
c – Cod, hake, haddock (FAO Group 32) catch
d – Alaska pollock catch (included in c)
e – Mackerel (FAO Group 37) catch
f – Atlantic and chub mackerel catch (included in e)
g – Jacks, mullets, etc. (FAO Group 34) catch
h – Redfish, basses, etc. (FAO Group 33) catch
j – Tunas etc. (FAO Group 36) catch
k – Shellfish (FAO Groups 41–47 and 51–58) catch
l – Catch of all other marine species

Source: as in table 3.1.

Antarctic. (Well over 95 percent of world marine fishery landings come from the productive waters on or over continental shelves.) This relationship suggests the possibility of development in other areas, especially in the Indian Ocean and other parts of the Southern Hemisphere.

For example, the annual potential of bottom fishes in the Western Indian Ocean has been estimated to be in the order of 2 million tons, three times the present amount (FAO, 1979). And while the Southwest Atlantic produced only about half as much catch in 1981 as did the Northwest Atlantic, it has roughly twice the continental shelf area. Potential landings from the Southwest Atlantic have been estimated at over 4 million tons, as opposed to the present production of about 1 million tons (FAO, 1979). One reason that the Southern Hemisphere has not received a full share of fisheries attention is that the heavily populated major fishing nations are almost all in the Northern Hemisphere (table 3.3).

It is generally conceded that most of the world's stocks of large tunas are fully exploited or overexploited. But it is also agreed that skipjack tuna are probably not fully utilized. An estimate by the South Pacific Commission places the potential catch of skipjack in the lightly populated Central Pacific at several million tons, enough to double the world tuna landings (*Tuna and Billfish Assessment Programme, Technical Report No. 8, 1983*).

The distribution of mollusc fisheries is particularly interesting from a human demographic point of view. More than half of the world's mussels come from four European countries. Half of the world's clams and oysters come from the Northwest Pacific, as do more than half of the squids (*FAO Yearbook of Fishery Statistics*, vol. 52). These figures represent the distribution of mollusc-consuming humans and their food preferences, rather than the distribution of the animals. There are certainly many mollusc resources remaining in the world to be brought to full utilization. It has been estimated, for instance, that the world catch of squids and octopuses could be increased to over 10 million tons a year, as opposed to the present 1.5 million or so (*The Fish Resources of the Ocean*, FAO, 1971).

Seventy percent of the world's crabs came from the North Pacific in 1981. Nearly half of the world's shrimp in 1981 came from only three areas – the Western Central Atlantic, the Western Indian Ocean, and the Northwest Pacific (*FAO Yearbook of Fishery Statistics*, vol. 52). It is likely that there are substantial underexploited crab and shrimp resources elsewhere in the world.

There is a wild card in the deck when dealing with possible future production from shrimp-like resources – the Antarctic krill. The maximum sustainable yield has been estimated at from 25 to 150 million tons (*Global 2000*, page 111), but catches have been less than 1/2 million tons per year. The resource could probably contribute enough to double or triple the present world take of marine species. There are several serious impediments to utilization of this resource – developing acceptable products that can be sold at a profit, fishing it in the remotest part of the earth where operations are only possible a few months of the year, and not least, the problem of interaction with the great whales. Krill is the principal food of these whales, and an intense krill fishery could block recovery from their present low levels of abundance. For this reason there is opposition from many conservationists to attempts to develop the resource fully.

Some experts have estimated that the total sustainable harvest of all marine species could be as high as 150 million to 300 million tons. There have been some estimates running to the thousands of millions (billions) of tons. All of these projections depend on radical changes in fishing practices and consumer acceptance, since they involve the harvest of types of marine animals unfamiliar to many, such as squids and plankton organisms.

The widely-accepted (except by *Global 2000*) estimate of possible yields reaching 100–120 million metric tons of conventional species first got wide circulation in FAO's *Indicative World Plan* published in 1970. It was elaborated in *The Fish Resources of the Ocean*, published by Fishing News (Books) Ltd. for FAO in 1971. The estimate represented the thinking of a major body of experts as of the late 1960s.

There has been some puzzlement and confusion about just what was meant by "conventional species." Species that are considered delicacies by one culture are often considered distasteful or even inedible by another – octopus and shark, for instance. And there are other reasons why people will not eat certain seafood. Moslems and Jews are enjoined by religious law from eating molluscs and crustaceans. But exotic or proscribed species make up a small part of the total; marine landings are made up of a surprisingly small number of kinds of fish. Herring- and cod-like fishes have accounted for some 40 percent of the total catch for as long as world statistics have been assembled (table 3.4). Although FAO reports on nearly 700 separate species, only 20, all marine finfish, make up 40 percent of the total and 50 percent of the marine finfish landings (*FAO Yearbook of Fishery Statistics*, vol. 52).

Many re-examinations of the FAO estimate have appeared in the last 10 years or so. The most comprehensive and credible is FAO's own *Review of the state of world fishery resources* – FAO Fisheries Circular No. 710, first published in 1977 and its revisions in 1979 and 1981. The conclusions are that the catches of familiar types of fish might be nearly doubled. About 20 million tons of increase could be expected from improved management of depleted stocks, and 30 million tons from those stocks now lightly or moderately exploited.

Another recent re-examination is that by Rothschild (*BioScience*, March 1981). He concludes that the production of oceanic marine fish is probably several times greater than present landings, but that the primary control occurs in the market.

Pollution and the Environment

Pollution and most other man-induced changes of the environment have had little or no measurable effect on large-scale marine fisheries. Some local effects have been severe, but they have been limited to small areas – individual bays and harbors, for instance. The Mediterranean Sea is a case in point – pollution in many coastal areas is a serious problem. But fisheries have increased nearly 50 percent during the most recent 10 years, at a rate of over 4 percent per year (*FAO Yearbook of Fishery Statistics*, vol. 52).

The major changes associated with human activities have been caused by fishing itself, as mentioned for the Peruvian anchovy and the Atlantic cod. The damming of rivers has caused serious decreases in salmon fisheries.

The predicted disastrous consequences for fisheries of oil spills have not materialized. Their effects, if any, on important fisheries have been below the measurable level. Even their influence on local small-scale fisheries have usually been transitory. See, for example the discussion in *Science*, 8 July 1983, of the effects of a spill of nearly a quarter of a million tons of oil off the Brittany coast.

Environmentalists and governments have shown a curious ambivalence to some of the realities of marine fisheries and environmental change. There are loud noises from the environmental community when a company proposes to drill small holes in the seabed to prospect for oil. The culprit is required to defend itself in multi-volume environmental impact statements and even in court, on the grounds that drilling the holes might alter the marine environment. If, on the other hand, a company, a government, or an international organization proposes to develop a new fishery or complex of fisheries – an enterprise which if successful will certainly cause major alterations in the ecosystem – in most cases the environmental community is silent.

Aquaculture

Fishing on wild stocks is a kind of hunting. It is a deceptively facile transition from this thought to the idea that aquaculture is the best way to provide food from aquatic sources. A substantial fraction of the world marine science community has reservations about the commercial feasibility of large-scale marine aquaculture, but the drafting of studies is done by aquaculturists, that is by advocates, and the reservations do not appear in the reports.

Examples of success in aquaculture in Japan are often held up as models of how an industrious people can show the way to increase world food supply. A closer look often reveals that what the industrious Japanese aquaculturists are doing is raising high-value species by feeding them low-value species. They are turning cheap fish into expensive fish for consumers who are willing to pay the world's highest prices. There is nothing wrong with this practice from an economic point of view; it is like using corn to fatten beef. But it does not have much to do with increasing world food supplies.

Aquaculture is sometimes regarded almost mystically as a special case. Governments and universities set up dedicated laboratories, and planners are influenced to stress aquaculture rather than the general goal of increasing food supply. But mysticism and confusion of means and ends should have no place in setting food policy. The decision tree should look something like what follows.

Given that we need more protein to feed the population, should this protein come primarily from vegetable sources, from land animal sources, or from aquatic sources? Having decided that the protein or a large part of it should come from aquatic sources, there are then three choices. Should it be imported, should it be caught by fishing, or should it be raised by aquaculture? The answer or set of answers is by no means easy. Availability of resources, geography, economics, manpower, food preferences, other cultural considerations, etc., must all be weighted appropriately. With luck, the correct answer or set of answers will be found.

Going directly to aquaculture because aquaculture enthusiasts have the ear of government, or because "aquaculture works in China", is not a sensible approach. For example, it is not a good choice for the U.S. Many U.S. aquaculture studies are based on the dubious premise that the country needs more protein from aquatic sources, and that aquaculture is the best way to obtain it. This premise is difficult to reconcile with the facts that:

(1)   the U.S. is a net exporter of protein foods;

(2)   the U.S. permits the taking by foreigners of over 1.5 million metric tons of edible fish in its Fishery Conservation Zone each year; and

(3)   the U.S. converts another 1.5 million metric tons of fish to fish meal each year, mostly for animal feedstuffs.

The edible fish production of the U.S. could be doubled by taking the fish now allocated to foreigners. It could be doubled again if fish converted to meal were used directly for human food. Aquaculture is only practical if it can produce protein more economically than can expansion of fishing or conversion of fish meal to human food.

The Fish Meal Question

Since the mid-1960s, about 30 percent of all the fish caught in the world has been used to make fish meal. This is a convenient place to dispel three widely held but wrong ideas about fish meal. The first is that fish meal is made from by-products. A tiny fraction is, but nearly all of it is made from whole fish caught for the purpose, almost always herring-like fish. The second is that fish meal is used for fertilizer. Fish meal would be good fertilizer, but it is much too expensive. The third is that fish used to produce meal are "wasted." Since there is currently no human food market for the species, there is presently no other use for them. Also, most are eventually converted to human food as feedstuffs for chickens, pigs, and cattle.

The 30 percent of the world fish catch now processed into fish meal represents a large potential for direct use as human food if ways can be found to make acceptable products from it. The need in this case is for post-production systems and post-harvest technology. There is a major possibility for augmented production of food from the sea without increasing exploitation of marine resources and without turning to aquaculture. The increase would be less than 30 percent, since the conversion efficiency factor of 10–20 percent in transformation through animals must be discounted.

Other Ways of Increasing Food from the Sea

The terms "catch" and "landing" are frequently used interchangeably. But a substantial part of the fish caught by fishermen is not landed. It is discarded at sea for one reason or another, usually because of market considerations (sometimes because of "conservation" laws or regulations). While there are no reliable evaluations of the total, there is a recent estimate that 3 to 5 million tons of fish are discarded by shrimping fleets alone each year (*Fish By-catch . . . Bonus from the Sea*, International Development Research Center, Ottawa, 1981). Probably at least as much is discarded by other fleets. Few if any of these discards get into national or international statistics, but it is possible to surmise that a

10–15 percent increase in the total could be obtained if ways were found to utilize catches that are now discarded.

There is, as in all food products, a considerable amount of wastage and spoilage after landing – how much is impossible to estimate at present.

The Bottom Line

What then can we say realistically about the prospects of increased food supplies from the sea by the year 2000 and beyond?

Production will probably continue to grow for the next 20 years at close to the present rates, which are equal to, or higher than, the rate of human population growth. It will reach the predicted 100–120 million tons of conventional species around the turn of the century.

If practical ways are found to fish the Antarctic krill and to turn it into commercial products, total production may well double. Other unconventional species may make large contributions, and the possibility of discovering ways to utilize species now used for fish meal directly as human food offers the chance of yet another large increase. Elimination of discards at sea, and more efficient processing with less spoilage and wastage, could lead to substantial increases in food production even without increases in fishing. It is evident that tripling or even quadrupling the present level of production of food from marine sources before the end of the twenty-first century is a reasonable possibility.

Such projections must be tempered by economic reality. Consumers must be able and willing to buy seafood. Producers must be able to supply products at acceptable prices. Seafood prices have increased in constant dollars since 1960 – edible finfish and crustaceans are up about 70 percent, although molluscs are up less than 40 percent (table 3.5). What will happen to prices in the future is difficult to estimate. They may decrease in the short term, since fuel is a large part of the cost of fishing – as much as 30 or 40 percent in some cases.

Future production of food from the sea will also depend on the national policies and economies of the less than ten countries (out of over 200) which have accounted for half or more of the total catch since world statistics have been assembled (table 3.3).

Projections by aquaculture enthusiasts notwithstanding, it is unlikely that aquaculture will increase its contribution to the world food supply very much by the year 2000. Restoration of overfished stocks by management and the development of new fisheries on unfished or lightly fished stocks can produce food at a lower cost. New developments in aquaculture are likely to be aimed at producing high-priced commodities such as shrimp and lobster in relatively small quantities. These enterprises will

TABLE 3.5 UNITED STATES PRICES FOR FISH AND SHELLFISH, 1960–81

Year	a	b	c	d	e	f	g	h	j
1960	0.252	0.284	0.184	0.207	0.431	0.486	0.779	0.878	88.0
1961	0.258	0.288	0.205	0.229	0.432	0.482	0.795	0.887	89.1
1962	0.262	0.289	0.185	0.168	0.524	0.578	0.769	0.849	89.9
1963	0.265	0.289	0.206	0.225	0.475	0.518	0.896	0.822	91.2
1964	0.227	0.244	0.158	0.147	0.497	0.535	0.743	0.800	92.4
1965	0.206	0.218	0.250	0.237	0.501	0.530	0.780	0.825	94.4
1966	0.321	0.330	0.262	0.270	0.543	0.559	0.735	0.756	99.1
1967	0.330	0.330	0.251	0.251	0.516	0.516	0.827	0.827	132.9
1968	0.369	0.354	0.256	0.246	0.598	0.574	0.905	0.868	103.6
1969	0.418	0.381	0.295	0.267	0.726	0.661	0.871	0.793	108.9
1970	0.435	0.374	0.351	0.302	0.676	0.581	0.848	0.729	114.9
1971	0.497	0.410	0.327	0.270	0.816	0.673	0.884	0.729	118.4
1972	0.564	0.450	0.363	0.290	0.934	0.745	1.028	0.820	123.5
1973	0.699	0.525	0.483	0.363	1.131	0.850	1.065	0.800	141.4
1974	0.673	0.456	0.521	0.353	0.950	0.643	0.955	0.647	161.7
1975	0.744	0.462	0.523	0.324	1.195	0.741	1.194	0.741	175.4
1976	0.924	0.542	0.626	0.367	1.484	0.870	1.863	1.093	180.8
1977	0.994	0.548	0.673	0.371	1.510	0.832	1.979	1.090	192.2
1978	1.136	0.581	0.760	0.389	1.802	0.922	2.294	1.174	211.4
1979	1.315	0.581	0.910	0.419	2.134	0.982	2.617	1.204	234.5
1980	1.203	0.487	0.837	0.339	1.907	0.773	2.952	1.196	254.6
1981	1.355	0.504	0.943	0.351	2.260	0.840	2.530	0.941	272.5

Notes: Prices are "ex-vessel," that is, as paid to the fisherman at first sale. Consumer prices are about three times this amount for finfish and two times for shellfish. Weights are for the whole animal as removed from the sea, except for molluscs, which are for edible portion only. "Edible" in "a" and "c" is total landings less California anchovy and menhaden. Does not include landings of tuna by U.S. vessels in Puerto Rico.

a – Total edible, price per kilogram
b – "a" adjusted by CPI
c – Edible finfish, price per kilogram
d – "c" adjusted by CPI
e – Crustaceans, price per kilogram

f – "e" adjusted by CPI
g – Molluscs, price per kilogram
h – "g" adjusted by CPI
j – Food component of the CPI

Sources: Prices in U.S. dollars from *Fisheries of the United States*, appropriate years. Consumer price Index (CPI) from *Statistical Abstract of the United

be based in many cases on feeding cheap fish to the animals cultured. They may be profitable, but they will contribute little to increasing production of food from the sea.

The *Global 2000* Fisheries Projections

Unfortunately, the world harvest of fish is expected to rise little, if at all, by the year 2000 . . . The world catch of naturally produced fish leveled off in the 1970s at about 70 million metric tons a year (60 million metric tons for marine fisheries, 10 million metric tons for freshwater species). Harvests of traditional fisheries are not likely to increase *on a sustained basis* . . .

It seems unlikely . . . that the generally accepted annual potential of 100 mmt of traditional marine species will be achieved on a sustained basis. It is more likely that the potential is nearer the present catch, or about 60 mmt . . .

It is difficult to imagine how these statements could be made in the face of available facts. But a close look at the fisheries predictions in the *Global 2000* report shows that they suffer from two major defects. The first is that they are frequently simple assertions, unsupported by analysis. The second is the inconsistencies in the projections, and the careless handling of facts and figures. Some examples:

Global 2000 indicates that world fish production "leveled off in the 1970s at about 70 million metric tons a year . . .". In fact, the average production in the 1970s was around 65 million tons, and it was nearly ten percent higher in 1979 than it was in 1970 – over 30 percent higher if the Peruvian anchovy is excluded (table 3.1).

Global 2000 says, on p. 105, that it seems unlikely that the generally accepted potential of 100 million metric tons of traditional marine species will be achieved on a sustained basis – it is more likely that the potential is nearer the catch in 1975, 60 million tons. But on p. 111 the report indicates that the potential is probably greater than the 1975 catch, noting that the increased yield from lightly exploited areas has been estimated at 30–50 million tons. The increased yield plus the 1975 catch add up to 90–110 million tons, bracketing the 100 million disavowed just a few pages earlier. And the figure on p. 106 (which does not agree with the table on p. 105) seems to predict catches in the order of 90 million tons for the year 2000.

Global 2000 predicts on p. 106 that if pollution continues unabated, "as appears to be the prognosis" (whose prognosis?), the effect will be a significant reduction in fishery yields. Earlier on *Global 2000* had said only that yields are not likely to increase. It says on p. 111 that ". . . the estimated increase . . . in yield is made up of hakes . . . and croakers . . ." but also that "the present world harvest of marine fish . . . will not increase . . .". How is the reader supposed to figure out what is really meant?

The pollution theme is elaborated on p. 111, where *Global 2000* says that coastal zones are being changed at ever-increasing rates to the detriment of productivity. But on p. 112 *Global 2000* says that inshore aquaculture shows possibilities for enormous expansion. How can aquaculture in inshore areas be successful if coastal zones are being degraded at increasing rates? (The point is raised on p. 23, where it is noted that "increasing pollution" is "likely to be a serious impediment" to the growth of aquaculture.)

An example of careless treatment of data may be found on p. 105, where *Global 2000* says that the catch of crustaceans has been nearly constant since 1970, and that molluscs have increased, but only in small amounts. The table on the same page shows the catch of crustaceans increasing 18 percent during 1970–5, and the catch of molluscs increasing 12 percent. In *Global 2000* terms, an increase of 18 percent is nearly constant, while an increase of 12 percent is small.

There is a comparison on p. 106 between the amount of protein furnished in 1975 by the 60 million ton marine catch to 4 billion people and the amount of protein to be furnished by a possible 100 million tons to 6 billion people in 2000. The conclusion is that the supply will decrease in relative terms. Ignoring the confusion generated by comparing marine animal catch with aquatic yield, would not a 67 percent increase in catch at least keep pace with a 50 percent increase in human population? Another version of this curious arithmetic occurs in the summary on p. 23, where 17.6 kg per capita in 2000 (112 million tons/6.35 billion people) is held to be less than 17.5 kg per capita in 1975 (70 million tons/ 4 billion people).

TABLE 3.6 *GLOBAL 2000* PREDICTIONS,
AND ACTUAL VALUES

Prediction (based on data to 1975)	Actual 1975–81 (%)
Marine catches will not increase	+13.5[a]
Marine finfish catches will not increase	+11.4[b]
Crustacean catches nearly constant	+32.0
Mollusc catches increasing by small amounts	+26.8

Notes: [a] 17.3% if the Peruvian anchovy is excluded. [b] 15.7% if the Peruvian anchovy is excluded.

In summary, *Global 2000* is inaccurate and inconsistent with respect to fisheries. On detailed examination it is not clear just what *Global 2000* has to say, except that the outlook is gloomy and that catches will not increase (or maybe they will, unless they decrease).

In any case, 6 years, nearly a quarter of the forecast period, have passed (*Global 2000* used fisheries data only to 1975), and the *Global 2000* predictions can be compared with what has really happened (table 3.6).

Trends observed several years after the *Global 2000* predictions were made are opposite to those predicted. This fact speaks louder than any analysis about the credibility of *Global 2000* with respect to fisheries.

4

Global Forests

ROGER A. SEDJO AND MARION CLAWSON

Forests are important natural resources in the world today; they always have been and they always will be. They cover a large proportion of the world's land surface, they produce a large volume of varied goods and services, and they touch the lives of everyone. In any resource review, forests must be considered carefully and critically.

It is part of today's conventional wisdom that the world's forests, particularly the tropical forests, "are disappearing at alarming rates as growing numbers of people seek land to cultivate, wood to burn, and raw materials for industry" (Council on Environmental Quality, p. 66). But it is also the case that some deforestation may be necessary to best meet the full range of social, environmental, and developmental goals.

In this chapter we examine the evidence regarding the current rate of deforestation and the long-term prognosis. We conclude that the most recent and best evidence suggests that while serious *local* problems of excessive deforestation do exist in some regions of the tropics, the overall picture is not nearly as gloomy as portrayed in *Global 2000* (Barney, 1980). The actual rates of deforestation are considerably below those used in the *Global 2000* projections and better forest management – which is already becoming prevalent – makes massive deforestation less likely.

Important Questions Concerning Forests

In any analysis of resources in 2000 or any other future year, there are four major questions which need to be addressed concerning forests. The assembly and analysis of data should be directed toward illuminating these questions:

(1) Will there be enough wood fiber on a global or international basis to provide the lumber, plywood, fiberboard, paper, chemical feedstock, and other forest products needed by the presently

economically developed countries and for the rapidly industrializing ones as well, at reasonable costs?

(2) Will there be enough wood fiber locally available, especially in
low-income countries, to meet the needs for local construction,
fuel and other locally used products?

(3) Do present or prospective forest management practices pose
serious environmental problems, locally or globally?

(4) Do present or prospective forest management practices seriously
threaten the genetic inheritance of the world, and what are the
consequences if they do?

Forests in Transition and the Common Property Problem

A few thousand years ago humans in large parts of the world were faced
with vast inherited forests – forests which had become established, grown,
and matured with little or no input of human management activities.
Humans in many regions were forest-dwellers and in other regions they
lived on the edge of the forests and utilized the forests to some extent.
These vast forests were both important assets and serious obstacles to
more intensive utilization of the land. As assets, they provided building
materials and wood for other purposes, such as furniture, and above all
provided fuel. The latter was used not only for residential space heating
but also for industrial production. The wood was used directly in some
areas and for some uses, and as a source of charcoal in other areas and for
other uses.

In substantial parts of the world – for example, Western Europe and the
British Isles – the original inherited forests were cleared, beginning
relatively early in the history of those regions. Indeed, clearing was
essential if the land was to be used for the growing of cultivated crops.
The ability to clear forests was limited but not unimportant in the days of
relatively crude hand tools and no power tools. Forest land clearing
always involves substantial ecological changes in the area; that is its
purpose. The soil surface is opened to sunlight and to direct impact of
rain; changes in soil temperature, in soil microbiology, and in nutrient
cycling take place. In the temperate zones these changes are generally
milder and quite different than in tropical and subtropical zones. The
cleared forest land can then be used for the growing of farm crops. While
the initial crop agriculture following forest clearing may have been primitive in comparison with the crop agriculture practiced today on those
same areas, yet it produced vastly more food for humans than did the
forests. One need not argue that forest clearing triggered population
increases but one may assert that without the forest clearing the increased
human population would have lacked food to sustain the population

increases. Wildlife species in the original forests were reduced, some-times eliminated, by the forest clearings.

While these early (over 300 years ago) forest clearings were basic to the development of agriculture and of industry in the regions concerned, it is also true that much forest clearing took place which, in retrospect, was unwise. For example, the Mediterranean region in general once was heavily forested. As early as Greek and Roman times, much of the forest had been cut, the land was experiencing erosion, and forest reproduction was inhibited or prevented by extensive grazing of domestic livestock. In modern times (the past 100 years), governments and other organizations have sought to reforest some parts of the Mediterranean region. Tree planting must be accompanied by fire control and by animal grazing control if the tree seedlings are to survive and grow to reasonable maturity. In spite of some success achieved in many areas, much of this region is still deforested.

Forest clearing for the purpose of establishing cultivated crop agri-culture has taken place in many parts of the world, temperate and tropical zones alike, where the combination of soils and climate was unsuitable for successful continued crop farming. More detail will be provided on this point for the United States and for some of the moist tropical forests today in later sections of this chapter.

These early inherited forests in many parts of the world were, in practice, common property resources; i.e. they were the property of no-one and hence the property of all. Forest and nearby dwellers were able to use the wood and other outputs of the forests without approval from any owner or from any governmental agency. While the demand for the resource was light, this system was adequate; natural regeneration was sufficient to replace the disruptions caused by humans. In this environment artificial reforestation was unnecessary. However, as demand for the resource rose institutions were required to insure that resource was not destructively exploited. Such institutions were needed to provide reasonable assurance that investments in maintaining and improving the resource were allowed to reach fruition. Where adequate institutions arose, the resource was managed. Where appropriate insti-tutions failed to develop, the resource was over-exploited and resource degradation occurred. There was little or no incentive for any individual user to replant trees, or to protect natural regeneration from fire or from premature utilization by others. If one user did not take the available wood, someone else would do so. This is the classical common-property dilemma or "tragedy of the commons" (Hardin, 1968). At one time or another it has plagued efforts at reforestation in many parts of the world, including areas within the Mediterranean Basin, China, and desert areas in Africa today.

The common-property dilemma has been solved in extensive parts of the world in either or both of two ways: by the extension of private ownership to the forests, and/or by the establishment of adequate governmental controls and management on the ground for public forests. It is not a serious oversimplification to maintain that regions of the globe that have no serious current problems with deforestation are also the regions of the globe where the common-property problem has been dealt with in a satisfactory manner. The United States, for example, has handled this problem in forestry both with the institution of private property and also through public ownership of timber lands. The same is true for most if not all countries in the important forested regions of the temperate zones of the Northern Hemisphere. To a large extent this is not true for the tropical forests, and for much of the other forests in the Southern Hemisphere, including many of the desert "forests."

One need not espouse private property as the sole route to purposeful and successful forestry; competent and forceful public forest management within the context of either a private or socialistic economy may achieve more or less the same ends. But one can say, with confidence, that unless effective means of protecting the seedling until it grows up are established, there is little to be gained by putting the tree seedling into the soil.

Humans throughout all of the world were once foragers and hunters, utilizing the crops and the animals which appeared naturally, without their help and often in spite of their actions. Agriculture, in the sense of crop cultivation and livestock care and management, began to arise at least 6,000 years ago in some regions. It has spread until today human gatherers and hunters are but remnants in remote regions. Science, technology, and arts for agriculture had to be developed, slowly at first, more rapidly later; and they had to spread to all users of the land.

Forestry was once a hunting-and-gathering form of human activity also. People sought natural stands of trees, harvested those kinds and those parts of trees they could use effectively, with little or no consideration for another crop from the same area. While this kind of forestry was beginning to yield to managed forestry concerned with continued crops of trees from the same area in some parts of Western Europe a few hundred years ago, the hunting–gathering system of forestry prevailed nearly everywhere until fairly recently, and still prevails in many parts of the world. As we shall show in a later section, hunting–gathering forestry was dominant in the United States until perhaps 1920 or later. Forest utilization in much of the tropical forests is still a matter of searching for valuable species and valuable trees and harvesting them with little or no concern for regeneration. The same is true for many of the desert and semi-desert areas of the world.

It is also true, however, that managed forestry is beginning to be important in many areas where is was unknown a generation or so ago.

Plantation forestry is beginning to emerge in Latin America, in the Pacific Basin, and elsewhere outside of the northern temperate zone where it is also increasing in area and in importance. As with agriculture, managed crop production involves vastly more inputs of labor, capital, and managerial competence on the same area of land, than does hunting–gathering: but it should also result in vastly more output. Whether or not it is profitable in the economic sense depends on many factors including, above all, the price at which the output can be sold.

Managed forestry encounters some problems that typical crop agriculture does not. Trees have long growing cycles – a few years at the minimum, half a century to a century or more for many species and many locations, compared with mostly annual cropping for farming. Both forestry and crop farming have many common problems of production (diseases, pests, etc.), of marketing, or economic instability and price variation, and others. On the technical side, crop farming can adjust vastly more quickly than can forestry. The economic barriers to adjustment may be severe for both but are hardly less so for forestry than for cropping. One must expect, therefore, that the results of intensive or managed forestry will show up slowly and gradually. This fact increases, rather than diminishes, the importance of a careful look at the future.

Forestry today is experiencing a transition similar to that experienced two or three millennia ago in agriculture. Just as agriculture evolved from gathering and hunting to cropping and livestock raising, similarly forestry is beginning to evolve from the gathering of natural inventories to the cropping of forest plantations. For the transition to occur, a number of changes must occur simultaneously. First, the increasing pressures on the natural resource must result in its increasing economic scarcity, i.e. either higher market prices or increasing costs of foraging and hunting to obtain the resources as reflected in returns to that activity per unit of inputs expended. Second, certain changes in social institutions must occur to preclude the destructive features of the common property problems. For example, planters must have a reasonable expectation that they will be able to collect the fruits of their investments in the form of a harvest of the crop. Likewise, herders must have a reasonable expectation they will reap the fruits of their efforts in raising livestock. Similarly, some form of institutional arrangement must be developed to allow investors in forests, whether public or private, to have some degree of certainty that they, or their designated successors, will be in a position to capture the bulk of the benefits of the forest investment.

Thus some form of institutional arrangement must be developed to allow the common-property type of resources, such as wildlife, natural forests, foraging foods, genetic resources, and environmental services, to accrue predictably to individuals who are willing to make the necessary investment in establishing and maintaining these resources or in preserving habitats necessary to maintain these resources. Numerous such human institutions have developed. These include the institution of private property and property rights, as well as the other institutions for collective action, or that require collective agreements.

In addition to the establishment of appropriate social institutes, incentives must be present to induce either the private or public owner-manager to undertake investments in forestry. The incentives may be of various types. For example, protection forestry may be undertaken to avoid the costs associated with excessive water runoff, erosion, silting and downstream flooding. More direct financial returns will also encourage tree planting and forest management. Of all the natural resources examined by Potter and Christy (1962) and Manthy (1978), wood was the only one that experienced a continuous long-term upward trend in its real price in the U.S. (table 4.1). Evidence indicates that a similar trend was experienced in Europe (Sivonen, 1971). This trend suggests that wood, or at least certain types of wood, has become increasingly scarce in an economic sense. This rising scarcity has created financial incentives which have been manifest in the rapidly increasing rate of investments in tree planting and forest management.

While, as noted above, the countries of the temperate climate Northern Hemisphere appear to have largely resolved problems of excessive deforestation, in some areas of the tropics and Southern Hemisphere problems continue to exist and these problems appear to be related to the common-property features of the land and/or the forest. For example, the most common source of forest destruction in these regions appears to be the institutions of "slash and burn" agriculture. In a world where the demands on the resource are minor, serious common-property problems do not arise. Thus, in the context of light population pressures, a situation in which small tracts of forest are cleared, typically through burning, used for agriculture for a few years and then left unattended, revert to forest, and at some future date are once again used temporarily for agriculture, does not put undue pressure upon the ecological system. However, just as in the "tragedy of the commons" where the common-property pasture will be utilized in excess, so too, as pressures increase, the "slash and burn" approach may be overused in both an ecological and economic sense, with deleterious results if access is unrestricted and pressures large. Much of the contemporary problem of deforestation in tropical regions is the result of its "common-property" characteristics. In addition to the slash and burn agriculture just mentioned, regions experiencing excessive deforestation typically have other common-property-induced difficulties. For example, firewood gathered in the context of a common-property environment and population pressures could be expected to contribute to the problem of excessive deforestation.

TABLE 4.1 FOREST PRODUCTS, DEFLATED PRICES (DEFLATED BY THE 1947–9 WHOLESALE PRICE INDEX)

Year	Sawlogs[a] ($/m B. ft) (1)	Pulpwood[b] ($/cord) (2)	Veneer Logs[c] ($/m ft³) (3)	Minor Products ($/m ft³) (4)	Fuelwood ($/m ft³) (5)	Turpentine ($/gal) (6)	Rosin ($/cwt) (7)	All forest Products ($ millions) (8)
1870	7			47				1965
1871	8			50				1133
1872	8			50				1148
1873	8			51				1167
1874	8			51				1159
1875	8			49				1185
1876	8			49				1178
1877	8			50				1137
1878	8			50				1139
1879	8			54				1218
1880	8			52				1188
1881	9			56				1272
1882	9			57				1298
1883	9			57				1298
1884	9			61				1379
1885	10			62				1485
1886	10			64				1448
1887	10			64				1453
1888	10			62				1486
1889	10			62				1486
1890	10			63				1436
1891	10			63				1424
1892	10			65				1473
1893	10			65				1464
1894	11			71				1685
1895	10			67				1524

Year							
1896	1600				71		11
1897	1536				68		10
1898	1557				69		11
1899	1599			180	71	15	11
1900	1568				65		10
1901	1648	2			65		10
1902	1787	2			72		11
1903	1768	3			69		11
1904	1788	3		217	62	18	9
1905	1621	5		176	71	14	11
1906	1966	5	1	221	81	18	13
1907	2068	5	1	238	82	19	13
1908	2278	4	1	253	106	20	16
1909	2226	5	1	242	104	20	16
1910	2128	6	1		94		14
1911	2391	7	1		114		18
1912	2251	7	1		138		17
1913	2289	4	1		128		16
1914	2311	4	1	246	116	20	18
1915	2298	4	1		118		18
1916	1881	5	1	195	98	16	15
1917	1682	3	1	179	84	15	13
1918	1852	6	0	202	85	16	13
1919	2953	8	1	219	92	18	14
1920	2168	6	1	234	99	19	15
1921	3189	3	1	391	118	32	18
1922	2775	4	1	318	116	26	18
1923	2663	3	2	306	113	25	17
1924	2833	4	1	311	135	25	21
1925	2886	7	1	284	162	23	25
1926	2846	8	1	284	155	23	24
1927	2796	6	1	282	155	23	24
1928	2586	6	1	266	138	22	21
1929	2748	5	1	261	168	21	26
1930	2657	4	1		154		24

TABLE 4.1 (Continued)

Year	Sawlogs[a] ($/m B. ft) (1)	Pulpwood[b] ($/cord) (2)	Veneer Logs[c] ($/m ft³) (3)	Minor Products ($/m ft³) (4)	Fuelwood ($/m ft³) (5)	Turpentine ($/gal) (6)	Rosin ($/cwt) (7)	All forest Products ($ millions) (8)
1931	23	23		152	285	1	4	2726
1932	20			131		1	3	2532
1933	20	17		129	213	1	4	2192
1934	20	16		129	196	1	4	2889
1935	19	15		121	181	1	4	1948
1936	19	15	186	126	181	1	5	1987
1937	20	14	174	138	175	0	6	1965
1938	19	16	188	127	196	0	4	2855
1939	21	16	197	137	193	0	5	2114
1940	20	16	202	131	193	0	4	2080
1941	22	14	203	142	174	1	4	2061
1942	24	16	178	155	195	1	5	2233
1943	32	18	190	205	217	1	6	2672
1944		19	192		235	1	8	2771
1945	30	19	198	195	236	1	9	2754
1946		19	204		238	1	9	3112
1947	42	18	267	273	228	1	8	3235
1948	39	17	295	251	215	0	7	3033
1949	43	16	309	278	197	0	7	3097
1950	41	16	341	278	283	1	6	3116
1951	37	18	303	238	226	1	8	3034
1952	41	19	332	264	234	0	7	3242
1953	42	18	351	272	219	0	7	3238
1954	42	18	344	271	219	0	7	3225
1955	44	18	351	286	225	1	8	3354
1956	43	19	347	288	230	0	7	3338
1957	40	18	322	262	217	0	7	3135
1958	39	18	315	252	219	0	7	3074

Year								
1959	41	18	317	264	217		8	3147
1960	42	18	328	271	222		12	3278
1961	40	18	312	262	219		10	3159
1962	39	18	316	255	217	0	9	3188
1963	40	18	293	258	224	0	9	3133
1964	41	18	294	266	221	0	9	3168
1965	41	18	389	269	224	0	9	3212
1966	40	18	380	268	226	0	8	3168
1967	41	18	323	264	220	0	8	3176
1968	43	18	320	279	227	0	8	3298
1969	46	18	362	297	224	1	9	3458
1960	39	18	334	253	219	1	11	3158
1971	46	17	313	299	213	1	12	3373
1972	52	17	322	336	209	1	13	3586
1973	64	19	582	415	235	1	14	6489
1974[a]	56	19	460					
1975	48	17	384					
1976	55	17	506					
1977	63	16	407					
1978	68	16	524					
1979	81	16	594					

Notes:
[a] Douglas fir, average
[b] Southern pine, Southeast
[c] Douglas fir, average
[d] Data after 1973 obtained from "U.S. Timber Production, Trade, Consumption, and Price Statistics 1950–80."
Source: Manthy (1978), p. 95.

Casual observations of the tropical countries where the problem exists suggest that the common-property view of the problem appears applicable to many countries where fuelwood is experiencing excessive depletion. Likewise, many of the countries in the Sahel which have fuelwood problems appear to have situations where the resource is treated as a common-property resource, either because institutions have not been developed to limit access or because the existing institutions do not have sufficient power actually to restrict effectively (Thomson, 1981).

A second situation where rapid rates of deforestation are occurring appears to reflect a conscious decision, typically by the local government, that the particular forest resource ought to be utilized for its commercial values. This type of situation might be said to obtain in much of the region of Southeast Asia and the East Indian Archipelago, e.g. the Philippines, Indonesia, and Malaysia, where the forest resource is logged and traded for foreign exchange. Here the critics charge that the rate of deforestation is excessive, the wood use inefficient, and the environmental damages substantial. On the other hand one might reasonably ask what is the desired rate at which the resource ought to be utilized, given the high quality of the forest resources for wood products and the ready markets, and whether some environmental costs are justified. We might note here that in the case of some of these areas non-forest land uses have been designated which are part of the country's economic development strategy, e.g. the transmigration scheme in Indonesia, which calls for major population migrations to the outer islands – the islands where the forests are largely located.

The final type of situation might be illustrated by the Amazonian case in which the commercial timber values of many of the natural forests are small and deforestation has been, at least during some period, encouraged by official governmental policies aimed at regional development and finding alternative uses for the forest lands. Such a situation presents the dilemma of a trade-off of benefits from alternative land uses. We should note here that, despite international concerns, the aggregate rate of deforestation for the Amazon has been quite modest, perhaps reflecting the unfavorable economics inherent in many of these types of schemes.

The History of U.S. Forests

The history of the U.S. forests is in many respects an excellent example of the generalized history of world forests presented above. U.S. forests are obviously important to U.S. citizens but they are also important to people in other countries because the high productivity of U.S. forest lands make this country a potential source of wood for other industrial countries.

While data on U.S. forests are neither as complete nor as reliable as some of us would like, they are nevertheless far better than data on forests in many other parts of the world.

As recently as 400 years ago – which from a historical point of view is little more than yesterday – the United States had extensive areas of mature forests, inherited from the operation of natural forces over centuries (Clawson, 1979). In Lillard's phrase (1947), the early colonists from various European countries were confronted with a sea of trees. About 45 percent of the total area of the "lower 48" states was covered with what the Forest Service today calls "commercial forests."

In addition to these 380 million hectares of commercial forest, the land within what are now the 48 states contained a substantial area of more sparse or "non-commercial" forests. The land within the present United States also included substantial areas of prairie and open plains with few or no forests. Thus, in the broad general regions where forests were found, the forests were dominant, almost all-inclusive, as a land use. The areas east of the Mississippi River were mostly fully forested; so were extensive areas in the Rocky Mountains and along the Pacific Coast.

While it is true that many of these forests were fully mature, it is also true that forests are dynamic and constantly changing. Natural processes – including fire, disease, insects and storms – continually swept over these forests destroying some, usually the older more decadent stands, to make way for new vigorous forests. However, for substantial areas of the inherited forest the volume of standing timber was near the maximum the site and the species could produce, with little or no net annual growth. Such growth as did take place was largely or wholly offset by mortality from weather and age. These magnificent forests were storehouses, not growth machines.

As in Western Europe, these vast heavily stocked inherited forests in the United States were both great assets and great problems to the first settlers in every area. Ready availability of wood for building materials, for tools and implements of many kinds, and for fuel was a great asset to the early settlers; but the forests had to be cleared if crops were to be grown; and the size of the trees which was so awe-inspiring also made them very difficult to clear. Many times the trees were simply girdled and allowed to die and eventually to fall over, and crops were grown in the land around them.

Clearing of forests proceeded slowly for many decades and as late as 1800 had taken only a few million hectares out of the original forest. The rate of clearing accelerated during the nineteenth century, especially during the latter part of it, and was active as late as 1920. The peak probably occurred around 1905. The rate of clearing, or the shrinkage in the original forest area, was almost exactly matched by an expansion of crop agriculture until prairies and plains were reached, after which crop

acreage could be increased at the expense of grazing land rather than at
the expense of forest land. Wherever and whenever there was a market or
a use for the wood from the cut trees, the wood was used. In many areas,
however, there was no local market and no need for the volumes of wood
so made available, and the trees were burned on the ground where they
lay.

The volume of timber standing when the colonists first came was
reduced by half because nearly half of the forested land was cleared for
farming, and the volume on the lands remaining in forests was also
reduced by half again, as timber harvest proceeded faster than regrowth
could replenish it. The owners of the forest land were simply converting
the capital from standing trees to more liquid forms, investable in other
forms of capital.

The timber harvesting of the nineteenth and early twentieth century
was often a brutal ecological process. Trees were all cut – "clearcut" we
would say today, although that term seems not to have been used during
much of this process, or the trees not cut often were damaged by the
cutting of other trees. Areas were burned, often repeatedly; there was a
general belief that the land would go into farming, hence burning to
prevent tree regrowth was economically and socially sound and productive. The harvest of the trees changed the ecology of the areas concerned – indeed, that was its purpose, for those areas taken into crop
agriculture. The process may have been a brutal one, but it was also
necessary if crop agriculture was to expand to provide food for the rapidly
growing population.

· The loss of forest area, the reduction in volume of standing timber on
the areas not converted to farming, the devastated appearance of the
harvested areas, and the slow recovery of the natural forests greatly
disturbed and alarmed many observers of the forest scene during those
decades. Out of their concern emerged the processes for the establishment of public forests on which it is hoped much better forest management could be practiced. In the United States today about a third of all
the commercial forests are publicly owned, most by the federal government but some by states and some by countries.

By about 1920 the process of forest clearing had largely run its course
and since then the area of forest land has remained relatively stable in the
United States. Some land continues to be taken out of forests, for
highways, power line rights of way, reservoirs, urban expansion, and
even for agriculture. But some land which had been used for other
purposes reverts to forest or is planted to forest. Reversion of farmed
land back to forest began very early – before the Revolution, for the
tidewater areas along the Chesapeake Bay and adjoining waters, as
worn-out tobacco land was allowed to revert to trees. While abandonment of farm land and reversion to forest began in New England and the

TABLE 4.2 NET VOLUME OF GROWING STOCK AND SAWTIMBER ON COMMERCIAL TIMBERLAND IN THE UNITED STATES, BY SOFTWOODS AND HARDWOODS AND SECTION, 1952, 1962, 1970 AND 1977

Growing stock (million cubic feet)

Section	All species				Softwoods				Hardwoods			
	1952	1962	1970	1977	1952	1962	1970	1977	1952	1962	1970	1977
North	111,275	137,402	155,862	173,145	27,629	34,332	39,661	44,574	83,645	103,070	116,201	128,571
South	136,484	156,038	176,819	202,009	58,245	71,553	84,896	97,136	78,238	84,485	91,923	104,873
Rocky Mountain	91,435	97,606	99,290	99,814	87,457	93,104	94,413	94,935	3,978	4,502	4,877	4,879
Pacific Coast	264,201	256,737	248,456	236,000	251,614	241,833	230,820	219,134	12,587	14,904	17,636	16,866
United States	603,394	647,783	680,427	710,968	424,946	440,822	449,790	455,779	178,448	206,961	230,637	255,189

Sawtimber (million board feet, International 1/4-inch log rule)

Section	All species				Softwoods				Hardwoods			
	1952	1962	1970	1977	1952	1962	1970	1977	1952	1962	1970	1977
North	248,629	282,153	319,662	359,021	58,756	69,877	82,877	96,504	189,873	212,276	236,785	262,517
South	409,191	465,093	534,596	614,709	196,556	245,712	295,804	341,023	212,635	219,381	238,791	273,686
Rocky Mountain	389,779	399,458	393,350	390,169	380,795	389,825	383,386	380,380	8,984	9,633	9,964	9,790
Pacific Coast	1,464,624	1,369,754	1,290,773	1,215,042	1,430,096	1,327,344	1,239,606	1,167,503	34,527	42,410	51,167	47,539
United States	2,512,222	2,516,458	2,538,379	2,578,940	2,066,203	2,032,758	2,001,673	1,985,408	446,018	483,700	536,706	593,532

Note: Data may not add to totals because of rounding.
Source: An Analysis of the Timber Situation in the United States 1952–2030, U.S. Dept. of Agriculture, Forest Service, Forest Resource Report No. 23, December 1982, p. 133.

Middle Atlantic States before the Civil War, the really large reversions came after World War I, in the South particularly but also in the Lake States. The 1920 Census of Agriculture records the high water mark of cropping in much of the South.

The dramatic changes in U.S. forestry in the past 60 years have not been in land area, but in annual growth of wood. Average annual growth today is 3½ times what it was in 1920 (Clawson, 1981). Each successive timber inventory and appraisal by the Forest Service has shown a substantially higher total annual wood growth than its predecessor, and between 1952 and 1977 the total forest inventory (growing stock) increased almost 18 percent (table 4.2). The capacity of American forests to regenerate naturally, and to grow wood, has been repeatedly and seriously underestimated by foresters generally and by the Forest Service in particular. In a series of major studies since 1900, and more particularly since 1930, the Forest Service has estimated future wood growth. Every such estimate has been wrong – too low, and by a substantial amount. In large part, this persistent tendency to err has been due to concentration on biological factors with little or no regard for the effect of economic factors on the willingness of forest owners to grow more timber in response to favorable economic conditions. For the periods for which data are available, there has been a high correlation between annual wood growth on private lands and wood prices 20 years earlier. Since real prices of wood have continued to rise, one may reasonably judge that wood growth will continue to rise in the future in response to prices already evident in the market.

As a result of this dramatically higher wood growth in the United States, and as a result of timber harvest at a rate less than growth, inventories of standing timber in the United States have increased significantly since 1920. A popular view is that the United States is consuming its wood faster than it is growing, and that we are denuding our forests. In fact, exactly the reverse is happening – we are building them up.

What lessons does the U.S. forest history have to offer to the economically less developed countries of the world? Clearly, ecological and environmental conditions are different, and hence one would not want to overdraw the parallel between the experience of the U.S. and that of the countries of the developing world. However, it is clear that dynamic growing societies will generate pressures on, and changes in, the forest resource base. The experience of the temperate climate world indicates that forests and forestlands need not inevitably continue the process of destruction and reduction. Despite the continuing dynamism of temperate climate countries, their forested area has remained remarkably stable in recent years. In the U.S. a period of forest harvest which at the time seemed wasteful, rapacious, and brutal actually turned out to have been a necessary step in natural resource development – not a perfectly conducted or even a wisely managed step, but a necessary part.[1] The need for a long look, the recognition that times will change, the recognition that forests can be made to grow, and that other aspects of a forest situation change over time, are all necessary in any developing country. It is highly probable that some actions will be taken which in retrospect will seem to be mistakes – but inactions may be mistakes also.

Overall World Forest Summary

Forests cover about 20 percent of the world's land surface. Most (66 percent) of this forested area is closed forest, meaning that there exists a substantially complete cover of trees over the whole surface of the land (table 4.3). Closed forests vary greatly, from totally closed forests in the moist tropical forests, where very little sunlight reaches the ground, to comparatively open forests in many temperate zones. The open forests are also highly variable from region to region, varying from tree stands which at a distance seem both continuous and pervasive on the landscape, to areas where trees or large shrubs occur at wide intervals with truly open areas between the individual trees.

For the world as a whole 60 percent of the forest land area, both closed and open, is classified as hardwood and the remainder as softwood. This varies greatly across the globe. In the Northern Hemisphere by far the greater part of the total forest land area is composed of softwood species; in the Southern Hemisphere and the tropics the reverse is true. There are, of course, exceptions to this generalization, both within hemispheres and within countries. About 84 percent of the softwood closed forests are located in the U.S.S.R. and North America, while about 54 percent of the hardwood closed forest land is found in South America and Asia (table 4.4). In general, softwoods are more readily viable for commercial purpose.

When it comes to current standing volume of timber, the overall picture is generally similar but somewhat different in details than the picture of the land area. While timber volumes vary from region to region and site to site, the aggregate region timber volumes correspond roughly with the forest land area. The U.S.S.R. and North America have about 85 percent of the world's coniferous growing stock, while Latin America and Asia have about roughly 60 percent of the world's closed forest growing stock of hardwoods (Persson, 1974).

Table 4.5 indicates the world's production (harvest) of wood in 1980 by major region. About 40 percent of the total production is produced in the temperate regions of North America, Europe, the U.S.S.R. and Oceania alone. If fuelwood is excluded, as in table 4.6, this jumps to 75 percent.

TABLE 4.3 WORLD FORESTED AREA BY REGION, 1973

	Millions of hectares				Closed forest (percentage of land area)	Total forest (percentage of land area)
	Forest land	Closed forest	Open woodland	Total land area		
North America	630	470	(176)	1,841	25	34
Central America	65	60	(2)	272	22	24
South America	730	530	(150)	1,760	30	41
Africa	800	190	(570)	2,970	6	27
Europe	170	140	29	474	30	36
U.S.S.R.	915	785	115	2,144	35	43
Asia	530	400	(60)	2,700	15	20
Pacific area	190	80	105	842	10	23
Total world	4,130	2,655	(1,200)	13,003	20	31

Source: Global 2000 Report to the President, Technical Report, vol. II, p. 118.
Data on North American forests represent a mid-1970s estimate. Other data are from Persson (1974); they represent an early-1970s estimate. Forest land is not always the sum of closed forest plus open woodland, as it includes scrub and bushland areas which are neither forest nor open woodland, and because it includes deforested areas where forest regeneration is not taking place. In computation of total land area, Antarctic, Greenland, and Svalbard are not included; 19 percent of arctic regions are included.

TABLE 4.4 LAND AREA (MILLION HECTARES) OF WORLD FOREST RESOURCES BY REGION AND TYPE

Region	Coniferous		Broadleaf		Combined coniferous and broadleaf forests[a]	
	Land area	Percentage	Land area	Percentage	Land area	Percentage
North America	400	35.2	230	14.1	630	22.3
Central America	20	1.8	40	2.4	60	2.1
South America	10	0.8	550	33.6	560	19.8
Africa	2	0.2	188	11.5	190	6.7
Europe	75	6.6	50	3.0	140	5.0
U.S.S.R.	553	48.7	175	10.7	765	27.1
Asia	65	5.7	335	20.5	400	14.2
Oceania	11	1.0	69	4.2	80	2.8
Total world	1,136	100.0	1,637	100.0	2,825	100.0

Note: Closed forests.
Source: Persson (1974).
[a] The totals for combined coniferous and broadleaf forests do not always add, because no breakdowns have been given for areas in Europe and the U.S.S.R. excluded by law for exploitation.

Roger A. Sedjo and Marion Clawson

TABLE 4.5 ROUNDWOOD PRODUCTION – 1980

Region	Coniferous		Nonconiferous		Total	
	1000 m³	Percentage	1000 m³	Percentage	1000 m³	Percentage
Africa	12,537	1.1	379,662	21.7	433,851	14.4
North America						
(U.S. and Canada)	380,283	32.5	103,349	5.9	433,631	16.0
North						
Central America	17,358	1.5	28,618	1.6	47,208	1.6
South America	41,164	3.5	236,628	13.5	315,202	10.4
Asia	187,602	16.0	812,379	46.4	1,017,100	33.7
Europe	222,802	19.0	111,496	6.4	334,346	11.1
Oceania	12,520	1.1	20,287	1.2	32,968	1.1
U.S.S.R	297,500	25.4	58,500	3.3	356,000	11.8
World	1,171,766	100.0	1,750,919	100.0	3,020,306	100.0

Forests in the Temperate Regions

Over half of the world's forestlands are located in the temperate climate regions (table 4.3). These include the forests of North America, Europe, the U.S.S.R., China, and Oceania.[2] While these regions have large volumes of both hardwood and softwood, the softwoods are predominant. Table 4.7 presents FAO data on the forested area for the temperate area between 1949 and 1980. While the individual regions show fluctuations over the period, the aggregate picture is one of

TABLE 4.6 INDUSTRIAL ROUNDWOOD PRODUCTION – 1980

Region	Coniferous		Nonconiferous		Total	
	1000 m³	Percentage	1000 m³	Percentage	1000 m³	Percentage
Africa	7,380	0.8	43,050	10.1	50,430	3.6
North America						
(U.S. and Canada)	376,001	38.9	87,957	20.6	463,958	33.3
North						
Central America	7,505	0.8	3,453	0.8	10,958	0.8
South America	28,007	2.9	37,915	8.9	65,922	4.7
Asia	76,601	7.9	130,095	30.5	206,696	14.8
Europe	212,744	22.0	78,577	18.4	291,321	20.9
Oceania	12,115	1.3	13,872	3.3	25,986	1.9
U.S.S.R	246,900	25.5	31,300	7.3	278,200	20.0
World	967,252	100.0	426,219	100.0	1,393,471	100.0

Source: Food and Agriculture Organization of the United Nations, *1980 Yearbook of Forest Products*, 1969–1980.

substantial stability. Over the 30-year period the land area reported in the temperate forests increased about 2 percent. The regions experiencing the largest increases in growth were Europe, China, and Oceania. Growth in these areas offset declines in North America while the total forested area in the U.S.S.R. was reported to remain constant. The regions which the data indicate are expanding their land area in forests are generally the regions experiencing active reforestation efforts. For example, China has had a massive reforestation effort under way for the past two decades which involves tens of millions of hectares. Similar reforestation and afforestation efforts are under way on a more modest scale in Oceania and parts of Europe.

Taken on a global scale, the temperate regions have something in excess of one-half of the world's land area in forest as well as about the same percentage of the world forest timber volume. This region produces about one-half of the total wood production (table 4.5). Thus the temperate climate region's share of forest land area and forest volume is roughly proportional to its wood production for all uses.

Even as the forest land area of the temperate regions has remained stable, this region has also been the world's principal supplier of industrial wood, providing, as noted, about 75 percent of the world total in 1980 (table 4.6). North America and the U.S.S.R. alone supply well over one-half of the world's total industrial wood.

Overall, the forestry situation appears to be in an acceptable steady state in the temperate regions of the world. The land area in forests, and probably the forest volumes, are largely stable. In regions where economic (such as Oceania) or ecological (such as China) conditions dictate, reforestation has been undertaken, often with great zeal.[3] The temperate regions are not only providing the vast majority of the world's industrial wood but their wood-growing stocks and potential appear to be increasing. Simultaneously, by and large, the temperate regions appear to have successfully dealt with their most pressing ecological problems related to the forest resource, although it must be acknowledged that the problems are less complex than those of the tropics. Apparently, the institutions that have been developed, whether in the market or planned economies, are dealing in a passable manner with the common-property and other aspects of the forestry problem.

Forests in Deserts and Semi-Deserts

A substantial part of the world's surface – a quarter or a third, depending upon precise definitions – is desert or semi-desert in character. There are extensive deserts on almost every continent. Much of northern Africa is desert; there are extensive deserts in South America; much of Australia is

TABLE 4.7 FORESTED AREA IN TEMPERATE REGIONS (1000 HECTARES)

	North America (U.S.[a] and Canada)	Europe	Mainland China	U.S.S.R.	Oceania	Temperate area total	World total (temperate and tropical)
1949	650,318	124,000	81,974	628,000	31,568	1,515,860	3,523,000
1950	654,021	128,000	81,859	920,000	75,227	1,859,107	4,024,000
1951	653,738	128,000	81,859	920,000	75,510	1,859,107	4,007,000
1952	610,528	128,000	81,859	920,000	63,510	1,863,897	3,869,000
1953	669,476	127,000	81,859	920,000	64,569	1,862,904	3,843,000
1954	660,975	127,000	82,211	920,000	64,225	1,854,411	3,947,000
1955	660,975	135,000	82,211	920,000	64,225	1,862,411	3,949,000
1956	668,801	136,000	80,520	742,600	87,225	1,715,146	3,864,000
1957	668,512	138,000	80,520	742,600	54,514	1,684,146	3,839,000
1958	668,512	148,000	80,520	880,317	54,514	1,831,863	3,985,000
1959	668,512	148,000	80,520	880,317	53,514	1,830,863	3,987,000
1960	744,222	148,000	76,600	880,317	53,000	1,902,139	4,069,000

Year							
1965	745,429	137,000	76,600	880,317	79,000	1,918,346	4,105,000
1966	745,429	138,000	76,600	910,009	82,000	1,952,038	4,015,000
1967	738,718	139,000	76,600	910,009	82,000	1,946,327	3,997,000
1968	739,229	139,000	76,600	910,009	82,000	1,946,838	3,994,000
1969	739,229	140,000	76,600	910,009	82,000	1,947,838	4,068,000
1970	739,229	139,000	76,600	910,009	82,000	1,946,838	4,091,000
1971	739,229	140,000	76,600	910,009	81,000	1,946,838	4,028,000
1972	748,987	140,000	96,000	910,009	82,000	1,976,996	4,041,000
1973	735,551	140,500	118,000	910,009	84,892	1,988,952	3,990,643
1974	735,551	143,144	111,800	914,900	86,599	1,991,994	4,034,755
1975	626,971	148,648	147,700	920,000	85,606	1,928,925	4,052,550
1976	626,671	152,787	151,800	920,000	186,008	2,037,266	4,156,350
1977	616,129	153,444	155,500	920,000	135,950	2,031,023	4,145,215
1978	615,629	154,656	121,500	920,000	155,173	1,966,958	4,077,000
1979	616,229	154,670	115,000	920,000	155,457	1,961,356	4,056,670
1980	616,889	154,585	115,700	920,000	151,227	1,958,401	4,107,980

Note: [a] Includes Alaska and Hawaii
Source: FAO Production Yearbooks. The data given for a particular year are the data given for that particular yearbook; it is not the result of forest surveys taken in that particular year.

desert in character; so is much of Mongolia, adjacent Russia and China and the Middle East; as well as deserts in the southwest U.S. and Mexico. The distinguishing characteristics of deserts is the lack of moisture; many are hot but some are cold, and desert-like conditions exist on many high mountain areas, such as Tibet and the Andes.

With virtually no exceptions, deserts lack true forests; they may have some trees, in very scattered stands and shrubs. A substantial number of people live in desert and semi-desert conditions around the world; many are livestock raisers, often nomadic in life-style, moving where forage exists at a season or in a year, for their livestock. Many of them require wood for fuel; often it is the only source of energy for food preparation.

In nearly all deserts, private ownership of land is nonexistent; various forms of communal land tenure, including simple use rights on land owned by the nation, exist. The nomadic form of life is one reason for the origin and the continuance of the various group tenures. Many of the claims to use of land have developed over generations, sometimes as a result of armed struggles. Given the demand for wood, the mobile character of the population, and the land tenure situations, the stage is set for the classic common-property situation. Everyone has an incentive to harvest whatever wood that grows; no-one has an incentive to try to grow more wood. The ecology of most desert areas would make wood growth difficult in any case; but the economic and social situation makes tree-growing nearly impossible. All in all, the wood supply situation in the desert and semi-desert areas is one of the most serious and discouraging of any of the forest situations in the world. The technical problems of wood-growing are great; the social problems of wood-growing are extremely difficult with alternative sources of fuel generally lacking.

Tropical Moist Forests

Lying on each side of the equator around the world is an immense area of tropical moist forests, which have special characteristics and present special problems. A third of these are in Brazil – the Amazon Basin – and another quarter are in other Latin American countries; some are in west Africa, while others are in Asia and the islands of the East Indies. There are, of course, some biological differences among these areas and there are many significant economic and political differences among the countries in which these forests lie.

Most of these tropical moist forests are characterized by extremely high volumes of vegetation per unit of area, and by great diversity in the vegetative cover in each area. The vegetation is often so dense that the forest floor is in perpetual twilight. The soils of these areas are, for the most part, relatively infertile, and the largest pool of existing nutrients is tied up in the vegetation. The available plant nutrients are recycled from soil to plants and back to the soil as plants die and decompose, with relatively little nutrient storage in the soil. These forests are the home of an enormous variety of life forms – insects, reptiles, birds, and mammals – among which exist numerous and complicated biological interrelationships. Biologists, ecologists, and other natural scientists have long expressed a particular interest in these unique forests; but at the same time there has been a lack of sustained serious research on them.

When many of these tropical moist forests are cleared, the resultant ecological change in the soil and vegetation is often severe. For a small portion of tropical forest soils, the heating effect of direct sunlight results in major chemical changes (laterization) which are, for practical purposes, irreversible and seriously downgrade the soil capability. A more common problem on some soils is the accelerated rate of organic matter decomposition associated with deforestation which reduces the soil's ability to capture and retain nutrients (Allen and Cady, 1983). Partly because of the great variety of trees grown, the number of trees of a particular species per hectare is generally low, which severely handicaps efforts at commercial exploitation of these stands of timber. While there has been commercial timber harvest in some areas – notably in certain countries of Southeast Asia and the East Indies – most of the clearing of these tropical moist forests has been for agriculture. When some forests are cleared, farmed for a year or two using the plant nutrients released by burning the trees, and then the forest allowed to grow back for a period of years, the damage to the soils and to the whole ecology may be slight and bearable. If the cycle of this slash and burn farming and forestry is shortened too much, serious damage may occur. If an effort is made to convert even the best of these soils to permanent crop agriculture, special soil management practices are needed to maintain fertility.

While the unsuitability of the soils of the tropical moist forests for continued crop farming is generally asserted, there is evidence that this difficulty can be overcome. Sanchez *et al.* (1982) have shown that some soils in the Amazon Basin can be cropped continuously and indefinitely, yielding high outputs of cultivated crops without soil erosion or fertility loss. However, this result is obtainable only by heavy application of fertilizers and by application of highly sophisticated agronomic techniques – conditions impossible for native dwellers of these forests to meet, but these conditions may not be beyond the capabilities of competent governments of economically rapidly developing countries such as Brazil. There is reason to believe that some of the same results are obtainable in the forested areas of west Africa.

Plantation Forestry

While less than 1 percent of the forests of Latin America are industrial plantations, about one-third of the region's industrial wood output comes from industrial forest plantations. Furthermore, the total area in industrial forest plantation is projected to increase 300 percent between 1979 and the year 2000. In addition, other forest plantations, such as protection and fuelwood, are also expected to increase in number and land area. By the year 2000 it is expected that more than half of the greatly expanded industrial wood production of Latin America will be produced from plantation forests (InterAmerican Development Bank, p. 17). The foregoing not only attests to the potential of forest plantations to replace the natural forests as the principal source of industrial wood, but also indicates the extent to which relatively small areas of highly productive forest plantations can substitute for natural forests as producers of society's industrial wood needs. Therefore, simple comparisons of areas deforested and areas in forest plantations must be interpreted with care.

It is only in very recent times that plantation forestry has been a factor affecting the world's forests. Although some conscientious tree planting took place in parts of Europe and the Far East before the twentieth century, the vast bulk of reforestation that occurred was through natural regeneration. However, the incidence of artificial regeneration has increased dramatically since World War II and particularly after 1960.

Today forestry is experiencing a transition similar to that which occurred in agriculture much earlier in human history. Just as humankind has progressed from foraging and hunting to cropping and livestock raising, we are currently experiencing a transition from having our wood needs met from wild forests to a situation in which conscious decisions are made to plant, manage and havest wood.

In a world where wood is readily available from naturally regenerated forests, there would be little incentive for investments in plantation forests. However, increases in demand together with a reduction in accessible and merchantable natural timber stands provides upward pressures on wood prices. Higher wood prices, together with improved tree-growing techniques, have combined in the post-1960 period to provide an environment conducive to both private and public forestry investments. It is interesting to note that in some regions of the world, e.g. New Zealand and Chile, forest plantations are being established on lands that were formerly used for agriculture.

As table 4.8 indicates, by the mid-1970s the area of artificially regenerated forest worldwide totalled about 90 million hectares or roughly 3 percent of the world's closed forest area. Most of these forests were located in Europe, North America and the U.S.S.R., with nearly

TABLE 4.8 PLANTATION FOREST BY REGION (CIRCA 1975)

Economic class and region	Million hectares
Developed	
North America	11
Western Europe	13
Oceania	1
Other	10
Total	35
Developing	
Africa	2
Latin America	3
Asia	2
Total	8
Centrally planned	
Europe and the Soviet Union	17
Asia	30
Total	47
Total world	90

Source: Food and Agriculture Organization of the United Nations. Development and investment in the forestry sector. FO: COFO-78/2. Rome, 1978.

one-third of the plantation area found in China.[4] Another study estimates that almost 10 million hectares per year of artificially regenerated forests were being established worldwide in the late 1970s.[5]

While the data indicate that most forest plantations are situated in the temperate climate regions of the Northern Hemisphere, in recent years increased attention has been given to plantation activities in the tropics and subtropics, and in the Southern Hemisphere temperate climate regions. Today major forest plantation activities are under way in Brazil, Chile, Venezuela, South Africa, India, Indonesia, the Philippines, Australia, New Zealand, and a host of other tropical and Southern Hemisphere countries. Brazil alone established over 250,000 hectares per year of forest plantations during the decade of the 1970s. Tables 4.9 and 4.10 summarize a study of forest plantations in the tropics (Lanly and Clement, 1979) which estimated that the tropic and subtropic regions of Central and South America, Africa, and Asia had about 11.8 million hectares of plantation forest in the mid-1970s. Of this, about 6.7 million hectares were industrial forest plantations. By 1980, only 5 years later, the industrial forest plantations were projected by Lanly and Clement to

154   *Roger A. Sedjo and Marion Clawson*

TABLE 4.9   AREAS OF PLANTATIONS IN CENTRAL AND
SOUTH AMERICA, AFRICA, AND ASIA (THOUSAND HECTARES)

Region	1975
Central and South America[a]	3,589
Africa, south of Sahara[b]	1,578
Developing Asia[c] and the Far East	6,709
Total	11,876

Source: Lanly and Clement, 1979.
[a] Includes nonindustrial plantations, e.g. protection forests.
[b] Excluding South Africa.
[c] From Pakistan east, excluding the People's Republic of China and Japan.

have increased by 36 percent to 9.1 million hectares, and projections for the year 2000 indicated the industrial plantations in that region will cover over 21 million hectares or 3 times the area of the mid-1970s.

While the land areas involved in plantation forestry are modest relative to the total forested land area of the globe, their effect is potentially profound. Since industrial plantation forests are highly productive and are specifically located in regions that facilitate access to markets, their influence upon the worldwide availability of wood is likely to be significant. Sedjo (1980, 1983b) estimates the substantial potential for industrial forest plantations in regions which have not traditionally been major producers of wood. For example, Brazil has the potential to be a major force in world wood pulp markets before the end of the century.

While industrial forest plantations are sometimes viewed as a threat to the natural forest, the opposite is likely to be near to the truth. To the extent that plantation forests meet society's needs for industrial wood the

TABLE 4.10   INDUSTRIAL PLANTATIONS – TROPICAL AND
SUBTROPICAL AMERICA, AFRICA, AND ASIA
(THOUSAND HECTARES)

Region	1975	Projected 1980	Projected 2000
Central and South America	2,786	4,128	10,705
Africa south of Sahara[a]	997	1,248	2,180
Developing Asia[b] and the Far East	2,892	3,719	8,265
Total	6,675	9,095	21,150

Source: Lanly and Clement, 1979.
[a] Excluding South Africa.
[b] From Pakistan east, excluding the People's Republic of China, Mongolia, and Japan.

pressures upon the natural forests as a source of industrial wood will be reduced. Given yields readily obtainable in plantation forests (10–20 cubic meters per hectare per annum), wood volumes equivalent to the world's projected industrial wood needs for the year 2000 could be met by the sustained yield production of just 100–200 million hectares of plantation forests or only 3.5–7.0 percent of the world's closed forestland area (Sedjo, 1983a). In addition, to the extent that nonindustrial protection forests are being artificially established, environmental damage that was being generated in the absence of protective forest is being reduced.

Tropical Deforestation

Information about the tropical moist forests is relatively scant. What information we do have comes more from anecdotal evidence – provided by isolated investigations at single times and places – than from systematic studies conducted over large areas and lengths of time. As a result, there is little agreement as to the reliability and appropriateness of much of the data relating to these forests. Competent, honest, and unbiased scientists may differ considerably in their understanding of just what is happening to these forests as a whole; it is easy to be influenced greatly by observations of particular and perhaps unusual situations, or to assume trends from measurements at one point in time.

The general opinion is that the tropical forests "are disappearing at alarming rates" largely as the result of "slash and burn" agriculture and also as a result of commercial forest operations, highway and dam building, and clearing for more permanent pasture and cropping. It is maintained that the results of this land clearing are, in general, disadvantageous or even critical to the areas involved; that the soils of these tropical moist forest lands are unsuitable for crop agriculture; and that the continued existence of many species of life is threatened by clearing of these forests.

A hard look at the available data supports the view that some regions are experiencing rapid deforestation. However, the view that this is a pervasive phenomenon on a global level is questionable. The *Global 2000* report indicates that the range of estimates of loss in forest land area – mostly tropical area – was from 4 million to 10–12 million hectares annually. The report then chose to use a higher figure (18–20 million hectares) to discuss the problems and treated these figures as if they were fully reliable.

What are the best estimates of what is happening to tropical forests worldwide? Perhaps the most thorough compilation of the various data sets on the extent of the world's deforestation was undertaken by Allen and Barnes at Resources for the Future (1982).[6] They analyzed the data for a wide array of estimates of forested area and underlying concepts relevant to the issue of deforestation.

Table 4.11 and figure 4.1 present the estimates assembled by Allen and Barnes combined with an earlier estimate (Zon and Sparhawk, 1923) of the world's forests. As Allen and Barnes note, these estimates, coming from different sources and utilizing different forest definitions "are probably not very reliable as indicators of deforestation." Nevertheless, there is certainly nothing in the data to suggest that the world is experiencing significant net deforestation.

Focusing on the tropical forest areas of Africa, Asia, and Latin America, Allen and Barnes compared four sets of estimates of the size of the forests in tropical regions: Persson (1974), Lanly and Clement (1979), Sommer (1976) and the recent estimates of the FAO/UNEP (1982). Using definitions for both closed forests and other formations their results are presented in figure 4.2. Again, although the data are probably not very reliable indicators of deforestation, since they combine country data from different sources and cover only a 7-year period, the data certainly do not support the hypothesis that the tropical regions are experiencing major aggregate deforestation.

Allen and Barnes go on to use three sources of somewhat inconsistent data to estimate trends in forest area on a country-by-country basis over a period of 4 years or more (table 4.12). These sources are the *FAO Production Yearbook* (UN FAO, 1979), the recent Lanly directed FAO/UNEP study (1982) and a report to the National Academy of Sciences (Myers, 1980). The *FAO Production Yearbook* measures deforestation as the change in total forest land area over the period 1968–78, the FAO/UNEP study measures deforestation as the change in natural closed forest area – thereby excluding forest plantations – over the period 1976–80, and Myers measures deforestation as the conversion of moist tropical forest to *any other uses*, even naturally regenerated forest, over various periods of time. Also, Myers provided quantitative estimates for only selected tropical countries.

Of these three studies the 1982 FAO/UNEP study is the most recent and most thorough. In it Lanly provides the latest examination of the extent and rate of tropical deforestation utilizing a common conceptual framework and set of definitions. This study involved large numbers of specialists examining a wide variety of data, both official and unofficial, for 76 countries. In addition to normal techniques, the study made use of satellite imagery for a number of countries where other data were absent or suspect. The FAO/UNEP study estimated the rate of deforestation of the closed tropical broadleaf forests at 7.1 million hectares per annum (0.60 percent) for 1976–80 or 30–50 percent of Myers' estimates of 20–24 million hectares per annum. The rate of deforestation is almost identical for Latin America, Africa and Asia. Due to the larger area of

Source and year	Million ha	Source and year	Million ha
Zon and Sparhawk, 1923[f]	3,031	Whittaker and Likens, 1973[b]	4,850
Weck, 1961[b]	2,477	Bruning, 1974[b]	4,150
WFI, 1963[d]	4,126	Windhorst, 1974, 1976[b]	2,393
Olson, 1970[a]	4,800	Olson, 1975[b]	4,800
Bazilevich et al., 1971[b]	5,290	Eckholm, mid-1970s	2,657
Bruning, 1971[b]	3,590	Eyre, 1978[b]	6,050
Whittaker and Wordwell, 1971[b]	5,000	Smith, 1978[e]	2,563
FAO, 1972[a]	3,800	Steele, 1979	3,799
Lieth, 1972[a]	5,700	FAO, n.d.	4,300
Lieth, 1972, 1975[b]	5,000	Openshaw, n.d.	3,712
Persson, 1973[c]	4,030		

Note: n.d. = no date
[a] Taken from Earl, 1975.
[b] Taken from Leith, 1979.
[c] Taken from World Bank, 1978.
[d] Taken from Persson, 1974.
[e] Estimate of closed forests only.
[f] Zon and Sparhawk, 1923. Forest Resources of the World. Volume I, McGraw Hill Book Company Inc., New York.

Source: N.I. Bazilevich, L.F. Rodin and N. N. Rozov, "Geographical aspects of biological productivity," Soviet Geography Review Translation, 12, 293–317 (1971); E. F. Bruning Forstliche Produktionslehre (Europaische Hochschulschriften XXV/1, Bern, Frankfurt, 1971); E. F. Bruning, "Okosysteme in den Tropen," Umschau, 74, 405–10 (1974); D. E. Earl, Forest Energy and Economic Development (Oxford, Clarendon Press, 1975), p. 43; Eric Eckholm, Planting for the Future: Forestry for Human Needs (Washington, D.C., Worldwatch Institute, 1979). p. 11; S. R. Eyre, The Real Wealth of Nations (New York, St. Martins Press, 1978); Helmut Lieth, "Uber die Primerproduktion der Pflanzendecke der Erde," Angew. Botanik, 46, 1–37 (1972); Helmut Lieth, Primary Productivity of the Biosphere (New York, 1975); Helmut Lieth "Forest uses in global and regional (USA) perspectives," in Stephen G. Boyce, (ed.), Biological and Sociological Basis for a Rational Use of Forest Resources for Energy and Organics, proceedings of an international workshop sponsored by The Man and the Biosphere Committees of Canada, Mexico, and the United States held at Michigan State University, 6–11 May 1979, p. 70; J. S. Olson, World Ecosystems (Washington, D.C. Seattle Symposium, 1975); Keith Openshaw, "Woodfuel—A time for Re-Assessment," Natural Resources Forum, 3, (1) (1978), 35–51; Reidar Persson, World Forest Resources: Review of the World's Forest Resources in the Early 1970's (Stockholm, Skogshogskolan, Royal College of Forestry 1974) p. 222; Nigel Smith, Wood: An Ancient Fuel with a New Future (Washington, D.C., Worldwatch Institute, 1981) p. 134; R. C. Steele, "Some social and economic consequences and constraints to the use of forests for energy and organics in Great Britain," in Stephen G. Boyce (ed.), Biological and Sociological Basis for a Rational Use of Forest Resources for Energy and Organics: Proceedings of an international workshop sponsored by The Man and the Biosphere Committees of Canada, Mexico, and the United States, held at Michigan State University, 6–11 May 1979, p. 31; U.N. Food and Agriculture Organization, Forestry for Rural Communities (FAO Forestry Department, n.d.), p. 8; J. Weck and C. Wiebecke, Weltfurstwirtschaft und Deutschlands Forst-und Holzwirtschaft (München, 1961); R. H. Whittaker and G. E. Likens, "Primary production: the biosphere and man," Human Ecology, 1, 357–69 (1973); H. W. Windhurst, "Das Ertragspotential der Walder der Erde," in Studien zur Waldwirtschaffgeographic. Beihefte zur Geographischen Zeitschrift H. 39 (Wiesbaden, 1974); H. W. Windhorst, "The forests of the world and their potential productivity," Plant Research and Development, 3, 40–9 (1976); The World Bank, Forestry Sector Policy Paper (Washington, D.C., World Bank, 1978) p. 26; World Forest Inventory, 1963 (Rome, Food and Agriculture Organization, 1963).

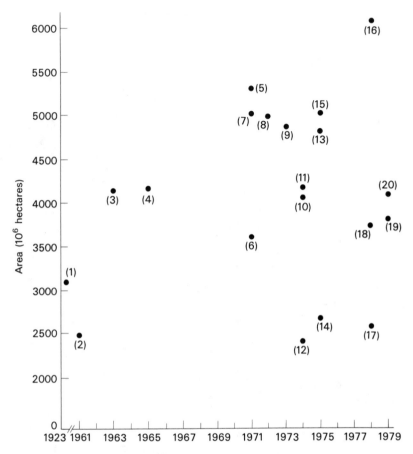

Figure 4.1 Estimates of world forest area (closed forest and forestland), arranged chronologically.

Sources: Numbers in parentheses refer to sources listed in table 4.1.

closed broadleaf forest in Latin America, this region accounts for about 56 percent of the total tropical area deforested. When open and coniferous forest types in the tropics are included, the total area deforested annually is estimated to be 11.3 million hectares with the percentage decline in all tropical forests falling slightly to 0.58 percent per annum due to the larger total forest land areas involved. As table 4.10 shows, the study's results are not substantially at variance with the data of the *FAO Yearbook*.

Importantly and somewhat surprisingly, the study indicates that the undisturbed or "virgin" broadleaved closed forests have a far lower rate

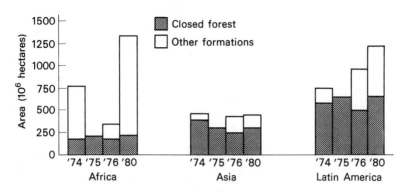

Figure 4.2 Estimates of tropical forest area in Africa, Asia, and Latin America.
Sources:1974 estimates are from Persson, 1974; 1975 estimates from Lanly and Clement, 1979; 1976 estimates from Sommer, 1976; and 1980 estimates from UNFAO/UNEP, 1982.

of deforestation than the total, being only 0.27 percent annually as compared with 2.06 percent annually for logged over secondary forest (p. 78). This figure indicates that deforestation pressure on the more pristine and generally more genetically diverse tropical forests is quite low. These findings are in sharp contrast to the conventional view that the tropical forests "are disappearing at alarming rates," and suggest that concerns over the imminent loss of some of the most important residences of the world's diverse genetic base, based on rates of tropical deforestation, are probably grossly exaggerated.

Ecological and Environmental Consequences of Tropical Deforestation

While it is uncontested that the clearing of tropical moist forests undoubtedly results in the destruction of most forms of vegetation and wildlife on that particular tract, very little is known about the connection between the disappearance of the tropical moist forest and the extinction of species (Harrington and Fisher, 1982). At the least one can say that frequently quoted extreme statements have no basis in historical experience but rather represent an extrapolation to the future. There are several possibilities for error in the estimates of large-scale loss of species. Clearing of one site does not mean that the same species may not continue on adjoining forest sites. Gentry (1978) has noted "that most species are wide-ranging despite sharp ecological limits on their distribution greatly complicates evaluation of potential endangered status." Therefore, it is

TABLE 4.12 DEFORESTATION BY COUNTRY ACCORDING TO THREE DIFFERENT SOURCES (FROM ALLEN AND BARNES, 1982)

Country	(1) FAO Yearbook Rank	Annual change (%)[a]	(2) FAO/UNEP Rank	Annual change (%)[b]	(3) Myers Rank	Annual change (%)[c]
* Ivory Coast	1	−3.7	1	−5.4	1	−5.3
* Haiti	2	−3.1	4	−3.2	—	—
* * Togo	3	−2.4	27	−0.64	—	—
* * Philippines	4	−2.2	22	−1.02	8.5	−1.25[d]
Swaziland	5	−1.9	—	—	—	—
* Sri Lanka	6	−1.8	18	−1.42	5	−1.8[e]
* Liberia	7	−1.66	14	−1.89	6	−1.41[f]
Niger	8	−1.61	—	—	—	—
* Upper Volta	9	−1.56	—	—	—	—
* * Rwanda	10	−1.46	10	−2.13	—	—
Brunei	11	−1.4	12	−1.99	—	—
* Ecuador	12	−1.14	13	−1.94	—	—
* * Somalia	13	−0.94	32	−0.225	—	—
* * Congo	14	−0.90	36	−0.103	—	—
* Mexico	15	−0.78	20	−1.09	—	—
* * Malaysia	16	−0.75	21	−1.05	7	−1.28[g]
* Thailand	17	−0.54	6	−3.15	2	−4.3[h]
Afghanistan	18	−0.50	—	—	—	—
Vietnam	19	−0.46	25	−0.71	—	—

*	Costa Rica	22	-0.38	5	-3.19	—	—
	Sierra Leone	23	-0.36	24	-0.75	—	—
	Belize	24	-0.344	26	-0.647	—	—
*	Surinam	25	-0.338	37	-0.0168	—	—
*	Brazil	26	-0.246	29	-0.406	11	-0.342[j]
*	Zaire	27	-0.232	33	-0.156	—	—
*	Indonesia	28	-0.113	28	-0.47	8.5	-1.25[j]
*	Nepal	29	-0.111	2	-3.68	—	—
*	Argentina	30	-0.093	—	—	—	—
*	Zambia	31	-0.087	19	-1.26	—	—
*	Paraguay	32	-0.082	3	-3.39	—	—
*	South Korea	33	-0.079	—	—	—	—
*	Bangladesh	34	-0.067	23	-0.83	10	-0.83[k]
*	Jamaica	35	-0.016	11	-2.05	—	—
*	Madagascar	36	-0.001	17	-1.50	4	-2.21[l]
*	Benin	37	0.004	7.5	2.83	—	—
	Botswana	38	0.04	—	—	—	—
	Kenya	39	0.05	16	-1.62	3	-2.6[m]
	Uruguay	40	0.56	—	—	—	—
*	Ethiopia	41	0.68	31	-0.227	—	—
*	El Salvador	42	0.69	7.5	-2.83	—	—
*	India	43	0.4	30	-0.28	—	—
	Guinea	44	0.5	15	-1.64	—	—
	China	45	0.6	—	—	—	—
	Burundi	46	1.6	9	-2.4	—	—
	Cuba	47	2.83	35	-0.136	—	—

[For Notes and Sources see overleaf.]

Notes: Dash indicates data not available. * indicates countries which are included in later regression analyses. Turkey, Morocco, Uganda, Burma, Dominican Republic, Guatemala, Nicaragua, and Panama are not listed in the table but are included in the later analyses.

Sources: (1) U.N. Food and Agriculture Organization, *1979 Production Yearbook* (Rome, U.N. Food and Agriculture Organization, 1980), pp. 45–57; (2) Jean-Paul Lanly, tables compiled for the Forest Resources Division, U.N. Food and Agriculture Organization, 1981; and (3) Norman Myers, *Conversion of Tropical Moist Forests*, a report prepared for the Committee on Research Priorities in Tropical Biology of the National Research Council (Washington, D.C., National Academy of Sciences, 1980), pp. 62–167.

a Average annual percent change in forests and woodland over the period 1968–78, using 1968 as a base year. Only complete removal of forest cover is measured. Forest and woodland refers to land under natural or planted stands of trees, whether productive or not, and includes land from which forests have been cleared but that will be reforested in the foreseeable future. Forests and woodland are not defined consistently in actual measurement practice by all countries nor over all years.

b Average annual percent change in natural woody vegetation in the form of closed broadleaf, coniferous or bamboo forest over the period 1976–80. Excludes forest plantations. Only complete removal of forest cover is measured. Includes tropical countries only.

c Average annual percent change in tropical moist forest over various periods. This measure includes all types of forest conversion, including logging. Tropical moist forest includes evergreen or partly evergreen forests, with or without some deciduous trees, but never completely leafless, forest savanna mosaic where forests are not confined to streamsides, and coastal savanna mosaic. According to the FAO Committee on Forest Development in the Tropics, interpretation of the term "tropical moist forest" should be left to individual countries (Sommers, 1976, p. 6). Conversion of tropical moist forest can range from marginal modification to fundamental transformation (Myers, 1980, p. 9). Where Myers has no reliable figure for total forest area FAO/UNEP estimates of closed forest or natural woody vegetation was used as a base to calculate deforestation rates. See explanatory notes.

d "Forestlands . . . disappearing each year," 1971, p. 98.

e Forest "degraded" each year by shifting cultivation, 1950–80, p. 102.

f "Primary forest converted to degraded forest . . . or bushland by shifting cultivation," annually, 1980, p. 162.

g Actual rate of clearing in proposed agricultural lands, 1975–80, p. 83.

h "Loss of forest cover," 1961–78, p. 110.

i "Forests eliminated" 1966–75, according to Brazilian development office (SUDA), p. 128.

j Estimate of forest "eliminated," "by shifting cultivation annually, 1980, p. 71.

k "Forest in the central and northern parts . . . declining, primarily through shifting cultivation . . . ," p. 65.

l Moist forest "disrupted and impoverished through shifting cultivation" annually 1980, p. 162.

m Net rate in Nandi Forest only, 1966–76, p. 159.

n Near East and Far East, excludes centrally planned.

doubtful that a 10 percent loss in tropical moist forest area – should this occur – would result in anything like a 10 percent loss in forest species, as was suggested in *Global 2000*. Since some ecological zones foster a disproportionately high degree of genetic diversity the question of species loss is related not so much to the rate or percentage of forest destruction, but rather to the extent to which forest destruction occurs in areas of large genetic diversity and limited geographic range. With this perspective Gentry has observed that

the short term picture for plant species preservation in much of Latin America is surprisingly good. Thus the vast forest expanses of much of Amazonia are virtually untouched despite the considerable effort being expended to develop them. Similarly large regions of the steep forested slopes on either side of the Andes remain inaccessible and essentially untouched by virtue of their rugged topography.

However, he goes on to caution that

In some other parts of Latin America the situation is much more acute, especially in Central America where great biological diversity is compressed into a small area all of which is relatively accessible to exploitation.

Two measures are available to conserve the world's biological resources. *In situ* approaches leave species where they are found in nature, preserved in more or less natural setting, and *ex situ* approaches include removal of species from their natural habitat for preservation in permanent collections such as zoos and botanic gardens and the preservation of seed and other genetic materials in a controlled environment (Harrington, 1982). Progress is being made on both fronts. Developing countries are becoming increasingly concerned about the preservation of natural habitats. The Brazilian government recently purchased a section of primary forest in the state of Bahia that is especially rich in endemic species, and several new conservation areas have been created in Brazil. Additional signs of positive responses include Costa Rica's establishment of Corcovado National Park on its wet forest Osa Peninsula; efforts by Ecuador to establish a national park near Puerto Lopez and other efforts to establish preserves in genetically rich forest. In addition, Indonesia recently has announced a plan to set aside 5 percent of the nation's land area in parks and natural reserves (Goodland, 1981).

Today numerous activities are under way to collect and maintain germplasm. These involve not only private collection but also, for example, the National Seed Storage Laboratory operated by the U.S.

Department of Agriculture and the National Plant Germplasm System. In addition, about 40 germplasm banks around the world are now part of the International Board of Plant Genetic Resources and store over one million varieties of crop plants (Griggs, 1982). Recently, at the initiative of private timber interests and affected national governments, the Central America and Mexico Coniferous Resources Cooperative was established to collect and preserve endangered seed of the tropical pines resource of Central America. One activity will be to establish tropical pine orchards elsewhere, to insure permanent genetic preservation.

Nevertheless the problem of the protection of the world's genetic resources remains a serious concern. It is estimated that 25–50 percent of the world's species reside in tropical forests. While documentation of actual tropic species extinction is rare, the common property characteristics of many of these forests suggest susceptibility to over-exploitation. It is clear that the habitats of some unique genetic resources are threatened, particularly in coastal Brazil and Madagascar. These genetic resources are like an unopened treasure chest in that their long-term value to humanity is quite uncertain. To the extent that these tropical forests are overcut, so too the genetic resources residing in these forests are unlikely to be adequately protected.

Concern has also been expressed repeatedly and strongly by some observers about the dire effects on world climate resulting from increased CO_2 in the atmosphere and the warming effect this will have upon the world's climate, and the role that forest clearing may play in this process (see Landsberg, chapter 10 of this volume). While a consensus on the effect of more CO_2 in the atmosphere is emerging, there remains a great deal of uncertainty on the sources and severity of this problem. For one thing, the role of the oceans in absorbing CO_2 is most imperfectly understood (Clark, 1982). Even if it be conceded that CO_2 does have all the harmful effects argued by many observers, there are clearly many sources of CO_2 aside from forest clearing; for example the extensive burning of fossil fuels. In fact, the authoritative *Carbon Dioxide Review 1982* (Clark *et al.*, 1982) states flatly, "No one any longer suggests land-use changes will produce a significant fraction of man's total future releases of CO_2. If there is a carbon dioxide problem in the future, it will be due to the burning of fossil fuels; *not the burning of forests*" (italics added).

The tropical forests are a great natural resource, large in area, unique in characteristics, home for considerable (but not large) numbers of people who have unique lifestyles, and with an enormous number and variety of plant and animal species. Thus far in human history they have been more storehouses of unknown and uninventoried wealth than they have been of annual outputs of goods and services. In this respect, they are similar to the old growth mature forests of the United States 400 years ago. Utilization of the tropical moist forests for an annual stream of goods and services to an outside world cannot follow closely the U.S. pattern of forest clearing, exploitation, and regeneration because the ecological base is so different. A rapid, unthinking exploitation of the tropical moist forests might well be a disaster, not only to the people who live there and to the natural resources themselves, but to the world as a whole. An attempt to remove large areas of the tropical moist forests from many types of human utilization, however, almost as if the areas involved were somehow exported to the moon or to another planet, might be equally foolish.

Why the Differences?

How might we explain the difference between the conclusion of the *Global 2000* report that the annual rates of deforestation of the moist tropical forests are about 20 million hectares and the prognosis of the massive destruction of much of the world's principal tropical forests by the early twenty-first century, and the relatively reassuring results, both in the rate of tropical deforestation and in the long-term prognosis for tropical forests, that emanate from Lanly's work? One explanation may be found by examining the very influential work of Myers in his National Academy of Sciences study (1980). To some extent the differences between Myers and the FAO/UNEP studies reflect different definitions of what constitutes "deforestation." As noted, Myers' estimates are of conversion or disturbance, even if the land remains in tropical forest. In addition, while Myers discusses a large number of countries in his study, his empirical estimates of the rates of deforestation are limited, and Allen and Barnes report a subgroup of only eleven countries (table 4.12).[7] For most of these countries the annual average rate of deforestation is relatively high, with several being over 2 percent. However, Myers' estimates varied considerably among countries. For example, while he estimates the Ivory Coast rate of deforestation at 5.3 percent, his estimate for Brazil is just 0.342 percent. If these rates continued, by the end of this century the Ivory Coast forests would totally disappear while Brazilian forests would be reduced by only 6 percent.

However, the major confusion appears to result from Myers' aggregate estimate of the rate of conversion of tropical forests which is not based upon his empirical estimates (Lugo and Brown, 1982; Sedjo and Clawson, 1983) but rather is the result of suppositions about the rate at which forest farmers are converting forestlands together with other factors which contribute to conversions (pp. 25–6 and p. 175). Using a speculative process Myers estimates the rate of tropical deforestation to total 20 million hectares per year, a rate that corresponds closely with the figure used in the *Global 2000* projections. This rate is 80–180 percent above the empirically derived estimates of the FAO/UNEP.

As noted, Myers does not make numerical estimates of the rate of deforestation for several important individual regions and countries. For example, the central African forest of Zaire and Gabon is one of the major tropical forests of the world. While Myers does not estimate the rates of deforestation for these countries, Lanly's FAO/UNEP study shows their rates of deforestation to be so small that "on the whole the limit of the closed forest appears, therefore, to be stable and corresponds to a balance between savannas maintained by fires and forests capable of regeneration in present conditions" (p. 82).

Nevertheless, it is clear that some countries are experiencing a rapid net loss of tropical moist forests. However, while the local effects of the rapid deforestation may be severe, the evidence does not support the view that either the world or the tropics are experiencing rapid aggregate deforestation. Furthermore, the evidence shows that current rates of deforestation are quite modest in much of the world's virgin tropical forests, for example, those of the Amazon (Brazil); and therefore they are probably in little danger of wholesale destruction in the foreseeable future.

Summary

We summarize the results of this consideration of world forestry by going back to the major questions posed at the beginning:

(1) The data suggest little possibility of the world running out of forests, or even of major regions being dramatically denuded in any reasonable time horizon. The recent stability of forested area in most of the temperate climate world, following a period of intensive exploitation and destruction, demonstrates the lack of inevitability in extrapolating deforestation trends. Nevertheless, there appear to be excessive rates of deforestation occurring in certain regions, particularly in some tropical areas.

(2) There will be, for the foreseeable future, an adequate supply of wood for the industrialized and rapidly industrializing countries. As with every natural resource, there will be some problems of supply, processing, transport, demand, and other aspects; and some environmental problems to be faced. But forestry and forest products pose no insurmountable or critical problems. The situation is, by and large, a reasonably comfortable one. The problems can be both faced and met.

(3) The local and regional forest situation is much more variable and, in general, less happy. There are some regions of the world today where local wood supply is inadequate, where wood is urgently needed as fuel, and where the prospects for improvement are not good, for ecological or sociological reasons or both. In many of these areas people are poor, governments are weak, and social infrastructure is lacking in large degree. While this unfavorable situation does not exist everywhere in the less developed world, unfortunately it is often common and serious. Typically, excessive deforestation reflects the existence of a common-property type problem which occurs due to the absence of an appropriate institutional setting.

(4) The threat of serious environmental damage from forest utilization is local and *not* global. The local threat is primarily to water and soil quality. Yet this threat is not inevitable or unmanageable. While concern has been expressed as to the effect of deforestation on the global climate via the route of increased CO_2 and global warming, the scientific consensus is that deforestation will not significantly change future global CO_2 levels.

(5) The potential also exists for serious depletion of the world's genetic resources, especially in the moist tropical forests; but the probability of really serious damage is much less, and the risks have been exaggerated. Nevertheless, there are reasons to believe that unique genetic resources, particularly those confined to limited areas of tropical forests, may experience socially excessive rates of destruction. There are modest measures which can reduce the risk of irrevocable loss. However the possibilities of loss must be weighed against the possibilities of gain from utilization of the forests.

Notes

The views expressed herein are personal, not organizational.

1 It should be noted that recent studies by Johnson and Libecap (1980) and Berck (1979) have suggested that the rate of drawdown of old growth inventories in the Lake States and the Pacific Northwest was actually far less exploitive than commonly believed, and approximated the social optimal rate.

2 It should be noted that some areas that should be defined as the temperate region have been omitted. These include temperate parts of Africa, South America, and Asia excluding China. The temperate parts of these regions are included with the continental data.

168   *Roger A. Sedjo and Marion Clawson*

3   Most estimates place forest plantations in China at about 30 million hectares. Reforestation in 1979 was estimated at 4.489 million hectares (*World Wood*, 1982, p. 44).
4   Opinions about the success of China's reforestation efforts vary considerably. A recent World Bank assessment (1982) of China's environmental problems presents a pessimistic appraisal.
5   This estimate is obtained by summing the separate estimates of artificially regenerated forests by regions as presented in *World Wood* (1981).
6   An extensive analysis of the rate of tropical deforestation was also undertaken by Lugo and Brown (1982) as part of a critique of the Norman Myers' report "Conversion of tropical moist forests" (1980).
7   Lugo and Brown (1982) report Myers' numerical estimates of deforestation for eighteen countries.

References

Allen, Julia C. and John G. Cady (1983) "Impact of forest soils on the biochemistry outlook in developing countries," Discussion Paper D-73N, Energy in Developing Countries Series, Resources for the Future, Inc., Washington, D.C.

Allen, J. C. and Douglas F. Barnes (1982) "Deforestation, wood energy and development." Unpublished paper, Resources for the Future, Inc., Washington, D.C.

Barney, Gerald O. (1980) *Global 2000 Report to the President*. Entering the Twenty-First Century, a report prepared by the Council on Environmental Quality and the Department of State, vol. II: Technical Report. Washington, D.C.: U.S. Government Printing Office.

Berck, Peter (1979) "The economics of timber: a renewable resource in the long run," *The Bell Journal of Economics*, **10** (2), (Autumn), 447–62.

Clark, William C. (ed.) (1982) *Carbon Dioxide Review 1982*. Oxford University Press, New York.

Clark, William C., Kerry H. Cook, Gregg Marland, Alvin M. Weinberg, Ralph M. Rotty, P. R. Bell and Chester L. Cooper (1982) "The carbon dioxide question: perspectives for 1982." In W. C. Clark (ed.), *Carbon Dioxide Review 1982*, p. 4.

Clawson, Marion (1979) "America's forests in the long sweep of history," *Science*, **204** (4398), 1168–74.

—— (1981) "Past and future use of land in agriculture in the United States," *Journal of Forest History*, **25** (4), 222–7.

Council on Environmental Quality (1981) United States Department of State. *Global Future: Time to Act*. January.

Gentry, Alwyn (1978) "Extinction and conservation of plant species in tropical America: a phytogeographical perspective." In Igna Hedberg (ed.), *Systematic Botany, Plant Utilization and Biosphere Conservation*, pp. 110–26. Almquist and Wiksell International, Stockholm.

Goodland, Robert (1981) "Indonesia's environmental progress in economic development." In V. H. Sutlive, N. Altschuler, and N. Zamora (eds), *Where

Have All the Flowers Gone? Deforestation in the Third World. Studies in Third World Societies No. 13 (Department of Anthropology, College of William and Mary, Williamsburg, Va., 1981).

Griggs, Tim (1982) "FAO Acts to strengthen seed conservation." *International Agricultural Development* (June), p. 14.

Hardin, Garett (1968) "The tragedy of the commons," *Science*, **162**, 1243–8.

Harrington, Winston (1982) "Endangered species – a global threat." In *Resources*, October. Resources for the Future, Washington, D.C.

Harrington, Winston and Anthony C. Fisher (1982) "Endangered species." In P. R. Portney (ed.), *Current Issues in Natural Resource Policy*. Resources for the Future, Johns Hopkins Press, Baltimore.

Inter-American Development Bank (1982) "Forest industries development strategy and investment requirements in Latin America: Technical Report No. 1." Prepared for IDB conference on Financing Forest-Based Development in Latin America, Washington, D.C., 22–25 June.

Johnson, R. and Gary N. Libecap (1980) "Efficient markets and Great Lakes timber: a conservation issue reexamined," *Explorations in Economic History*, **17**.

Lanly, J. P. and J. Clement (979) "Present and future natural forest and plantation areas in the tropics," *Unasylva*, **31** (123), 12–20.

Lillard, R. G. (1947) *The Great Forest*. Knopf, New York.

Lugo, Ariel E. and Sandra Brown (1982) "Conversion of tropical moist forests: a critique," *Interciencia*, **7** (2), 89–93.

Manthy, Robert (1978) *Natural Resource Commodities – A Century of Statistics*. Johns Hopkins Press, Baltimore.

Myers, Norman (1980) "Conversion of tropical moist forests," a report prepared for the Committee on Research Priorities on Tropical Biology of the National Research Council (Washington, D.C., National Academy of Sciences).

Persson, Reidar (1974) *World Forest Resources; Review of the World's Forest Resources in the Early 1970s*. Research Notes No. 17 (Department of Forest Survey, Royal College of Forestry, Stockholm).

Potter, Neal and Francis T. Christy (1962) *Trends in Natural Resource Commodities*. Johns Hopkins Press, Baltimore.

Sanchez, Pedro A., Dale E. Bandy, J. Hugo Villachica and John J. Nicholaides (1982) "Amazon Basin soils: management for continuous crop production," *Science*, **216**, 21 May, pp. 821–7.

Sedjo, Roger A. (1980) "Forest plantations in Brazil and their possible effects on world pulp markets," *Journal of Forestry*, **78** (1), 702–5.

—— (1983a) "The potential of U.S. forest lands in the world context." In R. A. Sedjo (ed.), *Governmental Interventions, Social Needs and Forest Management*. Resources for the Future, Inc., Washington, D.C.

—— (1983b) *The Comparative Economics of Plantation Forestry: A Global Assessment*. Resources for the Future, Inc., Washington, D.C.

—— and Marion Clawson (1983) "Tropical deforestation: how serious?" *Journal of Forestry*, **81** (12).

Sivonen, S. (1971) "Havusahapuun Rantohinnan paa Sunntrainen Rehitya Suomessa vuosina 1920–67." (Report of the Committee on the Costs of Forest Planting and Seeding, Annex 5, pp. 116–20. *Folia Forestalia*, **109** (Helsinki, Finland).

Sommer, Adrian (1976) "Attempt at an assessment of the world's tropical moist forests," *Unasylva*, **28** (112 and 113), 5–24.

Thomson, James T. (1981) "Public choice analysis of institutional constraints on firewood production strategies in the West African Sahel." In C. S. Russell and N. K. Nicholson (eds), *Public Choice and Rural Development*. pp. 119–52. Resources for the Future, Inc., Research paper R-21.

U.N. Food and Agriculture Organization (1980) *1979 Yearbook of Forest Products, 1967–1979*, pp. 2–50. Food and Agriculture Organization, Rome.

UNFAO/UNEP (1982) *Tropical Forest Resources*, by J. P. Lanly. FAO Forestry Paper No. 30, Rome.

U.S. Interagency Task Force on Tropical Forests (1980) "The world's tropical forests: a policy, strategy and program for the United States," a report to the President. Washington, D.C., U.S. Government Printing Office.

World Bank. (1978) Forestry Sector Policy Paper, pp. 18–19, 33–4. Washington, D.C., World Bank.

——— (1982) "The People's Republic of China: environmental aspects of economic development," pp. 4–8. Office of Environmental Affairs, Projects Advisory Staff.

World Wood. (1981) *1981 World Wood Review*, **22** (8).

Zon, R. and W. N. Sparhawk (1923) *Forest Resources of the World*, McGraw Hill Book Company, Inc., New York (2 vols).

5

On Species Loss, the Absence of Data, and Risks to Humanity

JULIAN L. SIMON AND AARON WILDAVSKY

Introduction

The Global 2000 Report to the President expressed concern over the possible loss of species between now and the year 2000. Its "Major Findings and Conclusions" section says: "Extinctions of plant and animal species will increase dramatically. Hundreds of thousands of species – perhaps as many as 20 percent of all species on earth – will be irretrievably lost as their habitats vanish, especially in tropical forests (*Global 2000*, vol. I, p. 3). *Global 2000* also expressed concern about deforestation, especially in the tropics, both for itself and as related to the loss of species. "The projections indicate that by 2000 some 40 percent of the remaining forest cover in LDCs will be gone" (*Global 2000*, vol. I, p. 2).

This concern is widespread now. For example, *Science* referred to "the near-catastrophic state of deforestation" (Waldrop, 1981, p. 914), and Myers (1979) and Ehrlich and Ehrlich (1981) have written about these matters. This ending sentence in a recent lead article in *Science* surely is typical of many other writings: "We cannot afford the extinction of '15 to 20 percent of all species on earth' by the year 2000, as predicted in Global 2000" (Fyfe, 1981, p. 105). And the concern is "official": *Global 2000* "was the U.S. government's analysis of probable changes in world population, resources, and environment through the end of the century" (*Global Future*, p. iii).

The analysis reaches beyond deforestation: "The deforestation will be caused by a combination of population increase and economic growth" (*Global 2000*, vol. II, p. 332). And following on the analysis in *Global 2000*, the, new *Global Future: Time to Act* Report to the President presented suggestions for "a vigorous response" to these and other purported "urgent global problems" (p. iv), devoting almost a fifth of its pages to "Tropical Forests" and "Biological Diversity."

In our judgment, however, the available facts are not consistent with the level of expressed concern in *Global 2000*, and do not provide support for the various policies suggested to deal with the purported dangers. To show that this is so is one aim of this chapter. Furthermore, various considerations, biological and otherwise, suggest that the extinction of a species is not necessarily a bad thing for humankind and for biological development generally. To attempt to maintain the present biological composition of the world can have far-reaching negative as well as positive effects which must be considered along with the short-run costs of saving species from possible extinction. To discuss these risks is a second aim of this chapter.

It is not our intention, however, to suggest that our society, and humanity at large, should ignore possible dangers to species. Individual species, and perhaps all species taken together, constitute a valuable endowment, and we should guard their survival just as we guard our other physical and social assets. But we should strive for a sensible view of this set of assets in order to make the best possible judgments about how much time and money, and human welfare, should be spent in guarding them in a world in which this valuable activity must compete with other valuable activities, including the guarding of other valuable assets and of human life.

Species Loss Estimates

With respect to loss of species, *Global 2000*'s "projection" is: "Efforts to meet basic human needs and rising expectations are likely to lead to the extinction of between one-fifth and one-seventh of all species over the next two decades" (vol. II, p. 328). The projection is based on this statement by Lovejoy:

> What then is a reasonable estimate of global extinctions by 2000? Given the amount of tropical forest already lost (which is important but often ignored), the extinctions can be estimated. . . . In the low deforestation case, approximately 15 percent of the planet's species can be expected to be lost. In the high deforestation case, perhaps as much as 20 percent will be lost. This means that of the 3–10 million species now present on the earth, at least 500,000–600,000 will be extinguished during the next two decades. (vol. II, p. 331)

This extract summarizes a table of Lovejoy's which shows a range between 437,000 and 1,875,000 extinctions out of a present estimated total of 3–10 million species. The table in turn is based on a linear relationship running from zero percent species extinguished at zero percent tropical forest cleared, to about 95 percent extinguished at 100 percent tropical forest clearing. The main source of differences in the range of estimated losses is the range of 3–10 million species in the overall estimate.

The basis of any useful projection must be some body of experience collected under some range of conditions that encompass the expected conditions, or that can reasonably be extrapolated to the expected conditions. But none of Lovejoy's references contains any scientifically impressive body of experience. The only published source given for his key table (Table 13–30, p. 331) is Myers' *The Sinking Ark* (1979), which was written under the auspices of a committee of which Lovejoy was one of three members, and whose prologue is a motto of the World Wildlife Fund, on whose staff Lovejoy serves. Myers' and Lovejoy's writings, which are by no means independent, are apparently the only source of the widely-discussed forecasts of species extinction.[1]

The basic source is Myers' summary:

At least 90 percent of all species that have existed have disappeared. But almost all of them have gone under by virtue of natural processes. Only in the recent past, perhaps from around 50,000 years ago, has man exerted much influence. As a primitive hunter, man probably proved himself capable of eliminating species, albeit as a relatively rare occurrence. From the year A.D. 1600, however, he became able, through advancing technology, to over-hunt animals to extinction in just a few years, and to disrupt extensive environments just as rapidly. Between the years 1600 and 1900, man eliminated around seventy-five known species, almost all of them mammals and birds – virtually nothing has been established about how many reptiles, amphibians, fishes, invertebrates and plants disappeared. Since 1900 man has eliminated around another seventy-five known species – again, almost all of them mammals and birds, with hardly anything known about how many other creatures have faded from the scene. The rate from the year 1600 to 1900, roughly one species every 4 years, and the rate during most of the present century, about one species per year, are to be compared with a rate of possibly one per 1000 years during the "great dying" of the dinosaurs.

Since 1960, however, when growth in human numbers and human aspirations began to exert greater impact on natural environments, vast territories in several major regions of the world have become so modified as to be cleared of much of their main wildlife. The result is that the extinction rate has certainly soared, though the details mostly remain undocumented. In 1974 a gathering of scientists concerned with the problem hazarded a guess that the overall extinction rate among all species, whether known to science or not, could now have reached 100 species per year. [Here Myers refers to *Science*, 1974, pp. 646–7.]

Yet even this figure seems low. A single ecological zone, the tropical moist forests, is believed to contain between 2 and 5 million species. If present patterns of exploitations persist in tropical moist forests, much virgin forest is likely to have disappeared by the end of the century, and much of the remainder will have been severely degraded. This will cause huge numbers of species to be wiped out . . .

Let us suppose that, as a consequence of this man-handling of natural environments, the final one-quarter of this century witnesses the elimination of 1 million species – a far from unlikely prospect. This would work out, during the course of 25 years, at an average extinction rate of 40,000 species per year, or rather over 100 species per day. The greatest exploitation pressures will not be directed at tropical forests and other species-rich biomes until towards the end of the period. That is to say, the 1990s could see many more species accounted for than the previous several decades. But already the disruptive processes are well underway, and it is not unrealistic to suppose that, right now, at least one species is disappearing each day. By the late 1980s we could be facing a situation where one species becomes extinct each hour. (Myers, 1979, pp. 4–5)

We may extract these key points from the above summary quotation:

(1)   The estimated extinction rate of known species is about one every 4 years between the years from 1600 to 1900.

(2)   The estimated rate is about one a year from 1900 to the present. No sources are given for these two estimates, either on the page from which the quote is taken or on pages 30–31 of Myers' book where these estimates are again discussed.

(3)   Some scientists have (in Myers' words) "hazarded a guess" that the extinction rate "could now have been reached" 100 species per year. That is, the estimate is simply conjecture and is not even a point estimate but rather an upper bound. The source given for the "some scientists" statement is a staff-written news report (C.H., 1974). It should be noted, however, that the subject of this guess is different from the subject of the estimates in (1) and (2), because the former include mainly or exclusively birds or mammals, whereas the latter includes all species. While this

difference implies that (1) and (2) may be too low a basis for estimating the present extinction rate of all species, it also implies that there is even less statistical basis for estimating the extinction rate for species other than birds and mammals than it might otherwise seem.

(4)   Even this guessed upper limit in (3) is then increased and used by Myers, and then by Lovejoy, as the basis for the "projections" quoted above. In *Global 2000* the language has become that economic developments "are likely to lead" to the extinction of between 14 and 20 percent of all species before the year 2000 (*Global 2000*, vol. II, p. 328), which calculates to about *40,000* species lost per year. Observe that an upper limit for the present that is pure guesswork, and that is 100 times the observed rate in the recent past, has become the basis of a forecast for the future, which is 40,000 times greater than at present, and which has been published in newspapers to be read by tens or hundreds of millions of people and understood as a scientific statement.

The two historical rates as stated by Myers, together with the yearly rates implied by Lovejoy's estimates, are plotted together in figure 5.1. It is clear that without explicitly bringing into consideration some additional force, one could extrapolate almost any rate one chooses for the year 2000, and the Lovejoy extrapolation has no better claim to belief than a rate, say, one-hundredth or one-forty-thousandth as large. Looking at the two historical points alone, many forecasters would be likely to project a rate much closer to the past than to Lovejoy's, on the basis of the common wisdom that in the absence of additional information, the best first approximation for a variable tomorrow is its value today, and the best second approximation is that the variable will change at the same rate in the future that it has in the past. This conventional wisdom may well be mistaken, but we are given no reason to depart from it.

Projected change in the amount of tropical forests implicitly underlies the differences between past and projected species-loss rates in Lovejoy's diagram. But to connect these elements logically, there must be systematic evidence relating an amount of tropical forest removed to a rate of species reduction; no such empirical evidence is given to Lovejoy, Myers, *Global 2000*, the Ehrlichs, or other sources we have checked. This implies that there is no basis to choose between Lovejoy's projected rates, and rates about the same as those in the past; yet this is the difference between recommending national policies to reduce extinction rates and not making any recommendations at all. Again, this is not to say that no protection policies should be undertaken. Rather, it implies better data to estimate extinction rates are needed as the basis for policy decisions.

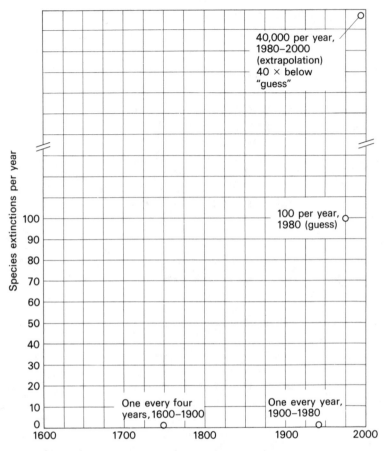

Figure 5.1 Myers–Lovejoy estimates of species extinction and their extrapolations to the year 2000.

Deforestation Estimates

We might logically stop here, with the case considered complete: there is no convincing case for the rapid extinction of species and therefore no need for a solution to what may be a non-existent problem. Let us, however, go further. Even if there were a known link between amounts of deforestation and amounts of species extinction of the sort simply speculated about by *Global 2000* – which there is not – the data on deforestation would not support estimates of extinction anything like the sort *Global 2000* asserted.

Lovejoy asserts that there is now, and will be in the future, a rapid rate of deforestation (though we must say again that even if the rate of deforestation were indeed rapid, there would still be little or no basis for inferring a rate of species extinction of Lovejoy's projected magnitude). *Global 2000* says "Significant losses of world forests will continue over the next 20 years . . ." (vol. I, p. 2). But *Global 2000* presents no time-series data on such losses. In fact there is no historical evidence to support a projection of such rapid deforestation, as is shown in the article in this volume by Sedjo and Clawson (chapter 4).

Please keep in mind that only a historical series of comparable observations can establish the existence of a trend. Observation at one given moment can convey only impressions about a trend. The impressions may be sound because they are made on the basis of first-hand contact, previous wide experience, and wise judgment. But impressions are a very different basis for policy decisions than are well-grounded statistical trend estimates.

In *Global 2000*, Lovejoy, Myers, and others say that *tropical* forests (rather than the world's forests as a whole) are particularly crucial with regard to the extinction of species, and also are especially liable to deforestation. *Global Future* opens up this topic by asserting that "The world's tropical forests are disappearing at alarming rates . . . tropical deforestation is an urgent problem . . ." (*Global Future*, pp. 66 and 67). The earlier quote from *Global 2000* also clearly attributed species loss to having their "habitats vanish, especially in tropical forests."

Calculations of species loss with two assumed deforestation rates for tropical forests were made by Lovejoy. The "low" projection assumed a 50 percent rate between 1980 and 2000 for Latin America, a 20 percent rate for Africa (the least important in terms of total species), and 60 percent for South and Southeast Asia. The "high" projection assumed 67 percent deforestation for all regions between 1980 and 2000. Lovejoy cites chapter 8 in *Global 2000* as his source for the alternative assumptions; but no trend data are given there to support any such estimate, and the main sources given (*Global 2000*, vol. II, p. 134) are Persson (1974) and Whittaker and Likens (1975). The latter contains no original survey data; and Persson's data are for a world rather than tropical forest inventory. Neither gives support for Lovejoy's assumptions about tropical deforestation, either high or low, or, for that matter, can serve as the basis for any trend of deforestation. The Sedjo–Clawson chapter in this volume provides solid evidence that such assumptions are very far from the mark (chapter 4).

Such aggregated figures might mask the regional situation in rain forests. Brazil and its Amazon region attract most concern. An article by

Rohter (1979)[2] – a newspaper piece in the *Washington Post* about
Landsat photographs – seems to be the main source for Lovejoy's loss
estimates in Brazil's Amazon region.

> Even the deforestation projected in Chapter 8 [of *Global 2000*] may
> have been underestimated. Warwick Kerr predicts the loss of all
> Amazon forests (B. Dickson, "Brazil Learns Its Ecological Lessons
> the Hard Way," *Nature*, vol. 275, 1978, pp. 684–85), and
> P. W. Richards (op. cit.) predicts the loss of all untouched rain
> forests by the century's end. Very recently, however, some new
> information has become available for the tropical forests of the
> Amazon basin. According to Larry Rohter (op. cit.), Brazil's
> national Space Research Institute analyzed 32 photographs taken
> from a Landsat satellite and estimated in late 1978 that as much as
> one-tenth of the Brazilian Amazon forest has been razed. This is an
> area larger than the state of Texas and probably does not include
> areas that are now forested but are no longer diverse, virgin forest.
> On the matter of future cutting, the Brazilian Government is
> reported to be studying the use of "risk contracts" for the large-
> scale logging in the Amazon basin. The Superintendency for the
> Development of the Amazon (SUDAM) has identified approxi-
> mately 100 million additional acres (between 5 and 10 percent of the
> total area of the Amazon basin) for timber exploitation. (Lovejoy in
> *Global 2000*, vol. II, p. 330)

Even if the data discussed by Rohter – an unusual source to rely upon for
an estimate of such manifest importance – are reliable, the data would not
be relevant here because that article describes observations at only one
moment. So even if the measurement method is sound, it gives no clue
about the rate of change of forests in Brazil, or even whether the forest
cover is decreasing or increasing, because the "razing" seen from the
Landsat satellite includes the cumulative results of all forest clearing that
has ever been done in the region. The equivocal term "as much as," in the
quote from Lovejoy means that the number mentioned is not a point
estimate but only a bound. This expository technique appears frequently
in *Global 2000*.

Another of the sources frequently referred to is Sommer (1976). This is
Sommer's method for predicting future deforestation in Brazil's Amazon
region:

> A comparison of the road networks in the Amazon region for 1964
> and 1974 gives some indication of the changes planned or now
> taking place. Between 10,000 and 20,000 km of roads have been
> constructed, are under construction or are planned during this

period. Assuming that along all these roads a strip of 4 km (1 walking hour) on both sides would be cleared in the first stage, an area of 0.8–1.6 million ha or 0.3 to 0.6% of the total estimated area would be taken over per year. (p. 17)

In our judgment, Sommer's method is a flimsy evidential basis for any prediction at all, and certainly for any policy recommendations.

With respect to the estimates of deforestation rates given by Myers, upon which *Global 2000* relies heavily, the Sedjo–Clawson chapter in this volume digs deeply into the entire issue, and concludes that they are much too high.

Over-exploitation of local areas near transportation networks may or may not be ugly, painful, and a serious problem in Brazil or other countries. But with respect to species loss, such local exploitation would not seem to constitute a cause for action just as long as there are isolated similar habitats nearby where the species can continue to exist. Of course there may be some species that can live in only one small area, but such species are likely to be less important to man and the rest of nature for that very reason.

Risks from Species Loss

To give the species-preservation argument the best possible hearing, let us assume – contrary to the best evidence – that much tropical forest will be totally or largely destroyed, and that a large number of species will therefore be extinguished by the year 2000. Would the implications be simply negative?

Let us begin by asking: Why should we worry about these species? "The point is," *Global 2000* says,

that the already narrow genetic base of the world's major food crops may become even more narrow. . . . More extensive monoculture of food staples could lead to sudden unanticipated widespread losses in world food production. How likely and how serious is such a disaster? There is no easy or precise answer to the question. Past history suggests that the probability of a major genetic failure is low but increasing. (p. 288)

There are, according to *Global 2000*, two types of catastrophe — sudden and slow. Thus "present trends towards uniform strains and loss of genetic reserves could raise the frequency and severity of pest-related and disease-related crop failures significantly by 2000 . . .," which "may ultimately outweigh gains from genetically increased yields, even if major catastrophes do not occur. Such a development would be a catastrophe by itself, eventually" (p. 289).

The implication is that even a minor failure in agriculture is unbearable. Since error is part-and-parcel of life, modern agriculture, despite its appearance of abundance, is seen to be setting mankind up for a fall so steep that it might have been better off without new technology.

Let us turn the argument around by asking: Does limiting the extinction of species add to, or subtract from, the safety of human or animal or plant systems? The extinction of some species is an essential precondition of the development of newer and better versions, for if every species that exists at one moment must be maintained either at its existing level or at a level guaranteeing ample reproduction, there will be less room for new ones to emerge. The argument against extinction is not a position in favor of variety but rather in favor of old variety compared to new.

Ernst Mayr's seminal work on *The Growth of Biological Thought: Diversity, Evolution, and Inheritance*[3] states that biologists estimate the upper bound of current animal and plant species to be around ten million. And, "considering that life on earth began about 3.5 billion years ago, [and] also that a rather rich biota has existed for at least 500 million years, and allowing for a reasonable turnover in the species composition of the biota, . . . an estimate of one billion extinct species is presumably rather on the low side" (p. 139). If genetic extinction doomed mankind, presumably it would have died a billion deaths by now!

The argument that variety is enhanced by prohibiting all extinction cannot be sound. Rather, such a policy protects existing species against generations of species that will therefore not have the opportunity to emerge. Any single generation of species must be highly uniform in comparison to the variety of future generations that would come into the world if left unhindered.

Hundreds of millions of years have seen both enormous losses and gains of genetic diversity. While the gains may at times have more than compensated for the losses, it stands to reason that some of the losses have hurt. No doubt situations arose for which past genetic diversity might have been appropriate but for which it was no longer available. Yesteryear there was no way in which old diversity could be kept in reserve without diminishing the prospects for new variety. Today there is. Seed banks (or their equivalents) permit storage; and experiments with recombinant DNA may permit mankind to generate new forms under controlled conditions. To a greater (and growing) extent than ever before, mankind can simultaneously retain the old and generate new variety without paying a dear price. This extraordinary capacity comes from the very technology that is often portrayed as the source of catastrophe. Truly, as the aphorism has it, no good deed goes unpunished.

Conclusion

Biologists with whom we have discussed this material agree that the numbers in question are most uncertain; but they say the numbers do not matter scientifically. The conclusion would be the same, they say, if the numbers were different even by several orders of magnitude. But if so, why mention any numbers at all? The answer, quite clearly, is that these numbers do matter in one important way: they have the power to frighten in a fashion that numbers much smaller would not.

Some have said: But was not Rachel Carson's *Silent Spring* an important force for good even though it exaggerated? Maybe so. But the account is not yet closed on the indirect and long-run consequences of ill-founded concerns about environmental dangers; and it seems to us that, without some very special justification, there is a presumption in favor of statements that lead to the facts as best we know them, especially in a scientific context.

Still, the question exists: How should sound policies be formulated with respect to species extinction? One should not propose saving all species in their natural habitats, at any cost, even if it were desirable to do so, any more than one should propose a policy of saving all human lives at any cost, for the cost is counted in human welfare forgone because limited resources were devoted to lesser uses. Certainly we must try to establish some informed estimates about the social value present and future of species that might be lost, just as we find that we must estimate the value of human life in order to make rational policies about public health-care services such as hospitals and surgery, and about indemnities to accident survivors. And just as with human life, valuing species relative to other human assets will not be easy, especially because we must value some species about which we do not know much if anything, and others that do not now exist. The evaluational task is made even less accessible for the standard modes of analysis because some guess must be made about the nature and value of new species that might arise in response to the extinction of present species, as well as of the value of species which may be extinguished. This task approaches, or surpasses, the limits of any existing human knowledge. It may be almost impossible in principle to think quantitatively about this matter, because the cascade of feedback mechanisms and species in response to changes in species composition is ever-expanding in complexity and in foreignness from what we now know. The threat here is that we may overestimate our powers and underestimate our ignorance, and take counter-productive steps based on dangerously (perhaps necessarily) incomplete knowledge. Yet if policies are to be sensible, explicit evaluation of possible consequences must be made, even if that evaluation is that we are so ignorant that we should at least try to avoid doing harm by ill-founded policies.

We should certainly try to get more reliable information about the number of species that might be lost with various forest changes. This is, of course, a very tough task, too; one that might exercise the best faculties of a statistician and designer of experiments. One suggestion: if the population sizes of selected species could be measured in a series of periods along with experimental or non-experimental changes in habitats, extrapolation might teach something about conditions which would cause species to approach or reach extinction.

Lastly, any policy analysis concerning species loss must explicitly evaluate the total cost of the safeguarding activity; for example, cessation of foresting in an area. And such a total cost estimate must include the long-run indirect costs of reduction of economic growth to a community's education and general advancement, as well as the short-run costs of forgone wood or agricultural sales. To ignore such indirect costs because they are hard to estimate would be no more reasonable than ignoring the loss of species that we have not as yet identified. The analysis must also take into account the possibilities of safeguarding species with protected park habitats, and with "banks." It must also take into account the possibilities for human-made genetic variation. Perhaps the key question is: Might radical change in species occur before our expanding techno-logical capacities in this area can step in to protect us sufficiently? It might, but there is no good evidence to suggest this claim.

Our conclusion is that there is now no *prima facie* case for any expens-ive species-safeguarding policy without more extensive analysis than has been done heretofore. But the warnings that have been sounded are persuasive that the problem deserves deeper thought, and more careful and wide-ranging analysis, than has been done until now.

Notes

James Karr read an earlier draft and gave valuable criticism. Richard Sullivan provided helpful research assistance.

1   Lovejoy says (p. 422), that "support for a curve of this sort [relating deforestation and species loss] is suggested in A. Sommer" but Sommer, so far as we can tell, does not even discuss species loss.
2   The Rohter article's correct date is 1979 rather than the 1978 given by Lovejoy. We are grateful to Alexander R. Brash of the World Wildlife Fund – U.S. for the correct citation.
3   Ernst Mayr, *The Growth of Biological Thought: Diversity, Evolution, and Inheritance* (Cambridge, Mass.: Belknap Press of Harvard University Press, 1982).

References

Ehrlich, Paul and Anne (1981) *Extinction*, (New York: Random House).

Fyfe, W. S. (1981) "The environmental crisis: quantifying geosphere interactions," *Science*, **213**, 105–10.

C.H. (1974) "Scientists talk of the need for conservation and an ethic of biotic diversity to slow species extinction," *Science*, May, pp. 647–8.

Muthoo, M. K. (1978) "Brazil," *World Wide Review*, May, pp. 51–3.

Myers, Norman (1979) *The Sinking Ark* (New York: Pergamon).

Persson, R. (1974) *World Forest Resources* (Stockholm: Royal College).

Rohter, Larry (1979) "Amazon Basin's forests going up in smoke," *Washington Post*, 5 January, A14.

Sommer, Adrian (1976) "Attempt at an assessment of the world's tropical moist forests," *Unasylva*, **28**, 5–27.

U.S. CEQ and Department of State (1980) *The Global 2000 Report to the President*, Vol. II (Washington: GPO).

U.S. CEQ and Department of State (1981) *Global Future: Time to Act* (Washington: GPO).

Waldrop, M. Mitchell (1981) "Wood: fuel of the future?", *Science*, 27 February, p. 914.

Whittaker, R. H. and Likens, G. E. (1975) "The biosphere and man," In H. Lieth and R. H. Whittaker (eds), *Primary Productivity of the Biosphere* (New York: Springer).

6

The World Supply of Agricultural Land

ROGER REVELLE

Editors' Note

Whereas chapters 2, 7, and 9 deal with trends and economics of world agriculture, this chapter concerns the physical input factor of land (and a later chapter deals similarly with water). The relationship between the two approaches is as follows: the physical data provide an indication of whether the constraints upon physical activity are, and will be in the foreseeable future, fundamentally different from what they were in the past. If the answer is "no" (as this chapter suggests), it is reasonable to conclude that the economic forces operating in the past will continue to operate in a similar fashion in the future in such a manner that the trends observed in the past will continue in the same direction.

The world's food problem does not arise from any physical limitation on potential output or any danger of unduly stressing the environment. The limitations on abundance are to be found in the social and political structures of nations and in the economic relations among them. The unexploited global food resource is there, between Cancer and Capricorn. The successful husbandry of that resource depends on the will and actions of men. (David Hopper, 1976)

One of the purposes of this essay is to demonstrate the truth of Dr. Hopper's eloquent statement, not only for future food supplies in Asia, Africa and Latin America, but also, by extension, for supplies of another resource – energy – that is essential for the welfare of the world's poor people.

During the past three decades, food production in many poor countries has grown somewhat more rapidly than population. But can this rate of growth continue in the future? These are some long-range aspects of the world food problem.

To gain a deeper understanding of the problem, we should first ask ourselves whether the physical resources of land, water and energy in the poor countries are adequate to allow them to grow enough food for their own future needs. And if they are, as we shall show, then what biological research and development is needed, and what social and economic measures should be taken, to ensure enough food for all human beings in times to come?

Land and Water Resources for Agriculture

A comprehensive assessment of the earth's climate and land resources for agriculture was made by the panel on the World Food Supply of President Johnson's Science Advisory Committee (PSAC) in 1967, based on a world soil map prepared by the U.S. Soil Conservation Service, and on climatic information compiled from time-series of weather reports. A series of "agro-climatic regions" was established, depending on the number of months in which temperatures were sufficiently above freezing to allow plant growth and precipitation plus soil moisture exceeded evapotranspiration. Maps showing the location and extent of these zones were superimposed on the soil map (Revelle *et al.*, 1967).

It was found that potentially arable land (land that, under cultivation, can produce an acceptable level of food crops) makes up 24 percent of the total ice-free surface of the earth, or about 3.2 billion hectares, well over twice the land area that has been cultivated at some time during recent decades, and more than three times the area actually harvested in any given year. (With the prevailing low levels of agricultural technology in many poor countries, land must be left fallow, often for several years, to recover its fertility – Young and Wright, 1980). In the remaining 10 billion hectares, climates are too cold or too dry, the land surfaces are too stony, rough or hard, or the soils are too thin, too sandy and unstable to hold water, or are unsuitable in other ways for agricultural use.

Of the 3.2 billion net cultivatable hectares, one rain-fed crop could be grown on 2.17 billion hectares; two crops under rain-fed conditions on an additional 180 million hectares; and the equivalent of three four-month crops could be produced, if suitable technology could be developed, on 510 million hectares within the humid tropics, where precipitation exceeds potential evapotranspiration throughout the year. Irrigation is needed to grow even one crop on 350 million hectares.

The three continents of Africa, South America, and Asia contain, respectively, 23, 21 and nearly 20 percent of the potential net cultivated area of 3.2 billion hectares, followed by North America with 15 percent, the Soviet Union with 11 percent, and Australia and Europe each with 5 percent. Outside the humid tropics, for which high-level agricultural technology is not yet well developed, Africa contains 500 million hectares where at least one crop could be grown with available rain or river water, Asia has 470 million hectares, and South America has 375 million hectares.

With sufficient water, the potential net irrigated area could be 2.0 billion hectares, with a gross cultivated area of 3.5 billion hectares (gross cultivated area = number of crops grown per year × net cultivated area). However, examination of the volumes of discharge from 69 major rivers throughout the world and estimates of the total discharge from each continent (Revelle *et al.*, 1968) show that, even if all available water were used, the gross cultivated irrigated area would be much smaller – about 1.1 billion hectares. The principal reason is that the distribution of potential irrigation water supplies and of irrigable land is very uneven among continents and in different regions of the same continent. Nearly one-third of the total river discharge comes from South America, the smallest of the less developed continents, where only 80 million gross cultivated hectares can be irrigated. In Africa, on the other hand, 290 million gross hectares could be irrigated by utilizing all available river waters, whereas 610 million gross hectares are irrigable.

Outside the humid tropics, the ultimate gross cultivated, irrigated and rain-fed area in all the continents could be 3.6 billion hectares. Assuming an average yield of 3 tons of cereal-grain equivalent per gross cultivated hectare devoted to food crops, and 13 percent of production going to seed and waste, about 35 billion people could be fed at an average caloric intake of 2,350 kcal per day. The assumed average yield is less than half the present average in the "corn belt" of the United States (FAO, 1980a).

If the equivalent of three crops per year could be grown in the humid tropics, the gross cultivated area would rise to 5.2 billion hectares and, in the less developed continents alone, to about 3.75 billion hectares. Outside the humid tropics, the ultimate potential for these continents is about 2.3 billion gross cultivated hectares. Even if only half the river run-off were utilized for irrigation, the gross cultivated area in the less developed continents could be 1.85 billion hectares, enough to feed 18 billion people under the assumptions made above. For comparison, the UN "high" estimate (Tabah, 1981) of the ultimate stable population size in the less developed regions is 12.6 billion, a level that could conceivably be reached 150 years from now.

Future Food Supplies for Africa

A more detailed and precise computation of potential agricultural production is being made for the developing countries of Africa by the Food and Agricultural Organization of the United Nations, in co-operation with the UN Fund for Population Activities (FAO, 1980). The same basic methodology is used as in the PSAC study. Agro-climatic zones are classified in different temperature and rainfall regimes during the crop-growing period, and are further divided by lengths of growing season in days. The climatic groups include those with temperatures of more than 20°C in the warm tropics and subtropics, 15–20°C in the moderately cool tropics and subtropics, and 5–15°C in the cool tropics and subtropics. A growing period is defined as the length of time in days during which the available moisture is half or more than half of potential evapotranspiration, and mean daily temperatures exceed 5°C. The growing period zones comprise duration of less than 75 days, 75–89 days, then by 30-day intervals to 329–64 days, 365– days and 365+ days. The last category corresponds to the "humid tropics" designation used by PSAC, in which precipitation exceeds potential evapotranspiration throughout the year. A map showing contours of equal length of growing period is superimposed on the FAO–UNESCO *Soil Map of the World* (Revelle, 1979), which gives the location and extent of 26 major soil groups broken down into 106 different units. The soil map depicts associations of soil units, called "mapping units," in which there is a dominant soil, plus associated soils that make up less than 50 percent of the total area of the mapping unit. Each mapping unit is further classified by soil texture, as coarse, medium or fine, and by characteristic slope: level to gently undulating – dominant slope between 0 and 8 percent; rolling to hilly – 8 to 30 percent slopes; and deeply dissected to mountainous – slopes greater than 30 percent. Some soil mapping units may also have deleterious characteristics, called "phases," such as stoniness, salinity or alkalinity, a shallow hardpan or a high calcium carbonate content.

The degree of suitability of each growing period zone, climate type and soil unit is evaluated for 17 crops commonly grown in Africa (wheat, sorghum, millets, phaesolus bean, maize, soybean, cotton, white potato, sweet potato, sugarcane, cassava, bunded rice, upland rice, banana/plantain, peanut, barley and oil palm). If all characteristics are optimal for a particular crop, the area is evaluated as very suitable for it; otherwise as suitable, marginally suitable, or unsuitable. These evaluations depend to some extent on the assumed level of agricultural technology. Three levels are considered, referred to as low-, intermediate- and high-input levels. At the low-input level it is assumed that farm production is subsistence-oriented, with low capital and high labour intensity. The only power source is manual labour with hand tools. Only local cultivars are utilized, with no chemical fertilizers or chemical pest and disease controls. Fallow periods are used to enable the soil to recover its fertility, but other soil conservation measures are minimal. Land holdings are small and sometimes fragmented. At the high-input level, farm production is market-oriented, capital intensity is high and labour intensity low, and mechanization is employed at all stages, including harvesting. High-yielding cultivars are utilized, with optimal applications of chemical fertilizers and chemical pest and disease controls. Extensive land conservation measures are practised, and there is a high level of advisory services, leading to early application of research findings. Land holdings are consolidated and may be large.

At high-input levels on suitable soils, the assumed yields for the crops vary with lengths of growing period. Optimal growing periods for each crop and the corresponding yields in terms of cereal-grain equivalents (caloric content equal to a given tonnage of wheat, milled rice or maize) are given in table 6.1. It will be seen that the expected yields of most of these crops, in terms of cereal-equivalents, significantly exceed 3 tons per hectare. The only exceptions are rice, white potato, banana/plantain and

TABLE 6.1 EXPECTED YIELDS FOR AFRICAN CROPS ON SUITABLE SOILS UNDER RAIN-FED CONDITIONS WITH HIGH TECHNOLOGY

Crops	Optimum temperature during growing period (°C)	Optimum growing period A (days)	Yield (metric tons/ ha of maize equivalent)
Winter barley	5–20	150–179	3.7
Winter wheat	5–20	180–209	4.9
Spring wheat	5–20	180–209	5.6
Highland phaesolus bean	5–20	180–209	3.0
White potato	5–20	180–209	2.9
Highland sorghum	15–20	210–239	4.1
Highland maize	15–20	210–239	6.5
Pearl millets	20	150–179	3.9
Lowland sorghum	20	150–179	5.1
Lowland maize	20	150–179	7.1
Lowland phaesolus bean	20	180–209	3.4
Soybean	20	180–209	3.9
Paddy rice	20	210–239	2.5
Peanut	20	210–239	3.2
Sweet potato	20	240–299	3.9
Upland rice	20	240–299	2.7
Cassava	20	300–329	4.5
Banana/plantain	20	365+ (humid tropics)	2.7
Sugar cane	20	365–	1.5 (dry sugar)
Oil palm	20	365+ (humid tropics)	16.7

Source: FAO, 1980b

sugarcane. Yields of maize, spring wheat, lowland sorghum and oil palm are more than 5 tons/hectare. For winter wheat, highland sorghum and cassava, expected yields are between 4 and 5 tons. These high yields of most crops commonly grown in Africa give confidence in our computations of the numbers of people who could be fed with average yields of 3 tons.

Estimated yields for low-input levels are one-fourth of those we have given for high inputs. But at low-input levels, the estimated carrying capacities per hectare discussed below (numbers of people who could be fed per hectare of land area in African countries) are only one-sixth of the carrying capacities for high-input levels. The reason is that, without chemical fertilizers, parts of the farm areas must be left fallow to allow the soil to recover its fertility. When the need for fallowing is taken into account, the productivity of soils at low-input levels in the humid tropics may be less than 10 percent of that for high-input levels (Young and Wright, 1980).

Actual and potential future irrigation are considered in the FAO study. Because the time-horizon is limited to the year 2000, only about a 40 percent increase in the total net irrigated area is projected, from 8.7 million hectares in recent years to 12.4 million hectares in 2000. Assuming that two crops would be grown under irrigation, the gross irrigated area could be 25 million hectares. This is less than one-tenth of the estimated ultimate irrigation potential, given earlier, of 290 million gross hectares.

For areas with a relatively long or discontinuous growing period, double-cropping is projected, partly to ensure an optimal protein content in human diets. Crops considered for double-cropping under high-input conditions are lowland maize, upland rice, paddy rice, lowland phaesolus bean, lowland sorghum, pearl millets, soybean, peanuts, sweet potato and white potato. For growing periods between 300 and 365 days, annual production of calories and proteins per net cultivated hectare from double-cropped upland or paddy rice is higher than from any other single or double crop. Oil palm gives a higher caloric content, but it is lacking in protein.

On about 60 million hectares with winter rainfall, and 380 million hectares with summer rainfall, the length of growing period is less than 75 days. In these regions the FAO group considers that rangeland livestock husbandry may be more productive than settled agriculture. They calculate that, under high-input conditions, enough calories could be produced in milk and meat, in the total area of about 450 million hectares, for 41 million people, and enough protein for 114 million. These numbers are reduced to 10 million and 28.5 million under low-input conditions.

In areas of higher rainfall and longer growing periods, livestock husbandry, especially of ruminant animals, can be a productive supplement to field crop agriculture. Farm residues that are inedible for human beings can provide most of the diets of ruminant livestock. However, very large areas of sub-humid, tropical Africa are infested by tsetse flies, the vectors of trypanosomiasis ("sleeping sickness"), and here cattle husbandry is virtually impossible. Onchoceriasis, or "river blindness," which is also caused by species of flies, seriously limits human activity in tropical West Africa (Wortman and Cummings, 1978).

The results of the FAO assessment are given not in terms of arable land areas but as average human carrying capacity per hectare of the total land area of each country, and of less developed Africa as a whole. It is assumed that productive technology exists for the humid tropics. With a high level of inputs and a crop mix giving a balanced diet of calories and protein, the FAO group estimates that the average carrying capacity for the 2.84 billion hectares of less developed Africa is 3.37 persons per hectare, sufficient for a total population of 9.6 billion people.

In the PSAC study for all of Africa, the gross cultivated, rain-fed area outside the humid tropics was 490 million hectares. Adding 290 million gross irrigated hectares, and the equivalent of 110 million triple-cropped hectares in the humid tropics, gives a gross cultivated area of 1.11 billion hectares. Here we follow FAO in assuming the existence of a productive technology for the humid tropics. Corrected for the omission of South Africa, the gross cultivated area for less-developed Africa is about 1.06 billion hectares. With our assumption that cereal-equivalent yields per gross cultivated hectare are 3 tons, that 10 percent of the cultivated area is devoted to non-food crops, 13 percent of production is lost or saved for seeds, and average calorie requirements are 2,350 kcal/day, we arrive at a potential future population of 10.16 billion people, 6 percent higher than the FAO estimate.

Both figures are more than 20 times the 1980 population of Africa, and about 4.5 times the UN medium estimate of the ultimate stabilized population of 2.2 billion in 2110 (Tabah, 1981). With the low-input level of most present-day African agriculture, the FAO group estimates that only 0.55 persons per hectare can be fed, corresponding to a total population of about 1.5 billion persons. It is expected that this population size will be reached by 2025 – 45 years from now (Tabah, 1981).

In fact, the foods needs of some 11 African countries with populations of more than one million people already exceed the FAO's estimate of the production capacity of their land at a low level of inputs. These include Morocco, Algeria, Tunisia, Libya and Somalia in North Africa, Mauritania and Niger in the Sahel, and Burundi, Kenya, Lesotho and Ruanda in southern and central Africa. Their total populations are nearly 80 million people, or more than 17 percent of the population of the continent. In most of these countries, food production per capita is declining. Algerian food production per person diminished by 25 percent between 1970 and 1979; in Mauritania the decline was 27 percent, in Morocco 20 percent, in Somalia 15 percent, and in Kenya 13 percent. Sharp declines in food production also occurred in Angola, Congo, Ghana, Mozambique, Togo, Uganda, Zimbabwe, and Ethiopia (FAO, 1980a). In several countries regression can be accounted for by political turmoil, but in others, such as Kenya, Algeria, and Morocco, it probably reflects a low level of investment of physical and human resources in agriculture.

The potential agricultural land and water resources of Africa are immense. It is clear that these resources must be more fully utilized within the next few decades if the people of the continent are to produce enough food for their own needs.

In the short run, increases in food production might be accomplished by bringing uncultivated land under the plough. But the FAO study demonstrates that, over the longer term, the productivity of cultivated land – yields per cultivated hectare – must be drastically improved. This can be done in part by developing irrigation, which would allow double- or triple-cropping. The necessity of fallowing must first be eliminated, however; otherwise double-cropping cannot be utilized. This will require maintaining the soil fertility through use of nitrogen and other fertilizers. The nitrogen supply does not have to come from chemical fertilizers, based on expensive fossil fuels; instead, it could come from plants with symbiotic nitrogen-fixing bacteria such as several species of fast-growing trees, leguminous crops or *Azolla* ferns.

Intensified biological research is a necessary, if not sufficient, condition for raising African agricultural productivity. This should be directed towards increasing biological nitrogen production, raising water use efficiencies, shortening the growing season of many crops to facilitate double- or triple-cropping, and developing biological controls for diseases and pests (Revelle, 1976a). The strengths and weaknesses of the traditional farming systems of tropical Africa should be studied scientifically to gain insights into possible improvements (Hopper, 1976).

Meeting Future Food Needs in Asia

Multiple cropping and increased yields on presently cultivated land

About 450 million hectares are cultivated, of which 130 million are irrigated (FAO, 1980a). Although much of the irrigation water is used very inefficiently, some irrigated fields are double-cropped, as are also some lands under rain-fed agriculture where the rainy season is sufficiently long. Consequently, the gross cultivated area (net cultivated area × number of crops grown per year) may well be over 500 million hectares.

The net cultivated area is 82 percent of the potentially arable area of 550 million hectares, including 80 million hectares in the humid tropics and 15 million hectares requiring irrigation for even one crop (Revelle *et al.*, 1967). With better use of available water resources, the irrigated area could be increased to 340 million hectares.

If all the potentially arable land, including the 80 million hectares of the humid tropics, were cultivated, one net cultivated hectare would need to feed 10.1 persons by the middle of the twenty-first century. (For comparison, the present population density of Bangladesh is 9.5 persons per cultivated hectare.) This would require an average annual production of 3.4 metric tons of cereal-grain equivalent per hectare – more than twice the present production of milled cereals of 1.5 metric tons per net cultivated hectare (FAO, 1980a). In making this calculation, we have assumed that 10 percent of the arable land must be used to produce cotton and other non-food crops, that seeds and wastage would be 13 percent of the harvested grain, and that the average diet would contain 2,500 kcal per person per day. For a more adequate diet, including sufficient high-quality protein – protein with the balanced content of amino acids required by human beings and all other warm-blooded animals except cattle and related ruminants – and "protective" foods such as fruits and vegetables, the equivalent in cereal-grain production should be at least 4,000 kcal per person per day. This would correspond to annual production of 5.4 tons of cereals per net cultivated hectare.

The Asian areas within the humid tropics, that is within the climatic zone where precipitation exceeds potential evapotranspiration throughout the year, occur very largely on the sparsely settled islands of Borneo, Sumatra and north-western New Guinea. A relatively small proportion exists in the Philippines, the Malay peninsula and on the island of Java (FAO, 1980c). Recent work by members of the Agro-Ecological Zones Project of the UN Food and Agriculture Organization indicates that only about 14 million hectares out of a total area of 85 million humid tropic hectares are suitable or marginally suitable for rice cultivation, even under a high level of technology. A much smaller area is marginally suitable for cultivation of cassava. The investments needed to bring the humid tropic regions under cultivation and to create new farming communities within them would seem to be better spent on raising the productivity of presently cultivated land, by increasing both the intensity of cultivation – that is, the number of crops grown per net cultivated hectare – and the yields per crop.

Under rain-fed conditions, agricultural modernization would enable two crops to be grown on about 50 million presently cultivated hectares (Revelle *et al.*, 1967). But a much more important step would be to enlarge the irrigated area. Indeed, additional water control through irrigation is essential to increase the production of rice (FAO, 1980c), the staple food of half the people of Asia. If 50 percent of the estimated total discharge of 6,750 km^3 in Asian rivers (Revelle *et al*., 1968) could be diverted for irrigation, the total irrigated area could be increased by 210 million hectares above the present level of 130 million hectares. This would provide for a "virtual" depth of irrigation at the point of diversion from the rivers of 1 metre over the entire irrigated area of 340 million hectares, enough on average for one additional crop. Counting the proposed double-cropped, rain-fed areas, two crops could be grown on 375 million hectares, and the total gross cropped area could be raised to 845 million hectares. For a diet of 2,500 kcal per person per day, the required yields to accommodate the population in 2050 would be 2.2 metric tons of cereal-grain equivalent per gross cultivated hectare – about 45 percent more than present cereal production per net cultivated hectare. For a diet of 4,000 kcal per person per day, average yields would need to be 3.5 tons per gross cultivated hectare.

With present-day agricultural technology under favourable environmental conditions, as in the "Corn Belt" of the mid-western United States, average yields are now nearly 7 metric tons per gross cultivated hectare (FAO, 1980a). There is no known physical or biological reason why equally high yields per gross cropped hectare could not be obtained from most Asian farmlands if adequate controlled water supplies were available. Thus, in principle, an alternative to maximizing the irrigated area would be to concentrate irrigation and other developments in the most favourable regions, with the objective of approaching the maximum yields attainable under existing technology. This might not be either politically feasible or socially desirable, if it resulted in very uneven development between countries or between different regions of the same country. However, in those developing countries where other energy resources are inadequate, it may be essential to obtain high food yields on limited land areas in order to make land available to produce biomass fuels (Revelle, 1979).

High yields of food crops may also become necessary in the future for some already-crowded Asian countries such as Bangladesh, whose population is projected by the UN Population Division to be 222 million people in 2025 (Tabah, 1981). Average yields of 4.1 and 6.6 tons per gross cropped hectare on the 8.1 million double-cropped hectares available for food production would be required to provide daily diets corresponding, respectively, to 2,500 and 4,000 kcal of grain-equivalent per capita. Further population growth expected after 2025 would demand either still higher yields or higher cropping intensities (triple-cropping). Here we face a paradox and a dilemma. The introduction and use of the required high level of agricultural technology implies a large measure of economic and social development. Such development would, in itself, probably result in a decline in birth rates and a stabilization of population size at a lower level than that projected by the UN Population Division. On the other hand, if Bangladesh does not become self-sufficient in food, large-scale, export-oriented industrialization would be necessary to provide foreign exchange for food imports; and this also would require economic and social development, presumably accompanied by rapidly declining birth rates.

An example: irrigation and modernization in the Ganges Plain

The possibilities for increased irrigation use of river flows are well illustrated in the Ganges Basin of India and Bangladesh (Revelle and Lakshminarayana, 1975). At present, a gross cultivated area of about 12.5 million hectares in the Indian part of the Basin is partially irrigated with 5.6 million hectare metres (2 hectare metre = 10^4 m³) of water diverted into irrigation canals from the Ganges and its tributaries or pumped from ground waters recharged by the rivers and the monsoon rains. This is 13 percent of the presumed river flows of 42 million hectare metres before the beginning of irrigation. With combined surface and ground-water development, the total consumptive use of water in irrigation could be increased more than four-fold to 24 million hectare metres, or 57 percent of the original Ganges flows, covering a gross cultivated area of 40 million hectares. A small part of this irrigated area would lie south of the Ganges Basin and would be supplied by transfer of 1.8 million hectare metres out of the Basin.

The key to the development would be surface and underground storage of a major part of the monsoon flows of the Ganges and its tributaries, which now run to the sea largely unused. Utilization of these high flows for irrigation throughout the year would have a further advantage in ameliorating flood damage.

The average depth of irrigation on the gross irrigated area would be only 60 cm, considerably less than the average depth of 1 metre we have computed for all of less developed Asia. More than half the gross irrigated area would be irrigated during the winter, or "rabi" growing season, when the difference between potential evaporation and precipitation is less than 35 cm over most of the Basin (White House, 1964). Rainfall provides a large fraction of the water requirement during the monsoon, or "kharif" growing season.

In computing the gross cultivated area, we have assumed that average evapotranspiration and drainage to maintain a salt balance on cultivated fields would be 50 cm, including non-beneficial uses. Other evaporative losses before the water reached the fields were assumed to be 17 percent of the water diverted from the rivers.

To take full advantage of the potential for increased production, considerable investments must be made to strengthen the agricultural infrastructure, in addition to construction of irrigation works. I estimated in 1976 (Revelle, 1976a) that costs would be close to $1,000, distributed as shown in table 6.2. With 1981 construction prices these costs should probably be doubled, to $1,900 per gross cropped hectare.

The energy required to produce 3 tons of food grains on a gross cultivated hectare would be about 38 percent of the food energy in the crop, or 4 million kcal, equivalent to 0.36 ton of petroleum-based fuel (see table 6.3). At 1981 prices the cost of this quantity of oil would be around $88 on the dock in Bombay, plus costs of refining, transportation and marketing. About half of the fuel requirements would go to producing the nitrogen, phosphate, and potash fertilizers that are essential for increased yields.

The annual farm operating costs, not counting farm labour but including interest and amortization of capital investments (farm tools and farm machinery, plus development costs described above), purchase of fertilizers, pesticides, high-yielding seeds, fuel for farm vehicles and electricity or diesel fuel for irrigation pumps, would be of the order of $350 per gross cultivated hectare. At $200 per ton, 3 tons of food grains should bring the farmers about $600 for each gross cultivated hectare. With an average farm size of 2 hectares, producing two crops per year, the income per farm household would be $1,000 less the costs of hired agricultural labour. (Production of two crops of 3 tons on 2 hectares gives

TABLE 6.2 ESTIMATED COSTS ($) OF STRENGTHENING AGRICULTURAL INFRASTRUCTURE

Tube-well construction	75
Construction of surface reservoirs and irrigation canals	350
Electrification for wells	90
Land-levelling, grading and field drains	150
Construction of fertilizer plants with capacity of 110 kg/gross cultivated hectare/year	36
Flood control and major drains	100
Construction of marketing, storage, food processing, research and extension facilities, and factories for tools, machinery and pesticides	50
Construction of farm-to-market roads	100
Total	951

Roger Revelle

TABLE 6.3 AVERAGE ENERGY REQUIREMENTS PER GROSS
CROPPED HECTARE (PIMENTEL, 1974; WHITE HOUSE, 1964)

	10^6 kcal
Irrigation water[a]	0.5
Chemical fertilizers	2.0
High-yielding seeds	0.1
Plant protection against diseases and pests	0.03
Construction of farm tools and farm machinery	0.2
Fuel for operating farm machinery	1.0
Crop drying	0.2
Total	4.03

[a] Assuming half of total irrigation supply is pumped from wells at an average depth of 10 metres
with diesel-powered pumps.

a return of 12 × $200 = $2,400; costs of $350 per crop = $1,400; net receipts are therefore $1,000.) But if the present urban–rural population distribution persists (Revelle, 1976b), about 20 people would inhabit the countryside for each farm family. With a probable size for a farm household of 5 persons, 15 people would be "landless labourers" under present socioeconomic conditions. It is clear that rural industrialization must accompany agricultural modernization if the rural population is to attain an adequate per capita income or even be able to purchase the food produced by the farmers (Revelle, 1980).

*Required capital investment for agricultural
modernization in Asia*

Assuming that average costs per gross cultivated hectare throughout Asia would be about the same as those we have estimated for the Ganges Plain, the total investment to bring irrigation and agricultural modernization to 210 million hectares not now irrigated, and to improve irrigation systems and farm productivity on 130 million presently irrigated hectares, would be close to 650 billion. Costs for modernization of the remaining 130 million cultivated hectares, which will continue to be farmed under rain-fed conditions, could be $900 per hectare, or about $115 billion. These expenditures for rain-fed areas would include land-levelling and grading, and construction of field drains, major drains and flood-control works, fertilizer plants, farm-to-market roads, factories for manufacturing farm equipment and pesticides, and other facilities. If the needed irrigation works and agricultural infrastructures are to be in place to feed the projected Asian population by the year 2050, these investments should be made within the next 60 years.

Evenly divided over this time-span, the annual capital expenditure would be $12.7 billion, about $5 per person per year for the 1980 population, or about 1.5 percent of the overall Asian gross product in 1980 of $851 billion (World Bank, 1980). Annual capital expenditures in the Asian countries are well over $100 billion – probably at least ten times the needed agricultural investments.

Without the productivity increases that should result from these investments, even larger expenditures may well be required over the next several decades to pay for food imports. The International Food Policy Research Institute has estimated (IFPRI, 1977) that, even by 1985, Asian imports of cereal-grains will be 50 million tons per year, at a likely cost of more than $10 billion. Thus, provided the political will exists, there should be no great difficulty in finding the needed capital for radical agricultural improvement.

A considerable fraction of these investments is already being made, as is evidenced by the fact that food production in Asia rose by about 30 percent between 1970 and 1979. Although some countries have fallen behind, the FAO production data show that, on average for all Asian countries, food production per capita also rose by about 8 percent over the past decade. These increases continue the trend of growing food production that started at the beginning of the 1950s. Much of the increase between 1950 and 1970 can be accounted for by an expansion of the cultivated areas, but since 1960 increases in yields have predominated (Wortman and Cummings, 1978).

The need for human resource development and
socioeconomic change

The most serious constraints on agricultural improvements are not lack of capital for investment in physical facilities, but the slow pace of development of human resources and of the economic and social conditions for successful market agriculture. More specialists are needed who can plan, design and operate irrigation facilities, both large and small. The farmers need to learn how to use irrigation water and other inputs more efficiently to attain high yields. Government price policies for agricultural products need to be adjusted to assure a healthy profit for efficient farmers. More credit on economically realistic terms must be provided, especially for "small farmers." Patterns of land-holding should be rationalized. And opportunities for non-farm employment in the countryside should be multiplied.

Effects of Increased Atmospheric Carbon Dioxide

By the middle of the next century, continued burning of fossil fuels as a source of energy is likely to result in a doubling of the carbon dioxide (CO_2) content of the atmosphere relative to the amount present in 1860, at an early stage of the Industrial Revolution. This increase will have two kinds of consequences: a direct effect on photosynthesis because of the greater quantity of carbon available to plants from the atmosphere; and marked changes in climate. Computer models in three dimensions of the general circulation of the atmosphere indicate that, on a global basis, average temperatures near the earth's surface will rise between 2 and 3°C with a doubling of atmospheric CO_2, and both evaporation and precipitation will increase by about 9 percent. The rise in average temperature will be much greater at higher latitudes, and changes in precipitation are expected to vary markedly with latitude.

Where solar radiation, water supply, soil nitrogen and other soil nutrients are adequate, increased atmospheric CO_2 should act as a fertilizer for crop plants, raising both photosynthetic production and water-use efficiency. Greenhouse experiments indicate that a doubling of CO_2 under high agricultural technology can increase total biomass yields by about 40 percent. Indeed, it is possible that part of the improvement in agricultural yields during the past 50 years has resulted from the 13 per cent increase in atmospheric CO_2 since the end of the nineteenth century. The effects should be especially important for crop plants such as rice, wheat, millets and potatoes, which have a C_3 photosynthetic pathway. Corn, sugarcane and sorghum, with a C_4 pathway, are likely to be limited by solar radiation rather than by CO_2.

Much research is needed to take full advantage of these expected effects on photosynthesis. Varieties of field crops need to be developed, through conventional breeding programmes, and modern methods of genetic manipulation, that will have higher net photosynthetic production and will use less water as the atmospheric CO_2 content increases, but will not respond to a warmer atmospheric temperature by an increase in respiration, which would cancel out the effect of CO_2 fertilization. We are concerned both with greater total plant production and an increase of the "harvest index," that is, the portion of the plant that can be used by human beings for food, fuel, fibre or other useful products. The effects of higher temperature and increased carbon dioxide on biological nitrogen fixation and on weeds, insects and microbiological pests must be taken into account. Programmes of genetic improvement should include greater resistance to pests, as well as to other environmental stresses.

Using both historical climate data and computations for "general

circulation" models of climate, the distinguished climatologist, Herman
Flohn, has recently estimated the changes in average surface temperature
and precipitation that are likely to occur by the year 2000 in different
latitude belts if atmospheric carbon dioxide goes up by 560–680 ppm
(Flohn, 1981), about twice the nineteenth-century value (NRC, 1977)
(see table 6.4).

These changes will have profound effects on the world distribution of
water resources. When precipitation exceeds evapotranspiration, the
total surface run-off from a river system is simply the difference between
precipitation and evapotranspiration (with a slight correction for underground seepage into the ocean). In the Colorado River system of the
United States, the major drainage basin is located around 40°N latitude.
At the present time, about 85 percent of the precipitation evaporates and
only 15 percent is carried by the river. Because potential evapotranspiration depends mainly on surface temperatures, the percentage change in
run-off owing to climatic change is likely to be much greater, other things
being equal, than the percentage change in precipitation. With a rise in
average air temperature of several degrees centigrade, and a 10–15
percent fall in precipitation, the average flow of the Colorado could
diminish by 50 percent or more. Yet even with large volumes of water
storage, the present flow of the river is barely sufficient to meet the
present demands of irrigation agriculture over a period of years.

Major changes in surface and underground water supply could also
occur elsewhere in the world. In northern Africa, the average flows of the

TABLE 6.4 LIKELY CHANGES IN
TEMPERATURE AND PRECIPITATION OWING
TO AN INCREASE IN ATMOSPHERIC CO_2

Latitude	Average annual change in surface temp. (°C)	Change in precipitation (%)
60°N	+7.5	+18
50°N	+6	+ 4
40°N	+6	−14
30°N	+4.5	0
20°N	+2.5	+20
10°N	+0.5	+20
Equator	+3	0
10°S	+4	−20
20°S	+4.5	− 5
30°S	+4	+ 5
40°S	+4	+12
50°S	+3	+12
60°S	+2.5	+12

Niger, Chari, Senegal, Volta and Blue Nile Rivers could increase by large fractions because of 10–12 percent more precipitation and only slightly higher surface temperatures. The flows of the Narmada and other South Indian rivers would also be expected to increase. On the other hand, the largest river in China (the Hwang Ho), the Amu Darya and Syr Darya in one of the prime agricultural belts of the Soviet Union, the Tigris–Euphrates system in Turkey, Syria and Iraq, the Zambezi in Zimbabwe and Zambia and the Sao Francisco in Brazil could greatly diminish in volume and flows. Somewhat smaller run-off and underground storage could also be expected in the Ganges of northern India, the Indus in Pakistan, the Danube in eastern Europe, the Yangtze in China and the Rio Grande in the United States. All of these rivers form the basis of very extensive and highly productive irrigation agriculture, and the projected diminutions in their flow could have potentially disastrous consequences. On the other hand, the expected considerable increase in the flows of the Mekong and Brahmaputra rivers could lead to frequent disastrous floods over large areas of Thailand, Cambodia, Vietnam, India and Bangladesh. Careful studies should be made of national and international actions, including investments in river basin development, that should be taken to mitigate these possible effects.

References

Bloodworth, L. J., E. Bossany, *et al.*, (1978) *World Energy Resources, 1985–2020*, pp. 212 –47. World Energy Conference, IPC Science and Technology Press.

Flohn, Herman (1981) *Major Climatic Events as Expected during a Prolonged CO_2-Induced Warming*. Report prepared for Institute of Energy Analysis, Oak Ridge Associated Universities, Oak Ridge, Tenn.

Food and Agriculture Organization of the United Nations/UNESCO (1974a) *Soil Map of the World*, UNESCO, Paris.

Food and Agriculture Organization of the United Nations (1980a) *FAO Production Yearbook, 1979*, FAO, Rome.

Food and Agriculture Organization of the United Nations (1980b) *Land Resources for Populations of the Future, FAO, Rome.*

Food and Agriculture Organization of the United Nations (1980c) *Report on the Agro-Ecological Zones Project, Vol. 4: Results for Southeast Asia* pp. vii, 39. FAO, Rome.

Hopper, W. David (1976) "The development of agriculture in developing countries," *Scientific American*, September, pp. 197–205.

International Food Policy Research Institute (1977) *Food Needs of Developing Countries*, Report no. 3, IFPRI, Washington, D.C.

National Research Council, Geophysics Study Committee (1977) *Energy and Climate*, National Academy of Sciences, Washington, D.C.

Pimentel, David (1974) *Energy Use in World Food Production*, Report 74–1, Dept of Entomology and Section on Ecology and Systematics, Cornell University, Ithaca, N.Y.

Revelle, Roger (1976a) "The resources available for agriculture," *Scientific American*, September, pp. 165–78.

Revelle, Roger (1976b) "Energy use in rural India," *Science*, **192**, 969–75.

Revelle, Roger (1979) "Energy sources for rural development," *Energy*, **4**, 969–87.

Revelle, Roger (1980) "Energy dilemmas in Asia: the need for research and development," *Science*, **209**, 164–74.

Revelle, Roger, Nyle C. Brady, Albert L. Brown, *et al.*, (1967) "Water and land," in *The World Food Problem*. *Report of the Panel on the World Food Supply*, President's Science Advisory Committee, The White House, May, pp. 405–69.

Revelle, Roger, and V. Lakshminarayana (1975) "The Ganges water machine," *Science*, **199**, 611–16.

Revelle, Roger, Peter Rogers and Harold A. Thomas, Jr (1968) "Some international aspects of water resources development," in *International Problems of Science and Technology*. US Dept of State, Washington, D.C.

Tabah, Léon (1981) "The world demographic situation: some current trends, emerging issues and perspectives." Paper prepared for Nobel Symposium, Oslo, September.

White House/Dept of Interior Panel on Waterlogging and Salinity in West Pakistan (1964) *Report on Land and Water Development in the Indus Plain*. Washington, D.C.

World Bank (1980) *World Development, 1980*, Oxford University Press, New York.

Wortman, Sterling, and Ralph W. Cummings. Jr (1978) *To Feed This World: the Challenge and the Strategy*. Johns Hopkins University Press, Baltimore.

Young, A. and A. C. S. Wright (1980) "Rest period requirements, tropical and sub-tropical soils under annual crops," Appendix V of *Land Resources for Populations of the Future*, pp. 197–208. FAO, Rome.

7

Soil Erosion in the United States

EARL R. SWANSON and EARL O. HEADY

Introduction

Soil erosion in the United States has been and continues to be an important consideration in agricultural production. The nature of the impacts that occur as a result of soil erosion and the economics involved in controlling this erosion presently are subjects of much debate.

The author of the *Global 2000* food and agriculture projections (chapter 6) concludes that the environmental difficulties likely to be associated with the projections appear, at least in theory, to be manageable:

> Management options within the agricultural sector are wide enough, particularly if supplemented with environmentally sensitive technology, to solve the problems inherent in using a larger proportion of the world's resources is an increasingly intensive manner to produce food. (*Global 2000*, p. 101)

There are two related questions that currently focus on the use of soil as a resource. First, there is the uncertainty about the need to maintain soil *productivity*. This uncertainty stems from questions about whether technology that increases production per unit of land will be generated and adopted at a rate fast enough to meet our future food and fiber needs. A second concern behind the current interest in soil conservation is found in *environmental quality* considerations, primarily concerned with the quality of water.

The soil resource implications of the agricultural projections in chapter 6 are treated in chapter 13 of *Global 2000*. Here soil erosion is viewed as a more serious problem than in chapter 6:

> By that time (the year 2000) many croplands that are now producing well will be facing serious soil problems if current cultivation

practices continue. Because corn (maize) is relatively poor at holding soil, the corn-growing lands – about 7.5 percent of all lands in cultivation, producing roughly one-fifth of the world's grain – will fare the worst. The United States, as the world's largest corn producer, is in particular danger. (*Global 2000*, p. 280)

In this chapter we focus on the productivity aspect of soil conservation and, although we restrict our analysis to the United States, we develop a substantially more optimistic perspective than that found in the second quotation from *Global 2000*. Our view is thus more consistent with that of the first quotation.

The *Global 2000* food and agriculture projections (chapter 6) were generated using a world grain–oilseed–livestock (GOL) model. This model does not explicitly consider the relationships between soil loss and productivity. Rather, one of the assumptions incorporated into the GOL model is that there will be no large-scale loss or degradation of arable land due to mismanagement or environmental deterioration (p. 547). In a later section of this chapter we present the results of a national model that considers the yield-reduction impact of soil erosion in making projections to the year 2000.

The relationship between productivity and soil conservation is a variation on an old theme that periodically has attracted the attention of economists, historians, and even Presidents. Rasmussen (1982) has pointed out that Thomas Jefferson advocated soil conservation, mainly through crop rotation, planting clover, and contour plowing. About 30 years ago the role of soil erosion in the decline of various civilizations throughout the world was reported in a publication by Lowdermilk (1953). He examined the ancient history of the Near East and of China, and concluded that civilizations have flourished or fallen, depending on how the soil was used or abused. His analysis of the U.S. situation in 1953 is largely in physical terms: "More than 300 million acres out of our 400-odd million acres of farm fields are now eroding faster than soil is being formed. That means destruction of the land if erosion is not controlled."

Although much remains to be learned about the physical consequences of soil erosion in terms of future productivity and environmental quality, economic assessments using available data for the purpose of public policy analysis must be made. Further, the monitoring of the trends in soil erosion rates is an important component of the information base for forming public policy.

Trends in Soil Erosion in the United States

On a national basis, sheet and rill erosion caused by water account for the vast majority of total erosion. Sheet erosion refers to soil movement that results from the splash action of raindrops and the force of shallow flow over sloping fields. Rill erosion is characterized by small channels.

It is difficult to assess the national trends in soil erosion and their consequences. First, there is the question of whether the focus should be on (1) the soil status in terms of current and potential productivity or (2) the annual rate of erosion per unit of area. Ideally, these elements are related and information is needed on both in order to assess national trends in the impacts of erosion. Another measure of the degree of soil erosion is the total tons of gross erosion per year for the entire U.S. This can be misleading because soils differ substantially in the impact of a given erosion rate on their potential productivity.

Another complicating factor is the shift in land-use patterns that may occur between surveys. This makes direct comparisons between surveys at different times more difficult. There is considerable variation in the change in annual erosion rates among areas due to changes in land-use patterns. For example, between 1967 and 1975, 53 million acres shifted from cropland to pasture and 32 million acres shifted from pasture to cropland (Dideriksen *et al.*, p. 3). During the same period about 8 million acres shifted from cropland to forest-land. These land-use changes represent responses to complex forces including crop price changes as well as attempts to maintain the productivity of the soil asset.

The first survey of soil erosion in the U.S. was the Reconnaisance Survey of 1934. The survey attempted to classify the kinds of erosion and to measure the degrees of severity of erosion and the proportion of topsoil which had been lost. Held and Clawson (1965) examined the results of this survey, the 1957 National Inventory of Soil and Water Conservation Needs, and other information, and concluded:

There are simply no clear-cut, well-designed data, especially on a historical scale, which are adequate to answer the critical questions about soil conservation achievements over the past thirty years or so. . . . To us, however, it seems fairly clear that substantial progress has been made since about 1930. All the evidence we have been able to find points in this direction; none to contradict this conclusion. (Held and Clawson, p. 232)

The National Summary Evaluation of the Agricultural Conservation Program (1980) indicates that, in 1977, 78.9 percent of the nonfederal land in the United States in all uses had erosion rates from sheet and rill erosion of less than 3 tons per acre per year and 86.7 percent had erosion rates from sheet and rill erosion of less than 5 tons per acre per year (table 3 of the National Summary Evaluation of the Agricultural Conservation Program). If wind erosion is included, 81.7 percent of nonfederal land had erosion rates in 1977 of less than 5 tons per acre per year (Summary of Appraisal, Soil and Water Resources Conservation Act, 1980). A comparison of these estimates in 1977 with those of Lowdermilk in 1953 indicates that rates of erosion have decreased. Lowdermilk indicated that about 75 percent of the farm fields were at that time eroding faster than the soil was being formed. A comparison of the 1934 Reconnaisance Survey with the 1977 National Resources Inventory has been made by Dallavalle and Mayer (1982). Data from these surveys show an increase in cropland with slight erosion from 47 percent to 77 percent. The estimated decrease in cropland with moderate erosion was from 38 percent to 13 percent, and for land with severe erosion from 15 percent to 10 percent. Dallavalle and Mayer concluded (p. 29): "Despite problems of measurement, however, there are indications that considerable progress has been made in the four and one half decades in which the Federal soil conservation programs have been in effect."

A comparison of the condition of nonfederal rangeland in 1963 and 1977 is reported by Mayer (1982). The percentage of nonfederal rangeland rated as good and excellent doubled, increasing from 20 to 40 percent during this period. The percentage of nonfederal rangeland rated fair and poor decreased from 80 to 60 percent. Again, there is an indication that, at least in some areas, improvement in soil condition is occurring. Increases in acreage in corn to include areas with high erosion potential occurred in the 1970s. However, a comparison of 1931 corn production with 1981 corn production indicates a reduction in total U.S. acreage that has concentrated corn production on the less-erosive soils (Schultz, 1982, table 3).

Crosson and Stout (1983) address the question of trends in the quantity of soil eroded from the nation's croplands. After comparing the decade of the 1930s with that of the 1970s (periods with approximately the same amount of total cropland), they conclude that there is strong circumstantial evidence that erosion per acre of cropland in the U.S. declined. Crosson and Stout considered a number of factors in their analysis: (1) shifts in the distribution of cropland among regions with varying amounts of erosion per acre; (2) changes in the percentage of cropland in the various crops; (3) technology; (4) institutional factors; and (5) soil conservation policies. The reduction in erosion per acre from the 1930s to the 1970s is due primarily to improvements in such technology as (a) conservation tillage and (b) the increases in plant canopy providing more protection for the soil. Changes in soil conservation policy were judged to have had a mildly favorable role in the reduction in soil erosion rates.

Crosson and Stout (1983) have also reviewed the results of various studies of the relationship between soil loss and crop yields, and conclude that if the soil erosion rates of 1977 were to continue over the next century, there would not be a major threat to the productivity of the nation's cropland. Further, they estimate that the impact of erosion on crop production costs would continue to be small relative to the effects of rising demand, input prices, and technological advance.

The need for altering the rates of soil erosion in the United States will depend on a complex set of food demand and agricultural productivity variables. These are not only domestic but also of world scope. The projected food demand, both domestic and export – and an ability to meet that demand – is treated in some detail by D. Gale Johnson in chapter 2 of this book. In a later section of this chapter we discuss past productivity trends in agriculture and assess the likely levels of productivity in crop and livestock production in the year 2000.

Soil Loss Tolerance as a Policy Goal

The view of soil erosion primarily as a physical phenomenon has influenced the statement of public policy goals in terms of an annual rate of soil loss. The "soil loss tolerance" values (T-values) that have been established for each soil are stated in terms of tons per acre per year, and are influenced by the concept of balancing annual soil loss with the annual rate of soil formation. These soil loss tolerances represent judgments about "the maximum level of soil erosion that will permit a high level of crop productivity to be sustained economically and indefinitely" (USDA, 1978, p. 12). The average soil loss tolerance for cropland, pasture, and forestland in the United States is about 5 tons per acre per year. An average acre-inch of topsoil weighs about 150 tons. If there were no soil formation, and if there were to be a soil loss of 15 tons per acre per year, an inch of top soil would be lost every 10 years.

In the United States the concept of limiting annual erosion rates to annual rates of soil regeneration has played an important role in establishing T-values. However, it has been noted by some authors that, at least on some soils, the currently accepted T-values are higher than rates of soil regeneration (McCormack et al., 1982). The rate of soil regeneration is highly variable and depends, among other things, on the nature of the parent material underlying the topsoil. For example, Bartelli (1980) indicates that on permeable unconsolidated material soil regeneration may occur at approximately ten times the tolerance level while topsoil above hard rock would have regeneration rates below the soil loss tolerance levels. The rate of regeneration on a number of Illinois soils exceeds the soil loss tolerance levels. McCormack and his colleagues indicate that the issues in establishing soil loss tolerance levels are not only technical but largely stem from the uncertainty about the demands that will be placed on the soil resources in the future. In the early 1960s, off-site damage also became a consideration in the estimation of soil loss tolerance levels.

Although the setting of soil loss tolerance levels provides a benchmark for a physical equilibrium, we must also consider the economics of the matter and view the demand for soil conservation as a derived demand. McConnell (1983) has pointed out that requiring annual soil loss to be no more than natural replenishment may have radical consequences for policy and cultivation practices. There are few, if any, natural resources for which the public policy is one of restricting use to the rate of replenishment. As a public policy goal, soil loss tolerance levels should be based on a comprehensive analysis including such factors as the role of technology as a land substitute and the expected future demand for food and fiber.

A National Model for Economic Analysis of Soil Erosion

The type of economic models needed to assess the implications of alternative national soil conservation policies is represented by the national and interregional modeling activity at the Center for Agriculture and Rural Development (CARD) at Iowa State University. It should be noted that the world grain–oilseed–livestock (GOL) model used in the analysis presented in chapter 6 of *Global 2000* does not explicitly address environmental and soil resource issues. The CARD models were used to analyze the soil conservation programs considered under the Soil and Water Resources Conservation Act of 1977 (RCA) and these models also will be used to provide the 1985 RCA assessment required under that act. An example (English and Heady, 1980) will serve to illustrate the general nature of the models and the results. The report by English and Heady examines the impacts of meeting various soil loss goals on agricultural production, and resource use, in the year 2000. The model used is a large-scale interregional linear programming model that includes 105 producing areas, 48 water resource regions, and 28 market regions. Alternative cropping systems with various soil conservation and tillage practices are considered in land groups which represent differences in soil productivity within each of the 105 producing areas. Gross soil loss is calculated for each alternative in the model, thus providing a means for assessing the aggregate consequences of meeting various soil loss tolerance levels.

The commodity demands are those prepared by the National Inter-regional Agricultural Projections (NIRAP) effort of the U.S. Department of Agriculture and are based on projected domestic demand for a U.S. population of 260.3 million in the year 2000 and projections of export demand in the year 2000 (English and Heady, tables 2–5). The following levels: corn, 7,451 thousand bushels and wheat, 2,892 thousand these demand assumptions. The total domestic and export requirements for two selected commodities for the year 2000 are projected at the following levels: corn, 7,451 thousand bushels and wheat, 2,892 thousand bushels (English and Heady, table 5).

The model provides some informative results. A base solution, with no restrictions on soil loss, resulted in a national gross soil loss of 1,191 million tons. To meet the soil loss tolerance levels (T-values), this amount would be reduced almost in half – to 678 million tons. As mentioned earlier, the T-values represent a judgment regarding the maximum level of soil erosion that will permit a high level of crop productivity to be sustained economically and indefinitely. A comparison of the solutions from the year 2000 base run (no imposed restrictions on soil loss) with those that meet the loss tolerance requirement, indicates, among other things, that the total land required to meet demands increased from 77.62 percent of land available for the entire U.S. to only 78.50 percent for the run which satisfied the soil loss tolerance levels.

However, the increased pressure on the land resource base under a program of meeting T-values is indicated by an increase in the average shadow price of land in the year 2000 as compared to the year 2000 base run (no restrictions) (English and Heady, table 11). The shadow price of land is an indicator of the relative scarcity of land in agricultural production. It is also interesting to note that under the base run assumptions there is a slight decline in the average shadow price of land from 1985 to 2000. The crop yields used for the year 2000 were determined within the model. Yields depend on soil loss and fertilizer use which were chosen by the cost-minimization process of the model. Two examples (English and Heady, table 13) indicate that the yield levels are clearly within the range of moderate expectations (see later section of this chapter on production potentials). Corn yields (bushels per acre) in 2000 under the base solution and the T-value solution are 123 and 120 bu./acre respectively. The corresponding values for soybeans are 42 and 40 bu./acre and the wheat yields are the same (44 bu./acre) under both the base and the T-value solutions.

The analysis of the CARD National Model indicates soil loss tolerance goals could be met by the year 2000 and, although costs of production would increase, the total fraction of available land used would increase only slightly. Further, the crop yield increases by the year 2000, determined by the CARD model, are well within the range predicted by research workers in the sciences related to crop production. In effect, these crop yield increases dampen the pressure on the soil resource.

Private Incentives for Reductions in Soil Erosion to
Soil Loss Tolerance Levels

There is evidence that the private economic incentive for a substantial reduction in soil erosion to meet T-values is, in general, rather weak or non-existent. Further, there is a wide variation from watershed to watershed in the consequences of soil erosion, in terms of both productivity and off-site damage to environmental quality. The current economic incentives to adopt conservation tillage practices, although still weak, are greater than they were in the 1960s and 1970s.

In order to assess the private economic incentive it is necessary to know the impact of soil loss on crop yields. Observations of increasing yield trends due to improved crop technology tend to mask the declines which otherwise would have taken place due to soil erosion. However, if the surface layer of the soil is eroded it becomes difficult, if not impossible, to apply known technology to restore crop yields. At that point the damage of the soil for crop production is apparent. Thus soil losses may occur for a long period of time before there are noticeable yield losses. The yield reduction due to soil loss alone, in general, increases at an increasing rate with yields declining more rapidly as the subsoil is approached (English *et al.*, 1982; Walker, 1982).

The yield loss impact does not suddenly occur over an entire farm or area. The visible consequences of severe soil erosion on small areas can thus serve as indicators to farmers and landowners of the economic need for soil loss control. There is some evidence that the land market takes into account the economic damage from yield reductions due to erosion. Miranowski (1982) reports that land purchasers in Iowa pay more for less eroded land and for land with less erosion potential.

Adoption of soil conservation farming practices in response to economic incentives depends very much on the length of time for which the farmer plans. Evidence on several important soil types in Illinois indicates that the cost of yield losses over a 50-year period into the future is not likely to be great enough to induce the farmer to reduce the present rate of soil loss to the soil loss tolerance levels (T-values) recommended by the Soil Conservation Service (Swanson and Harshbarger, 1964; Swanson and Maccallum, 1969). Discount rates used in these studies ranged from 5 to 20 percent.

Six watersheds were studied in Illinois in 1972–3 (Gunterman *et al.*, 1974; Lee *et al.*, 1974; Swanson, 1978). In the watershed with the most severe erosion, soil losses were approximately 10 times the tolerance levels suggested by the Soil Conservation Service (Lee *et al.*, 1974). Yet, an adequate soil conservation plan – as defined by meeting soil loss tolerance levels for 20 years into the future – would increase annualized private net farm income by only about 1 percent (Lee *et al.*, 1974, table 10). The discount rate used for these studies was 7.5 percent.

A study of five watersheds in Texas also shows a pattern of rather weak private economic incentives for soil conservation (Taylor *et al.*, 1978). Planning periods of 10, 100, and 200 years into the future were considered in the Texas study. Conservation practices that were not profitable with the 10-year plan often became profitable as the period of the plan extended to 100 years. Given the uncertainty of the future it is only natural that farmers do not always find that soil conservation competes well with other more profitable investments that can be made in the farm business.

Partly because of higher fuel costs and the desire to save time in field operations, many farmers have shifted from conventional tillage to conservation tillage in the last decade. Thus the incentive to reduce soil erosion over the long term is being reinforced by current cost–returns considerations. The percentage of total crop acres in conservation tillage (minimum and no-till) has increased from 17.8 percent in 1973 to 32.0 percent in 1981 (Christensen and Magelby, 1983).

In a study conducted by the Center for Agricultural and Rural Development (CARD), linear programming (LP) models were used to evaluate the economics of various soil and water conservation practices on 18 representative Iowa farms (Pope, *et al.*, 1983). The models incorporated five tillage systems, three supporting practices, and 15 crop rotations. Cost, return, and soil loss estimates were made for all practical combinations of the included practices on each farm. Profit-maximizing solutions were obtained under different scenarios which incorporate assumptions on soil loss constraints, terracing subsidies, soil loss taxes, farmers' willingness and ability to use conservation practices, the types of livestock raised on the farm, and other factors.

Results from this study indicate that under proper management, conservation tillage in combination with contour planting is the most economically viable means of reducing soil erosion to T-value levels on most Iowa soils. The use of reduced tillage means significantly lower levels of soil loss on many soils. On many of the steep soils, however, reduced tillage is not sufficient in reducing soil losses to tolerable (T-value) levels.

Additional practices are needed such as less intense crop rotations, strip cropping, and occasionally terracing. Use of these practices, however, tends to reduce farm profits in proportion to the potential erosiveness of the farm. The study concludes that the first step toward eliminating excessive soil loss should be the implementation of reduced tillage practices. Additional measures to reduce erosion further can be used, but only at a cost to farmers and/or the rest of society.

Menz and Sundquist (1983) have studied the policy of targeting public subsidies for soil conservation and conclude:

It appears that economic forces will ensure that the existing trend toward the adoption of conservation and no-tillage will continue. Direct, significant public subsidization of these techniques should not be necessary in the long run, although some subsidization might speed adoption which has been estimated to reach 60–70 percent in the Corn Belt by the year 2000.

Relative Importance of Productivity Loss and Sediment Damage

We now turn to the impact of soil erosion on environmental quality in terms of sediment damage. This will be discussed in terms of the damage done by sediment after the eroded soil leaves the farm. In both the Illinois and Texas watershed studies sediment damage showed considerable variation among watersheds. For example, in Texas the sediment damage in dollars per acre was nearly twice as high in the Lake Lavon watershed as in the Duck Creek watershed (Taylor *et al.*, p. 46). Variability in sediment damage among watersheds is also noted in the Illinois studies. In the Hambaugh–Martin watershed (Lee *et al.*, table 10) in western Illinois with a conventional tillage system and a corn–soybean rotation, sediment damage per acre is nearly 6 times greater than with the same system in the Upper Embarras River basin in eastern Illinois (Lee *et al.*, table 12). Finally, there is no clear-cut general relation between the extent of the impairment of long-term productivity and the sediment damage. Watersheds with high sediment damage from soil loss may suffer minimal productivity losses, and vice-versa. However, in the six watersheds in Illinois the general pattern indicated that the economic gains from reducing soil erosion were more important for lessening sediment damage than for productivity maintenance.

In the study of six Illinois watersheds, the off-site sediment damages from soil erosion were compared with the on-site reductions in private net income over a 20-year period (Gunterman *et al.*, 1975). With conventional tillage practices the off-site damage from soil erosion was approximately 15 times greater than on-site loss in private net income.

Production Technology and Soil Erosion

If improved technology and productivity growth in all of U.S. agriculture can be maintained over the next two decades, the need to reduce soil erosion would be lessened. Technology could thus serve as a substitute for land subject to high rates of erosion. On the other hand, if technological improvement in U.S. agriculture is rapidly approaching a limit, and yields and productivity growth are attaining a plateau, the public and private incentives for soil conservation need to be examined more closely. We first examine the aggregate productivity trends in U.S. agriculture. Aggregate agricultural productivity may be measured in terms of the total amount of products (outputs) generated *per year* and the total amount of resources (inputs) used in the same year to produce these products. Agricultural productivity is thus viewed as a ratio of the flow of products from agriculture in a given year divided by the flow of inputs into agriculture in that year.

When the various agricultural products are combined to form total output (the numerator of our total productivity measure) the weights used for each product are usually the market prices in some given year. In order to reflect only the changes in physical quantities over a period of time, these weights are held constant from year to year. A similar procedure is followed in combining the various inputs into total input, the denominator in our total productivity measure. Both inputs and outputs must be expressed in terms of annual flows; that is, amounts of inputs used during the year and the production for that year.

In brief then, changes in the total productivity measure for U.S. agriculture should tell us the rate of technical progress at the national level – the highest level of aggregation, considering all products and all resources. Although an interpretation of the total productivity index encounters a number of difficulties, both conceptual and empirical (USDA, 1980b), it does provide a summary statement of agricultural productivity trends.

Figure 7.1 indicates little, if any, support for the hypothesis that the increase in the productivity of U.S. agriculture slowed down in the 1970s. Do the limitations of the total productivity index seriously affect the conclusion that U.S. agricultural productivity has increased at a constant absolute rate in the last two decades? One of the principal defects in this measure of total productivity lies in its failure adequately to reflect improvements in the quality of the inputs. Thus there is an understatement of the "true" amounts of the various inputs and, because inputs are the denominator in the productivity measure, an overstatement of total productivity. The failure to take into account quality changes applies to the labor input (e.g. increases in manual skills and management capacity) as well as to some of the capital inputs. However, there is little evidence that the *degree* of underestimation of the inputs has changed during the 20-year period. Hence the lack of adjustment of inputs for quality does not appear to be a likely source of serious difficulty in interpreting the trend in productivity shown in figure 7.1. Another potential limitation

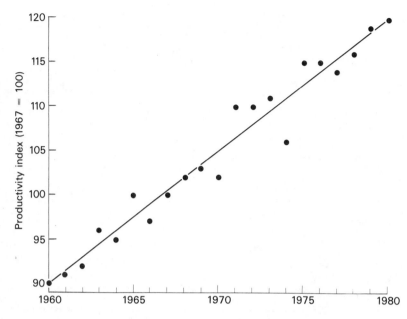

Figure 7.1 U.S. agricultural productivity, 1960–80.
Source: United States Department of Agriculture, Economic Research Service.

deals with the choice of base period weights that are designed to reflect the relative importance of the various inputs in the production process. The prices paid in 1967–9 for the various inputs are used as weights to construct the input index and all input prices have increased substantially since then. However, the input prices structure has changed only moderately and use of a more recent cost structure is not expected to alter drastically the general picture of a sustained increase in productivity shown in figure 7.1.

Questions of yield plateau

Several agricultural specialists have suggested that U.S. agriculture is approaching a yield plateau, or already has attained one. Even though the U.S. corn and soybean yields for 1950–72 published in a report by the National Academy of Sciences (1975, fig. 4, p. 6 and fig. 8, p. 11) indicate no levelling of yields of these crops, the report points to a number of biological limitations on crop production imposed by such factors as energy availability and the leaf area of plants, that will influence future yields. Crosson (1979) suggested that while yield increases had started to slacken in the mid-1970s, weather also had not been as favorable as in the 1960s. Lin and Seaver (1978) used data to the mid-1970s and found evidence of declines in the rates of yield increase. Thompson (1979) indicated that the rate of yield increase in the period 1955–70 accentuated due to the increased use of fertilizer, and believes that the yield from now to the end of the century might parallel trends over the period 1935–55. An initial assessment of Wittwer (1980) is that crop yields have plateaued. Ruttan (1979) has pointed out that the rate of growth of U.S. agricultural output since 1950 has averaged a little more than 1.7 percent per year – well below the 2–4 percent growth rates achieved by many developed and developing countries.

It is not quantitatively conclusive at this time that yields have attained a plateau. Most of the observations indicating a levelling of crop yields refer to a period which ended with somewhat less favorable weather and the movement of some idle land out of supply control into production during the mid-1970s. It is likely that this land was less productive than that already in crops. Swanson and Nyankori (1979 and 1981) using more recent observations and less aggregated data, find that yields have not reached a plateau. Similarly Heady (chapter 2 in Crosson, 1982) indicates that a statistical proof of a developing yield plateau is not evident if recent observations are included. Walker et al. (1982) found that soybean yields continue to increase. Duvick (1980) has analyzed the increase in corn yield in the U.S. since 1930 (figure 2.19) and found that there is little evidence to support the plateau hypothesis. Menz and Pardey (1983) have recently analyzed the impact of technology on corn yields, and find no evidence of a plateau in yields. Significant genetic diversity remains to be exploited. Before the end of the century, emerging biotechnologies are expected to increase corn yields significantly.

Regression studies of yield data at national, state, or county levels, or even with data from individual farms, are not apt to provide much additional insight. Improved understanding of the relative importance of the various sources of crop yield increase is more likely to come through studies of the combined effect of specific technologies such as the Sundquist et al. (1982) study of corn technology.

There are some logical reasons why we may not see a continuation of present crop yield trends. A major one is that fertilizer and pesticides were applied over most cropland during the period 1950–5 and much of this source of production increment has already been realized. Similarly, the opportunity to exploit groundwater for irrigation during that period cannot be repeated in the future. Conversely, it is expected that some shift from irrigated to dryland will occur over the next 30 years as water use must drop to recharge rates. Some agricultural specialists point to limits in use of solar energy and CO_2 as restraints on further large increases in crop yields. Further, some point out that improved efficiency in converting grain into beef has been very modest, and no great breakthroughs appear imminent. In order to provide a current assessment, we report below a part of the results of a symposium on future agricultural technology (English *et al.*, 1984).

Production potentials

Even if rates of productivity increase are, on the average, declining, it is the potential for the future that matters. A symposium held in December of 1982 convened two groups of scientists – one specialized in crops and the second in livestock – for the specific purpose of predicting the performance of crop and livestock technologies that are presently in the development stage and that are likely to be adopted by the year 2000. These scientists are, in general, active participants in the research and development processes that have generated the technological changes in agriculture in the last two or three decades. Many factors affect the actual on-farm performance of the emerging technologies, including the economic environment, regional patterns of production, rates of adoption, and other factors not of a purely technical nature. The scientists recognized these factors and, as far as possible, have attempted to take them into account.

The projected percentage increases in crop yields per acre from 1980 to 2000 are presented in table 7.1. The technology already exists to achieve the "most probable" projections for most of the crops listed. It is primarily a question of incentives for adoption, which, in turn, largely depend on the demand.

The animal scientists participating in the symposium developed estimates of the potential productive efficiency of various species by the year 2000 (table 7.2). Again these represent expected on-farm production conditions and will be conditioned by the economic environment. Although the animal scientists presented only one projection, it may be interpreted as the "most probable."

TABLE 7.1 YIELD INDEX PROJECTIONS FOR U.S. AVERAGE YIELDS FOR THE YEAR 2000 (1980 YIELDS = 100)

Crops	Low	Most probable	High	Optimistic
Corn, barley	120	140	160	200
Oats, sorghum	120	140	160	200
Wheat	125	150	175	200
Rice	150	200	250	300
Soybeans	130	160	220	250

Source: English, *et al.*, 1984.

216   *Earl R. Swanson and Earl O. Heady*

TABLE 7.2 POTENTIAL EFFICIENCY INDEX PROJECTION FOR
FOOD PRODUCTION FROM ANIMALS FOR THE U.S. FOR THE
YEAR 2000 (1980 EFFICIENCY = 100)

Animal/product	Unit	Potential efficiency index year 2000
Beef	Liveweight marketed per breeding female	125
Pork	Liveweight marketed per breeding female	135
Sheep	Liveweight marketed per breeding female	135
Broiler chickens	Liveweight marketed per breeding female	130
Turkeys	Liveweight marketed per breeding female	140
Dairy	Milk marketed per breeding female	140
Laying hens	Number of eggs per hen	120
Catfish	Daily rate of gain	150

Source: English et al., 1984.

A number of projections previously have been made and, in general, they have substantially understated the crop yields actually achieved. For example, projections for 1975 crop yields were made in 1960 (Rogers and Barton, 1960). The projected yields were made in a series of joint meetings with natural scientists and production economists in the U.S. Department of Agriculture. The "economically attainable" corn yield in the United States was estimated to be 53 bushels per acre in 1975. The actual 3-year average corn yield (1974–6) was 82 bushels per acre. In the same study wheat yields were underestimated 17 percent and the soybean yields were approximately correct.

The perspective that emerges from the 1984 reports of these two panels of scientists is that, in general, the past increases in the performance of agricultural technology are likely to continue at least to the year 2000. These scientists, somewhat reluctantly, also made projections to the year 2030. These increases in productivity are less predictable because they will come, in part, from concepts that are presently not well developed. Nevertheless, the general expectation of these scientists was a pattern of continued increases in crop yields, and livestock efficiency from 2000 to 2030. As in the past, improved technology will be expected to dampen the economic pressure to use soils that have high erosion rates.

The future outcome with respect to productivity growth will certainly be a function of the investment society makes in maintaining the number

Soil Erosion in the United States 217

of scientists and their equipment. Lu *et al.* (1979) predict that if expenditures on agricultural research only offset inflation over the next two decades, productivity growth will slow down to only 1 percent by 2000. With a real growth rate of 3 percent in agricultural research funding – the average rate since World War II – the productivity growth rate could be 1.1 percent; with a real growth rate in agricultural research funding of 7 percent, the productivity growth rate is predicted at 1.3 percent.

Land supplies

Another set of variables affecting the desired rate of soil erosion needed for economic agricultural production in future decades surrounds land supplies and use. Grain production in the North Central States increased 2.84 percent per year from 1937 to 1977 (Patrick and Swanson, 1979). Increased yields accounted for a large part of this production increase in all states in the region throughout the period. For the three states of Illinois, Indiana, and Iowa the contribution of increases in land area to increased grain output was greater in the first half of this period than in the second half. A continuation of this trend is expected, and thus there is a restricted scope for further expansion of grain production on land presently in farms.

Further, there is a perspective that the nation will have less land available for agriculture as this resource is transferred to non-agricultural uses and has its productivity eroded away through exploitative farming methods encouraged by high commodity prices and land values (Brown, 1979). According to projections by Barlowe (1975), if past trends in non-farm uses of land continue to 2000, urban areas will use only about 2 percent of total U.S. land area. This compares to 1.5 percent in urban areas in 1969. Transportation uses would require only 1.2 percent as compared to 1.1 percent in 1969. Frey (1979) shows only 2.7 percent or 61 million acres used for urban areas, highways, roads, railroads, and airports. This is not a mammoth transfer of land to non-agricultural uses if gauged against possibilities in zoning and a considerable supply of land which could be transferred to crops. John Fraser Hart (see chapter 8 of this book) presents an analysis of the estimates of the rates of conversion of agricultural land to non-agricultural uses.

The 1967 Conservation Needs Inventory (CNI) (USDA, 1971) estimated that a possible 265 million acres could be converted to the equivalent of Class I and II cropland. Under consideration of location and economic feasibility the 1977 National Resource Inventory (NRI) places this convertible supply at 127 million acres, with 40 million being readily convertible. Hence, it is our judgment that a net supply of land exists to expand crop production, albeit at higher unit costs, especially if adequate soil conservation measures are taken. The results of the CARD National

Model (see earlier section of this chapter) indicate that even if soil loss tolerance levels were satisfied, that there would still be land available for agricultural production in the year 2000.

Energy price effects

Energy price also represents a variable of uncertain magnitude in the future (see chapters 12 and 13 of this volume for an analysis of expected energy prices). If the real price of energy continues to increase over the next two decades, higher prices for energy and inputs derived from it should dampen the level of use of these factors in agriculture. Sloggett (1981) indicates that, in the eleven major irrigating states, rising energy prices are likely to have a greater influence on pumping costs than declining groundwater levels.

If higher real energy prices occur, the extent to which they cause a reduced use of energy-related inputs depends, among other things, on the elasticity of production for these inputs. The use of fertilizer in the United States is relatively high, and its elasticity at these levels of use is so low that slightly reduced use would cause a low percentage decrease in yields. A study of the impact of a substantial increase in the relative price of energy-related inputs in the Corn Belt indicated that corn acreage was reduced less than 4 percent with soybean acreage being the primary replacement (Swanson and Taylor, 1977). Similarly, there are some indications that water use levels are generally so high that production elasticities are very small – or perhaps that water marginal productivity is even negative (Ayer and Hoyt, 1981; Hexem and Heady, 1976). If the optimists with respect to possible future innovations and technologies are correct, and if there is sufficient investment in research and development, the new technologies could interact to increase greatly the marginal productivity of energy-based inputs (i.e. markedly raise the production surface for which energy-based materials and new technologies are inputs). In a similar vein, the new technologies can respond to the increased relative scarcity of energy and, in a sense, serve as partial substitutes for energy-based inputs, allowing yields still to increase with relatively less energy used in the input mix. In terms of the concept of induced innovations (Ruttan, 1982), this latter set of possibilities would seem to us to prevail within the resource pricing setting expected for the future.

The Prospects

We believe that there is a period of perhaps several decades when continuation of productivity trends in the U.S., and growth of agricultural production in developing countries, can maintain food supply fairly strongly against food demand. This will substantially reduce the pressure to use the more erosive soils for production. Further, the increasing adoption of conservation tillage by farmers illustrates that a practical method exists for producers to reduce the annual rates of soil losses on cropland that is used. In the past decade, land in conservation tillage has increased four-fold, and it has been estimated that by the year 2010 conservation tillage will be used on 50–90 percent of U.S. cropland (Ritchie and Follett, 1983).

An important characteristic of the remainder of this century is likely to be the volatility of farm prices and income such as that experienced in the decade 1972–82 with dampened prices during years of generally world-wide normal weather, and high prices in years of crop shortfalls in major world regions. Average real prices for U.S. agricultural products during the next two decades are not likely to increase. We judge that the prospects are good for maintaining an efficient, low-cost, agriculture in the United States and, at the same time, reducing the rates of soil erosion on our farmland. This is in contrast to the prediction in *Global 2000*: "Because corn (maize) is relatively poor at holding soil, the corn-growing lands . . . will fare the worst. The United States, as the world's largest corn producer, is in particular danger" (p. 280).

References

Ayer, H. W. and Hoyt, P. G. (1981) Crop water production functions: economic implications for Arizona. Bulletin No. 242. Tucson: Ariz. Agric. Exp. Sta.

Barlowe, R. (1975) Demands on agricultural and forestry lands to service complementary uses. *Perspectives on Prime Lands*, pp. 105–119. Washington: U.S. Department of Agriculture.

Bartelli, L. (1980) Soil development, deterioration and regeneration. Paper presented at the Soil Transformation and Productivity Workshop, Washington, D.C. National Research Council, National Academy of Sciences, Washington, D.C.

Brown, L. R. (1979) *The Worldwide Loss of Cropland*. Worldwatch Paper 24. Washington: Worldwatch Institute.

Christensen, L. A. and Magelsby, R. S. (1983) Conservation tillage use. *J. Soil Water Conserv.*, **38** (3), 156–7 (May–June).

Crosson, P. R. (1979) Agriculture and land use: a technological and energy perspective. In M. Schnepf, (ed.), *Farm Land and the Future*. Ankeny Iowa: Soil Conservation Society of America.

——, (ed.) (1982) *Cropland Crisis: Myth or Reality?* Baltimore and London: Johns Hopkins Univ. Press.

——, and Stout, A. T. (1983) *Productivity Effects of Cropland Erosion in the United States*. Washington, D.C.: Resources for the Future.

Dallavalle, R. S. and Mayer, L. V. (1982) Soil conservation in the United States: the Federal role. Congressional Research Service, Library of Congress. Report No. 80–144S.

Dideriksen, R. I., Hidlebaugh, A. R., and Schmude, K. O. (1977) Potential cropland study. Soil Conservation Service, U.S. Dept. of Agriculture Statistical Bulletin No. 578. Washington, D.C.

Duvick, D. N. (1980) Recent advances in maize breeding. Symposium on Production, Processing and Utilization of Maize (15–19 September 1980, Belgrade, Yugoslavia, Economic Commission for Europe, Committee on Agricultural Problems).

English, B. C. and Heady, E. O. (1980) Short and long-term analysis of the impacts of several soil loss control measures in agriculture. CARD Report No. 93. Center for Agricultural and Rural Development. Ames: Iowa State Univ. Press.

——, Alt, K. F., and Heady, E. O. (1982) A documentation of the Resource Conservation Act's Assessment Model of Regional Agricultural Production, Land and Water Use, and Soil Loss. CARD Report No. 107T. Center for Agricultural and Rural Development. Ames: Iowa State Univ. Press.

——, Matzold, J. A., Holding, B. R., and Heady, E. O. (eds) (1984) RCA Symposium: *Future Agricultural Technology and Resource Conservation, A Symposium*. Ames: Iowa State Univ. Press.

Food and Agriculture Organization of the United Nations. Agriculture, (1981) *Towards 2000*, pp. 6–64. Rome.

Frey, H. T. (1979) Major uses of land in the United States: 1974. Agricultural Economic Report No. 440. Economics, Statistics, Cooperative Service. U.S. Department of Agriculture, Washington.

Guntermann, K., Lee, M. T., Narayanan, A. S., and Swanson, E. R. (1974) Soil loss from Illinois farms: economic analysis of productivity loss and sedimentation damage. IIEQ Document No. 74–62. Illinois Institute for Environmental Quality, Chicago, IL.

——, Lee, M. T., and Swanson, E. R. (1975) The off-site sediment damage function in selected Illinois watersheds. *J. Soil Water Conserv.*, **30** (5), 219–24.

Heady, E. O. (1980) *Economic and Social Conditions Relating to Agriculture and its Structure to 2000*. Paris: Organization for Economic Cooperation and Development.

——, (1982) The adequacy of agricultural land: a demand–supply perspective. In Crosson, P. R. (ed.), *The Cropland Crisis: Myth or Reality?* pp. 23–56. Baltimore and London: Johns Hopkins University Press.

Held, R. B. and Clawson, M. (1965) *Soil Conservation in Perspective*. Baltimore: Johns Hopkins Univ. Press.

Hexem, R. and Heady, E. O. (1976) *Water Production Functions in Irrigated Agriculture*. Ames: Iowa State Univ. Press.

Lacewell, R. D. and Collins, G. S. (1982) Implications and management alternatives for western irrigated agriculture. Technical Article 17807. College Station, Texas: Texas Agr. Exp. Sta.

Lee, M. T., Narayanan, A. S., and Swanson, E. R. (1974) Economic analysis of erosion and sedimentation: Hambaugh-Martin watershed. AERR-127. Department of Agric. Econ. Urbana: Univ. of Illinois.

Lin, K. T. and Seaver, S. D. (1978) Were crop yields random in recent years? *S. J. Agr. Econ.* (December), pp 139–142.

Lowdermilk, W. C. (1953) Conquest of the land through seven thousand years. Agriculture Information Bulletin No. 99. U.S. Department of Agriculture, SCS.

Lu, Yao-chi, Cline, P. and Quance, L. (1979) Prospects for productivity growth in U.S. agriculture. Agricultural Economic Report No. 435. Washington: U.S. Department of Agriculture, ESCS.

Mayer, L. V. (1982) Farm exports and soil conservation. In Hadwiger, D. F. and Talbot, R. B. (eds), *Food Policy and Farm Programs*. New York, N.Y.: *Proc. Acad. Polit. Sci.*, **34** (3), 99–111.

McConnell, K. F. (1983) An economic model of soil conservation. *Am J. Agr. Econ.*, **65** (1), 83–9.

McCormack, D. E., Young, K. K., and Kimberlin, L. W. (1982) Current criteria for determining soil loss tolerance. Chapter 9 in *Determinants of Soil Loss Tolerance*. ASA Special Publication Number 45. American Society of Agronomy and Soil Science Society of America. Madison, Wisconsin.

Menz, K. M. and Sundquist, W. B. (1983) Targeting soil erosion control technologies in the Corn Belt. *N. Cent. J. Agr. Econ.* **5** (1), 65–72.

———, and Pardey, P. 1983. Technology and U.S. corn yields: Plateaus and price responsiveness. *Am. J. Agr. Econ.*, **65** (3), 558–62.

Miranowski, J. A. (1982) More federal government involvement in soil conservation. Presented at National Public Policy Education Conference.

National Academy of Sciences (1975) Agricultural Production Efficiency, National Research Council, Committee on Agricultural Production Efficiency, Board on Agriculture and Renewable Resources, Washington, D.C.

Patrick, G. F. and Swanson, E. R. (1979) Components of growth in grain production in the north central states: 1937 to 1977. *N. Cent. J. Agr. Econ.*, **1** (2), 87–96.

Pope, C. A., III, Bhide, S., and Heady, E. O. (1983) The economics of soil and water conservation practices in Iowa: results and discussion. CARD Report No. 109, SWPC Series II. The Center for Agricultural and Rural Development, Iowa State University, Ames, IA.

Rasmussen, W. D. (1982) History of soil conservation, institutions, and incentives. In Halcrow, H. G., Heady, E. O., and Cotner, M. (eds.) *Soil Conservation Policies, Institutions, and Incentives*. Ankeny, IA: Soil Conservation Society of America.

Ritchie, J. C. and Follett, R. F. (1983) Conservation tillage: where to from here? *J. Soil Water Conserv.*, **38** (3), 267–9 (May–June).

Rogers, R. O. and Barton, G. T. (1960) Our farm production potential, 1975. U.S. Dept. Agr. Agricultural Information Bulletin 233.

Ruttan, V. W. 1979. Inflation and productivity. *Am. J. Agr. Econ.*, **61** (5), 896–902.

———, (1982) *Agricultural Research Policy*. Minneapolis: Univ. of Minn. Press.

222   *Earl R. Swanson and Earl O. Heady*

Schnittker, J. A. (1981) Future of the United States Department of Agriculture. Address at the Sixth Annual Conference on Food, Agriculture, and Public Policy, Sioux City, NE, 10 November.

Schultz, T. W. (1982) The dynamics of soil erosion in the United States: A critical view. Agr. Econ. Paper No. 82:8. Univ. of Chicago.

Sloggett, G. (1981) Prospects for ground-water irrigation: declining levels and rising energy costs. Agr. Econ. Report No. 478. U.S. Department of Agriculture, ERS.

Sundquist, W. B., Menz, K. M., and Neumeyer, C. F. (1982) A technology assessment of commercial corn production in the United States. Special Bulletin 546. Agric. Exp. Sta. St. Paul: Univ. of Minn.

Swanson, E. R. Economic evaluation of soil erosion: Productivity losses and offsite damages. In Baker, M. (ed.) *The Economic Impact of Section 208 Planning on Agriculture.* Great plains Agricultural Council Publication No. 86. Nebraska Agr. Exp. Sta. Lincoln: Univ. of Nebraska.

——, (1981) Agricultural productivity and technical progress: Acceleration or atrophy? Univ. of Illinois Dept. of Agr. Econ. Staff Paper No. 81 E-152.

——, and Harshbarger, C. E. (1964) An economic analysis of effects of soil loss on crop yields. *J. Soil Water Conserv.,* **19** (5), 183–6.

——, and Maccallum, D. E. (1969) Income effects of rainfall erosion control. *J. Soil Water Conserv.,* **24** (2), 56–9.

——, and Nyankori, J. C. (1979) Influence of weather and technology on corn and soybean yield trends. *Agr. Meteorol.,* **20**, 327–42.

——, and Nyankori, J. C. (1981) Influence of weather and technology on corn and soybean yield trends – reply. *Agr. Meteorol.,* **23**, 175–80.

——, and Taylor, C. R. (1977) Potential impact of increased energy costs on the location of crop production in the Corn Belt. *J. Soil Water Conserv.,* **32** (3), 126–9.

Taylor, C. R., Reneau, D. R., and Harris, B. L. (1978) Erosion and sediment damages and economic impacts of potential 208 controls: A summary of five agricultural watershed studies in Texas. TR-93. Texas Water Resources Institute. College Station: Texas A & M Univ.

Thompson, L. M. (1979) Climate change and world grain production. Unpublished paper for Council on Foreign Relations. Ames: Iowa State Univ.

U.S. Council on Environmental Quality and U.S. Department of State, (1981) *The Global 2000 Report to the President,* vols I, II, and III.

U.S. Department of Agriculture (1971) *National Inventory of Soil and Water Needs,* 1967. Statistical Bulletin 466. Washington, D.C.

——, Science and Education Administration, (1978). *Predicting Rainfall Erosion Losses _ A Guide to Conservation Planning.* Agr. Handbook No. 537.

——, (1980) *Measurement of U.S. Agricultural Productivity: A Review of Current Statistics and Proposals for Change. Economics, Statistics, and Cooperatives Service,* Technical Bulletin No. 1614.

——, (1981) Soil and Water Resources Conservation Act – 1980 Appraisal, Part I. Washington, D.C.

Walker, D. J. (1982) A damage function to evaluate erosion control economics. *Am. J. Agr. Econ.,* **64** (4), 690–8.

Walker, W. M., Swanson, E. R., and Carmer, S. G. (1982) *Soybean Yields Continue to Increase. Better Crops.* Atlanta, GA (Spring).

Wittwer, S. H. (1980) Agriculture in the 21st century. Paper prepared for the Agricultural Sector Symposia, World Bank, 11 January, 1980. Washington, D.C.

Wittwer, S. (1982) New technology, agricultural production and conservation. In Halcrow, H. G., Heady, E. O., and Cotner, M. (eds). *Soil Conservation: Policies, Institutions and Incentives.* Ankeny, IA: Soil Conservation Society of America.

8

Cropland Change in the United States, 1944–78

JOHN FRASER HART

Back in the mid-1960s I was duly impressed by a speaker who proclaimed, "The American farmer is like the American Indian. He is the vanishing American. And if our cities keep growing the way they are, pretty soon we will have to start setting up reservations for farmers just the way we used to set them up for Indians." His words, as I said, were impressive, but his basic idea was dead wrong. The U.S. Census of Agriculture reports that the total area of cropland in the United States actually increased from 434 million acres in 1964 to 461 million acres in 1978, an average cropland gain of nearly 2 million acres a year.

The basic problem of American agriculture is an embarrassment of riches – the United States has far more good farmland than it needs to feed and clothe its people. Our surplus of farmland depresses the prices farmers receive for their products, and we constantly hear pleas from Washington for farmers to reduce their acreages of various crops, but rare indeed is a request for them to produce more. One way of coping with such a surplus is to abandon part of it; between 1910 and 1960 farmers in the eastern United States simply walked off and left an acreage larger than the entire state of Iowa, and they continue to abandon less productive land, especially in marginal areas.[1] Another way of coping with surplus farmland is to sell it abroad; the produce of one of every three acres of American cropland has been exported each year since 1975, and American farmers have become hostages to the whims of the international market and global power politics.

The surplus of farmland, and the surplus of crops it produces, have kept a fairly tight lid on the prices of farm products, but not, para-doxically, on the price of farmland itself during the 1970s. Unlike prices, the costs of farming have risen steadily, and far-sighted farmers have realized that the only way they could keep their heads above water was to increase the number of units they produced in order to compensate for their low returns per unit. Since World War II, and especially in recent years, the motto of American agriculture might have been "Get Bigger or Go Under."

A farmer can increase the number of units he produces (and thus expand his volume of production) by squeezing more out of every acre, and/or by farming more acres. Successful farmers have been doing both. The avidity with which American farmers have seized on technological breakthroughs to increase their production per acre is an oft-told tale. They are alert to the latest advances of the plant breeder's art. They need and use a whole arsenal of agrichemicals to kill weeds, control pests, and encourage the growth of crops. They keep buying bigger, better, and more expensive machinery; old-timers like to boast that picking a hundred bushels of corn by hand was a long, hard, back-breaking day's work, but nowadays a hundred bushels is only about 10 minutes work with a six-row, air-conditioned, $100,000 combine.

The new technology has put the farmer in an escalating spiral. His new machines enable him to farm more land, but he has to farm more land in order to pay for the new machines. (If he elects to specialize in livestock, as many farmers have done, he must invest heavily in new and better buildings – the dairy barns, the cattle feedlots, the hog houses, and the poultry sheds of 1959 are as outdated as the farm machines and the automobiles of 1959.) Most modern farmers need more land, but few can afford to buy it, and they have expanded by lease rather than by purchase. The price of farmland has soared, because the competition for it has been intense, not only from farmers, but from city investors who have seen it as a fine hedge against inflation.

Since World War II the American family farm has been transformed into a heavily capitalized, highly specialized, fully equipped, well-managed, and very efficient business. The farmer still works the land by himself, perhaps with some help from his wife and children. His base is the old home place, which he inherited or bought from his parents, but he rents three or four other farms of equal size. The net worth of his land, buildings, and machinery may be a million dollars, or much more, when he goes to the bank to borrow money for seed, fertilizer, pesticides, machinery, spare parts, gasoline, oil, taxes, insurance, and other necessary expenses. His debt load is frightening, and he pays a staggering amount of interest each year. He specializes in what he can do best, and the the old diversified farm operation has gone the way of the horse and buggy.

The impact of these changes on the availability and use of farmland in the United States can be summarized quite simply by looking at changes in crop yields. In 1959 the national corn crop averaged 53 bushels an acre, but by 1979 it had more than doubled, to 109 bushels an acre. Other crops showed similar increases. One can boast about growing two ears of corn where only one has grown before, but the other side of the coin is a potentially troublesome problem of surplus cropland. The acreage needed to produce a given quantity of any crop is cut in half when its production per acre is doubled, and the land that was used to raise the crop may be rendered surplus unless the demand for the crop is steadily increasing.[2] Regional variations in cropland change reflect the changing demand for the crops that have dominated different regions of the United States.

Regional Variations in Cropland Change

The primary source of data on agricultural land and its use in the United States is the Census of Agriculture that is taken at 5-year intervals. (The Statistical Reporting Service of the U.S. Department of Agriculture produces estimates of crop acreages, but its primary concern is the collection and dissemination of data on the production, marketing, and prices of agricultural commodities, which it does superbly well..These data are derived from sample surveys, and they do not lend themselves to satisfactory geographical disaggregation.) Taking a complete inventory of the use of land in a vast nation is a monumental task, and the results of each census will inevitably be marred by minor flaws and inaccuracies. For example, the 1974 Census of Agriculture somehow managed to miss about 6 percent of the nation's cropland.[3] One may quibble about the results of individual censuses, or about comparability between censuses, but any quibbler must produce a better set of data, and there is no better set. The student of agricultural land use cannot afford to ignore the census data, and I have elected to rely on them heavily, because they are far and away the best available.

In this chapter I have concentrated on cropland, which is defined as land that is regularly used to grow crops. The category of cropland includes land from which crops were harvested, land in rotation pasture, land in summer fallow, land under cover crops, land on which crops failed, and idle cropland. Cropland is only one category of farmland, which, in addition to cropland, includes all grazing land, woodland, wetland, and any other land that happens to be owned by farmers, even though such land may make only a modest contribution to the success of the farm operation.

Each component of cropland has a geography of its own and a history of its own. Each varies in different fashion in different parts of the nation, and each changes through time in a fashion independent of the other components. Each of these variations and changes has an interesting message, but the different messages may be no more than mere noise to anyone who is not intensely knowledgeable about the individual components, and this is hardly the place for a learned disquisition on cover crops or summer fallow.

Frey has shown that changes in census definitions and procedures since 1969 have overestimated the acreage of rotation pasture, and he believes that the acreage of rotation pasture should be subtracted from the total cropland acreage in order to ensure comparability with early censuses.[4] I have disregarded his advice because maps of total cropland are readily available in the map volumes that have been published as parts of each census of agriculture,[5] and the data require no further calculations, with the associated possibility of error (figure 8.1).

The total area of cropland in the United States has remained remarkably stable around a mean of 445 million acres since the end of World War II (table 8.1). It rose from 451 million acres in 1944 to a peak of 478 million acres in 1949, then declined steadily at a rate of about 3 million acres a year for the next 15 years to a low of 434 million acres in 1964, and has fluctuated between 440 and 460 million acres since 1969. The acreage of cropland in 1978 was 16 million acres less than in 1949, but 11 million acres more than in 1944. These figures give cold comfort to those who wail that the nation is losing its cropland at a rapid rate.

The national pattern of change in cropland acreage is merely the aggregate of many local changes, and it conceals divergent trends in

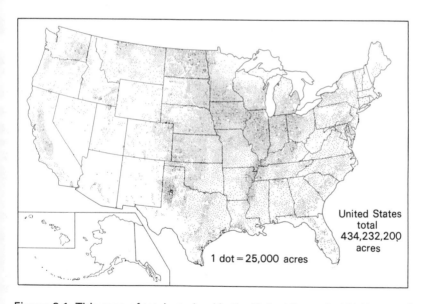

United States
total
434,232,200
acres

1 dot = 25,000 acres

Figure 8.1 This map of total cropland in the United States in 1964 is one of the finest maps of U.S. cropland that has ever been produced. After 1964 the Census Bureau started to use a computer to produce its dot maps. The saving in cost has been far more than offset by a pathetic deterioration in geographic and cartographic quality.
Source: *1964 Census of Agriculture*, vol. III, part 5, *Maps*, p. 25.

TABLE 8.1 TOTAL CROPLAND, BY MAJOR REGIONS, 1924–78

	United States	Northeast	Southeast	Middle West	Northern Plains	South Center	West
Thousands of acres							
1924	505,027	28,003	73,532	149,086	104,338	84,167	65,899
1929	522,396	26,287	73,993	150,184	112,567	90,188	69,176
1934	513,914	25,985	75,980	152,236	106,820	87,733	65,160
1939	530,151	25,815	78,246	153,907	109,879	92,855	69,430
1944	450,694	22,097	64,940	138,408	95,471	74,017	55,760
1949	477,838	21,726	68,102	142,366	100,666	78,270	67,175
1954	459,649	19,987	60,404	139,720	99,773	73,200	66,564
1959	447,563	17,826	54,190	138,586	99,323	70,079	68,084
1964	434,232	15,997	49,191	137,106	97,674	67,233	67,030
1969	459,048	14,683	52,137	138,978	103,287	79,438	67,523
1974	440,039	13,851	49,030	137,276	100,274	74,449	65,160
1978	461,341	15,095	53,078	143,826	100,087	80,314	68,939
1944 = 100							
1924	112	127	113	108	109	114	118
1929	116	119	114	109	118	122	124
1934	114	118	117	110	112	119	117
1939	118	117	120	110	115	125	125
1944	100	100	100	100	100	100	100
1949	106	98	105	103	105	106	120
1954	102	90	93	101	105	99	119
1959	99	81	83	100	104	95	122
1964	96	72	76	99	102	91	120
1969	102	66	80	100	108	107	121
1974	98	63	75	99	105	101	117

different parts of the country. Some areas have gained while others have lost, and cropland change is essentially a geographical phenomenon. A proper analysis of change should be conducted at the county level, because states are inappropriately large units for geographical analysis, but this discussion is constrained to regional groupings of states. It is based, however, on the dot maps of cropland change that have been published in the graphic summaries of each census of agriculture, and in special publications of the U.S. Department of Agriculture.[6]

The standard census divisions and regions are generally satisfactory, but the distribution of cropland and patterns of change suggest two modifications (figure 8.1). I have grouped Mississippi with the West South Central States (AR, LA, OK, and TX) as the South Center, and I have separated the four westernmost North Central States (ND, SD, NE, and KS) from the Middle West and identified them as the Northern Plains Staes (figure 8.2).

The Northeast

Pennsylvania and the states to the east and north, which had 5 percent of the nation's cropland in 1944 but only 3 percent in 1978, might seem to be the classic example of a region of cropland loss. The Northeast lost an average of a quarter of a million acres of cropland a year between 1944

Figure 8.2 The major regional groupings of the states of the United States that are used in this chapter.

and 1974 (figure 8.3). The region retained 1¼ million acres of cropland between 1974 and 1978, but it still was 7 million acres below its 1944 peak.

The Northeast is the most heavily urbanized part of the United States. It is quite tempting, and also completely wrong, to jump to the conclusion that cropland was lost to urban encroachment. Loss has been widely and evenly distributed, and it quite definitely has not been concentrated near urban centers (figure 8.4).

Cropland has been abandoned in the Northeast because this region is one of the poorest farming areas in the United States. The summers are short and uncomfortably cool for the major field crops, and much of the land is infertile, steep, stony, and difficult to till. The recent abandonment of cropland in the Northeast is merely the continuation of an ongoing process that began as soon as the early settlers finally realized that much of the land simply is not fit for cultivation.

It is all too easy for city folk to wring their hands in dismay about cropland that has been abandoned, but Hardscrabble Hill Farm begins to lose a lot of its glamor when you have to admire it across a plow attached to the rear end of a horse, and many fields are too small and too steep for

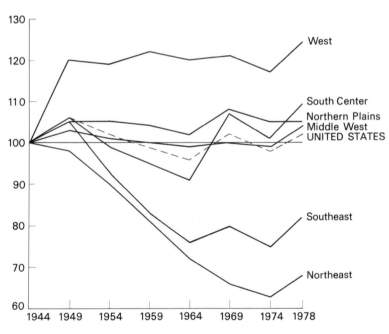

Figure 8.3 Changes in total cropland in the major regions of the United States between 1944 and 1978 (1944 = 100).

(a)

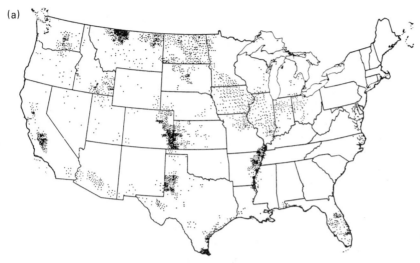

1 dot = 10,000 acre increase,
in counties which had a net
increase in cropland acreage

(b)

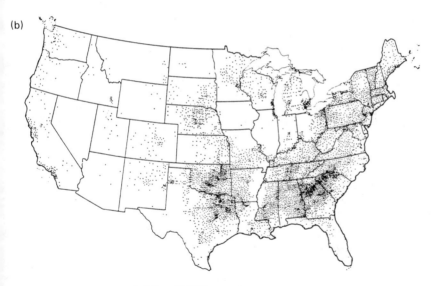

1 dot = 10,000 acre decrease,
in counties which had a net
decrease in cropland acreage

Figure 8.4 (a) Increase and (b) decrease in cropland in the United States
between 1944 and 1964. These maps exclude cropland pastured, which was
not excluded in figure 8.1.
Source: Krause, *Cropland Trends Since World War II*, see note 6.

efficient use of tractors and modern farm machinery. Anyone foolish enough to argue that such land should not have been abandoned should be sentenced to try to make his entire living by farming it.

The poorer marginal land of the Northeast has been allowed to go fallow, as well it should have been. It probably is not too much of an exaggeration to say that American agriculture would suffer no very great loss if the entire Northeast were paved over, because farmers in the rest of the nation could quickly and easily pick up the slack.

Paradoxically enough, urbanization probably has done more to encourage farming in the Northeast than to discourage it. Proximity to the city was important back in the horse and buggy, milk train, days of slow and inefficient transportation. Perishable products, such as milk, eggs, fruit, and vegetables, had to be sped to consumers before they spoiled. Bulky commodities, such as potatoes and hay, were too expensive to be hauled any great distance; hay for urban livery stables, in fact, was a major crop in some parts of the Northeast before the automobile replaced the buggy and substituted one form of urban pollution for another.

Farmers near the city have lost some of their advantage as transportation from more distant areas has improved, but they still are willing to pay a premium price for farm land, and they have shown a remarkable ability to survive and prosper in the nooks and crannies at the city's edge. Some of our most expensive farmland is at the margins of our built-up areas, but it derives its value from its location rather than from the inherent quality of its soil. The price of this land is also pushed up because it is ripe for urban expansion, and developers are casting covetous eyes upon it. Urban encroachment on this land is well-nigh inevitable, but such encroachment is no great catastrophe, because the area of high-priced farmland at the edge of the city will merely expand outward as the bow wave of the city's expansion.

Global 2000 repeated the persistent canard that "urban and industrial developments are often [sic] located on some of a nation's, or the world's best [italics in original] agricultural land."[7] The origin of this myth antedates the horse and buggy, and must be traced back to the days of the oxcart. Cities in medieval Europe had to be in good farming areas because transport was so poor. Food could only be hauled short distances in creaking oxcarts, and feeding any concentration of people was so difficult that only cities on navigable rivers could grow to any appreciable size before the advent of the railroad.

The largest cities of Europe before 1830 undoubtedly were in the best farming areas, and one would have expected their subsequent expansion to have removed large acreages of land from agricultural production, but in fact Best has concluded that Western Europe is very much like the United States: "one of the most serious problems facing European agriculture, both now and in the future, is the predicament of surplus production and the related dilemma of too much cropland rather than too little."[8]

The Southeast

The acreage of cropland in the Southeast attained its post-World War II peak of 68 million acres in 1949, then declined at a rate of about 1¼ million acres a year for 15 years, and since 1964 has wobbled around 50 million acres (table 8.1; figure 8.3). Cropland in the Southeast has been rendered surplus by a combination of increased yields per acre and no increase in demand for the traditional crops of the region. Farmers in the Southeast can grow the same amount of cotton, tobacco, and peanuts on far smaller acreages, but the demand for these crops has stabilized or even declined: cotton has lost ground to synthetic fibers, many people have sworn off smoking for fear of lung cancer, and after 1976 some Republicans stopped munching peanuts.

Farmers have few crops that they can profitably substitute for the traditional standbys. Soybeans have come to the rescue in some areas, but mainly on level land that is suited to large-scale machinery. Much of the land of the Southeast is mediocre, at best, for farming, with infertile soils and steep, choppy topography, and millions of acres that once produced cotton, tobacco, and peanuts have been allowed to grow up in broom sedge, brush, and old field pine. The new pine forests of the Southeast have been a bonanza for the pulp and paper industry, but foresters have begun to worry about the inferior quality of the forests that are replacing them once they have been harvested.[9]

The traditional crops were so hard on the land that many farmers regularly "rotated" cropland with woodland over a long time span.[10] They grew crops in small cleared areas – "patches" rather than fields – amidst the trees. A new patch of ground was cleared for crops when the old one wore out, and the old patch was allowed to recuperate under brush fallow and woodland before it was cleared once again.

The present area of cropland has shrunk back into "islands" of cleared farm land set in a dark monotonous sea of pine forest.[11] The traveler in parts of the Southeast today has to drive through mile after dreary mile of "pine tunnel," with only occasional patches of open land. The islands of cleared land are generally the better farming areas, and each island is dominated by a crop for which it has special advantages. The concentration of a particular crop in a particular island may have originated by accident of history in an environmentally suitable area. That concentration has been reinforced by the evolution of the necessary infrastructure – knowledge of production techniques and development of facilities for processing and marketing – and it may have been fossilized geographically by government acreage control programs that have been necessitated by price support programs.

Much of the land between the islands is used mainly, if at all, for rural residence, and many stretches of highway in the Southeast are cordoned by strips of new houses. Houses were spread fairly evenly across the land before World War II, when the countryside was a place of work and most rural people were farmers, but nowadays the countryside has become a place of residence for long-distance commuters, and houses are strung along the paved roads for easy commuting. Some of the people who live along the highways have moved out from town, but many of them are ex-farmers or farm children who have merely moved up to a new home on the blacktop highway from an old tumbledown farm shack on an unpaved road in the backcountry, where former cropland has been abandoned and allowed to grow up in brush.[12]

One might argue that some of the former cropland of the Southeast should never have been cropped, and it should remain under woodland, but part of it is an "acreage reserve" of cropland that could be brought back into production if ever the nation needs it. The swamps and marshes along the Atlantic and Gulf coasts are another vast "acreage reserve" that could be brought under cultivation by the simple, if expensive, expedient of clearing, draining, and desalinizing them. It probably is conservative to estimate that the cropland acreage of the Southeast could be increased by 50 million acres or so if ever the need justified the expense.

Any attempt to return land to agricultural production, however, might be constrained by problems of landownership. The Southeast has two quite distinctive traditions of landholding.[13] Some areas are dominated by large holdings, locally called plantations, that were fragmented into sharecropper units before World War II, but could easily be reconstituted into units large enough for modern farm operations. The problem areas are those that were dominated by the small yeoman farms so beloved of rural sociologists. The old forty-acres-and-a-mule cotton or tobacco farm is far too small for modern technology, but it has been just the right size for purchase by a doctor or lawyer or businessman who deemed land the best hedge against inflation. Some of these new owners have been trying to do something with their land, but the taxes on it have been so low that many of them have been quite content merely to hold it as an investment and to let it grow up in brush. It might be extraordinarily difficult to assemble enough of these small scattered parcels to make an efficient farming operation.[14]

The South Center

The area of cropland in the south central states (Texas, Oklahoma,

Arkansas, Louisiana, and Mississippi) increased by 4 million acres between 1944 and 1949, then decreased steadily at an annual average rate of about ¾ million acres for the next 15 years, and has bounced up and down since 1964, with an overall upward trend (table 8.1; figure 8.3). These fluctuations reflect the diversity of the region, which has two major areas in which the cropland acreage has increased fairly consistently, and two major areas in which it has declined. The aggregate regional trend has been dominated in some periods by the areas that have gained, and in others by those that have lost.

One major area of fairly consistent loss is in eastern Texas, western Arkansas and Louisiana, and eastern Mississippi (figure 8.4). This area is the western part of the erstwhile Cotton Belt, and it is similar to the former cotton-producing areas farther east. The soils have low inherent fertility, and they can no longer grow cotton competitively. There is no other crop to take the place of cotton, and much former cropland has been allowed to grow up in brush. Some of this land presumably could be returned to crop production if it were needed, but a goodly part of it has been acquired by pulp and paper companies, and it is managed for sustained production of forest products.

The poor farming area in the eastern part of the south central states is interrupted by the Delta, one of the world's finest agricultural areas, where the acreage of cropland has increased appreciably since World War II (figure 8.4). The Delta should not be confused with the true delta of the Mississippi River, which is in southern Louisiana, and remains fairly heavily wooded. The Delta is the local name for the broad alluvial bottomland, 25–125 miles wide and 400 miles long, that reaches southward from the Missouri Bootheel beyond Natchez, Mississippi.[15] The soils of the Delta were deposited by the floodwaters of the Mississippi River and its tributaries. They are deep, black, and fertile. The plantation tradition of very large landholdings is strong in the area, and the awesomely flat land is superbly well suited to modern farm machinery. The Delta has the largest farms in the eastern half of the United States, and a high percentage of the land is cultivated.

The problem of the Delta has been too much water. Dikes have had to be constructed to protect the land against floods, and massive drainage works have been necessary, but the soil is enormously productive once it has been drained. Nearly 4 million acres of bottomland forest in the Delta have been drained, cleared, and converted to cropland since World War II.[16] In many places the valuable hardwood trees were simply uprooted, bulldozed into windrows, and burned by landowners ignorant of their value.[17] Soybeans are the leading crop on the newly cleared land, but the Delta is one of the few areas in the South where cotton has been able to hold on as a major crop. Land reclamation in the Delta is possibly a model for what might be done in the coastal areas of the South if ever the nation's need for additional cropland were great enough to justify the enormous expense that would be necessary.

The second major area of cropland loss in the South Central States is the rolling plains of central Oklahoma and the Blackland Prairie that runs southward across eastern Texas from Dallas to San Antonio (figure 8.4). This area straddles the boundary between the humid East, which receives adequate amounts of rainfall for crop production, and the arid West, where irrigation is necessary. The soils are relatively productive, but mositure is a problem. In dry years there is not enough rain for most crops, but there are not enough dry years to justify the expense of irrigation. Cotton was once a major crop in this area, and it is still hanging on in parts of the Blackland Prairie, but cotton production is not competitive with irrigated areas farther west, and many farmers have switched to wheat. Some former cropland has been converted into pasture and grazing land, but mesquite and other undesirable plants have begun to invade marginal range land areas.

The other major area of cropland increase in the South Central states is the southern High Plains in the Texas Panhandle, from south of Lubbock to Amarillo (figure 8.4). This was an area of ranches and large dryland farms until the 1930s, when farmers began pumping water from shallow wells to irrigate their crops. The level land is well suited to large-scale farming, and farmers produced bumper crops of cotton, grain, sorghum, and wheat. The High Plains have become the nation's leading cotton-producing district, with the greatest concentration of irrigated land east of California.

The acreage of irrigated land on the High Plains has increased fairly steadily, but there are storm clouds on the horizon. Uncontrolled pumping has seriously depleted the water supply, and the groundwater table has been dropping at a rate of several feet per year. Irrigation water has to be pumped from ever greater depths, and the cost of energy to operate the pumps has been rising rapidly. The sinking water table and the rising cost of energy may force much of the irrigated acreage back into dry farming or range land before too many years have passed.

The South Central states are in the heart of the so-called Sunbelt, whose population has been swollen by migrants from other parts of the nation, and some of those who have looked only at regional aggregate data have jumped to the conclusion that in-migration and urban growth have somehow managed to remove land from agricultural production. Nothing could be farther from the truth. The most rapidly urbanizing areas in the South have not lost significant acreages of cropland. The areas of greatest cropland loss are so poor that they have not been able to support cities of any consequence, and they have had slight attraction for migrants.

The Middle West

The eight states of the Middle West are the agricultural heartland of the nation, with nearly one-third of its total cropland (table 8.2; figure 8.1). The acreage of cropland has remained remarkably stable at just under 140 million acres since the end of World War II (table 8.1; figure 8.3). The overall regional increase immediately after the war was the aggregate of two divergent trends. A general increase in cropland in the heart of the Corn Belt countered significant losses near major metropolitan centers and lesser losses in the dairy country to the north (figure 8.4). Since 1960 there have been no noteworthy concentrations of gain or loss.

The Middle West has been shifting away from the traditional rotation of corn, small grains, and hay to a greater emphasis on cash grains – corn and soybeans. The stepped-up production of corn and soybeans has been absorbed by a strong and steadily growing demand, both domestic and foreign. In recent years Midwestern farmers have exported a third of their cropland each year. An area that can export a third of its cropland annually would not seem to suffer from any serious shortage of same.

Some of those who advocate policies of agricultural land preservation in the United States have seized upon the export demand for U.S. food and fiber to support their position. They argue that we can sell our farm products abroad to improve our balance of payments, as indeed we can and should, but it becomes a bit confusing when the same people argue that the nation has a moral obligation to feed a hungry world by giving our farm products to countries that cannot afford to pay for them. Improving our balance of payments by giving away commodities would be a very neat trick indeed, if we could manage to pull it off.

TABLE 8.2   ACREAGE OF CROPLAND, BY REGION, 1978
(thousands of acres)

Region	Total area	Cropland	Percentage cropland
United States	2,265,661	461,341	20.4
Northeast	104,495	15,095	14.4
Southeast	255,132	53,077	20.8
Middle West	286,944	143,826	50.1
Northern Plains	194,255	100,087	51.5
South Center	304,073	80,314	26,4
West	1,120,762	68,939	6.2

Southeast = South east of Mississippi; Middle West = North Central minus Northern Plains; Northern Plains = North Dakota, South Dakota, Nebraska, and Kansas; South Center = Mississippi and West South Central.

A good healthy chunk of our farmland goes to Japan each year to pay for automobiles and cameras and television sets. The United States devotes more land – about 15 million acres – to feeding Japan than Japan devotes to feeding herself. Most of the rest of our agricultural exports are shipped to developed countries to feed livestock, not to Third World countries to feed hungry people. Should young American families "be asked to forego their homes in the suburbs so that American farmers can feed Russian cows"?[18]

It might be unwise to base national policies on the whims of the international market, because most countries are instinctively autarkic, and they become uneasy when they rely too heavily on foreign suppliers. It seems almost inevitable that sooner or later they will try to reduce imports by increasing their home production or by modifying their economies.

The Northern Plains

The Northern Plains states have 100 million acres of cropland, and the total has not changed more than a few million acres since 1949, despite considerable internal shifting (table 8.1; figure 8.3). These states are second only to the Middle West in cropland acreage, and the two regions together have more than half the nation's cropland. I have separated the Northern Plains states from the Middle West because they are so dry that they are dominated by wheat rather than by corn and soybeans.

The wheat farming areas of the Northern Plains are environmentally vulnerable and this region is the most likely candidate for sharp decreases in cropland in the foreseeable future. Wheat is even more subject to the vicissitudes of the foreign market than corn and soybeans, because more than half the crop normally is exported. It is a food grain rather than a feed grain, and export demand could suffer from the anticipated world shift from a cereal-based diet to a livestock-based diet. The long-awaited development of a successful hybrid could increase yields appreciably and thereby reduce the acreage needed to satisfy a volatile demand.

The Northern Plains straddle the western margin of unirrigated cropland, which runs along the 97th meridian through Dallas and Winnipeg, and they are subject to severe climatic stress. Much of the land might better be under grass and used to graze range livestock. Some farmers have tried to mitigate their risks by flirting with alternative crops, such as grain sorghums and sunflowers, which have become important secondary or even primary crops in some areas. Corn production has pushed westward in Nebraska with the help of center-pivot sprinkler irrigation, but questions have been raised about possible depletion of the groundwater resources on which it depends.

The Northern Plains states, in short, are a region where agriculture is on sufferance, and a major decline in the cropland acreage would not be surprising.

The West

The area of cropland in the West jumped from 56 to 67 million acres immediately after World War II, but it has not changed very much since 1949 (table 8.4; figure 8.3). Two-fifths of the cropland is irrigated, because few parts of the West have enough rainfall to grow crops without irrigation. Abundant supplies of cheap water for irrigation have been the very lifeblood of agriculture in the region.

Irrigated agriculture in the West is highly specialized and efficiently organized. Farms are large, and many are operated by corporations. Large-scale production, processing, and marketing systems are necessary, because farmers in irrigated areas have no monopoly on many of the crops they produce. They must compete with farmers 1000 miles closer to market who can grow the same crops without the expense of irrigating them.

Irrigated farming areas in the West have also felt the pinch of competition for a limited water supply from rapid urban growth. People can live only where water is available. The cities of the West are in the irrigated oases, and their expansion inevitably removes land and water from agricultural use. The West, in fact, provides many of the horror stories that alarmists have projected into frightening national estimates of the rate of urban encroachment on agricultural land. The citrus groves of the Los Angeles Basin, for example, have all but disappeared; the famous fruit orchards of the Santa Clara Valley have been replaced by the electronics plants of Silicon Valley; and other oases have had similar experiences.

Irrigation is essential for agriculture in the West, but critics have begun to ask serious questions about the wisdom of national irrigation policies and their implementation. The first irrigation projects were simple stream diversions – dams and ditches that were developed and paid for by the farmers who used them. Most of the cheap and easy projects had been developed by the turn of the century, however, and in 1902 Congress passed the Reclamation Act to authorize long-term loans of interest-free public funds for the development of large-scale irrigation projects that could not be financed privately. The original purpose of the Act was to encourage the development of the arid West by fostering the creation of prosperous family farms of 160 acres or less, but the 160 acre limit has been honored more in the breach than in the observance. In recent years users have taken public subsidy as a right rather than a privilege, and they have demanded ever-larger and more expensive projects.

The new projects are undeniably impressive – massive dams, vast reservoirs, and canals that look big enough to float a battleship – but they have also been fearfully expensive. For example, the price tag on the proposed Peripheral Canal project in California, which was rejected by the voters in 1982, was variously estimated at somewhere between $5.4 and $20 *billion!* Much of the cost of constructing such behemoths has been borne by taxpayers in the East rather than by the users in the West who benefit from them, because the Bureau of Reclamation charges scandalously low rates for the irrigation water it sells to farmers. In some years, in fact, the Bureau has not even recovered its short-run costs of operation and maintenance, despite its legal obligation to do so.

Yvonne Levy has made a meticulous analysis of the pricing of Federal irrigation water in California.[19] She identified three accounting doctrines that might be used in pricing irrigation water: *historic* (the original cost of constructing facilities); *replacement* (the current cost of replacing facilities); and *incremental* (the cost of the next scheduled project). The average price for an acre-foot of irrigation water in 1981 dollars should have been $23.77 if costed on a historic basis, $47.69 if costed on a replacement basis, and $324.00 if costed on an incremental basis. The Bureau of Reclamation was actually charging only $5.09, and American taxpayers were picking up the difference.

The pricing policies of the Bureau of Reclamation have encouraged profligate use of water and unwarranted expansion of irrigated land. A realistic pricing system would compel farmers to use more efficient irrigation methods and to shift to crops that require less water. The total acreage of irrigated cropland undoubtedly would decline, more water would be available for urban users from existing projects, and there would be less pressure for new water projects.

Potentially irrigable land does not deteriorate if it is not developed, but developed irrigation projects have a finite life expectancy because of reservoir siltation, sedimentation, and soil salinization. Perhaps the remaining irrigable land of the West should be held as a national reserve against possible future needs for cropland. Westerners will not take kindly to the idea, because they have a vested interest in continued subsidization of water projects, and they are happy to take advantage of the ignorance of people in the East, who are blissfully unaware of the enormous amounts of public money that have been, and are being, spent to subsidize irrigation projects that serve no clear and generally accepted national need.

Regional summary

The acreage of cropland in the United States has shown two general trends: first a steady decline between 1949 and 1964, and then upward fluctuation since 1964. Extrapolation of these two trends produces astonishingly different results. Extrapolation of the declining trend for 1949–64 might indeed give cause for alarm, because it suggests that the nation's cropland base would have declined from 478 million acres in 1949 to only 340 million acres by the year 2000. The error of this crude extrapolation is revealed by the fact that it underpredicts the actual cropland acreage in 1978 by 40 million acres. Extrapolation of the more recent trend for 1964–78 suggests little change from the 1978 cropland base of 460 million acres by the year 2000. It would be quite unrealistic, of course, not to expect the unexpected, but it would be even more unrealistic to try to guess what might possibly happen.

The impression of stability in the nation's cropland base is reinforced by a brief analysis of regional patterns and trends. The decline in the Northeast and the Southeast may have bottomed out. Former cropland in the East and South is an acreage reserve, and much of it could be brought back into cultivation if the need ever arose. Land drainage probably has just about run its course in the Delta, but extensive areas along the coast could be drained if the expense were ever justified. The Middle West and the Northern Plains rely heavily on export markets for corn, soybeans, and wheat. There is no reason to expect major cropland changes in the heartland, but environmental stress may cause fluctuations on the semi-arid Northern Plains. The acreage of cropland may be reduced by sinking groundwater levels in some irrigated areas, such as the High Plains of Texas, and by urban encroachment in others, such as the Los Angeles Basin and Silicon – neé the Santa Clara – Valley.

The Spectre of Urban Encroachment

Some people believe that urban encroachment is a major threat to our national cropland base.[20] They argue that agricultural land is being converted to non-agricultural land uses at a rate so unacceptably rapid that immediate action must be taken to direct and control it, and to halt it if at all possible. In many areas they have not been able to mobilize the necessary political support locally, and thus they have advocated the adoption of state and national land-use policies and legislation for farmland protection that will give them greater strength in local political frays.

Critics have charged that the advocates of farmland protection are elitists who favor the preservation of open spaces and abhor development. The farmland protection movement, say these critics, has used emotional arguments about food and fiber production as a smokescreen to conceal its ideological opposition to development. A threat to our ability to feed and clothe ourselves, or even to our responsibilities to feed a hungry world, are more persuasive political arguments than a threat to the pleasure of a Sunday afternoon drive through an unspoiled country-side. The adoption of regulations based on a national policy purportedly designed to protect farmland will be of limited value to most farmers, and it may actually hamstring some, but it will place powerful weapons in the hands of those who oppose development and wish to block it.

No-one can deny that urban encroachment on agricultural land is highly visible. Most Americans, if they bother to think about the matter at all, probably believe that our best farmland is rapidly disappearing, buried beneath a floodtide of subdivisions and shopping centers that is moving inexorably outward from our cities and towns. The popular press is full of articles reporting that urban encroachment on agricultural land is a serious problem, and we have the additional evidence of our own eyes, because each of us has seen the tentacles of urban growth snaking farther and farther into the countryside. These tentacles are largest and extend farthest from the largest cities, where the greatest number of people cannot help but see them.

Many Americans have a fairly strong anti-urban bias, and they see urban encroachment on rural land as a kind of morality play that pits the good guys on the land against the bad guys from the city. Our national ethos has always cherished farmers and the family farm, and it has harbored a certain ambivalence about cities, which are perceived as necessary evils at very best. Our forefathers placed the state capital and the state university outstate to protect the most easily corrupted members of society against the snares and temptations of the wicked and sinful metropolis, and they set aside national and state parks where good, honest, native-born citizens could find at least temporary refuge from the hordes of Newer Immigrants that were thronging into the cities. More recently all right-thinking Americans have headed for a home and lawn in the suburbs just as fast as they could, and sidewalks and apartment buildings are positively un-American.

Furthermore, we cannot escape signs of urban encroachment (in the form of new second homes, condominiums, motels, fast-food joints, and the like) even when we go on vacation, and of course it is the most popular vacation areas that attract the most blatant manifestations of urban influence, plus the greatest number of people who can react to them. It seems almost axiomatic to say that urban impact is greatest where there are the most people, but the less obvious corollary is that most people have an exaggerated idea of urban impact. Most of us assume that our own experience is representative, and we cannot resist the temptation to expand the limited sample of our own observations of the most populous and most popular areas into frightening national estimates.

Just how serious is the problem? The National Agricultural Lands Survey (NALS) estimated that "the United States has been converting agricultural land to nonagricultural uses at the rate of three million acres per year."[21] This estimate is grossly inflated. It was derived from a comparison of two surveys conducted by the Soil Conservation Service in 1967 and in 1975. The 1975 survey was conducted in great haste and without widespread consultation, it had different objectives, it used different objectives and a far skimpier sample, and it was never intended to be comparable with the 1967 survey.[22]

The errors that can result from an undersized sample are vividly illustrated in Florida. The NALS concluded that "Florida – producer of more than half the world's grapefruit and one-fourth of the world's oranges – will lose virtually *all* [italics in original] of its unique and prime farm lands by the turn of the century if present land loss trends continue."[23] That prospect would be frightening if it were true, but fortunately it isn't; it is merely the result of a clerical error. The clerk listed 6,500 acres of urban land in the Rural column and 367,850 acres of rural land in the Urban column.[24] This and other gross errors were expanded into an estimate of land loss trends that is approximately 50 times larger than it should have been, so we don't have to worry about our oranges and grapefruit after all.

The 3 million acre figure is a gross overestimate.[25] It is not confirmed by any independent data, and it has been challenged by those familiar with other sources of land-use data. Despite its inaccuracy, however, the 3 million acre estimate seems to have taken on a life of its own. Alarmists have bandied it about with great vigor and enthusiasm, often without citing the original source, and others have assumed that each mention was independent confirming evidence. The 3 million acre estimate has now been quoted so often that it has become enshrined in a whole corpus of alarmist literature.

Frey has analyzed a variety of data sources, and he has concluded that 1 million acres a year is a more reasonable estimate of the total rate of land conversion.[26] The 1980 Census of Population, for example, reported an urban population of 167 million persons on an urban area of 47.3 million acres. The urban area increased during the 1970s at an average rate of 1.27 million acres a year, as compared with 0.91 million acres a year in the 1960s, but the census definition of urban area has become increasingly generous, and it includes incorporated areas of low density that remain essentially rural. Furthermore, the figure of 1.27 million acres refers to total area rather than cropland. A classic study by Zeimetz *et al.* found that only about 35 percent of newly urbanized land had previously been used for cropland, which suggests that our average annual loss of cropland to urban growth in the 1970s was on the order of about 0.445 million acres.[27]

If the trend of the 1970s continues, urban growth will reduce the nation's cropland from around 461 million acres in 1978 to around 440 million acres by the year 2000, and to around 400 million acres by the year 2100. Julian Simon argues that the loss of cropland to urban encroachment will be countered, at least in part, by the "creation" of new cropland by drainage, irrigation, and more efficient use of existing cropland.[28]

This trend is cause for long-range concern but not immediate alarm. In the short run the psychological effects of urban encroachment on agricultural land may be more serious and more widespread than the actual physical conversion of land to other uses. For example, "leapfrog" development may be encouraged by zoning regulations and taxation policies that are intended to control growth in the urban fringe. The developer who considers one political jurisdiction too restrictive may simply move farther out in search of a more congenial jurisdiction.

Farmers in the city's shadow, whose land may soon be bought by a developer, may be reluctant to invest in desirable long-term improvements. Farmers who have been bought out by developers may move farther outward in search of land to buy if they wish to continue farming. They have an urban fringe sense of land values, they have been paid and are willing to pay more per acre than the local farmers against whom they are bidding, and they can have an inflationary effect on the price of land that ripples far outward from the city.

The Quality of Land

One final, and extremely important, question concerns the quality of agricultural land that is being converted to non-agricultural uses. Most Americans probably would agree that we should strive to protect our best farmland against non-agricultural development. We may take solace in the thought that our finest farmland is not especially attractive for residential development unless it happens to be near a city. Most city people are completely bored by the flat, treeless, and incredibly productive plains of our agricultural heartland. Residents of central Illinois, for example, complain that you can take a Sunday drive by going out to the edge of town, parking your car beside a cornfield, and racing its engine for half an hour.

Even near major cities in the Middle West the best farmland is no better than third choice for residential purposes. The well-to-do favor homes with a view in the lake-studded, wooded morainic hills; the flat, sandy, well-drained, but not particularly fertile outwash plains are best for large-scale tract development. The rolling till plains that farmers prefer are too flat to provide any kind of view, and they require drainage integrated at the scale of 40-acre fields rather than 1-acre lots. The same holds true for recreational development; the lakes and wooded areas that make attractive sites for recreation and second homes are generally inferior farmland.

These subjective observations demand more precise quantitative definition, but the concept of prime farmland has proven surprisingly elusive. Certainly it should be deep, flat, fertile, well-drained, and stone-free, so that it can produce sustained high yields of crops under careful management, but the productivity of land is a complex function of location, capital, and labor as well as the physical character of its soil, and there is much disagreement about the variables that should be considered in attempting to define prime agricultural land that should be protected against conversion to non-agricultural uses.

The Soil Conservation Service (SCS) of the U.S. Department of Agriculture is attempting to define and map prime farmland. The SCS program for the identification of "important farmlands" is based on the classification of individual soil mapping units.[29] It has developed national criteria for deciding whether a specific soil mapping unit should be classified as prime or not prime, but the process is completely mechanical after the mapping unit has been classified. The map of prime farmland is actually a map of the soil mapping units that satisfy the SCS criteria. Anyone can prepare a map of prime farmland from any soils map merely by coloring the areas of all soils that are included in the prime category. Areas with soils that fail to satisfy the criteria for prime may be classified as unique farmland if they are used for high-value crops, and local worthies may add areas that they think are of statewide or local importance.

The SCS maps of important farmlands are drawn on base maps of national accuracy standards. They look impressively final and authoritative, but their precision is illusory, and they are not appropriate for making policy decisions. Anyone who needs to identify prime farmland should use the original soil surveys from which the maps of important farmland have been derived, and anyone who cannot use the original soil survey is sure to be misled by the map of important farmland, because it rests on methodological quicksand.[30] The productivity of individual soil mapping units is not uniform. It varies geographically for specific crops, such as corn, in response to broad environmental gradients of precipitation, temperature, and topography, and it also varies locally from crop to crop. For example, soils in Georgia that are good for peanuts are not necessarily good for corn or tobacco, and vice-versa, and good rice soils in eastern Arkansas may be poor soils for cotton.

Furthermore, the simple dichotomous classification system developed by the SCS also arrogates the prerogatives of the decision-maker. The policy-maker, not the technician, should decide whether a particular soil mapping unit in a particular area is prime, or important, or critical, or worthy of protection. In order to make this decision the policy-maker needs a quantitative value that will indicate the relative quality of particular soils, and his options are limited when soils are classified merely as prime or not prime.

Some economists have suggested that we need not concern ourselves about prime farmland, because the land market will be able to control farmland conversion quite satisfactorily without the necessity for any social or political action, but they may have been a bit too insensitive to variations in the physical quality of land. Apparently one of the truisms of economics holds that there is no such thing as marginal land, and you can grow anything anywhere if only the price is right.[31] In theory, I suppose, a hard-working, right-thinking economist could grow bananas at the South Pole or paddy rice in the middle of the Sahara desert, but those of us who inhabit the real world probably would have to stop eating bananas or rice if we had to pay that kind of price for them.

Conclusion

The total area of cropland in the United States dropped from 478 million acres in 1949 to 434 million acres in 1964, and then rose to 461 million acres in 1978. The nation's built-up area expanded from 34.6 million acres in 1970 to 47.3 million acres in 1980, an average increase of 1.27 million acres a year. Approximately one-third of the newly built-up area had previously been used for cropland, so it is estimated that cropland was converted to urban uses at an average rate of about 0.44 million acres a year during the 1970s. This figure is minuscule in comparison with the nation's total cropland base of 460 million acres. The loss of even ½ million acres of cropland each year leaves no ground for complacency, to be sure, but the rate of conversion gives cause for thoughtful concern rather than immediate alarm.

Presumably no-one would argue that we should squander our patrimony of good farmland, but we need a far better accounting of it. The elusive concept of prime farmland must be refined and sharpened before it can be useful. Local decision-makers need a precise quantitative measure of the relative quality of particular soils in order to make enlightened decisions about the wisest allocation of land to various claimants. The basic question of how and by whom the use of land should be allocated comes down to a fundamental question of political philosophy: can we continue to rely on the operation of the marketplace, or is political action necessary to control and regulate the market in order to serve the best interests of society?

The conversion of agricultural land to non-agricultural uses is a highly localized geographic phenomenon. Farmland is being converted to urban uses at an impressive rate on the fringes of many cities, small as well as large, but extreme examples should not be extrapolated into national estimates whose scariness is exceeded only by their inaccuracy. Urban encroachment is not a national problem, and it does not appear to require nor warrant national action. Urban growth is inevitable, and urban land requirements must be balanced against the needs of agriculture. The adoption of national or even statewide policies for farmland protection would place a powerful weapon in the hands of those who wish to turn back the tide and halt all development. Preservationists should not be allowed to block development, but neither should developers be allowed to run roughshod over the sensitivities of those who cherish the non-economic value of land.

It would seem reasonable to concentrate on problem areas instead of essaying the awesomely difficult task of trying to formulate an equitable national policy. One might argue that decisions about the protection and preservation of agricultural land – or about any other use of land, for that matter – should be made at the same level of political responsibility where the political bills must be paid. Each polity should develop its own comprehensive growth management program, tailored to its own unique and distinctive character and needs, to decide how the use of its land should be allocated, to prevent premature or haphazard development, and to ensure balanced, rational growth.

Acknowledgements

I would like to express my appreciation for the advice and encouragement I have received from H. Thomas Frey and Philip J. Gersmehl; for the cartographic efforts of Gregory Chu, Carol Gersmehl, Patti Isaacs, and Reid Maier; and for the skill with which Margaret Rasmussen has mastered the word processor.

Notes

1   John Fraser Hart (1968), "Loss and abandonment of cleared farm land in the Eastern United States," *Annals of the Association of American Geographers,* **58**, 417–40; pp. 423–5.
2   John Fraser Hart (1978), "Cropland concentrations in the South," *Annals of the Association of American Geographers,* **68**, 505–17; p. 512.
3   H. Thomas Frey (1979), *Major Uses of Land in the United States: 1974,* Agricultural Economic Report No 440 (Washington: U.S. Department of Agriculture), p. 23.
4   H. Thomas Frey (1982). *Major Uses of Land in the United States: 1978,* Agricultural Economic Report No 487 (Washington: U.S. Department of Agriculture), p. 6.

5   For example, 1978 Census of Agriculture, vol. 5, Special Reports, part 1, Graphic Summary, pp. 49 and 50.

6   Orville E. Krause (1970). *Cropland Trends Since World War II: Regional Changes in Acreage and Use.* Agricultural Economic Report No. 177 (Washington: U.S. Department of Agriculture), and James Horsfield and Norman Landgren (1982), *Cropland Trends Across the Nation,* Agricultural Economic Report No. 494 (Washington: U.S. Department of Agriculture).

7   *The Global 2000 Report to the President,* vol. II. The Technical Report. Chapter 6, Food and Agriculture Projections, pp. 73–104. The Food and Agriculture Projections and the Environment, pp. 272–98; p. 281.

8   Robin H. Best (1979), "Land-use structure and change in the EEC," *Town Planning Review,* **50**, 395–411; p. 410.

9   Loblolly pine and slash pine are the two most desirable tree species for intensive forest management in the South. Since 1965 many small private landowners have been harvesting their pine stands without taking steps to ensure that their land would regenerate to pine, and millions of acres of pine forests have been transformed into inferior oak-pine and hardwood forests, especially on private land that is not owned by companies in the forest industry. Herbert A. Knight (1978), "The south is losing its pines," *Forest Farmer,* November–December, pp. 10–11; Stephen G. Boyce and Herbert A. Knight (1979), "Regeneration for the third forest," *Forest Farmer,* July–August, pp. 12–14; and idem. (1979), *Prospective Ingrowth of Southern Pine Beyond 1980,* Research Paper SE-200 (Asheville, N.C.: Southern Forest Experiment Station).

10 John Fraser Hart (1977), "Land rotation in Appalachia," *Geographical Review,* **67**, 148–66.

11 Hart (ibid., note 2), p. 507.

12 John Fraser Hart (1981), "Migration to the blacktop: population redistribution in the South," *Landscape,* **25** (3), 15–19.

13 John Fraser Hart (1982), "The role of the plantation in southern agriculture," *Proceedings, Tall Timbers Ecology and Management Conference,* **16**, pp. 1–19.

14 John Fraser Hart (1980), "Land use change in a Piedmont county." *Annals of the Association of American Geographers,* **70**, 492–527; p. 500.

15 William D. Thornbury (1965), *Regional Geomorphology of the United States* (New York: Wiley), p. 56.

16 H. Thomas Frey and Henry W. Dill, Jr. (1971), *Land Use Change in the Southern Mississippi Alluvial Valley, 1950–69: An Analysis Based on Remote Sensing,* Agricultural Economic Report No. 215 (Washington: U.S. Department of Agriculture), p. 6.

17 Herbert, S. Sternitzke and Joe F. Christopher (1970), "Land clearing in the lower Mississippi Valley," *Southeastern Geographer,* **10**, (1) (April), 63–6.

18 William A. Fischel (1982), "The urbanization of agricultural land: a review of the national agricultural lands study," *Land Economics,* **58**, 236–59; p. 258.

19 Yvonne Levy (1982), "Pricing Federal irrigation water: a California case study," *Federal Reserve Bank of San Francisco Monthly Review,* Spring 1982, 35–55.

20 John Fraser Hart (1976), "Urban encroachment on rural areas," *Geographical Review,* **66**, 1–17.

21 National Agricultural Lands Study (1981), *Final Report* (Washington: National Agricultural Lands Study), p. v.

22 H. Thomas Frey, (1982). "Farmland conversion: some comments on the potential cropland study," *Professional Geographer*, **34**, 342–5.

23 National Agricultural Lands Study (1981), *Where Have the Farmlands Gone?* (Washington: National Agricultural Lands Study), p. 14.

24 Richard Kleckner (1980). Office of Geographic Research, U.S. Geological Survey, "Trip Report, Iowa State University Statistics Laboratory, September 24, 1980."

25 The National Agricultural Lands Study has been ridiculed by Fischel (op. cit., note 18); Philip M. Raup (1982), "An agricultural critique of the national agricultural lands study," *Land Economics*, **58**, 260–74; Julian L. Simon (1982), "Are we losing our farmland?" *The Public Interest*, no. 67 (Spring), pp. 49–62; Julian L. Simon and Seymour Sudman (1982), "How much farmland is being converted to urban use?," *International Regional Science Review*, **7**, 257–72; and other serious students of land use in the United States.

26 H. Thomas Frey, personal communication.

27 Kathryn A. Zeimetz, Elizabeth Dillon, Ernest E. Hardy, and Robert C. Otte (1976), *Dynamics of Land Use in Fast Growth Areas*, Agricultural Economic Report No. 325 (Washington: U.S. Department of Agriculture), p. 21.

28 Simon (op. cit., note 25), p. 59.

29 R. M. Davis, Administrator, Soil Conservation Service (1977), Land Inventory and Monitoring Memorandum 3 (Rev. 1), dated 16 August.

30 Philip J. Gersmehl (1980), "Productivity ratings based on soil series: a methodological critique," *Professional Geographer*, **32**, 158–63.

31 John D. Black (1945), "Notes on 'poor land' and 'submarginal land'," *Journal of Farm Economics*, **27**, 345–74.

9A

Water Resource Adequacy: Illusion and Reality

GILBERT F. WHITE

This paper examines recent shifts in technical thinking which have altered prevailing views on how to assess the adequacy of fresh water supplies to satisfy future demand. From a study of recent national and international documents at least six concepts of water resources and its uses can be shown to be undergoing significant change. They are related to: constraints on drinking water adequacy; the alternatives to increasing physical supply; the relationship of population growth to industrial and agricultural water use; the meaning of flood and drought disasters; the risks to aquatic ecosystems; and the implications of possible climatic changes.

The emphasis in assessment has in turn shifted from an estimation of total supply and withdrawal towards an estimation of the effects on water quality and distribution resulting from changes in water and land use. The author shows that assessments of future supplies will have to take into account not only the total volume of water as related to growing demand but also an examination of the social and political conditions within which fundamental choices as to technologies and water management strategies will take place.

Introduction

Technical thinking about how to appraise the adequacy of fresh water to satisfy expected demands has been changing in ways that are strongly affecting prevailing views as to the resource and its wise management. These shifts are well illustrated by the evolving efforts to take the measure of the water situation on a world scale, including the recent *Global 2000 Report to the President*[1] and the United Nations Environment Programme (UNEP) assessment of *The World Environment, 1972–1982* (Holdgate *et al.*, 1982).[2] In those documents and in the body of national and international studies from which they draw are found at least six concepts of water resources and its uses that are undergoing significant change. To the extent these changes are accepted, the methods and policies for dealing with water problems also are altered.

None of the shifts in thinking is wholly new: each marks a different emphasis to take account of accumulating experience and to move away from certain widespread illusions about what determines the availability of water to serve human needs. They have to do with the principal constraints on drinking water adequacy, the alternatives to increasing physical supply, the relationship of population growth to industrial and agricultural water use, the meaning of flood and drought disasters, the risks to aquatic ecosystems, and the implications of a possible climate change. I call attention to them because I believe they ought to be in mind whenever water plans are in preparation. They are taken for granted, wholly or in part, in much planning today but they also are ignored in many instances.

As background for a discussion of each shift, the major attempts at appraisal of global water availability are noted. Each change in thinking then is examined briefly. The discussion is in no sense comprehensive, but is intended to state the change concisely and to outline the realities and illusions it confronts.

Evolving Efforts to Assess the World Water Situation

At the first United Nations conference on natural resources at Lake Success in 1947 the hydrologic data were so incomplete and scattered that there seemed little point in attempting a world-wide estimate of water supply and use (UN/DEA, 1950).[3] Instead, the discussions hinged on modes and effects of various types of water management within river-basin, national and sub-national units. The chief topics were hydrologic appraisal, water supply and pollution, water conservation strategies, flood control, navigation, irrigation and drainage, and hydroelectric power. The conference heightened interest in strengthening hydrological networks, in basin surveys, and in technical assistance for water planning at national levels.

By the time of the Water for Peace conference in 1967 a variety of international programmes to take stock of water resources had been launched, including the UNESCO arid zones research programme, the International Hydrological Decade (IHD), and a large number of surveys and studies funded by the United Nations Development Programme and bilateral assistance agencies in cooperation with developing countries. The papers at the Water for Peace conference canvassed much of this rapidly growing body of information on precipitation, stream flow, ground water, unconventional sources, water technology, water quality, water use, education, training, organization and financing (US Government, 1967).[4] A major paper ventured a global estimate (Doxiadis, 1967).[5] Doxiadis produced a projection of water supply and use by sectors for 1975, 2000 and up to 2090 without breaking it down by area or showing how it was computed.

During the next 15 years the calculations of the volume of fresh water available to the human race tended to converge. More data were collected, and the uncertainty as to how much surface and ground water is available, and its distribution in time and space narrowed. Knowledge as to ground water location remained rudimentary in many areas, and the estimates as to stream discharge were handicapped by the highly probabilistic evidence as to the magnitude and frequency of low and peak flows. However, the main physical parameters of surface supply came to be recognized with a moderate degree of accuracy for large continental areas. Information on groundwater and water quality and its trends is far less satisfactory.

In 1974, L'vovich completed a calculation of total supplies and withdrawal of fresh water by continental units (L'vovich, 1974).[6] The USSR Committee for IHD (1974)[7] also published a world-wide computation of water balance as did Baumgartner and Reichel a year later (Baumgartner and Reichel, 1975).[8]

It remained for the United Nations Water Conference in 1977 to bring together the immense body of information which had been accumulating in national and international records, and had been analyzed by a number of investigators (United Nations, 1972).[9] The review paper for that conference, on "Resources and Needs," compared the estimates of global water balance by Baumgartner and Reichel, L'vovich, and the USSR Committee for the IHD,[10] and reviewed the information in hand as to uses.

These reviews showed that the prevailing scientific consensus placed the total volume of fresh water at less than one-thirtieth of all water on the globe. The water moving in streams in a year was estimated at 40–47 trillion m³. Altogether, at any one time about 22 percent of the fresh water is in the soil or in the ground, 0.35 percent is in lakes and wetlands, 0.04 percent in the atmosphere, less than 0.001 percent is in the streams and about 77 percent is in snow and ice.[11] The point of giving these figures is to show that the great reserve of liquid fresh water, in contrast to snow and ice, is underground, while the running streams and lakes are a very small, rapidly circulating proportion of the total resource. There is doubt as to how much of the ground water is within economic pumping depth: perhaps only one-third at most.

The calculations of water use roughly agreed as to total but differed as to sectoral use. As of the mid-1970s the volume of fresh water withdrawn annually for human uses was believed to be of the order of the figures given in table 9.1. Withdrawals for other uses were not included in these

TABLE 9.1 ESTIMATES (MID-1970s) OF VOLUME OF FRESH WATER CONSUMED (BILLIONS M³)

	Reference		
	Doxiadis[a] *(1975)*	*Global* *2000[b]*	*USSR[c]* *1970s*
Domestic and municipal	228	201	150
Industrial	184	305	630
Irrigation	2000	1830	2100
Total	2412	2838	2880

[a]Doxiadis, *loc. cit.* (Ref. 5).
[b]*Global 2000*, p. 147 (Ref. 1).
[c]*The World Environment, 1972–1982*, p. 131 (Ref. 2).

computations and no figures were attached to in-stream uses such as for navigation, wildlife conservation, and waste dilution. The estimates were drawn from scattered national statistics or were estimated by assigning assumed per capita use to total population: the volumes for countries compiling national data were much more nearly accurate. In few cases was there a distinction between the volume of water withdrawn and the volume consumed in evaporation or transpiration and therefore not returned to the surface or underground water body. The proportion consumed has a profound effect upon subsequent availability: a power plant consuming less than one percent of the water it takes out of a stream for cooling has quite a different effect on stream flow than an irrigation project returning to the stream only 40 percent of the water diverted onto its fields. To arrive at the volume of water consumed would require taking 1–15 percent of domestic and industrial uses and 40–80 percent of irrigation uses.

The United Nations Conference on Desertification in 1978 focused attention on resource problems of the arid and semi-arid third of the continental land areas.[12] More details thereby were provided on the water-land situation in dry areas, and on management strategies appropriate to the high variability and prolonged droughts in those regions. One of the estimated produced at that time was the Swedish report on water in dry lands which carried forward the calculations of water availability per unit of land area.[13]

At the end of 1980 the *Global 2000* report in the United States built upon the previously published data to make projections of water availability by country for all purposes from 1971 or 1975 to 2000. The projections were made by taking the L'vovich calculations of the amount of annual surface runoff "plus groundwater flows" for each country and dividing this by 1971 populations.[14] The resulting per capita figures then were reduced in volume for the year 2000 in exact proportion to the projected increase in population made under the *Global 2000* population model.[15]

From this and from other GNP and resource projections it was concluded that "increases of at least 200 to 300 percent in world water withdrawals are expected over the period 1975–2000."[16] As indicated in two of its maps showing per capita availability, the report asserted that "population growth alone will cause demands for water to at least double relative to 1971 in nearly half the countries of the world. Still greater increases would be needed to improve standards of living."[17] Referring to FAO's 1977 estimates, it noted that by far the largest absolute increase in demand would be for irrigation. The study stressed the problems of meeting the needs for potable water and of using irrigation water effectively without causing soil and water deterioration.

A principal recommendation of the United Nations Water Conference was that the Secretary General should "make appropriate arrangements for organizing meetings of existing international river commissions, with a view to developing a dialogue between the different organizations on potential ways of promoting the exchange of their experience."[18] The first such meeting took place in Dakar in May 1981, and examined a wide range of legal, institutional, cooperative, and economic topics associated with river basin development.[19] In these discussions the growing complexity of carrying out effective water planning was recognized, and the fruits of exchanging experience were specified, but the comparison of total supply and projected use did not play an important role.

When UNEP undertook its review of changes in the world environment during 1972–82 it did not attempt any new projections of water use. Instead, *The World Environment* examined the principal ways in which the workings of the hydrological cycles were known to have been affected by human activities in the decade following the Stockholm Conference on the Human Environment, and identified trends which either enhanced or degraded the supplies of surface and ground water. The emphasis thus shifted away from total supply and total withdrawal and consumption over large areas towards the effects which changes in land and water use in particular areas were exercising on water quality and water distribution.

My thinking about the highly significant aspects of water adequacy on the world scene has been influenced by having shared in that UNEP review. It revealed numerous points at which gaps in scientific knowledge or basic monitoring inhibit wise resource management. It also showed how irrelevant any broad generalizations about water supply and use over large areas may be to understanding what, in fact, is happening to water resources as they affect human well-being. If these are to be meaningful, the descriptions of those features need to be stated in terms of the geographic realities of combinations of physical and biological factors in local areas, and with an eye to the effects of technology, social organization, and economic productivity upon the uses made of the physical resource.

Six Major Shifts in Thinking

After reviewing advances in evaluating water resources and in marshalling and forecasting techniques, the *World Environment* report presented the global water balance in terms of annual surface runoff and the ground water situation, noted efforts to augment supplies, and commented on changes in water use in major sectors. Further attention was given to alterations in water quality and aquatic ecosystems, and to developments in water planning and legislation. It attempted finally to sum up the 19 major changes of the decade as falling on either the positive or negative side. Its concluding observation was as follows:

> Efforts towards international co-operation accelerated during the 1970s, but the record was not one of unmixed improvement. In some places and in some ways the water resource was worse off in 1980 than when the Stockholm Conference called for a reversal of the then prevailing trends. Although water quality and accessibility improved in some regions, the absolute numbers of people without access to safe water grew. A rough balance of gains and losses suggests that the trends were generally – albeit slightly – favorable to the sustained use of the basic resource. (p. 161)

The trends and changes reported there were chiefly in information techniques, social organization, and the quality of the resource. In part implicit in them, and in part independent of them were the shifts in thinking that promise to have large impact upon the way in which water is managed in future. I have selected six of those.

Drinking water and sanitation for all

The task taken on as a goal in 1980 of providing safe drinking water and sanitation for all the human family marked a new recognition of public responsibility to meet those needs, and called for fresh approaches. It was immediately clear that a continuation of the level of improvement activity prevailing in the 1970s would increase the absolute numbers served with potable water but would leave the growing world population relatively no better off. A different type or magnitude of effort was needed.

Beginning on a revised programme with a comparison of water availability and increasing use reveals nothing of significance. The physical supply-use ratio per capita is unimportant in most areas: other factors govern the reliability and safety of supply. Somewhere in the neighborhood of 150–250 billion cubic metres of water is withdrawn for domestic purposes in a year. The mean annual flow of all of Italy's rivers is approximately the same magnitude.[20] Withdrawals for domestic purposes are less than 1 percent of the total flow of all continental rivers. This does not substract the heavy drafts made on ground water to supply numerous urban places.

Obviously not all the water occurs where and when it is needed, and the availability is set basically by the social cost of transporting and storing water so as to deliver it at the needed place and time in a quality suitable for drinking. Only about 43 percent of the population of developing nations were reported to have had reasonable access to safe supplies in 1980.[21] Physical supply is not the prime limiting factor in these areas. Nor is cost necessarily the chief constraint in many instances. The experience with programs to speed up the provision of improved supplies suggests that the rate and extent of improvement is affected by combinations of cost, financial capacity, trained personnel, and community organization that vary from country to country. The challenge is to find methods of mobilizing those resources appropriate for the particular natural and social environment of the country.

The populations of the industrialized nations are generally provided with potable supplies, but two conditions throw some doubt on their adequacy. The two conditions relate to the state of older systems and to the possible health effects of increasing loads of organic chemicals in surface and ground sources. In the industrialized countries many of the water and sewer facilities have deteriorated so that heavy expenditures are required for rehabilitation, quite aside from investment to extend storage or conveyance facilities to meet the needs of enlarged populations.

At the same time serious questions have been raised as to the possible public health effects of new chemical compounds, chiefly organic compounds, reaching surface and ground sources of supply for municipal users.[22] These leave uncertainty as to whether or not the conventional methods of treatment will be adequate in future to meet health standards. In neither case is the volume of supply a major constraint although here and there the technical and economic problems of enlarging supply are serious.

Increased supply and the alternatives

Where available supplies are judged inadequate to meet current or prospective demands the next step usually has been to explore the possibility of enlarging the supply, and here the illusions that may work against sound long-term solutions are that there are readily available technical means, especially new techniques, of increasing supply, and that management of demand is of secondary significance.

The need for seeking to enlarge supply may spring from degradation of the quality of supply, from competitive use of surface and ground supplies, or from pumping aquifers at a rate greater than recharge. As groundwater mining has expanded in some areas, pumping levels have increased and it is accurate to speak of exhaustion, oftentimes irreversible. The past decade saw heightened public concern with such depletion near a few cities and irrigation areas.

Among the unconventional technological fixes attracting attention in recent decades as a remedy for threatened water shortage have been cloud seeding, desalination, and towing icebergs. Weather modification efforts to augment precipitation after more than 30 years of trial still have not been shown to have consistently positive results, although their advocates continue to find them promising in a few areas. Desalting operations have grown only modestly. They have proven economically feasible principally in arid regions where heavy investment seems warranted for supplementing existing urban and industrial supplies, or, as in the case of United States' delivery of Colorado River water for irrigation in Mexico, where it is the most feasible means to meet a political commitment. Icebergs are still in the realm of science fiction. There should be no hesitation in exploiting these unconventional measures whenever they might help. However, they have been all too often an excuse to pass over other means of coping with rising demand.

In favorable circumstances such new technology may offer a promising local solution, but two sets of advanced techniques of greater impact and broader application are those relating to ground water exploration and extraction, and to re-use of water. Improved seismic and geological surveys, well drilling, and pumping methods are opening up a huge volume of water previously ignored or inaccessible. This has been of major importance in developing countries which could gain access to previously untapped supplies without building elaborate storage and conveyance works. Technical assistance has played an influential role in diffusing the new methods.[23] Rising energy costs, in contrast, have inhibited some new pumping projects.

As a result of advances in treatment methods and in system planning the re-use of water is beginning to be viewed as a practical measure in both urban and agricultural settings. With techniques that meet health requirements and are otherwise publicly acceptable, the diversion of a stream may lead to a sequence of uses without seeking a new source for each use.

A much wider range of previously tested alternatives is receiving appraisal in the search for adequate water. Pricing as a device for managing demand is increasingly recognized as a means of holding withdrawals to economically warranted levels.[24] Methods of locating leaks in urban water systems may identify losses claiming as much as one-half the total withdrawal. Water conserving devices in households and for lawn watering are reducing per capita use by as much as 20–40 percent in some cities.[25] Water conservation in irrigation encompasses canal lining, water application scheduling, drip irrigation, and choice of water-efficient crops.

Reduction of water use in industrial processes has been pursued with fresh vigor in response to increased water costs and public concern with stream pollution. Supply is rarely a limiting factor for industrial development. In a few cases water supply dictates choice of a site, but more often it is obtained as necessary to serve the site favored by other factors such as transport, raw materials and labor. Industrial location may, however, be strongly influenced by considerations of waste disposal, and the question of how much and what kind of burden the effluent places on receiving water may be pivotal in the design of manufacturing processes and in setting the required withdrawal.

One of the profound changes in thinking about water adequacy during the past decade has to do with industrial waste disposal. For many years the prevailing approach to effluents from manufacturing was to discharge them into water bodies capable of assimilating them without undue harm downstream, or to treat the waste sufficiently to meet some minimum standard of ambient quality in the receiving waters. The cost of maintaining water quality was seen as the construction and maintenance of waste treatment works. According to this view, projections of water use could assume that industrial demand would increase as rapidly or several times as rapidly as the population. Slowly, more emphasis was placed on altering the plant production process so as to reduce the volume of waste and of water used for cooling and material transport. Less waste thereby required dilution or treatment and the plants withdrew less water. Reports from France, Japan, the United States and the Soviet Union show decreasing use of water per capita for industry.[26]

Population growth and industrial and agricultural water use

The ideal of minimal water consumption and minimal production of waste material is far from achievement in many areas, but as it is sought in new housing and industrial installations and in rehabilitation of old facilities per capita use may decrease rather than increase. In these circumstances the notion that municipal and industrial water use will mount in direct proportion to population becomes illusory. The second United States national water assessment projected a decrease of as much as 60 percent in industrial withdrawals in the 25 years after 1975.[27]

In a strict sense the availability of surface or ground water sets the outside limits for agricultural development in the roughly 13 percent of cultivated lands dependent upon irrigation just as precipitation is a major limit to cultivation in more humid lands. In a relatively few semi-arid and arid areas such as the Indus and Rio Grande basins the water supply is already fully utilized for irrigation. Elsewhere, the prospect for agricultural development, where sparse and variable precipitation is a significant constraint, rests more heavily in the short run upon making full and effective use of available water supply than upon expansion of basic irrigation sources.

The indicative plans by the Food and Agriculture Organization for agriculture to 2000 give one assessment of the part which irrigation improvements are expected to play in enhancing the capacity of the growing population in 90 developing countries to feed themselves at a minimal level of nutrition.[28] One of that study's conservative projections estimated that only about 28 percent of desired increase in agricultural output would come from expansion of cropped area, and that irrigation would be a major factor in increasing crop yields and cropping intensity. It judged that about one-half of the land in irrigation schemes in those countries is fully irrigated. Some of the unused lands will never be suitable for irrigation, but others may become highly productive. And new lands may be developed. In Egypt, which depends almost exclusively upon irrigation for its agriculture, there is proposed a modest expansion in cropped area, but the primary increase in production is planned to derive from intensification of cropping in lands now watered from the Nile. The emphasis is less upon more water than upon making efficient use of water now within call.

Although there are no thorough statistics on the state of irrigation and drainage on lands already irrigated, the scattered and somewhat anecdotal evidence in hand suggests that a very substantial proportion of those lands are subject to different degrees of deterioration due to excessive water applications or inadequate drainage. Water logging, salinization, and alkalinization are widespread, but causes and remedies are known in many areas.[29] In those circumstances the critical needs are for improved management and for applying lessons from the presently cultivated lands to design and management of new projects.

The opportunities for conservation of agricultural water through improved conveyance and farm distribution systems, application methods, scheduling, crop selection, and cropping practices are large. So, too, are the opportunities to halt and reverse the degradation of irrigated lands beset by waterlogging and salinization. Such efforts are far less dramatic than the construction of a huge storage reservoir or a network of canals on a parched landscape. Yet, they offer solid economic returns in numerous projects and would warrant being undertaken regardless of the physical limits of supply.

Flood, drought and physical remedies

The occurrence of major floods or widespread droughts sometimes is cited as evidence water resources are out of adjustment to human needs. Floods are seen as indications of accelerated runoff rendering the supply less accessible in time, and droughts as evidence of dwindling water supplies. To varying degrees this is true, but often the disastrous social consequences are the products of changes in land and water use rather than of alterations in physical supply, and ideas are changing as to how best to cope with the threat of such disaster.

Flood frequency in numerous urban areas undoubtedly has increased as a result of buildings, paving, and channel encroachment. Likewise, in some mountain terrain the devastation of torrents and mud flows has expanded in the trail of deforestation and unsuitable cropping practices. In the greater number of areas reporting expanding flood disasters, the growth in damages is to be attributed to human invasion of vulnerable areas. To some extent the intensified use of floodplains may be warranted by the prospective economic returns, but elsewhere the remedy may be in revised land use, flood-proofing of buildings, insurance, or improved warnings rather than water control.

Drought disasters follow in the train of prolonged periods of unusually dry weather in areas where the pattern of land use and agricultural productions is ill-prepared for such dry periods, and as those patterns shift the magnitude of human suffering may grow. Thus far, there is no evidence that droughts themselves have increased in frequency. The appropriate preventative measures are seen as including such activities as land use regulation, limits on herd size, provision of alternative employ-ment, and market improvement as well as water conservation in suitable areas.

The accumulating experience with damaging floods and droughts suggests a basic observation about the course of water management. Reliance upon technological solutions to the exclusion of complementary changes in social and economic institutions and process may be counter-productive. A flood-control structure may lead to increased flood damages if land use in vulnerable areas is not managed at the same time. Providing more water wells to a drought-stricken pastureland may enlarge the destruction of both herds and vegetation. Thinking is moving away from primary reliance upon water control toward a combination of water development, land use management, and economic and social adjust-ments. When dry periods come water is not seen as the panacea.

Aquatic ecosystems at risk

In recent years the spectacular alterations in river regime effected by large man-made lakes have probably attracted more popular attention than any other type of water management. However, the interest often has focused on a few detrimental or allegedly detrimental consequences for human health or agricultural productivity, and has neglected some less dramatic but possibly more far-reaching consequences of water control activities for terrestrial and aquatic ecosystems.

In Western Europe, Australia and North America the era of building large storage works and canals for power, irrigation and related uses has nearly run its course: a large proportion of favorable dam sites and of unregulated flows have been claimed. A few promising sites remain. In certain regions of Africa, Asia and South America the physical conditions exist for large new developments. Over the past two decades a series of lessons have been learned the hard way as to how to plan and carry out a large water impoundment without provoking serious side effects.[30] While some of those lessons are still not followed adequately, the glaring social and environmental costs are recognized and minimized in many new projects. Net benefits from power production and irrigation thereby are increased.

On the other hand, unfortunately little attention has been paid to the maintenance of aquatic ecosystems in the path of water diversion, water storage, channel works, and inputs of fertilizer, pesticides, and other waste flows from non-point sources. The effects of altered stream flow patterns upon aquatic life are still not well understood: desirable in-channel flows are difficult to establish. The contributions of non-point pollutants to river pollution are now seen along many reaches to be more difficult than waste from point sources of city or factory.

The most dramatic of these changes in Western Europe and Eastern North America are in acidification of streams and lakes attributed to sulphur and nitrogen in precipitation.[31] While the processes of atmospheric transport and deposition in water bodies and soils are in controversy, it is apparent that this type of change is widespread.[32] The concept of availability of water for human use is being revised to recognize that the quality of water may be influenced by land uses in nearby or distant areas, and that these may be more troublesome to handle than simple deficiencies in physical supply.

Speculation on climate change and its effects

Amid the welter of speculation that has spread during the past decade on the likelihood of climate change, the possible consequences for water resources have received their share of attention.[33] *Global 2000* used an array of opinions solicited from competent meteorologists.[34] The speculation is in two stages. The first asks what shifts in climate pattern might be expected from anticipated changes in atmospheric CO_2, ozone, sulphur, and trace elements generated by human activity. The second, to the extent those alterations in temperature, precipitation and other parameters are indeed realized, inquires into what difference it would make to water resources distribution in time and place.[35]

Because of the dilemma attaching to the first stage of examination, it is difficult to judge how seriously the hypothetical future climate should be considered in looking into future water availability. If the change is sufficiently large to be measured by normal observations of temperature and precipitation it is likely then to be far enough advanced so that efforts to reverse the causes in energy generation and forest management would at best take many years to achieve. In view of the large uncertainties, water planners are cautious about taking explicit measures to cope with climatic alterations. Nevertheless, they are becoming sensitive to the possibility that if and when identified the effects on distribution of water, temperature and evapotranspiration in place and time might trigger severe reactions in economy and society.

The speculation, while causing anxieties in the next few years or decades, may turn out to foster readjustments in water management that would be beneficial in any event. It may be that the same kinds of measures – such as provision for additional carry-over storage or the encouragement of water conservation – which would be desirable in making current water uses less vulnerable to the vagaries of weather would be those which would be sought were climate change to render a region more arid. Some scientists think shifts in climate may be observed within a few years or a decade; others believe the processes are so complex it may be much longer. Whatever the time scale this consideration now is entering into water planning activity. Its pursuit is likely to have large influence in elevating the attention and priority given to water conservation measures.

New Orientations

In view of these shifts in thinking, the type of estimate of water availability presented in *Global 2000* for 1971 and 2000 may have little relevance to the actual situation, and, indeed, may promote action in unproductive directions. For example, the *Global 2000* calculations of "water availability per capita" for 1971 and again for 2000 show Egypt and Saudi Arabia in the class of nations having the least amounts, and assert that "the greatest pressure will be on those countries with low per capita water availability and high population growth, especially in parts of Africa, South Asia, the Middle East, and Latin America."[36] In both countries water as such is not likely to be the limiting factor in food production in the next few years: suitable land, agricultural services, capital, and other factors may be determinative.

Global 2000 recognizes that population growth is only one relatively crude measure among many important factors that could affect a country's water situation, but concludes that "population growth will be the single most significant cause of increased future demand. . . ."[37] As population grows, to be sure, the aggregate demand enlarges. Yet, for reasons given above, this need not imply that aggregate withdrawal will mount in the same degree.

The social complications of managing water do seem likely to increase. It is revealing that in the United States, where water science and technology are relatively sophisticated, a recent review by the National Research Council of the outlook for science and technology affecting water development did not dwell on issues as to the volume of potential supply.[38] After pointing out the need for future research on the process of deterioration in ground-water quality, and on the response of aquatic ecosystems to toxic inputs and non-point pollution, the National Research Council group directed urgent attention to the importance of exploring and appraising innovative ways of organizing water management at the sub-national level.

One of the observations emerging strongly in *The World Environment* was that the political stability of nations in the international economic system was a basic and often determinative factor in the application of scientific and technical knowledge to environmental management. In place after place the primary, guiding constraint on use of water for the public good is not information on stream flow or ability to pump ground water or knowledge of soil–water–plant relations although there are and will continue to be glaring gaps in that knowledge. The practical use of what already is known and the wily search for what it would be most important to learn in addition about water is dependent upon ability to marshal people and ideas in a consistent, effective fashion.

To learn how adequate the water resource is for a present or future society it is necessary to look into how the physically available waters are being used and what physical, social, economic and political constraints apply to further use. In some places the physical limits are severe, and changes in technology, as with central pivot irrigation, can alter the estimates drastically. More frequently, the crucial factors are social, economic and political. The capacity of a society to manage demand, to assure continuity in management policy, and to place values on environmental effects and the maintenance of the quality of surface and ground waters is more likely to influence the course of development.

Conclusions

There is bound to be continuing appeal in attempts to sum up the world water prospect in terms of the total volume of water available for the globe as a whole or for major regions as related to growing human uses. The arithmetic of fixed supply and growing demand is simple and therefore attractive. Yet, understanding of the current situation or skill in forecasting the future will be advanced only when the calculations are based upon the realities of the available alternatives for changing the location and form of use in relation to supply.

The contrast in approach is exemplified by the manner in which the *Global 2000* and *The World Environment* deal with water. Both canvass the basic evidence as to water supply and use, and both discuss some of the difficulties in promoting economic use and environmental quality. *Global 2000* emphasizes the ratio between physical supply and growing use as a curb on development. *The World Environment* report dwells on problems and trends in management of the supply. One finds grounds for concern in the diminishing volume of water per capita. The other derives cautious hope from improved methods of management.

Technicians and administrators looking to the future will do well to canvass the basic hydrologic facts so far as those can be ascertained, but their efforts will be prescient if they give equally discerning examination to the social and economic conditions within which fundamental choices as to technology and water management strategies are made. The likelihood of the world running out of water for sustaining its life is zero; the likelihood grows of its grossly mismanaging its water resource unless the proper political and technological decisions are made.

Notes

1   U.S. Council on Environmental Quality and the Department of State, Gerold O. Barney (Director) 1980. *The Global 2000 Report to the President: Entering the Twenty-First Century*. vols. I–III. U.S. Government Printing Office, Washington, D.C.

2   Holdgate, M. W., Kassas, M. and White, G. F. (eds.) (1982). *The World Environment 1972–82: A Report by the United National Environment Programme*. Tycooly International Publishing, Dublin (for the United Nations Environment Programme).

3   United Nations Department of Economic Affairs (1950). *Water Resources* Proc. United Nations Scientific Conf. on Conservation and Utilization of Resources, 17 August–6 September 1949, Lake Success, New York, vol. IV.

4   U.S. Government (1967). *Water for Peace*. Intl. Conf. on Water for Peace, 23–31 May, 1967. U.S. Government Printing Office, Washington, 8 vols.

5   Doxiadis, C. A. (1967). "Water and environment". In: *Water for Peace*, vol. 1, pp. 33–60.
6   L'vovitch, M. I. (1974). *Global Water Resources and Their Future*, Micl, Moscow (in Russian).
7   USSR National Committee for the International Hydrological Decade (1974). *World Water Balance and Water Resources of the Earth*. Hydrometeoizdat, Leningrad (in Russian).
8   Baumgartner, A. and Reichel, E. (1975). *The World Water Balance: Mean Annual Global, Continental and Maritime Precipitation, Evaporation and Run-off*. Elsevier Scientific, Amsterdam.
9   United Nations (1972). *Water Development and Management*. Proc. United Nations Water Conf., Mar del Plata, Argentina, March 1977. Pergamon Press, Oxford (for the United Nations) vols. 1–4.
10 Ibid., vol. 1, p. 14.
11 Ibid., vol. 1, p. 5.
12 United Nations, 1977. *Desertification: Its Causes and Consequences*. Proc. United Nations Conf. on Desertification, Pergamon Press, Oxford.
13 Falkenmark, M. and Lindh, G., 1976. *Water for a Starving World*. Westview Press, Boulder, CO.
14 *Global 2000*, vol. II, pp. 152–3.
15 Ibid. vol. II, pp. 7–28.
16 Ibid. vol. I, p. 26.
17 Loc. cit.
18 UN (1977). *Report of the United Nations Water Conference*, United Nations Publ. No. E.77.II.A.12, New York.
19 UN (1982). *Report of the Interregional Meeting of International River Organizations, Dakar, Senegal, 5–14 May 1981*. United Nations, New York.
20 Van der Leeden, F. (1975). *Water Resources of the World: Selected Statistics*. Water Information Center, Port Washington, NY, p. 2.
21 UN (1980). *International Drinking Water Supply and Sanitation Decade; Present Situation and Prospects*. United Nations Publ. A/35/367. New York.
22 U.S. Council on Environmental Quality (1981). *Contamination of Ground Water by Toxic Organic Chemicals*, U.S. Government Printing Office, Washington, D.C.
23 U.N. Department of Technical Co-operation for Development (1979). *A Review of the United Nations Ground-water Exploration and Development Programme in the Developing Countries, 1962–1977*. Natural Resources/ Water Ser. No. 7. United Nations Publ. No. 79.II.A.4. New York.
24 U.N. Department of Technical Co-operation for Development, 1980. *Efficiency and Distributional Equity in the Use and Treatment of Water: Guidelines for Pricing and Regulations*. Natural Resources/Water Ser. No. 8. United Publ. No. 80.II.A.11, New York.
25 Baumann, D. D. *et al.* (1979). *The Role of Conservation in Water Supply Planning*. Prepared for United States Army Corps of Engineers Institute for Water Resources. National Technical Information Service, Springfield, VA. U.S. General Accounting Office (1979). *Water Resources and the Nation's Water Supply: Issues and Concerns*. Rep. CED-79-69. U.S. Government Printing Office, Washington, D.C.
26 *The World Environment, 1972–1982*, pp. 415–28.
27 Water Resources Council (1979). *Second National Water Assessment*. U.S. Government Printing Office, Washington, D.C.

28 Food and Agriculture Organization of the United Nations (1979). *Agriculture: Toward 2000*. Proc. Conf., Twentieth Session, Rome, 10–29 November 1979. FAO, Rome.

29 FAO UNESCO (1973). *Irrigation, Drainage and Salinity: An International Source Book*. UNESCO, Paris, Hutchinson, London.

30 Ackermann, W. C. *et al.* (eds) (1973). *Man-made Lakes: Their Problems and Environmental Effects*. American Geophysical Union, Washington.

31 *The World Environment*, pp. 142–4.

32 Committee on the Atmosphere and the Biosphere (1981). *Atmosphere-Biosphere Interactions: Toward a Better Understanding of the Ecological Consequences of Fossil Fuel Combustion*. National Academy Press, Washington, D.C.

33 Panel on Water and Climate, Geophysics Study Committee (1977). *Climate, Climatic Change, and Water Supply*. Studies in Geophysics, National Academy of Sciences, Washington, D.C.

34 *Global 2000*, vol. II, p. 51–65.

35 For example, see: Kellogg, W. W. and Schware, R. (1981). *Climate Change and Society: Consequences of Increasing Atmospheric Carbon Dioxide*. Westview Press, Boulder, CO.

36 *Global 2000*, vol. II, p. 153.

37 *Loc. cit.*

38 National Research Council (1982). *Outlook for Science and Technology: The Next Five Years*. W. H. Freeman, San Francisco, pp. 255–85.

9B

On Water: A Critique of *Global 2000*

STEVE H. HANKE

Global 2000's alarming statements about the future state of the world's water resources are inconsistent with – in fact, are completely opposed to – the report's own analysis of what can be reasonably said about these resources. Since the materials on water represent such a clear example of the report's self-contradictory mode of analysis and presentation, our critique will devote more attention to the report's internal inconsistencies than do others.

Supply

We first examine the supply side of the analytical chapter, "Water Projections." The report states that

> The supply of water available to a given area, therefore, cannot be estimated on the basis of data now available, but a lower bound can be determined by measuring or estimating the total surface water discharge from the area. This volume of water is potentially available for withdrawal, although storage facilities might be required to satisfy certain patterns of withdrawal. Additional, unmeasured sources of supply include ground water that leaves the area in some way other than as surface discharge, net additions to ground-water storage, and return flows from other water users, but data are not available to determine the magnitude or significance of these additions to water supply. (p. 140)

> Unfortunately, calculations performed on the basis of nations and continents inevitably blur the inherent variation in the data. (p.140)

> The larger the land area of a nation, the larger the major river systems within the nations, and the more seacoast included, the

more seriously these data may understate the true availability of water. (p. 140)

As a result of the considerations discussed above it is impossible to make meaningful statements concerning the supply of water available across the world, or throughout any continent or nation. Meaningful statements describing supply can be made only for relatively small areas and then only after detailed on-site investigation of the nature and behavior of the actual water resources available to that area. Therefore, the data presented in this section are included only to illustrate the shortcomings of aggregate calculations and to provide some indication of the gross differences existing among the various regions of the world. (pp. 140–1)

The analytical section of *Global 2000*, therefore, makes it very clear that statements about water supply cannot be made in the context of the report. Furthermore, the report explicitly states that the water supply data that are presented are only for purposes of illustrating the shortcomings of aggregate water supply projections. In short, the analytical section of the report makes no water supply projections. Moreover, it presents a sound analysis which outlines why nothing can be said about the supply side of the demand–supply picture.

Demand

Next, we examine the demand side of the analytical chapter, "Water Projections." The report states that

Forecasts of future water withdrawals require consideration of all the various determinants of water demand. Ideally, each water-using sector would be considered separately, and the factors that influence water use would be identified, quantified, forecast, and combined, using an appropriate demand function, to yield a forecast of future water use. Thus domestic water use would depend upon future lifestyles, family income, family size, water-using appliance technology, and the future price of water for domestic purposes. Future industrial water use would be determined from assumptions regarding technology, industrial output, the price of water, etc. Similarly, agricultural use of water would be expressed in terms of crops, output, irrigation technology, price, and other factors. (p. 143)

Unfortunately, general demand relationships suitable for such estimates on a national and global basis are not available. . . . Little examination of demand for water has occurred, and that has tended to focus on relatively small aggregations. (p. 143)

Further, past management practices have produced historical data of dubious quality. (p. 143)

These problems do not preclude the development of suitable forecasting models; they merely underline the necessity of intensive sector by sector analysis prior to the postulation of such models. They also suggest some of the important deficiencies of forecasting methods that rely on extrapolations of past water-use data. Such methods are likely to produce forecasts seriously in error, especially where water scarcity may increase. Extrapolation alone cannot predict the various economic, technological, and social adjustments known to occur when water becomes, through scarcity, a higher-valued resource. Extrapolations have limited use but should be viewed as highly tentative forecasts. (pp. 147–8)

The analytical section of *Global 2000*, therefore, makes it very clear that statements about water demand cannot be made in the context of the report. However, unlike the supply section, the demand section continues with a rather extended and unguarded discussion of water use forecasts which are based on extrapolations.[1] It is at this point that we realize that the report suffers from internal inconsistencies.

Findings and Recommendations

If the report had followed its own arguments,[2] it would not have included empirical water-use forecasts. Indeed, it would have simply stated that: "based on our analyses, we must conclude that, in the context of this report, nothing can be said about the future water supply–demand situation."[3]

However, such a concluding statement was not forthcoming. Instead, even the analytical chapter, "Water Projections," includes a lengthy discussion on the future of water resources. For example, this chapter concludes that:

By the year 2000 population growth alone of the world will cause at least a doubling in the demand for water in nearly half the countries of the world. . . . Much of the increased pressure will occur in the developing countries when, if improved standards of living are to be realized, water requirements will expand several times. Unfortunately, it is precisely these countries that are least able, both financially and technically, to deal with the problem. (p. 158)

The total irrigated area of the world was 223 million hectares in 1975, and is expected to rise to 273 million hectares in 1990. As a result the demand for water for irrigation in developing market economies alone would increase between 1975 and 1900 by 438 cubic kilometers, or more than 30 percent of the current total world use of water for irrigation. (pp. 158–9)

The need for water resources, however, goes beyond quantity and must also consider quality. The harmful effects of waste disposal on quality are well known, but a major unseen problem is the increasing salinity of water resources with use – particularly irrigation use. Increasing salinity is an inevitable process in nature, but man has greatly accelerated it and, with continued increases in the intensity of use, the problem will become greater. (p. 159)

It is estimated that about half of all the irrigated lands of the world have been damaged by salinization, alkalinization and water-logging. . . . Past neglect of drainage, in conjunction with irrigation, has reduced the productivity of millions of hectares, which must now be reclaimed if at all possible. (p. 159)

As pressures on water resources increase, conflicts among nations with shared water resources are likely to intensify. Inter-state disputes between upstream and downstream users of multi-national river basins are particularly apt to occur over questions of water rights and priorities. Long-standing quarrels could easily worsen as pressures become critical. (p. 159)

It is indeed remarkable that these findings are presented in the same chapter that contains analyses that are devastatingly critical of statements about water supply and demand projections.[4] Indeed these alarming conclusions are not based on this chapter's analyses but rather on vague, unscientific language and powerful rhetoric.

Perhaps even more remarkable and more disturbing, are the alarming "findings" and recommendations about water resources that are presented throughout the non-analytical sections of the report, particularly since it is these summary sections that have been most widely read and reported on in the media. For example, the following excerpts are from the chapter entitled "The Study in Brief:"

The Global 2000 Study population, GNP, and resource projections all imply rapidly increasing demands for fresh water. Increases of at least 200–300 percent in world water withdrawals are expected over the 1975–2000 period. (p. 26)

The quality of the world's water resources is eventually certain to suffer from changes taking place between now and the year 2000. (p. 35)

As the use of water for irrigation increases water salinity problems are certain to increase. (p. 35)

Virtually all of the Global 2000 Study's projections point to increasing destruction or pollution of coastal ecosystems. (p. 35)

Concluding Observations

Global 2000 develops a sound analysis that finds that no reasonable or useful forecasts of the world's water supplies or demands can be made. However, the report then ignores its own analysis, and proceeds to offer forecasts and frightening conclusions about the future state of the world's water resources. This self-contradictory mode of analysis and presentation should cause us to reject the report's conclusions. But more importantly, it should cause us to reflect on the role played by ideology in shaping the final report.

Notes

1 It should be noted that the two global forecasts that are presented contain estimates of water use that differ by more than an order of magnitude. In addition, the assumptions underlying these forecasts are not publicly documented.

2 The analytical, water sections of the report, with the exception of the empirical forecasts presented in the demand section, are indeed based on the most advanced thinking of professionals in the water field.

3 A non-analytical summary chapter, "Renewable Resources," does contain language that is similar to that which we suggest: "Water is a fluid substance in more ways than one. On the supply side, it slips through all attempts to achieve a uniform definition of 'water supply' " (p. 564). "On the demand side, it is difficult to hold water to fixed relationships. . . . The amounts of water required to specific industrial processes often vary by a factor of two or more. . . . Per capita consumption in national cross sections does not closely follow per capita incomes. In short, there is very little to hang onto in making predictions; water use patterns are highly variable and could assume forms quite different from those we observe today should water scarcity become a problem" (p. 564).
   "Given this nebulousness, the methodology of global water forecasts is quite arbitrary, and the forecasts themselves not especially meaningful . . ." (p. 564).

4 The conclusions of the analytical chapter, in addition to being irreconcilable with the analysis in the chapter, cannot be supported by the empirical information that is presented (and note that these data are inconsistent with the chapter's analyses).

10

Global Climatic Trends

H. E. LANDSBERG

What Is Climate?

The earth has a unique gaseous envelope, the atmosphere. This atmosphere is a buffer between the earth and the universe. It transmits the sustaining energy of the sun and offers protection against excessive energy loss from the earth. It is essential for sustaining life on earth. There is continuous motion in the atmosphere. This serves to equalize the heat contrasts between the equatorial zones, where large amounts of solar energy are received, and the polar regions, which at times are entirely without radiation. Essential players in these energy exchanges are also the oceans (the hydrosphere) and the areas covered by snow and ice (the cryosphere). One of the major roles of the hydrosphere is the evaporation of water which in vapor form circulates in the atmosphere, moves latent heat, forms clouds, and eventually returns to the surface as rain or snow. This hydrological cycle is part of the unending atmospheric motions which create the diversity of weather. The manifestations of weather vary with latitude, distance from the ocean, elevation, and position in mountainous terrain. All the weather events over a period of time create the climate of a locality or region. Integrally, for the various elements of climate, such as temperature and precipitation, one can formulate the concept of a global climate.

It is essential to understand that climate is the composite of all weather events. It must also be noted that climate is not a constant. It fluctuates on all time scales: monthly, yearly, decadally, centennially, and millennially. It thus is a statistical collective and, while often described in terms of mean values of particular climatic elements, it also encompasses a wide range of values, including extremes. Although the atmospheric motions follow well-known physical laws, the day-to-day variations or those for longer time intervals can, for many purposes, be treated like quasi-random variables. Statistical analyses applicable to stochastic universes can result in useful predictions of climate.

Climatic conditions are best expressed as frequency distributions of single or complex climatic elements. Among these are: temperature, humidity, evaporation, radiation, wind direction and speed, cloudiness, precipitation form and amounts for specified time intervals, occurrences of thunderstorms or fogs, concentration of aerosols, wind chill value, and many others. Singly and in combinations they affect human activities, clothing, housing structures; they govern sizeable sectors of the economy including production of food and fiber, transportation, energy consumption, tourism, ski resorts, and other sport activities.

Even though the term "normal" is often used in connection with climate that word conveys an erroneous connotation. There is no such thing as a "normal" climate. The so-called "normal" is professional jargon for a 30-year mean value. While this is a value reflecting the central tendency (though often the median is a better statistic) without measures of dispersion, such as standard deviation and range, it conveys little information. The principal characteristic of climate is variability. In any given era the values of the climatic elements vary around an equilibrium position which reflects the balance of all the energies and forces acting on the earth's atmosphere. Should there be a major change in these governing physical parameters a new equilibrium will be established and one may speak of a climatic change. But even a fairly lengthy minor departure from an established mean does not necessarily reflect a climatic change. A time element of many thousands of years is involved in the natural changes of climate. Shorter-term ups and downs, while important enough, are fluctuations because, as will be demonstrated, in historical times there have been no sustained one-sided trends. But rhythms of decades and centuries are part of the global climate system.

Aside from the natural changes and fluctuations man has changed the face of the globe and his technologies have introduced new elements into the climate system. Their extent and influence have been a subject of much speculation and some exploration. The anthropogenic influences on climate had best be designated as "alterations" to distinguish them from natural changes.

What Governs Climate?

The principal forces governing climate, whether global or local, are radiative. There is the incoming radiation from the sun, part of which is directly reflected back by clouds and from the surface, especially if covered by ice and snow. The second great element is the infrared radiation flux from the earth back into space, which is governed by the temperature of the radiating surface. Some of the solar energy is also scattered back to space by atmospheric suspensions (aerosols). Contrasts in the radiation balance between various latitudinal zones set into motion the great planetary wind systems, resulting in the general atmospheric and oceanic circulation. Snow and ice, because of their great reflectivity, called albedo, have a major influence on climate. Other surfaces too have an albedo, fairly high for desert sands, lower for vegetated surfaces, and quite low for liquid surfaces.

In very general terms, anything affecting the solar energy received by the earth will produce a climatic change. It is now known from satellite observations that there are slight fluctuations of solar energy output from day to day but the period of observation is still too short to gage if this output changes more than the now observed 0.1–0.3 percent (Eddy et al., 1982). However, it is fairly certain that an active sun, characterized by many sunspots, is a "cool" sun and that a quiescent sun is a "hotter" sun. Time series analyses of long temperature records show some coherence with the sunspot rhythms but usually less than 10 percent of the variance is explained by this influence.

Of much greater importance for climate is the position of the earth with respect to the sun. This undergoes quasi-cyclic variations. All told, there are three major elements involved: the precession of the equinox, the inclination of the axis of the earth with respect to the ecliptic, and the eccentricity of the earth's orbit around the sun. This is not the place to go into the details of these changes; suffice it to state that they show quasi-periodic values around 21,000 years for the precession, 41,000 years for the inclination, and 97,000 years for the eccentricity. These time intervals are not constant but the values given convey an impression of the lengthy time intervals involved. Based on these periodicities the Serbian astronomer Milankovich calculated the changes of solar radiation received at various times in the past by the different latitudinal zones on earth. Geological evidence, principally obtained by cores from the ocean bottom, containing temperature-sensitive microfossils and by isotope analysis, shows coincidence between the cold periods thus established and the eras of lowered radiation calculated by the Milankovich model. It is now widely accepted that for about ½–1 million years before the present this model can explain initiation and dissipation of glaciated and interglacial warmer intervals on earth. The oribital elements are therefore indeed a basis for climatic changes (Kerr, 1983).

Celestial mechanics and output of solar energy influence climate. Terrestrial happenings too can cause aberrations. Volcanic eruptions of a certain type are the culprits. They have been well chronicled so that it is feasible to assess their effect (Simkin et al., 1981). The eruptive variety that brings large amounts of dust and gases into the atmosphere seems to affect the global temperature. This effect is particularly notable and lasting when volcanic material reaches the stratosphere. Sulfur gases released by volcanoes, reaching great heights, will form small droplets of sulfuric acid. These and microscopic dust will scatter some of the incoming solar radiation back to space and thus reduce the earth's beneficial energy income. A comparison of the occurrence of such dust veils from known major volcanic eruptions with observed temperatures suggests a "weak" signal in these. The massive eruption of Krakatoa in 1883 is credited with a 0.3°C global temperature drop (Mass and Schneider, 1977).

Low-level volcanic dust is usually rapidly eliminated but may at times lead to formation of a haze or dry fog. Such a case seems to have taken place in 1783 when Lakagigar (Laki) in Iceland started to erupt violently on 8 June. Explosions occurred off and on until February 1784 (Thorarinson, 1981). As it happens, 1784 turned out to be hemispherically the coldest year between 1616 and 1798. There has been considerable debate whether the low temperatures of 1816, "the year without summer" could be attributed to an explosion of the Tambora volcano in Indonesia in April 1815. However, cold years had already begun in 1799 and lasted with little interruption until 1818.

Volcanic activity is unpredictable, and knowledge of solar physics is inadequate to state if larger changes in the energy output of the sun have taken place and are likely to reoccur. However, energy balance models, which simulate at least some of the main characteristics of climate, have shown that a 1 percent increase or decrease of solar radiative power would cause major climatic changes on earth, principally in the high latitudes. These and other mathematical model simulations have made great progress in the past two decades thanks to increased computer capacity. They still suffer by their inability to simulate a host of feedback mechanisms and by the inadequacy of representing the ocean influence in the system. The albedo effects have been reasonably well incorporated but many others are still too complex to be accommodated adequately in these simulations. A diagram developed by Sellers (1974) conveys a good impression of the intricate interactions (figure 10.1).

The energy balance models are a handy tool for exploring what influences affect the equilibrium climate. They are inadequate for depicting the climatic fluctuations. These can be somewhat better reflected by General Circulation Models (GCM). These are similar to numerical models which are used for preparing the daily weather forecast, based on a set of dynamic equations representing the principal physical phenomena in the atmosphere. Modern computers permit running these equations, with a solar forcing function representing the annual variation, for several simulated years until a stable state is reached, roughly resembling the distribution of the climatic elements over the globe. Even these models must introduce a number of short cuts (called parameterizations). They also have been pressed into service for simulations of what would happen if some atmospheric elements are changed.

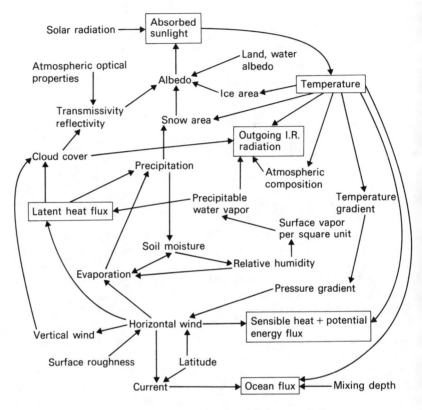

Figure 10.1 Causes and feedback linkages of climate.
Source: Sellers, 1974.

This is, of course, the case when there is a perturbation such as an injection of aerosol by a volcanic eruption or by some manmade compound. In some instances only the energy balance is perturbed by these influences but in others the atmospheric chemistry is altered. Then the time-dependent models have to project not only the transport of the intruding substance but also the chemical changes. The new dimension entering the system by a hierarchy of slow and rapid reactions, photochemical effects, disappearance of old chemical species and appearance of new ones, actions of sources, and sinks of species and their residence time in the atmosphere burdens the models to an extent that valid projections are not readily achieved.

The reason for the somewhat lengthy foregoing discussion is the fact that neither the nature of the climate system nor its representation by numerical models has been fully grasped by some who have drawn far-reaching conclusions from some ongoing research studies and have suggested sweeping policy changes. One can only view these suggestions with skepticism in the face of very substantial uncertainties. The difficulties of modeling the variations of the different climatic elements, even if realistic mean values are obtained, have been described by Hansen *et al.* (1983).

Climatic History

About 18,000 years ago there was the height of the last ice age. Global temperatures were about 5–6°C lower than at present. Major portions of northern North America and Northern Europe were under thick ice sheets. This ice age terminated about 11,000 years ago and the present (Holocene or Recent) geologic epoch started. It is an interglacial epoch.

A gradual warming accompanied by the melting of inland glaciers was aided by the reduction in albedo. This changed the landscape in the higher latitudes radically. Tundra turned into forest and previously glaciated areas became tundra. There were other notable changes of flora which, in turn, led to substantial changes in fauna. A fairly adequate gross picture in many localities can be obtained from the plant associations present. They are reconstructed by pollen counts in lake sediments. These can be dated for various layers in a core from lake bottoms by carbon fourteen analysis. One can see, for example, succession of pollen from subarctic species to warmth-loving plants and trees, from birches and firs to oaks and maples. Animal remains showed the retreat of musk ox and mammoth and their replacement by less woolly species. Sea level rises caused by the melting ice can be documented. Areas unburdened of thick ice masses, such as Scandinavia, rose isostatically out of the subcrustal material. All this culminated between 8000 and 5000 years before the present in a warm period, designated as the Hypsithermal or Climatic Optimum. Global temperatures were about 1.5°C warmer than presently. Since that time some cooling has occurred again. The northern tree line has receded about 300 km. Old tree trunks can still be found in the Canadian tundra. The northern glaciers have advanced but since about 2000 years before the present the global climate has become fairly well stabilized. But because of the cooling since the Hypsithermal the geologists have dubbed the era since, the "Little Ice Age" (Matthes, 1939).

In historical times there are fairly good documentary sources in Europe, North Africa, and China that depict climatic conditions not very far from the present. In western North America tree rings carry us fairly far back for that era. In other parts of the world there is less information but none of the floristic, faunistic, or archeological data suggest any radical climatic changes.

Since the fourteenth century there are a variety of sources of direct and indirect information about weather and climate. Some are proxy data such as dates of freezing of lakes, blossoming of cherry trees in Japan, wine harvest dates in France, tree rings in many areas of the globe. All these can be calibrated by comparison of similar simultaneous observations with instrumental weather records of temperature and precipitation and using the "transfer functions" to infer conditions before such instrumental data are available. Also in the pre-instrumental era there are some systematic weather diaries, one as early as 1337 to 1344 for a locality near Oxford, England. In later centuries, especially since 1700, more such information is available. All of it suggests that there have been no major changes for the localities where such information was recorded. But it must also be noted that substantial fluctuations, as are observed presently, took place. An impression can be gained from a summer temperature index derived from the grape harvest dates in France and Germany and the maximal recorded glacier advances in the Alps since 1453 (Bray, 1982); see figure 10.2. Incorporated since 1659 are central England summer temperatures, representing the longest available continuous instrumental record (Manley, 1974). The main purpose of this presentation is to convey two things: (1) the absence of overall trends, and (2) the oscillatory character of this climatic curve. It is representative of any other climatic time series.

Since the middle of the eighteenth century there have been an increasing number of instrumental observations which, in conjunction with suitable proxy data, principally tree rings, can be used to yield an approximation of Northern Hemisphere temperatures. (For the southern hemi-

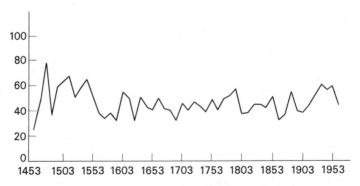

Figure 10.2 A summer temperature index for Western Europe, 1453–1973, as decadal averages
Source: based on data by Bray, 1982.

sphere there is not enough information that one could safely use for a global estimate.) Many climatologists have placed more faith in observations made since the establishment of the national weather services than in earlier records. Hence the century from 1881 onward has become a sort of standard for judging climatic fluctuations and trends (Mitchell, 1963; Borzenkova *et al.*, 1976). This material, still restricted to temperature, formed the basis for the National Defense University study (1981) and its extrapolations, used as basis for climatic estimates in *Global 2000*. Considering the fact that a century is only about 1 percent of the time which has elapsed since the end of the last glaciation one must wonder how well this represents the nature of a widely fluctuating natural environmental factor such as climate.

By judicious use of older instrumental observations and proxy data, and exploiting known teleconnections of climate the record can be extended to the sixteenth century. The uncertainty grows with temporal distance from the present but it shows internal consistency. The year-to-year fluctuations can be somewhat smoothed out by using decadal averages, which are shown in figure 10.3 (Groveman and Landsberg, 1979). Using the 1881–1975 period as a baseline one can first see that during the 400-year interval from 1579 to 1980 the decadal values have only fluctuated in a narrow range of, all told, a little less than 1°C. There is an irregular sequence of colder and warmer intervals. The coldest decade was from 1810 to 1819, with the year 1812 having the dubious distinction of having the lowest estimated temperature in the Northern Hemisphere. The warmest intervals were in this century from 1930 to 1942. Analysis of the 400-year series for periodicities, at the level of 99 percent significance, shows only one longer component of 99-year length. One might identify this with the Gleissberg rhythm of solar activity, but with only four waves

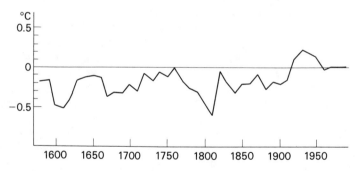

Figure 10.3 Mean temperatures of the Northern Hemisphere for successive decades.
Source: from 1579 to 1880 after a reconstruction of Groveman and Landsberg, 1979; from 1881 to 1975 after Borzenkova *et al.*, 1976.

in the sample this must be viewed with great caution. The only other highly significant peak is an iteration of between 2 and 3 years, well known to meteorologists as the quasi-biennial oscillation. It is noted in nearly all long meteorological time series.

There have been a number of more recent studies which confirm the general conclusions of the reconstruction of 400 years of temperature fluctuations in the Northern Hemisphere.[1] In Western Europe Bray (1982) used the long records of German and French grape harvesting dates to construct a summer temperature index and compared it with observations of alpine glacier conditions. Summer temperatures are key factors for glacial advances or retreats because they govern the melting of the snow fallen in the preceding seasons. Glacial maxima, usually lagging general temperature decreases by several years, were fixed for the intervals 1599–1607, 1618–22, 1818–20, and 1845–60. Tree ring data were used to reconstruct the time of freezing for Hudson Bay in autumn for a period starting in 1680 and calibrated by recent observations (Jacoby and Ulan, 1982). The material clearly shows the oscillatory nature of climate and confirms that there has been no substantial change in north-eastern Canada since the end of the seventeenth century.

Using only instrumental data from the best collection of such information, the World Weather Records, Lauscher (1981) formed decadal means for the period 1730–1980. From this material he derives an overall warming trend of about 0.5°C per century, with a standard deviation of the 25 individual decadal values of about 0.5°C. His warmest decade was 1931–40 and the coldest 1871–80. According to this work 1934 was the warmest year in recent climatic history and 1917 the coldest.

All the available temperature studies, and there are many more for individual localities and regions, show that irregular short-periodic oscillations dominate climate. Longer swings or trends are buried in this "noise." One more example will illustrate this. Figure 10.4 shows an integrated, areally weighted time series of winter temperatures (December–February) for the United States (Center for Environmental Assessment Services, 1982). These temperatures have been closely watched in recent years because of the fuel problems. Harsh, especially snowy, winters have had very adverse effects on the economy. Individual winters, such as that of 1976/7, have been singled out for special attention because of its cruel impact. It was a rare event; yet statistical analysis shows that such an occurrence has to be expected once in a century in a time series showing quasi-random distribution of its elements. From time to time there have also been statements that the variability of climate has increased. The record shows that there are decades with high variability and others which show less fluctuations. In the current century the 1930s were the most turbulent in the climatic manifestations, but recent decades have been more quiescent.

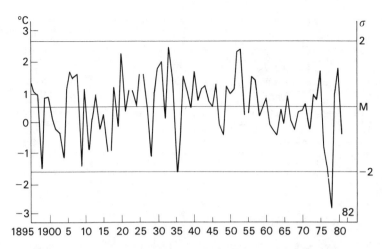

Figure 10.4 U.S. winter temperatures 1895–1982, weighted areal averages.
Source: Environmental Data and Information Service, National Oceanographic and Atmospheric Administration, 1982.

If oscillations govern temperature this tendency is even more pronounced in precipitation. In many regions of the world this most fickle of climatic elements fluctuates from inundation to drought and back. Some of the most populous regions of the world are subject to the monsoonal vagaries; and considering the intimate relation of crop production to rainfall and irrigation, rainfall governs the nutritional status of the vast majority of mankind. Let me caution in this context that average or even median values of precipitation are almost meaningless for purposes of projection. A coefficient of variation is a minimal additional piece of information required for analytical work.

Precipitation must be looked at in terms of local or regional conditions. It does not lend itself to combination on a continental, hemispheric, or global scale. For the human condition drought is probably the most important aspect of precipitation. It was drought that focused public attention on the climate problem. In 1973 the Sahel drought, in 1974 the Russian drought, in 1975/6 drought in southern England, and 1977 drought in California made headlines. The list shows that all regions of the world can have drought. Those close to deserts are more prone to it than others. The economic losses are often huge but in every case one can readily show that these events are not unique and not beyond statistical expectation. The drought in southern England, which had been designated as "unprecedented," could be shown on the basis of a precipitation measure going back to 1698 to be exactly what one would expect to happen once in 300 years in a stochastic universe. If one looks at a somewhat larger area, namely England as a whole, one can see notable percentage variations of annual precipitation from 1725 to 1973 (Craddock, 1976), as shown in figure 10.5. There are large oscillations, a number of very dry years, but filtering by 10-year overlapping means shows some longer waves but no trends (Schönwiese, 1979). The same is true of all areas where longer precipitation records are available, including the monsoon regions of eastern and southern Asia (Hakkarinen and Landsberg, 1981). There have been pessimistic reports that the Indian monsoon has been failing and that it has become more variable. An analysis of the long record at Madras, which started in 1817, showed the greatest variability from that year onward to 1832 and the lowest in the more recent time from 1961 to 1976. Again the "no trend" verdict is valid.

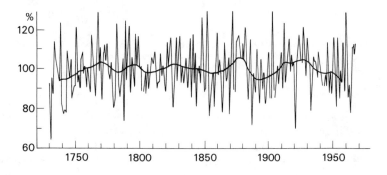

Figure 10.5 Annual totals of precipitation, as percentages of the average, 1725–1973.
Source: after Craddock, 1976; with 30-year overlapping smoothing (solid curve) after Schönwiese, 1979.

The fluctuations of precipitation have been subject to searches for regularities and there are, indeed, indications that rhythms are hidden in the "noise." There is little question that the quasi-biennial oscillation, a 2–3-year phenomenon, is present at many locations. There is also a slight tendency for compensation of a large excess in one direction to be followed by a sizeable excess in the other, i.e. a very wet year may succeed a drought year. But it could not escape attention that in the North American Great Plains there seemed to be some regularity in the occurrence of drought. As early as 1787 the fur traders who had to rely on water transport were hampered by low water in the rivers. Then in 1804/5 Central North America was dry again (Kemp, 1982). The long rainfall record in Muscatine, Iowa, which started in 1846, shows a drought in 1854–5, (figure 10.6) (Diaz, 1980). Other parts of the Great Plains were dry in 1877. There were conspicuous droughts around 1900; 1910/11 and 1921 were dry, and then 1934–6, the dust bowl years, were the driest on

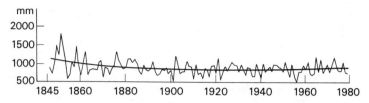

Figure 10.6 Total annual precipitation at Muscatine, Iowa, 1846–1979. Line of least square polynomial fit shows almost no trend
Source: after Diaz, 1980.

record so far. The year 1956 was also dry, and in 1977 there was the western drought. The intervals suggested a solar influence and an investigation of the drought areas indicated by tree rings implied on average interval of 20 years between major droughts (Mitchell *et al.*, 1978). There was a strong coherence with two solar rhythms, the 22-year Hale cycle and the Gleissberg cycle, set at about 90 years, in over 300 years of tree growth. Although both the solar rhythms and the western drought rhythms are irregular, they seem to be quite persistent, so that one can count on future repetitions, even if they cannot be precisely timed. It appears that another cycle of 18.6 years, lunar in origin, causes some irregularity (Currie, 1981). In South Africa a similar rhythm in rain occurrence has been noted since 1840, between 16 and 20 years in length

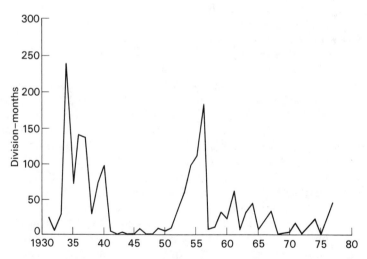

Figure 10.7 Great Plains drought area 1931–77 (based on Palmer drought index, April through August) in terms of numbers of Great Plains climatic divisions reporting severe or extreme drought
Source: from Warrick and Bowden, 1981.

(Tyson, 1981). But when all is told, scrutiny of the long precipitation records, even in the periodically dry parts of central North America, show only the familiar irregular seesaw patterns.

Climate or Climatic Impacts?

Many of the recent writings about climate are not really dealing with climate but with the impacts of climate on human activities, economics, and ecology. In fact, closer inspection shows that these impacts are often produced by extreme weather events. These are quite transitory but can be extremely damaging. Persistent weather aberrations, including lack or excess of precipitation, extremely high or low temperatures, sustained high winds, or lengthy periods of stagnation are, of course, the cause for many ills. They affect health and survival, cause failure of crops, damage or destroy property, fan fires, and cause air pollution episodes. The important climatic aspect is the frequency of such extreme events and any time-dependent changes in this frequency (Flohn, 1981).

The impacts of extreme weather events are often tragic. Major outbreaks of tornadoes, onslaughts of hurricanes or typhoons, and ice storms cause deaths and injuries as well as much property damage. While in recent years these have been mitigated by timely warnings and forecasts, they still cause thousands of casualties annually on a worldwide basis. Similarly Santa Ana winds promote widespread fire damage and often claim burn victims. There are few studies of economic losses due to these weather events. The major insurance carriers have, however, made actuarial studies of losses produced by hail and by floods.

Longer weather anomalies have always been assessed for their economic impact in the production of food and fiber. Crop statistics readily reflect the weather factor after correction for changes in technology. Seasonal weather conditions, as noted in yields, have many facets: rainfall and soil moisture, growing degree days, humidity and dew causing fungus growth, winds blowing rust, and other factors. They have been watched for years and crop-weather models for all principal crop plants are available (Baier, 1977). The second phase of the impact assessment for crop yields as influenced by a potential climatic change by the year 2000 in the National Defense University study (1981) concentrates on five crops in eight major producing countries. An "opinion" poll of 24 climatologists and 35 agricultural experts guessed what might happen to yields under several climate "scenarios." These experts thought that agricultural technology will be the overriding element in production of crops. They dealt with the output of climatic response models based on many simplifying assumptions. In particular, these models cannot cope well with climatic extremes.

Fortunately there is solid evidence that, even if the models cannot, the people generally cope quite successfully with climatic vagaries. History shows that in the United States there is a tapering off of drought impact on crops and individuals (Warrick and Bowden, 1981). Malnutrition has been radically diminished, yields have declined less in recent droughts than earlier ones, fewer farms have been abandoned or transferred in recent droughts, but there has been an effect of public assistance (see also figure 10.7). All this is perhaps best illustrated by the change in relative wheat yield declines during droughts in the U.S. (Warrick, 1980):

Drought decades	1890s	1910s	1930s	1950s	1970s
Percentage decline of wheat crop from trend	26	24	29	19	17

Even though some have argued that advanced technology might make the farm system more vulnerable to drought, the figures speak for a lessening of impact.

In contrast, the effects of climatic fluctuations on energy consumption and costs have increased. They have just begun to enter the economic models. The severe winter of 1976/7 with its $40 billion losses prompted the late Senator Hubert Humphrey to remark in February 1977: "The weather report has become the latest addition on the list of economic indicators" (Hughes, 1982). The less severe winter of 1981/2, with only a very cold January, caused 350 fatalities and economic losses of $8.2 billion. (Center for Environmental Assessment Services, 1982). The damages to transportation, including railroad and highway losses, were estimated at $2 billion. This included a $100 million loss to Conrail from a single snowstorm. There were $2 billion property damages, $1.8 billion production losses, a $1.1 billion increase in energy consumption, and a $1.3 billion agricultural damages.

It is not only in winter when energy costs are greatly affected by weather. The neglect of this element in summer in the *Business Week* weekly economic index distorts the correct interpretation of index fluctuations (Maunder, 1981). Power consumption can increase dramatically when hot days require more cooling, which can raise it by billions of kilowatt hours for a single week. Maunder cogently pleads for explanatory climatic models to take their place next to the predictive climatic models to permit objective climatic impact evaluations. The predictive models have, as Kates (1980) put it, "no complete rationale or objective way to foresee the future even though people are discussing the climatic impacts in the years 2000, 2050, or 2400." He correctly characterizes climate as a "hazard" but rejects current possibilities of acquiring enough climatic knowledge to use it for decision-making. The principal point of this discussion is to prepare the reader to use the existing climatological knowledge in an actuarial sense, a topic to which we will return.

In concluding this brief discussion on climatic impacts it is well to heed a note of caution set forth by Bowden et al. (1981). They comment that the fact that certain climatic aberrations became catastrophes is attributable to a "combination of factors: political and social instability, an absence of technological innovation, and, to a limited extent, climatic and hydrological stress." This applies, of course, principally to the so-called developing countries.

Man's Impact on Climate

Man has had an influence on climate, albeit on a local scale, since time immemorial. On every occasion when a forested area was turned into agricultural fields, when swamps were drained, or when fields were irrigated the local climate, often referred to as the microclimate, was altered. Most of the time these changes, although measurable, only affect the spots where man altered the landscape. His doings altered the albedo, and in response, the heat balance was affected. The direct consequences were effects on the air temperature and its extremes, relative and absolute humidity, windspeed, evapotranspiration and other elements important for the climate of that all-important atmospheric boundary layer where we live, raise our crops, and build our dwellings. As mankind increased in number there were corresponding local alterations of microclimates, some beneficial and some detrimental.

There is little doubt that urbanization and industrialization have affected the climate of fairly substantial areas occupied by man. The urban changes, still essentially local, have been well documented (Landsberg, 1981). The notorious *urban heat island* has raised the average urban temperature by 1–2°C and can exceed the rural surroundings on occasion by 10°C. The urban fabric leads to rapid run-off of precipitation and raises the flood danger. Summer rainfall increases, especially downwind from cities, are likely. The air composition has been notably altered, visibility is lowered, and fogs are more numerous, aided by the lowered wind speeds in the urban area. Sunshine is notably attenuated and pollution episodes are a nuisance and an occasional menace. In some countries abatement efforts have been moderately effective, including the U.S., but some localities are virtually hopeless because of their orographic setting. Notable among them are Mexico City and Los Angeles but they are, fortunately, not the prototypes of cities.

The example of the urban heat island (which is only in part due to anthropogenic heat production but mainly due to an altered heat balance) has led to the question how much influence *heat rejection* to the atmosphere from human activities could have on climate. Ultimately all energy conversions result in heat. Most common is chemical conversion, principally the combustion of fuels. Much of this takes place in widely dispersed places, including furnaces for space heating or engines of vehicles. This heat is rapidly dissipated in the atmosphere and has little, if any, influence on the massive heat transactions of the atmosphere. The same is true of the conversion of electricity for lighting, cooking, and other electric appliances. The heat rejected by air conditioning also diffuses rapidly but all these processes, especially in the winter of higher-latitude cities, will contribute up to one half of the temperature rise of the heat island. More concentrated and more massive is the heat rejection of power plants, whether using fossil fuels or fissionable material. The cooling tower has become their visual emblem. At present most of them are not more than 40–45 percent efficient. Thus over half of the energy converted goes either directly into the atmosphere or indirectly from heated river waters or cooling ponds. There are some observable effects on cloud formation and it is conceivable, even if probably rare, that near multi-megawatt installations, a local storm might become intensified (Landsberg, 1980). There is, however, clear evidence that other effluents from power plant stacks and other industries can influence local cloud systems and affect visibilities in the vicinity. There have been fears expressed that with the assumed great increases of energy use by the end of the century (or a little later) global climate changes might take place. Even with a scenario of a growth rate at 3 percent per annum the anthropogenic heat rejection would stay puny in comparison with solar energy received by the earth. Using a general circulation model and creating a large heat-injection perturbation at the likely places in the world did not seem to affect the circulation of the atmosphere (Washington and Chervin, 1979). Although this is only a simulation, there are no adequate physical reasons to expect any but local effects from energy uses by man.

A still controversial alteration centers around the chemistry of precipitation water, the *acid rain* problem. Man seems to be running a notable competition with nature in this case. Let us first establish that since measurements of rain acidity were first made in the 1930s there were always some occasions when it was quite acid even at remote locations. The matter came into the foreground when ecological changes in Scandinavian lakes and some soils in the 1950s and 1960s revealed damage. These were attributed to advected acids from industrial establishments in other European countries. This resulted in organized surveillance, with a suspicious finger pointed at coal-fired power plants, emitting both oxides of sulfur and of nitrogen which turned into acids in the cloud formations. Recent estimates claim that 17 percent of the acidity is of local Scandinavian origin, 56 percent is advected from other countries, and 27 percent is of unknown origin (Hinrichsen, 1982).

Canada and the United States have their own dispute about how much acidity they mutually export to each other. Here again network observations have been instituted because ecological changes in the lakes of Ontario and of New York State have been attributed to power plant and smelter effluents. It is hard to see trends in rain acidity. Measurements in the early 1950s in the vicinity of Boston showed a substantial number of cases of highly acid precipitation then (Landsberg, 1954). There is also substantive evidence that there is acid precipitation in the immediate vicinity of a coal-fired power plant (Anderson and Landsberg, 1979). Most of these stack effluents seem to be deposited or washed out at relatively short distances of 100–200 km.

Recent comprehensive reviews of the problem reveal that it is not very clear what the trends are, what the partitioning of man-made and natural acidity is, and what the ecological consequences of acid precipitation are (Szabo et al., 1982; Record et al., 1982). There are undoubtedly some localities where advective processes have caused increases in rainfall acidity and the subsequent run-off into lakes. Peters et al. (1982) indicate that although sulfate concentration in western New York State has decreased between 1965 and 1978, acidity has increased by about 0.3 pH units. Some have interpreted the observed increased rainfall acidity since the 1950s in the U.S. as caused by the absence of calcium- and magnesium-bearing dusts, caused in the earlier years by dust storms. These dusts would neutralize some of the acidity (Stensland and Semonin, 1982). Even at remote sites rainfall is, on an average, more acid than expected (expected about pH 5.6–5.7). Thus, for example, both Bermuda and Amsterdam Island show average values of pH of 4.8 (Galloway et al., 1982). One can accept the presence of an advective anthropogenic component in Bermuda but at Amsterdam Island in the middle of the Indian Ocean (approx. 37S, 77E) one must doubt the presence of any such component. What and where, then, is the mix of man-made and natural components?

The natural components are also ubiquitous. Some are of marine origin and some result from plant decay but the largest, if sporadic sources, are volcanic eruptions. Prodigious amounts of sulfur dioxide transform to sulfuric acid and are injected into the stratosphere where they spread throughout the globe. They reach earth again over a period of years. Greenland ice cores show that eruptions in pre-industrial times brought sulfuric acid with the snow that fell subsequently. Thus the famous Laki volcano eruption of 1783 in Iceland raised the snow acidity to 50 times its average value (Josephson, 1982). Etna, the Italian volcano which shows almost continuous activity, brings daily between 142 and 1600 tons of sulfur dioxide into the air (Jaeschke et al., 1982). El Chichon, Mexico, in its 1982 eruption, belched 10^7 tons of sulfur into the atmosphere (Zoller, 1982). Yet future increase in the combustion of high-sulfur coal cannot but aggravate local and regional acid deposition.

Juxtaposed to the volcanic eruptions are possible anthropogenic *aerosols*, which by intercepting and scattering of solar energy might cause climatic alterations. This has been seriously suggested as a result of past and future increased industrialization. Observations indicate that the residence time of aerosols released at the surface is quite short, usually not more than 7–10 days. It is also encouraging that there is no increasing trend of atmospheric turbidity in general. There are now over seven decades of atmospheric transmission observations available at Physical–Meteorological Observatory in Davos, Switzerland. Their annual report for 1980 clearly states that there are no measurable turbidity trends and that the record contains only temporary disturbances by large volcanic eruptions. This report also states that inspection of the data obtained at other radiation stations, widely distributed over the globe, do not show any trends (Physikalisch-Meteorologisches Observatorium, 1981).

Over the past decade there has also been much worry about man-made interference with the stratospheric ozone layer. First, there were the oxides of nitrogen expected from a massive fleet of supersonic transport aircraft. Learned articles and Academy reports were written, based on very inadequate knowledge of stratospheric chemistry. But this stimulated a massive research effort. It resulted in the augmentation from very few reactions first assumed to well over 100. The oxides of nitrogen appear now to be exculpated and the supersonic transport fleets have not materialized. Next came the chlorofluoromethanes as culprits. Again the

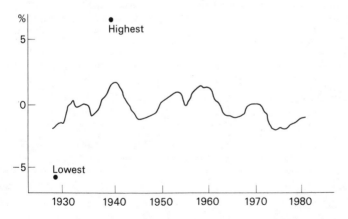

Figure 10.8 Time-series of total atmospheric ozone, 1926–80, as observed
in Arosa, Switzerland
Source: Dütsch, 1981.

knowledge was inadequate but as a precaution the U.S. Government prohibited their use as a propellant in spray cans. Continued improvements in the study of the intricate chemistry of the stratosphere have led Academy Committees to decrease their estimate of a 9–24 percent stratospheric ozone reduction (Panel on Stratospheric Chemistry and Transport NRC, 1979) to a depletion of only 5–9 percent (ibid., 1982). There is no expectation that even if such a reduction were to result, any appreciable alteration of climate at the earth's surface can be expected. (The medical problem of a potential increase in skin cancer goes beyond the scope of this chapter.) Time-series analyses of stratospheric ozone observations have yielded no trends so far. The natural fluctuations are quite appreciable and there is no hope of discovering anthropogenic influences until they exceed about 5 percent (figure 10.8) (Dütsch, 1981). The extent of effects of natural oxides of chlorine is still obscure and the models offer only partial solutions. The definite trend of low-level ozone increase in many areas also has not been assessed. Recent discoveries of massive production of methane and oxides of carbon by insects have yet to be evaluated for their impact on atmospheric chemistry (Zimmerman *et al.*, 1982).

By far the most troublesome atmospheric alteration has been the steady increase in *carbon dioxide* (CO_2). This and a few other minor gases have been lumped together under the term "greenhouse" gases. Their action is supposed to increase surface temperature, somewhat analogous to the glass panes of a greenhouse (actually an incomplete interpretation of greenhouse action). Undeniably CO_2 has steadily increased on a global basis, probably since the 1860s, and at an accelerated rate since the end of World War II. Systematic global measurements started during the International Geophysical Year 1957/8. Since then it has risen about 7 percent. The total increase since 1860 has been from 280 ppmV (parts per million by volume) to 335 ppmV. These are the established facts. They have prompted a staggering amount of literature pertaining to the climatic consequences of a continuing increase in atmospheric CO_2. The potential of a rising CO_2 level in the atmosphere to raise global temperatures at the surface has been discussed on and off ever since Svante Arrhenius advanced the idea in 1896. There is general agreement that the infrared-absorbing qualities of this gas will reduce the outgoing radiation from earth to space and thus raise the surface temperature. At the same time the radiation from the gas itself would cool the stratosphere.

The question about this temperature rise is how much, how soon, and with what regional distribution. There is no agreement on that. Some of it is a result of the initial uncertainties. These include principally the projections for future CO_2 increases. There had been the contention that this is primarily due to the increases in the use of fossil fuels. The calculations had shown that the past increase of CO_2 corresponded to about one-half of the CO_2 produced by combustion of the reasonably well-known consumption of fossil fuels. This was extrapolated to the future with scenarios of exponential increases in the use of fossil fuels. It must be said here that not all the CO_2 increase is caused by fossil fuel use. There have also been some decreases in uptake of CO_2 by vegetation, caused by deforestation especially in tropical areas. According to some estimates the depletion is presently at the rate of nearly 8 million hectares annually (Tolba, 1982). However, the potential increase of other biomass as a result of additional CO_2 remains to be fully quantified (Olson, 1982; Woodwell, 1982).

The whole carbon cycle and the transfers from the various reservoirs soil, sea, and plant cover have not been adequately represented in past considerations, as pointed out in an excellent recent review by Bolin (1982). He points out that the regional biogeochemical processes are important for climatic models and have so far been inadequately considered: "Important feedback mechanisms may therefore have been overlooked, some of which may possibly cause natural climatic oscillations. Important also are the man-made changes in the surface of the land and the fact that on longer time scales ecosystems are hardly static."

The whole CO_2–climate problem is, in the words of Kellogg and Schware, (1981) a "cascade of uncertainty." There is recognition that the prime problem lies with the scenarios. Kellogg and Schware proceed with the assumption that by the year 2000 atmospheric CO_2 will have risen to 360 ppmV and that it will have doubled from the pre-industrial level by 2035. While they admit the need for research to improve knowledge they proceed to discuss dire consequences. They are quite conservative compared with more alarming views by Flohn (1980). He writes "the possibility of a drastic rapid climatic modification on a large scale must be envisaged," setting a critical limit at 450 ppmV with "catastrophic" possibilities at higher levels. Without much reference to the uncertainties this is elaborated in a report of the International Institute for Applied Systems Analysis (1981). It is partly based on a paleoclimatic scenario, the hypsithermal of the Holocene, when global temperatures were estimated to have been 1.5°C above the present. CO_2 and the infrared-absorbing trace gases methane, nitrous oxide, and the chlorofluoromethanes are expected to constitute 70 percent and 30 percent, respectively, of the absorbing mixture. By the year 2050 the pre-industrial CO_2 has doubled and a 4°C global temperature rise is projected. Rain belts will be shifted, some areas will have more droughts, the polar ice will melt rapidly, coastal areas will become submerged. Doom will be there.

Such views prompted some scientists to propose policy changes that would postpone the evil day. Many of the scenarios had envisaged an annual use increment for fossil fuel of 4 percent. It was thus natural to urge a "low-risk" energy policy (Bach and Breuer, 1980). Actually there had already been a slow-down to an annual increase of 2¾ percent, presumably due to economic factors. Yet the predictions of temperature increases of several degrees in 50–70 years continued with adverse effects on the United States, the Soviet Union, and China (Kellogg and Schware, 1982): "It now appears that the possible global climate change may be very disruptive to some societies. It may trigger shifts in agricultural patterns, balances of trade, and habitual ways of life for many people – and eventually, a few centuries from now, may even force abandonment of low-lying land due to a rise in sea level".

With such prospects being bandied about it is not surprising that legislative concern is being aroused. Thus subcommittees of the U.S. House of Representatives held hearings on carbon dioxide research and the greenhouse effect. Fortunately there was very cautious scientific testimony. It brought out that there are widely different results from various models used to simulate the CO_2 effect. It also indicated that it would probably take centuries to melt the Western Antarctic ice sheet. Even though there is a fair amount of consensus that the greenhouse effect is real, there remains a wide range of opinion as to the magnitude and the rate at which climatic change will occur and, in particular, about the changes that will take place on the all-important regional scale (Hansen, 1982).

Because so many conclusions are based on the mathematical–numerical modeling of climate, it is imperative to take a critical look at the various models. The fact that they appear in the exact framework of mathematics is deceiving because they can only simulate nature successfully if they represent all variables and their interactions. With the present state of knowledge that is virtually impossible. Hence it is also not surprising that various modelers have used different approaches and parameterizations to achieve approximations. The tests of validity have usually been that they present a fair representation of the current mean value of a climatic element and its annual variation. Yet when they are employed to project, say, the global mean temperature for the case of doubled atmospheric CO_2 the answers vary widely. An excerpt from a comparison of the results for various models shows a wide range of estimates (figure 10.9) (Schlesinger, 1982). Twenty-eight model experiments, based on three categories of models, scatter from a fraction of 1°C to nearly 10°C. The majority of them cluster in the range of 1.5–4.5°C for doubled CO_2. This has been called the "consensus estimate" (Thompson and Schneider, 1982). But one should not overlook that a substantial minority, 25 percent of the estimates, is 1°C or lower. One scientist places the global warming at less than 0.26°C for a doubling of CO_2 (Idso, 1982).

Where lie the problems? There are many. The question of the biospheric reservoir has already been pointed out (Bolin, 1982). The study also clearly stated the inadequate consideration of storage and circulation

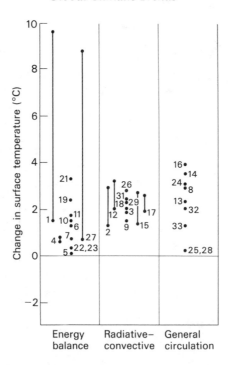

Figure 10.9 Global temperature changes, calculated from various climatic models, for a hypothetical doubling of atmospheric CO_2
Source: after Schlesinger, 1982.

of CO_2 in the ocean. It is quite clear, as others have also pointed out, that the circulation of the deep sea is not well known and the available data are insufficient to verify current theories about that circulation. We know very little about the CO_2 transfer to greater depths in the ocean and the depth of the thermocline and its role in this transfer remains to be explored. In a recent study of the turn-over of the deep waters of the world oceans it was concluded that their replacement-time is between 200 and 500 years (Stuiver *et al.*, 1983). No such time lag appears in any of the climate models. The question of evaporation from the ocean and its thermal effect, the role of increased water vapor in the atmosphere, the proper cloud cover for a higher-temperature earth and its albedo effect, other surface albedo changes with numerous inter-element feedbacks, both positive and negative, call for intensified efforts for modeling, observations for the verification of models, and a highly conservative attitude with respect to conclusions.

There have been a number of statements that a CO_2-induced warming has already occurred and that there is observational evidence for it. These refer particularly to shrinkage of the Antarctic ice sheets (Kukla and Gavin, 1981) and sea level changes (Gornitz *et al.*, 1982). However, there is no detectable decrease of Antarctic sea ice in 9 years of satellite observations (Zwally *et al.*, 1982). There are, as in all such elements, notable fluctuations. In satellite observations between 1967 and 1981 there are ice increases of considerable magnitude. These obscure any CO_2-induced trend and the postulate of such a trend is purely speculative. Also calculated temperature rises of 0.14°C because of CO_2 and 0.1°C because of other trace gas increases for the 1970–80 decade (Lacis *et al.*, 1981) simply disappear in the noisy climatic temperature pattern. There has been an estimate of sea-level rises (Gornitz *et al.*, 1981). These amount to about 10 cm in a century, (figure 10.10), and are probably due to some general melting of the earth's ice and snow cover. Natural warming since the last decades of the nineteenth century is probably a major cause. It is unlikely that clear evidence of a CO_2-induced temperature rise, if it occurs, will be discovered before 2000. The difficulties have been well discussed by Thompson and Schneider (1982).

   The current stand of the CO_2–climate question has been lately comprehensively discussed again (Clark, 1982). It is worth noting here that the eminent atmospheric scientists F. K. Hare (1983), in his review of this book for *Science*, states the only thing agreed upon is the atmosphere CO_2 increase. He then states:

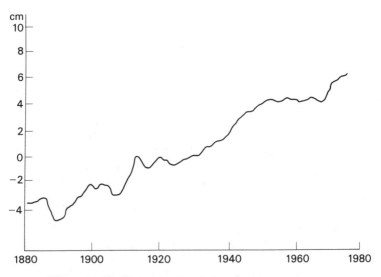

Figure 10.10 Global sea level rises in the past century
Scource: adapted from Gornitz *et al.*, 1981.

The volume is a long litany of uncertainties – of the internal transport processes in the ocean, of ocean atmosphere interaction, of the magnitude of forest and soil carbon wastage, of the future course of fossil-fuel consumption.

He also notes the many "ifs" that lead to the uncertainties. Were the models right, were CO_2 increase to continue, were the present assumptions of the role of the oceans correct, then an unprecedented post-glacial climatic change in global climate could occur next century.

At the end of this brief review of the CO_2 problem it is perhaps worth while to quote the laconic opinion of the members of the Executive Committee of the World Meteorological Organization. At its 34th meeting (Geneva, 7–24 June, 1982) this committee noted

that [the] increasing amount of CO_2 released into the atmosphere as a result of human activity may have far-reaching consequences on the global climate, but that the present state of knowledge does not permit any reliable prediction to be made of future CO_2 concentrations or their impact on climate.

Opportunities for Beneficial Modification

There have been many proposals and many attempts to influence weather and climate to improve natural conditions and mitigate damages (Hess, 1974). Some of them have been successful, others have failed. The successful manipulations have generally been on a small or moderate scale and most of them have been not only beneficial but economically valuable.

Probably the earliest attempts to manage the atmospheric vagaries were made in the hydraulic civilizations of the Near East and China. They introduced the practice of irrigation. In regions of great seasonal differences of precipitation, water is stored during the rainy season and released, principally for agriculture, in the dry season. Use of reservoirs is still an essential practice today. The Romans built large aqueducts from areas with water surplus to those with deficiencies. Engineering has vastly improved these procedures but the principles have remained the same. Use of ground water also is an ancient art. A more doubtful practice is the mining of fossil water, which is, of course, exhaustible. It might be noted here that about 17 percent of the world crop acreage is under irrigation.

Another early artificial weather modification has been the use of windbreaks. In agriculture this has taken the form of shelter belts which are very effective in reducing evaporation and modifying the daily temperature variations.

In areas with much snowfall windbreaks and snow fences are installed along the roads to decrease accumulations from wind-driven snow on the highway. Similarly, special windbreaks have been used to reduce sand motion from dunes on beaches and the fringes of deserts. On the beaches the cabanas also reduce the wind to increase the comfort of bathers. We could include here all housing and clothing which is designed to exclude or modify the atmospheric conditions immediately surrounding persons.

Also very successful on a small scale have been the methods to modify the radiation balance. The principal applications have again been in agriculture. Some of them change the local albedo by use of, for example, white dust to reduce soil temperature or black dust to increase it. Black dust has also been used to hasten the melting of snow covers and of river ice in spring. Into this category also falls the use of black or transparent plastic sheets between or over crops. These are either arranged in rows to conserve soil moisture or used as blankets to provide a greenhouse effect over whole fields. In orchards and vineyards both radiative and sensible heat is produced by artificial heaters to ward off frost. In some areas wind machines are used for that purpose with the aim of destroying a ground inversion of temperature.

Fog has also been successfully controlled if it is composed of super-cooled water droplets, i.e. they are liquid at temperatures below freezing. Some are made to freeze by dry ice or liquid propane and then the difference of vapor pressure over ice and water creates a mass transfer which causes the water drops to disappear and the ice crystals to grow sufficiently large to fall out. The same technique can be applied to low supercooled stratus clouds which will dissipate when so treated. This is a full-fledged technology which is applied at higher-latitude airports during the cold season to improve visibilities.

Less successful have been attempts to augment precipitation by various methods of cloud seeding. Although numerous attempts have been made to add to precipitation in semi-arid lands only few unequivocal successes have resulted. The reason is the inadequately understood physics of clouds, and indiscriminate seeding of clouds with various chemical substances has not advanced the science. Similarly, claims that hails have been dissipated must be viewed with skepticism; attempts to modify severe storms and hurricanes have also been distinctly premature. There is hope that by strictly long-sustained scientific approaches some progress can be made in the future. However there is little hope of alleviating droughts because they are characterized by clear skies with few, if any, modifiable clouds in the sky.

There have also been a number of proposals to modify climate on a large scale. Most of them are extremely expensive engineering schemes with rather unpredictable outcome. Among them are the Russian schemes to reverse the northward flow of Siberian rivers to the south, and another Russian idea that a dam across the Bering Strait would lead to reduction of the Arctic Sea ice. In this class also belongs the French proposition to bring Mediterranean waters into a big depression in the Sahara desert.

Actually the best plan for a beneficial modification of climate is reforestation on as substantial a scale as feasible. This will not only have a good influence on the albedo of the areas so treated but will, at least partially, mitigate whatever threat the CO_2 increases may pose.

The Outlook

There have been a number of predictions of how climate will evolve in the near and more distant future. Some of them are based on the assumed relations of climate to solar variations. Most of them, however, are focused on the CO_2-induced, man-made changes that are expected. The latter usually find their support in models of the atmosphere, calculating the future state on the basis of scenarios of anticipated use of fossil fuels and other economic elements. It is absolutely essential to view any such prediction with a clear understanding of the uncertainties. Figure 10.11 represents these in a schematic fashion. Past performance of a variable is a good, but by no means perfect, guide; models are only as reliable as their realistic representation of nature. The present models all have flaws and yield predictions which are almost an order of magnitude apart. Scenarios can, of course, be constructed at will. They are probably even more afflicted with uncertainties than the atmospheric models. They must project demographic, economic, and political developments, each one having its own uncertainties. This further reduces the climatic prediction to a conditional one: if – then –. Finally we have to contend with speculation both about natural events and human activities. In the natural realm there are volcanic eruptions which in the next few decades can range from massive activity to quiescence. On the human side there are wars, revolutions, and, last but not least, unexpected technological developments.

With the foregoing in mind, let us review some of the predictions. On the natural side it has been stated that there has been a cooling trend in the United States, particularly in the Central region and somewhat less in the East, while the West has warmed. This has been ascribed to the 90-year solar Gleissberg rhythm (Agee, 1982a,b). There is some belief that an upturn is expected in the next few decades. Chances are that this will not be very perceptible in the continuous climatic noise.

The opinion of the National Defense University experts has already been noted, with a majority expectation of slight warming to the end of the century and some increase in U.S. drought frequency. The foremost

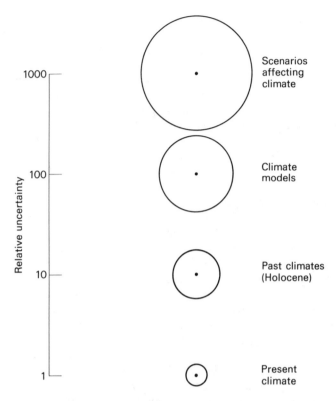

Figure 10.11   Relative uncertainties of climate projections into the twenty-
first century, based on various procedures.

Russian expert in the field is also an advocate of modest warming
(Budyko, 1982). He and his collaborators believe they have noted some
decrease in the Arctic Sea ice, with the rising atmospheric CO_2 as cause.
Budyko's most recent book contains projections for the years 2000 and
2025 of both temperatures and precipitation for the U.S.S.R. He also
projects heat sums above 10°C, a quantity useful for estimating crop
responses. Budyko's projections, with maps of anticipated changes,
based on heat balance models, are by far the most specific ones yet in the
literature. For temperatures the greatest rises for the year 2000 are
presented to be in the Arctic, ranging for winter from about 1.5°C at the
Arctic Circle to 2.5°C near the North Pole. Other seasons and latitudes
are much less affected. For the 2020s not only would the annual heat sums
above 10°C rise by 1500°C in the high latitudes of the Soviet Union but the
water balance (precipitation −evaporation) would also rise notably by

several hundred millimeters. In an elaborate discussion this author places considerable confidence in his projections, all based on the conviction that atmospheric CO_2 will rise inexorably.

Others stick essentially to global values with only relatively vague references to regional impacts. Bach and Breuer (1980) foresee a doubling of CO_2 by the year 2025 and expect a global temperature rise of about 2°C. Flohn projects about 1°C rise for the interval 2000–2010, and 2.5°C for some time between 2020 and 2050, and toward the end of the twenty-first century 4°C global temperature rise.

The mathematical modelers, especially those using three-dimensional general circulation models, do not indulge in dating their predictions. They only show model outputs "if CO_2 doubles or quadruples." They leave it to others to say when this will happen, if it will happen at all.

In spite of frequent citing of a "consensus" about the CO_2 influence on climate (CO_2/Climate Review Panel NRC, 1982) there are still doubts about the final outcome. The principal unsolved problem is the role of the ocean, as has been discussed above (see also Newell and Dopplick, 1979). The main effect could be on the rate at which a temperature rise may occur. The slower the process, the better the chance for other than fossil-fuel energy production. There is no doubt at all that the ocean question needs substantially more work for realistic simulations (Bryan *et al.*, 1982; Thompson and Schneider, 1982).

Clearly, most individuals and certainly most policy-makers do not generally care to make decisions to affect events that may afflict our unborn successors two or three generations removed. There are too many unknowns and uncertainties. One may even raise the question: Is there need to act now? As far as weather and climate are concerned these are some reasonable statements one can make. These presuppose the absence of any major natural calamity, such as a major change in the energy output of the sun, a sudden mass outbreak of volcanoes, or the impact of an asteroid. As we have noted the climate, both globally and locally, has not radically changed in the past few centuries. It is therefore not unreasonable to assume that it will stay within the range of the previously observed values and events. To the year 2000 this is a safe expectation. It is likely to hold also to 2025. Should a 0.5°C global temperature rise occur (from CO_2 or any other cause), it is unlikely to cause ecological upsets. Similarly should it get globally 0.5°C cooler it would be entirely within the realm of experiences of the not-too-distant past. Mankind has been able to cope with such variations. There is little doubt that technology can remedy any difficulties which may arise.

As has been pointed out, the weather extremes are the troublesome factors. It is axiomatic that any extreme that has been observed in the past can be repeated in the future. This applies to temperatures, rain or the lack thereof, snow, high winds, stagnation, or any other weather element, or any combination of elements. Thus, it is perfectly reasonable to project that before the end of the century a severe drought will plague the U.S. Great Plains. It is equally likely that some major hurricanes will strike the Gulf and Atlantic coastlines. One cannot state when such events will occur but it is certain that they will occur. Using the accumulated past climatic data, especially annual extreme values, one can fit suitable distributions to them and make probability estimates for frequency of occurrence. This type of analysis also permits a probability assessment of chances that a prior record value will be exceeded. Information of this type can be used by design engineers, planners, and economists. It is not a deterministic forecast but a stochastic one. The data base for most parts of the earth is readily available and reasonably adequate to turn the past climatic experience into forecasts without date. If properly used they can protect from foolish actions (such as groundnut schemes in East Africa or Aswan dams in Egypt). They can permit us in the climate sector to look with confidence toward the year 2000.

Global 2000 – Critique of the Climate Section

Various sections of this work deal with climate. The term climate, as understood by the authors, is nowhere defined. The text is essentially based on a National Defense University study (NDU, 1978). The main purpose of that study was the assessment of the effects of potential future climatic changes on world food supplies. Again, the term change remained undefined.

The NDU study was predicated on a segment of information for the recent past of temperature and precipitation, for the interval 1880–1975. A group of experts was asked to give individually an estimate of probability of temperature changes for the Northern Hemisphere in five categories. These ranged from no change to large warming and large cooling, all quantitatively expressed. Based on their individual estimates, the experts were also to assess precipitation changes, drought probabilities in mid-latitudes and the Sahel, as well as influences on Asiatic monsoons. The length of growing season was also included. Carbon dioxide and turbidity influences on climate were to be specified as anthropogenic climatic parameters. The responses were then combined by a Delphi technique based on self-rating and peer-rating of the expertise of the respondents. The principal result was a weighted estimate that by the year 2000 a moderate warming of the Northern Hemisphere could be expected, with a tendency of views leaning toward slight warming placing it at 0.5°C. Much of this was based on a scenario of increasing atmospheric carbon dioxide caused by rising use of fossil fuels and increasing deforestation. The effects of increasing particulates as a counterbalancing influence appeared to be a less important factor in the global heat balance but other anthropogenic trace gases would add to the CO_2 burden in the atmosphere. These were also anticipated to reduce the stratospheric ozone concentration. There was no clear-cut projection of precipitation trends although a "sentiment" to anticipate more frequent drought in the central U.S. was noted.

The report does contain critical views on the climate projections because it used too short a segment of the past, especially for judging the effect of weather on crops. But one must credit it with a few statements that cannot be faulted, such as: "Because of the difficulty of climatological modeling, it is not possible currently to produce generally agreed-upon quantitative climate projections." That should have appeared in bold type. And the conclusions of the section "Climate Changes and the Environment" state:

Both the National Defense University survey of expert opinion and the analysis of the possible climatic implications of the Global 2000 Study's other projections lead to the same general conclusions: (1) Climate will continue to vary in the future, just as it always has in the past, in a largely unpredictable manner. (2) Apart from this characteristic variability, no substantial net trend of climate in the direction of either warming or cooling is anticipated between now and 2000.

That is an admirable statement in the face of the ignorance in the year 1980 when it was presumably written.

In the executive summary, the section on "Impacts on the World's Atmosphere and Climate," we read that air quality is likely to worsen and that emission of sulfur and nitrogen oxides lead to acid rain. It states clearly: "The effects of acid rain are not yet fully understood," but cites observations of ecological damage attributed to it. Then the text turns to the effects of CO_2 and estimates the increase by the year 2000 "by nearly a third higher than preindustrial level." This would bring CO_2 to about 370 ppmV, an extrapolation based on a growth rate of fossil fuel use increase of 2 percent per year. It is then stated that if this were to continue at this rate the atmospheric CO_2 concentration would double by the middle of next century. Should deforestation substantially reduce the tropical forests the doubling would occur sooner. And:

The result could be a significant alteration of precipitation patterns around the world, and a 2 to 3°C rise in temperatures in the middle latitudes of the earth. Agriculture and other human endeavors would have great difficulty in adapting to such large, rapid changes of temperature. Even a 1°C increase in average global temperatures would make the earth's climate warmer than it has been at any time in the last 1,000 years.

Again, we jump far ahead of 2000. The projected changes in precipitation are based on uncertain models but no mention of this uncertainty is made. It would appear that there is a contrast between a 2–3°C rise of temperature in middle latitudes and a global rise of 1°C, but both are essentially equivalent. Agriculture in high latitudes would have a "field" day and such a change in five to seven decades seems hardly a "rapid change" in a fast-moving world.

The report then proceeds to be concerned about a tripling and quadrupling of CO_2 in the atmosphere with great rises in polar temperatures leading to melting of ice and flooding of coastal cities. This certainly carries us far beyond the year 2000, presumably to the twenty-second century. There seems to be a bit of the "Jupiter Effect" that has crept into the report.

Finally, the problem of emissions of nitrous oxides and chlorofluorocarbons and their potential effect on the ozone layer is briefly summarized. The resulting increase of solar ultraviolet at the surface of the earth is mentioned but no other climatic consequences are mentioned. The effects on skin cancer rates and crop damage are the main consequences cited.

Unfortunately, the letter of transmittal extrapolated also to 2050 and stated:

Atmospheric concentrations of carbon dioxide and ozone-depleting chemicals are expected to increase at rates that could alter the world's climate and upper atmosphere significantly by 2050. Acid rain from increased combustion of fossil fuels (especially coal) threatens damage to lakes, soils, and crops.

Note that this excludes the presumed small atmospheric changes and consequences to 2000.

Obviously such statements as cited above had further rippling effects and thus the Council on Environmental Quality and the Department of State in a report issued in January 1981 called for action to avert the climatic disaster.

Their text essentially copies the wording from *Global 2000*, with a doubling of atmospheric CO_2 due to fossil fuel consumption, the 2–3°C middle-latitude temperature rise. It then adds: "Such climate changes could in turn lead to widespread agricultural, ecological, social, and economic disruption." They hedge then: "At present, the nature, time and onset, and regional distribution of these impacts are not at all well understood." Nonetheless, they recommend consideration of the CO_2

problem in developing energy policy and examination of alternative energy futures.

Dealing with the ozone depletion again *Global 2000* is quoted verbatim (without quotation marks) and it is recommended piously that "further domestic and international action is called for." This should principally take the form of research on the problem, encouragement of international bodies with tasks in this field, and the promulgation of regulations limiting ozone-depleting emissions.

Finally, they deal with acid precipitation: "The extent to which acid rain will adversely affect food production is still unknown, but it could be significant over the next 20 years." The text also refers to the cross-border transport of acid rain ingredients between the United States and Canada. It envisages a "threat" by acid precipitation and then recommends research into identification of natural and man-made sources and transport patterns, as well as bilateral agreements between Canada and the U.S. The report urges further intensified efforts under the Clean Air Act to reduce this hazard.

The text notes that "the results of scientific research on the atmosphere have been useful to policy makers in dealing with these [climate] problems, but too often the information available is too thin a foundation of basic knowledge to provide unequivocal answers." The acute need for climate knowledge to formulate policies for energy, food production, and other activities requires that knowledge, and hence U.S. support of the World Climate Program, is advocated. Climatologists who designed these programs can only applaud this sentiment.

Although much of the climate portion of *Global 2000* and its sequel is quite sound, the conclusions drawn from them in the news media picked only the frightening aspects up for communication to the public: a dangerously heated earth, deluges, and crop-damaging rains.

There has been little technical critique. Clearly the time interval for the climatological analysis must be lengthened and extended to all reliable items of information. Clear definitions of terms must be used. There is need to stress the uncertainties and point out the failures of some of the past speculative projections. The dire tone of impending doom has little place in a scientific analysis. *Global 2000* has also too little emphasis on the role of feedback mechanisms in the climate system and its statistical nature. Further, how far into the future should we project? Is the cut-off point 2000, 2025, 2050, 2100?

Much new relevant material has accumulated in the past 2 years, since *Global 2000* appeared. It will throw some light on the issues.

Appendix: Tables

Long time series of data used for climatological analysis: these are partially derived from meteorological observations and partially proxy data covering earlier years but are parallel with meteorological observations in recent years. The examples given are:

Table 10.1   Index of Western European summer temperatures, 1453–1973 (from Bray, 1982).

Table 10.2   Northern Hemisphere annual temperature anomalies, 1881–1975 (from Borzenkova *et al.*, 1976).

Table 10.3   New interpretation of Northern Hemisphere annual temperature anomalies, 1881–1978 (from Vinnikov, K. Ya., G. V. Grusa, V. F. Zakharov, A. A. Kirilov, N. P. Kovynena and E. Ya. Rankova (1980) *Soviet Meteorology and Hydrology*, **6**, 1–10).

Table 10.4   Reconstructed Northern Hemisphere temperature departures, 1579–1880 (from Groveman and Landsberg, 1979).

Table 10.5   Standard errors of estimate applicable to data in table 10.4 (ibid.).

Table 10.6.   Atmospheric concentrations of CO_2 in the atmosphere in ppmV, 1958–1980 (from Keeling, C. D., R. B. Bastacow, and T. P. Whorf; Measurements of the concentration of carbon dioxide at Mauna Loa Observatory, Hawaii. In W. C. Clark (1982), pp. 377–85.

(There are many other long climatological time series and tree ring series available that could be added or listed.)

TABLE 10.1 PERCENTAGE SUMMER TEMPERATURE (JUNE–AUGUST) BASED ON MAINLY PROXY DATA. A.D. 1453–1973. VALUES FOR 1453–1483, 1623–1658, AND 1880–1973 ARE BASED ON ONE DATA SET ONLY

0–49	50–99	1450–99	1500–49	1550–99	1600–49	1650–99	1700–49	1750–99	1800–49	1850–99	1900–49	1950–99
0	50	—	86	68	8	32	25	44	61	41	61	62
1	51	—	31	74	12	54	50	28	58	32	61	43
2	52	—	37	81	29	48	35	36	48	52	27	57
3	53	0	58	67	89	56	38	51	54	29	24	50
4	54	0	83	53	39	28	59	30	54	37	46	21
5	55	0	57	6	79	54	44	45	35	40	54	76
6	56	0	71	91	10	44	63	28	51	41	55	23
7	57	50	56	38	60	58	54	50	64	67	11	56
8	58	50	55	75	49	32	45	41	62	60	40	48
9	59	0	75	42	31	49	41	61	27	67	18	77
10	60	0	70	42	78	55	40	59	39	18	35	51
11	61	100	6	29	65	47	39	53	56	49	86	42
12	62	50	51	74	59	40	43	69	22	36	27	30
13	63	75	48	19	47	36	19	52	26	29	35	38
14	64	100	71	63	29	52	43	64	28	39	52	45
15	65	50	19	43	77	48	34	38	41	71	37	32
16	66	0	90	25	92	67	29	42	3	44	31	43
17	67	100	25	79	13	50	36	26	26	46	54	52
18	68	25	71	16	51	54	70	39	68	80	41	44
19	69	0	63	18	60	62	70	35	54	54	34	58
20	70	75	26	12	60	48	33	23	35	68	21	61
21	71	—	77	35	19	53	35	35	23	44	69	41
22	72	50	76	78	59	39	36	55	82	49	13	24
23	73	100	83	7	52	35	49	41	17	47	44	56
24	74	100	36	17	62	25	54	47	32	55	30	
25	75	100	80	73	32	6	2	53	62	47	58	

0–49	50–99	1450–99	1500–49	1550–99	1600–49	1650–99	1700–49	1750–99	1800–49	1850–99	1900–49	1950–99
26	76	33	23	65	44	76	65	37	73	52	56	
27	77	50	11	17	14	44	61	31	49	44	36	
28	78	100	66	50	8	52	62	59	52	53	37	
29	79	100	7	10	66	57	47	63	32	16	40	
30	80	100	53	47	60	46	36	59	36	47	51	
31	81	0	74	11	56	48	53	77	60	33	35	
32	82	100	77	45	26	27	47	35	45	29	59	
33	83	100	18	52	38	46	56	64	44	33	87	
34	84	69	79	76	46	62	51	41	67	61	68	
35	85	22	68	13	46	37	29	41	50	33	70	
36	86	80	92	42	46	62	62	42	40	44	50	
37	87	49	65	12	82	34	53	34	48	67	58	
38	88	2	37	32	80	35	45	59	36	12	49	
39	89	22	72	40	54	29	43	37	38	44	50	
40	90	23	88	79	44	35	15	40	41	21	58	
41	91	1	65	19	36	47	48	49	31	34	58	
42	92	0	0	57	30	19	37	41	59	27	53	
43	93	64	65	42	30	39	43	48	24	75	56	
44	94	82	45	15	66	29	39	68	43	32	57	
45	95	88	88	35	66	10	28	42	25	48	58	
46	96	60	78	65	44	36	44	35	79	55	35	
47	97	44	73	7	44	32	54	48	48	63	87	
48	98	23	32	20	34	12	42	67	39	45	38	
49	99	73	50	89	22	47	37	26	44	85	75	

TABLE 10.2 NORTHERN HEMISPHERE ANNUAL TEMPERATURE ANOMALY (°C) REPORTED BY BORZENKOVA, et al. (1976) (DATA CURRENT AS OF OCTOBER 1981)

Decade	\multicolumn{10}{c}{Year of decade}

Decade	0	1	2	3	4	5	6	7	8	9
1880		−0.10	−0.17	−0.20	−0.50	−0.51	−0.46	−0.40	−0.32	−0.07
1890	−0.13	−0.18	−0.32	−0.31	−0.30	−0.20	−0.17	−0.02	−0.20	0.01
1900	0.03	0.00	−0.35	−0.33	−0.33	−0.35	−0.12	−0.34	−0.16	−0.17
1910	−0.30	−0.04	−0.32	−0.29	0.01	0.02	−0.12	−0.35	−0.25	−0.10
1920	0.02	0.13	0.05	0.10	0.08	0.15	0.19	0.14	0.18	−0.02
1930	0.22	0.22	0.22	−0.12	0.23	0.15	0.16	0.36	0.43	0.26
1940	0.25	0.15	0.19	0.31	0.27	0.08	0.13	0.18	0.16	0.17
1950	0.09	0.12	0.11	0.32	0.08	0.07	−0.12	0.12	0.20	0.21
1960	0.20	0.13	0.16	0.11	−0.28	−0.24	−0.15	0.10	−0.11	−0.17
1970	0.15	0.05	−0.35	0.17	0.11	0.13				

TABLE 10.3 NORTHERN HEMISPHERE ANNUAL TEMPERATURE ANOMALY (°C) REPORTED BY VINNIKOV, et al. (1980) (DATA CURRENT AS OF NOVEMBER 1981)

Decade	0	1	2	3	4	5	6	7	8	9
1880		−0.14	−0.28	−0.21	−0.50	−0.50	−0.42	−0.42	−0.30	−0.08
1890	−0.15	−0.27	−0.28	−0.31	−0.29	−0.18	−0.16	−0.05	−0.18	0.03
1900	0.03	0.03	−0.30	−0.28	−0.28	−0.32	−0.08	−0.32	−0.16	−0.19
1910	−0.27	−0.06	−0.26	−0.21	0.00	0.04	−0.12	−0.32	−0.23	−0.10
1920	−0.01	0.17	0.05	0.12	0.09	0.16	0.24	0.16	0.23	−0.09
1930	0.27	0.29	0.26	−0.11	0.30	0.15	0.17	0.39	0.53	0.33
1940	0.32	0.17	0.26	0.35	0.33	0.07	0.18	0.29	0.20	0.16
1950	0.05	0.22	0.21	0.41	0.12	0.09	−0.12	0.11	0.22	0.24
1960	0.22	0.15	0.16	0.13	−0.19	−0.11	−0.07	0.15	−0.05	−0.19
1970	0.15	−0.01	−0.29	0.17	0.11	0.14	−0.12	0.17	0.08	

TABLE 10.4   RECONSTRUCTED NORTHERN HEMISPHERE
TEMPERATURE DEPARTURES

Year	0	1	2	3	4	5	6	7	8	9
1570										+0.04
1580	−0.28	−0.23	−0.16	−0.13	−0.29	−0.13	−0.09	−0.10	−0.32	−0.16
1590	−0.25	−0.09	−0.09	−0.01	−0.06	−0.21	−0.08	−0.36	−0.03	−0.40
1600	−0.31	−0.55	−0.43	−0.28	−0.34	−0.36	−0.43	−0.75	−0.66	−0.72
1610	−0.69	−0.48	−0.52	−0.43	−0.41	−0.67	−0.63	−0.51	−0.50	−0.43
1620	−0.51	−0.44	−0.47	−0.39	−0.36	−0.30	−0.32	−0.42	−0.32	−0.34
1630	−0.28	−0.35	−0.20	−0.26	−0.25	−0.12	−0.09	−0.08	−0.14	+0.05
1640	+0.04	−0.14	−0.21	−0.12	−0.31	−0.11	−0.09	−0.11	−0.18	−0.15
1650	−0.19	−0.19	−0.16	−0.05	−0.08	−0.13	−0.09	−0.08	−0.02	−0.15
1660	−0.09	−0.10	−0.05	−0.10	−0.04	−0.17	−0.08	−0.30	−0.17	−0.31
1670	−0.26	−0.27	−0.32	−0.39	−0.40	−0.53	−0.43	−0.47	−0.43	−0.39
1680	−0.55	−0.44	−0.26	−0.36	−0.41	−0.24	−0.04	−0.29	−0.47	−0.26
1690	−0.20	−0.30	−0.30	−0.17	−0.25	−0.50	−0.50	−0.43	−0.44	−0.36
1700	−0.29	−0.24	−0.06	−0.15	−0.05	−0.17	−0.24	−0.24	−0.22	−0.49
1710	−0.20	−0.29	−0.34	−0.32	−0.20	−0.25	−0.32	−0.33	−0.33	−0.35
1720	−0.35	−0.26	−0.17	−0.07	−0.19	−0.09	+0.23	+0.03	−0.01	+0.03
1730	−0.01	−0.19	−0.26	−0.24	−0.39	−0.33	−0.18	−0.22	+0.03	−0.18
1740	−0.36	−0.12	−0.06	+0.14	+0.02	−0.06	+0.09	0.00	−0.08	−0.17
1750	−0.08	−0.25	−0.11	−0.04	−0.01	−0.21	−0.02	−0.14	−0.20	−0.05
1760	+0.03	+0.08	−0.04	−0.11	−0.14	+0.09	+0.30	+0.11	0.00	−0.35
1770	−0.30	−0.33	−0.16	−0.14	−0.16	+0.04	−0.17	−0.33	−0.24	−0.07
1780	−0.02	−0.10	−0.48	−0.33	−0.58	−0.34	−0.33	−0.01	−0.33	−0.42
1790	−0.20	−0.21	−0.21	−0.37	−0.31	−0.38	−0.13	−0.37	−0.22	−0.78
1800	−0.63	−0.42	−0.49	−0.35	−0.13	−0.57	−0.63	−0.55	−0.56	−0.58
1810	−0.61	−0.59	−0.87	−0.62	−0.69	−0.58	−0.78	−0.57	−0.48	−0.27
1820	−0.41	−0.05	−0.04	−0.04	−0.08	−0.08	+0.40	+0.24	+0.41	+0.17
1830	+0.21	−0.02	−0.05	−0.30	−0.14	−0.35	−0.49	−0.37	−0.38	−0.33
1840	−0.32	−0.39	−0.26	−0.31	−0.51	−0.39	−0.25	−0.11	−0.42	−0.26
1850	−0.32	−0.22	−0.05	−0.20	−0.19	−0.30	−0.12	−0.07	−0.13	−0.47
1860	−0.29	−0.03	−0.13	−0.25	−0.20	−0.11	−0.27	−0.32	−0.20	−0.25
1870	−0.20	−0.24	+0.09	−0.05	−0.11	−0.23	−0.01	−0.02	+0.03	−0.16
1880	−0.09									

TABLE 10.5 STANDARD ERROR OF ESTIMATE FOR MULTIPLE
REGRESSION EQUATIONS USED IN RECONSTRUCTION OF
NORTHERN HEMISPHERE TEMPERATURE

Equation used for reconstruction of the years:	Standard error of estimate (SEE) (°C)
1579–1658	0.162
1659–1705	0.147
1706–37; 1741, 1764	0.143
1738–40; 1742–56	0.138
1757–74	0.134
1775–7	0.130
1778–80; 1787	0.131
1781–6; 1788–96	0.127
1797–1801	0.118
1802–16; 1821–2	0.123
1817–20	0.120
1823–5	0.117
1826–31	0.114
1832–40	0.128
1841–5	0.120
1846–65	0.122
1866–71	0.119
1872–80	0.114

TABLE 10.6 ATMOSPHERIC CONCENTRATIONS OF CARBON DIOXIDE AT MAUNA LOA OBSERVATORY, HAWAII, IN PPM (DATA CURRENT AS OF JANUARY 1982)

Year	Jan.	Feb.	Mar.	Apr.	May	June	July	Aug.	Sept.	Oct.	Nov.	Dec.	Ave.
1958	mv	mv	315.58	317.18	317.43	mv	315.71	314.71	313.04	mv	313.07	314.34	mv
1959	315.16	315.97	316.37	317.40	317.96	317.82	316.23	314.54	313.60	313.03	314.57	315.32	315.66
1960	316.10	316.68	317.37	318.79	319.63	319.29	317.86	315.55	313.85	313.64	314.61	315.81	316.59
1961	316.54	317.34	318.12	319.06	320.20	319.44	318.24	316.52	314.57	315.13	315.75	316.73	317.30
1962	317.70	318.29	319.37	320.25	320.84	320.43	319.35	317.13	316.01	315.19	316.42	317.47	318.20
1963	318.45	318.82	319.72	321.06	321.87	321.22	319.44	317.48	315.89	315.83	316.72	317.98	318.71
1964	319.17	mv	mv	mv	322.08	321.92	320.42	318.58	316.68	316.65	317.60	318.49	mv
1965	319.32	320.36	320.82	322.06	322.17	321.95	321.20	318.81	317.82	317.37	318.93	319.09	319.99
1966	319.94	320.98	321.81	323.03	323.36	323.11	321.65	319.64	317.86	317.25	319.06	320.26	320.66
1967	321.65	321.81	322.36	323.67	324.17	323.39	321.93	320.29	318.58	318.60	319.98	321.25	321.47
1968	321.88	322.47	323.17	324.23	324.88	324.75	323.47	321.34	319.56	319.45	320.45	321.92	322.30
1969	323.40	324.21	325.33	326.31	327.01	326.24	325.37	323.12	321.85	321.31	322.31	323.72	324.18
1970	324.60	325.57	326.55	327.80	327.80	327.54	326.28	324.63	323.12	323.11	323.99	325.09	325.51
1971	326.12	326.61	327.16	327.92	329.14	328.80	327.52	325.62	323.61	323.80	325.10	326.25	326.47
1972	326.93	327.83	327.95	329.91	330.22	329.25	328.11	326.39	324.97	325.32	326.54	327.71	327.59
1973	328.73	329.69	330.47	331.69	332.65	332.24	331.03	329.36	327.60	327.29	328.28	328.79	329.82
1974	329.45	330.89	331.63	332.85	333.28	332.47	331.34	329.53	327.57	327.57	328.53	329.69	330.40
1975	330.45	330.97	331.64	332.87	333.61	333.55	331.90	330.05	328.58	328.31	329.41	330.63	331.00
1976	331.63	332.46	333.36	334.45	334.82	334.32	333.05	330.87	329.24	328.87	330.18	331.50	332.06
1977	332.81	333.23	334.55	335.82	336.44	335.99	334.65	332.41	331.32	330.73	332.05	333.53	333.63
1978	334.66	335.07	336.33	337.39	337.65	337.57	336.25	334.39	332.44	332.25	333.59	334.76	335.20
1979	335.89	336.44	337.63	338.54	339.06	338.95	337.41	335.71	333.68	333.69	335.05	336.53	336.55
1980	337.81	338.16	339.88	340.57	341.19	340.87	339.25	337.19	335.49	335.51	336.63	337.74	338.36

Note

1   Recently Fritts and Lough (1983) have presented another estimate for northern hemisphere temperatures based on western U.S. tree ring data. While there are considerable differences between the two reconstructions in part of the record, the total range estimates are closely alike.

References

With exception of some older citations, all references given here are material which has appeared since *Global 2000* was written.

Agee, E. M. (1982a) Terrestrial cooling and solar variability, NASA Contractor Report (NASA CR-161985). Marshall Space Flight Center, Alabama.

——, (1982b) Diagnosis of twentieth century temperature records at West Lafayette, Indiana. *Climatic Change*, **4**, 399–418.

Anderson, D. E. and H. E. Landsberg (1979) Detailed structure of pH in hydrometeors, *Env. Sci. Technol.*, **13**, 992–4.

Arrhenius, S. (1896) On the influence of carbonic acid in the air upon the temperature of the ground, *Phil. Mag.*, **41**, 237–75.

Bach, W. and G. Breuer (1980) Wie dringend ist das CO_2 Problem? *Umschau*, **80**, 520–1.

Baier, W. (1977) Crop weather models and their use in yield assessments, World Meteorological Organization, Technical Note No. 151, Geneva.

Bolin, B. (1982) "Biogeochemical processes and climatic modelling." International Meteorological Institute in Stockholm, Report DM-39.

Borzenkova, I. I., K. Ya. Vinnikov, L. P. Spirina, and P. I. Stechnooskii (1976) Izmenenie temperatury vozducha severnogo polushariya za period 1881–1975. *Meteorologiya i Gidrologiya*, no. 7, pp. 27–35.

Bowden, M. J., R. M. Kates, P. A. Kay, W. E. Riebsame, R. A. Warrick, D. L. Johnson, H. A. Gould and D. Weiner (1981) The effect of climate fluctuations of human activities: two hypotheses. In T. M. L. Wigley, M. S. Ingram, and G. Farmer (eds), *Climate and History*, pp. 479–513. Cambridge University Press.

Bray, J. R. (1982) Alpine glacial advance in relation to a proxy summer temperature index based mainly on wine harvest dates. *Boreas*, **11**, 1–10.

Bryan, K., F. G. Komro, S. Manabe and M. J. Spelman (1982) Transient climate response to atmospheric carbon dioxide. *Science*, **215**, 56–8.

Budyko, M. I. (1982) *The Earth's Climate: Past and Future*. Academic Press (Int'l. Geophysics Series, vol. 29.). New York.

Center for Environmental Assessment Services, U.S. Economic impact of the severe winter of 1982, Env. Data & Info. Service, NOAA, Washington, D.C.

Clark, W. C. (ed.) (1982) *Carbon Dioxide Review: 1982*. Oxford University Press, New York.

CO₂/Climate Review Panel (1982). *Carbon Dioxide and Climate: A Second Assessment*. National Academy Press, Washington, D.C.

Council on Environmental Quality and the Department of State (1980) *The Technical Report*. Government Printing Office, Washington, D.C.

Council on Environmental Quality (1981) *Global Energy Futures and the Carbon Dioxide Problem*. Government Printing Office, Washington, D.C.

Craddock, J. M. (1976) Annual rainfall in England since 1725, *Q. J. R. Meteorol. Soc.*, **102**, 823–40.

Currie, R. G. (1981) Evidence for the 18.6 year M_N signal in temperature and drought conditions in North America since 1800 A.D. *J. Geophys. Res.*, **86**, 11055–64.

Diaz, H. F. (1980) "A Long Record of Weather Observations in Southeastern Iowa 1839–1979," NOAA NCC (Historical Climatological Series), Asheville, NC.

Dütsch, H.-U. (1981) Die Ozonschicht der Atmosphäre, ihre Erforschung und ihre Bedeutung. *Annal. d. Meteorol.*, N.F. no. 17, pp. 16–22.

Eddy, John A., R. L. Gilliland, and D. V. Hoyt (1982) Changes in the solar constant and climatic effects. *Nature*, **300**, 689–93.

Flohn, H. (1980) Geophysikalische Grundlagen einer anthropogenen Klimamodifikation, Veröff. *Joachim Jungius – Gesellschaft d. Wissenschaften, Hamburg*, **44**, 191–218.

——, (1981) Short-term climatic fluctuations and their economic role. In T. M. L. Wigley, M. J. Ingram, and G. Farmer (eds), *Climate and History*, pp. 310–18. Cambridge University Press.

Fritts, H. C. and J. M. Lough (1983) Estimating average Northern Hemisphere annual temperatures from 1602 to 1982 using western North American arid site tree rings, Second Conference on Climate Variations, American Meteorological Society, 10–14 January 1983, New Orleans: Abstracts, p. 44.

Galloway, J. N., G. E. Likens, W. C. Keene and J. M. Miller (1982) The composition of precipitation in remote areas of the world, *J. Geophys. Res.*, **87**, 8771–86.

Gornitz, V., S. Lebedeff, and J. Hansen (1981) Global sea ice trend in the past century. *Science*, **215**, 1611–14.

Groveman, B. S. and H. E. Landsberg (1979) Simulated northern hemisphere temperature departures 1579–1880. *Geophys. Res. Lett.*, **6**, 762–9.

Hakkarinen, I. M. and H. E. Landsberg (1981) "Precipitation Fluctuations in Monsoon Asia During the Last 100 Years," University of Maryland, Department of Meteorology, Publication No. 81–191, College Park, MD.

Hansen, J. E. (1982), Global climatic changes due to increasing atmospheric CO_2 and trace gases. Testimony presented at Joint Hearing on Carbon Dioxide Research and the Greenhouse Effect. U.S. House of Representatives, Subcommittee on Natural Resources, Agriculture Research and Environment and the Subcommittee on Investigations and Oversight of the House and Technology Committee, 25 March, 1982.

——, G. Russel, D. Rind, P. Stone, A. Lauis, S. Lebedoff, R. Ruedy, and L. Travis (1983), Efficient Three Dimensional Global Models for Climate Studies: Models I and II, Monthly Weather Review, **III**, 609–62.

Hare, F. K. (1983) The Buildup of CO₂ (book review of W. C. Clark (ed.), *Carbon Dioxide Review 1982*, Oxford University Press). *Science*, **219**, 283.

Hess, W. N. (ed.) (1974) *Weather and Climate Modification*. John Wiley & Sons, New York.

Hinrichsen, D. (1982) Acid indigestion in Stockholm, *Ambio*, **11**, 320–1.

Hughes, P. (1982) Weather, climate and economics. *Sea Technology*, June 1982, pp. 32–4.

Idso, S. B. (1982) *Carbon Dioxide: Friend or Foe?* IBR Press, Tempe, AZ.

International Institute for Applied Systems Analysis (1981) "Life on a Warmer Earth – Possible Climatic Consequences of Man-Made Global Warming," Executive Report 3 (based on research by H. Flohn at IIASA), Laxenburg.

Jacoby, G. C. and L. D. Ulan (1982) Reconstruction of past ice conditions in a Hudson Bay estuary using tree rings. *Nature*, **298**, 637–9.

Jaeschke, W., H. Berresheim, and H.-W. Georgii (1982) Sulfur emissions from Mt. Etna. *J. Geophys. Res.*, **87**, 7253–61.

Josephson, J. (1982) Air pollution baselines from glacier studies. *Env. Sci. Technol.*, **16**, 437A-440A.

Kates, R. W. (1980) Climate and society: lessons from recent events. *Weather*, **35**, 17–25.

Kellogg, W. W. and R. Schware (1981) *Climatic Change and Society – Consequences of Increasing Atmospheric Carbon Dioxide*. Westview Press, Boulder, CO.

——, and R. Schware (1982) Society, science and climatic change. *Foreign Affairs*, **60** (5), 1076–1109.

Kemp, D. D. (1982) The drought of 1804–1805 in Central North America. *Weather*, **37**, 34–41.

Kerr, R. A. (1983) Orbital variation – ice age link strengthened. *Science*, **219**, 272–274.

Kukla, G. and I. Gavin (1981) Summer ice and carbon dioxide. *Science*, **214**, 497–503.

Lacis, A., J. Hansen, P. Lee, T. Mitchell and S. Lebedeff (1981) Greenhouse effect of trace gases, 1970–1980. *Geophys. Res. Lett.*, **8**, 1035–8.

Landsberg, H. (1954) Some observations on the pH of precipitation elements, *Arch. Meteorol., Geophys., Biokl.*, Ser. A, **7**, 219–26.

——, (1980) Meteorological effects of rejected heat. *Ann. N.Y. Acad. Sci.*, **339**, 569–74.

——, (1981) *The Urban Climate*. Academic Press, New York.

Lauscher, F. (1981) Säkulare Schwankungen der Dezenniemittel und extreme Jahreswerte der Temperaturen in allen Erdteilen, Zentralanstalt für Meteorologie und Geodynamik, Publikation 252, Wien.

Manley, G. (1974) Central England temperatures: monthly means 1659–1973, *Q. J. Roy. Meteorol. Soc.*, **100**, 389–405.

Mass, C. and S. H. Schneider, (1977) Statistical evidence on the influence of sunspots and volcanic dust on long-term temperature records. *J. Atmos. Sci.*, **34**, 1995–2004.

Matthes, F. E. (1939) Report of the Committee on Glaciers. *Trans. Am. Geophys. Un.* **20**, 518–23.

Maunder, W. J. (1981) National economic indicators: the importance of weather. In L. D. B. Hunan and E. W. Kinsley (eds), *Man, Environment and Planning*, pp. 41–60. (Essays in Honor of Ronald Lisler). Department of Geography, University of Otago.

314   *H. E. Landsberg*

Mitchell, J. M., Jr. (1963) On the world-wide pattern of secular temperature change. *UNESCO Arid Zone Res.* **20**, 161–81.

——, C. W. Stockton and D. M. Meko (1978) Evidence of a 22-year rhythm of drought in the Western United States related to the Hale solar cycle since the 17th century. In: B. M. McCormac and T. A. Seliga (eds) *Solar–terrestrial Influences on Weather and Climate*, pp. 125–43. Reidel, Dordrecht.

National Defense University, Research Directorate (1978) *Climate Change to the year 2000*. Fort Lesley McNair, Washington, D.C.

National Defense University, Research Directorate (1981) *Crop Yields and Climatic Change in the year 2000*. Fort Leslie McNair, Washington, D.C., vol. I.

Newell, R. E. and T. G. Dopplick (1979) Questions concerning the possible influence of anthropogenic CO_2 on atmospheric temperature. *J. Appl. Meteorol.*, **18**, 822–5.

Olson, J. S. (1982) Earth's vegetation and atmospheric carbon dioxide. In W. C. Clark (ed.), *Carbon Dioxide Review 1982*, pp. 388–98. Oxford University Press.

Panel on Stratospheric Chemistry and Transport (1979) *Stratospheric Ozone Depletion by Halocarbons: Chemistry and Transport*. National Academy of Sciences, Washington, D.C.

——, (1982) *Causes of Effects of Stratospheric Ozone Reduction: An Update*. National Academy Press, Washington, D.C.

Peters, N. E., R. A. Schroeder, and D. E. Troutman (1982) Temporal trends in the acidity of precipitation and surface waters of New York; Geological Survey Water – Supply Paper 2188, U.S. Gov't. Printing Office, Washington, D.C.

Physikalisch-Meteorologisches Observatorium und Weltstrahlungszentrum (1981), *Jahresbericht 1980*, Publikation no. 582, Davos-Dorf, Switzerland.

Record, F., D. V. Bubenick, and R. J. Kindya (1982) *Acid Rain Information Book*, Noyes Data Corporation, Park Ridge, NJ.

Schlesinger, M. E. (1982) "CO_2-induced climate warming: a review of model research and prospectus for first detectability." Climate Research Institute, Oregon State University, Report No. 36, Corvallis, OR.

Schönwiese, C. D. (1979) *Klimaschwankungen*. Springer Verlag, Berlin.

Sellers, W. (1974) "Climatic Cause-and-Effect (Feedback) Linkages;" The diagram was designed by Sellers for a symposium on climate but first published with attribution in: Kellogg, W. W. and S. H. Schneider, (1974) Climate stabilization: for better or for worse?, *Science*, **186**, 1163–72.

Simkin, T., L. Liebert, L. McCelland, D. Bridge, C. Newhall and J. H. Latter (1981), *Volcanoes of the World*. Hutchinson Ross, Stroudsburg, PA.

Stensland, G. J. and R. G. Semonin (1982) Another interpretation of the pH trend in the United States. *Bull. Am. Meteorol. Soc.*, **63**, 1277–84.

Stuiver, M., P. D. Quay, and H. G. Ostlund (1983), Abyssal water carbon-14 distribution and the age of the world ocean. *Science*, **219**, 849–51.

Szabo, M. F., M. P. Esposito, and P. W. Spaite (1982). "Acid Rain: Commentary on Controversial Issues and Observations on the Role of Fuel Burning." DOE Contract Report DE82-016914, Pedco Environmental, Inc., Cincinnati, Ohio.

Thompson, S. L. and S. H. Schneider (1982) Carbon dioxide and climate: has a signal been observed yet? *Nature*, **295**, 645–6.

——, and S. H. Schneider (1982) Carbon dioxide and climate: the importance of realistic geography in estimating transient temperature response. *Science*, **217**, 1031–3.

Vinnikov, K. Ya., Gruza, G. V., Zakharov, V. F., Nirilov, A. A., Konyneva, N. P. and Rankova, E. Ya. (1980) "Current Climatic Changes in the Northern Hemisphere," *Soviet Meteorology and Hydrology*, **6**, 1–10.

Thorarinson, S. (1981) Greetings from Iceland – ashfalls and volcanic aerosols in Scandinavia. *Geografiska Annaler*, **63** A (3–4), 109–118.

Tolba, M. K. (1982) The global environment: retrospect and prospect. *Mazingira*, **6**, (2), 24–31.

Tyson, P. D. (1981) Climate and desertification in Southern Africa, *Geo-Journal*, Supplementary Issue 2, 3–10.

Warrick, R. A. (1980) Drought on the Great Plains: A case study of research on climate and society in the U.S. In J. Ausubel and A. K. Biswas (eds), *Climatic Constraints and Human Activities*, pp. 93–123. IIASA Proceedings Series, Vol. 10, Pergamon Press, Oxford.

——, and M. J. Bowden (1981) The changing impacts of droughts in the Great Plains. In M. P. Lavern and M. E. Baker (eds), *The Great Plains Perspectives and Prospects*, pp. 111–37. Center for Great Plains Studies, University of Nebraska, Lincoln.

Washington, W. M. and R. M. Chervin (1979) Regional climatic effects of large-scale thermal pollution: simulation studies with NCAR general circulation model. *J. Appl. Meteorol*, **18**, 3–16.

Woodwell, G. M. (1982) Earth's vegetation and the carbon dioxide question. In W. C. Clark (ed.), *Carbon Dioxide Review 1982*, pp. 399–400. Oxford University Press.

World Meteorological Organization (1982) Thirtyfourth Session of the Executive Committee, 7–24 June 1982, WMO No. 599, Geneva, p. 126.

Zimmerman, P. R., J. B. Greenberg, S. O. Wandiga and P. J. Crutzen (1982) Termites: a potentially large source of atmospheric methane, carbon dioxide, and molecular hydrogen. *Science*, **218**, 563–5.

Zoller, W. H. (1982) Personal communication.

Zwally, H. J., C. L. Parkinson and J. C. Comiso (1982) Variability of Antarctic Sea ice and CO_2 change, *Science* **220**, 1005–1012.

11

Global Trends in Non-Fuel Minerals

HAROLD J. BARNETT,
GERARD M. VAN MUISWINKEL,
MORDECAI SHECHTER, AND JOHN G. MYERS

Herein we review and supplement *Global 2000* with respect to non-fuel minerals. We focus on five policy questions with respect to resources which are important for national and global economic welfare in the long term:

(1) *Trends in economic scarcity of minerals* – that is, trends in mineral costs and prices – are the fundamental concern. Substantial increases in mineral costs would make us poorer than we would otherwise be.

(2) *Efficient international production and trade in minerals.* The whole world benefits from using least-costly mineral supplies.

(3) *Ocean mineral resources policies* may greatly influence future minerals costs and prices.

(4) *Incentives are necessary for innovation and discovery* to replace or substitute for depleted deposits.

(5) *Environmental protection and land withdrawals* influence both mineral costs and environmental amenities.

We shall not discuss still other important categories of minerals policies – those concerned with supply disruptions, urgent defense requirements, stockpiles, and business cycles and related regional economic dislocations. These are primarily short-term phenomena rather than long-term trends. There is a considerable literature which suggests that stockpiles are usually a preferred solution for supply disruptions and urgent defense requirements. (See, for example, H. Landsberg and J. Tilton, in several Resources for the Future publications, 1982).

Trends in Economic Scarcity

There is widespread belief that minerals become increasingly scarce during economic growth. Two elements of the belief are that: (1) physical endowments of mineral resources are a fixed total as compared to the increased demands from economic growth; and (2) we tend to use the best economic resources first. Like agriculture, minerals are conceived to be a decreasing returns or increasing cost industry; formal economic literature goes back to Smith, Malthus, Ricardo, and Mill. In addition, the limited minerals resources are subject to depletion from use, and this is believed further to restrict returns. W. S. Jevons was one of the first to write on this, in 1863. A well-known Hotelling theorem treats minerals as a capital asset subject to withdrawals. Resources writings of the past hundred years, ranging from early literature on *lebensraum* and colonialism to the new international economic order, generally affirm the theory of increasing economic scarcity of minerals related to physical limits.

A number of writings, however, have questioned relevance of the theory of increasing mineral scarcity in the modern world, in concept and in fact. The economists'.classroom principle of diminishing returns is static and not necessarily applicable in long-term trends. It omits consideration of increases in knowledge; improvements in techniques of production, transportation, and use; discoveries of new resources and substitutes; growth in international trade; recycling; and other social–technical changes.

With respect to the facts, a study from Resources for the Future covering the period 1870 to 1957 discovered contrary evidence (Barnett and Morse, 1963). In the United States, over a period of almost a century, minerals production was not subject to increasing costs, either absolutely or relative to labor of nonextractive goods. Figures 11.1 and 11.2 summarize the data. In figure 11.1 we see that the opportunity cost of minerals in terms of man-days of labor to produce them declined persistently. In figure 11.2 we observe that the opportunity cost of units of minerals in terms of other goods forgone did not increase. Another recent study marshalled factual evidence from geology and technology on potential mineral supplies and substitutions to cast doubt on the concept of inelectable, pervasive, increasing economic scarcity (Goeller and Weinberg, 1978).

In the United States, during the period 1870–1970, the theory of increasing economic scarcity of minerals is not supported by the facts.[1] This is important evidence. The period is a long one; the USA is the largest minerals producer and consumer; and the studies were carefully done.

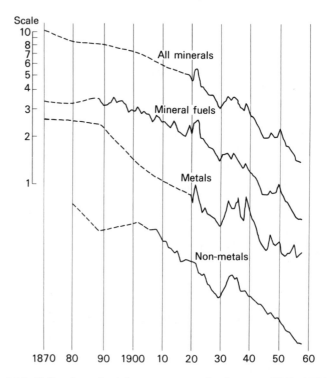

Figure 11.1 U.S. minerals: labor cost per unit of output 1870–1957. Note: Solid lines connect points in annual series; dashed lines connect points over a year apart.

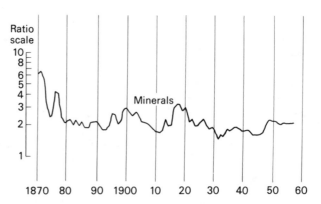

Figure 11.2 Unit prices of mineral products relative to non-extractive products in the U.S., 1870–1957.

Global Trends, 1950–80

We now undertake to extend the investigation in two ways: to the present, and to world minerals markets. We confine ourselves to the major non-fuel minerals. Other chapters of this book focus on fuels; and we reported on fuels in a previous paper (Barnett, van Muiswinkel and Shechter, 1982). We also exclude ubiquitous, unlimited resources such as sand, gravel, and cement which are not significant in international trade.

Our basic measure will be the trends of world mineral market prices, essentially the same scarcity measure which we reported for the U.S.A. in figure 11.2. In all cases, unless otherwise explicitly stated, the mineral prices are expressed relative to overall prices. For the Organization for Economic Cooperation and Development (OECD) industrial countries as a group, our deflator is the price of Gross Domestic Product (GDP) in OECD, based on domestic currencies converted into dollars. When we turn to individual countries the appropriate corrections for exchange rates will be made, and our usual deflator will be the country's GDP price index. The effect will be that the deflated prices express economic scarcity trends of minerals, taking into account the economic situations of individual countries and the fact that minerals are sold for dollars in international markets.

The essence of the question is whether we can discover evidence of increasing economic scarcity in deflated price trends, or whether (as in the 1870–1957, figure 11.2, for the U.S.A.) the data fail to support the increasing scarcity hypothesis. We consider first the following aggregate minerals price indexes, published by the United Nations and UNCTAD:[2]

YA – (minerals, ores, metals), composed of iron ore, manganese ore, phosphate, aluminum, copper, lead, zinc, tin, and tungsten;
ANF – (non-ferrous base metals), composed of aluminum, copper, lead, zinc, tin and nickel;
FTR – (crude fertilizers), composed of phosphate rock and potash.

Has there been an increasing trend of deflated world market prices for non-fuel minerals groups from 1950 to 1980? The answer appears to be no. Has there perhaps been an increasing trend in these deflated price series in more recent years, even if not since 1950? The answer again appears to be no. The data are given in table 11.1 (see also figure 11.3).[3] They contradict widespread belief that these minerals have been becoming increasingly expensive. The trend data support the findings in U.S.A. mineral statistics of 1870–1957, in figure 11.2.

There was a speculative non-fuel mineral price boom in 1973–4, but this was reversed by a later decline and the greater inflation of prices

320　　　　　　　　　*Harold J. Barnett*, et al.

TABLE 11.1 WORLD NON-FUEL MINERAL PRICES X
(OECD FE/GDP DEFLATOR); 1970 = 100

	YA Minerals, ores, metals	ANF Non-ferrous base metals	FTR Crude fertilizers
1950	98	92	189 [a]
1960	88	81	142
1970	100	100	100
1980	93	83	149

Notes: [a] 1955. FE is the OECD foreign exchange rate relative to dollars.
The data in the table are the respective mineral price indexes multiplied by the OECD foreign
exchange rate and divided by the GDP deflator, in index terms, 1970 = 100

generally in the 1970s. The boom as such was not exceptional, because
the same has happened in 1950–1, 1954–5, 1963–6, and 1967–9 (see
figure 11.3).

Individual Non-fuel Minerals

We have fourteen individual minerals and metals on which to present
evidence and therefore simplify. About twelve minerals had a net decline
or only a small net rise in deflated price from 1950 to 1980 (see
table 11.2). In some cases high peak values were reached during the three

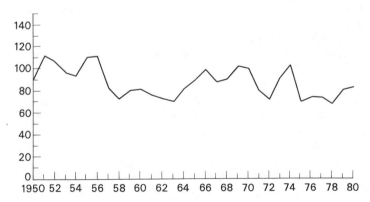

Figure 11.3 OECD, deflated price of non-ferrous base metals (ANF)
(1970 = 100).

TABLE 11.2 MINERAL AND METALS PRICES
× (OECD FE/GDP DEFLATOR); 1970 = 100

	1950	1960	1970	1974	1980
Copper	69	66	100	99	60
Nickel	65	79	100	92	115
Aluminum	100	119	100	83	111
Lead	182	90	100	127	117
Zinc	202	113	100	248	99
Tin	107	81	100	148	175
Iron ore	117	143	100	92	79
Chrome ore	121[b]	117	100	87	130
Manganese ore	276[b]	206	100	125	100
Manganese	448	218	100	140	108
Mercury	38	71	100	47	37
Tungsten ore	104[a]	55	100	113	104
Phosphate rock	253	161	100	335	157
Potash	166[a]	123	100	130	141

Notes:
[a] 1955
[b] 1954

decades, characteristic of the short-term, inelastic, cyclical movements of the minerals sector. But the peak prices did not hold. Only two of the fourteen minerals, nickel and tin, increased substantially in relative price during the 30-year period. The general trend of deflated prices of the fourteen minerals was not increasing.

While the 30-year cost trends are favorable, similar to the overall mineral groups presented, the decade of the 1970s reveals substantial cost increases for four of the fourteen minerals: tin, chrome ore, and the two fertilizers, phosphate rock and potash. The data appear in table 11.2, where 1980 values may be compared with the 1970 base year (= 100).

We conclude as follows: in general, cost trend evidence for non-fuel minerals fails to support the increasing scarcity hypothesis. The evidence includes both group indexes and price series for individual commodities. While several of the minerals have increased substantially in price since 1970, the periods of increase are as yet too short or too inconsistent to be termed "trends," and may be related to transient market control efforts by producer associations.

Impacts on Individual Countries

The foregoing analysis has treated the mineral scarcity hypothesis – the supply price conditions for the OECD economies as a whole. We now consider what these have meant for some individual countries. To do this in full degree is beyond our capability. It would require that we compare the changes in the prices of mineral inputs with changes in the prices of other goods, then observe shifts in minerals use and factor proportions induced from changes in prices and technology, and then appraise a variety of macro and parameter change effects, finally leading to effects on income and output per capita.

At this time we can only do the first of these steps. We compare changes in prices of imported minerals with changes in prices of GDP in individual countries. Since international mineral prices (P_i) are expressed in dollars and domestic prices (GDPP) in domestic currency, we make them comparable by employing a foreign exchange conversion factor (FE). This is the number of units of domestic currency per dollar in each year. Thus we can compare $(P_i \times$ FE) with GDPP. Alternatively, we can express the relationship as P_i versus FE/GDPP. We can look at the real cost of minerals in terms of domestic goods generally by observing $P_i \times$ FE/ GDPP. In the differences among countries this multiplicative deflator index (FE/GDPP) plays a substantial role in calculations of deflated mineral prices among countries. We illustrate with figure 11.4 for Germany (FGR). It shows the trend of the nominal world market prices of non-fuel minerals. These prices are then adjusted by the rising value of the Deutschmark (DM) relative to the dollar, and then this price is further adjusted by the price of GDP in the FGR. The result is the price of the imported minerals relative to the price of all other economic goods in Germany, both expressed in DM and converted to index numbers.

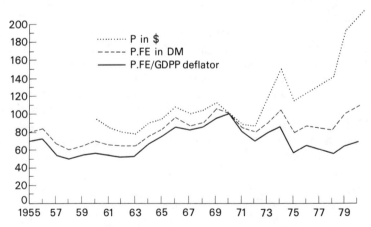

Figure 11.4 West Germany, prices of non-ferrous base metals (ANF) (1970 = 100).

We have compiled such data for about forty individual countries, but it would be repetitive and tedious to present them here. Instead, we try to summarize our findings.

OECD comprises the twenty-four industrial countries of the world outside the Soviet bloc, nineteen in Europe and five elsewhere. Their aggregate GDP is probably in excess of three-quarters of the world total. They consume by far the bulk of the world's minerals. For OECD as a group, price trends of non-fuel minerals relative to other prices have not been increasing.

This conclusion is based on international mineral prices and the deflator index of the aggregate of all the OECD nations. The deflator index represents, in effect, an average of these nations' price levels and exchange rates, weighted in proportion to the size of each nation's GDP.

TABLE 11.3 AVERAGE ANNUAL PERCENTAGE CHANGE IN DEFLATED PRICES OF MINERALS, PURCHASED BY OECD INDUSTRIAL COUNTRIES 1950–80

	YA	ANF	FTR
OECD – Total	−0.8	−0.8	−1.0
OECD – Europe	−2.1	−2.0	−2.3
Large			
France	−0.6	−0.5	−1.0
Germany (FGR)	−2.9	−2.8	−3.3
Italy	−1.6	−1.6	−1.9
Japan	−2.7	−2.5	−3.1
United Kingdom	−0.9	−0.8	−0.9
U.S.A.	0.3	0.4	0.3
Other			
Australia	−1.6	−1.6	−1.7
Austria	−2.0	−2.1	−2.2
Belgium	−1.4	−1.3	−2.3
Canada	0.2	0.3	0.1
Denmark	−2.7	−2.7	−3.3
Finland	−0.6	−0.5	−1.3
Greece	0.2	0.3	−0.7
Ireland	−1.5	−1.4	−1.6
Netherlands	−3.1	−3.2	−3.4
Norway	−1.1	−1.1	−1.5
New Zealand	−0.3	−0.2	−0.9
Portugal	−0.5	−0.4	−1.2
Spain	−2.2	−2.0	−2.8
Sweden	−2.0	−1.9	−2.4
Switzerland	−3.1	−3.0	−4.2

In such an average, the larger nations statistically dominate. It is therefore desirable to observe the national differences. Table 11.3 does this for the mineral aggregates YA, ANF, and FTR. It shows the average annual percentage changes in deflated mineral prices from 1950 to 1980. The percentages are the compound annual rates of change, as represented by the slopes of logarithmic, least squares, trend lines fitted to the annual price data.

Among large nations the U.S.A. and France has performed less well than average, and Japan and Germany much better. The differences reflect relative capability in managing their economic affairs in this period, especially foreign exchange, productivity, and inflation. Among smaller industrial nations, Switzerland and Netherlands have done well and Canada, Finland, Greece, and New Zealand less well in deflating the dollar prices which are paid for foreign minerals.

The related question arises, how have the less developed countries (LDCs) fared in prices paid for foreign minerals as compared with the

TABLE 11.4 AVERAGE PERCENTAGE CHANGE IN DEFLATED PRICES OF MINERALS PURCHASED BY LDCS, 1950–80

OECD	YA	ANF	FTR
Total	−0.8	−0.8	−1.0
Europe	−2.1	−2.0	−2.3
Middle-income, developing			
Argentina	1.7	1.8	0.7
Brazil	1.4	1.3	0.1
Chile	1.9	1.9	2.2
Colombia	3.2	3.3	2.3
Egypt	1.2	1.1	1.3
Israel	2.9	2.9	1.3
Republic of Korea	0.6	0.8	−0.1
Malaysia	0.5	0.4	1.4
Mexico	1.0	1.1	−0.6
Philippines	3.2	3.3	2.9
South Africa	−0.5	−0.5	−0.8
Syrian Arab Republic	−0.4	−0.4	0.7
Thailand	0.7	0.9	0.4
Turkey	1.4	1.4	1.6
Venezuela	1.6	1.7	1.1
Yugoslavia	3.4	3.4	4.0
Median	1.4	1.4	1.3
Low-income, developing			
India	1.6	1.5	1.6
Pakistan	3.6	3.4	5.6

industrialized OECD countries? Table 11.4 presents the data for the purchases of the YA, ANF, and FTR minerals. It will be seen that the group as a whole experienced less favorable trends in deflated costs of purchased minerals. Most of the LDCs experienced moderate increases in such costs during 1950–80. By comparison, OECD experienced moderate decreases. The primary reason is unfavorable relative trends in the LDC foreign exchange rates. The terms of trade of the LDCs developed unfavorably in most cases.

Minerals Availability or Scarcity Relative to Labor

In the preceding discussion we asked whether prices of minerals were trending upward relative to prices of other economic goods. This is obviously a useful measure: it tells whether minerals are becoming increasingly scarce *as compared with other products*. It tells whether we have had to give up more and more other goods to get a ton of desired minerals. The answer has been "No."

It is also obviously sensible economics to ask whether minerals have become increasingly scarce as compared with labor. It tells whether we have had to divert more and more labor effort to get each unit of minerals. Useful discussion of this alternative concept – economic availability or scarcity of units of minerals relative to units of labor – have been published (Barnett and Morse, 1963; Smith, 1979; Barnett and Van Muiswinkel, 1980; Simon, 1981; citations earlier in this chapter and in these publications). J. Simon, in the Editors' Introduction to this volume, argues that the trend of mineral cost relative to labor is an even more significant test of increasing scarcity than mineral cost relative to other goods.

There are several ways to measure for increasing economic scarcity of minerals relative to labor. One – the units of labor required to produce a unit of minerals – was presented for the U.S.A. in figure 11.1. It shows that the labor cost per unit of minerals output declined persistently from 1870 to 1957. As noted earlier, Johnson, Bell and Bennett (1980) have extended the declining trends to 1970.

Another way of testing for economic scarcity of minerals relative to labor is to ask: "what is the trend of the ratio, price of minerals relative to price of labor?" If minerals have become increasingly scarce then the ratio would have trended upward, showing that minerals prices have risen as compared with wage rates.

We have compiled wage rates (WGR) for the individual countries in their local currencies and compared these with international mineral prices converted to local currencies, PM × FE. That is, for the period 1965–80, we have computed trends for each of about forty countries of

$$PM \times FE \div WGR$$

or

$$\frac{PM \times FE}{WGR}$$

with respect to PM, the price of the aggregate mineral index YA.[4] The results are as follows:

(1) In all but one of the industrial countries these trends have declined significantly, about 4 to 11 percent per year. The U.S.A. is the notable exception: mineral price relative to wage rate declined by less than 1 percent per year (this was apparently due to low productivity growth in the U.S.A.).

(2) In most of the LDCs the trends of mineral prices relative to wage rates were downward, but the rates per year are more variable. A few – Argentina, Chile, India, Pakistan, and Philippines – had rising trends of 1–5 percent per year.

The overall conclusion is that non-fuel minerals in international post-World War II markets have not become increasingly scarce relative to labor; the same conclusion was reached from figure 11.1 trends.

What implications do our trend findings have for global and national policies? These constitute the remainder of our chapter. We present both objective policy analyses and also our own policy preferences.

Proposals for a New International Economic Order (NIEO) and Cartels

Third World countries have proposed that a New International Economic Order (NIEO) is needed in the world economy. Under leadership of the LDCs in the United Nations General Assembly, the Charter of Economic Rights and Duties of States Resolution 3281, 29th UN General Assembly, 27 December 1974, was adopted by a vote of 120 in favor and six against, with ten abstentions. We quote, emphasizing resources provisions:

It is a fundamental purpose of this Charter to promote the establishment of the new international economic order. . . . Every State has and shall freely exercise full permanent sovereignty, including possession, use and disposal, over all its wealth, natural resources and economic activities. Each State has the right: (a) To regulate and exercise authority over foreign investment. . . . (b) To regulate and supervise the activities of transnational corporations. . . . (c) To nationalize, expropriate, or transfer ownership of foreign property, in which case appropriate compensation should be paid by the State adopting such measures, taking into account its relevant laws and regulations and all circumstances that the State considers pertinent. In any case where the question of compensation gives rise to a controversy, it shall be settled under the domestic laws of the nationalizing State and by its tribunals. . . . All States have the right to associate in organizations of primary commodity producers. . . . Correspondingly all States have the duty to respect that right. . . . States shall take measures aimed at securing additional benefits for the international trade of developing countries . . . a balance more favorable to developing countries . . . measures designed to attain stable, equitable, and remunerative prices for primary products.

The "Dakar Declaration" of 3–8 February 1975, Conference of Developing Countries on Raw Materials, states (in UN-ECOSOC document E/AC.62/6 of 15 April 1975):

1. The present structure of international trade, which had its origins in imperialist and colonialist exploitation, and which has continued in force up to the present day . . . needs to be replaced by a new international economic order. . . . A powerful weapon which the developing countries can use to change this state of affairs is to defend their natural resources . . . by combining their forces. . . . 22. The inequities and weaknesses of the present economic system are particularly glaring in the conduct of world trade in raw materials. Those who control the levers of the price mechanism have successfully denied to the producers of a number of raw materials their due profit from their labor and from their natural endowment, while they themselves have continued to make excessive profits by charging high prices for the finished products.

There have been further declarations, meetings, and institutions. There were four Conferences on International Economic Cooperation (CIEC) in Paris and elsewhere, until the end of 1976, concerned with energy, raw materials, finance, and development. The Nairobi Conference completed in May 1976 had statements that natural resources are to be used to redistribute the world's wealth and income, promote justice and equity, bring fairness to the conduct of economic trade, etc. The U.S. Secretary of State has proposed an International Resources Bank to provide investment funds to the LDCs for their natural resources. Other measures are

Harold J. Barnett, et al.

to provide for moratoria or cancellation of LDC debts, which have shot upward due to five-fold increases in oil prices and inflation; to finance buffer stocks, in order to improve markets for LDC exporters of raw materials; and to transfer technology to the LDCs.

Briefly, the argument summarizes as follows. Each nation should take over its indigenous mineral resources from private owners, especially foreigners and multi-national companies. International free trade in minerals is "unfair" – improperly exploitive of the Third World countries. International mineral markets have been highly unstable in prices, production and consumption during business cycles, inflicting great damage on LDC mineral exporting economies. Instead, minerals development and trade should be conducted by governmental international cartels, with the objective of increasing prices and stabilizing them at higher levels, and increasing rents and profits for the state owners of the resources.

The strong and active drive by LDCs for the NIEO doctrine has been generated in significant degree by the example of OPEC, although the view itself preceded OPEC. A substantial number of public, political and press leaders in Western developed countries believe that central planning, direction, and control of mineral resources in national and international mineral markets is needed. Socialist doctrine for 100 years has been that mineral resources should be owned and controlled by the state in both domestic and world markets. The rejection of belief in private investment and free international trade in minerals is very widespread.

We think this dominant view is in error. Apart from our value preference for political and economic freedom over central authority and direction, there is powerful economic evidence for free international trade in minerals.

Free trade has been substantially "economically efficient." Our statistical evidence on favorable mineral cost trends proves this. In the international economy, increased world demands for non-fuel minerals have been met with plentiful economic availability, i.e. without increase in costs relative to other goods and services. In this result, private enterprise, economic efficiency, competitive international trade and investments, and free markets have played a major role. There have been persistent explorations for lower-cost mineral resources, frequently in the LDCs. Exploration and technology efforts have been demonstratively successful: despite the physical limits of the earth and exhaustion of some deposits, relative prices of minerals have not risen. The lower-cost minerals have been a price-reducing influence in the flow of finished goods and services, bought by all peoples and nations.

Thus, the competitive, international free trade system has reduced costs of minerals by aiming at lower-cost resources and by pumping investments and advanced technologies into development of resources, and then transportation from the LDCs. The utilization of low-cost LDC minerals has increased.

The benefits of the greater efficiency in mineral supply have been shared among all peoples in complex ways. All countries buying fertilizers, metals, chemicals, and industrial products, have benefitted from access to competitive low-cost, international supply of non-fuel minerals. It is especially true that the economic systems of the industrial nations depend on, and have benefitted from, access to international minerals. LDCs having valuable natural resources of non-fuel minerals have a special stake in preserving open access to international markets for inputs, capital, and sales. The benefits are widespread and long-term. The trends in price and availability of non-fuel minerals under the existing system of free trade, open access, and international investments have been favorable for consumers, producers, and international trade and relations.

In the NIEO cartel alternative, higher-cost resources would be developed, inefficient production arrangements fostered, and political acquisitions of wealth increased. Observe the model for the scheme – OPEC – and the economic and political damages inflicted on the world, the maldistribution and inefficiencies of the "benefits" from the oil monopolies, the economic dislocations, and especially the effects of $30 oil (increased more than 10-fold) upon the desperately poor of India, Pakistan, South America, and Africa. Most nations have lost grievously; and even most of the OPEC countries may yet regret their short-term extravagances with petro dollars and power. Certainly the poor in the OPEC countries have not equitably shared the windfall gains of the monopolies, and the poor elsewhere have been hurt.

Monopoly is inefficient. It fosters power for small groups and poverty for the mass of people. It has no real relation to equity; it unjustly enriches; and it is inimical to the political freedom of people and nations. The efforts to cartelize the world's supplies of non-fuel minerals are unlikely ultimately to succeed – there are too many alternative sources and products, especially if ocean resources are available. But the efforts at cartelization, even though abortive, can do great harm, as OPEC illustrates. They should be opposed in their inception. Already the expropriations of the 1970s, hostility and threats against multi-national companies, and denials of profits to risk-takers have warned off international investors. Already investments in non-fuel minerals are flowing to "safe" countries like Australia, U.S.A., and Brazil, and bypassing LDCs which desperately need the funds for employment and development (Barnett, 1980).

Ocean Resources

The recent International Law of the Sea Conferences addressed a number of issues. One of them was the useful idea that ocean mineral resources beyond national boundaries should be developed for *benefit* of all peoples. This implied two valid economic propositions. First, the minerals should be efficiently developed, produced, and supplied at low cost to almost 5 billion consumers world-wide, most of them poor. Second, economic rents, if any, from "ownership" of these ocean areas should, in some way, be distributed to *benefit* all peoples of the world.

But in the conferences these worthy objectives were distorted into a proposal *to socialize and cartelize* the world's ocean mineral resources beyond national boundaries. This was a powerful and dangerous effort at monopolization. It would have delivered considerably more than half of the world's mineral resources to a World Cartel Authority. Moreover, the design and program was pernicious. The World Authority was to collaborate in a super-cartel with the national governments owning land-based resources. The super-cartel would have controlled access to, and restricted output of, the ocean mineral resources so as to foster monopoly prices for all minerals in international trade, land-based as well as ocean.

The great danger here was that the super-cartel would have been created *by treaty* among all nations of the world, as a World Governmental Authority. It was as if an international UN agency for energy were set up by treaty to collaborate with OPEC so as *to restrict* development and output of oil, coal, gas, and nuclear fuels in all of Alaska, U.S. mainland and waters, North Sea, Mexico, Asia, Africa, the whole world – so as to limit supply and foster monopoly energy prices. The danger was that the usual competing alternatives – substitute minerals, alternative companies, multiple countries, new discoveries, technical advance, etc. – which normally doom cartels to failure, would have been denied by treaty. The World Governmental Cartel Authority edicts would be enforced on citizens of each nation in perpetuity.

For the present the danger has been avoided. But the proposal to socialize and cartelize all the world's ocean resources will likely rise again, in the guise of benefitting the poor, international amity, and political cooperation, as before. The effect, if adopted, would be greatly to restrict supplies of minerals, in order to increase and maintain monopoly supply prices. The primary beneficiaries would probably be private interests and the international agency bureaucracy and controllers. The losers would be the consumers of minerals and the finished goods which are made from minerals, as well as prospective LDC suppliers of minerals from their national resources.

It is a major task of public policy to prevent cartelization of ocean resources, while at the same time providing for a socially desirable distribution of economic rents from the common property ocean resources.

Incentives for Innovation

A major policy problem for the nation and world is to provide incentives for innovation in non-fuel minerals production. For a variety of reasons it is inevitable that the non-fuels minerals industries are subject to considerable regulation: taxation; environmental controls; utilization of public land and water resources; the need for public investment in transport facilities and infrastructure; the highly cyclical markets in which minerals are traded. These problems lead to regulation, and inevitably the policies chosen impinge upon industry efficiency, profitability, and incentives for innovation. The danger is that the regulatory process may unnecessarily impair these.

Innovation in the minerals industries involves not only technical change (as in other industries) but also exploration, discovery, and development. Since developed reserves inevitably are used up, it is necessary to bring other resources – the same, similar, or very different substitutes – into a usable state. This is the economic equivalent of invention, the creation of *new* production functions from new resources.

In all invention activity, the number of unsuccessful tries, experiments, and unsuccessful discoveries greatly exceeds the number of successful discoveries. The windfall gains from a success must cover the numerous losses. Such gain in the successful discovery is not merely an ordinary return on investment. It must also be the compensation for all the unsuccessful tries. The incentives in invention and exploration activities must include exceptional gains for the occasional success, sufficient to more than cover the numerous failures. The excess reward is for Schumpeterian innovation – the creation of *new* resources, products, or techniques.

A major tendency in present societies is to tax the gains from discovery in mineral finding and development activities as if these were simply a usual economic activity, which merited a profit rate only moderately higher than the interest rate on bonds. This would be a sufficient return to operate the enterprise in its existing form with existing resources. But it does not provide funds to reimburse for failures in discovery efforts. The result for mineral enterprises is that there is inadequate net financial incentive for exploration, discovery, and development. The difficulties have been starkly revealed in recent years in the LDCs. In LDC take-over from the mining companies, when they have paid at all, after much delay, it has been the net book value of the successful properties. Payments for the unsuccessful (dry or empty hole) outlays have been omitted. In such cases the companies are unlikely to explore and develop in those jurisdictions again.

The problem also occurs in advanced economies, when the gains of mining companies are too heavily taxed. The incentives in such a case are to avoid the more risky explorations for entirely new, less accessible resources or technical changes, and instead to extend existing, known, declining-quality resources. An example is U.S. tax policy for oil. Incentives to find new oil resources from high-risk efforts have been reduced by the windfall profit tax, while secondary and tertiary pumping of old deposits are not subject to the windfall tax. Similarly, Canada has greatly impaired incentives to develop tar sands. Sometimes even more perverse incentives operate. When newly discovered resources are taxed *when developed*, it becomes desirable for tax purposes to hold and trade resources as capital assets rather than spend to develop them.

Part of the difficulty is that public policies view the windfall of discovery as an "economic rent" or "unearned increment," which can be taxed away without adverse effect on the mining industry or society's allocation of economic resources. After the fact the windfall can be viewed as an economic rent related to the *particular* discovery. But it is not really a Ricardian economic rent to the company or minerals industry, but is the necessary risk return for the larger array of exploratory and discovery efforts.

Environmental Implications

It is now well understood that non-fuel minerals supply – exploration, development, production, and transportation – may generate adverse externalities or spillovers. These include surface mines (stripping of overburden and open pits); accumulations of tailings and other wastes; pollution of water, air, and surrounding land areas; and other effects. It is now well-accepted in the United States and most of the advanced countries that the costs of avoidance or damage should be included in the supply price of the commodities, in an efficient way.

The trend in developed countries during the past dozen years has been to require that the producers and consumers of minerals internalize these costs. The present price trends in these countries include these recent costs, and so the favorable cost trend record we observed earlier already incorporates environmental protection.

However, environmental protection in non-fuel minerals production is not well developed in the LDCs. This is usually considered to be an internal matter for the LDC. In the LDC trade-off between income and jobs, on the one hand, and environmental protection on the other, the latter may have been given small value. Therefore the favorable cost trend record we observed may not include environmental protection costs in adequate degree.

The relative price trends of minerals produced in LDCs may be lifted slightly in the next several decades by improved environmental protection measures. In general, the multi-national companies in the LDCs are impelled to install stronger environmental protection measures than are native or State companies. We think the effect on mineral prices will not be significant; efficient environmental protection for production of non-fuel minerals need not be costly. Actually, the total externalities (environmental and other) of minerals production by multi-nationals in LDC might be favorable on balance. They cannot conduct a major minerals operation in an LDC without some investment in schools, roads, improved sanitation standards, water purification, environmental protection education, and an array of other improvements in infrastructure.

A policy question in the U.S.A. and possibly other advanced nations concerns land withdrawals and reservations. This is the "zoning" of major portions of U.S. government lands as off-limits for minerals exploration and development. During the 1970s there were great increases in the volumes of government lands and offshore waters withdrawn or proposed to be withdrawn. In recent years there have been protests by the mining industry, unions, local governments, and regional economic development groups that the withdrawals were excessive. The contest is primarily political and propaganda war, without much valid economic analysis.

The economic realities are less confusing. First, as we observed, the trends of world costs and prices of non-fuel minerals to American users have been favorable, even with the substantial land withdrawals of the 1970s. It is clear that at least moderate withdrawals of U.S. lands may be made without impoverishing the U.S. economy.

Second, a considerable portion of U.S. minerals consumption is from foreign sources, because of lower prices. There is no reason to deny ourselves this access – the countries from whom we buy (frequently from American companies abroad) in turn use the dollars to buy other goods from us. This trade is mutually enriching, and promotes international cooperation and development in addition. The argument is sometimes made by some domestic mining firms, unions, and States that this endangers our national security, and therefore we should develop and use expensive domestic resources instead. This is in error. For such conceivable national security danger, we could stockpile the modest amounts necessary for the time of war and to develop our own resources. This has been repeatedly proven in policy research and analyses.

Third, the arguments for the sanctity of every actual and proposed withdrawal have been greatly overstated. It is simply untrue that every exploration effort at every time would be destructive or highly disturbing to the withdrawn sector. Nor is it true that every acre, perimeter as well as internal, is sacred to the objective of the withdrawal. Such absolutist argument is on a par with absolutist national security and budget arguments, and both should be firmly rejected. Decisions on land protection must be made in the context of environmental and economic alternative benefits and costs.

Comments on *Global 2000*

The principal findings and conclusions of *Global 2000* reflect the global beliefs and concerns of the sponsors and authors. These preceded the project: population is growing too rapidly, exceeding carrying capacities of the land and waters. LDC income remains too low and the gap between rich and poor nations widens. Real food prices will double, arable land is insufficient, and hunger will increase. The energy outlook is bleak. The rich nations will preempt the bulk of energy and mineral supplies. Water shortages will become more severe. Deterioration of agricultural soils, forests, and atmosphere will occur worldwide. Extinctions of land and animal species and tropical forests will increase dramatically. Poverty, ill-health, hunger, and disease will claim more children, and more of the survivors will be handicapped. All these global effects will occur if present U.S. national policies continue. The need is to change national and internationl policies by central planning, world cooperation, international mechanisms for the global commons, to improve ". . . decisions of worldwide significance that the President, the Congress, and the Federal government as a whole must make. . . . Prompt and vigorous changes in public policy around the world are needed."

In this panorama of vaulting concerns and visions interest in non-fuel minerals virtually disappears. There are occasional pages and paragraphs, and also a 20-page chapter, primarily from publications of the Bureau of Mines, Geological Survey and Malenbaum's projections. These are organized and presented poorly in *Global 2000*, but nevertheless the conclusion generally emerges that non-fuel mineral resources have been, and are likely to be, sufficient to meet growing demands without increase in real prices: "Economic growth will not be restricted by mineral availability or price; in fact, real mineral prices may decline in the future." There is some inconsistency among the parts – different authors wrote different pages. We quote the entire statement concerning non-fuel minerals from the Major Findings and Conclusions:

Non-fuel minerals generally appear sufficient to meet projected demands through 2000, but further discoveries and investments will be needed to maintain reserves. In addition, production costs will increase with energy prices and may make some non-fuel mineral resources uneconomic. The quarter of the world's population that inhabits industrial countries will continue to absorb three-fourths of the world's mineral production.

The ambivalence and the low level of interest in the non-fuel minerals sector make it difficult for us to comment on *Global 2000*'s treatment of non-fuel minerals. Most of what they present is unexceptional: LDCs depend upon purchases by industrial countries; consumers should bear the cost of environmental protection, which will be fully manageable; the effects of deep sea mining upon ocean organisms in the long run is unknown, and should be researched; reserves and resources, which greatly exceed current rates of output, are listed.

Unfortunately, *Global 2000* does not competently address the major questions concerning non-fuel minerals: multi-national companies and private enterprise vs. the NIEO and state socialized enterprise; cartels vs. competition; socialization and cartelization of seabed resources in an international seabed authority; international investment in minerals; etc.

The merit of *Global 2000* with respect to non-fuel mineral is that it has not said much that is wrong. The defect is that it has not said anything that was not well-known, and it failed to identify and discuss the major policy issues.

Appendix: Sources of Data

Description	Source
Minerals, ores, metals (YA): phosphate rock (11%), manganese ore (2%), iron ore (21%), aluminum (13%), copper (33%), lead (2%), zinc (4%), tin (12%), tungsten (1%)	UNCTAD
Non ferrous base metals (ANF): copper (44%), nickel (10%), aluminum (28%), lead (4%), zinc (8%), tin (7%)	UN
Fertilizers (FTR): phosphate rock (50%), potash (50%)	UN
Copper: U.S.A. f.o.b. Atlantic (9%), LME wirebar (91%)	UN
Nickel: Canda producer price f.o.b.	UN
Aluminum: U.S.A. producer (18%), Canada del. U.K. (82%)	UN
Lead: U.K. LME (86%), Canada (14%)	UN
Zinc: U.K. LME (73%), Canada (27%)	UN

Tin: Malaysia, ex works Penang (73%), U.K. LME (27%)	UN
Iron ore: Brazil (45%), Canada (25%), Sweden (18%), Liberia (11%)	UN
Chrome ore: Turkey, c.i.f. euroports	UN
Manganese ore: India, c.i.f. euroports	UN
Manganese: India, U.S. ports	IFS
Mercury: Spain	EMJ
Tungsten: c.i.f. Europe	UNCTAD
Phosphate rock: f.a.s. Casablanca	UN
Potash: Canada	IFS

The prices or price indexes are from five different sources. All series have been transferred into indexes with 1970 = 100 and are based on U.S. dollar prices. They can be found in:

"Methods used in compiling the U.N. indexes for basic commodities in international trade," U.N. Statistical Papers, Series M, No. 29, Rev. 2 of 1979. These series have been updated with the "U.N. Monthly Bulletin of Statistics." Weighting patterns are adjusted every 5 years (latest 1975) and are based on trade patterns.
"International Financial Statistics" of the IMF, Yearbook 1979 and subsequent issues.
Commodity Price Forecasts, World Bank.
Monthly Commodity Price Bulletin, Special Supplement and Handbook, UNCTAD, Geneva.
Engineering and Mining Journal.

Exchange rates

"International Financial Statistics" (IMF) quotations of the period averages (yearly) of par rate/market rates (line rf.) were used. For countries that express dollars in local currency reciprocals were taken. All exchange rates were converted into index numbers with 1970 = 100.

Wage rates

Sources are the ILO Yearbooks 1975 and 1979, and the most recent ILO Quarterly Bulletins and Supplements. The wages are for manufacturing (all industries), either expressed as earnings or rates per month, week, hour, or day. The data are annual averages except for some of the 1979–80 values, where the latest monthly data were taken. All wage rates were converted into indexes with 1970 = 100.

Implicit GDP deflators

These deflators are from the UN Yearbook of Rational Account Statistics 1977, table 8A. For the years 1976–80 the deflators are based on IFS series, by dividing GDP (line 99b) by GDP in 1975 prices (line 99bp). These series were rebased to 1970 = 100 and linked to the UN data. The OECD–Europe GDP deflator was computed from OECD "Main Economic Indicators."

Growth rates

The growth rates are the slopes of log-linear trend lines.

Notes

This chapter forms part of a continuing project, "Mineral Scarcity and Economic Change." The authors are happy to acknowledge assistance from several sponsors: the NAS in a grant to IIASA, Vienna-Laxenburg, for work by Messrs. Barnett and van Muiswinkel; NSF to Professor Barnett, Washington University, St. Louis, Grant DAR 78-15705; Neaman Institute, Technion University, Israel to Professor Shechter, University of Haifa; and RFF to Professor Myers, Southern Illinois University, Carbondale, Illinois. The present chapter, in part, incorporates and revises selected elements from a 1980 conference paper, "Are minerals costing more?" published in *Perspectives on Resource Modeling* (ed. R. Amit and M. Avriel; Ballinger Publishing, 1982) and in *Resource Management and Optimization*, September 1982.

1 For further discussion of various economic scarcity measures, see Smith (1979) and Barnett and van Muiswinkel (1980). Johnson, Bell and Bennett (1980) and Manthy (1978) have updated the measures in figures 11.1 and 11.2 to 1970. They observe that the U.S.A. trends continue.
2 See Appendix: Sources of Data.
3 Data sources for these indexes and other statistics are described in the Appendix following this chapter.
4 This is the slope of log-linear trend lines, 1965–80 of the series, price of minerals × foreign exchange rate ÷ wage rate.

References

Barnett, H. J. and C. Morse (1963) *Scarcity and Growth*, Johns Hopkins University Press; Barnett, H. J. (1979) "The bauxite cartel in the new international economic order," in *Advances in the Economics of Energy and Resources II* (ed. R. S. Pindyck; JAI Press); Barnett, H. J. and G. van Muiswinkel (1980) "Minerals scarcity and economic change: design and discussion," WP–80–100, IIASA, Laxenburg; Barnett, H. J., G. van Muiswinkel, and M. Schechter, "Are minerals costing more?", in R. Amit and M. Avriel (eds), *Perspectives on Resource Modeling* (Ballinger Publishing, 1982) and in *Resource Management and Optimization*, September 1982.

Barney, G. O. *et al.* (1980) *The Global 2000 Report to the President,* Penguin Books.

Goeller, H. E. and A. M. Weinberg (1978) "The age of substitutability," *American Economic Review,* 5 (68), 6.

Johnson, M. H., F. W. Bell, and J. T. Bennett (1980) "Natural resource scarcity: empirical evidence and public policy," *Journal of Environmental Economics and Management,* 7, 256–71.

Manthy, R. S. (1978) *Natural Resource Commodities – A Century of Statistics.* Johns Hopkins University Press.

Simon, J. (1981) *The Ultimate Resource.* Princeton University Press.

Smith, V. (ed.) (1979) *Scarcity and Growth Reconsidered,* Johns Hopkins University Press. (See essays by Smith and Krutilla, Brown and Field, Fisher and Barnett.)

12

World Demand for Oil

S. FRED SINGER

This chapter discusses the outlook for energy in general, and for oil in particular. The consumption of energy, in relation to the availability of various suitable fuel resources at reasonable prices, does not appear to provide any kind of limit to future economic growth, nor even an important brake. Contrary to popular views, the availability of oil presents no major problem. The increase in oil consumption has often been considered as the crucial limit to future growth; but it is clear that fuel substitutions based on purely economic decisions provide an automatic adjustment to higher oil prices.

The so-called energy crisis of the 1970s can be traced to various governmental interferences with free-market pricing. In the United States, shortages were produced by price controls on natural gas and by price allocation controls on oil. The world oil crisis was partly psychological and partly due to a sudden price rise in 1973, following the takeover of oil concessions by the host countries.

The recent (1979–80) large increase in oil prices, together with fears of even higher prices, has greatly speeded up the back-out of oil for heat and steam applications by gas, coal and nuclear energy. Once up-front capital investments are made, these become "sunk costs"; even lower prices will not fully restore the use of oil. We estimate that OECD oil demand will fall by half before 2000. Oil prices will weaken. The inherent instabilities will cause severe problems for OPEC, and especially Saudi Arabia.

The Historical Use of Energy

Energy has always been used by human beings in the form of food, and even in prehistoric times in the form of fire for cooking and for warmth. The energy rates necessary to maintain the human metabolism amount to approximately 100 watts, depending, of course, on climate and on the level of activity. For comparison, the average per capita energy consumption in the United States is currently at the level of 12,000 watts. [1,2]

S. Fred Singer

Over recorded human history, energy consumption has increased steadily, but probably with large jumps (figure 12.1). The development of agriculture brought with it the use of animal power as a form of energy. Pre-industrial man, i.e. before about 1800, began to use energy in increasing amounts, including not only firewood and animal power, but also wind and water power and, where available, coal. Energy intensities were low since there was no easy way to transport energy and concentrate it in one location.

The industrial revolution brought with it a large and sustained increase both in energy intensity and in consumption rates, but only in the industrializing countries. As a result, it no longer makes sense to speak of (world) average energy consumption rates. Most observers consider that the world is now in a period of transition. While energy consumption rates in the most heavily industrialized countries, such as the U.S., may have topped out, large increases can still be expected in the newly industrialized countries. For lack of better estimates, and considering the introduction of energy conservation measures, a figure of 10,000 watts appears to be a reasonable estimate of per capita energy consumption in the future. When multiplied by the world population, it represents an upper bound for total world energy consumption.

Figure 12.2 shows the types of energy resources which have been used since the beginning of recorded history. Food, firewood, and draft animals can all be considered as *biomass* (to use the modern term) – or

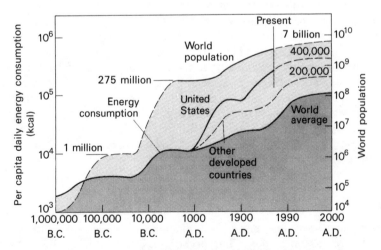

Figure 12.1 Human population and energy use have grown in surges representing revolutions in man's control of energy, from the discovery of fire through reliance on hunting, agriculture, industry, and technology. Note the logarithmic scales.
Source: Earl F. Cook, *Man, Energy, Society*, W. H. Freeman and Company, San Francisco, 1976.

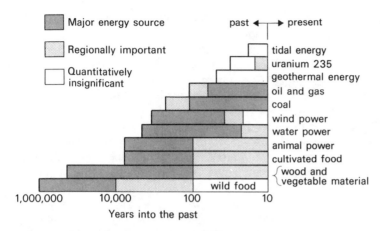

Figure 12.2 Man's energy sources during the past million years are represented on this chart, which has a logarithmic scale. Only in the past 150 years have non-renewable resources become more important than the renewable resources on which man depended for so long.
Source: Earl F. Cook, *Man, Energy, Society*, 1976.

more precisely, as solar radiation converted by means of photosynthesis into chemical energy, which is released as work or just heat energy through oxidation. The oxidation can occur *internally*, as in the metabolism of food, or *externally* by burning of firewood or agricultural waste material. Biomass can also be processed into more convenient energy fuels, such as methane, methanol, or ethyl alcohol.

For the sake of completeness it should be mentioned that water power and wind power are simply other aspects of solar energy. Peat, coal, petroleum, and natural gas are fossil fuels, i.e. solar energy which has been stored in the form of chemical energy. Nuclear energy, whether generated by fission of uranium or by the fusion of hydrogen isotopes, is a fundamentally different energy source, which is not a consequence of solar radiation. It should be pointed out, however, that naturally occurring nuclear fusion provides the fundamental energy source which heats the sun's interior and ultimately produces the solar radiation that sustains life on earth.[3] Natural radioactivity in the earth's interior is believed to be the source of geothermal energy.

Projections of Energy Demand

The projection of future energy demand has become a popular pastime, consuming much effort and resources. It is, of course, motivated by

S. Fred Singer

people's desire to know whether there will be a "shortage," i.e. whether "demand will exceed supply." To those who believe that prices in a free market can allocate available fuels efficiently, and bring forth the necessary resources, the idea of a long-term shortage makes no sense whatsoever; the projection of energy demand without considering price changes should be viewed as an academic exercise without much policy content.

This view is reinforced by the fact that energy projections in the past have been widely off-base for a variety of reasons. They have been misused by politicians and others to create the specter of a "crisis," and have served to involve the government in dubious interventions into the energy market.

It is encouraging to me, therefore, that even recent authoritative projections – for example, the National Academy of Sciences' study *Energy in Transition* – give energy consumption rates for the United States for the year 2010 which vary by a factor of three between the low and high estimates! (see also figure 12.3).[4]

The key parameter will always be the price of energy. And since energy resources are *owned* – i.e. since property rights can be established and freely brought and sold – the management of energy resources in a reasonably free market should present no long-term problems. It certainly would not require any intervention by government – unlike the management of environmental quality of un-owned (common) resources, such as water and air.

The conventional method for projecting energy demand relies on a coefficient, empirically determined, between energy use and GNP. Energy demand forecasts depend therefore on forecasts of population growth and economic growth. More sophisticated projections allow for the fact that the energy/GNP ratio has been decreasing in industrialized countries, and is likely to decrease further as energy prices rise and conservation becomes more prevalent (figure 12.4). It is likely that the asymptotic value of this ratio will depend on the fraction of the GNP devoted to paying for energy, as well as on structural changes in the economy. For example, the relative increase of the high-technology and services sectors in post-industrial countries reduces the energy consumption/GNP ratio. On the other hand, less-developed, industrializing countries which are expanding their manufacturing sector require a great deal more energy.

For all of these reasons – and particularly since it is not possible to forecast with certainty the degree of industrialization of the less-developed countries (LDCs) – it is probably sufficient to assign a value of 10,000 watts to the average per capita energy consumption rate in an industrial country.

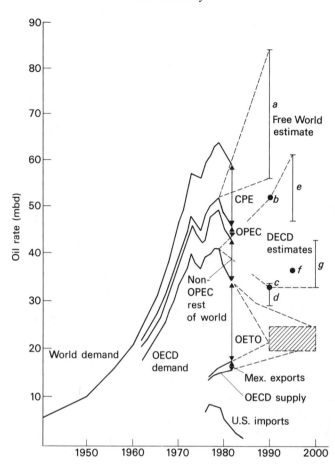

Figure 12.3 Oil demand – rise and fall.
The demand of OECD (industrialized nations), non-OPEC rest-of-the-world, OPEC members, and the CPE (centrally planned economies) are shown cumulatively and add up to the world demand. Also plotted are OECD supply, OECD supply plus Mexican exports, and US imports (for comparison). Line *a* encompasses seven different estimates (made between 1977 and 1980) for Free World demand in 1990; *b* through *g* show the wide range of OECD demand estimates. Micro-sectorial analysis (see text) yields a much lower range of demand estimates. The rectangle (cross-hatched) indicates the approximate uncertainty in the eventual OECD demand and in timing. Note that the estimated end point is *not* an extrapolation of the 1979–82 downward trend of OECD demand. The long-term estimate is therefore independent of cyclical recessions and recoveries, and of stockpiling and destocking.

Projections of Energy Mix

The projection of the energy mix (i.e. the percentage of different energy resources used), is also uncertain. In a rational world system the mix will

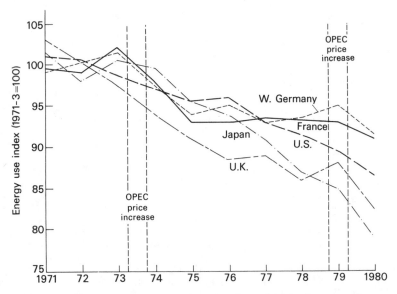

Figure 12.4 Energy efficiency in selected countries. This measure of energy efficiency is referred to as the energy/GNP ratio. Put simply, it is the ratio of an economy's total energy consumption to its real economic output (correcting for inflation). Even more striking is the decline in the ratio of oil use/GNP. Japan reached an index of 67 in 1980, and 61 in 1981.
Source: Institute of Energy and Economics, Tokyo, 1982.

be determined by the relative costs of various energy resources. Depending on geographic location, coal, nuclear fission, and natural gas are reasonably competitive with each other for producing electric power, provided we properly amortize the up-front capital costs, be they nuclear reactors, gas pipelines or other transport systems. Oil is in an anomalous situation: its current price is too high, while its marginal cost is quite low. On a heat basis, oil is now about twice as costly as gas or coal, at least in the United States, while its marginal cost in the Middle East is only a fraction of the resource cost of coal. This situation, of course, can and will lead to instabilities which are discussed in more detail below.[5]

Some remarks are in order about more exotic energy sources, such as nuclear breeder reactors, nuclear fusion reactors and solar energy. I would judge that their competitiveness – hence entry into the market – depends very much on further technology developments and the resultant economics. Most analysts would agree that breeders are not competitive currently – and will not be for the rest of this century – because uranium prices are too low. With respect to nuclear fusion there seems to be little possibility of any commercial activity during this century. And while nuclear fusion energy may provide an inexhaustible resource, there is no guarantee that the energy will be of low cost and competitive with other energy sources.

It is difficult to draw overall conclusions abour solar energy. Leaving aside hydro and wind power, solar (radiation) energy for heating has been competitive for many years and will continue to expand and occupy a wider niche. These applications include domestic water heating, space heating, and industrial applications of hot water. With the development of "solar ponds," hot water could become even cheaper, and low-temperature steam will become available for applications such as desalination and air conditioning. Many expect an eventual break-through in the cost of photovoltaic cells and in other methods for directly using the high-quality solar radiation, for example by the direct generation of hydrogen. The success of such technologies would open up a very wide market to solar energy; there will be many applications where solar energy will be the preferred energy source and be most economic. But it is doubtful whether solar energy would supply more than a small percentage of total world energy use by the end of the century.[6]

Global Energy Autarky

Taking a world point of view and applying free-market thinking, it does not matter very much which energy sources will capture a larger share of the market. The mix will always represent some kind of lowest-cost solution. But from a geographic view, and from the point of view of national development – as against international – it matters very much. Certain countries are favored with low-cost and extensive coal resources (e.g. the United States, U.S.S.R., Australia, and South Africa), while other countries have large and easily developed resources of oil and gas.

In this connection I would venture a prediction: that the world will become *less* interdependent on natural resources rather than *more*. The underlying reasoning is that low-cost fuel (and mineral) resources will be developed first – before high-cost, poor-quality resources are tackled. But such lower-grade resources are more widely distributed throughout the world, while high-quality resources are found only in unique locations. For example, every sedimentary basin should have some oil and gas, but only the Persian Gulf has a truly spectacular and unique hydrocarbon resource. Yet within a few decades, and certainly some time in the next century, most of the world's high-quality resources will be depleted, leaving behind a wider distribution of poor-quality resources.

With an increasing degree of autarky for fuels and minerals, countries will be less inclined towards conflicts based on competition for natural resources. Forced to fall back on low-quality resources – energy as well as non-fuel minerals – the challenge will be to use brain power and innovative technology to learn how to produce energy at a reasonable cost. And since technology is relatively easy to transfer, advances anywhere should produce benefits worldwide.

Misconceptions About Oil

Crude oil is currently the most important energy resource in the world. It also has been very much in the news, largely because of the existence of OPEC and of two rapid price increases during the decade of the 1970s. In 1970 the world price was of the order of $2 a barrel but doubled by the middle of 1973 (see figure 12.5). Following the October 1973 war and the Arab oil embargo, the price jumped to $12 a barrel, as producing countries took over production decisions from the major international oil companies. The price again rose following the fall of the Shah of Iran. From about $13 a barrel, at the end of 1978, the spot price reached a peak of about $40 by the middle of 1980, before falling to about $30. (The posted price for Light Arabian Crude was $34 in 1982.)

Much concern has been expressed about the adequacy of the oil resource. At various times, especially during the past decade, it has been predicted that the world would "run out of oil." In 1977, President Carter predicted an oil crisis for 1983, during which the "demand for oil would exceed production"! Various studies then available seemed to support such a viewpoint.[7] It is still widely believed that some time in the future, perhaps in the 1990s, the available supply of oil will not be adequate to meet the demand.[8] Such views, of course, do not make economic sense: the consumption of oil must always equal what is produced – if one neglects the storage of oil. In fact, the existence of strategic stockpiles can avoid even the short-term dislocations from sudden interruptions in the oil supply, be they accidental or political.

The longer-term balance between supply and demand can always be achieved by means of prices. In case of a "shortage," the price would rise sufficiently both to dampen the demand and encourage the development of alternative sources of energy and of additional supplies of oil.

There are a number of additional misconceptions that have bedeviled plain thinking about the oil problem: the fear of running out of oil; the fear of an Arab oil embargo; the concern about "access" to oil; the fear of not being able to recycle petrodollars, etc.[9] Misconceptions also exist concerning ways of achieving oil independence: throughout the 1970s there have been strong advocates for synfuels, particularly for making synthetic oil from coal or from shale. It has become clear, however, that synfuels are not required. The market is choosing another method of replacing oil, namely in particular sectors rather than across the board.[10]

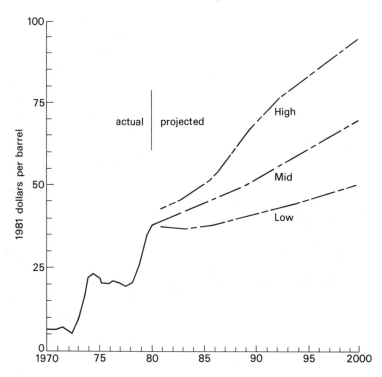

Figure 12.5 World oil price projections, published by DOE in July 1981, assuming high and low GNP growth rates, high and low OPEC production, and high and low non-OPEC production. (The individual scenario forecasts are not shown.)

The price is expected to increase under all combinations of assumptions and to reach between $50 and $100 in the year 2000. A 1982 report projected the world oil price for 2000 as $75 (in 1980 dollars per barrel), following a reasonably flat price out to 1986.

A compilation dated December 1982 was produced by the Stanford (University) Energy Forum's International Energy Workshop. Of the 17 respondents listed, 16 gave the real 2000–price as greater than the 1980 price. The median was 56 percent higher, although one expert gave 240 percent. The Institute of Energy Analysis, Oak Ridge, gave the 2000 price equal to 1980. These results may be contrasted to those of Figure 12.6

Source: U.S. Department of Energy, *Projections to the Year 2000*, 1981, pp. 2–21.

Oil remains the preferred fuel for transportation uses while being replaced in its applications to produce heat and steam. Refineries have noticed this trend and are adjusting their output accordingly.

This skeptical approach to synfuels, founded on the presence of cheaper fuels and doubts about OPEC's ability to maintain a higher price, was expressed by the author at the onset of the "energy crisis," in January 1974:[11]

In the author's view we should be very cautious before going ahead on a full-scale basis with high-cost energy resources, such as oil shale and coal liquefaction. The reasons are as follows.

A huge investment locks the U.S. into a high-cost energy resource. Once the capital expenditures have been made, it becomes important to amortize them by maintaining production and of course by selling the oil at a high price. In the author's view, the world situation is one in which we may not only have self-sufficiency for oil in the United States in a few years, but a continuing surplus in the world. There are vast resources which have not yet been drilled up, and many discoveries which have not yet been made but will be made because of the increased price of oil. The markets for high-priced oil are very limited. Overproduction must therefore lead to pressure on the world price. The only question is to what level will it go down and how soon.

The OPEC countries are in a difficult position because a monopoly is not stable. If in their greediness they keep the price too high, they will thereby encourage the setting up of high-cost domestic resources in the consumer countries which will then be protected by their respective governments. This could then lead to an oversupply of oil and a collapse of the price to a very low value set by the basic cost of lifting oil plus transportation.

History of Oil Use

The use of oil in the world has undergone a spectacular increase in this century (see figure 12.3). This was brought on by the convenience, versatility, and low cost of oil and its ready availability in different parts of the world due to the relatively low transportation cost (as compared to coal or gas). The development of the automobile, of course, gave a tremendous boost to oil consumption, especially in the United States, and since World War II also in Europe and in developing countries. Around 1970, oil use spurted upward in the United States for a number of reasons: the Clean Air Act discouraged the use of coal, while at the same time the regulation of wellhead prices of natural gas created an artificial scarcity. Oil was able to replace both of these fuels quite easily, but this replacement found a great increase in oil imports.[5]

The first major price increase of 1973–4 introduced a certain measure of conservation in the use of oil. It stimulated the development and use of more efficient conversion devices, including smaller cars. When oil consumption increased after 1973, it increased at a slower rate than before 1973 (see figure 12.6). But the price of oil was not yet high enough to

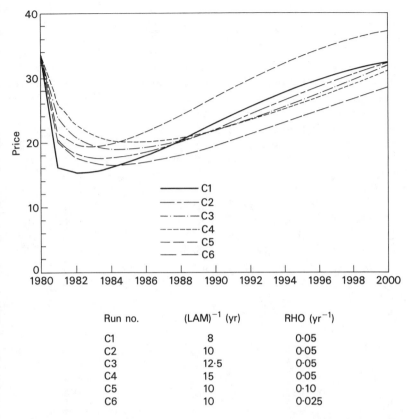

Run no.	$(LAM)^{-1}$ (yr)	RHO (yr^{-1})
C1	8	0·05
C2	10	0·05
C3	12·5	0·05
C4	15	0·05
C5	10	0·10
C6	10	0·025

Figure 12.6 Optimal oil price model. The graphs show the optimum price for the OPEC core (Saudi Arabia, etc.) to maximize their (discounted) stream of future profits – beginning with a 1980 price of $34 per barrel. All prices are in 1980 dollars. Note that these price patterns yield a lower profit stream than those in which there was no price increase in 1979–80.

force major fuel substitutions. For nuclear energy, coal and natural gas, the initial capital costs were high enough to discourage wide-scale fuel switching; gas pipelines are very costly and the transport of LNG (liquefied natural gas) involved only a minute fraction of gas use in the world. For all practical purposes, gas was a major fuel only in the United States where pipelines had been constructed before and after World War II.

Recent History of Oil Prices

In the past decade we have experienced two periods of rapidly rising prices for oil – in 1973–4, following the initiation of the Arab oil embargo; and in 1979–80, following the fall of the Shah of Iran. The first increase can be explained in terms of a structural change in the world oil market. Producer countries took control of production decisions from the multinational oil companies and then restricted growth in output. In 1979, however, there was no structural change; the price rise was largely psychologically based and resulted from an artificial increase in demand, beyond actual consumption needs, as oil users stockpiled oil in anticipation of even higher prices – thus producing a self-fulfilling prophecy.[5]

We have seen a weakening of the price between 1974 and 1978, and a well-pronounced drop in the real price starting in 1981. It is generally agreed that we are now in the period of an oil glut, i.e. the present price of oil is too high to be supportable by the market. Unless production of oil is restricted, either by design or by accident, the price will continue to weaken for the next decade or so.[5]

Since 1974 the world has seen the largest transfer of wealth (over $1,300 billion in 8 years) from oil importers to oil exporters. To make the economic impact even greater, industrialized nations have invested heavily in high-cost alternative energy sources – certainly an important factor in lowering the rates of economic growth and growth in the standard of living. The impact on the LDCs, of course, has been calamitous.

Mid-term Outlook for Oil Demand and Oil Prices

The future price of oil is the parameter of crucial importance for all kinds of decisions regarding energy supplies and investments. Unfortunately – to quote Niels Bohr, the Danish Nobel Prize winner in Physics – "it is very difficult to make an accurate prediction, especially about the future." In fact, it is altogether possible that the world oil market will have changed dramatically before this analysis appears in print.

What we can say is this. The sudden tripling in the oil price during 1979–80 is an event which carries important implications for the future, mainly for OPEC, and especially for Saudi Arabia. The current price is far removed from the price pattern which would constitute an optimum for Saudi Arabia, namely one which would produce a maximum of profits over time.[5] (see Appendix A).

Instead, the price jump is effectively killing a large part of the future oil market. For many applications, such as heat and steam production, it is now more economical to use cheaper fuels, such as natural gas, coal, or nuclear energy. It is even cost-effective to replace oil in *existing* installations and make the necessary capital investments. For example, heavy fuel oil can be replaced by newly-developed coal–water mixtures at about half the cost. Existing oil-fired boilers can also be retrofitted by fluidized-bed combustion units. Light fuel oil, which is used for the heating of homes and commercial establishments, can be economically replaced by natural gas and even by electricity in many cases.

To estimate future oil demand, one must take into consideration also the improvement in automobile efficiency, and even the introduction of such substitutes as compressed natural gas, alcohol, and methanol as transportation fuels. Altogether, various forms of conservation can cut oil use considerably, by more than a factor of two in the industrialized nations (OECD)[5] (see Appendix B, and figure 12.3).

It is safe to assume that the oil consumption of the OECD countries reached its peak in 1978 at about 42 million barrels per day. By the next decade OECD oil consumption could conceivably be as low as 20 mbd, if all of the economic replacements are put into effect. I will not consider the consumption of oil within OPEC, which is highly subsidized, nor within other developing countries. (In order to maintain or increase their oil consumption, these non-oil-producing developing nations will have to work out some concessionary arrangements with producing countries – perhaps long-term, loan or barter agreements.) Thus, for purposes of estimating future oil price, it is more relevant to focus on the oil consumption of "hard currency countries," i.e. industrialized nations.

This prospective decrease in demand for oil in the world would normally lower the price. However, continuous reductions in the supply of oil, mainly by Saudi Arabia, have kept the price near the present level for many months. But there are instabilities because of different objectives of OPEC members. Saudi Arabia and the Gulf sheikhdoms, with large oil reserves and small populations, must be concerned about the long-term market for oil. Other OPEC members, with small reserves and pressing budgetary needs, have short-term concerns.

In spite of decreasing OECD demand, the world price did not drop right away – since OPEC also decreased its production accordingly. (Its output dropped to 18 mbd in late 1982 from its 1978 peak of 32 mbd.) Normally, most of OPEC would want to produce all-out and sell at the highest possible price, while Saudi Arabia and the other Arabian sheikhdoms with similar long-term objectives would adjust their production to maintain an optimum price level that yields them the maximum of discounted profits.

It would be in Saudi Arabia's long-term interest to increase its production greatly and lower the price sufficiently so as to discourage OECD nations from investing in alternatives to oil. On the other hand, there is great pressure from Saudi Arabia to reduce its production so as to keep up the world price of oil for the benefit of the other OPEC producers.[12]

My guess is that this pressure on Saudi Arabia has been successful, since the price has remained approximately level through 1982. Saudi Arabia has cut its production continuously from 10.5 down to 4 mbd, and has been willing to reduce its income, in order to maintain the price level.

But world demand may continue to fall. With a general expectation of higher prices and future oil interruptions, and with concerns about embargoes, OECD nations will likely continue to make the investments which switch them away from oil permanently, such as nuclear reactors, major gas pipelines, and possibly even shale oil and tar sands projects, etc. Actual interruptions in the oil supply, producing short-lived price increases, would further urge consuming nations to make investments away from oil.

A particularly crucial problem could develop for Saudi Arabia whenever Iraq and Iran decide to stop fighting and concentrate on exporting oil in order to replenish their treasuries. In order for them to be able to sell on the world market, someone else would have to cut production.[13] This may cause additional pressures on the Saudis; by then they may not be able to cut production any further without serious damage to their economic welfare and to their internal stability. But if they do not cut production, there could be substantial price breaks on the world oil market.[12]

If the price should collapse, industrialized nations may no longer be willing to switch back to cheaper oil. After having made substantial investments they would want to protect them, partly for internal political reasons. For example, the United States, to protect domestic oil producers, may wish to establish a (variable) import fee on imported oil. Other countries with substantial capital investments may take similar action.

Long-term Outlook for World Oil

Such a price break would be a bonanza for the Third World non-oil-producing nations who may not have had the capital to invest in alternatives to oil. They would benefit from lower oil prices. But this happy situation cannot last for very long. Cheap oil will be depleted eventually, even in Arabia, and oil prices will then be held at levels which will be determined to a large extent by the available alternatives, mainly gas, coal and nuclear power.[5]

In the process it appears likely that more than half of the oil resources of the world will be bypassed, so that by the year 2050 perhaps three trillion barrels of oil will have been used and four trillion barrels will remain behind. Part of this oil will be in old fields where oil has been incompletely recovered; part of it will be in inaccessible regions of the world; and much of it will be in the form of heavy oil and tar sands where production costs are too high to justify exploitation. Again, this view is not new, as the following quote attests:[11]

> As the world moves towards abundant and presumably low-cost nonfossil-fuel energy sources after the year 2000, an interesting question can be raised: Which hydrocarbon resources will be by-passed? Will it be U.S. coal (as has almost happened twice earlier), or oil shale, or the Canadian or Venezuelan tar sands, gas in the arctic, or the vast oil and gas resources of Siberia?

The *Global 2000* projections for energy demand are in line with the "official" projections published by the Department of Energy. This is not surprising since *Global 2000* relied on DoE data and methodologies.

The DoE projections underwent great changes within a few years. For example, the DoE in 1977 projected a free world oil demand for 1990 of 84 mbd. By 1981 DoE estimates for OECD oil demand had dropped to about 33 mbd.

Global 2000 itself, published in 1980, projects OECD oil demand for 1990 at 51.8 mbd. In my view, OECD oil use in 1990 will be about half that amount, near 26 mbd.

Appendix A: Recent Runs (March 1982) of the UVA OPEC Oil Model

(1) These runs are *not* price forecasts.[14]
(2) The runs represent "optimum" price paths for the OPEC core (Saudi Arabia, plus sheikhdoms). "Optimum" means a price pattern over time which maximizes the profit stream to the core, starting with 1980 conditions and price. Profits are discounted to the present (1980).
    i.e.

$$\max \sum_{t=0}^{\infty} (D - S)(P - C)(1 + \varrho)^{-t}$$

D	is world demand;
S	is competitive supply of price takers;
$(D - S)$	is supplied by core as swing producers
P	is world price;

C is production cost of core, starting at \$0.50 and growing exponentially;

ϱ (rho) is the (inflation-free) discount rate.

Demand and supply functions are linear functions of the lagged price P^*. The lag adjustment parameter is LAM and expressed in (years)$^{-1}$. We specify long-run elasticities of demand and supply. (The short-run elasticities are the (long-term values) × LAM.) We also specify: DEL, the growth rate with time in demand D due to income growth; and SIG, the depletion rate with time of the competitive supply S.

(3) The plots of figure 12.6 indicate merely the sensitivity of price to the assumed economic parameters and initial conditions. *They are not price forecasts.*

(4) The actual price patterns to be expected depend on the actual production decisions and on political scenarios which cannot be forecast with any degree of certainty.

In addition, we must factor in: (1) sudden supply interruptions due to various causes (planned cut-off; sabotage, and other third-party interference, or accidental cut-off); (2) psychologically based over-shoots in price (both up and down); (3) possible OPEC competition, leading to price cutting and "price wars," together with suitable responses by importing countries.

Appendix B

A microsectorial analysis has been carried out according to the outline (dated March 1981). (For details see Ref. 5.) This study looks at seven different oil products in some twenty applications and in nine different geographic areas, mainly for the industrialized countries (OECD). Table 12.1 summarizes the results of this analysis. It is evident that the need for OPEC oil imports by OECD is declining rapidly over the medium term and could reach zero after 1990. (See figure 12.3.)

A low oil use scenario (March 1981)

(Outline of study to estimate world oil demand and supply in the 1990s)

I *Assumptions*

(1) The price increase of 1979 has set into motion irreversible economic forces whose consequences will now be felt.

TABLE 12.1 OECD OIL DATA (MBD)

	1978–9	*1981*	*1990*	*2000*
OECD oil demand	42	36	28–30	20+
OECD production plus non-OPEC (Net)	18	20	24–25	28

(2) Oil is fungible, i.e. oil displaced (backed out) becomes available elsewhere in the world.

(3) The world price of oil is set by supply and demand, with supply restricted by the production decisions of Arabian producers. Departures from this market will occur as noted below.

(4) Refineries can and will keep up with changing product demands. World coal production can expand to meet whatever is demanded. World nuclear expansion rate will reach 25 GW/yr. or 1.0 mbd oil equivalent per year.

II *Base case* (with world oil prices assumed to be roughly constant)

(1) Oil will be replaced in all applications where cheaper alternatives are available, principally for the production of heat and steam. New capacity will not use fuel oil.

(2) In the transportation sector, both efficiencies and activity will increase with time. Hence total oil consumption must be estimated for each country (region), under the assumption of different technologies. (For example, in the medium term consumption may decrease, and in the longer term it may increase.)

(3) The supply response throughout the world to the oil price increase of 1979 will be felt in the mid-1980s. It may involve the production of heavy oil, tar sands, and shale oil.

(4) In some parts of the world, where natural gas is available at low cost, it may pay to produce methanol or gasoline, which would displace oil.

III *Scenarios of world oil price*

(A) *Likely price scenario – (short term) (1981–3)*

(1) Saudi Arabia tried to depress the price (to around $32) by maintaining high production, in order to get OPEC agreement on its price strategy.

(2)   The realization that prices are dropping (in constant dollars) becomes widespread. This serves as a psychological trigger and produces two consequences:
      (a) the reduction of oil inventories in the consuming countries;
      (b) full-scale production by OPEC members and other producers.
(3)   The net effect of (2) would be to produce a downward price spiral based on self-reinforcement, abolishing much of the price increase of 1979 (which was due to a similar upward spiral).
(4)   The actual price will depend on Saudi reaction, on their own production decision, and on whether they can enforce discipline, i.e. production cutbacks, on OPEC members.
(5)   Complicating this picture (and reinforcing the price drop) will be the (partial) comeback of production by Iraq and Iran. Both countries will want large revenues.

(B)   *Likely price scenario – (medium term) (1985–95)*

(1)   Dropping world demand and rising world production should cause a crunch for OPEC by about 1983–5, if not before. Even if Saudi Arabia persuades other Arab producers to cut production, they may lose control over prices when they cannot cut any further.
(2)   World price will then fall, unless military actions or sabotage reduce oil exports from the Middle East. (For example, it would be to Iran's economic advantage to eliminate Saudi oil exports in order to maintain high prices for themselves.)
(3)   Consuming countries may either:
      (a) admit the cheaper OPEC oil, delay conversions to coal and nuclear and give up the investments already made;
      or
      (b) more likely, impose tariffs or import quotas to protect resources (e.g. tertiary oil, shale oil, nuclear reactors);
      or
      (c) both (a) and (b), causing international trade problems

(C)   *Likely price scenario (long term)*

(1)   In the long term, beyond 1995–2000, the medium-cost oil resources outside of Arabia may be pretty well exhausted, including Alaska, North Sea, and other OPEC production (such as Indonesia, Iran, Nigeria, Algeria, etc.)
(2)   Arabian oil will gradually re-establish itself, at a price set by the price of coal and nuclear, probably close to the present price (in real dollars). That is, with alternatives to oil pretty well estab-

lished, even in the transportation sector, people would not pay a great premium for oil.

IV   *Backout of heavy fuel oil*

Residual fuel oil will be replaced in (a) electric utility boilers, (b) industrial boilers, (c) heating installations, (d) marine transport, by cheaper coal and nuclear energy. Replacement of existing oil-fired capacity will proceed at different rates in different countries, depending on economics, availability of capital, environmental and safety considerations, desire for self-sufficiency. We can extrapolate current coal and nuclear trends towards saturation.

Leading technological candidates for speeding up the replacement of oil are:

(a)   highly-loaded (70 percent) coal–water mixtures, designed to replace No. 6 fuel oil in existing boilers (including marine boilers);

(b)   fluidized-bed combustion units designed for retrofit applications;

(c)   mass-production techniques being adopted for nuclear reactor manufacture (in U.S.S.R. and elsewhere);

(d)   powdered coal to replace oil in marine diesels;

(e)   low-temperature nuclear for district heating (e.g. Canadian "Slowpoke;" Russian systems).

V   *Back-out of medium fuel oil*

(1)   Medium and light fuel oil will be replaced in residential and commercial heating applications by whatever technology or fuel is cheaper. Candidates are:

(a)   natural gas, which should become plentiful, once it is de-regulated (in the U.S.) and backed out of utility and industrial use by cheaper coal;

(b)   electricity (produced by coal and nuclear); various uses of heat pumps;

(c)   district heating based on coal, nuclear (see IV(e)), or geo-thermal energy (where appropriate);

(d)   solar energy (where appropriate);

(e)   biomass, municipal waste.

It should be noted that conservation in the residential–commercial sector has not yet reached its economic limits and can be relied on to reduce demand further.

VI   *The transportation sector*

Transportation, which now consumes about one-third of world oil, mainly as gasoline, jet fuel and diesel fuel, should become the major oil user by 1990. Therefore, its worldwide requirements need to be estimated rather carefully.

(1)   Private cars: gasoline consumption will decline greatly (in the U.S.) in the near and medium term, with some increase in diesel fuel, as more efficient cars enter the fleet and improve average fleet mileage. Outside of North America, where gasoline has always been heavily taxed, the effect will be smaller. If minicars (50 to 60 mpg) become widely accepted, or even electric cars, then consumption can decrease much further and even beyond 1995–2000.

(2)   Trucks: conservation effects will be important but less so than for cars. Vehicle miles will grow.

(3)   Aircraft: conservation effects will be of some importance. Better scheduling and higher load factors could achieve significant savings.

Editors' Appendix

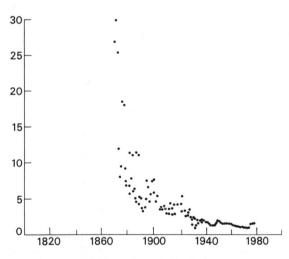

Figure 12.7 The price of oil relative to wages.

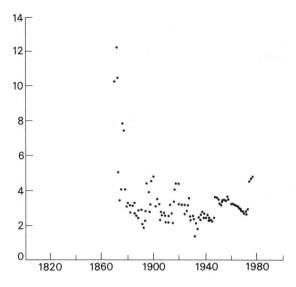

Figure 12.8 The price of oil relative to the consumer price index.

References and Notes

1 About half of this energy is lost, mainly in electricity generation and transportation uses. Improvements in efficiency can capture some of these losses.
2 Earl F. Cook. *Man, Energy, Society.* W. H. Freeman and Company, San Francisco, 1976.
3 S. Fred Singer (ed.) *Energy.* W. H. Freeman and Company, San Francisco, 1979.
4 *Energy in Transition, 1985–2010* (Final Report of the Committee on Nuclear and Alternative Energy Systems), National Academy of Sciences, Washington, D.C.) W. H. Freeman and Company, San Francisco, 1980.
5 S. Fred Singer, "The price of world oil." In *Annual Reviews of Energy.* **8.** Annual Reviews, Inc., Palo Alto, 1983.
6 Petr Beckmann (chapter 15, this volume).
7 "The international energy situations: outlook on 1985," CIA Report ER77-1024U, April 1977; Carroll Wilson (ed.), Workshop on Alternative Energy Sources (WAES), 1977 – the study is reviewed in convenient form by Andrew R. Flower, "World oil production," *Scientific American*, **238**, March 1978; Mason Willrich *et al.*, "Workshop Report." International Division, Rockefeller Foundation, New York, 1978.
8 *World Energy Outlook.* International Energy Agency (IEA/OECD) Paris, 1982.
9 S. Fred Singer, "Limits to Arab oil power," *Foreign Policy*, No. 30, Spring 1978; "The many myths about OPEC," *Wall Street Journal*, 18 February 1977; Douglas J. Feith, "The oil weapon de-mystified," *Policy Review*, no. 15, Winter 1981.

10 S. Fred Singer. "The coming revolution in world oil markets," *Wall Street Journal*, 4 February 1981.

11 S. Fred Singer, "Domestic resources can satisfy the energy needs of the United States," *Energy Systems and Policy*, vol. 1, no. 1, 1974.

12 S. Fred Singer, "Oil pricing blunders now have Saudis in a jam," *Wall Street Journal*, 28 May 1981; idem., "Saudi Arabia's oil crisis," *Policy Review*, no. 21, Summer 1982; idem., "What do the Saudis do now?" *Wall Street Journal*, 18 March 1983.

13 The Iranian oil minister, Mohammed Gharazi, has stated that his country would do anything to defend its recently increased share of OPEC production – "even if it has to resort to force. . . . Getting back Iran's share should come from those who grabbed it at the occasion of Iran's revolution. . . this means it should be reduced from Saudi Arabia and nobody else" (*Washington Post*, 12 July 1982).

14 For details see Appendix 2 of Singer, "The price of world oil."

13

The Outlook for Future Petroleum Supplies

WILLIAM M. BROWN

Introduction

If the present consensus about the remaining extractable amounts of conventional crude oil and natural gas is correct, the world is likely to exhaust nearly all of these resources within roughly the next 50–60 years. However, such claims – which have appeared in similar forms for over 100 years and have always been wildly wrong (see table 13.1) – should be tempered by the known potential of *unconventional* alternatives. These alternatives can provide both oil and gas, and are huge compared to the conventional ones.

The technologies for producing oil and gas from the many unconventional sources are now under active development and will be phased in more or less gradually over the coming decades – hopefully, fast enough to provide a smooth transition away from conventional petroleum sources. Also, during the next few decades technological developments in the extraction of conventional oil and gas should make great progress. That progress might substantially increase current estimates of available supplies over the longer term, and help to stretch out and smooth out the long-term transition to other energy sources.

An examination of the outlook for the production of petroleum in the non-OPEC countries during the rest of this century suggests that in most areas with adequate resources the output is likely to rise. A growing worldwide exploration effort is expected to occur in nearly every region with reasonable petroleum prospects. The main stimulus for that prolonged effort was provided by the recent oil crises and the concerns it created about future supplies. Most countries which have petroleum resources are strongly motivated to reduce their present dependence on oil imports and are moving to accomplish that result.

The presently anticipated short-term decline in oil prices is unlikely to have a large impact on existing programs to reduce oil-import vulner-

TABLE 13.1 PAST PETROLEUM PROPHECIES AND REALITIES

Date	U.S Oil Production Rate (10^9 bbl/yr)	Prophecy	Reality
1866	0.005	Synthetics available if oil production should end (U.S. Revenue Commission)	In next 82 years the U.S. produced 37 billion bbl. with no need for synthetics
1885	0.02	Little or no chance for oil in California (U.S. Geological Survey)	8 billion bbl. produced in California since that date with important new findings in 1948
1891	0.05	Little or no chance for oil in Kansas or Texas (U.S. Geological Survey)	14 billion bbl. produced in these two states since 1891
1908	0.18	Maximum future supply of 22.5 billion bbl. (Officials of Geological Survey)	35 billion bbl. produced since 1908 with 26.8 billion reserve proven and available on 1 January, 1949
1914	0.27	Total future production only 5.7 billion bbls. (Official of U.S. Bureau of Mines)	34 billion bbl. produced since 1914 or six times this this prediction
1920	0.45	U.S. needs foreign oil and synthetics: peak domestic production almost reached (Director of U.S. Geological Survey)	1948 U.S. production in excess of U.S. consumption and more than four times 1920 output
1931	0.85	Must import as much foreign oil as possible to save domestic supply (Secretary of the Interior)	During next 8 years imports were discouraged and 14 billion bbl. were found in the U.S.
1939	1.3	U.S. oil supplies will last only 13 years (Radio Broadcasts by Interior Department)	New oil found since 1939 exceeds the 13 years' supply known at that time
1947	1.9	Sufficient oil cannot be found in United States (Chief of Petroleum Division, State Department)	4.3 billion bbl. found in 1948, the largest volume in history and twice our consumption
1949	2.0	End of U.S. oil supply almost in sight (Secretary of the Interior)	Recent industry shows ability to increase U.S. production by more than a million bbl daily in the next 5 years

Source: Presidential Energy Program, Hearings before the Subcommittee on Energy and Power of the Committee on Interstate and Foreign Commerce House of Representatives. First session on the implication of the President's proposals in the energy independence act of 1975. Serial No. 94-20, p. 643. 17, 18, 20, and 21 February, 1975.

ability. As it generally takes from 10 to 20 years to discover and develop a significant fraction of a nation's petroleum potential the emerging national policies for reducing import dependence cannot reasonably fluctuate very much in response to short-term price trends. This conclusion appears to be valid for both the developed and developing nations.

The relatively great extent of both conventional and unconventional petroleum resources, combined with the impressive technological progress expected to occur in all important aspects of energy production and the strong desire of most countries to reduce their import dependence, suggests that in the future indigenous oil and gas supplies should gradually, if somewhat unevenly, come into better balance with demand. That could result in a gradual diminution of the markets now supplied by OPEC and in lower-than-expected international oil prices.

The views expressed above are diametrically opposed to some more pessimistic ones presented in the late 1970s and even the early 1980s.[1] In recent years it became tempting for many studies, including *Global 2000* in particular, to bemoan the world's energy predicament. Nevertheless, adjustments to the new energy realities since 1973 have been occurring more rapidly than was expected by nearly all analysts. Consequently, institutional projections of future supply and demand made during the mid- and late 1970s, have quickly become outdated.

The Outlook for Future Petroleum Supplies

Long-term prospects for petroleum

For many decades those committed to the preservation of non-renewable resources – in this case, petroleum – have generally held a relatively simple image of the world's geological potential, perhaps something like the following hypothetical quotation:

> The earth contains within its upper crustal layer a limited amount of crude oil and natural gas pools. These pools are being continuously tapped to provide society with fuels and petrochemical feedstocks. Well-known geological experts and major oil companies have recently estimated that about 20 percent of the earth's extractable crude oil and perhaps 10 percent of its natural gas have already been consumed. According to a consensus of these experts, only a little over half – a much more difficult half – of the original oil resources are still to be discovered, and perhaps 70 percent of the natural gas.
>
> Recently drilling for oil and gas reached an historically high rate. Worldwide, over 2.5 million wells have been drilled in search of these hydrocarbons, with about 96,000 during 1981 alone. Because

of rapidly rising consumption during this century, the combined production of oil and gas has reached about 90 million barrels per day (of crude oil equivalents). Therefore, even a low growth in future consumption of these fuels, say 2 percent annually, implies that the earth's crust will have been nearly sucked dry within a few decades and very little would then be left for posterity. Consequently, our grandchildren, if not our children, are likely to inherit an earth almost barren of these fuels and will be forced to employ extreme and expensive energy conservation measures. They will also have to make enormous investments in order to convert the environmentally-dangerous solid fossil fuels into desirable fluids. But, as even those costly resources are limited, it will still leave the question, what about fuels for their children and grandchildren?

Although the image given above has the appeal of simplicity and clarity, we should remember that in similar forms it has been more or less in vogue ever since petroleum was discovered in the U.S. in 1859. Prior to that time preservationists were almost always concerned with the possible exhaustion of the prevailing commercial fuels such as wood from forests – or even whale oil, when its use became widespread, and its cost high in the nineteenth century.

Some of the past concerns about petroleum availability in the United States is reflected in table 13.1, which shows that the fears of the preservationists have often been sympathetically expressed in official government pronouncements over the last hundred years. However, it is also clear from the table that human ingenuity, perhaps combined with a little luck, has managed to confound all of those long-range prophecies. Indeed, with today's hindsight we can see that all those prophecies about the inadequacy of future supplies were not only wildly wrong, but always on the low side.

Nevertheless, such evidence about past errors has not deterred today's preservationists from making similar gloomy forecasts. The argument that the world will soon exhaust its petroleum resources, if present consumption trends continue, has probably been as strong during the last 10 years as it has ever been. The current concerns often rely upon estimates from expert opinion, which asserts that roughly 1.5 trillion barrels of crude oil remain to be produced in the world.[2] This quantity would last about 75 years at current rates of consumption (about 20 billion barrels annually), but only 45 years with a 2 percent annual growth in consumption. A roughly similar amount of natural gas (in energy equivalents) remains to be extracted and would last about 150 years at the current rate of consumption, but not quite 60 years at the 3 percent growth rate commonly projected.

Although there appears to be a growing belief that the demand for crude oil will not increase much, if at all, during the 1980s, most oil analysts appear to believe that its growth will resume during the 1990s and continue until much higher prices appear once again to deter further expansion of consumption.[3] In any event, even with modest increases in worldwide demand, it is doubtful that there would be enough crude oil – according to the conventional wisdom about ultimate oil reserves – to last for more than 40 or 50 years. Natural gas resources may last a little longer, but with continually rising demand presumably they, too, could be largely used up within 60 years.

Whether the available time before exhaustion of conventional oil and gas supplies occurs would be sufficient for the world's energy industries to develop and phase in enough alternative energy supplies is also part of a continuing debate. Clearly, if the above projections are reasonably correct, then before long consumers must again be faced with a persistent upward pressure on oil and natural gas prices. Indeed, if those estimates could be trusted, production of oil and gas should provide excellent long-term investments, as the value of any new or existing reserves should continue to increase over time.

But the above perspective has some serious inherent uncertainties that must be considered. For example, suppose the present expectation of higher future prices, plus new technological developments, combined with a little bit of luck, should result in an extra trillion barrels of crude oil becoming available worldwide, and perhaps an equivalent amount of natural gas. That outcome is well within the range of uncertainty of the consensus estimate (see figure 13.1) At current consumption levels the postulated extra amounts would add another 50 years of petroleum supplies, and about 100 years of natural gas supplies. However, assuming continued accelerating usage, the additional trillion barrels of oil might only last for about another two or three decades.

Nevertheless, an extra 20–30 years before exhaustion of conventional supplies is not to be lightly dismissed. It could provide more than enough time for the world to develop satisfactory commercial petroleum substitutes on a large scale and at tolerable prices. If that is a reasonable conclusion, long-range investments in petroleum or natural gas might be no better than many other opportunities. Indeed, even at present it is widely anticipated that many commercial alternatives to conventional oil and gas will be developed over the next 30–40 years from resources which are now called *unconventional*. The most serious near-term impediment to that development seems to be the concern about future prices. The recent soft market for petroleum shook the astonishingly widespread belief in ever-rising prices that existed prior to 1982, and led to the postponement or cancellation of many large energy supply projects whose viability evidently depended on firm if not rising oil prices.

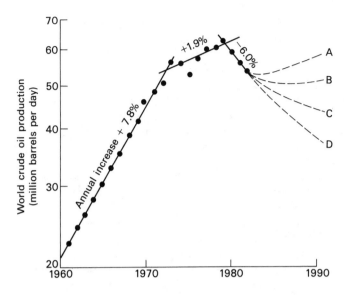

Figure 13.1 World crude oil production, 1960–90.
Source: data through 1982 compiled from Department of Energy publications.

Unconventional sources for oil and gas

Some of the more likely candidates for alternatives to conventionally produced oil and gas include (1) heavy oil deposits, (2) tar sands, (3) "tertiary" oil recovery – especially the extraction of crude from existing depleted fields – and (4) synthetic fuels, the liquids and gases that can be produced from the *solid* fuel deposits: oil shale, coal, and peat. In the U.S. the potential of each of the above alternatives is large but the fourth, synthetic fuels, is enormous compared to conventional petroleum resources. Still other unconventional possibilities exist for the production of both crude oil and natural gas. For natural gas the better-known U.S. sources include (1) selected low-permeability formations (especially those of the Rocky Mountain region), (2) the drainage of methane from existing coal beds, and (3) the Eastern gas shales. Within the U.S., the potential from each of these three sources appears to be comparable to, or larger than, the known natural gas reserves.[4] Data concerning the potential of similar unconventional resources in the rest of the world are much poorer, in large measure because of the relatively sparse amount of exploration that has occurred outside the U.S. However, no intrinsic technical reasons now exist to support the notion that the U.S. was nature's single preferred repository for such resources. Consequently, from simple geographical considerations alone (the U.S. has only about 6 percent of the world's land area) the world's unconventional fossil fuel resources, assuming that they become commercially developed, should eventually be able to provide at least *ten times* as much fuel as the consensus estimate of the remaining conventional petroleum resources – that is, at least *40 trillion barrels* of crude oil equivalents. Clearly such numbers are speculative, but not without support. Duncan and Swanson of the U.S. Geological Survey have estimated that the world's oil shale resources, considering only that portion which can yield 10 or more gallons of oil per ton of shale, theoretically could produce over 300 trillion barrels of oil.[5]

Two important points need to be made about the alternatives to conventional petroleum supplies. The first is that two or three decades, perhaps more, will be needed in order to phase in a large commercial industry in the United States. The second is that although the unconventional resouces mentioned above are estimated to be very large compared to conventional ones – at least ten times as large – even they do not exhaust all of the possibilities. From time to time other speculative possibilities appear that offer immense new potentials for additional supplies. Two such possibilities are (1) the extraction of natural gas from the hydrates (or *clathrates*) of the polar regions and (2) a possible but still very speculative potential for finding enormous deposits of *abiogenic* methane in non-sedimentary basins.[6]

In the hope of making the above alternatives commercial, many new technologies are now being investigated or developed. For any of them it may take 10–20 years, perhaps more, before much confidence can be placed in the profitability of commercial operations. Even after 20 or more years, their economic outlook will probably continue to change (to improve, very likely) in response to normal technological progress. Indeed, a reasonable possibility exists that technological breakthroughs could substantially reduce the costs of producing such fuels. It is often conjectured, for example, that *in-situ* methods for extracting oil and gas from coal or shale deposits could, over time, become relatively impressive. During this transition period the energy industry will also be trying to develop competitive processes to produce fluid fuels based upon other new technologies, as well as improving those used in conventional oil and gas production. Changing technology in the petroleum industry may become crucial, and is discussed below.

Petroleum technologies

Energy chemistry Every student of elementary chemistry and physics soon learns that energy cannot be destroyed; that it can exist in many basic forms and that these forms are interchangeable, in principle. That is, energy may exist as heat, light, motion, or it may be bound up chemically within many substances, or it may exist in the form of potential electric power from dammed-up rivers. The principle implies that sunlight can be converted into gasoline, water power into natural gas, or coal into either of these or into light or motion. This inherent interchangeability of energy from one form to another is not debatable among scientists; what has been omitted is that there are *costs* involved in making any of the desired transformations. Thus, the energy in coal can be converted into liquid fuels or electric power, but the conversion is not free. Indeed, we can, in principle, make coal out of electric power or from the sunlight. Those conversions would also involve substantial costs, even though relatively high-grade forms of energy are being changed to a low-grade form.

Obviously, successful commercial ventures are generally those which, at acceptable costs, produce relatively high-grade forms of energy from lower-grade ones. Still, it is important to understand the interchangeability concept in principle. It implies that there can never be any real danger of running out of any of the preferred forms of energy such as oil, gasoline, electricity, or natural gas. As long as there are sufficient basic sources of energy – and for millions of years these obviously will exist in the form of sunlight, geothermal energy, and nuclear energy (both fission and fusion) – society can be assured, in principle, of adequate supplies. It is the economic feasibility which will usually be society's major concern for any particular technology.

However, as our primary concern in this chapter is with petroleum, the discussion of new technologies will be limited to a few notable developments in the petroleum industry.

Advances in petroleum technology   During the last several years possibly the most spectacular of many impressive technological developments in the oil and gas industry has been the amazing progress in the application of computers to seismic techniques in exploration. Successful oil and gas exploration increasingly relies on the ability of computers to process an enormous amount of data contained in vibrations reflected from deep-earth strata and recorded by large surface arrays of seismic instruments. Because data-processing progress in this field has been so spectacular (see figure 13.2), seismic exploration systems can now furnish "pictures" depicting the nature and geometry of deep rock formations with very high resolution. Indeed, specially designed computers can now create such images rapidly in three dimensions and color them artificially.

Those developments have been credited for making possible many recent petroleum discoveries. In some areas (for example, the Overthrust Belt in the U.S.), geologists have flatly stated that the discoveries would

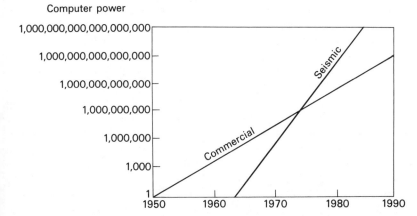

Figure 13.2 The ever-growing computer power. The seismic computers referred to in this figure are ones which have been and are being designed for the specific high-speed "number-crunching" tasks required in processing the data produced by the large arrays of seismometers routinely used in petroleum exploration. *Computer power* is defined as the product of computational speed and the size of the direct-access memory.
Source: Carl. H. Savit, "Future Trends in Petroleum Exploration," in *Petroleum 2000*, published by the *Oil & Gas Journal*, August, 1977.

not have occurred without the new seismology. Seismic techniques not only facilitate the discovery of new fields, but are also now used routinely to delineate the boundaries of the underground reservoirs and thus enable the contained hydrocarbons to be extracted more completely with fewer dry holes.

Although the relatively spectacular advance in the adaptation of computers to oil and gas exploration has been stressed, this is only one of many developing technological areas in the industry. Indeed, since World War II this industry has been involved in a profound technological transition. It could hardly have been otherwise in such a complex, competitive industry which may be the world's largest. The trade literature regularly reports technological advances in such areas as drilling rigs, production platforms, deep sea well-completion technology, advanced designs for drill bits, the capability for directional driling (which now permits *horizontal* boreholes to be drilled at almost any depth), "logging" tools which enable the presence of hydrocarbons to be sensed through the steel casing of either new or old wells, instruments for measuring important borehole parameters (pressure, temperature, conductivity, etc.) while the drilling continues, new catalysts for extracting 80 percent or more of light petroleum products from crude oil (where perhaps only 40 percent was available just a few years ago), etc.

The newer exploration technologies are helping to find greater quantities of hydrocarbons and, in some cases, are opening up vast new regions with great potential for production. The newer regions are the frontiers of petroleum exploration. They include the usual frontiers such as the jungles, mountains, and polar regions where physical access is difficult. They also include the offshore petroliferous basins of the continental rises in which ocean drilling may be required in water depths of 2–3 miles. Those deep ocean areas may yet yield as much petroleum as all the land areas of the world, according to some respected geologists.[7] Another promising region – relatively unexplored even in the U.S. – exists in the deeper horizons of known petroleum basins. That is, for economic reasons over 95 percent of the existing basins have not been explored below 15,000 feet. As incentives for such exploration increased sharply with the higher prices for oil and gas during the last few years, so did deeper drilling. It is still much too soon to estimate the ultimate potential of the deeper horizons. There is little doubt that they will be significant. There is a reasonable chance that they will prove to be astonishingly productive as improving technology makes them economic to explore. At present, much less than half of the world has been adequately explored to even 10,000 feet. However, in my judgment, by the year 2100 nearly all of the world's petroleum resources at depths of up to 40,000 feet, perhaps deeper, are likely to have been examined and delineated.

Because of ongoing technological progress in exploration the world's need for commercially competitive alternatives to oil and gas may be pushed further into the future, perhaps by more than a decade or two. Steadily improving technological capabilities for new supplies, coupled with flat or only slowly rising demand for crude oil, should help to bring a relative long-term stability to the international oil market.

The estimated quantities of conventional oil and gas which might eventually be extracted from the earth tend to reflect the optimistic or pessimistic views of the forecaster. We have shown that consensus views of industry and government tend to be conservative. It may take 10 years or more before a new consensus emerges that potentially could be much larger than the current one. There is little doubt but that the technological explosion which is now under way, and shows no signs of abating, will bring forth significantly larger amounts of these preferred fuels, as well as the ability to produce them at lower cost.

We referred above to estimates of the world's total petroleum reserves and potential resources (figure 13.3). If oil and gas are combined, the present consensus estimate is that the world's past production, 600 billion barrels (of oil equivalent), is about one-third of the discovered *proven and probable* reserves to date. Adding the *undiscovered* potential for conventional oil and gas suggests that about one-seventh of the total

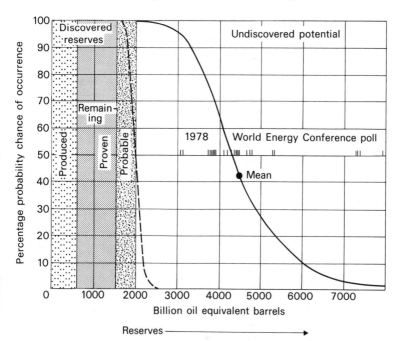

Figure 13.3 World total petroleum reserves potential. Note: the word *petroleum* refers to both crude oil and natural gas.
Source: *How Much Oil and Gas?*, Exxon Background Series (N.Y.: Exxon Corporation), May 1982, p. 9.

ultimate production (4.5 trillion barrels of oil equivalent) has already been produced.

However, some of the experts who were part of that consensus take a somewhat more conservative view – namely, that the world has already consumed as much as one-fifth of the total potential. Others are more optimistic and prefer to believe that less that one-tenth has been consumed. The optimistic view of ultimate production is at least twice that of the pessimistic view; the difference is an enormous 3 trillion barrels of crude oil equivalents. The world's economic development during the next century is likely to depend significantly upon the resolution of these differing estimates. Over time, the developing exploration and production technologies should allow a much more accurate projection of this crucial quantity to be made, perhaps well before the year 2000.

My view now leans toward the more optimistic side of the above supply projections. In part this guarded optimism is based on the historical evidence that "official" long-range estimates of ultimate oil supplies have consistently been gross underestimates (see table 13.1). I have also observed that the consensus forecasts emanate mostly from personnel associated with large institutions, such as international oil companies and government agencies. These institutions are not only traditionally conservative but also tend to avoid projections based upon radical improvements in technology. Yet it is just such developments in technology which have made all of the older forecasts obsolete. Conclusion: petroleum may be somewhat more expensive in the year 2050 but adequate supplies will be available nearly everywhere.

The mid-term outlook for non-OPEC production

United States   During the past few years, projections for U.S. oil production during the 1980s have generally varied from relatively flat – that is, about 10 million barrels per day (mbpd), including natural gas liquids – to steadily declining volumes fallowing below 7 mbpd within this decade.[8] The more pessimistic of these projections might have been somewhat undermined by the enormous response in 1980 and 1981 to higher oil prices. In those two years the number of active drilling rigs just about doubled. Moreover, recent data indicate that oil production is holding up quite well and, in fact, rose perceptibly in the first three quarters of 1982. However, after prices began to weaken in 1982 the number of active drilling rigs fell dramatically to levels well below those of 1981.

Forecasters are now somewhat uncertain about future U.S. drilling activity. The more optimistic view in the oil and gas industry is that drilling will once more become relatively active, and that steady growth in this activity soon should resume and continue during the rest of the decade. That projection appears to be based on the belief that oil prices will soon become firm and encourage the desired response. Few industry spokesmen have openly discussed the possibility that oil prices might fall considerably from current levels and induce another substantial drop in U.S. drilling activity. That outcome is an important possibility that should not be ignored. The drilling decline in 1982 and early 1983 suggests that many potential investors will be hesitant about making commitments while oil prices and the cost of leases and services appear likely to fall further, in real terms. If a large oil-price drop should occur it is likely to be a "short-term" experience, but still could last for several years. During that time oil investments in the U.S. would probably be somewhat restrained.

A severe, prolonged drought in U.S. oil and gas drilling would not only tend to increase our dependence on foreign imports in the 1980s and 1990s, but would have other earlier repercussions, including a demand by that industry for some kind of protection. Undoubtedly, political forces would then arise that would attempt to alleviate the problem through "appropriate" goverment intervention. In particular, a relatively strong lobby could arise to promote the imposition of an oil-import fee. That action could keep internal oil prices substantially above international ones. It would probably be supported by a number of special interests, including the oil and gas industry, the international banks, the auto industry and the conservationists. Indeed, there are also some powerful national security arguments to support that type of intervention.[9]

Canada In Canada the national government and provincial governments are both actively involved in exploration and production of oil and natural gas. The provinces own the minerals within their boundaries and demand substantial royalties and taxes from oil and gas production. The national government controls the exploration and production in the northern territories and the offshore regions. In addition the national oil company, PetroCanada, is active and expanding in most phases of the oil and gas industry.

Changing policies with regard to such matters as prices, royalties, taxes, export permits, exploration and production incentives, and the rights of foreign companies have recently created a considerable amount of turbulence in the Canadian petroleum industry. In fact, during 1981 and 1982, new policies led to an abrupt decline in exploration and development activity, just when those activities were accelerating in most other countries. Although there are important signs that the Canadian government may be softening some of its recent attitudes, there have been insufficient changes as yet to offer great encouragement for new investments. It appears likely that modifications in Canadian energy policy, in addition to those begun in 1983, will soon be made in an attempt to relieve many of the burdens which have restrained their industry's recent efforts.

The 1980 change in Canadian oil policy was supposed to have been designed to make the country self-sufficient in oil by 1990. To reach that goal will require about a 30 percent increase in production, to perhaps 1.8 mbpd. This is about 10 percent above the current consumption level, including imports. Since the 1980 policy substantial declines in drilling and production have thrown a considerable cloud on Canada's prospects for meeting its self-sufficiency goal.

Although Canada is not a major factor in the world oil market it imported about 0.4 MBPD during 1982, causing a cash outflow of about $5 billion. To stem that outflow I expect that the government will act soon to reinvigorate oil production exploration. In particular, the potential super giant fields in the Beaufort Sea and offshore in the eastern Maritime provinces should help bring about the political adjustments which will permit a relatively vigorous exploitation of these promising areas, although little oil can be delivered from them before 1990. Still, if the government acts soon, its self-sufficiency goal might be achieved by 1995. After that it could then contemplate the desirability of becoming an oil exporter.

Progress toward those goals would not only help the Canadian economy; it would also help to reduce the dependence of the free world on OPEC supplies. Another Canadian contribution to reduced dependence on OPEC could come about by rising exports of Canadian natural gas to the U.S. Estimates of increases in potential exports during the next several years vary from 1 to 2 TCF annually (equivalent to 0.5–1.0 MBPD of crude oil). Toward that end the Canadian government has indicated that it might soon become receptive to price reductions which would make Canadian gas competitive in the U.S. markets.

Mexico   The troubles of the Mexican economy have made headline news recently. Somehow, in a prototypical Third World manner, Mexico's government has managed to "turn a silk purse into a sow's ear." With enormous continuing success in petroleum exploration and production, in principle it should have been relatively easy to absorb the small (10–15 percent) downward adjustment in oil prices during 1981–2, especially with their oil and gas export markets essentially unlimited by anything except their own choices.

In retrospect it is hard to conclude that their economic troubles did not stem from "normal greed and corruption" entrenched in their political system. Evidently earlier wishful expectations about ever-increasing oil prices and export volumes helped to buttress the government's expenditure commitments. However, 1982's modest decline in oil prices, coupled with accelerating financial obligations of their overheated economy, soon revealed Mexico's fragile economic underpinning and brought on their financial crisis.

So severe did the 1982 cash crunch become that expenditures were even reduced in petroleum exploration and development, probably the only major hope for overcoming their debt problems – assuming that the government's spending spree has stopped and does not resume soon. Mexico's past borrowing had grown so fast (by $24 billion last year alone – *The Wall Street Journal*, 4 October, 1982) that it will now require about 80 percent of their current 1.5 mbpd petroleum exports just to pay the estimated $12 billion annual interest on its accumulated foreign debt (roughly $80 billion for both public and private debt). Even this estimate depends upon firm oil prices in the 1980s, an unlikely outcome in my judgment.

Given the severe financial strains, in part brought about by rosy interpretations of their future oil income, almost any practical solution will require a substantial increase in Mexico's exports of oil and natural gas. However, with reasonable management of its future budgets those exports probably can be increased by as much as 0.5 mbpd (oil equivalent) each year for several years. At current prices that would provide them with, roughly, an *additional* $5 billion after 1 year, $10 billion after 2 years, etc.

There is little question but that Mexico has enough petroleum resources to maintain a healthy growth in oil exports (see figure 13.4). Indeed, they may well have the world's best potential outside of Saudi Arabia. If they meet the export goals suggested above, and set aside part of that potential additional income to reduce their debt to a more comfortable level over the next several years, they could still have a substantial and growing income – assuming reasonably stable oil prices – to devote to industrialization and modernization.

In whatever way their president (Sr. Miguel de la Madrid Hurtado who assumed the office on 1 December, 1982) might wish to handle the

(a)   The boom years in figures

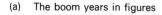
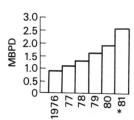

* Pemex reported early in
June that production had
reached this level on average

(b)   The growing slice of exports
         (percentage of total exports)

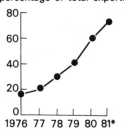

* First quarter

(c)   Proven reserves
         (in billions of barrels)

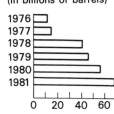

Figure 13.4 Mexican petroleum data.
Source: Latin America regional reports, Mexico and Central America, RM-81-06, 10 July 1981, p. 5; reserves data from Banamex, Banco de Mexico and Pemex.

present debt, pressures to produce more oil and gas for export now appears to be irresistible. Any future declines in nominal oil prices would only make that conclusion stronger. Fortunately, the oil fields in southern Mexico are so prolific that their production costs must be quite low (perhaps $2 per barrel) compared to market prices (now about $30 per barrel for light crude). Moreover, at current production levels their estimated potential reserves of more than 200 billion barrels would last over 200 years. However, their reserve estimates, which have been adjusted sharply upward almost every year for the last 10 years, are almost certain to increase substantially during the 1980s and 1990s.

Rising Mexican oil exports during the 1980s would add downward pressure on world oil prices. Without a resurgence of demand in the free world some OPEC members would have to reduce their export volumes in order to accommodate Mexico's need for a growing share of the international market. This must be a disturbing prospect for the oil exporters. It could become an especially difficult problem for OPEC if the fighting between Iraq and Iran stops and both those countries attempt to export more.

North Sea   A few years ago production of oil and gas from North Sea resources – mainly by the U.K. and Norway – was expected to make a growing contribution to supplies during the 1980s, and thereby to help reduce the world's imports from OPEC significantly. However, following the period of rising prices in 1979 and 1980, coupled with an astonishing worldwide unanimity in the belief that prices were inevitably headed upward in the 1980s and 1990s, the U.K. and Norwegian governments became increasingly cautious about their oil and gas depletion policies. They also demanded a greater share of the income from existing oil concessions, thus discouraging or delaying new investments by the major international oil companies.

As a result, any former expectations of rapidly rising North Sea oil production have now become slowly rising ones which appear likely to top out within the next few years, and may even be declining significantly by the end of the 1980s. However, natural gas production should continue to rise slowly for the rest of the 1980s and 1990s.

Although estimates of the potential petroleum resources in the North Sea vary substantially, the most conservative estimates are typically taken by governments as a basis for their production and export policies. In particular, governments are prone to assume that it is foolish to base such policy decisions upon any reserves that are not proven – that is, reliably indicated by specific engineering data from actual field measurements. Historical trends, geological potential, expanding technological capabilities, or unexplored promising territories are all typically prevented from exercising any significant impact upon policy considerations.

This "banker's" approach prevails despite the almost certain likelihood that any policy based upon it will be short-lived and possibly counter-productive.

A recent study for the Pentagon of the North Sea production potential concluded that the official estimates of its resources were grossly pessimistic[10] – a conclusion that has been held and promoted for years by "maverick" forecasters such as Professor Peter O'Toole of the Netherlands. But such non-official external studies seldom have much influence on government policy-makers and should not be expected to in this instance. The conservative assumptions on which such policies are based tend to restrain new exploration, and in that way may be inherently self-fulfilling, at least in the short run.

As we have seen (table 13.1), for over 100 years the U.S. government has periodically claimed that the U.S. was on the verge of exhausting its oil supplies. The U.K. and Norway are relative newcomers who have only had a few years of growing oil and gas production but are now making similar claims about their resources. Their administrations are unlikely to be swayed by technical arguments about future potential.

To be fair, it should be mentioned that nearly all governments (as examples: Canada, Mexico, Kuwait, Australia, Argentina) have exhibited the same kind of conservative syndrome. Therefore we should expect it to be repeated in the future as potential petroleum resources become changed to reserves in some of the luckier countries.

Fortunately for the oil-importing countries, the anticipated flattening of North Sea production during the 1980s no longer appears to be critical. Even without an increase in non-OPEC supplies, growing downward pressures on international oil prices now seem to be likely. Even with a North Sea slowdown non-OPEC near-term oil supplies are likely to grow (according to the projections of major oil companies and by the International Energy Agency), perhaps by 4–5 mbpd by 1990. If those forecasts are accurate the pressures on OPEC's members will escalate accordingly.

Developing countries (non-OPEC)   A few of the non-OPEC developing countries are important oil exporters – for example, Mexico, Egypt, and Oman. Nevertheless, there is no reason to believe that *any* developing country is now content with its present energy situation. The oil exporters generally find that they need more income than they are currently receiving, while the oppressive outflow of hard currency continues to undermine the modernization hopes of those which import oil. Consequently not only are the developing countries trying (with some success) to reduce their oil imports through conservation and substitution, but those with potential petroleum resources are increasingly finding it possible to arrive at acceptable exploration arrangements with the international oil companies. Consequently, the number of active drilling rigs in some of these areas has continued to rise despite the recent softness in oil prices, a trend which should expand in the years ahead.

Many prospective new areas are now being explored in Third World regions, but it is too early to predict with confidence which of them might blossom into giant producers. The results of exploration in recent years indicate that in the near term substantial increases are expected in many of these countries – for example Brazil, Egypt, Ivory Coast, Cameroon, Angola, Sudan, etc. For example, since 1979 Brazil's daily oil production is up about 60 percent to 250,000 barrels and the government expects to double that in the next 3 or 4 years; production in Cameroon almost quadrupled to 120,000 barrels per day (bpd) and is climbing rapidly; Egypt's production has been climbing steadily and is up 40 percent during the last 3 years to over 700,000 bpd and could reach 1 million in 1986; and India has demonstrated its interest in reducing its imports by increasing its 1979 production of 240,000 bpd to 400,000 bpd by the end of 1982. Although the promise may be great, exploration has started in rank wildcat territory such as Sudan and the Ivory Coast, but accurate quantitative results will generally not be known for several years.

Projections of new petroleum supplies from any one of these regions are necessarily highly uncertain. Aggregate projections of future production for the Third World as a whole are also not reliable, but should be much better because of statistical aggregation and because investment capital will tend to flow toward the more successful regions. However, there is no approach that does not involve considerable uncertainty. Potential changes in Mexico's export policies alone could swing the oil production in the developing countries by as much as 2–3 mbpd just during the 1980s. This is roughly 30–50 percent of the recent total combined production in these countries (about 6.3 mbpd in 1981).

Estimates by major institutions (e.g. oil companies, DoE, World Bank, IEA) generally foresee a long-term growth of Third World oil production, although the forecasts vary and are hard to compare because the statistical aggregations differ among these institutions. Still, the DoE's 1982 forecast may be reasonably representative of these institutions. It projects for the developing countries production of 8.4 and 9.9 mbpd in 1985 and 1995, respectively. During that 10-year period about half the total output is expected to come from Mexico. The most recent IEA forecast (from their second World Energy Outlook, as reported in the *Oil and Gas Journal*, 25 October, 1982) is similar, except that it shows a range instead of a single number for each of the years as shown in table 13.2.

Their estimates begin to look somewhat grim after 1990. Presumably, the overall growth in oil output will be substantially less than projected growth in its consumption, implying an ever-increasing dependence upon

TABLE 13.2 INTERNATIONAL ENERGY AGENCY FORECAST

	1980	1985	1990	1995
Non-OPEC developing countries				
Oil demand (MBPD)	7.9	9–10	11–13	17–22
Oil production	5.3	8– 9	8–11	9–13

imports. That is not a happy prospect for the developing countries, especially if – as the IEA expects – oil prices will be rising over most of that prolonged period of dependence.

I believe that at least a small likelihood exists that the post-1990 dependence of these countries will *not* grow as much as shown in the above table. The outcome for Third World oil production will depend partly upon chance factors in exploration and technological progress, and partly upon reasonable government investment policies. The latter is obviously the more worrisome. Still, reality factors will undoubtedly tend to restrain Third World oil dependence from becoming and remaining excessive. The above DoE or IEA projections might seem to be reasonable now, but neither organization has a good track record for short-term, let along long-term, forecasts.[11]

Communist Countries   For many years there has been a net outflow of oil from the communist countries. The Soviet Union has been by far the largest producer, supplying over 80 percent of the total output in recent years. Recent evidence that the former steady growth of Soviet oil production may be ending has had a strong effect upon many analysts – especially after a 1977 CIA study asserted that the communist countries would become oil importers in the early 1980s.[12] However, since then the results have shown that those CIA conclusions were unwarranted. Although the growth rate of Soviet oil production has slowed considerably, their output has risen, even during 1982. Now it appears likely to remain flat at about the current level of just over 12 mbpd, or to grow only very slowly, at least during the next several years.

However, Soviet natural gas production continues to rise at about 6–8 percent annually and now is beginning to challenge oil production for first place in fuel-equivalent terms. Currently natural gas provides about two-thirds as much energy as their oil production does, and it may move into the lead before 1990. This rapid growth in its natural gas supplies is clearly one of the major factors that has enabled the Soviet Union to continue and even to expand its oil shipments to the West. Indeed, during 1982 its estimated volume of petroleum exports to OECD countries increased by a surprising 40 percent, according to the International Energy Agency (*Wall Street Journal*, 18 February, 1983).

Although many institutions may prefer to assume that Soviet oil exports to the West will soon vanish, I believe that a continuation of those exports is a more likely result. Their strong need for Western currencies is likely to keep oil exports to the West steady, if not growing. In addition, beginning in 1984 additional natural gas exports to Western Europe should also add significantly to their hard-currency income. Those exports are made feasible by their enormous natural gas reserves which are greater, in terms of fuel-equivalents, than the oil reserves of Saudi Arabia. Moreover, their proven reserves have been growing steadily as exploration and development continue.

In addition, it is well known that the Soviet Union has a very large potential for fuel conservation, a potential which they have only recently begun to address seriously. At present prices the economic benefits of conservation can hardly fail to impress the Soviet leaders. It has already been reported that they have sharply increased gasoline and some other fuel prices. Still, there is not sufficient information available to make accurate quantitative estimates of the effectiveness of their conservation efforts. Also, their policy of raising prices for oil and gas exports – roughly in accordance with changing international prices – to their Eastern European satellites has certainly helped to restrain demand in those countries.

Finally, it is certainly possible, after a pause of a few years, that Soviet oil production will once more begin to rise significantly. Many geologists believe that their potential oil resources are still enormous and that what the Soviet Union mainly needs – in addition to greater allocations of capital – is access to modern technology in order to exploit those resources. They are just beginning to get such help from European countries (and even some from the U.S.). The trade journals have reported that the Soviet Union has sharply accelerated its investments in both production and exploration. More money, more outside assistance, and good geological prospects could add up to a resurgence of production – and larger exports – in the 1990s.

China also is known to have excellent petroleum prospects and, during recent years, has moved decisively to develop them with the help of the international oil companies. Because their principal attractive prospects are offshore, it is doubtful that their oil output before 1990 will become significantly greater than it is at present. However, current Chinese economic policy appears to be bent upon Western-style modernization and it will need all the hard currency that can be obtained. Certainly their potential oil exports are one of the more promising near-term avenues toward such income.

How much might China contribute to world supplies? That is, of course, highly uncertain. It is optimistic, but still possible that with good luck their oil exports during the 1990s could reach the level of 2–3 mbpd.

To accomplish that result, a lot of confidence must be established in their political reliability (and stability). Most of the investment capital in oil production almost certainly will have to come from the large international oil companies. The rate at which any initial investments can be increased will depend upon the confidence which, over time, can be placed in China's compliance with its contractual obligations. The outward evidence suggests that China has at least made a good start. Any progress which occurs during the next several years will be closely watched.

Conclusions

(1) Perhaps it has always been relatively difficult to believe that adequate new oil and gas supplies for the longer term would be found, while it is always easy to estimate the rate at which known reserves are being depleted. Thus, as the historical record clearly indicates, petroleum experts – particularly those associated with larger institutions, both public and private – have generally underestimated the potential for future production. Consequently I expect that most supply estimates for the 1990s and beyond are apt to be somewhat pessimistic and the projected oil prices to be unduly high.

(2) During the last 10 years each oil-importing country has twice faced the painful consequences of unexpected sharp price escalations, coupled with threats to the security of its fuel supplies, even at those high prices. Moreover, similar threats are likely to persist – at least in most people's perceptions – probably for decades. The obvious simple scenario is easy to write. Lower world oil prices in the 1980s increase demand, reduce investments, gradually increase dependence on imports, and set the stage for another round of price hikes. Those higher prices could occur gradually through normal market forces as the world's excess production capacity dwindles, or relatively suddenly after a major interruption in supplies, whether willful or inadvertent.

However, the "once burnt, twice shy" maxim – in regard to petroleum – may now need to be replaced by "twice burnt, forever shy." The implication is that most countries now seek to reduce their dependence on oil imports and to increase their domestic energy supplies. The result should be growing long-term efforts in the production of alternative energy supplies as well as in exploration for oil and gas. Although the results will undoubtedly be erratic, especially in exploration, overall I do not expect that the prior level of dependence upon imported petroleum on a world scale will be repeated, even if oil prices should decline drastically in real terms during the next few years.

(3) For most countries the importance of reducing dependence upon oil imports is usually much greater than for reducing dependence upon other commodities such as copper, sugar, or steel. That follows, in part, because the international petroleum trade is larger than that of all other commodities combined. Another contributing factor is the widespread belief that the growing impact of governments – especially of the OPEC governments – in all phases of petroleum markets will keep those petroleum consumers dependent upon imports and highly vulnerable to new price shocks. Rising petroleum prices can severely damage the entire development program of an oil-importing nation – by extracting from it a large fraction of its hard currency income. Indeed, some economists have asserted that the two oil-price shocks constitute the single most important reason for the recent worldwide recession. Whether that proposition can be demonstrated or not there is little disagreement about the assertion that the oil price shocks were significant contributors.

In recognition of the potentially great economic impact of petroleum prices upon world trade and prosperity, the policies of nearly all private consumers and public institutions now include measures to reduce their vulnerability associated with oil imports. Moreover, an impressive portion of the world's technological talent has become dedicated to that same goal.

Because the development of indigenous energy supplies on a large scale usually requires a long time – perhaps decades – a nation's energy-supply policies and programs cannot be expected to fluctuate rapidly with changes in market prices. Offshore oil production in a difficult region (e.g. as in the North Sea) will generally take 10 or more years to attain a substantial production capacity. Despite the recent softening in oil prices, the international effort in oil and gas exploration outside of North America is still strong. Over the decade ahead it should continue to expand as long as oil-importing countries see a potential threat to their energy security and reasonable prospects exist for increasing domestic oil supplies.

Except for Mexico, which has huge undeveloped oil reserves, new oil and gas investments in non-OPEC countries generally can only affect their indigenous oil supplies to a significant degree after the 1980s. The evidence seems clear that such investments are still being encouraged and that production of both oil and gas in the non-OPEC countries of the free world will be increasing. The major question each country must face is whether its production will rise as fast as its demand.

(4) The recent sharp decline in North American oil field activity, first in Canada and then the U.S., should not be interpreted as a harbinger of similar changes in other countries. In each of these two countries some difficulties in financing new petroleum ventures occurred for reasons

peculiar to its own political, economic, geological, and institutional "structures" and have little relevance for other countries. Indeed, in most other countries decisions about investing in energy supplies are almost entirely a formal *government* function and are unlikely to change rapidly in response to fluctuating oil prices. Even in Canada and the U.S. it is generally believed that the special conditions which led to the sharp declines in drilling activity are being adjusted and that a resurgence should soon occur in both countries, although the very rapid earlier expansions are unlikely to be repeated.

(5) There is now a spectrum of opinions available about the future supply–demand balance. Some forecasters believe that Free-World demand will rise faster than supplies, and that OPEC will be called upon to provide the difference. Others believe that demand will rise more slowly than supply, thereby reducing OPEC's production and prices over time. For the 1980s and 1990s my position is firmly with the latter group. The reasons related to supply are presented in this chapter; those related to demand are discussed by S. Fred Singer in chapter 12.

Because the authors accepted the DoE's projections of late 1977 as a basis for their forecasts, the conclusions in *Global 2000* about the outlook for future supply–demand relationships were misleading before it was issued. For example the opening sentence in its Energy section (vol. I, p. 27) states: "The Global 2000 Study's energy projections show no energy relief from the world's energy problems." We all know now that early relief started early in 1980 as both consumption and prices started to fall. In fact, spot prices started to fall from their peak in the fourth quarter of 1979 (see figure 13.5). In its second sentence about energy *Global 2000* said: "The projections point out that petroleum production capacity is not increasing as rapidly as demand." The facts are that since 1979 non-OPEC production capacity has been rising steadily – at about 4–5 percent annually in the Free World – while worldwide demand has been declining at an even faster rate (figure 13.1).

Indeed, the *Global 2000* statements in vol. I about energy supply or demand that can be checked by facts generally appear to be quite incorrect. "Per capita energy consumption is projected to increase everywhere. The largest increase – 72 percent over the 1975–90 time period is in industrialized countries other than the United States." In the United States and Europe per capita energy consumption has *decreased* since the Global 2000 study began. "While prices for oil and other commercial energy sources are rising, fuelwood – the poor person's oil – is expected to become far less available than it is today." Clearly we will not know about the fuelwood projection for some time but the explicit assumption about rising oil prices is wrong.

Expectations about future demand for energy, especially petroleum,

are discussed by Fred Singer in chapter 12. I examine the prospects for future supplies of petroleum (and natural gas) in this chapter. The portrayal is considerably different from the one found in *Global 2000*. The international energy trade is so huge that the appropriate responses to a major price shift cannot be expected to occur rapidly. Even under the best of circumstances a full response is likely to require decades. In my judgment, governments of most countries impede rather than facilitate desired economic responses. This "obvious fact" is not recognized in *Global 2000*, a government study which urges that *governments* take the lead in promoting solutions to projected energy problems – rather than urging governments to reduce their roles, in favor of private efforts. Thus *Global 2000* asserts that "an equally important priority for the United States is to cooperate generously and justly with the other nations – particularly in the areas of trade investment and assistance – in seeking solutions to the many problems that extend beyond our national boundaries."[13] However noble the intention, no mention is made of evidence that actions by governments may have created many energy-related problems, rather than led to their solutions.

To sum up my criticisms of the Energy section of *Global 2000*: its projections are incorrect; it ignores the important role of economics in providing solutions; and it leans almost exclusively upon government for assistance to prevent imagined difficulties.

In its executive summary, *Global 2000* states: "a world transition away from petroleum dependence must take place, but there is still much uncertainty as to how this transition will occur." I would much prefer the following: "During the next hundred years a world transition away from increased dependence on petroleum seems likely: however there is still much uncertainty as to if, when, where, or how this transition will occur."

My preferred statement may seem a bit heretical to some people who believe that "everybody knows" that petroleum consumption must be phased out relatively quickly. My view is that the outcome will be determined largely by economics, technology, geology, and sheer luck. Very little in the history of energy allows confidence to be placed in statements about long-term future developments (see table 13.1).

Notes

1 For example: *Global Insecurity: A Strategy for Energy and Economic Renewal*, edited by Daniel Yergin and Martin Hellebrand (Houghton Mifflin, 1982).
2 For example see *Energy: Global Prospects 1985–2000*. Workshop on Alternative Energy Strategies. (New York, McGraw-Hill, 1977).
3 "Predicting long-term oil demand," *Petroleum Economist*, July 1983.

4   U.S. natural gas reserves are currently about 200 TCF, the equivalent of
    about 30 billion barrels of petroleum.
5   *U.S. Mineral Resources.* D. A. Brobst and W. P. Pratt (eds). U.S. Geological
    Survey. Washington, Government Printing Office (1973).
6   There is convincing evidence for the existence of methane hydrates in quantities
    that dwarf the conventional gas resource. Daniel J. Milton of the U.S.
    Geological Survey reported that Soviet calculations of the amount of methane
    in hydrate formations exceeded 10^{18} m^3. That is equivalent to the energy of
    approximately 6,000 trillion barrels of oil – that is more than 1,000 times
    greater than the consensus estimate of total conventional petroleum re-
    sources. (See *The Future Supply of Nature-Made Petroleum and Gas*; Report
    of an international conference sponsored by UNITAR and IIASA, Pergamon
    Press, 1976, chapter 53, p. 928.)
        However, the abiogenic methane potential rests mostly on an imaginative,
    but unproven, theory that has been developed by Dr. Thomas Gold, a
    prominent physicist–astronomer at Cornell University. Investigation of that
    theory is now being supported by the Gas Research Institute and the Swedish
    government.
7   For example, see John M. Hunt, *Petroleum Geochemistry and Geology.* San
    Francisco: W. H. Freeman and Company, 1979. Part 12, pp. 534–41.
8   Exxon Company, *U.S.A.'s Energy Outlook* (December 1979) projects 6.1
    MBPD of conventional oil production in the U.S. during 1990.
9   See William M. Brown, *A Perspective on the Near-Term Outlook for Oil
    Prices.* Croton, N.Y.: Hudson Strategy Group, Research Memorandum No.
    119, June 1982. A similar view is expressed by economists Paul L. Joskow and
    Robert S. Pindyck in a recent *N.Y. Times* article (1 May, 1983, Business
    section).
10 "Alternative Strategies for Natural Gas in Western Europe." Report Com-
    missioned by the Department of Defense, Economics and Science Planning
    Department, Washington, D.C. Geneva, Switzerland: Energy Advice, 1982.
11 I was pleased to notice the emergence of a more optimistic view in a recently
    published energy book *OPEC Behavior and World Oil Prices*, ed. by J. M.
    Griffins and D. J. Teese (London: George Allen and Unwin, 1982).
12 Central Intelligence Agency (1977), *The International Energy Situation:
    Outlook to 1985.*
13 P. 4 under "Major Findings and Conclusions."

14

Nuclear Power

KARL COHEN

Nuclear fission power is unique among man's potential future sources of energy in the following combination of qualities:

(1) the impact on public health of large-scale deployment is far less than that of other already deployed sources, from the standpoints of air pollution, fuel mining, transport of fuel and waste, and waste disposal[1] (table 14.1);
(2) it offers a potentially inexhaustible supply of energy by well-understood technology;
(3) its fuel is highly concentrated and thus transportation is not a hindrance to its use any place on the globe, including underwater;
(4) nuclear electric power is generally economical compared to conventional fossil-fueled power stations;
(5) it is deployed on a substantial scale, and an industry and technical manpower exist ready to expand its use.

It also has unique drawbacks:

(1) the generation of fission power is accompanied by the production of radiation six orders of magnitude larger than any other human activity;
(2) fission reactions use as fuel, and have as products, the materials of man's most destructive weapons;
(3) because of these two circumstances, fission power is subject to unprecedented governmental regulation, based on considerations of national security, foreign policy, health, and safety;
(4) further, because of all the above, it arouses considerable public apprehension which can easily be turned into hostility.

In the twenty-first century the aspiration of the approximately 10 billion inhabitants of the earth cannot reasonably be met without a vast supply of

TABLE 14.1 HEALTH EFFECTS AND ACCIDENT HAZARDS OF DIFFERENT FUEL CYCLES[a]
(normalized to the production of 1 GW/yr of electrical energy)

(a) Comparison of health effects[b]

Fuel cycle	Workers		Population		Total	
	Deaths	Diseases	Deaths	Diseases	Deaths	Diseases
Coal	0.1 (5)	1.5 (2)	3 (10)	1000 (20)	3 (10)	1000 (20)
Oil	~0	0.01	3 (10)	1000 (20)	3 (10)	1000 (20)
Gas	~0	~0	~0	~0	~0	~0
Uranium	0–0.2	0–0.2	0–0.1	0–0.1	0–0.3	0–0.3

Note: Best estimates are accompanied by uncertainty factors in parentheses.

(b) Comparison of accident hazards[c]

Fuel cycle	Workers		Population		Total	
	Fatal	Non-fatal	Fatal	Non-fatal	Fatal	Non-fatal
Coal	1.40 (1.5)	60 (1.5)	1.0 (1.5)	1.8 (2.0)	2.40 (1.5)	62 (1.5)
Oil	0.35 (1.5)	30 (1.5)	?	?	0.35 (1.5)	30 (1.5)
Gas	0.20 (1.5)	15 (2)	0.009	0.005	0.21 (1.5)	15 (2)
Uranium	0.20 (1.5)	15 (2)	0.012	0.11	0.21 (1.5)	15 (2)

Notes: Best estimates are accompanied by uncertainty factors in parentheses.
[a] The tables cover the hazards caused by the activities of extraction, processing, transport, conversion to electricity and waste management. They are from W. Paskievici[1] who reviewed the findings of nineteen different studies dated from 1974 to 1980.
[b] Table 14.1a covers occupational fatalities and diseases, and fatalities and chronic disease in the general population due to normal working conditions and operations.
[c] Table 14.1b covers occupational fatalities and injuries, and fatalities and injuries to the general population due to accidents.

energy, which could easily be furnished by nuclear power. Despite the hopes and desires of many well-intentioned people to develop alternative large energy sources – solar, fusion, or a full-spectrum coal economy – it would be imprudent for mankind to abandon a certain solution to its energy problem for uncertain future solutions, whose properties and drawbacks are only dimly perceived. It would not, however, be uncharacteristic of mankind to avoid difficult decisions, and in view of the concerns with nuclear power, to avoid definitive commitment to large-scale nuclear power unless and until it becomes evident that no other course is possible.

This is *a fortiori* true for the United States. In the U.S. the need for great future expansion of energy production to accommodate the needs of the rest of the world is not high on our priorities, and the reality of a great expansion of energy for the U.S. itself is still being debated. Further, the U.S. is in a privileged situation with respect to fossil energy. The need for commitment to an infinite energy source based on nuclear fission appears less pressing for the U.S. than for the world as a whole.

These viewpoints underlie the expected figures for nuclear energy expansion in the next decades. World build-up of nuclear power plants is now at a rate about a third of that projected only 5 years ago (tables 14.4 and 14.5). By the year 2000 we project that about 500 GWe of nuclear power stations will be deployed globally, a small fraction of the ultimate nuclear potential. The increase will be at the rate of 20 GWe/year. In the U.S., absent a resurgence of public support for nuclear plants, and a subsequent recasting of governmental–industry relations, the rate of growth will be negligible.

History of Nuclear Power Expansion

In the 15 years following the discovery of uranium fission in 1939, civilian nuclear applications were suppressed in favor of military applications.[2] They were bottled up in government establishments and stifled by secrecy. Nevertheless, in the course of developing nuclear weapons, important technical progress was made in the physics of reactor cores, in nuclear cross-sections, in control and instrumentation, in production of special materials such as pure graphite and heavy water, in the chemistry and metallurgy of uranium and plutonium, and in winning uranium from ore. Facilities were built for isotopic enrichment of uranium and for reprocessing spent fuel elements chemically to extract the plutonium. A small, relatively high-temperature submarine propulsion reactor, water-cooled and water-moderated, became (in 1954) the first practical nuclear power application. The whole constituted a substantial, publicly-owned but secret infrastructure upon which a nuclear power enterprise could be erected.

By 1954 it was plain that attempts to maintain a monopoly of nuclear weapons by withholding information had failed. Weapons states then altered their policies in concert to exchange cooperation with non-weapons states in peaceful nuclear applications for their pledges not to produce nuclear weapons.[3]

A period of active promotion and encouragement of nuclear power ensued. Much information was declassified. Industry was encouraged to participate. The perception at the time of both the participants and the public was that nuclear power generation presented few technical difficulties and no serious safety problems. In the U.S. manufacturers and small electric utilities with no prior experience in power generation were actively recruited by the Atomic Energy Commission, under mandate to avoid a feared monopoly by the largest corporations and private utilities.[4]

There was early experimentation with a variety of reactor types.[5] The nations with large diffusion plants, whose capacity became surplus in the mid-1960s[6] by the advent of hydrogen weapons and other improvements in weapons technology, eventually settled on water-cooled and water-moderated reactors (pressurized water reactors and boiling water reactors) which use enriched uranium as fuel (the U.S. and the U.S.S.R.). Nations with no, or little, uranium enrichment capability (Canada, the U.K., France) developed heavy water-moderated and -cooled reactors, or graphite-moderated, CO_2-cooled reactors, which use natural uranium fuel. Early concerns about uranium supply, which had stimulated breeder reactor development in the late 1940s,[2] had been dissipated by the development of uranium reserves and supplies to feed the weapons complexes. Breeder reactors became a long-term research goal, not a commercial product.

Table 14.2 shows the historical profile of the global spread of nuclear power plants through the year 1982. The U.S., the rest of the Free World, and the Centrally Planned Economies, are separately listed.[7] Expansion in the CPEs lagged for about a decade, as they struggled to recover from the war. In 1979, after the moratorium on reactor licensing which was caused by the Three Mile Island accident, the U.S. relinquished the lead in nuclear power deployment to the rest of the Free World. The last column shows an impressive growth. Note, however, that compounded annual growth over the period 1971–6 was 29 percent, while for the period 1976–82 it was down to 12 percent. This is just the reverse of what might have been expected in view of the improved economics of nuclear power following the precipitate rise in oil prices which began in 1973.[8] In the U.S. electric energy production grew over the period 1950–73 at a compound rate of 7.2 percent. This fell to 2.09 percent for the period 1973–82.[8,9] Although there are other factors in the slowdown, such as

Year	U.S.[b] No.	U.S.[b] MWe/Yr	U.S.[b] GWe cum.	Free World ex U.S. No.	Free World ex U.S. MWe/Yr	Free World ex U.S. GWe cum.	CPE[c] No.	CPE[c] MWe/Yr	CPE[c] GWe cum.	World Gwe cum.
56	—	—	—	2	92	0.1	—	—	—	0.1
57	1	60	0.1	—	—	0.1	—	—	—	0.2
58	—	—	0.1	3	127	0.2	6	600	0.6	0.9
59	1	207	0.3	3	105	0.3	—	—	0.6	1.2
60	1	175	0.4	1	40	0.4	—	—	0.6	1.4
61	—	—	0.4	—	—	0.4	—	—	0.6	1.4
62	7	519	1.0	6	576	0.9	—	—	0.6	2.5
63	1	61	1.0	—	—	0.9	—	—	0.6	2.6
64	2	76	1.0	4	620	1.6	2	310	0.9	3.5
65	—	—	1.0	8	1,694	3.3	1	50	1.0	5.2
66	2	900	1.9	5	1,110	4.4	1	80	1.0	7.3
67	3	1,068	2.9	6	1,121	5.5	1	200	1.2	9.6
68	—	—	2.9	2	366	5.9	—	—	1.2	10.0
69	4	2,534	5.4	6	1,612	7.5	1	365	1.6	14.5
70	4	2,402	7.8	2	661	8.1	—	—	1.6	17.5
71	5	3,693	11.5	7	3,284	11.4	1	440	2.0	24.9
72	6	4,224	15.7	11	4,745	16.2	2	552	2.6	34.4
73	12	9,246	24.9	3	1,162	17.3	4	2,030	4.6	46.9
74	14	11,752	36.6	7	4,230	21.6	2	880	5.5	63.7
75	3	2,965	39.6	7	4,335	25.9	3	1,880	7.4	72.9
76	7	6,258	45.8	10	7,205	33.1	2	1,405	8.8	87.7
77	4	3,715	49.6	9	6,138	39.2	1	1,000	9.8	98.6
78	3	2,608	52.2	11	9,268	48.6	2	880	10.7	111.4
79	—	—	52.2	11	9,046	57.6	2	2,000	12.7	122.5
80	4	4,013	56.2	8	6,560	64.2	6	4,480	17.2	137.6
81	3	3,412	59.6	15	12,895	77.1	5	2,917	20.1	156.8
82	5	5,383	65.0	11	9,201	86.3	5	3,228	23.3	174.6

Notes:
  [a] Not corrected for plants withdrawn from service.
  [b] In U.S., operating license dates.
  [c] CPE = Centrally Planned Economies.
  All figures are net output.

the rise of public opposition in the 1960s and 1970s, reduction in electric energy growth (which was not limited to the U.S.) is clearly a major factor.

The 1973 watershed is most strikingly exhibited in table 14.3, which shows nuclear plant orders and cancellations in the U.S.[7] Over 20 percent of the cancelled plants had already received construction permits, and one or two were 27 percent complete.[10]

Nuclear Power Capacity Projections to 2000

Past projections of nuclear generating capacity in 1990 and 2000 are now an embarrassment to their authors. In February 1975 the median forecast of ERDA for U.S. nuclear electric capacity was 375 GWe by 1990 and 940 GWe by 2000.[11] The December 1975 median forecast prepared jointly by the CECD and the IAEA for the Free World as a whole was 940 GWe by 1990 and 2240 GWe by 2000.[12] These forecasts were made before account was taken of the phenomenon illustrated in table 14.3. The appended forecast, table 14.4, is based, so far as the Free World is concerned, on a country-by-country appraisal of planned additions by NUEXCO, and in the case of the U.S., on a utility-by-utility survey of generating expansion needs and plans.[13] The NUEXCO survey covers the period 1982–91. Since all the plants which will be operating by the end of this period are under construction or in advanced planning, one can have some confidence in these figures.

TABLE 14.3 ORDERS AND CANCELLATIONS,
U.S. NUCLEAR PLANTS

	Orders		Cancellations	
	No.	*MWe*	*No.*	*MWe*
1970	14	14,275	0	0
1971	21	20,873	0	0
1972	38	41,492	6	5,738
1973	41	46,840	0	0
1974	26	30,944	8	8,290
1975	4	4,180	11	12,291
1976	3	3,790	2	2,328
1977	4	5,040	9	9,862
1978	2	2,240	13	13,333
1979	0	0	8	9,476
1980	0	0	16	18,085
1981	0	0	6	5,711
1982	0	0	18	22,019

TABLE 14.4 WORLD NUCLEAR ELECTRIC GENERATING CAPACITY FORECAST
(NET ELECTRICAL GIGAWATTS, END OF YEAR)

	1982	1983	1984	1985	1986	1987	1988	1989	1990	1991	1999
United States	58	64	72	78	87	92	97	102	110	112	110 ± 25
Europe[a]	60	68	73	82	92	103	110	115	121	127	190 ± 25
Far East[b]	21	21	24	27	30	33	36	40	43	47	70 ± 15
Other Free World[c]	8	9	10	12	14	16	17	20	22	24	40 ± 15
Free World Total	146	162	179	200	224	243	260	277	295	310	410 ± 40
CPE[d]	25	30	34	38	41	45	48	51	56	60	100 ± 30
World Total	171	192	213	238	265	288	308	328	352	370	500 ± 50

[a] Europe excludes Comecon countries.
[b] Far East: Japan, Korea, Philippines, Taiwan.
[c] Other Free World: includes Canada, Argentina, Brazil, India, Pakistan.
[d] CPE: Centrally Planned Economies including China.

The plans of the Centrally Planned Economies, inferred from the vague schedules reported by the Atomic Industrial Forum,[7] with some discounting for underfulfillment of plans, were added to the NUEXCO tables. The values given for 31 December 1999 were then derived from the 1982–91 schedules by

(1)   assuming the U.S. nuclear capacity will not increase in the 1990s;
(2)   projecting the 1982–91 growth for other countries into 1991–9 using a compromise between linear and exponential extrapolation.

Assumption (1) describes the present U.S. trajectory. A rebirth of the nuclear industry in the U.S. is of course possible, and even necessary. If this were to occur in the early 1990s the effects would not be significant until the twenty-first century.

Table 14.5 lists, for comparison, some recent forecasts by the IEA/NEA (Paris), the IAEA, and the U.S. DoE.[14] *Global 2000* gave no clear projection. In the summary section it did not separate nuclear and hydropower, and projected only as far as 1990. It quoted in chapter 10, without endorsing them, projections by other bodies (the Workshop on Alternative Energy Strategies, the World Energy Conference, and others[15] which were current in 1977–8. These are also listed in table 14.5.

The 500 ± 50 GWe projected in table 14.4 would generate about 0.33 TWyr of electricity, consuming about 1 TWyr of primary energy. Using Häfele's Low Scenario energy projections for 2000,[16] namely 1.7 TWyr of electricity production and 13.6 TWyr of primary energy, nuclear power would be 19 percent of the world's electricity production and 7 percent of its primary energy. The last figure is in fairly good agreement with the Marchetti and Nakicenovic prediction, made in 1979, of a 6 percent nuclear share of primary energy in the year 2000.[17] In some industrialized countries (e.g. France), the proportion of electric energy production will exceed 50 percent. The nuclear portion of electric energy production in some countries is already substantial. Table 14.6 gives values for 1981.[7]

Nuclear Power Economics

In 1955, when civilian power became for the first time a priority item, the largest steam-electric generating unit in operation in the U.S. was 217 MWe; the average was 107 MWe.[18] The 28 coal-fired plants greater than 200 MWe showed costs in the range of $160 ± 25/kWe.[6,19] The average mine-mouth price of coal was less than 20¢/MMBtu. The stations produced power at about 6 mills/kWh or better. A 200 MWe light water reactor generating station was estimated to cost $250/kWe. The fuel cycle

TABLE 14.5 EARLIER ESTIMATES OF WORLD NUCLEAR GENERATING CAPACITIES[a] (ELECTRICAL GIGWATTS, END OF YEAR)

	1980	1981	1985	1990	1995	2000
1981 IAEA (14)						
Free World		135	261	346	365	
CPE		18	40	81	90	
World Total		153	301	427	455	
1982 IEA/NEA (14)						
United States	55		90	121		135–165
Europe	44		91	133		180–240
Japan	16		25	47		60–90
Canada	5		10	15		20–25
OECD Total	119		216	316		395–505
1980 INFCE Low (14)						
Free World			245	373	550	850
1982 US DoE (31)						
U.S. mid-range	55	57	85	118	142	140–160
1977 WAES (15)						
U.S., Case C1						420
U.S., Case C2						560
Free World, C1						960
Free World, C2						1540
1977 WEC (15)						
Free World						940
CPE						420
World Total						1360
1977 SRI (15)						
U.S. base case						510
U.S. low case						370

[a] Numbers in parentheses refer to References.

TABLE 14.6 NUCLEAR POWER SHARE (PERCENTAGES) OF ELECTRICITY PRODUCTION, SELECTED COUNTRIES, 1981

Belgium	25.4	Sweden	35.8
Canada	10.0	Switzerland	28.1
Finland	34.5	Taiwan	31.3
France	37.7	United Kingdom	12.8
Germany (F.R.G.)	14.6	United States	11.7
Japan	15.0		

cost, containing multiple unknowns, was estimated at 3+ mills/kWh, giving (paper) power costs of more than 9 mills/kWh.[19]

These figures, assuming they were correct for the nuclear plants (and they were not), were close enough to sustain the hope that nuclear power could be competitive, either in regions of the U.S. where coal transportation costs were high, or overseas where coal prices were more than twice as high, or by anticipated technical improvements in nuclear power generation.

The second round of British graphite reactors, which went into service in 1961/2, were considerably larger than the small Calder Hall reactors, with which they had obtained an early lead in civilian power application. They indicated that plant costs vary as the 0.6 exponent of the rating, and pointed the way for attempts to achieve economic nuclear power by increasing plant sizes. Table 14.1 shows the increases in average size of nuclear plants worldwide, paced by increases in maximum turbogenerator sizes (in the U.S., 500 MWe in 1960; 1000 MWe in 1965).[18] Light water reactors continued to increase in size to obtain economy of scale until the USAEC established a licensing limit of 4000 MWt to encourage plant standardization. Heavy water reactors increased in size from 200 MWe at Douglas Point to 740 at Bruce, with 880 MWe units planned for Darlington. The British graphite reactors show an evolution from 35 MWe at Chapel Cross to 660 MWe under construction at Torness Point. The Russian light water-cooled, graphite-moderated reactors have progressed from 100 MWe to 1500 under construction at Ingolinskaya.[10]

As nuclear power plant sizes increased their neutron economy improved and nuclear fuel costs dropped. Table 14.7 lists the evolution of utility nuclear fuel costs and coal costs over the period 1966–81 (U.S. data).[20] The price of uranium (yellowcake) is also listed.[13] Since utilities usually buy their uranium some years before it is used, the recent break in yellowcake price will not be seen until late in the 1980s. The present spot market price of uranium, deflated by the Producer Price Index, is lower than in 1968; while deflated coal prices are three times as high as in 1968.

The gap in fuel costs between coal and nuclear plants since 1970 has outweighed the capital cost advantage of coal plants and made nuclear power cheaper. In Europe, where coal costs are typically twice as high as in the U.S., the advantage has been particularly marked. Table 14.8 shows the comparative generating costs of coal and nuclear plants in France (units are centimes/kWh).[21] Of the 28.2 c/kWh shown therein as the generating costs for coal plants in 1981, 18.8 c/kWh is for coal, or $3.30/MMBtu.[22]

In the U.S., where coal is $1.75/MMBtu (per table 14.7), the results are much closer. Table 14.9, based on data reported annually by the nation's utilities to the Energy Information Administration of the Department of Energy, shows that for large nuclear and coal plants now in operation, on

TABLE 14.7 U.S. UTILITY FUEL COSTS, CURRENT DOLLARS
(FOR REFERENCE, INCLUDES MARKET PRICES OF U_3O_8)

Year	Nuclear fuel	Coal	Yellowcake	Producer's price index
1966	23	23		98
1967	22	23		100
1968	21	23	6.35	103
1969	18	26	6.15	106
1970	16	32	6.15	110
1971	14	38	5.95	114
1972	11	39	5.95	118
1973	14	41	6.50	126
1974	15	64	12.50	154
1975	18	81	26.00	172
1976	25	85	41.00	182
1977	29	94	42.40	195
1978	32	113	43.25	209
1979	39	132	42.20	237
1980	50	153	28.50	275
1981	55	175	23.50	304
1982			17.00	311

Note: Fuel costs in cents per million Btu delivered; yellowcake prices in dollars per pound.

TABLE 14.8 GENERATING COST OF FRENCH POWER STATIONS
(COSTS IN CONSTANT 1981 FRANCS)

Year	Conventional c/kWh	Operating hours	Nuclear c/kWh	Operating hours
1973	12.1	4,980	18.7	4,993
1974	19.0	4,398	17.0	4,832
1975	19.7	3,985	12.7	6,004
1976	17.0	5,107	15.6	5,594
1977	19.0	3,793	14.3	4,679
1978	17.4	4,071	11.6	5,798
1979	19.1	4,222	12.0	5,221
1980	21.7	4,015	12.4	5,958
1981	28.2	2,943	14.8	5,470

Note: First large PWRs came into service in 1977.

TABLE 14.9 NATIONAL AVERAGES OF U.S. INVESTOR UTILITY
NUCLEAR AND COAL-FIRED POWER PLANT GENERATION
COSTS FOR 1980 AND 1981

	Average Unit Costs (mills/kWh)	
Cost category	*Nuclear*	*Coal*
1980		
Fuel (actual)	4.99	12.73
O&M (actual)	5.69	2.46
Capital (estimated)	14.00	8.35
Generating (estimated)	24.68	23.54
1981		
Fuel (actual)	5.46	16.64
O&M (actual)	6.23	2.86
Capital (estimated)	14.40	9.41
Generating (estimated)	26.09	28.91

Notes: Capital costs estimated using a fixed charge rate of 18%; capacity factor of nuclear plants, 1980: 59.6%; 1981: 62.4%; capacity factor of coal plants, 1981: 59.7%

the average there is no clear advantage to either.[23] Since construction costs and coal deposits vary regionally, this conclusion is not valid regionally. Nuclear power costs two-thirds of coal power in the East North-Central region, while coal power costs two-thirds of nuclear in the Far West.[23] (It is worth noting here that at $30/bbl, an oil-fired plant of 50 percent thermal efficiency has a fuel cost alone of 30 mills/kWh, clearly not competitive.)

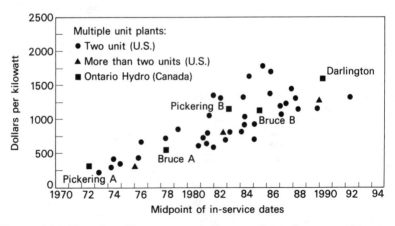

Figure 14.1 Electric utility cost group data: nuclear plants: graphic comparison of total project cost/kW (North American data).

Generating costs of operating plants are of course subject to question on the basis of the accounting ground rules chosen, but at least the annual costs and the total capitalization are known. It is when we try to predict future generating costs of plants not yet committed that we encounter the greatest uncertainties. To begin with, see the raw data of plant capital costs (figure 14.1, which combines Canadian and U.S. data[24]). Plants commissioned the same year may have specific costs which differ by a factor of two. This variation may be partially accounted for by regional differences, plant sizes, etc., but even after careful analysis there remains much residual variation. Figure 14.2 shows the costs of plants under construction, as reported quarterly in current dollars to the DoE.[25] The costs shown are a combination of actual plus estimated expenditures to

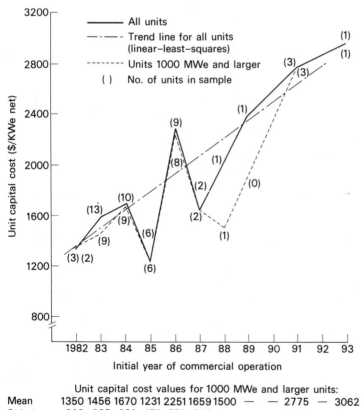

Unit capital cost values for 1000 MWe and larger units:

Mean	1350	1456	1670	1231	2225	1659	1500	—	—	2775	—	3062
Std. dev.	368	385	389	175	879	293	—	—	—	300	—	—

Figure 14.2 Estimated LWR power plant unit capital costs by year of entry into service (reported as of 30 June 1982).

complete. The Trend Line indicates an increase of 8.5 percent/year, which is less than the expected escalation rate of the Handy–Whitman construction index. The projections are of course minimums, since they do not include costs for plant changes yet to be mandated by the Nuclear Regulatory Commission. Analysis of this data confirms regional cost differences as large as ± 30 percent of the national average.[25]

Some economists (e.g. Mooz[26] and Komanoff[27]), noting that pre-construction cost estimates have had little relation to actual experience, even after allowing for intervening economic factors (inflation, escalation etc.) (compare figure 14.3[28]), prefer to predict future costs by extrapolating trends derived from statistical analysis of real cost experience. This method is unable to account for technical progress or changes in standards.

The utility industry as a whole has relied on the DoE cost analyses.

The U.S. DoE and its predecessor agencies have been tracking coal and nuclear construction costs with assistance from United Engineers

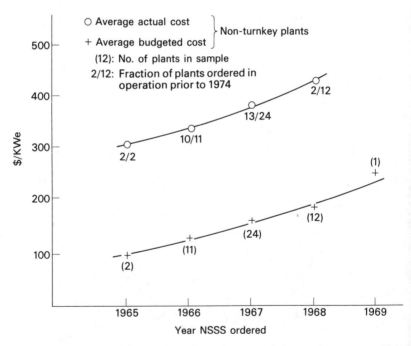

Figure 14.3 Expected and actual cost trends of nuclear plants (NSSS = nuclear steam supply system).

and Constructors Inc. for over 15 years. This effort has resulted in the development of a rigorous or engineered approach to cost estimating for stations under construction, and a large data base of nuclear and coal power plant economic models. The estimating approach constructs the cost estimate by defining the equipment, material and labor requirements for a specific plant of a specific size at a specific point in time. . . . The data base, known as the United States DoE Energy Economic Data Base (EEDB) contains capital, fuel, and operating and maintenance costs for 11 different types of nuclear and coal power plants.

The costs are presented in two main categories: physical plant costs (direct and indirect construction costs plus contingency) and time-related costs (escalation and interest during construction).[29]

Table 14.10 recapitulates these cost analyses over a period of 15 years. In comparing nuclear vs. fossil, the total costs are the relevant data, since the schedules and hence the time-related costs are different. For the nuclear plants the physical plant costs, and the physical plant costs deflated by the Handy–Whitman index, are also listed. The deflated costs show the cost inflation which can be attributed to increasingly rigorous design and construction standards – at least those standards recognized at the project start. The last column shows actual cost experience (or latest cost estimates) of the nuclear plants, which is disconcertingly different from the engineering estimates (the same is true for the fossil plants in the data base). The differences are usually attributed (by the industry) to more rigorous standards and regulations imposed *after* the project start. Of course it is difficult to distinguish regulatory changes from other differences between preliminary and final design, such as design changes dictated by operating experience with other plants, by construction problems, or even by financing difficulties.

The EEDB procedure identifies at best design-related costs which are known at project inception. The cost estimates differ from real life (even assuming no design changes) principally in the assumption of efficient and orderly construction. Other uncertainties include necessarily imprecise assumptions about inflation and escalation rates, the evolution of fuel prices, plant capacity factors, interest rates, and the structure and cost of capital.

Projections of Fossil and Nuclear Power Costs

The evident uncertainties of cost projections, and their past history of unpleasant surprises, have made them highly suspect and highly sub-

TABLE 14.10 ANALYTICAL COMPARISON OF COAL AND NUCLEAR PLANT CAPITAL COSTS, U.S. (SINGLE 1000 MWe PLANTS, CURRENT DOLLARS)

Document	Experience to	Project Start	Commercial operation	Total Costs Coal	Total Costs Nuclear	Overnight costs nuclear	Deflated overnight costs nuclear	Actual nuclear
Wash 1082	3/67	3/67	Late 1972	110	134	110	105	350
Wash 1150	6/69	6/69	Mid-1975	195	240	165	143	450
Wash 1230	1/71	1/71	Jan. 1978	275	345	220	167	600
Wash 1230 Rev.	1/73	1/73	Jan. 1981	450	500	320	213	750
Wash 1345	1/73	1/74	Jan. 1983	625	700	375	237	1,400
Wash 1345 Rev.	1/75	1/75	Jan. 1985	750	925	430	229	1,700
Nureg	6/76	6/76	Mid-1986	925	1,130	600	291	1,800
EEDB-I	1/78	1/78	Jan. 1988	1,050	1,500	700	300	2,100
EEDB-III	1/80	1/80	Jan. 1992	2,149	3,192	1,050	374	2,600
EEDB-IV	1/81	1/81	Jan. 1993	2,545	3,999	1,082	351	2,800
EEDB-IVa	1/81	1/81	Jan. 1993	2,545	4,307	1,165	378	2,800
EEDB-V	1/82	1/82	Jan. 1994		3,932	1,480	437	3,080

Notes: Overnight costs include direct and indirect construction costs plus contingency, but no allowance for time-related costs; that is, escalation and interest during construction. The deflated overnight costs are deflated using the Handy–Whitman Index of Utility Construction Costs (Whitman et al., Baltimore, Md.) for the year of project start. "Actual" costs to 1982 are average observed costs for nuclear plants put in operation on the dates given in column 4. Project start dates generally do not correspond. For dates after 1982, "actual" costs are present best estimates from the trend line shown on figure 14.2. EEDB means Energy Economic Data Base of the DoE. "Actual" costs should be compared with total costs nuclear (column 6).

jective. Nevertheless, they remain a necessity for economic decision-making.

Let us consider first the economics of existing plants in the U.S. Table 14.9 shows that operating and maintenance (O&M) costs of nuclear plants are now more than half the production costs: they exceed nuclear fuel costs. They have increased from 2.5 mills/kWh in 1977 to 6.2 mills/kWh in 1981, and are now over twice the O&M costs for coal.[23] The cost increase reflects new regulatory requirements, which have increased personnel costs and mandated plant modifications. In part this is the immediate impact of Three Mile Island. Equipment failures also contribute to the O&M costs. In France O&M costs for the same type of plants are less than for coal plants.[22] Nevertheless, the production costs (fuel plus O&M) of existing nuclear plants are roughly 60 percent of those of coal plants, and nobody expects coal prices to go down. One can conclude that it is unlikely that nuclear plants now in operation will be shut down.

Overseas, in countries where fossil fuel costs (in 1982 dollars) are $3.00/MMBtu and up, and where nuclear plant capital costs are contained by disciplined construction and a reasoned regulatory process, future nuclear power plants will be unarguably economic. In the U.S., where none of these conditions apply, the relative economics of future coal and nuclear plants is obscure. Emission controls on fossil plants, and the tendency of coal prices to follow oil prices (the ratio has varied narrowly, per Btu, between 2 and 3 over the last 15 years),[8] have kept nuclear power economic, even though the original goals of the nuclear plant designers have not been met. The further evolution of regulatory requirements on both fossil and nuclear plants is very uncertain (the acid rain issue is an example). The most recent study by the EIA of the projected costs of electricity from plants ordered now for initial operation in 1995[30] indicates a mid-case economic advantage of at least 5 percent for nuclear plants in New England and the South Atlantic states, and a similar advantage for mine-mouth coal-fired plants in the old Southwest and the North Central states. The two plant types are projected to be competitive within the error of estimation in the rest of the country. The U.S. DoE has accordingly projected that nuclear and coal plants will be built in the decade 1990–2000 in the ratio of one to three, leading to their nuclear capacity projection of 150 GWe in 2000 shown in table 14.5.[31]

However, the nuclear plant cost advantages projected can be challenged by not implausible assumptions. The economic advantage of future nuclear plants cannot be proved beyond a reasonable doubt, and in the face of organized public opposition few utilities, and fewer public utility commissioners, will try to make the case. Although in the U.S. it now takes about 12 years from order to place a nuclear plant in operation, no plant has been ordered in the last 4 years, and no orders are now planned. This chapter accordingly projects no new nuclear plants in the decade 1990–2000. (The phenomenon of public opposition is discussed below, in the section "The Future of Nuclear Fission Power").

Uranium Supply

In this section we are obliged to confine ourselves to the Free World, since no data have been released by the U.S.S.R., its satellites, or China. The operative assumption is that no, or little, fuel or services will cross the boundaries.

The Free World's uranium resources are very imperfectly represented by published estimates, such as table 14.11, prepared by NEA/IAEA for the International Uranium Resources Evaluation Project. The tables reveal only the present state of exploration.[32] There is no reason to believe that North America is unique in its ratios of resources at higher prices to resources at lower prices, nor in the ratio of estimated additional resources to reasonably assured resources. The resource base, with present technologies and in the price range given, is generally considered to be perhaps five times as large. It is thus not necessary to consider higher-price resources.

More to the point is the ability of the mining industry to extract uranium in the quantities needed. The annual consumption in reactors can easily be derived from tables 14.2 and 14.4, and the known mix of reactor types. Table 14.12 is adapted from tables by NUEXCO[13] which combine such numbers with their knowledge of production figures. The

TABLE 14.11   ESTIMATED WOCA URANIUM RESOURCES
BY CONTINENT AS OF JANUARY 1979
(IN 1000 TONNES U)

Continent	Reasonably assured resources		Estimated additional resources	
	Up to $80/kg U	$80 to $130/kg U	Up to $80/kg U	$80 to $130/kg U
North America	752	224	1,145	759
Africa	609	167	139	124
Australia	290	9	47	6
Europe	66	325	49	49
Asia	40	6	1	23
South America	97	5	99	6
WOCA total (rounded)	1,850	740	1,480	970

WOCA = World Outside of Centrally Planned Economies areas.

TABLE 14.12 FREE WORLD URANIUM SUPPLY–CONSUMPTION BALANCE
(MILLIONS OF POUNDS U_3O_8 EQUIVALENT)

	1969	1970	1971	1972	1973	1974	1975	1976	1977	1978	1979	1980	1981
Production		49	49	51	51	48	49	60	74	88	100	111	112
Consumption[a]		19	22	26	30	33	37	40	43	46	48	51	57
Inventory[b]	(60)	90	117	142	163	178	190	210	241	283	335	395	450
Relative Inventory[c] (years)	(2.7)	3.4	3.8	4.0	4.2	4.3	4.3	4.4	5.2	4.9	5.1	5.3	5.5
Nuclear Generation (TWh)[d]		61	107	153	189	226	334	389	471	556	571	620	731

Forecast

	1982	1983	1984	1985	1986	1987	1988	1989	1990	1991	1999
Production	103	90	94	95	100	100	100	100	100	106	160
Consumption	63	74	83	91	94	100	107	105	106	110	145
Inventory	490	506	517	522	528	527	520	515	509	505	487
Relative Inventory	5.4	5.3	5.2	5.1	5.0	4.9	4.7	4.6	4.4	4.2	3.0

[a] Consumption is defined as uranium entering the reactor fuel cycle. It is calculated from the gross generation of nuclear electricity. Not the same as utility acquisitions.
[b] Inventory at year's end. Initial value assumed to be 2.7 years.
[c] Relative inventory is number of years forward consumption which could be supplied by the previous year's ending inventory.
[d] Gross nuclear electrical generation from ref. 9. Given for reference. For generation forecast, see ref. 13.

author has added the 1999 column by extrapolation, and made adjustments to the inventory figures to reconcile pre- and post-1981 figures.

Production in the U.S. comes from mines averaging 2–2.5 pounds of uranium per ton of ore. Some Canadian and Australian ores run from 25 to 50 lb/ton. Over the period 1982–2000 U.S. production will decline from its present rate of 26 million lb/yr, as high-cost producers gradually leave the market, while first Canadian, and then Canadian and Australian, uranium dominates the market.

Table 14.12 indicates that inventories will hang over the market for the rest of this decade, during which period one would expect prices to remain low. The production expansion required in the decade 1990–2000 will probably be accompanied by price increases (the price projections are the author's).

There is clearly an adequate uranium supply for the limited growth of nuclear power here forecast. Because some short-sighted breeder advocates have justified the breeder program on a near-term shortage and high prices of uranium, nuclear power opponents have concluded that a breeder program is unnecessary. This is an equally short-sighted view, since it ignores the probable need for large-scale expansion of nuclear power in the next century as billions of presently deprived people enter the energy market.

Enrichment requirements may be derived from table 14.12 by observing that 0.26 separative work units are added to each pound of yellowcake delivered to a separation plant to produce LWR fuel (at 0.25 percent tails concentration). Using INFCE[33] data on Free World enrichment capacity, we then construct table 14.13. From this table it is apparent that enrichment capacity will exceed demand for the foreseeable future, and that the planned capacity (and even some of the committed) will not be built.

The Future of Nuclear Fission Power

Eighty-six percent of all the world's reactors – operating, under construction, or planned – are light water reactors.[34] The majority are American designs, or designs based on American licenses. Almost all the rest are of Russian design, which are similar to American designs in layout, rating, power density and pressure. Therefore almost all the world's reactors have the same operating and safety characteristics, the same fuel cycle, and the same economics. The national plans for deployment of nuclear power, which result in the projections shown on table 14.4, show a geographic diversity between different industrialized and nuclear-capable states, which is not entirely explicable by economics,

TABLE 14.13 FREE WORLD ENRICHMENT SUPPLY
AND DEMAND (MILLIONS OF SEPARATIVE WORK UNITS)

Year	Supply		Demand
	Committed	Planned	
1982	36		16
1983	37		19
1984	39		22
1985	41	1	24
1986	41	2	24
1987	41	3	26
1988	42	5	28
1989	43	8	27
1990	44	10	28
1991	46	10	29
1992	47	11	30
1993	49	11	31
1994	49	12	32
1995	49	13	33
1999			38

resource availability, or technology. We have seen that the U.S. is opting strongly for fossil-fired rather than nuclear power plants, with no convincing economic arguments to support this trend. The Soviet Union, on the other hand, with an even richer resource base of coal, oil and gas, plans a strong nuclear building program for the decade 1990–2000 (economic estimates are, of course, unavailable).

The difference is usually attributed (in the U.S.) to prudent risk aversion to the following concerns:

(1) the spread of nuclear power plants will lead to the spread of nuclear weapons;
(2) nuclear power plant accidents might have catastrophic consequences;
(3) there is no safe means of disposal of nuclear wastes.

The first concern was considered, on the initiative of the U.S., in the International Fuel Cycle Evaluation.[33] This study lasted 2½ years (1977–80), and was participated in by fifty-six nations and five international organizations. The concern was, by and large, rejected.

It should be noted that building nuclear power plants *in the U.S.* in no way contributes to the spread of nuclear weapons, either vertically or horizontally. U.S. weapons are produced – are continuing to be produced – in an entirely separate military production complex. Horizontal proliferation might conceivably result from furnishing reactors or information to other countries, but cannot result from purely U.S. activities.

The argument was advanced during the Carter administration[3] that by setting an example of eschewing certain kinds of civilian nuclear activities (e.g. reprocessing and breeder reactor development) we would set a moral example which would induce other nations to take the same actions. (The administration did not consider the moral example produced by reprocessing fuel for military purposes *only*.) At all events, nobody followed our example, and the next administration scrapped the policy. There remains a Congressional majority for unilaterally imposing conditions on other nations' nuclear activities. They evidently feel that division of the world into nuclear haves and nuclear have-nots is both moral and maintainable. The principal consequence of the Nuclear Non-Proliferation Policy Act of 1977,[3] which responded to Congressional pressure, has been to reverse the U.S. position as the preferred nuclear supplier.

The second concern, about the safety of nuclear power plants, has been addressed in a number of admirably unbiased reports (e.g. the 1975 study of the American Physical Society, the 1979 Kemeny Commission report on the Three Mile Island accident, the H. W. Lewis review of the Rasmussen report, and a corresponding number of foreign reports).[35] In all these studies ([1,35]) the answer comes out that the risks from nuclear power plants, while not zero, are less than those from available alternate power generating methods (particularly coal) which have not aroused the same opposition.

The principal deleterious effects of the famous Three Mile Island accident were:

(1) psychological stress to the citizens of Middletown, Pa., caused by erroneous reports originating with the Nuclear Regulatory Commission, and spread with relish and embellishments by the media;

(2) a new wave of regulatory burdens on all nuclear plants, whose stated purpose is to avoid further events like TMI, and whose certain result is to increase costs;

(3) a tremendous financial loss to the utility owner – the owner was not protected by the Price-Anderson Act, which turned out to be almost irrelevant.

The third concern relates principally to the disposal of high-level radioactive wastes (spent fuel or wastes from fuel reprocessing). Studies of the disposal of high-level wastes in deep geological repositories, which include those by the U.S. Interagency Review Group during the Carter administration,[36] of the American Physical Society, of the National Academy of Sciences, and of numerous foreign groups,[37] agree that

Overall scientific and technological knowledge is adequate to proceed with region selection and site characterization, despite the limitations in our current knowledge and modeling capability. Successful isolation of radioactive wastes from the biosphere appears technically feasible for periods of thousands of years provided that the systems view it utilized rigorously.[36]

The recent enactment of a program for high-level waste disposal signals a concurrency by Congress with this conclusion. Although this is a hopeful indication that the waste disposal concern, which has been used by the State of California as a barrier to the deployment of nuclear power, may ultimately disappear, we may confidently expect a decade of legal challenges to the execution of the program. A single quotation[38] encapsulates the public attitude: "A key unsolved technical problem is the millennia-long management of the extremely toxic radioactive nuclear wastes."

Technically speaking, spent fuel is not waste. Not only does it contain the valuable heavy elements uranium and plutonium, but the high-level fission products themselves are useful. For example, the City of Albuquerque plans to use radioactive cesium, the most active gamma-ray emitter for the first 100 years, to sterilize raw sewage. Other uses of fission products are to sterilize food and surgical dressings; Americium is used to make smoke detectors; and so on. Plutonium is popularly believed to be the most lethal substance known. On an equal-molecular basis it is 80,000 times less toxic than botulism virus.

We have accepted without a debate a patronizing view of our descendants. According to the EPA we must protect them for 10,000 years from the consequences of their posited unawareness of radioactivity. No other activity, from oil drilling to water engineering, has a 10,000-year planning horizon. The addition of one more function to a digital watch would make the measurement of radioactivity as common place as time-keeping, and eliminate the most extreme human intervention scenarios. Is this unlikely in 100 years? Will the consequences of a given dose of radiation be unreduced by 100 years of medicine, not to say 1,000? It was only slightly over 100 years ago that the germ theory of disease was discovered.

The pressure for immediate demonstration of deep geologic burial likewise has no rational basis. Both France and Sweden plan to store their fission products at ground level for 40–50 years. The thermal power of spent fuel decreases by a factor of 100 in 100 years. Retrievable storage for this period would eliminate one of the major uncertainties in geologic disposal, and allow recovery in the interim of economic values. The theory of plate tectonics, now indispensable to explain mountain formation, earthquakes and volcanoes, was not widely accepted until 1963. Geological science, traditionally backward-looking, will be able to handle 10,000-year forward predictions much better in 100 years.

The French Commissariat à l'Energie Atomique discovered the remains of a 1.8 billion-year-old naturally occurring nuclear reactor in a uranium deposit at Oklo, Gabon.[39] Analysis of the position of the reaction products is strong evidence that the plutonium formed remained in place (within a few microns) for hundreds of thousands of years. This finding makes further demonstration of long-term geologic disposal unnecessary – a demonstration which, because of the long time scale, might otherwise seem impossible.

The arguments summarized above have evidently not disarmed the nuclear critics. To understand this we look more closely at the anatomy of the opposition. Some psychiatrists have diagnosed the opposition to nuclear power as the phenomenon known as displacement. According to them, fear of death from nuclear weapons becomes fear of death from nuclear power.[40] Indeed, anti-nuclear organizations have, since 1963, periodically switched back and forth from opposing weapons to opposing nuclear power plants. Certainly their practice of exaggerating the health effects of low-level radiation[41] – a practice which dates back to the campaign against atmospheric testing of nuclear weapons – serves to reinforce fear of nuclear power.

Dr. Lifton approves of displacement as an expression of the "wisdom of the body." This "wisdom" manifests itself differently in different parts of the world and in different sectors of society. Japan, despite a long seismic history, and a population density over ten times our own, still manages to find sites for its nuclear plants and to complete them far more rapidly than we do. Perhaps the Japanese have a better appreciation of the distinction between a nuclear weapon and a nuclear power plant. In Spain and France nuclear power protest movements have been associated with Basque and Breton separatist movements. In the U.S. it is most noticeable in sectors of the populace associated with other protests: the old anti-Viet Nam War cohorts, the (white) civil rights marchers, the public power and consumer movements, the anti-draft movement.[42] It is also strong in back-to-nature and anti-growth circles, who believe low energy use will compel the adoption of more frugal life-styles.

Thus Paul Ehrlich:[43] "giving society cheap abundant energy at this point would be equivalent to giving an idiot child a machine gun." Amory Lovins[44] has a similar viewpoint: "if nuclear power were clean, safe, economic, assured of ample fuel, and socially benign *per se*, it would still be unattractive because of the political implications of the kind of energy economy it would lock us into." Given the environmental qualities of nuclear power, this is a curious stance for a Friend of the Earth.

One would have to be excessively naive to believe that those opposed to the potential benefits of nuclear power can be persuaded that their concerns are unfounded. Nuclear power, because of its emotional associations, is a useful rallying point for a number of disparate grievances.

We should not expect the opposition to nuclear power to disappear separately from the discontents it symbolizes. The strongest argument by pro-nuclear advocates is the centrality of electricity to economic progress. This has not escaped the anti-nuclear movement. The electric utility industry, now a hostage to the movement, is too valuable to be released before the other grievances are settled. Thus the future of nuclear power depends on the resolution during the next decade of a number of social issues for which nuclear power is merely the symbol.

The nuclear power issue, however, is not unimportant *per se*. This has been well expressed by Andrei Sakharov:[45]

Policymakers always assume, not without reason, that one of the many factors in determining the political independence of a country, its military and diplomatic strength and its international influence is the level of economic development of a country and its economic independence. This assumption is doubly valid in the case of two world systems opposing each other. But the level of a country's economy is determined by its energy technology: that is, by the utilization of oil, gas and coal at present; of uranium and thorium in the near future and, perhaps, deuterium and lithium in the more distant future. . . .

Therefore I assert that the development of nuclear technology is one of the necessary conditions for the preservation of the economic and political independence of every country – of those that have already reached a high development stage as well as those that are just developing. For the countries of Western Europe and Japan, the importance of nuclear technology is particularly great. If the economy of these countries continues to be in any important way dependent on the supply of chemical fuels from the U.S.S.R. or from countries which are under her influence, the West will find itself under constant threat of the cutting off of these channels. This will result in a humiliating political dependence. . . .

Is the present campaign against the development of nuclear power inspired by the U.S.S.R. (or other countries of Eastern Europe)? I know of no reliable facts supporting this. If this were so, then insignificant and unnoticeable efforts are sufficient substantially to influence the dimensions of this campaign because of widespread anti-nuclear prejudice and lack of understanding of the inevitability of the nuclear era.

References

1   Starr, C. (1969). Social benefit versus technological risk. *Science*, **165**, 1232–8. Inhaber, H. (1979). Risk with energy from conventional and nonconven-

tional sources. *Science,* **203**, 718–23. List, E. J. (1972). Energy use in California: implications for the environment. *Environmental Quality Laboratory, California Institute of Technology,* Report no. 3. UK Health and Safety Executive (1980). *Comparative Risks of Energy Production Systems.* London: H.M. Stationery Office. Paskievici, W. (1982). Health hazards associated with electric power production. In *A Global View of Energy,* Kursunoglu, B. N. *et al.* (eds), chap. 23, pp. 249–74. Lexington, Mass.: Lexington Books. Hubert, P. (1982). Comparison of the Health Effects of Energy Systems: an assessment for France. In *A Global View of Energy,* (as above), chap. 22, pp. 233–47.

2   Hewlett, R. G. and Anderson, O. E. Jr. (1962). *The New World, 1939/1946.* University Park: Pennsylvania State University Press. Hewlett, R. G. and Duncan, F. (1969). *Atomic Shield 1947/1952.* University Park: Pennsylvania State University Press.

3   Egen, G. (1978). *Origins of the U.S. Non-Proliferation Policy.* Washington: Atomic Industrial Forum.

4   Joint Committee on Atomic Energy (1977). *Atomic Energy Legislation.* Washington: U.S. Govt. Printing Office.

5   Joint Committee on Atomic Energy. (1976). *ERDA Authorizing Legislation, FY 1977,* Part 2, Appendix 12. Washington: U.S. Govt. Printing Office.

6   Waterman, M. H. (1966). *Ohio Valley Electric Corporation.* Ann Arbor: Grad. School of Business Administration.

7   Atomic Industrial Forum. (1982). *Historical Profile of U.S. Nuclear Power Development.* Washington. Idem. (1982). *Nuclear Power Facts and Figures.* Washington. Idem. (1983). *International Survey.* Washington.

8   General Electric Co. (1980). *U.S. Energy Data Book.* Fairfield, CT.

9   U.S. Dept. of Energy (1983). *Monthly Energy Bulletins.* Washington.

10 American Nuclear Society. 1982. World List of Nuclear Plants. *Nuclear News* **26**: no. 2, no. 10. Idem. (1982). World List of Nuclear Plants. *Nuclear News,* **25**: no. 2, no. 10. Idem. (1981). World List of Nuclear Plants. *Nuclear News,* **24**: no. 2, no. 10.

11 U.S.ERDA (1975). *Total Energy, Electric Energy, and Nuclear Power Projections* (February 1975). Washington.

12 OECD and IAEA (1975). *Uranium Resources, Production and Demand* (December 1975) Paris and Vienna.

13 NUEXCO (1983). *Monthly Report on the Nuclear Fuel Market.* No. 173. Idem. (1982). Ibid. nos. 162, 168, 172. Menlo Park, CA.

14 IAEA (1981). *Nuclear Engineering International* 27, 330, p. 3, Aug '82 Suppl. IEA/NEA (1982). *Nuclear Energy Prospects to 2000.* Paris: OECD. INFCE (1980). *Projected Nuclear Generating Capacity in WOCA.* INFCE Summary Volume INFCE/PC/2/9 p. 4. Vienna: IAEA. US DoE (1982). *Energy Projections to the Year 2000, July 1982 Update.* DE82 022523. Washington.

15 *The Global 2000 Report* (1980), chap. 10: "Energy Projections". Harmondsworth: Penguin Books.

16 Hafele, W. (ed.) (1980). *Energy in a Finite World,* pp. 522, 580. Cambridge: Ballinger.

17 Marchetti, C. and Nakicenovic, N. (1979). *The Dynamics of Energy Systems and the Logistic Substitution Model.* RR-79-13 Laxenburg: IIASA.

18 Ebasco Services, Inc. (1973). *Business and Economic Charts.* New York.

19 Cohen, K. and Zebroski, E. L. (1959). Programming for Economic Power. *Proceedings of the American Power Conference,* **XXI**, 100–19. Chicago.

20 Brandfon, W. W. (1979). *Comparative Costs of Coal and Nuclear Electricity Generation*. Testimony before Subcommittee on Energy and the Environment, House Committee on Interior and Insular Affairs. Washington, 12 July.
21 News Review (1982). *Nuclear Engineering International*, **27**, (327), 9.
22 Balaceanu, J. C. (1890). *French Energy Policy for the 1980s*. Institut Français du Petrole, Ref. 28 572-A. Paris.
23 US DoE (1982). *Update Nuclear Power Program Information and Data*. April–June.
24 Ontario Hydro (1982). *Ontario Hydro's CANDU Projects*. Toronto.
25 US DoE (1982). *Update. Nuclear Power Program Information and Data*. July–September.
26 Mooz, W. E. (1980). Cost analysis for LWR power plants. *Energy* **6**, 197–225. Oxford: Pergamon.
27 Komanoff, C. (1981). *Power Plant Cost Escalation*. New York: Komanoff Energy Associates. Idem. (1981). Sources of Nuclear Regulatory Requirements. *Nuclear Safety*, **22**, 435–48.
28 Bupp, I. C., Derian, J. C., Donsimoni, M.-P. and Treitel, R. (1974). *Trends in Light Water Reactor Capital Costs*. Center for Policy Alternatives, MIT Cambridge. CPA 74–8.
29 Crowley, J. H. (1978). Power plant cost estimates put to the test. *Nuclear Engineering International*, **23** (273), 39–43. Crowley, J. H. and Griffith, J. D. (1982). *US Construction Cost Rise Threatens the Nuclear Option*. N.E.I. **27** (328), 25–8.
30 Reynolds, A. (ed.) (1982). *Projected Costs of Electricity from Nuclear and Coal-Fired Power Plants*. DoE/EIA-0356/1. Washington: U.S. GPO.
31 US DoE (1982). *Energy Projections to the Year 2000, July 1982 Update*. DE82 022523. Springfield: NTIS.
32 NEA/IAEA (1978). *World Uranium Potential, An International Evaluation*. IUREP Study. Vienna.
33 Beckjord, E. S. (1979). *Nuclear Power Projections*. Letter to Ambassador G. Smith, 23 May 1979. Washington, US DoE. IAEA (1980). *International Nuclear Fuel Cycle Evaluation*. Vienna.
34 IAEA (1982). *Nuclear Engineering International*, **27** (330), 3.
35 Report to the APS by the study group on light-water reactor safety. 1975. *Rev. Mod. Phys.*, **47**, Suppl. 1. Report of the President's Commission on the Accident at Three Mile Island (1979). Washington. Rasmussen, N. C. (ed.) (1975). *Reactor Safety Study*. WASH-1400 (NUREG-75/014). Springfield VA:NTIS. Lewis, H. W. (ed.) (1978). *Risk Assessment Review Group Report*. NUREG/CR-0400. Springfield VA:NTIS. Norwegian Nuclear Power Commission (1978). *Nuclear Power and Safety*, NOU 1978: 35C. Oslo: Universitetsforlaget.
36 Report to the President by the Interagency Review Group on Nuclear Waste Management (1979). TID-29442 UC-70. Springfield VA:NTIS.
37 Report to the APS by the study group on nuclear fuel cycles and waste management (1978). *Rev. Mod. Phys.* **50**, no. 1, pt. II. Committee on Radioactive Waste Management (1970). *Disposal of Solid Radioactive Wastes in Bedded Salt Deposits*. Washington: National Academy of Sciences. Cohen, B. L. (1977). High-level radioactive waste from light-water reactors. *Rev. Mod. Phys.* **49** (1), 1–20. Petrosyants, A. M. (1974). *From Scientific Search to Atomic Industry*, 2nd edn (translated), chap 9. Danville IL: Interstate.

Norwegian Nuclear Power Commission (see Reference 35). Klingberg, C. and Duguid, J. (1980). *Status of Technology for Isolating High-Level Radioactive Wastes in Geologic Repositories.* DoE/TIC 11207 (Draft). Clelland, D. W., Bonniaud, R., Corbet, A. D. W., Detilleux, E. and Krause, H. (1976). Review of European high-level waste solidification technology. Paper read at International Symposium on the Management of Waste from the LWR Fuel Cycle, Denver, Colorado, 11–16 July. Carter, L. J. (1982). The Radwaste Paradox. Science, **219**, 33–6. (News article. "Public health and safety does not require early disposal".)

38 Brown, J. M. (1976). Health, safety and social issues. In *The California Nuclear Initiative.* Stanford: Institute for Energy Studies.

39 Naudet, R. (ed.) (1974). Le Phenomène d'Oklo. *Bulletin d'Informations Scientifiques et Techniques*, **193**. Cowan G. A. (1976). A natural fission reactor. *Scientific American*, **235** (1), 36–47.

40 Pahner, P. D. (1976). *A Psychological Perspective of the Nuclear Energy Controversy.* RM-76-67, Laxenburg: IIASA. Lifton, J. R. (1976). Nuclear energy and the wisdom of the body. *Bull. At. Sci.,* **32** (7), 16.

41 Cohen, B. L. (1980). Radiation fantasies. *Reason*, March, pp. 24–35. Medical Research Council (1975). *The Toxicity of Plutonium.* London: H.M. Stationery Office. High Background Radiation Research Group, China (1980). Health Survey in High Background Radiation Areas in China. *Science*, **209**, 877–80.

42 Nuclear Information and Resource Service (1982). *A Fresh Portrait of the Anti-Nuclear Movement. Groundswell.* McCracken, S. (1982). *The War Against the Atom.* New York: Basic Books.

43 Ehrlich, P. (1975). *An Ecologist's Perspective on Nuclear Power.* Fed. of American Scientists, Public Issue report 5/6.

44 Lovins, A. B. (1977). *Soft Energy Paths*, p. 56. Cambridge: Ballinger.

45 Sakharov, A. (1978). Nuclear Power: Necessary and Inevitable. *Los Angeles Times*, 28 May, 1978, Pt. VI, p. 5.

15A

Solar Energy and Other "Alternative" Energy Sources

PETR BECKMANN

Solar energy and its derivatives (wind, waves, biomass) will continue to play a major role in the world's undeveloped countries: woodfuels, dung and crop waste constitute the principal cooking fuel for 56 percent of the world's population. In many countries, including Tanzania, Nigeria, and Bolivia, fuelwood accounts for 90 percent or more of the total energy budget.[1]

In the developed countries, even under very optimistic assumptions, solar energy will supply an insignificant fraction of the energy budget in the year 2000. The reason why this can be forecast with a confidence that would be misplaced for other energy sources is that direct, unaccumulated solar energy suffers from an inherent, purely physical constraint: low energy density. Though the total insolation of the globe is enormous (178,000 terawatts, or some 4,500 times mankind's present rate of consuming energy), its maximum power density is a little over one kilowatt per square meter, and no amount of technical innovation can change that diluteness. (Power is the rate of energy flow; power density is the spatial density of that flow through a unit cross-section. 1 terawatt = 1 million megawatts; 1 megawatt = 1 million watts.)

In separating the physics of solar energy from its popular–political image, it is well to begin by clearing up a misleading terminology.

Solar energy is highly efficient and abundantly available when nature has accumulated it in space or time, and man taps it at the points where nature has concentrated it. Solar energy accumulated over time – over millions of years – is concentrated in fossil fuels; solar energy accumulated over space – millions of acres – is concentrated via rainfall and drainage at the points where hydroelectric dams can tap it. Hydropower is thus no more "solar" than fossil fuels, though it is often classified that way simply to boost the "solar" energy percentage in paper plans and projections.

Nor is "renewable" a correct characterization of the sources the solar advocates have in mind, for nuclear fuel is just as "renewable" as sunshine: not just because of breeding new fuel, but because of the uranium carried into the sea by rivers at a rate 25 times higher than needed by present world electrical consumption; if necessary, it could be extracted from the sea at a cost well below $1,000/lb, which would contribute less than 1 percent to the cost of electricity.[2]

Finally, these sources are not "soft" in the sense of "gentle on the environment." The construction of a concentrated solar electric plant needs no less than 1,000 times as much copper, steel, chromium, and other materials as a coal-fired plant of equal capacity, and 500 times as much concrete as a nuclear plant.[3,4] If the conversion is not performed centrally, but is distributed over many small consumers (rooftops), the ratio becomes even more adverse, as it always does when mass production is compared with a cottage industry.

Thus the "soft" or "renewable" sources might perhaps more fittingly be called "on-stream solar and derivatives," and whatever the name, this is what will be considered here. By derivatives we mean wind, ocean waves, and biomass, including alcohol fuels. Although biomass, in a sense, represents *accumulated* solar energy, it differs crucially from fossil fuels or hydropower in that the producer forgoes other uses of the land where this energy is being accumulated – quite unlike the energy of hydropower, which accumulates by draining water from millions of acres not belonging to the producer.

A third source, often classified as "solar," Ocean Thermal Energy Conversion (OTEC) uses the temperature difference between the upper strata and the depths of tropical sea. This is certainly a case of tapping what nature has accumulated, and does not belong with windmills or biomass; in any case, by the year 2000 its contribution to the world's (or any one country's) energy supply will be an insignificant fraction.

The Essence: Diluteness

If unobstructed by clouds, solar energy arrives at the earth's surface at the rate of roughly 1 kW/m^2; when night hours and cloudy days are considered, the average insolation in moderate latitude drops to 100 W/m^2, which is the starting point that must be multiplied by the efficiency of the convertor (from 0.00008 for biomass to 0.7 for heat collectors) to arrive at the power available from a square meter (11 sq. ft); storage requirements then reduce this value by another factor depending on the sunless period to be tided over with high probability, typically a value of 5.

The result is a conversion that is valuable for space heating, warm water, and special applications (space and other remote, unelectrified places), but one that cannot achieve the economy of conventional sources, and in some cases (such as transportation) cannot achieve their performance at any price.

Another general disadvantage of solar energy that makes it unlikely to be widely adopted if the decision is left to a free market is its diseconomy not only in dollars, but also in Btu. One of the characteristics of an energy source is its energy yield – the ratio of useful energy extracted from it during its life to the energy that went into its construction. For a nuclear plant, with a life of 20 to 30 years, the energy yield is in the range of 15 to 20; for a solar hot-water collector, assuming that it will last for 15 years without maintenance, the yield is 1.8,[5,6] and in some climates without abundant sun (such as the U.S. Northeast), it may never return the energy invested in it.[7] Moreover, that invested energy was high-grade, whereas the collector turns sunlight into low-temperature heat incapable of doing significant mechanical work.

This last disadvantage does not apply to photovoltaics, whose energy payback time is also somewhat shorter (about 5 years). However, the electricity produced by them is not self-sustaining. While coal-fired or nuclear electricity is abundant enough to be used in the manufacture of further power plants of that type, photovoltaic electricity cannot, in the foreseeable future, supply the amounts of steady, reliable electric power needed for the furnaces and purification processes in the manufacture of solar grade silicon (figure 15.1).[8]

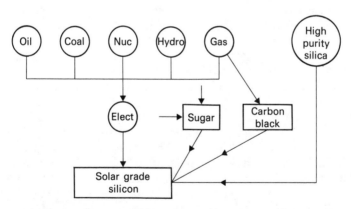

Figure 15.1 Resource flow diagram for the production of solar grade silicon, showing that solar electricity is not self-sustaining. The abundant, steady electric power needed to manufacture solar grade silicon is available only from conventional power plants.[8] (An alleged "solar breeder" in Maryland which runs on photovoltaics does not produce the silicon, but only assembles the cells.)

The history of man's energy use is a history of increasing energy concentration. As man went from sun and wind to wood, to coal, to oil, and to uranium, the energy per unit volume (or mass) became more concentrated at every step. The Industrial Revolution of the eighteenth and nineteenth century, for example, could not have taken place without the higher energy density of coal.

Conversely, the density of energy consumption, that is, the energy consumed per square meter in the urban areas of the world – which host an ever increasing fraction of its population (figure 15.2) – cannot be supplied by an energy source as dilute as solar power.

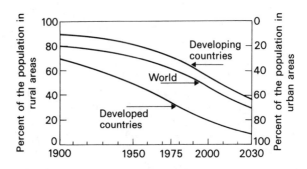

Figure 15.2 Historical and projected percentages of the world's population in rural and urban areas.[9]

In a sense, this imbalance between power density generated and consumed is even more important for the developing countries. Their energy consumption per head is smaller than in the West, as is the fraction of the population living in urban areas; however, this is at times so over-compensated by the crowding in Third World cities that they end up with higher densities of power consumption that the urban areas of the West.

For example, the average density of power consumption in the urban areas of West Germany is 7.5 W/m²; in the urban areas of India the average is 12 W/m², and there are examples where it reaches 30 W/m².[9] This cannot, of course, be met by an input power density of 100 W/m² by the time achievable efficiencies and storage requirements are taken into account. Careful studies have, in fact, shown that urban settlements with population densities of more than 1,000 persons/km² (London: 1,100; Rhine–Ruhr area: 1,280) cannot exist without some sort of centralized power, quite apart from any cost considerations.[9] If solar power is centralized – collectors in the country supplying energy to the cities – it loses its main attraction for those who wish to "disconnect from the utilities," and most of the solar-social engineers, including Nader, Lovins, and Brower, do, in fact, *oppose* centralized solar power.

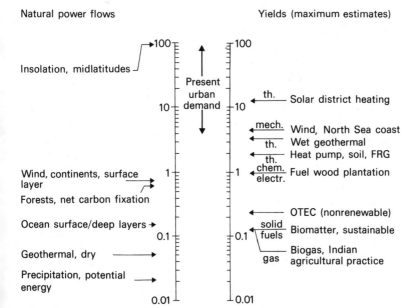

Figure 15.3 Power densities of solar energy – incoming and extractable. The power density of consumption in New York City is 6.4 W/m², and can reach 30 W/m² in the crowded cities of the Third World.[9]

These are the general underlying reasons why solar energy – barring improbably drastic government coercion – will not amount to a significant energy source in the developed countries in 2000; we now proceed to the individual forms of its use.

Space Heating

Most of the increase in solar energy use in the developed countries will come from space and domestic water heating, though even here installations are expensive. The fact that in sunny states like California or Colorado users rarely break even, though up to 70 percent of the cost is paid by the government in federal and state tax credits, does not bode well for the economics of even this simplest and most advantageous application of solar energy.

In a drastically different field, where solar energy is the obvious type of energy to use, namely power satellites beaming power to space defenses, solar energy convertors cannot affect the terawatts of the global energy budget, no matter how powerful they are. (Neither can a space-earth civilian power system affect it in the unlikely event that it overcomes the many obstacles facing it before the end of the century.)

Though space and domestic water heating will very likely show the largest increase of solar energy in the industrialized countries, the actual contribution to the energy budget will be quite small. The CONAES Report,[10] in a highly optimistic chapter on solar energy, considers two scenarios. The "low" scenario assumes that current tax credits remain in force, but that nothing else interferes in the market. The "high" scenario assumes that "a national policy mandates vigorous incentives to bring about the use of solar energy. This scenario is driven not by economic forces, but by government intervention in the energy market. It is assumed that this government policy mandates, regardless of cost, adoption after 1990 of solar energy for heating all new buildings and for all industrial process heat where feasible . . . [I]t is assumed that public policy requires the use of specified amounts of solar electric capacity for new generating capacity regardless of cost" (pp. 348–50).[10]

Under the low (tax subsidy) scenario of the report, the contribution of space heating in the U.S. in the year 2000 will be zero; but even under the draconian measures of a government-regimented economy defined by the "high" scenario, its contribution would remain under 2 percent of the U.S. energy supply.

Solar Electricity

At present, and probably to the end of the century, large thermal solar power plants (with mirrors focusing the sun's rays onto a "receiver" for generating steam) are considerably more efficient than central photovoltaic plants (converting sunlight directly to electricity).

However, once again the diluteness of solar energy causes both types of plant to be uneconomically large. A 1,000 MW conventional plant (coal-fired or nuclear) occupies about 25 acres; a solar plant of the same capacity would occupy some 50 square miles. This follows from a straightforward computation considering the insolation, efficiency, spacing between mirrors or collectors and capacity power (i.e., available rather than peak power), and is confirmed by the solar plants now in operation in New Mexico, Spain and California. Although the largest of them has a peak power of only 10 MW ("Solar One" in southern California), they pro-rate to that order of land use, even though they have only very limited storage capabilities.

The economics must inexorably follow the laws of physics, and it does:

"Solar One" in California, built with the greatest economy of size and the longest available experience of all contemporary central solar generating plants, cost more than $14,000 per installed kilowatt;[11] that is, more than 14 times as much as coal-fired power, and some 7 times as much as nuclear power even at a time when most of nuclear construction costs come from delays and litigations.

The diseconomy of concentrated solar electric power, together with the lack of a political constituency (the "solar advocates" usually oppose it) will prevent concentrated solar power generation from making a significant contribution to the energy, or even electricity, budget of the world in the year 2000. "Solar One's" peak power, for example, represents 0.00002 of the U.S. electric capacity.

For the reasons given earlier, we do not consider hydroelectric power a "solar" source that belongs with thermal or photovoltaic solar plants; however, we may note incidentally that in the worldwide energy budget, hydropower will increase in total capacity, but as a fraction of the total energy mix, it will not significantly change from its present roughly 6 percent. The reason is that the building of new dams in the developing countries, such as the giant 12,600 MW Itaipu plant on the border of Brazil and Paraguay, will roughly keep pace with the general growth of energy use. Eventually, of course, the developing countries will run out of usable sites, as the developed countries largely already have. The IIASA study[12] expects 0.83 terawatts from hydropower in the year 2000, which is 5–6 percent of its global energy forecast.

As for distributed (small-scale, domestic) electricity, significant advances are to be expected, especially price reductions in the field of amorphous semiconductors. However, this will not affect the fundamental diseconomy of distributed solar electricity, which is even more inefficient than central generation (mostly for the usual disadvantages of small-scale vs. mass production), and far more costly than solar space heating.

If the price does come down to below $1 per peak watt, it still means an investment of $1,000 per kilowatt (plus installation and conversion equipment, even without storage facilities), i.e., roughly $1,000 for a toaster or pressing iron, as against 5¢ to 10¢ per kilowatt-hour for using these appliances for 1 hour, and without being responsible for the maintenance and reliability of the power supply.

Domestic solar electricity is thus essentially going to be a toy of the affluent; but regardless of whether the bill is footed by the taxpayers or not, it cannot have a significant effect on the energy budget of the developed countries, let alone of the entire world. Even the high (government regimentation) scenario of the CONAES Report predicts less than 0.5 percent for this source in the U.S. in the year 2000, and the low (tax-subsidy) scenario estimates it at zero.

Wind and Waves

Wind evens out atmospheric pressure differences caused by uneven heating of the earth's surface; it is therefore derived from solar energy and even more dilute than its primary cause. In addition, it is more irregular and unpredictable than sunshine, and the energy flux available from it varies as the third power of its velocity, which makes it a very poor source at low velocities, and a very difficult one to use at high ones. These formidable disadvantages are partly counterbalanced by the advantage that wind energy is high-grade energy, convertible to electricity or mechanical work with an efficiency of up to two-thirds.

Wind-driven generators are useful in inaccessible places far from the power grid; but their gross lack of economy and environmental quality is obvious from the giant windmills that have been built in America and Europe. The 250-ft blades mounted on 150-ft towers, built at enormous expense, give about 2 MW – when the wind blows. Tens of thousands of these expensive giants would be needed to displace an appreciable fraction of primary fuels in America – an economically and environmentally unthinkable project.

Small-scale, domestic wind-driven power generation runs into the same difficulties as photovoltaic power; in addition, its installation is more complicated, its use less suited for urban areas, and its operation more dangerous.

Wave power is even less promising. The total wave power pounding Britain's shores, for example, is almost 5 times the British power consumption, but it is too dilute to be useful: not more than some 70 MW/km (112 MW per mile) is extractable,[13,14] which would mean a 9-mile chain of rafts or other equipment to harness – when the waves are high – as much as a single 1,000 MW coal-fired or nuclear unit produces. Britain, which was furthest along with research of harnessing wave energy, has now all but abandoned it. It takes no great powers of prophecy to see that the percentage of this type of energy in the total mix will be virtually zero.

Biomass

Biomass refers to the utilization of the solar energy accumulated in plants by burning them or by extracting fuel from them thermally, physically (pressing) or by fermentation.

Here again, the "theoretical" or "potential" amount of energy available is stupendous, but its diluteness makes its use unsuited for an industrial economy; in the undeveloped countries, to the contrary, it is a source that is being abandoned as the Third World's forests are being depleted.

If one simply adds up the calories of the world's existing plantable forests, one obtains something like 6 terawatts extractable without depleting them, which is roughly twice the world's present energy use. But exploiting this amount of biomass without depleting it, notes the Executive Summary of the IIASA Energy Group Report,[12] "would correspond to managing 30 million square kilometers of forests, more than twice the land area devoted to agriculture worldwide in 1975. It would mean managing the habitats of thousands of species, and it would mean dealing with more familiar problems on an unprecedented scale – problems of soil erosion, managing water systems, and the decreasing resistance of cultured plants to pests. In short, it would mean operating a worldwide herbarium."

There are more immediate problems with biomass, however. It competes with food production for land use, and its diluteness gives rise to considerable transportation problems. The diluteness of this type of energy, even when used most efficiently by direct burning, is obvious from the mere units: the rate of growth is half a cord of wood per acre per year, or 120 milliwatts per square meter – a conversion efficiency of 0.0008.[15] (120 mW is roughly the power consumption of a pocket calculator.)

In the developed countries, burning wood waste for energy is a valuable way of cutting costs, just as burning municipal wastes may yet turn out to be a good way of garbage disposal; but neither will have a significant effect on the energy budget.

The pitiful efficiency of directly burnable biomass is further reduced by extraction of fuels from it by fermentation, thermal treatment (charcoal, gasification, etc.) or physical methods (pressing and filtering for oil); however, this is counterbalanced by a significantly reduced transportation problem and by the production of motor fuels – alcohol, methane and diesel fuel.

In the industrialized world, alcohol fuels and gasohol mixes have made little progress in spite of subsidies and tax breaks, often very considerable ones (as in Iowa). The leader in this field is Brazil, which has had some success in fueling cars with alcohol, but which is also something of a special case: it has no fossil fuels, is advanced enough to provide the necessary capital investment, and above all, has no competition with growing food, since the feedstock is vegetation with high sugar content growing in Brazil's jungles. (Grain or corn is used in the U.S., and potatoes in some European countries.)

Once again, the impact of biomass on the energy budgets of the industrialized countries is likely to be tiny or non-existent if economic decisions are left to a free market; but it is likely to be small even if biomass production is mandated by the government. For example, even by the "high" CONAES scenario,[10] representing "the upper bound of what is technically feasible" at an investment of "around 3 trillion dollars, perhaps 2 to 3 times the cost of obtaining the equivalent energy from conventional nonrenewable sources," this upper limit regardless of cost is predicted at 5.4 quads (quadrillion Btu) for biomass in the U.S., or less than 5 percent of its energy supply even if economic growth is curtailed and energy use curbed.

But whatever the change in the use of biomass in the industrialized countries, it will be insignificant compared to the change in its use in the underdeveloped countries, where wood is the major energy source other than human and animal muscle power. Firewood, carried to its destination by man or beast, is getting scarce as the distance of carrying it is increasing with the progressive depletion of the forests. In Nepal, woodfuel is consumed at an annual rate of 600 kg per head, but regrown at only 80 kg/head/year; in Upper Volta, firewood cannot be found any more within a radius of 50 miles of the capital city; Senegal, if it continues its deforestation at present rates, will be treeless in 20 years, and Burundi by 1987; Sri Lanka has lost half its forest cover in the past 20 years, and Thailand is losing it at the rate of 10 percent a year.[1]

Table 15.1 gives an idea of the magnitudes involved, though it does not include the depletion rates.

The growing scarcity of fuelwood near populated localities in the Third World (forcing inhabitants to go ever further for their fuel supply) is what really will cause a change in the world's use of biomass energy;[17] in part because it will simply grow short of it under its present bad management with ill-defined property rights, in part because wood will be replaced by the concentrated and efficient energy that has fueled the unprecedented prosperity in the industrialized world.

An IIASA Report on "soft/decentralized" energy in the Third World[18] concludes that under "upper limit" conditions (including "well-organized,

TABLE 15.1 FIREWOOD CONSUMPTION[16]

Region	Millions of cubic meters	Percentage of wood production
North America	18	4
Central and South America	196	75
West Europe	6	8
East Europe	46	19
U.S.S.R.	74	19
Asia	522	73
Africa	297	87
Australia and Oceania	7	22

large and persistent efforts" by the governments of the region) as much as one-quarter of the Third World's energy demand could be covered by "soft" sources by the year 2030. For biomass, this would mean "intensive energy plantations even before the turn of the century." Thus even this overly optimistic report does not foresee substantial change by the end of the century; the investment, in any case, is no easier than for conventional energy sources.

The recommendations by the affluent West that the Third World live on sunshine and windmills will in all probability prove as useless as they are offensive; economic needs will force the less developed countries to adopt the same energy sources as used in the countries that, by industrializing, have left the Third World or are about to leave it – South Africa, Taiwan, South Korea, Brazil or Argentina. The industry of these countries could not, of course, operate on windmills; its chief sources by the end of the century will be nuclear and coal, supplemented by natural gas.

This inevitable process will lead to a significant *reduction* of the world's use of biomass by the year 2000 in favor of more concentrated and efficient fuels.

Geothermal and Tidal Energy

There are two more "alternative" (but non-solar) sources, neither of which will be much of an alternative in the year 2000.

Tidal energy is harnessed by trapping the high tide in a bay or inlet on shutting floodgates in a dam, then letting the water escape through hydraulic turbines. There are two such tidal electric plants in operation now, in France on the Atlantic, and in the U.S.S.R. on the White Sea, but there are few places in the world suited to this type of power, and fewer still where it would be economical. (A giant site with a potential capacity of more than 60,000 MW is located in northwest Australia where there is no demand for electricity.) There is therefore no significant contribution to the world energy budget to be expected from this source.

There are similarly only few places in the world where abundant hot steam or hot water is sufficiently close to the surface to be tapped for electricity generation or heat, and some of these places, e.g. the geysers in New Zealand, may be seriously depleted by the year 2000.

On the other hand, the virtually unlimited heat in the earth's interior, generated by radioactive decay and tappable in places where the molten rock comes within drilling depth of future technology, may be a significant alternative energy source in the mid-twenty-first century; but it will not have developed to a significant stage by the year 2000.

426 *Petr Beckmann*

Conclusion

The only major change in today's use of solar energy by the year 2000 will be a significant reduction in the use of biomass fuels in the Third World.

In the industrialized world, it would take drastic measures of government regimentation to boost this type of energy to even a few percent of the total energy budget.

By the year 2000 there will be no abundant alternatives to the main sources of energy in the developed countries, nuclear fission, coal, and natural gas.

References

1 N. L. Brown, "Solar energy in the third world," *Annual Reviews of Energy,* **5** 1980, 389–413.
2 B. L. Cohen, "Breeder reactors – a renewable energy source," *Amer. J. of Physics*, Nov/Dec 1982.
3 K. A. Lawrence, "Review of environmental effects and benefits of solar energy technologies," Solar Energy Research Institute (SERI) Report, Golden, Colo., 1978.
4 P. Beckmann, *Why "soft" technology will not be America's energy salvation*, Golem Press, Boulder, Colo., 1979.
5 F. Cap. "Energie und die Arbeitsfähigkeit von Kraftwerken" (Energy and the operating capacity of power plants), *Osterr. Z. f. Elektrot* (Austria), Feb. 1982, pp. 43–5.
6 W. Seifritz, *Sanfte Energietechnologie – Hoffnung oder Utopie?* (Soft technology – hope or utopia?), Verl. K. Thiemig, Munich, 1980.
7 S. Baron, "Solar energy – will it conserve nonrenewable resources?" *Publ. Util. Fortnightly*, 28 Sept. 1978.
8 C. Kikuchi, "Up front natural resource investments for energy conservation and pollution control," *J. Energy and Environment* (Michigan), Sept. 1982, pp. 21–36.
9 W. Sassin, "Urbanization and the global energy problem," contained in *Factors Influencing Urban Design*, Sijthooff, Alphen (Netherlands), 1980. (Extract published in IIASA *Options*, no. 3, 1980.)
10 National Academy of Sciences, Committe on Nuclear and Alternative Energy Systems (CONAES), *Energy in Transition*. Freeman, San Francisco, 1980.
11 Total cost of plant was $141 million (Southern California Edison news release of 14 April 1982).
12 *Energy in a Finite World*, Report by the Energy Systems Group of the International Institute of Applied Systems Analysis (IIASA), Wolf Häfele, Program Leader: Ballinger, Cambridge, Mass., 1981. Executive summary by A. McDonald, IIASA, Laxenburg, Austria, May 1981.
13 D. Ross, *Energy from the Waves*, Pergamon, Oxford (England), 1979.

14 F. Hoyle, *Energy or Extinction?* Heinemann, London, 1977.

15 H. C. Hayden, "Rossetta stones for energy problems," *Physics Teacher*, Sept. 1981, pp. 374–85.

16 Data from West German Federal Statistical Office, as quoted in *Mensch und Energie*, May 1981.

17 A. Sedjo and M. Clawson, "Global Forests," chapter 4 in this volume.

18 A. M. Khan, *Possible share of soft/decentralized renewables in meeting the future energy demand of developing regions*, Report RR-81-18, IIASA, Laxenburg, Austria, Sept. 1981.

15B

Coal

PETR BECKMANN

In the year 2000, coal use and production will have substantially increased; yet as a fraction of the total energy mix, coal can be expected to continue the steady decline which has been in progress for the last half century, and which has registered only small and temporary deviations from the general trend during such periods as World War II or the two "oil shocks" of the 1970s (figures 15.4 and 15.5).

Although coal, in terms of presently known reserves, is the most plentiful fossil fuel, it will continue to yield some of its market share to other fuels – primarily uranium, but also natural gas. This trend may be slowed, but is unlikely to be reversed, by the use of coal for synthetic fuels and by the use of pipelines for the transportation of coal.

Reserves, Resources, and Use

The world's coal reserves (economically recoverable at present energy prices) amount to about 660 billion (10^9) tons, or about 200 years of present coal use.

The world's coal resources, known to be in place, but not economically mineable at present prices, are several times greater (at least twice, and in many places more than ten times, as great).[1]

These resources are not, however, uniformly distributed through the world: Four countries – the U.S.S.R., the U.S.A., Mainland China, and Australia, have about 90 percent of the world's coal resources, and 60 percent of its reserves. The same three countries account for 60 percent of total world production; a further 25 percent were produced by only six countries in 1977: Poland, West Germany, Britain, Australia, South Africa, and India (table 15.2).

Coals is, above all, a fuel for electric power generation. Worldwide, 60 percent of all coal mined is burned in electric power plants (in the U.S., the fraction reaches 81.5 percent).[2] Conversely, about one third of the

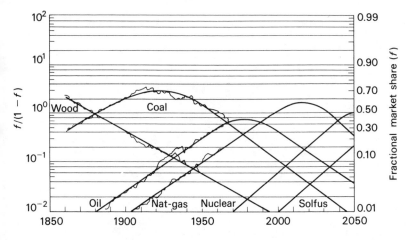

Figure 15.4 Fractions of world primary energy use, historical and forecast by the logistic law which fits the historical data well.[5]

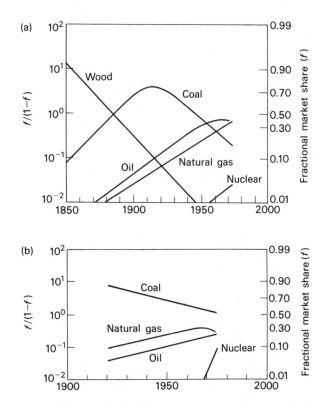

Figure 15.5 Fractions of United States primary energy use, historical and forecast as in figure 15.4; (a) total, (b) primary inputs to electric power generation.[5]

TABLE 15.2 THE DISTRIBUTION OF GLOBAL COAL RESOURCES IN BILLIONS OF TONS OF COAL EQUIVALENT (10^9 tce)[1]

Greater than 10^{12} tce (1000×10^9 tce)		Between 10^{11} and 10^{12} tce (100 and 1000×10^9 tce)		Between 10^{10} and 10^{11} tce (10 and 100×10^9 tce)		Between 10^9 and 10^{10} tce (1 and 10×10^9 tce)	
U.S.S.R.	4860	Australia	262	India	57	G.D.R.	9.4
U.S.	2570	F.R.G.	247	South Africa	57	Japan	8.5
China	1438	U.K.	163	Czechoslovakia	17.5	Columbia	8.3
		Poland	126	Yugoslavia	10.9	Rhodesia	7.1
		Canada	115	Brazil	10	Mexico	5.5
		Botswana	100			Swaziland	5.0
						Chile	4.6
						Indonesia	3.7
						Hungary	3.5
						Turkey	3.3
						Netherlands	2.9
						France	2.3
						Spain	2.3
						North Korea	2.0
						Romania	1.8
						Bangladesh	1.6
						Venezuela	1.6
						Peru	1.0

electric energy consumed in the OECD[3] countries is coal fired, with two countries high above the average – the U.S.A. (52.4 percent) and Australia (66 percent).

The other important use of coal, though less than half that of power generation, is in metallurgy (25 percent), and a smaller part (10 percent) in other industries, including railroad transportation in many countries. Residential and commercial use is gradually disappearing; in the U.S. it has dropped below 1 percent.

Reasons for Expanded Use

Coal is an abundant energy source with proven technology; beyond that there are two major reasons why the total amount of coal use will increase over the next two decades: first, the need to maintain the present order of energy consumption per head in the industrialized world, and drastically to increase it in the developing countries; and second, the need to substitute for oil.

The fertility rate, which has dramatically dropped in the developed countries, is a statistic whose effect is not felt in the same generation; in the United States, for example, the fertility rate has dropped below the "Zero Population Growth" level, but its population is still expanding, and so is its energy consumption. In the developing world, where fertility rates have not yet drastically dropped, coal will often be the fuel replacing wood.

The second reason, substitution for oil, will be important in some countries, of which the U.S. may be one, and South Africa (generating 60 percent of all electric power on the African continent) will certainly be another.

However, this is unlikely to be the case in Europe or in the industrialized countries of the Far East (Japan, South Korea). In Europe, oil for electric power generation is largely being replaced by nuclear power and natural gas; the European "coal revival," considered a possibility only some five years ago,[4] has so far not materialized. Indeed, in Europe coal use is declining not only as a fraction of the energy mix, but also in absolute terms, even in such former coal giants as Britain and Germany.[5] With the cost of a kilowatt-hour of nuclear power in West Europe close to half that of a kWh of coal-fired power,[6] it is unlikely that Europe will see much of a coal revival.

In the U.S. government pressures and incentives to convert oil-fired plants to coal-fired ones have not been successful. One of the obstacles is the great cost of conversion; however, it is entirely possible that technical innovations will enable oil-fired plants to be retrofitted for burning coal at reasonable cost. Particularly promising are coal-water mixes (with

432 *Petr Beckmann*

chemical additives to reduce the viscosity and prevent the crushed coal from settling out). Such mixes may be able to be pumped through pipelines to power plants and to be burned without first separating the coal from the water; the plants would have to be retrofitted with comparatively inexpensive furnaces and nozzles.

Impediments to Coal Use

Against these two major forces favoring coal use – demography and oil replacement – stand three continuing disadvantages: high labor intensity, troublesome transportation, and hazard to health and environment. All three are a consequence of insufficient energy density (Btu per pound or cubic foot), a property in which coal's chief alternative, nuclear power, exceeds it by a factor of several million.

Of the three drawbacks, environmental impact is probably the best known, but likely to be the smallest obstacle. This judgement is based on public acceptance over the last decade or so. While per unit of energy produced, coal demonstrably represents a far greater health hazard, involuntary risk, and environmental impact, the simple fact is that at present coal is politically far more acceptable than nuclear power. A political campaign has, for example, succeeded in frightening the public over a minuscule quantity of temporarily toxic nuclear wastes while glossing over an annual billion tons (in the U.S.) of coal wastes with an infinite lifetime, a considerable part of which is disposed of into the atmosphere. Now that the worst excesses of coal – the air pollution episodes of the 1940s and 1950s (figure 15.6) – have been cleaned up, it is unlikely that a new fuel such as uranium will be introduced merely because it is healthier and safer.

Nor is the carbon dioxide issue likely to affect the use of coal significantly by the year 2000. Although there is no doubt that fossil-fired power plants inject masses of carbon dioxide into the atmosphere, (about 300 kg per second for a 1,000 MW coal-fired unit), the global atmospheric CO_2 budget remains unclear; deforestation in the Third World, for example, could play a significant role in reducing its absorption. The extent of a change in average temperature due to CO_2 is unknown, and its effects now unpredictable. Most important of all, worldwide (or even country-wide) drastic changes in the economy because of perceived environmental dangers in the distant future run counter to all historical experience, and since this is not a report on what is desirable, but on what is probable, worldwide action against coal burning (a single country is not enough) as a measure against the increasing atmospheric CO_2 content can confidently be ruled out.

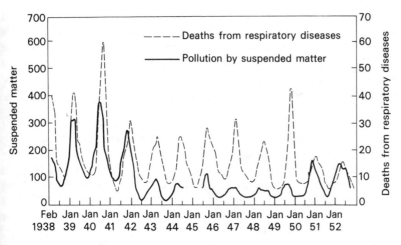

Figure 15.6 Air pollution and death rates in Dublin, Ireland, 1938–49 (from R. Wilson *et al.*)[7] This type of directly attributable loss of life persisted well into the 1950s in Europe and America, and has now been sharply reduced, though not eliminated – the median number of premature deaths correlated with coal burning in the U.S. is still 50,000 per year.[7,8]

Acid rain, contrary to popular opinion, has not yet been reliably linked to coal as such:[9] the fact that in the U.S. as much coal is burned now as in the 1950s (and in Europe less), while the damage from acid rain is now apparently much larger, suggests that either coal is not the culprit, or that the alkaline emissions which used to neutralize the acid precursors are being cleaned up too thoroughly. Whatever the outcome, the acid rain issue may affect pollution control, but is not likely to curtail coal use. (This topic is amply covered in chapter 10 of this volume.)

Far more decisive for coal use will be the economic factors that caused its decline in the first place: high labor intensity and troublesome handling.

The labor intensity in mining, transporting and handling coal and its wastes is for obvious reasons far higher than for liquid and gaseous fuels, which are not only far easier to transport per unit weight, but which concentrate more energy within that weight. For nuclear fuel, the ratio becomes quite dramatic: mining uranium ore for the same energy reduces the personnel by a factor of 10 and transportation of the fuel (for the same generated electric power) by a factor of hundreds.[10]

This high labor intensity drives up the price of coal, and also troubles utilities and other coal users with labor strife. Coal users seek to protect themselves by stocking up, but once more the lower energy density makes storage of coal more costly than oil or gas, not to mention nuclear fuel.

Transportation and handling coal may have been an even more important factor in its decline. In part, this is again linked to high labor
intensity, but there are additional difficulties, chief of which – certainly in
the U.S. – is the decline of the railroads, an entirely separate industry
over which neither coal producers nor users have any control.[11] Doubling
or tripling coal use in America by the end of the century, as has been
suggested, would put a high investment demand on the transportation
sector: even a 50 percent increase would need 800 trains, 100 barges, 7000
trucks, and 220 new mines.[12] In the U.S. the railroads, with deteriorating
tracks, are already working near capacity, and a switch to river transportation has begun.[13]

Even greater than the technical and economic restraints (in the U.S.)
are the restrictions placed on the mining and burning of coal by government regulation and environmental legislation, which makes a trebling of
coal production quite unrealistic.[11,14,15]

Synthetic Fuels

There are, however, two factors that may slow the decline of the market
share of coal among energy sources: synthetic fuels and transportation of
coal by pipeline.

The first of these is technically feasible in many ways,[16] including the
processing of coal underground (*in situ*). This process, which involves no
mining or human presence underground, is environmentally sound, but
as yet inefficient and not price-competitive with other fuels. Also,
virtually all of the coal gasification and liquefaction processes use large
amounts of water, which may not be readily available in all places where
coal is abundant, such as the Western U.S. (figure 15.7).

The most successful case of synthesizing fuel from coal on a large scale
is that of the three SASOL plants in South Africa, which use their own
liquefaction process, and which have reduced the country's energy
dependence on imported oil to 25 percent; when the third SASOL plant is
completed in 1983, this is expected to drop below 15 percent.[17]

The constraint on fuels synthesized from coal is almost exclusively
economical. In the U.S., energy corporations quickly flocked to the
Synfuel program with its $10 billion promise under the Carter admin-
istration, and left almost as quickly when the program was strongly
curtailed by Reagan. Even in South Africa, where SASOL is making a
consistent profit, the capital was put up by the government or through
government-guaranteed loans (70 percent of SASOL I is now publicly
owned, with a similar plan for SASOL II and III to be bought out from the
government), and the slightly higher price of gasoline is protected from
the imported competition by a tax.

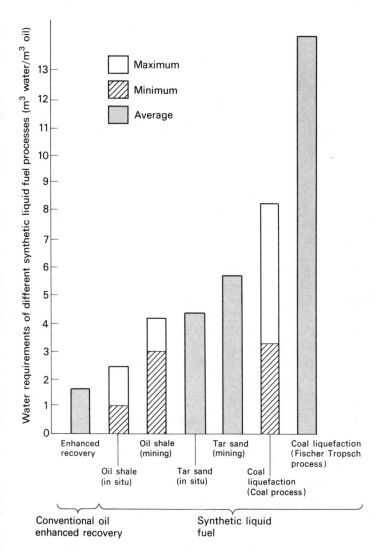

Figure 15.7 Water requirements for different synthetic liquid fuels and enhanced recovery of oil.[14]

Coal liquefaction and gasification, then, remain an abundant and environmentally sound energy source which can be put on stream with a lead time of some 5 to 6 years; however, the chances that they can beat the economy of presently used energy sources without massive government subsidies remain slim.

Pipelines

Far more encouraging is the outlook for pipelines carrying coal.

For the last four decades, there has been a consistent move away from solid fuel to pipelines carrying liquid and gaseous fuel, and to grids carrying energy, mainly as electricity, but also as heat (as in district heating). It now seems plausible that pipelines can take the place of railroads and trucks for transporting coal, too.

The furthest developed type of pipeline is the slurry line, in which pulverized or crushed coal is suspended in water and pumped through a pipeline.[18] At the destination, the coal is separated from the water, or in more advanced technology, the mixture goes almost directly into the furnace nozzles.

The technical drawback of such pipelines is the loss of water at the source, which may be located in a place that can ill afford it.[19] This has led to the development of a vacuum pipeline in which compressed air moves capsules on wheels carrying coal, essentially in the same way as internal mail is passed through the vacuum tube system of a bank. With a throughput of several million tons per year (tens of millions if the pipe diameter is made large enough), this system is likely to be economically more attractive, as well as safer and environmentally sounder than the present methods of coal transportation.[20]

The obstacles to coal pipelines, slurry or vacuum, in the world's biggest coal user – the United States – are entirely institutional and artificial. Dreading the competition, the railroads are refusing to let pipelines cross their tracks, and their lobbies in Washington are putting up an intense resistance to curbing their power to do so under their present "eminent domain" privileges.

However, it is improbable that the railroads will be able to hold out for long against a new technology that threatens them only by doing a better job. Both the coal industry and the electric utilities would welcome pipeline competition with the railroads. By the year 2000, therefore, we may assume that consumers will benefit from an expanding network of coal carrying pipelines (figure 15.8).

Other methods of evading the coal transportation problem include mine-mouth power plants which transmit electricity rather than shipping coal by railroad to the distribution center. This method has until recently been inefficient for long distances. High-voltage direct current for transmission and semiconductor technology for conversion have brought about a marked improvement, but even so, the method requires a considerable investment in the transmission line and it has so far proved economical only for low-grade coal (lignite)[21] – a consequence of the low

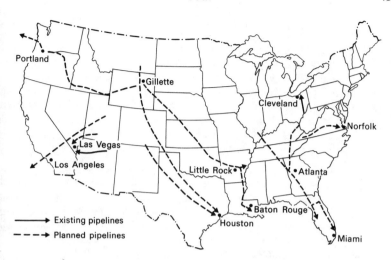

Figure 15.8 Existing and planned pipelines in the U.S. (1982).
Source: Slurry Transport Association, Washington, D.C.

price of the fuel at the mine mouth, and of the high price of transporting it by rail (more tons, fewer Btu).

Conclusion

The world's proven, presently economical coal reserves would suffice for two centuries at present rates of coal use, and the geological coal resources would last for many centuries beyond that – if they were needed.

The world's use of coal will increase to some 5 billion tons by the year 2000, in part due to the pressure to replace oil, in part due to the growing demand in the developing countries.

The share of coal in the total energy mix will, however, decline as nuclear power replaces coal in electric power generation in the industrialized countries, first in West Europe, and by the early 1990s, in the United States.

References

1   Report of the World Coal study (WOCOL), *Coal – Bridge to the Future,* Ballinger, Cambridge, Mass., 1980.
2   Unless otherwise noted, U.S. figures refer to 1981.

3   Organization of Economic Cooperation and Development, an organization of the industrialized countries with a market economy.

4   *Medium Term Aspects of a Coal Revival: Two Case Studies*, Report of the Coal Task Force, Interntnl. Inst. for Applied Systems Analysis (IIASA), Report CP-77-5, Laxenburg, Austria, Aug. 1977.

5   C. Marchetti, N. Nakicenovic, *The dynamics of energy systems and the logistic substitution model*, IIASA Report RR-79-13, Laxenburg, Austria, Dec. 1979.

6   K. P. Cohen, "Nuclear Power" in this volume (chapter 14).

7   H. E. Landsberg, "Global Climatic Trends", in this volume (chapter 10).

8   *The Direct Use of Coal* (1979) Conpressional Office of Technology Assessment, GPO Stock no. 052-003-0064-2. R. Wilson, S. D., Colome, D. G. Wilson, *Health Effects of Fossil Burning*, Ballinger, 1980. For comparison with nuclear power, see Amer. Medical Assn. Council of Scientific Affairs, "Health evaluation of energy generating sources," *J.A.M.A..*, vol. 240, no. 20, pp. 2193–95 (10 Nov. 1978); D. J. Rose, P. W. Walsh, L. L. Leskovjan, "Nuclear power – compared to what?" *Amer. Scientist*, vol. 64, p. 291 (1976); *Nuclear Power and Safety*, Norwegian Govt. Study, 1980, (available through Columbia Press, New York); *Comparative Risks of Energy Production Systems*, UK Health and Safety Executive, H.M. Stationery Office, London 1980; B. L. Cohen, "Health risks from electricity generation," *Comment on Molecular and Cellular Biophysics* (in print). The higher health hazards of coal have not been seriously disputed even by the antinuclear radicals, see the Union of Concerned Scientists' *The risks of nucelar power reactors* (1977) by its director H. Kendall.

9   M. Szabo *et al.*: *Acid Rain: Commentary on Controversial Issues and Observations on the Role of Fuel Burning*, Report DoE/MC/19170-11680, Tech. Info. Center, US DoE, Oak Ridge, Tenn.

10 *Energy in a Finite World*, IIASA Energy Systems Program Group, W. Hafele, Program Director, Ballinger, Cambridge, Mass., 1981.

11 E. Guccione, "Why coal will not be America's energy salvation," *Reason*, Oct. 1977.

12 K. E. Yeager, "Coal Clean-Up Technology," *Ann. Rev. Energy*, vol. 5 1980, pp. 357–88.

13 W. R. Hibbard Jr., "Policies and constraints for major expansion of US coal production," *Annual Rev. of Energy*, vol. 4 (1979), pp. 147–74.

14 *Energy Data*, General Electric Co., San Jose, Calif., 1980.

15 *Energy in Transition*, U.S. National Academy of Sciences Committee on Nuclear and Alternative Energy Sources, Freeman, San Francisco, 1980.

16 P. Nowacki, *Coal Liquefaction Processes*, Noyes Data Corp., Park Ridge, N.J., 1979.

17 R. W. Johnson, "South Africa's SASOL Project," *Coal Mining and Processing*, February 1981.

18 *Coal Slurry Pipelines*, Congressional Office of Technology Assessment, Govt. Prtg. Off., Washington, D.C., March 1978.

19 *Ground Water and Energy*, National Workshop, Albuquerque, US DoE Report CONF-800137, May 1980.

20 *Pipeline transportation for solid cargo*, Tubexpress Systems, Inc., Houston, Tex., 1978; Ampower Corp., Bergen, N.J., 1981.

21 "Special issue on Lignite," *Coal Age*, May 1981.

16

Long-Run Trends in Environmental Quality

WILLIAM J. BAUMOL
WALLACE E. OATES

When we undertook this study several years ago, we had definite pre-
conceptions about the general trends in environmental quality.* Because
of growth in population and industrial activity, we were convinced that
virtually all forms of environmental damage were increasing and that, in
the absence of powerful countermeasures, they would continue to accel-
erate more or less steadily. A preliminary study of available data seemed
to support this view.[1] However, a more careful and extensive re-
examination of the evidence has led us to revise this simplistic view of the
course of environmental decay. We have found on closer study that the
trends in environmental quality run the gamut from steady deterioration
to spectacular improvement. This chapter presents our accumulated data
on environmental trends.

Collecting Evidence about the Environment[2]

Because widespread and systematic concern about environmental issues
is relatively recent, it was not surprising that we found it difficult to obtain
reliable evidence on environmental trends extending back more than a
few years. Since the experience of a short period of time often can be
deceiving and heavily colored by transient, irrelevant influences, we
could not rely on easily accessible, short-term information.[3] The process
of tracking down longer-term evidence took us beyond libraries to repositories of dusty records, to the Swedish Fisheries Bureau in Gothenberg,
to the offices of St. Paul's Cathedral in London, and to the conservationists' offices in the Louvre. We want to emphasize that our survey in

---

* This chapter was written at an earlier date for another volume. The authors are happy to
have it reappear here, but note that they should not be assumed to subscribe to all the
conclusions reached in this report. As environmentalists, it is their conviction that public
policy must play an active role in the protection of our natural resources. [The editors,
and probably all the other contributors also, are not in principle against government
intervention in any particular situation requiring environmental protection. – *Ed.*]

this chapter presents *all* the long-term data that we have been able to discover; systematic evidence over past centuries (or even decades) is, indeed, very scarce. However, what we have found is, in some instances, quite intriguing. Our searches often led to dead ends, but in other cases turned up evidence that revealed that broad statements reported in the popular press were often either misleadingly simplistic or completely untrue.[4] This has forced us to revise our earlier, naive view that environmental deterioration has been a universal, accelerating process whose source is modern industrialization and population growth.

Environmental deterioration caused by natural processes. Some environmental damage, whose source at first appears to be industrial pollution, is in fact primarily the result of natural forces. An instructive illustration is the quality of the deeper waters of the central Baltic Sea. The data in figure 16.1 indicate that, in the central waters of the Baltic roughly midway between Stockholm and Helsinki, the oxygen content has been falling steadily from about 300 ml/l at the beginning of the century to virtually zero today. The data depicted in the diagram give the figures for only one of the sampling stations, but nearby stations show very similar trends. From such figures, some observers have concluded that the Baltic is becoming a "dead sea;" the inference has been that the pollution from its shores is destroying the Baltic.[5]

Yet it is by no means clear how closely the trends in oxygen content are related to pollution. For example, the northern part of the Bothnian Gulf

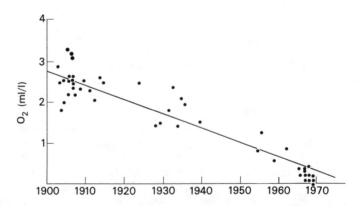

Figure 16.1   Oxygen content of the Baltic Sea (in milliliters per liter), Station
F 74 (depth of approximately 150 meters).

Source: Compiled from data from: (a) Conseil Permanent International pour l'Exploration de la Mer (ICES), *Bulletin des Résultats acquis pendant les Courses Périodiques*, Copenhagen (up to 1959); (b) *ICES Oceanographic Data Lists*, Copenhagen (1959–62); and (c) *Hydrographical Data*, Harsfiskelaboratorret, Göteborg (1963–69). For the actual figures from which this graph was drawn, see Appendix, table 16.8.

of the Baltic, which is quite shallow, receives a considerable influx of pollutants from nearby paper plants[6] and is consequently one of the portions of the Baltic most heavily subjected to oxygen-demanding effluents. Yet the data on the oxygen content of this portion of the Baltic (see figure 16.2) seem to exhibit no trend such as that displayed in the previous diagram. According to Stig H. Fonselius, the primary reason for the decrease in oxygen content in the central Baltic has been an increase in salinity.[7] Moreover, he attributes this rise in salinity to meteorological factors.[8] Specifically, "The main reason[s] . . are changes in the atmospheric circulation which have been observed over a long period . . . [causing] a decrease in precipitation resulting in a corresponding decrease in runoff [that is, a diminution in the inflow from rivers feeding into the Baltic]."[9] Examining the data on three rivers in the eastern Baltic region going back to the nineteenth century, he concludes, "There seems to be a general decreasing trend of the runoff in all three rivers from the beginning of the 20th century. If this is a true trend and it does continue there is not much hope for improved oxygen conditions in the Baltic deep water."[10]

Another rather curious illustration of environmental deterioration not

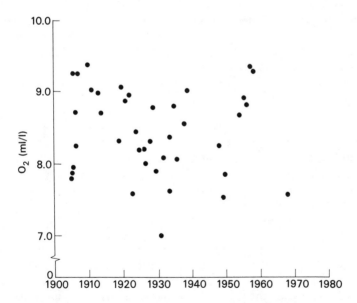

Figure 16.2 Oxygen content (in milliliters per liter) at 100 meters depth at Station F 12 in the Bothnian Bay of the Baltic Sea between 1900 and 1968.
Source: Stig H. Fonselius, *Hydrography of the Baltic Deep Basins, III*, Fishery Board of Sweden Series Hydrography Report No. 23 (Lund, Sweden: Carl Bloms Boktryckeri, 1969), p. 46.

attributable to recent human abuse is the case of "Cleopatra's Needle," the obelisk now standing in New York City's Central Park. Three sides of this monument are badly eroded, and the damage is often attributed to air pollution and continuous vibration from nearby traffic. We learned, however, that the obelisk, which originally stood at Heliopolis on the east bank of the Nile River, was tipped over by Persian invaders and remained on its side for some five and a half centuries until the Roman emperor, Augustus, had it moved and re-erected at Alexandria. From there it was brought to New York in 1880. According to E. M. Winkler, "The present east (undamaged) face probably faced downward during the monument's prostrate position between 500 B.C. and about 43 B.C." During that period there was "capillary migration from the iron-rich ground water on the flood plain silt of the Nile River."[11] That is, the stone absorbed Nile water and accumulated salt, which through normal capillary action was stored in the portions of the stone farthest away from the point of entry (that is, close to the other three sides). As a result "more than a few hundred pounds of granite flakings off the obelisk were cleaned up after a few years of exposure to the moisture-loaded atmosphere of New York City, which caused the hydration and expansion of the salts entrapped in the capillaries."[12] Much of the remaining damage to the monument is probably attributable to "the strong abrasive action of drifting sand" while the monument stood in Heliopolis and Alexandria. Thus, Winkler concludes that "the disastrous disintegration of granites in city atmospheres, as exemplified by Cleopatra's Needle, is a myth. It is therefore hoped that the obelisk will be eliminated from textbooks of physical geology as 'a good example of weathering in cities.' "[13]

Not all damage to our environment can be traced to economic growth and industrialization.

Environmental deterioration as an historical phenomenon. Another thing history makes very clear is that pollution is not a modern invention; technological developments have not always been an unmixed curse upon the environment. When the automobile began to replace the horse and rid the streets of odorous dungheaps, it was hailed as a major contributor to public health and sanitation. Certainly the modern city, whatever its state of cleanliness, is an improvement on the relatively tiny, but incredibly filthy, streets and waterways of medieval and Renaissance cities. It is reported that in about 1300 under Edward I, a Londoner was executed for burning sea coal in contravention of an Act designed to reduce smoke. During the reign of Edward I's grandson, some seventy years later, we find the following proclamation, one of many designed to protect the cleanliness of late medieval rivers and streets, all apparently equally unsuccessful (the reader will note especially the remarkable, if not wholly credible, assertion which we have italicized):

Edward, by the grace of God etc., to our well-beloved, the Mayor, Sheriffs, and Aldermen, of our City of London, greeting. *Forasmuch as we are for certain informed that rushes, dung, refuse, and other filth and harmful things, from our City of London, and the suburbs thereof, have been for a long time past, and are daily, thrown into the water of Thames, so that the water aforesaid, and the hythes thereof, are so greatly obstructed, and the course of the said water so greatly narrowed, that great ships and vessels are not able, as of old they were wont, any longer to come up to the same city, but are impeded therein*; to the most grievous damage as well of ourselves as of the city aforesaid, and of all the nobles and others of our people to the same city resorting; we, wishing to provide a fitting remedy in this behalf, do command you, on the fealty and allegiance in which unto us you are bound, strictly enjoining that, with all the speed that you may, you will cause orders to be given that such throwing of rushes, dung, refuse, and other filth and harmful things, into the bed of the river aforesaid, shall no longer be allowed, but that the same shall be removed and wholly taken away therefrom; to the amendment of the same bed of the river, and the enlarging of the watercourse aforesaid; so behaving yourselves in this behalf, that we shall have no reason for severely taking you to task in respect hereof. And this, as we do trust in you, and as you would avoid our heavy indignation, and the punishment which, as regards ourselves, you may incur, you are in no wise to omit. Witness myself, at Prestone, the 20th day of August, in the 46th year of our reign in England, and in France the 33rd."[14]

A description of the quality of the atmosphere in London in 1700 reminds us of its state two and a half centuries later:

the glorious Fabrick of St. Paul's now in building, so Stately and Beautiful as it is, will after an Age or Two, look old and discolour'd before 'tis finish'd, and may suffer perhaps as much damage by the Smoak, as the former Temple did by the Fire.[15]

The author goes on to point out:

By reason likewise of this Smoak it is, that the Air of the City, especially in the Winter time, is rendred very unwholesome: For in case there be no Wind, and especially in Frosty Weather, the City is cover'd with a thick *Brovillard* or Cloud, which the force of the Winter-Sun is not able to scatter; so that the Inhabitants thereby suffer under a dead benumming Cold, being in a manner totally depriv'd of the warmths and comforts of the Day . . . when yet to them who are but a Mile out of Town, the Air is sharp, clear, and healthy, and the Sun most comfortable and reviving.[16]

It is thus important to recognize that modern, industrialized society has no monopoly on pollution and environmental damage from either human sources or natural forces. Evidence of significant environmental damage does not necessarily mean that the damage is growing, and evidence that deterioration is growing may not mean that the source of the problem is human activity. We do not intend here to deny the seriousness of environmental decay, but rather to point out the complexities besetting an understanding and interpretation of levels and trends in environmental quality. With this in mind, we turn to the presentation of our accumulated data on these trends.

Cases of Mixed or Improving Environmental Trends

As we said at the beginning of the chapter, our examination of the available facts suggests that the trends in environmental damage are far less uniform than we had initially expected. This section presents some examples in which environmental quality is actually improving or in which a varied pattern of deterioration and/or improvement is apparent.

The Great Lakes. The deteriorating water quality of two of the most vulnerable of the Great Lakes (in terms of population and water volume), Lake Erie and Lake Ontario, has received widespread attention. Figures 16.3–16.5 show trends for these two lakes in the concentrations of three substances closely tied to industrial and municipal pollution: dissolved solids, sulfates, and calcium.[17] The figures show very clearly that, at least since early in the twentieth century, these concentrations have been increasing dramatically. Figures on concentrations of other substances in these lakes (chloride, sodium, and potassium, also associated with industrial wastes) tell much the same story (see figure 16.6). But the water quality of Lakes Erie and Ontario differ sharply from that of the other Great Lakes. Although Lakes Michigan and Huron have suffered from an increase in dissolved solids (see figure 16.7), this growth has been far slower than in Lakes Erie or Ontario. Moreover, Lake Michigan has suffered no growth in calcium content, and its concentrations of sodium and potassium leveled off soon after the turn of the century. Lake Superior's purity seems to have been increasing rather steadily or holding constant, at least in terms of the dissolved solids for which we have data. Figure 16.6 shows the great diversity in calcium, chloride, sodium, and potassium concentrations over time in the Great Lakes, with these chemicals apparently presenting an increasing problem only in Lakes Erie and Ontario. Sulfates, on the other hand, have

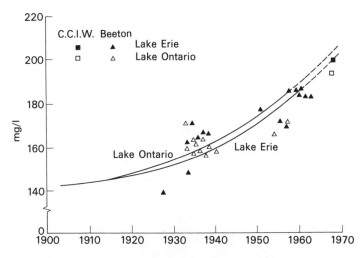

Figure 16.3 Changes in the concentrations of total dissolved solids in Lakes Erie and Ontario.

Source: Proceedings of the Conference on Changes in the Chemistry of Lakes Erie and Ontario, 5–6 November, 1970, *Bulletin of the Buffalo Society of Natural Sciences* **25** (2), (1971). In the key, C.C.I.W., refers to Canada Centre for Inland Waters: Beeton refers to A. M. Beeton, "Eutrophication of the St. Lawrence Great Lakes," *Limnology and Oceanography* 19 (1965): 240–54; and Kramer refers to J. R. Kramer, "Theoretical Model for the Chemical Composition of Fresh Water with Application to the Great Lakes," in *Great Lakes Research Division* (Ann Arbor, Michigan: University of Michigan, 1964): 147–60.

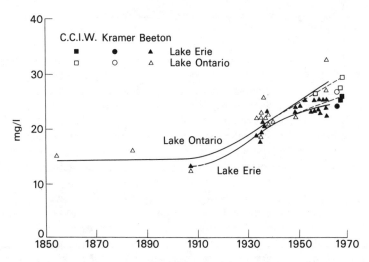

Figure 16.4 Changes in the concentrations of sulfate in Lakes Erie and Ontario.

Source: see figure 16.3.

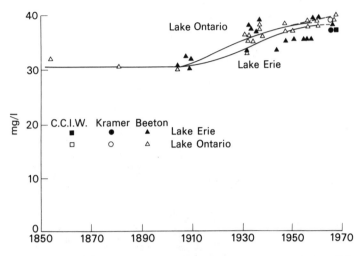

Figure 16.5 Changes in the concentrations of calcium in Lakes Erie and
Ontario.
Source: See figure 16.3.

increased in concentration in every one of the lakes except Lake
Superior, the largest, deepest, and most isolated of the lakes.[18] A
reporter could paint the most dismal picture of the state of the Great
Lakes by singling out Lakes Erie and Ontario, while the investigator who
chooses to study only Lake Superior could easily conclude that there is no
cause for alarm.[19]

Water quality in the New York City Harbor.   The quality of the waters
surrounding New York City has a mixed history. Figure 16.8 shows the
trend in dissolved oxygen concentrations in five waterways surrounding
the city for the years 1910–70.[20] (Any biodegradable emissions such as
human wastes, food products, or waste paper are gradually transformed
and assimilated by natural processes that use up oxygen. A waterway
heavily polluted by biodegradable emissions will, therefore, tend to have
a relatively low dissolved oxygen content.)[21] The decline indicated by the
graph for the period prior to 1920 suggests that oxygen-using pollution in
the city's waterways increased rapidly during the first years of the
twentieth century. In about 1920, however, the process of deterioration
suddenly halted. For the next three decades, the dissolved-oxygen level
remained relatively stable, or even improved slightly. It has been suggested that the decrease in dissolved oxygen up to 1917 was the result, not
of increased industrial activity in the area, but of rapid population
growth. This population growth increased the amount of sewage dumped

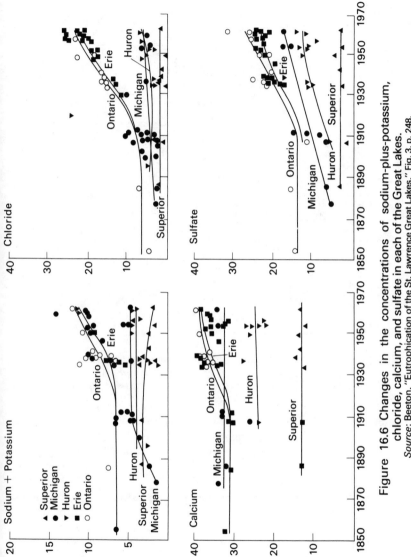

Figure 16.6 Changes in the concentrations of sodium-plus-potassium, chloride, calcium, and sulfate in each of the Great Lakes.
Source: Beeton, "Eutrophication of the St. Lawrence Great Lakes," Fig. 3, p. 248.

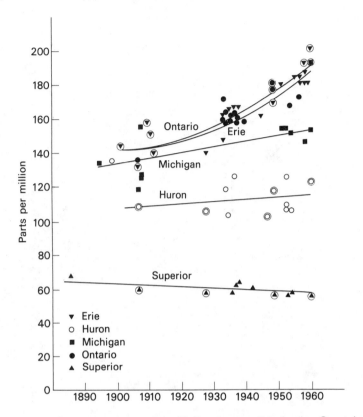

Figure 16.7 Concentrations of total dissolved solids in the Great Lakes
(circled points are averages of 12 or more determinations).
Source: Beeton, "Eutrophication of the St. Lawrence Great Lakes," Fig. 1, p. 246.

virtually untreated into the city's waterways. According to this view, it
was the restriction of immigration from abroad that accounted for the
stabilizing of water quality in New York's rivers. Unfortunately this
explanation is only partly tenable at best, since the population of the city
did continue to grow at least until 1930.[22]

In any event, by the early 1950s a major expansion in waste treatment
facilities was begun, first in the East River and later in the Hudson. By the
middle of the 1960s, dissolved oxygen concentrations had increased
sharply in all five of the waterways described in the graph. Indeed, there
was observable improvement throughout the Hudson River:

almost all fishermen, marine biologists, environmentalists and
government officials [are] agreeing that the river is cleaner now than
it has been in recent years.

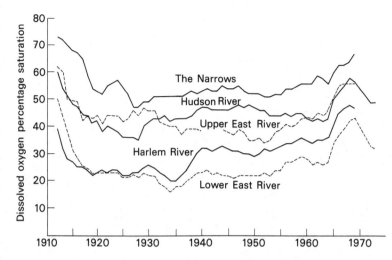

Figure 16.8 Five-year moving averages of the annual dissolved oxygen (as percentage of saturation) for the main branches of New York Harbor.
Source: New York Harbor Water Survey, 1970, provided by City of New York, Environmental Protection Administration, Department of Water Resources, Bureau of Water Pollution Control. For actual figures, see Appendix, table 16.5.

By almost every measure available – amount of money spent, number of sewage treatment plants constructed, number of crabs returning, number and size of fish, visibility of sewage, number of people swimming – the 155-mile-long main stem of the Hudson River between New York City and Troy is improving.

In the fishing season just ending, fishermen took in more and bigger blue-claw crabs, hauled in bigger weakfish, caught large numbers of "lafayettes" for the first time in 30 years. . . .[23]

U.S. air quality trends. New York City's air quality has shown similar improvement in terms of certain pollutants. Figure 16.9 shows the trends in settleable particulate matter (soot) for all five boroughs of the city during the post-war period. The change is certainly startling. In Brooklyn the figure has fallen to about one-sixth of its 1945 level, and in Manhattan it has declined by more than two-thirds. Similarly, there has been a decline in the sulfur dioxide content of the atmosphere, not only in New York but in other major cities as well. The data depicted in figure 16.10 show a dramatic improvement in New York and Chicago and more modest gains in the other cities such as Boston and St. Louis (although the latter two cities exhibited something of a reversal between 1971 and 1972). This sort of evidence suggests that environmental policy can be effective and can produce results that are both rapid and substantial.[24] Table 16.1 summarizes national emission trends for five major air pol-

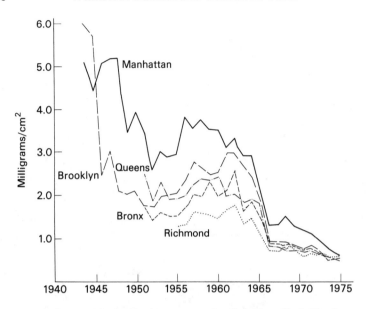

Figure 16.9 Settleable particulate matter for five New York City boroughs
(milligrams per square centimeter).
Source: Department of Air Resources, New York.

lutants for the period 1940–74. The figures indicate that between 1940 and 1970 emissions of these pollutants were steadily and significantly increasing. The Council on Environmental Quality writes, "Since 1970, however, air pollution control programs appear to be stemming that growth. The estimated total nationwide emissions of particulates and carbon monoxide have been reduced significantly, and the other major regulated pollutants have remained near 1970 levels."[25] Table 16.1 shows "that between 1970 and 1974 particulate emission levels dropped by about 29%, sulfur dioxide declined 8%, carbon monoxide dropped 12%, and hydrocarbon emissions declined about 5%. On the other hand, nitrogen oxide emissions have increased an estimated 10% over the same period."[26]

London: air and water quality trends. Air quality in London displays striking parallels to the New York experience. London's long history of air pollution was largely the result of the heavy use of coal fires for both industrial and domestic heating. One of the consequences was the prevalence of filthy fogs, sometimes in garish colors produced by the chemical content of the air; such fogs became as much a symbol of London as Westminster Abbey and Big Ben. Only after the disaster of December 1952, during which in a 2-week period abnormally high concentrations of

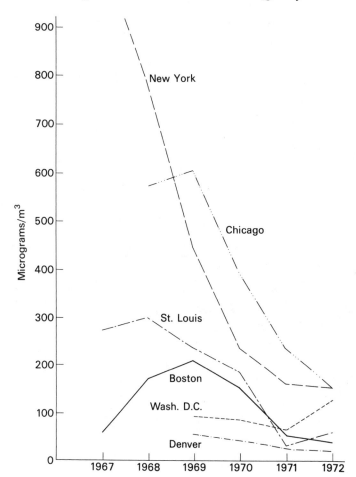

Figure 16.10 SO$_2$ air quality data for six U.S. cities (micrograms of SO$_2$ per cubic meter).
Source: Derived from *Environmental Quality, The Fourth Annual Report of the Council on Environmental Quality* (Washington, D.C.: U.S. Government Printing Office, 1973), p. 273. They cite as their source: EPA data from the National Air Sampling Network.

sulfur dioxide and smoke resulted in an estimated 4,000 excess deaths,[27] did Parliament adopt more stringent regulations for the protection of the atmosphere. The Clean Air Act of 1956 and subsequent legislation established smoke-control zones in which strict codes governed allowable smoke emissions.[28] The results have been impressive: pea-soup fogs have disappeared, and the number of hours of sunshine in London has climbed significantly. Figure 16.11 shows that there has been a 50 percent increase in winter sunshine in Central London since 1950. More generally,

TABLE 16.1   NATIONWIDE AIR POLLUTION EMISSIONS, 1940–74
(MILLIONS OF TONS)

Year	Sulfur dioxide	Particulates	Carbon monoxide	Hydrocarbons	Nitrogen oxides
1940	22	27	85	19	7
1950	24	26	103	26	10
1960	23	25	128	32	14
1968	31	26	150	35	21
1969	34	27	154	35	22
1970	34.3	27.5	107.3	32.1	20.4
1971	33.5	25.2	104.9	31.4	20.8
1972	32.6	23.2	104.9	31.3	22.2
1973	33.2	21.0	100.9	31.3	23.0
1974	31.4	19.5	94.6	30.4	22.5

Note: The CEQ cautions: "The techniques used to calculate these 1970–4 emissions differ from those used for 1940–70. Consequently, although recent emissions appear lower, the pre-1970 estimates are not truly comparable with the post-1970 calculations" (*Sixth Annual Report*, p. 305).

Sources: For the 1940–69 period, *Environmental Quality, The Third Annual Report of the Council on Environmental Quality* (Washington, D.C.: U.S. Government Printing Office, August 1972), table 2, p. 6; for the 1970–4 period, *Environmental Quality, The Sixth Annual Report of the Council on Environmental Quality* (Washington, D.C.: U.S. Government Printing Office, December 1975), table 32, p. 440.

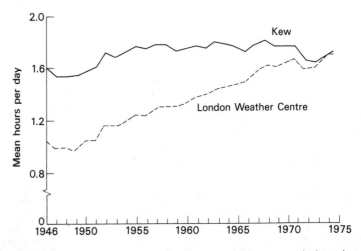

Figure 16.11 Trend in hours of winter sunshine recorded at London Weather Centre and Kew Observatory. Graph shows ten-year moving averages, December through February, plotted on last year of period.
Source: Cabinet Office, Central Statistical Office, London; letter from R. W. Freeman, 24 February, 1977. For data from which graph was drawn, see Appendix, table 16.6.

Table 16.2 indicates that emissions of smoke and, to a lesser extent, of sulfur into the atmosphere throughout the United Kingdom have fallen fairly steadily since the early 1960s.[29]

The English have also made considerable progress in the cleanup of some rivers and estuaries. We noted earlier the marked increase in recent years in the dissolved-oxygen content of New York City's rivers.

TABLE 16.2   EMISSION OF SMOKE AND SULFUR
DIOXIDE (SO_2) IN UNITED KINGDOM, 1955–75
(MILLIONS OF TONS)

Year	Smoke	SO_2	Year	Smoke	SO_2
1955	2.35	5.05	1971	0.61	5.83
1962	1.51	5.89	1972	0.50	5.63
1968	0.89	5.74	1973	0.49	5.87
1969	0.79	5.99	1974	0.46	5.43
1970	0.72	6.12	1975[a]	0.39	5.11

Source: Cabinet Office, Central Statistical Office, London SW10 3AQ, letter from R. W. Freeman, 24 February 1977.

[a] Provisional

Figure 16.12 depicts similar trends in levels of dissolved oxygen in the Thames near London. In contrast to the period of deterioration from the 1930s until 1954, when the dissolved oxygen content of the Thames just downstream from the City was close to zero, the curve for 1969 indicates a marked improvement. The Royal Commission on Environmental Pollution reported:

> The oxygen content of the Thames for some 10 miles above and 30 miles below London Bridge had been diminishing for decades, and the consequences were beginning to be very serious. In 1949 the Water Pollution Research Laboratory began an investigation into the causes of the deterioration. When these were diagnosed, the Port of London Authority launched a programme to improve the quality of the water. The success of this programme has been shown by the return of many kinds of fish. In 1957–58 a survey showed no fish between Richmond (15 miles above London Bridge) and Gravesend (25 miles below). By 1967–68 some 42 species were present and migratory forms were able once again to move through the polluted zone.[30]

These cases support the view that environmental policy can work. It does not follow, however, that the battle against pollution is essentially

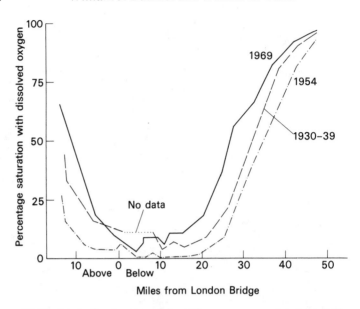

Figure 16.12 Analysis of water of river Thames: percentage saturation with dissolved oxygen at high water (average July–September).
Source: Royal Commission on Environmental Pollution, *First Report* (London: Her Majesty's Stationery Office, February 1971), p. 20.

won or that improvement is universal and unambiguous. There are important and documented instances of progressive decline in environmental quality. In the next section, we will discuss some evidence of growing human abuse of the environment.

Cases of Deteriorating Environmental Quality

Another look at urban air quality.   In the previous section we described the decreasing levels of atmospheric sulfur dioxide and particulate matter in New York and other cities as an example of improving air quality.[31] The trends in other measures of air quality are not so satisfying. Figure 16.13, for example, shows that concentrations of carbon monoxide in New York City have, apart from short-term fluctuations, remained constant since 1958. This is also largely true for most European cities. Similarly, figure 16.14, which depicts trends in the levels of suspended particulates in five major cities over a recent five-year period, shows that other cities have not done as well as New York in this respect. Indeed, the air in Denver has apparently been growing steadily more polluted in terms of particulate matter.[32]

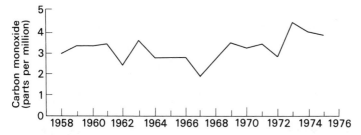

Figure 16.13 Carbon monoxide concentrations in New York City, 1958–75
(parts per million).
Source: Department of Air Resources, New York. Figures represent average annual measurements taken at Station Laboratory 121 (located at 121st Street) fifteen feet above street level. This
station was chosen because it is the oldest in the city and its data are more complete. Most of the
air pollutant measuring stations in New York City began operation after 1969. For figures from
which graph was drawn see Appendix, table 16.7.

Trends in atmospheric lead pollution. A striking case of increasing
environmental deterioration is the steady growth of lead concentrations
in the earth's atmosphere. Analyses of ice layers in the Arctic and
Antarctic regions have produced estimates of long-term trends in lead
concentrations (and other pollutants). Figure 16.15 shows the findings of
one of the most recent, and apparently most systematic, of these

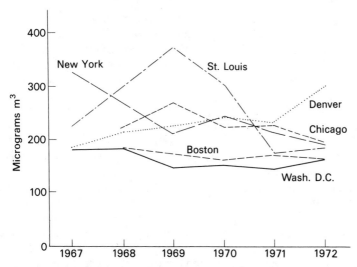

Figure 16.14 Total suspended particulates for six cities, 1967–72 (micro-
grams per cubic meter).
*Source: Environmental Quality, The Fourth Annual Report of the Council on Environmental
Quality* (1973), p. 273.

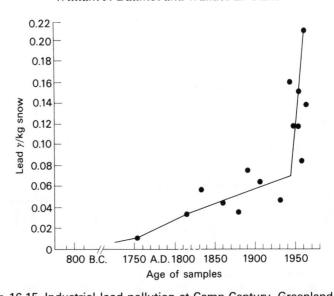

Figure 16.15 Industrial lead pollution at Camp Century, Greenland, since 800 B.C., γ/kg (micrograms per kilogram).
Source: M. Murozumi, T. J. Chow, and C. Patterson, "Chemical Concentrations of Pollutant Lead Aerosols, Terrestrial Dusts and Sea Salts in Greenland and Antarctic Snow Strata," *Geochimica et Cosmochimica Acta* **33**, 10 (October 1969), p. 1285.

studies.[33] The graph, which covers over twenty-five centuries, is certainly startling. It shows that, even in the remote regions of northern Greenland, there has been a persistent, accelerating rise in lead pollution; today lead concentrations at Camp Century, Greenland, are well over five-hundred times "natural" levels.[34] The study's measurement of other "impurities" in the ice samples showed no discernible trends; that is, of the seven items whose concentrations were estimated as far back as 800 B.C., it was lead alone that exhibited any long-term growth pattern. It should be noted that even the carefully gathered evidence of the Greenland study has been criticized on two grounds: first, similar results were not obtained in the Antarctic samples, and, second and perhaps more serious, the Greenland figures may reflect a very special source of lead contamination: "a major U.S. military base was established in Thule, Greenland, during World War II and a large camp was set up between 1959 and 1960 at Camp Century. This is only 80 [kilometers] from the Virgin Trench site where samples of snow, dated 1952–1965, were collected. The base was supplied by aircraft using leaded fuel . . . [thus] snow at the Trench site may well have been contaminated by these activities" (A. L. Mills, "Lead in the environment," *Chemistry in Britain,* **7** (April 1971), 161). It may be relevant to note that Mr. Mills is chairman of the Institute of Petroleum's advisory committee on health. Both charges have evoked responses. The difference in the results for the Northern and Southern studies has been attributed to "barriers to north–south tropospheric mixing . . . which hinder the migration of aerosol pollutants from the northern hemisphere to the Antarctic" (Murozumi, Chow, and Patterson, "Chemical concentrations," p. 1247). As for the second charge, an authoritative defender of the Greenland study has replied, "Firstly, the greatest amounts of lead were found to be deposited in the winter months when precipitation was heaviest and air traffic lightest. Secondly, the lead levels from sites between the Virgin Trench and the bases showed no elevation attributable to significant contamination from the bases. Thirdly, the Virgin Trench site was predominantly upwind from the bases. It is also worth noting that the major increase in ice-lead levels began about 20 years before the closer base was established" (D. Bryce-Smith, "Lead pollution from petrol," *Chemistry in Britain*, 7 (July 1971), 285).

The figures constitute grounds for genuine concern. Lead has been described as

one of the most insidiously toxic of the heavy metals to which we are exposed, particularly in its ability to accumulate in the body and to damage the central nervous system including the brain. . . . It inhibits enzyme systems necessary for the formation of haemoglobin . . . and has been said to interfere with practically any life-process one chooses to study. Children and young people appear specially liable to suffer more or less permanent brain damage, leading [among other things] . . . to mental retardation, irritability and bizarre behavior patterns. . . . More serious occupational exposure can lead to insanity and death. . . .[35]

Further evidence of long-term increases in lead concentrations is provided by a recent study in Peru comparing the lead content of six-century-old human bones with more modern samples. Lead concentrations in the modern bones were, on the average, over ten times as high as those in the earlier ones.[36] On the other hand, a Polish study showed ". . . that the levels of lead in modern Polish bones do not differ significantly from those found in bones from the 3rd century, although levels in the Middle Ages were often very high."[37] While there is strong evidence that the prevalence of this poison has increased markedly over the centuries, it is still impossible to reach completely unqualified conclusions.

The accumulation of solid waste.   We turn next to a source of indisputable environmental deterioration: the burgeoning *quantity* of solid wastes which society produces. Growth in population and in output per capita can be expected to increase the amount of solid waste. While time series for long-term trends in this area are not easy to obtain, the evidence available indicates that this has, indeed, been true. It is reported, for example, that in recent years the flow of solid wastes in New York City has been increasing 4 percent per year.[38] We have collected some data for Cincinnati that go back more than 40 years. Figure 16.16 indicates that the amount of solid waste collected in Cincinnati has grown at an average rate of about 4.5 percent per year.[39] If records were obtained for other cities, they would no doubt show very similar results. There is no question that this trend poses ever-increasing problems for society. Already many cities are having trouble disposing of the mounting heaps of trash. Neighboring areas are reluctant to serve as the cities' dumps, and locations near cities that are suitable for landfill operations are getting scarce. Other methods of waste disposal are now recognized to create problems of their own. Burning garbage pollutes the air, while treatment of liquid wastes leaves a sludge which must be disposed of. Moreover, we are learning that dumping wastes into the ocean nearby is not costless to society; sludge dumped into the sea can kill or contaminate marine life and pollute nearby waters and beaches. The changing composition of solid wastes also adds to the problem of disposal. For example, plastics (which are nondegradable and often have harmful combustion properties) make up an increasing percentage of solid wastes. All in all, the problem of solid waste disposal can hardly be viewed with equanimity; it surely represents a major environmental problem that is likely to grow worse.

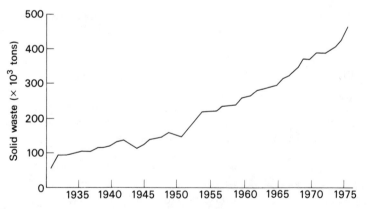

Figure 16.16 Total tonnage of solid waste received at city disposal sites, Cincinnati, Ohio, 1931–76.

Source: City of Cincinnati, Department of Public Works, Division of Waste Collection, Letters of 9 November 1973, and 17 February 1977, from R. D. Behrman, Administrative Assistant, and A. H. Schuck, Acting Superintendent. For data see Appendix, table 16.4.

Conclusions

The trends in environmental deterioration are varied and uneven. While the evidence presented in this chapter may undermine some of the more rash and unqualified predictions of imminent ecological disaster, there is no justification for complacency and inaction. Unquestionably, various types of environmental damage directly associated with human activity have grown rapidly and without interruption for a very long period of time. Some of them, with little doubt, produce serious consequences. Certain forms of pollution, besides making existence uglier and far less pleasant, have almost certainly increased the frequency of illness and added significantly to death rates. Some forms of pollution may even pose serious hazards for human survival. In recent decades facts have often caught up with and surpassed the inventions of science fiction; some of the more bizarre horrors threatened by environmental abuse cannot be ruled out with any high degree of confidence. But scare tactics are not necessary to make a case for strong environmental policy. The demonstrable ill effects of pollution on health and longevity, despite the untidy diversity of trends that accompany them, surely justify the adoption of effective countermeasures.

Appendix A: A Lesson from Very Long Time Series: the Case of the Nile

This chapter has presented a number of time series for environmental data, some of considerable duration. Yet from a historical point of view they are relatively brief; few of them extend more than 75 years.

In one area, the study of climate, time-series data are available over extraordinarily long periods of time.[40] From the evidence of tree rings, glaciers, and other sources, experts have accumulated figures spanning hundreds of years. One of the most remarkable of these series provides the annual figures on the height of the Nile River. They seem not to have been assembled by scientists, but rather by tax authorities who based their tax levies on these data as an indicator of the agricultural prosperity of the Nile valley. Before presenting a graph that summarizes a substantial portion of the data (which extend more than seven centuries), let us consider briefly the data in figure 16.17, which gives, in five-year averages, the behavior of the annual low-water mark of the Nile River. The pronounced and steady downward trend over the period of more than thirty years should be clear enough. It may suggest the onset of a period of drought. Surely, the consistency of its decline presages unpleasant things for the succeeding years. An observer looking at this

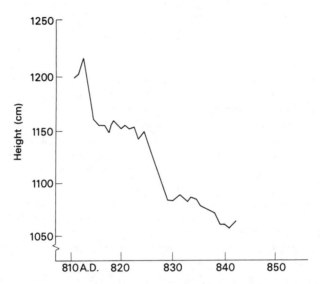

Figure 16.17 Five-year moving averages of the minimum height of the Nile river, 810–50.

Source: Prince Omar Tousson, "Mémoire sur l'Histoire du Nil," Mémoires présentés, à l'Institut d'Egypt et Publiés sous les Auspices de sa Majesté Fouad Ier, Roi d'Egypt, 10 (Cairo: Institut Français d'Archéologie Orientale, 1925), pp. 361–411. See table 16.3 for the data.

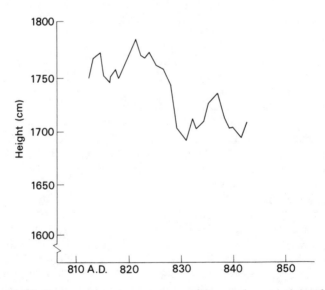

Figure 16.18 Five-year moving averages of the maximum height of the Nile river, 810–50.

Source: see figure 16.17.

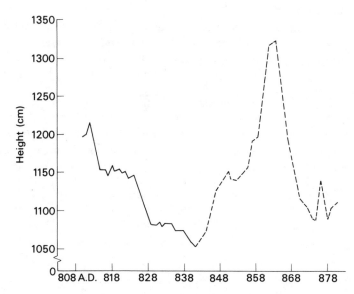

Figure 16.19 Five-year moving averages of the minimum height of the Nile river, 808–78.
Source: see figure 16.17.

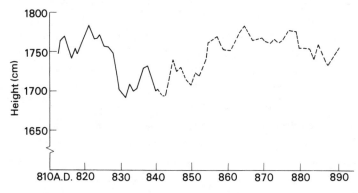

Figure 16.20 Five-year moving averages of the maximum height of the Nile river, 810–90.
Source: see figure 16.17.

trend might well project dire consequences for the future of the river valley and its inhabitants.

Yet the companion figure 16.18, which gives the trend of the *high-water* levels over the same period, already provides grounds for doubt. There is still something of a downward trend, but it is not nearly so pronounced or persistent as the annual minima. Moreover, figures 16.19 and 16.20 tell quite a different story; they repeat the data of figures 16.17 and 16.18 along with their sequels. The time paths can hardly be described as steady downward trends.

The full history, however, is revealed by our last graph, figure 16.21 which shows the variations in the height of the Nile from 641 through 1451. It is certainly not easy to discern any sharp trends in the data. The moral should be clear: it is dangerous to extrapolate from a consistent trend in a data series, even one persisting over decades.

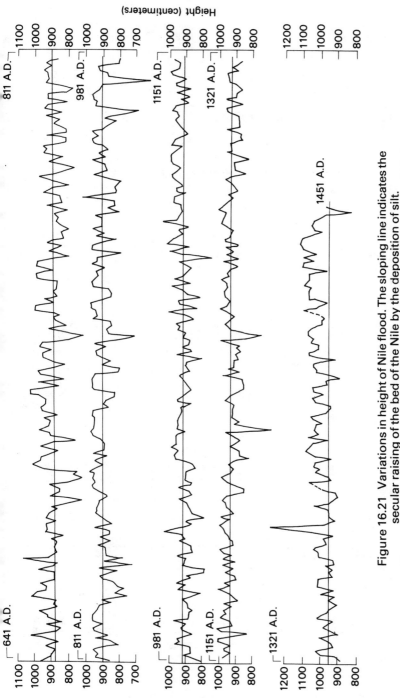

Figure 16.21 Variations in height of Nile flood. The sloping line indicates the secular raising of the bed of the Nile by the deposition of silt.
Source: C. E. P. Brooks, "Periodicities in the Nile Floods," *Memoirs of the Royal Meteorological Society,* **2** (12) (January 1928), p. 10.

TABLE 16.3   FIVE-YEAR MOVING AVERAGES OF THE HEIGHT OF THE NILE RIVER (CENTIMETERS)

Year	Minimum	Maximum	Year	Minimum	Maximum	Year	Minimum	Maximum
811	1196		840	1062	1700	869	1149	1771
812	1202		841	1055	1701	870	1125	1766
813	1217	1746	842	1054	1696	871	1111	1765
814	1183	1767	843	1065	1692	872	1107	1769
815	1159	1773	844	1072	1718	873	1092	1766
816	1153	1749	845	1085	1741	874	1090	1765
817	1152	1742	846	1102	1724	875	1094	1772
818	1145	1756	847	1122	1733	876	1142	1781
819	1156	1746	848	1227	1728	877	1113	1781
820	1152	1762	849	1137	1712	878	1090	1783
821	1153	1775	850	1144	1709	879	1105	1758
822	1150	1782	851	1153	1725	880	1106	1757
823	1152	1769	852	1139	1720	881	1065	1757
824	1143	1767	853	1138	1731	882	1103	1757
825	1148	1771	854	1143	1753	883	1139	1747
826	1140	1758	855	1151	1764	884	1143	1763
827	1122	1756	856	1153	1769	885	1148	1752
828	1106	1756	857	1179	1767	886		1735
829	1091	1727	858	1194	1759	887		1733
830	1081	1702	859	1196	1755	888		1744
831	1081	1695	860	1224	1755	889		1752
832	1088	1687	861	1276	1764	890		1764
833	1080	1712	862	1295	1770			
834	1085	1700	863	1316	1778			
835	1085	1706	864	1319	1786			
836	1077	1722	865	1299	1787			
837	1076	1732	866	1250	1771			
838	1073	1735	867	1205	1768			
839	1073	1713	868	1176	1771			

Source: E. A. L. Prince Omar Toussoun, "Mémoires sur l'Histoire du Nil," Mémoires Présentés à l'Institut D'Egypt et Publiés Sous Les Auspices SA

TABLE 16.4 TOTAL TONNAGE OF SOLID WASTE RECEIVED
AT CITY DISPOSAL SITES, CINCINNATI, OHIO

Year	Combustible waste	Year	Combustible waste
1931	66,682.4	1954	215,959.9
1932	95,536.9	1955	218,108.8
1933	95,415.1	1956	218,753.1
1934	99,225.5	1957	230,714.8
1935	103,037.8	1958	231,169.5
1936	107,016.6	1959	235,622.2
1937	107,474.9	1960	253,871.8
1938	116,860.8	1961	259,743.7
1939	118,314.4	1962	271,585.0
1940	121,022.5	1963	278,582.6
1941	130,897.7	1964	281,376.0
1942	138,114.5	1965	287,922.1
1943	124,507.4	1966	307,333.8
1944	116,483.4	1967	315,054.2
1945	120,625.1	1968	335,732.5
1946	138,072.4	1969	360,388.0
1947	142,786.9	1970	360,843.1
1948	147,390.6	1971	379,080.0
1949	158,023.6	1972	379,066.0
1950	150,803.5	1973	384,576.0
1951	144,543.8	1974	404,097.7
1952	171,628.4	1975	415,432.5
1953	195,201.9	1976	469,086.8

Note: Corresponds to figure 16.16 in text.
Source: City of Cincinnati, Department of Public Works, Division of Waste Collection, Letters of
9 November 1973, and 17 February 1977, from R. D. Behrman, Administrative Assistant and
A. H. Schuck, Acting Superintendent.

TABLE 16.5 FIVE-YEAR MOVING AVERAGES OF THE ANNUAL DISSOLVED OXYGEN FOR THE MAIN BRANCHES OF NEW YORK HARBOR, HUDSON RIVER AND LOWER EAST RIVER (PERCENTAGE OF SATURATION)

Year	Hudson River	Lower East River	Year	Hudson River	Lower East River	Year	Hudson River	Lower East River
1912	60	50	1933	44	18	1954	44	24
1913	54	44	1934	42	16	1955	44	24
1914	51	38	1935	43	18	1956	45	27
1915	48	32	1936	43	18	1957	44	27
1916	47	28	1937	43	20	1958	45	28
1917	44	25	1938	44	21	1959	45	29
1918	44	24	1939	46	23	1960	43	28
1919	41	22	1940	47	23	1961	42	26
1920	42	23	1941	47	24	1962	43	27
1921	38	23	1942	46	22	1963	42	26
1922	40	23	1943	46	23	1964	43	37
1923	39	23	1944	46	22	1965	50	33
1924	38	23	1945	46	22	1966	53	37
1925	36	22	1946	47	21	1967	55	39
1926	36	22	1947	48	22	1968	58	42
1927	36	22	1948	47	22	1969	57	43
1928	35	21	1949	48	22	1970	55	40
1929	40	23	1950	47	22	1971	52	37
1930	42	22	1951	46	22	1972	49	33
1931	43	22	1952	46	23	1973	49	32
1932	43	19	1953	44	22			

TABLE 16.6 HOURS OF WINTER SUNSHINE (DECEMBER TO FEBRUARY) AT LONDON WEATHER CENTRE AND KEW OBSERVATORY

Year	Mean hours per day Kew	Mean hours per day London	Year	Mean hours per day Kew	Mean hours per day London	Year	Mean hours per day Kew	Mean hours per day London
1939	1.64	1.19	1952	1.73	1.18	1965	1.77	1.55
1940	1.58	1.15	1953	1.71	1.18	1966	1.75	1.57
1941	1.56	1.11	1954	1.75	1.20	1967	1.80	1.64
1942	1.55	1.06	1955	1.78	1.25	1968	1.83	1.69
1943	1.57	1.05	1956	1.77	1.24	1969	1.79	1.69
1944	1.54	1.04	1957	1.78	1.30	1970	1.80	1.70
1945	1.56	1.04	1958	1.78	1.31	1971	1.79	1.73
1946	1.58	1.05	1959	1.74	1.32	1972	1.70	1.64
1947	1.53	1.00	1960	1.76	1.35	1973	1.67	1.62
1948	1.53	1.00	1961	1.78	1.41	1974	1.72	1.69
1949	1.54	0.98	1962	1.76	1.43	1975	1.77	1.72
1950	1.59	1.05	1963	1.80	1.51			
1951	1.62	1.06	1964	1.79	1.53			

Note: Corresponds to figure 16.11 in text.
Source: Cabinet Office, Central Statistical Office, letter from R. W. Freeman, 24 February 1977.

TABLE 16.7   CARBON MONOXIDE CONCENTRATIONS
IN NEW YORK CITY, 1958–75 (PARTS PER MILLION)

Year	Carbon monoxide	Year	Carbon monoxide	Year	Carbon monoxide
1958	3	1964	3	1970	3.2
1959	3.4	1965	3	1971	3.4
1960	3.5	1966	3	1972	2.7
1961	3.5	1967	2	1973	4.5
1962	2.5	1968	3	1974	4.1
1963	3.7	1969	3.5	1975	4.0

Note: Corresponds to figure 16.13 in text.
Source: see figure 16.13.

Date	(m) Depth	Oxygen	Percentage of saturation	Date	(m) Depth	Oxygen	Percentage of saturation
30 May 1903	162	286	33.4	10 Jul 1932	173	232	27.3
6 Aug 1903	159	178	20.8	13 Jul 1933	161	138	16.1
28 Nov 1903	141	250		13 Jul 1934	155	207	24.4
23 May 1904	150	254	29.7	16 Jul 1935	147.5	192	22.9
7 Nov 1904	155	198	23.2	8 Jul 1939	157	150	18.0
17 Aug 1905	146	324	38.2	23 Jul 1954	185	82	10
24 May 1905	150	218		26 Jul 1955	155	123	14.7
	155	259	30.3	19 Jul 1958	143	52	6.2
11 Nov 1905	140	257		20 Jul 1959	155	13	1.5
6 May 1906	150	313		21 Jul 1961	150	85	10.3
	167	311	36.3	14 Jul 1965	150	33	
8 Aug 1906	150	255			170	21	2.5
	175	239		20 May 1966	150	37	
12 Nov 1906	140	249		19 Nov 1966	165	36	4.3
15 Aug 1907	143	218		6 Nov 1967	140	8	0.9
17 Aug 1908	150	232	27.2	10 Dec 1967	150	41	
11 Jul 1909	175	252	29.5	14 Feb 1968	150	12	
28 May 1911	155	316	36.7		160	18	
6 Oct 1911	150	233	27.3	18 Apr 1969	150	14	
20 May 1913	172	257	30.2		170	10	
20 May 1914	167	245	28.8	18 Jul 1969	150	0	
8 Jun 1923	146	246	29.1		175	0	
18 Jul 1928	160	142	16.9		150	0	
13 Jul 1929	159	145	17.3		175	0	
13 Jul 1931	135	180					

Source: See figure 16.1.

EDITORS' APPENDIX

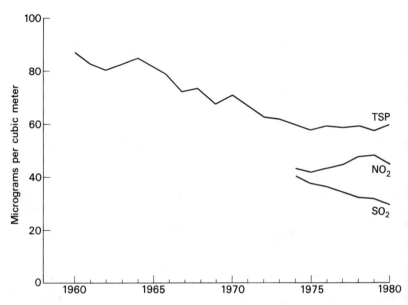

Figure 16.22 National ambient concentrations of total suspended particulates, nitrogen dioxide, and sulfur dioxide, 1960–80.
Data may not be strictly comparable. TSP (total suspended particulates data) for 1960–71 are
based on 95 sites. Data for 1972–76 are based on more than 3,000 sites. For 1977–80, there were
1,925 sites. The annual standard for TSP is 75 micrograms per cubic meter. SO_2 (sulfur dioxide)
data are based on 84 sites, all in urban areas. The annual standard for SO_2 is 80 micrograms per
cubic meter. NO_2 (nitrogen dioxide) data are based on 338 sites. The annual standard for NO_2 is
100 micrograms per cubic meter.
Source: U.S. Environmental Protection Agency.

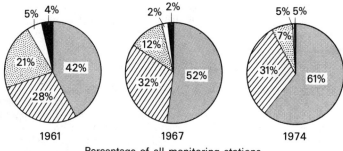

Percentage of all monitoring stations

Percentage of all observed levels exceeding criteria or reference levels

◼	Severe: 80–100%	▨	Fair: 20–40%
☐	Very poor: 60–80%	▦	Good: 0–20%
▦	Poor: 40–60%		

Figure 16.23   Trends in the quality of drinking water in the U.S.
Source: U.S. Council on Environmental Quality, Annual Report, 1975, p. 352.

References and Notes

1   See William J. Baumol, "Environmental protection, international spillovers and trade," *The Wicksell Lectures for 1971* (Uppsala, Sweden: Almquist & Wiksells Boktryckeri Ab, 1971), pp. 15–16. These pages also represented the view at that time of Oates, who had read and commented extensively on the manuscript during its preparation.
2   In this chapter we shall present numerous graphs and other figures to summarize the data that we have assembled. For anyone who wants to study the data more closely, we have either placed the actual numbers in an appendix or, where they are readily available, specified the source.
3   For an illustration of the dangers in drawing conclusions about trends from data spanning even many decades, see Appendix A which examines water-flow figures for the Nile River that cover many centuries.
4   A case in point, although not of major importance to this volume, is the matter of the progressive deterioration of works of art that are located out of doors. We had assumed from numerous studies in the press that there had been a marked acceleration in decay in recent years coincident with growing pollution. However, interviews with some of the world's leading authorities soon made our naiveté apparent. Where there is deterioration of these works of art, the causes are not completely understood and in some cases are clearly attributable in good part to natural phenomena. Even where

visible deterioration has increased sharply in recent years, it is not safe to assume that the cause is recent. For example, a piece of stonework may have been decaying beneath its surface for centuries; when the weakened structure finally collapses, it hardly can be blamed on twentieth-century abuse. The experts did *surmise* that chemicals emitted into the atmosphere do increase the incidence of "stone sickness" which leads to the crumbling of buildings and sculptures, but repeatedly emphasize the absence of conclusive evidence confirming this plausible conjecture.

There are, of course, a few noteworthy exceptions – cases in which the evidence of accelerating deterioration is persuasive. For example, there are the casts of some portions of the Parthenon Frieze made by Lord Elgin in the early nineteenth century. A comparison of those casts with the originals in Athens confirms that, in the sixteen decades since Elgin was in Greece, the marbles have indeed suffered enormous visible deterioration relative to what they underwent in the more than twenty centuries before. Details that were sharp and clear in 1800 are virtually unrecognizable today (see the photographs in H. J. Plenderleith, *The Conservation of Antiquities and Works of Art*, 2nd edn. (London: Oxford University Press, 1971), plates 40A and B, p. 316). However, except for catastrophes such as the Florentine flood, there are few other documented examples of recent acceleration in deterioration.

Despite all that has been printed and said about the threat of modern industry to our artistic heritage, we were able to find very little *conclusive* evidence on the subject one way or another. Most of the authorities with whom we spoke were not even willing to conjecture that matters were getting worse. A notable case in point was St. Paul's Cathedral. London, at the end of the seventeenth century when St. Paul's was under construction, could hardly boast about the purity of its atmosphere. For example, a German tourist reported in 1710 that in order to see the vista from the tower of the cathedral, he had to get there very early in the morning "in order that we might have a prospect of the town from above before the air was full of coal smoke" (*London in 1710, From the Travels of Zacharias Conrad von Uffenbach*, trans. ed. W. H. Quarrell and Margaret Mare (London: Faber and Faber, 1934), pp. 31–2). It is not surprising, therefore, that the new cathedral had to be cleaned within three decades after construction was started and before it was even finished. How, then, can one conclude with any degree of confidence that architectural stonework in London is being damaged more heavily today than it was three centuries ago?

5   See, for example, Stig H. Fonselius, "Stagnant Sea," *Environment*, 12 (July–August 1970), 2–3, 6, 28, 40.
6   Ibid., p. 42.
7   Stig H. Fonselius, *Hydrography of the Baltic Deep Basins, III*, Fishery Board of Sweden Series Hydrography Report No. 23 (Lund, Sweden: Carl Bloms Boktryckeri, 1969), p. 91. He lists, as the secondary reason for the increase, a rise in phosphorus concentrations which may well be related to the influx of sewage (pp. 90–1).
8   Ibid., p. 90.
9   Ibid., p. 56.
10 Ibid., p. 62. There is also some evidence suggesting that low-oxygen problems may have plagued the Baltic in the middle of the nineteenth century, well before the onset of extensive industrial activity. For the Vuoksi River in Finland, the uninterrupted data on runoff go back to 1847. While the

Vuoksi does not itself flow into the Baltic, its runoff figures since 1900 follow a time pattern very similar to those for the two other rivers for which data are available only since 1900, a relationship that is hardly surprising since they are all presumably replenished from the same regional sources. This is significant, because it suggests that the behavior of the other rivers feeding into the Baltic could be expected to have paralleled that of the Vuoksi for the second half of the nineteenth century. Moreover, the figures suggest that, during the period 1847–1900, the runoff of the Vuoksi exhibited something of a rising trend. Indeed, in the 1850s the runoff was almost as low as it has been in recent times; this raises the likelihood that stagnation may have occurred in the Baltic in earlier periods too.

11 E. M. Winkler, "Decay of Stone," *International Institute for Conservation, 1970 New York Conference on Conservation of Stone and Wooden Objects, I* (London: The International Institute for Conservation of Historic and Artistic Works, 1971), p. 6.
12 Ibid.
13 E. M. Winkler, "Weathering rates as exemplified by Cleopatra's Needle in New York City." *Journal of Geological Education,* **13** (2) (1965), 50–52.
14 "Royal Proclamation against the Pollution of the Thames," *Memorials of London and London Life in the XIIIth, XIVth, and XVth Centuries, Being a Series of Extracts, Local, Social, and Political, from the Early Archives of the City of London, A.D. 1276–1419,* select., trans. and ed. Henry Thomas Riley (London: Longmans, Green and Co., 1868), pp. 367–8. A reviewer comments, "I assume that what seems incredible about the quote is that the refuse could block navigation. I think this was probably a legally necessary assertion even if not an objective truth. If my offhand memory of legal history serves me well, the King's power over the condition of the waterways stemmed from a navigational servitude in favor of the crown which gave the crown such powers over the waterways as were necessary to preserve the crown's right of navigation thereon" (letter from Professor Marcia Gelpe, University of Minnesota Law School, 3 February 1977).
15 Timothy Nourse, *Campania Felix* (London, 1700), p. 352.
16 Ibid. Perhaps the quotation should be taken with a grain of salt since Nourse was a violent critic of cities, but the evidence from other sources certainly suggests that his description was based on fact.
17 For a table listing the major air and water pollutants with their sources, characteristics, and effects on human health, see W. Baumol and W. Oates, *Economics, Environmental Policy and the Quality of Life,* ch. 3.
18 The table below represents the latest figures on total dissolved solids, sulfates, calcium, chloride, and potassium available from the Great Lakes Basin Commission, Ann Arbor, Michigan, May 1977 (parts per million).

	Superior	Huron	Michigan	Erie	Ontario
Total Dissolved Solids	52	118	150	198	194
Sulfates	3.0	15	16	26	29
Calcium	13	25	32	37	40
Chloride	1.2	5.4	6	25	28
Potassium	0.5	0.8	1.0	1.0	1.0

19   Environmental programs have apparently produced some recent improve-
      ments in the purity of some of the Great Lakes. See *New York Times*, 23 May
      1974, p. 1 and 9 June 1974, Sect. 4, p. 2. The quality of Lake Superior,
      however, has been threatened by discharges of the Reserve Mining
      Company, which pours some 67,000 tons of taconite tailings into the lake
      every day. Besides just dirtying the lake and its shores, it has been alleged by
      some experts that "the asbestos-like fibers emptied into the water – which is
      used in its pure form as drinking water by Duluth and other communities – are
      a health hazard, since they have been known to cause diseases such as cancer
      among asbestos workers in other parts of the country, though sometimes not
      until 20 years after inhalation" (*New York Times*, 9 June 1974, Sect. 4, p. 2).
20   To eliminate from the data the confusing and irrelevant year-to-year fluctu-
      ations that are heavily influenced by fortuitous meteorological conditions,
      the graphs represent five-year averages rather than the raw annual data from
      which the averages are derived. That is, the figure shown for 1912 actually
      represents an average of the data for 1910–14, the figure for 1913 is an
      average of the data for 1911–15, etc. For the raw data and the average data
      see Appendix, table 16.5.
21   We should emphasize that the level of dissolved oxygen is only one determi-
      nant of water quality; as we saw in the case of the Great Lakes, there are other
      important elements affecting the quality of a body of water. More on this will
      be said later.
22   The population of the city as given by U.S. Census figures from 1900 to 1950
      was: 1900, 3.4 million; 1910, 4.8 million; 1920, 5.6 million; 1930, 7.3 million;
      1940, 7.5 million; 1950, 8.0 million (Ira Rosenwaike, *Population History of
      New York City* (Syracuse: Syracuse University Press, 1972), p. 133).
23   *New York Times*, 29 September 1973, p. 1. However, the reader will note in
      figure 16.8 that the most recent data for two of the rivers, the Hudson and the
      Lower East Rivers, indicate a reversal of this trend with dissolved-oxygen
      levels declining in the early 1970s.
24   Allen Kneese, in a letter to us, attributes much of the improvement in air
      quality, not to environmental policy, but to economic considerations which
      led to the substitution of oil and natural gas for coal "first in home heating
      (which was a terrible low level source of harmful and damaging substances)
      and later in industrial and electrical power generation. . . . This raises some
      interesting questions about what will happen when large scale reconversion to
      coal occurs." As we will discuss in a later chapter, the fuel crisis of the 1970s
      has brought great pressure for resumption of the use of fuels with higher
      sulfur content, and there is already some evidence of a concomitant deterio-
      ration of air quality in some U.S. cities.
25   *Environmental Quality, The Sixth Annual Report of the Council on Environ-
      mental Quality* (Washington, D.C.: U.S. Government Printing Office,
      December 1975), p. 305.
26   Ibid., p. 305.
27   Lester B. Lave and Eugene P. Seskin, *Air Pollution and Human Health*
      (Baltimore: Published for Resources for the Future by The Johns Hopkins
      University Press, 1977), chap. 9, p. 188.
28   Albert Parker, "Air Pollution Research and Control in Great Britain,"
      American Journal of Public Health 47 (May 1957): 569.
29   However, a reviewer points out that the decrease in smoke pollution may

have resulted in an increase in photochemical smog (the formation of which requires sunlight) and, perhaps, even in the incidence of skin cancer.

30 Royal Commission on Environmental Pollution, *First Report* (London: Her Majesty's Stationery Office, February 1971), p. 23.

31 It now seems evident that in fact, sulfur dioxide pollution is not as serious a threat to human health as are sulfate concentrations. Though SO_2 pollution in the cities has decreased markedly in the last decade (apparently largely because of the relocation to less populated areas of the main sources of urban SO_2, the municipal power plants), national ambient sulfate levels have remained fairly stable. This difference in the trends in sulfate and sulfur dioxide concentrations is apparently rather mysterious, since sulfates are a product of SO_2.

32 The evaluation of the overall pollution content of the atmosphere of a particular city or of a waterway is a complex matter, and data on any single pollutant or group of pollutants can easily be misleading. This point was made forcefully in a letter to us from Thomas McMullen of the Monitoring and Reporting Branch of the Environmental Protection Agency. Commenting on the data underlying figure 16.9, he remarked, "This measurement can in no way be interpreted as an index of general air quality because the complex character of air pollution has been changing over recent decades. Dustfall levels have been diminishing as restrictions on use of soft coal, conversions of home heating systems to gas, and changes in industrial practices have reduced the quantity of larger particles emitted. However, concurrent growth in vehicular traffic, expansion of urbanization, and the burgeoning diversity of industrialization has increased the volume of other pollutant emissions and multiplied the variety of trace pollutants. I think it might be difficult to specify an index, implying reference to a base year or to some common denominator, applicable to the evolving nature of air pollution over the last several decades."

33 See M. Murozumi, T. J. Chow, and C. Patterson, "Chemical Concentrations of Pollutant Lead Aerosols, Terrestrial Dusts and Sea Salts in Greenland and Antarctic Snow Strata," *Geochimica et Cosmochimica Acta* 33, No. 10 (October 1969): 1247–94.

34 Ibid., p. 1285.

35 D. Bryce-Smith, "Lead pollution – a growing hazard to public health," *Chemistry in Britain*, 7 (February 1971), 54. In a later note Bryce-Smith adds the significant point that "no other toxic chemical pollutant appears to have accumulated in man to average levels so close to the threshold for potential clinical poisoning" ("Lead pollution from petrol," p. 286).

36 See "Lead in ancient and modern bones," *Scientist and Citizen*, **10** (3) (April 1968), 89.

37 Mills, "Lead pollution," p. 161, citing a study by Z. Jaworoski.

38 *New York Times*, 27 March 1970, p. 49.

39 The figure of 4.5 percent was computed from data supplied by R. D. Behrman, Administrative Assistant, and A. H. Schuck, Acting Superintendent, Department of Public Works, Division of Waste Collection, City of Cincinnati, in letters of 9 November 1973, and 17 February 1977.

40 A good source on this subject is Emmanuel Le Roy Ladurie, *Histoire du Climat Depuis l'An Mil* (Paris: Flammarion, 1967).

17

Air and Water Quality
UNITED NATIONS ENVIRONMENT PROGRAMME

Editors' Note

To deal with the topics of air and water pollution, which arouse so much interest and concern, we have decided to include the following selections from the recent comprehensive report *The World Environment, 1972–82* by the United Nations Environment Programme, rather than a statement by an individual author. These are excerpts from a long report and should be examined in that context. We must emphasise that the selection of material for inclusion in this chapter is entirely the responsibility of the editors of this volume, and in no way reflects a judgement by the three editors of the UNEP report.

Measurements of urban pollution (total suspended particles and sulphur dioxide) began in the last century. In the 1950s there was a substantial increase in the number of cities and pollutants monitored; carbon monoxide, for example, being measured at seven stations in Los Angeles since 1955 (Tiao *et al.*, 1975). A few measurements of background levels of trace substances in rural and remote areas in Europe were also made before the middle of the present century. However, the results are often confusing because the analytical and calibration procedures were not generally comparable with those used today. Because of these problems, most of the time series available for study are short, the following being the most significant:

(1) *Carbon dioxide*: The record dates back to 1957 at Mauna Loa, Hawaii, and in Scandinavia some stations operated from 1955 to 1960, with other baseline stations being established in the 1970s.

(2) *The chemical constituents of precipitation*: A special observation network began in Europe in 1954 under the auspices of Stockholm

University's International Meteorological Institute. There is information, for example, about the sulphate content of rainfall in Norway, the Federal Republic of Germany, the U.S.S.R. and Eastern Europe, from this time. Systematic observations of chemical constituents of precipitation began in the U.S.S.R. in 1957, and by 1980 samples were taken at 70 stations over the whole country (Petrenchuk, 1980). In the United States, a network of stations was operated for a short period in 1955–6 and the data have been widely used for comparison with later measurements beginning in one small basin in 1964 and across North America in the 1970s. Recently networks were established in Canada, and in 1978 a special network was set up to monitor long-range sulphur transport in Europe.

(3) *Background monitoring of trace substances*: In 1970 the WMO decided to organize a Background Air Pollution Monitoring Network (BAPMoN) which includes sampling of the chemical constituents of precipitation, and in 1980 this comprised about 110 stations in about 60 countries. The United States associated with BAPMoN its own network of baseline stations (GMCC: Geophysical Monitoring for Climate Change) located at Mauna Loa, Hawaii; Point Barrow, Alaska; Samoa; and the South Pole (see for example, GMCC, 1978). Other national baseline stations, including those at Cape Grim, Australia, and Mount Kenya, were also associated with the network.

Trends in Smoke and Sulphur Oxides Concentrations

Neither sulphur oxides nor aerosols accumulate indefinitely in the atmosphere. The health problems they have created in the past arose from exposure to high local concentrations in urban areas where fossil fuels were burned inefficiently. In urban zones today, annual mean sulphur dioxide concentrations of 50 micrograms per cubic metre ($\mu g/m^3$) are still common (see table 17.1), whereas in rural regions figures of below 10 $\mu g/m^3$ are typical. Sulphate aerosol concentrations similarly range from 5–15 $\mu g/m^3$ in cities to under 2 $\mu g/m^3$ in rural areas. For smoke particles, typical values range from 20 to 100 $\mu g/m^3$ and below 10 $\mu g/m^3$ respectively. In unpolluted oceanic situations still lower values are to be expected. These figures do not reflect the pollution of indoor environments. The latter conditions received more attention during the decade (CEQ, 1980 [*Global 2000*]; see also Holdgate *et al.*, 1982, ch. 10). Urban air quality trends can be estimated from networks of monitoring stations or may be inferred qualitatively from economic data relating to fuel and

478   *UNEP*

TABLE 17.1 AVERAGE CONCENTRATIONS OF SUSPENDED
PARTICULATE MATTER (SPM) AND SULPHUR DIOXIDE
(SO_2) DURING 1973–7 IN SEVEN CITIES (AMOUNTS IN $\mu g/m^3$)

City	Commercial		Residential		Industrial	
	SPM	SO_2	SPM	SO_2	SPM	SO_2
Brussels	24	87	20	71	18	91
Calcutta	397	14	392	18	298	7
London	24	126	23	75	29	69
Madrid	170	116	44	47	214	112
Prague	170	108	112	100	133	49
Tokyo	43	68	47	42	52	77
Zagreb	147	117	112	40	144	49

Source: Akland *et al*. (1980).

power production, etc. Using the second approach, Brimblecombe (1977) inferred that smoke and sulphur dioxide concentrations in London rose steadily from AD 1600 to the late nineteenth century, and then slowly declined with the introduction of more efficient methods of combustion, cleaner fuels, smoke removal equipment and taller chimneys. No serious pollution episodes have been reported in London since the early 1960s.

The London experience is typical of cities in developed countries. In cities where·control policies have not been implemented, pollution has naturally increased with population growth. In Ankara the incomplete combustion of coal and lignite had raised both sulphur dioxide and smoke concentrations to over 250 $\mu g/m^3$ by the late 1960s and the situation continued to deteriorate during the 1970s. In the cities of the developing world, smoke concentrations in urban areas also remained high because of the use of wood as a home fuel and because of the many open incinerators. Table 17.1 shows that suspended particulate concentrations in Calcutta were much higher than in any other city listed. In countries such as Bangladesh the smoke concentrations continued high as a result of inefficient burning of fossil fuels, the popularity of firewood for fuel, and the prevalence of coal-burning brickfields.

First results of the World Health Organization/United Nations Environment Programme (WHO/UNEP) urban air monitoring project (Akland *et al.*, 1980) showed that the changes between 1973–5 and 1975–7 in the concentrations of suspended particulate matter and sulphur dioxide in seven cities were mainly downward. However, the period of record was rather short. A longer time series (1970–6) for sulphur dioxide in twenty-four localities, most of them cities, published by OECD (1979) showed comparable results, with a halving or more of concentrations in Montreal, Toronto, Tokyo, Osaka, and Nagoya and a deterioration in only three places. In the U.S.S.R., records from more than 350 cities showed that the maximum concentration of particles and sulphur dioxide varied between 150–300 and 80–160 $\mu g/m^3$ respectively at the beginning of the 1970s, and had decreased considerably by the end of the decade.

The effects of these changes on human health and on biological productivity are discussed in Holdgate *et al.* (1982, chs. 10 and 7). One effect not discussed there which claimed special attention during the 1970s is the corrosion of stone and metal on historical monuments: a particularly serious problem was the deterioration of marble in the Acropolis at Athens (Greece, 1981).

Trends in Photochemical Oxidant Concentrations

Photochemical oxidant smog is formed in urban areas as a result of reactions between nitrogen oxides and reactive hydrocarbons in the presence of sunlight. Ozone and numerous organic compounds are produced. The phenomenon was first investigated in Los Angeles during the 1950s. Since then it has been found in many parts of the world, especially in towns with high traffic densities and warm, sunny climates. Mexico City and Lima, Peru, for example, have frequent episodes. Significant oxidant concentrations were also reported in Tokyo, Sydney and Melbourne in Australia, London and other cities in northern Europe, Edmonton in Canada, and the north-eastern United States. In some of these areas the photochemical pollution considerably reduces visibility, and the aerosol in the polluted air mass has been observed to reduce the intensity of sunlight reaching the ground to one-tenth of the incident value.

It was formerly believed that photochemical oxidants give rise only to a local problem in the large urban areas because of either topography or population distribution. However, recent evidence from field studies conducted in Europe and Eastern North America has established that photochemical pollutants and their precursors can be transported up to several hundred kilometres. This long-range transport implies that emission control on a local scale may be grossly insufficient in Europe and Eastern North America (OECD, 1978).

General conclusions about oxidant trends over the last two decades are difficult to make. The data are sparse, particularly from rural areas and from cities in developing countries. In addition, measurement techniques changed during the period. It is likely, however, that oxidant levels rose:

(1) in areas where automobile use increased substantially;
(2) in areas with strong control programmes for suspended particulates (e.g. emissions from open incinerators) without a cor-

responding programme to reduce oxides of nitrogen and reactive hydrocarbons. (This was the case in some European cities.)

In contrast, where effective controls had been imposed, concentrations fell. In 1965 the average monthly maximum oxidant concentration in downtown Los Angeles was 0.27 parts per million (ppm); in 1974 it was 0.17 ppm. In the San Francisco Bay region the concentrations fell from 0.13 to 0.09 ppm during the same period (CEQ, 1976). In Japan, the number of days when the hourly average of photochemical oxidant concentrations exceeded the threshold at which "warnings" were issued (0.12 ppm) peaked at 330 alerts in 1973, and fell to around 150 warnings in 1978 and to 84 in 1979 (EAJ, 1980). No alarms for concentrations of 0.24 ppm or higher were issued in the latter year.

Sulphate and Nitrate Hazes

During fine summer weather the emissions of sulphur dioxide and nitrogen oxides from tall chimneys (power stations, smelters) are gradually converted to sulphate/nitrate hazes, which augment the haze and organics from forests, and sometimes cover areas as large as Western Europe and Eastern North America.

There were many personal testimonies to the lessening of occurrences of exceptionally high visibilities in the fifty years preceding the decade. These recollections were supported by analyses of visibility records at weather stations (Vickers and Munn, 1977; Husar *et al.*, 1979). For example, the frequency of summer haziness in the Canadian Atlantic Provinces increased sixfold since the 1950s, with winds blowing from the states of New York and New Jersey; with north-east winds off Newfoundland and Labrador, there was no change in the frequency of summer haziness (Vickers and Munn, 1977). Special attention was being given to this problem in the United States (Costle, 1980) but successful control strategies had not been developed by the end of the decade. Summer haziness was also reported from a variety of other countries, including Bangladesh.

A haze layer of interest to atmospheric chemists occurred over the Arctic Ocean from time to time (NIAR, 1977; Rahn *et al.*, 1979; Larssen and Hanssen, 1980). The haze was imported from more southerly regions but the dynamics of the phenomenon were not yet fully understood.

Domestic

The domestic water supply picture varied. Whereas the proportion of the urban population in developing countries with access to safe water supply rose from 67 percent in 1970 to 77 percent in 1975 and then declined slightly to 75 percent in 1980 (as shown in table 17.2), the proportion of rural people served by safe water supply increased from 14 percent in 1970 to 29 percent in 1980 (UN, 1980). During that period the number of countries reporting changed, and enumeration methods varied. The data therefore are of uneven quality and when aggregated as shown in table 17.3 may be misleading. A less rough picture of changes may be gained from comparing countries reporting in both 1970 and 1980. Table 17.2 excludes the developing country members of the ECE. Among the major regions, only the Economic and Social Commission for Asia and the Pacific (ESCAP) members – the most numerous in population – reported significant gains in the proportion of both urban and rural populations covered by safe water supply. The Economic Commission for Africa (ECA) members reported an extension of coverage for rural dwellers but no increase in urban coverage. In Latin America and Western Asia the proportions remained the same or declined (see table 17.3).

Although the estimates are rough (and are not based on a uniform definition of what constitutes safe water and reasonable access) a few aspects of domestic supply became apparent as the decade drew to a close. Massive improvements were made in the availability of supply. The number of rural dwellers served increased by 157 percent. The urban dwellers served expanded by 66 percent. However, considering the total population in need of service, the urban gains were modest, and while the rural proportion doubled it still left more than two-thirds without safe service. In only one major region was the rate of improvement in excess of the rate of population growth. A continuation of the 1970–80 trends would leave the total population only slightly better off. A disturbing aspect of the situation not revealed by the statistics (and indeed not precisely documented) was the probably large number of rural improvements that had fallen into disrepair. In addition many urban systems, such as those in Nepal and Pakistan, provided only intermittent service (ESCAP, 1980).

The waste water situation was even less heartening. While a high proportion of the developed urban populations had adequate services, the proportion of developing country urban population served by sewers, latrines or other sanitary measures for excreta disposal declined during the decade from 71 percent to 53 percent (Table 17.4). In rural areas the numbers served were 11 percent in 1970 and little better in 1980. Regional data are so incomplete that comparisons between 1970 and 1980 are not warranted. In 1980, however, it appeared that the proportion of urban populations covered was: Africa 56 per cent, Latin America 54 percent, Western Asia 70 percent and Asia and the Pacific 50 percent, For the rural populations the estimates were: Africa 15 percent. Latin America

TABLE 17.2 ESTIMATED SERVICE COVERAGE FOR DRINKING WATER SUPPLY IN DEVELOPING COUNTRIES, 1970–80[a]

	1970		1975		1980	
	Population served (in millions)	Percentage of total population	Population served (in millions)	Percentage of total population	Population served (in millions)	Percentage of total population
Urban	316	67	450	77	526	75
Rural	182	14	313	22	469	29
Total	498	29	763	38	995	43

Source: UN (1980).
[a] Figures do not include the People's Republic of China.

Region	Number of countries	1970 Total population (millions)	1970 Water coverage	1970 Percentage of total population	1980 Total population (millions)	1980 Water coverage	1980 Percentage of total population	Change in percentage covered
Africa (ECA) members)								
urban	29	62.8	51.5	82	96.2	78.9	82	0
rural	23	187.8	40.2	21	239.6	64.6	27	+6
Latin America (ECLA members)								
urban	18	153.1	115.6	76	212.6	157.8	74	−2
rural	15	110.6	25.2	24	129.1	27.8	22	−2
Western Asia (ECWA members)								
urban	9	13.9	13.3	96	22.5	19.8	88	−8
rural	7	18.0	6.1	34	18.4	6.2	34	0
Asia and the Pacific (ESCAP members)								
urban	14	220.5	130.2	59	300.3	209.5	70	+11
rural	12	737.3	77.6	11	917.3	298.6	32	+21

Source: WHO (1973) and UN (1980).
[a] The European (ECE members) region countries qualifying for technical assistance under UNDP procedures are not included as only one country reported in both years, and the figures listed for it for 1970 are not consistent.

TABLE 17.4 ESTIMATED SERVICE COVERAGE FOR SANITATION IN DEVELOPING COUNTRIES, 1970–80[a]

	1970		1975		1980	
	Population served (in millions)	Percentage of total population	Population served (in millions)	Percentage of total population	Population served (in millions)	Percentage of total population
Urban	337	71	437	75	372	53
Rural	134	11	209	15	213	13
Total	471	27	646	33	585	25

Source: UN (1980).
[a] Figures do not include the People's Republic of China.

23 percent. Western Asia 20 percent, and Asia and the Pacific 10 percent. Urban sanitation efforts clearly had not kept up with population growth (the special problem of squatter settlement is discussed in Holdgate *et al.*, 1982, ch. 9), and rural improvement had barely kept pace.

Pollution from Urban and Industrial Discharges and Land Drainage

The most critical problems of water pollution arise in the vicinity of centres of high population density and extensive industrial development. Waterborne sewage, storm drainage from city streets, and effluents from smaller industries combined to flow from municipal outfalls in mounting volumes. Industries frequently referred to as being significant polluters of water include pulp and paper, chemical works and food industries. Their progress or failure in coping with waste is described Holdgate *et al.* (1982, ch. 11).

Among industrial pollutants, mercury caused particular alarm during the late 1960s and the 1970s because of its conversion to the more toxic methyl form by bacteria in freshwater (and marine) sediments and accumulation in animal tissues. In several regions accumulations above a minimum safety level were detected in freshwater fish, which had to be withdrawn from human consumption. In Sweden, a ban imposed in 1967 on the use of mercury in the pulp and paper industries was followed by reductions in environmental concentrations (Olsson, 1976). In Lake Erie, Canada, the mercury originated from mercury-cell chlor-alkali works, and could be detected in sediments and fish (Thomas and Jaquet, 1976). Examples elsewhere in the world are given by D'Itri and D'Itri (1977).

In the early years of the decade, emphasis was placed upon urban and industrial sources of freshwater pollution, but by 1980 attention was turning to non-point sources as the cause of more intractable problems. This general trend was well illustrated by experience in OECD countries which reported that (1) levels of suspended solids and oxidizable matter (as measured by biological oxygen demand, BOD) commonly levelled off or decreased while micropollutants, pathogenic micro-organisms and thermal pollution caused increasing concern; and (2) while pollution from point sources was under progressively better control, non-point pollution was on the increase (OECD, 1979). The intensive use of fertilizer was a major factor in eutrophication. Other problems arose from the mis-application of pesticides and careless storage and handling of manure.

Another growing source of water pollution resulted from the expanding use of petroleum and petroleum products. Rapidly increasing road

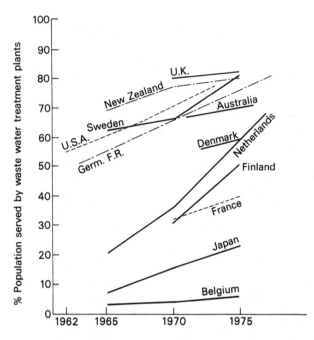

Figure 17.1 Domestic waste water treatment: selected countries, 1965–75.
Source: OECD, 1979.

travel, the mechanization of agriculture, and the increased transport of
oil on inland waters contributed to further pollution of both surface and
ground water. A potential future source of pollution is spills from vulnerable pipelines at high latitudes, as in Canada, although these have not yet
been serious (Sage, 1980; see also Holdgate *et al.*, 1982, ch. 13).

The most readily available indicator of effluent loading is provided by
the statistics on the proportion of population in selected industrial
countries served by some kind of waste water treatment. Figure 17.1
shows the 1965–75 trends in twelve countries. In all of them the
percentage increased, but the proportion of population served ranged
from less than 10 percent in Belgium to more than 80 percent in the
United Kingdom. No distinction is made as to type of treatment or the
nature of the receiving water and these are crucial in determining the
effects upon the aquatic system. In the developing countries about half of
the urban population were covered by sewer service (table 17.4). Only
scattered data are available on treatment facilities for the existing sewer
systems, but treatment beyond the primary stage of removal was rare.

Details are available of the changes in the biological oxygen demand

and nitrate load in major streams in OECD countries. BOD decreased between 1970 and 1975 in many streams, but mounted in the Scheldt, Tagus, Rhone and lower Rhine. Nitrate concentrations increased in all the selected streams except the Red and Nelson in Canada, and the Loire. As a consequence in those countries "almost all important freshwater bodies deteriorated during the 1965–75 period" (OECD, 1979).

In many United States streams, non-point pollution from nitrogen and phosphorus increased, whereas coliform bacteria, oxygen-demanding organic materials, and the level of suspended solids, salinity and acidity showed a decreasing trend. More rivers were moderately polluted in this decade than in the last decade, but fewer rivers were highly polluted.

The United Kingdom reported improvement in the quality of non-tidal rivers in recent years. The Thames was notable for restoration of quality as reflected in the re-establishment of fish populations. The improvement of water quality is attributed to intensified construction of purifying plants and facilities. In Sweden 99 percent of the sewage from urban areas was treated by 1975 (UNWC, 1978, p. 1965) and BOD levels had decreased after peaking in the previous decade. The biochemical oxygen demand in the Rhine rose between 1965 and 1975 but then fell and in 1978 was only 74 percent of the 1965 figure. On the other hand, the salinity of the Rhine increased. Large lakes respond to treatment very slowly. It was estimated, for example, that it would take thirty years for Lake Varen in Sweden to respond fully to the present-day reduction of industrial pollution.

Pollution of Groundwater

Groundwater, in its percolation through soil and rocks, leaches out soluble salts; it is thus typically mineralized, and sometimes heavily so. The vulnerability of groundwater to contamination is determined by the hydrological setting of the aquifer, the nature of the contaminant and the effectiveness of regulatory action. Of all the activities of man that influence the quality of groundwater, agriculture is probably the most important, as a diffuse source of pollution from fertilizers, pesticides, and animal wastes. Of the main nutrients in nitrogen, phosphorus, and potassium fertilizers, nitrogen in the form of nitrate is the most common cause of degradation of groundwater near agricultural lands (UNEP, 1981). Industrial wastes include a wide spectrum of materials from all types of industry, and contain many organic and inorganic chemicals which are potential pollutants. Industrial wastes reach groundwater from impoundments or lagoons, spills, pipeline breaks, and land disposal sites.

Septic tanks and cesspools contribute filtered sewage effluent directly to the ground, and are the most frequently reported sources of ground water contamination, especially in rural, recreational, and suburban areas. An increasing percentage of the municipal sewage is, however, not being processed in primary and secondary sewage treatment plants. In many areas, the solid residual material known as sewage sludge – which contains a large number of potential contaminants – is spread on agricultural land. In some regions liquid sewage that has not been treated or that has undergone partial treatment is sprayed on the land surface. Such application of liquid sewage and sewage sludge to the land provides valuable nutrients such as nitrogen and phosphorus to the soil, with benefits to agriculture. However, the waste water or sludge can add to the contamination of groundwater. The soil profile shows a considerable ability to remove or detoxify several of the compounds found in the waste water, but some may nonetheless affect groundwater quality. The soil may also effectively eliminate the pathogenic bacteria through filtration and soil microbiological processes, but survival of viruses is still an open question.

References

Akland, G. *et al*. (1980) "Air quality surveillance: trends in selected urban areas," *WHO Chronicle*, **34**, 147.

Brimblecombe, P. (1977) "London air pollution, 1500–1900," *Atmos. Environ.*, **11**, 1157.

CEQ (1976) *Environmental Quality*. 7th Annual Report. Washington, D.C.: Council on Environmental Quality.

CEQ (1980) *The Global 2000 Report to the President*. Washington, D.C.: Council on Environmental Quality.

Costle, D. M. (1980) "Visibility protection – a proposal," *J. Air Poll. Control Assoc.*, **30**, 632.

D'Itri, P. A. and F. M. D'Itri (1977) *Mercury Contamination: A Human Tragedy*. New York: John Wiley.

EAJ (1980) *Quality of the Environment in Japan – 1980*. Tokyo: Environment Agency.

ESCAP (1980) Economic and Social Commission for Asia and the Pacific, United Nations, Document E/ESCAP/7/1.

GMCC (1978) *Summary Report 1978, Geophysical Monitoring for Climatic Change*, no. 7. Washington, D.C.: Env. Res. Labs, NOAA, Department of Commerce.

Greece (1981) *Problems and Protection Measures for Monuments: The Acropolis Case*. Greek Review of Environmental Policies, reference document submitted by Ministry of Coordination. Athens.

Holdgate *et al*. (eds.) (1982) *The World Environment, 1972–1982*. United Nations Environment Programme.

Husar, R. B. *et al*. (1979) *Trends of Eastern US Haziness since 1948*. 4th Symposium on Atmospheric Diffusion and Air Pollution. Boston, Mass.: American Meteorological Society.

Larssen, S. and J. E. Hanssen (1980) *Annual Variation and Origin of Aerosol Components in the Norwegian Arctic-Subarctic Region.* Proceedings of the WMO Technical Conference on Regional and Global Observation of Atmospheric Pollution. WMO Report no. 549. Geneva: World Meteorological Organization.

NIAR (1977) *Sources and Significance of Natural and Man-made Aerosols in the Arctic.* Report of a workshop. Lillestrøm, Norway: Norwegian Institute for Air Research.

OECD (1978) "Photochemical oxidants and their precursors in the atmosphere," *Environment,* **78**, 6.

OECD (1979) *The State of the Environment in OECD Member Countries.* Paris: Organization for Economic Co-operation and Development.

Olsson, M. (1976) "Mercury level as a function of size and age in Northern Pike, one and five years after the mercury ban in Sweden," *Ambio,* **5**, 73.

Petrenchuk, O. P. (1980) *The Chemical Composition of Precipitation Studies at Background Stations.* Proceedings of the International Symposium on Integrated Global Monitoring of Pollution of the Natural Environment, Riga, U.S.S.R., 1978. Leningrad: Gidrometeoizdat.

Rahn, K. A. *et al.* (1979) "Long-range impact on desert aerosols of atmospheric chemistry: two examples," In C. Moreles (ed.), *Saharan Dust: SCOPE 14.* Chichester: John Wiley.

Sage, B. (1980) "Rupture in the Trans-Alaska oil pipeline: causes and effects," *Ambio,* **9**, 262.

Thomas, R. L. and J. M. Jaquet (1976) "Mercury in the surfacial sediments of Lake Erie," *J. Fish. Res., Canada,* **33**, 404.

Tiao, G. C. *et al.* (1975) "A statistical analysis of the Los Angeles ambient carbon monoxide data 1955–1972," *J. Air Poll. Control Assoc.,* **25**, 1129.

UN (1980) *International Drinking Water Supply and Sanitation Decade; Present Situation and Prospects.* A/35/367. New York: United Nations.

UNEP (1981) *The State of the Environment – Selected Topics – 1981.* Nairobi: United Nations Environment Programme.

UNWC (1978) *Proceedings of the United Nations Water Conference, Mar del Plata, Argentina, 1977.* 4 vols. Oxford: Pergamon Press.

Vickers, G. G. and R. E. Munn (1977) "A Canadian haze climatology." *Climatic Change,* **1**, 97.

WHO (1973) *World Health Statistics Report 26, 11.* Geneva: World Health Organization.

18

Nutrition and Health in the Changing Environment

A. E. HARPER

"The health of the American people has never been better."
(Surgeon General's Report, 1979)

It is anomalous, at a time when the health of the U.S. population is reported to be better than it has ever been (USDHEW, 1979), that fears about the safety and nutritional adequacy of the food supply should abound, and that there should be "a public preoccupation with disease that is assuming the dimension of a national obsession" (Thomas, 1977). This phenomenon is not unique to the United States; it appears to be prevalent throughout the rich highly industrialized nations of the world. The possibility that "residues" and "additives" in foods may be a threat to health arouses "irrational fears" among European consumers (Ferrando, 1981b). The governments of Australia, Canada, and the Scandinavian countries have all developed dietary guidelines for disease prevention, in large measure in response to fears of food and fears for health among their populations (Harper, 1981a). Even in Japan, the country that has made the greatest strides in diet and health improvement of any nation during the past 40 years, concern is being expressed over the possibility that changes in the incidence of chronic and degenerative diseases, such as diabetes and heart disease, are associated with changes that have occurred in the food supply (Hosoya, 1982). This widespread public perception that changes in the environment are responsible for deterioration of the food supply, which in turn becomes a threat to health, seems illogical in the light of evidence that health status in the United States, Japan, and other industrialized nations has improved throughout this century. Even in the poor, less industrialized countries where malnutrition is prevalent, the available information on death rates, which provides a crude measure of health status, indicates that, with very few exceptions, health has improved generally throughout the world (DeMaeyer and Bengoa, 1971), despite the persistence of widespread malnutrition among infants and children.

The problem of childhood malnutrition – protein–energy malnutrition as it is commonly called – is a major health problem of the poor countries of the world. It is not the result of environmental hazards impacting on the food supply. It is a problem that, paradoxically, is exacerbated by improvements in medical care. These reduce mortality, and thereby increase the rate of population growth in countries where economic development is slow; incomes are low; public investment in education, sanitation, and health care is limited; and access by much of the population, to the benefits of what development there is, is restricted owing to the dearth of opportunities for remunerative employment. Widespread childhood malnutrition is largely a socio-economic problem that has tragic health consequences. It can be treated successfully but it is prevented effectively only through measures that increase the purchasing power of the population. It is a problem of a very different type from those attributed to deterioration of the quality of the food supply and the environment.

In the highly industrialized countries, perceptions that there have been serious adverse effects of the environment on food and health are largely the result of misconceptions about current health status and exaggerations of the nature and complexity of the problems associated with ensuring the safety and nutritional adequacy of the food supply. It is undoubtedly possible to create hazards to health by misuse of even the best food supply. It is also possible to examine information about the characteristics of the food supply and the current state of health and, thereby, establish whether or not there is cause for apprehension. It is also possible, through careful and critical evaluation of this information, to identify the real problems that need attention.

Among the indicators we have of the safety and nutritional quality of the food supply and the health status of the population are:

illness and mortality from food-borne diseases;
illness and mortality from toxicants in foods;
illness and mortality from nutritional deficiency diseases;
infant, childhood and maternal mortality;
mortality from childhood diseases;
days lost from work;
obesity as a health hazard;
disability and mortality from degenerative diseases in relation to diet;
proportion of infants born surviving to old age;
changes in life expectancy over time and as compared to that of other populations.

If we examine each of these briefly in turn, noting the changes that have occurred over the years in the nature of the food supply and in the state of health, we should be able to assess the accuracy and validity of assumptions about relationships between food and health.

Safety and Nutritional Adequacy of the Food Supply

The U.S. Food and Drug Administration considers that contamination of food with bacteria and other micro-organisms that cause human diseases is a much greater threat to health than the presence in food of environmental contaminants such as pesticides; and that food additives rank last and are of least importance among potential hazards of the food supply (Hall, 1973). According to a National Research Council Committee (1982b) there is no evidence to suggest that food additives or environmental contaminants in the food supply have contributed significantly to risk of cancer for humans. Also, Ames (1983) states that human intake of mutagens and carcinogens that occur naturally in food is probably at least 10,000 times higher than the dietary intake of man-made pesticides.

Humans must have learned early during their development that food spoiled within a short time, especially in warm climates, unless special precautions were taken to preserve it. It is not possible to identify the time of origin of food processing and the use of additives to protect food from soilage, but both were practiced in antiquity and are used today by peoples who still live as did the early hunter–gatherers in prehistoric times. They knew that meat and fish could not be stored unless they were smoked or dried in the sun or over a fire. In ancient China meats were preserved by curing them with salt, pounding them with spices, or fermenting them with wine (Pyke, 1970). It has been estimated that in Africa today, where fish must be transported from undeveloped areas to urban markets, as much as 40 percent of the catch may be spoiled through improper packaging, transport, and storage.

Storage of foods has been crucial for survival, particularly in northern latitudes where many foods are available only during certain seasons of the year, and food generally is in short supply during the winters. Ice was gathered in antiquity in the more northerly areas to preserve foods at low temperature, and in far nothern areas foods could be kept frozen, without deterioration, merely by leaving them outside the dwelling places. In arid areas where milk spoiled readily, dehydration was practiced by precipitating the curd and salting it to give cheese in which micro-organisms were unable to grow, except on the surface. Fruit has been preserved by boiling it with sugar to reduce the moisture content, converting it to jams and jellies, and, thereby, preventing growth of micro-organisms also except on the surface (Pyke, 1970). When agriculture was developed, cereal grains, which were harvested only once or twice a year, had to be stored for many months to ensure a supply of food during times when little was available. Ordinarily seeds are dry at harvest time; if not, they may spoil owing to the growth of molds. Drying moist seeds in the sun and storing them in moisture-repellant vessels has also been practiced since antiquity.

During more recent times the problem of storing food has become more critical. In 1800 in the United Kingdom, only 25 percent of the people lived in large urban centres, whereas by 1900 over 75 percent lived in cities and large towns. In the United States, as recently as 1875, 75 percent of the population lived in rural areas; by 1950 the rural:urban ratio had reversed. This phenomenon has occurred throughout the world in more recent times. Thus, preservation, storage, and transport of food under conditions that will maintain nutritional quality and prevent losses has become increasingly critical to ensure an adequate supply of food for large urban populations. As this has happened technological advances have been required to ensure that a safe and nutritious food supply will be available at reasonable cost throughout the year for urban communities. It is concern about the nature of processing required to accomplish this that has contributed greatly to the current fear of food.

Microbiological safety

During the last century, and the early part of this one, most food in the U.S. was processed in the home when it was seasonable, and stored for later use. As the result of unsanitary conditions and improper preservation methods, serious food-borne diseases, including botulism, were common. Milk was frequently a carrier of tuberculosis and other pathogenic organisms. Even today in areas where milk is not pasteurized, food-borne disease outbreaks may be widespread (CDC, 1983). Incidents of food spoilage, and evidence that some manufacturers were producing food under unsanitary conditions, led to enactment of Pure Food and Drug Laws in 1906. Standards for sanitation were also established in cities and states. The Federal laws have been revised and expanded five times, the most recent revision being 1958.

As urbanization accelerated, the food industry developed. Production of processed foods increased; distribution was extended; and storage time was lengthened. This served as a stimulus for improving knowledge of food processing and the microbiology of foods. The result was an increasingly safe food supply.

The potential for outbreaks of food-borne diseases remains, nevertheless, the major current food safety problem. There have been three instances of botulism in the U.S. from commercially produced food during the past few years. These are tragic when they occur but, because of the ability of the regulatory agencies and the food industry to respond rapidly in such emergencies, none has come close to the potential there is for tragedy. Despite these failures, the safety record of the food industry is impressive. With 800 billion containers of food produced between 1940 and 1978, the number of deaths from botulism from processed food averaged about one per 5 years (Chou, 1979). The number from home-canned products is still five or more per year (figure 18.1) and was much higher prior to 1960 (CDC, 1981).

It is important in evaluating the effectiveness of food safety measures to distinguish clearly between hazards attributable to the food supply and hazards attributable to improper handling of the food supply (Chou, 1979). Most outbreaks of food-borne diseases (about 95 percent) are due to improper preparation and handling of foods after purchase by food service personnel, caterers and in the home (table 18.1). In 1980 the Center for Disease Control (CDC, 1983) found that of 136 reported outbreaks of food-borne disease, only four were attributable to food from an unsafe source. All the rest were from inadequate food preparation or

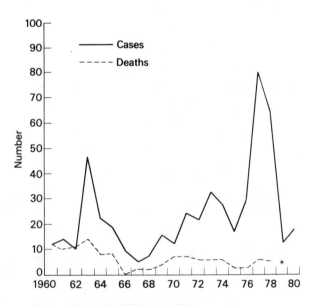

*Not available for 1979 and 1980

Figure 18.1 Botulism (foodborne) – reported cases and deaths by year, U.S., 1960–80. The fourteen outbreaks of foodborne botulism in 1980 involved eighteen people and were all related to home-canned or home-processed foods. There were eleven males and seven females representing ten states. Nine outbreaks were due to type A, three to type B, and two to type E toxin.

Source: Center for Disease Control (1981), p. 25.

TABLE 18.1   FOOD POISONING, 1979
(PERCENTAGE OF OUTBREAKS)

Food services	73
Homes	22
Food processors	5

After Chou (1979).

storage in homes, restaurants, schools, churches, or other food-handling establishments.

The microbiological safety of the modern American food supply is an accomplishment in which the food industry can take pride. Compared with many other hazards of life, e.g. automobile accidents which take some 50,000 lives a year to say nothing of the injuries, the hazards of the food supply are miniscule. There can be no doubt about the improvements that have occurred in the microbiological safety of the food supply in the industrialized nations of the world during this century, despite the fact that food-borne diseases are still a health problem owing to improper handling of food. The situation is perhaps best appreciated by comparing it with that of travellers in the less technologically developed parts of the world who must take unusual precautions to avoid food-borne diseases.

Chemical safety

During the nineteenth century, and the early part of this century, there were irresponsible food producers who added such hazardous substances as copper salts to canned vegetables to ensure that they would remain green. Adoption of food and drug laws in the U.S. was stimulated by such practices as well as by failure to maintain sanitary conditions. By 1938 standards were developed for chemical safety of foods and between 1951 and 1958 standards of identity were established for many foods; also long-term toxicity testing of food additives was instituted. These regulations were adopted not only for the protection of the consumer, but also to protect responsible food producers against the practices of those whose scruples were questionable. Similar regulations have been adopted in Japan and most European countries, and the World Health Organization has established many international standards (Ferrando, 1981a).

Despite the actions that have been taken through legislation and regulation to protect the consumer against chemical toxicity, much concern about the safety of food additives has been, and continues to be, voiced in many industrialized nations. There is fear of chemicals with strange names. Yet, Benarde (1981) could state that there has not been a single documented case of human illness or death attributable to additives included in foods. On the other hand, there have been deaths from overconsumption of Vitamins A and D when those essential nutrients have been used without following guidelines for their safe use. They, of course, are also chemicals with strange names, as are the myriad substances occurring naturally in foods.

Estrogenic, carcinogenic, mutagenic, antithyroid, antienzyme, anti-vitamin, and other potentially toxic substances occur naturally in some foods (FNB, 1973; Ames, 1983). Among the most toxic of these are compounds produced by molds, the aflatoxins, which are potent carcino-gens (FNB, 1973). They are found on peanuts and corn, when these crops are stored under moist conditions. Regulations to control these naturally occurring toxicants are much less stringent than those directed toward control of intentional additives and information about them is limited despite the fact that we may be exposed to relatively large doses of them (Ames, 1983). Hall (1973) has pointed out that many of these potentially toxic substances are naturally present in foods in quantities far in excess of most additives. Sugar, salt, corn syrup, and dextrose make up the major portion of the additives in foods; most others are used in only small amounts. The cases of chemical food poisoning reported by CDC in 1980 were from substances that occurred naturally in the food – mainly toxins in fish – not from substances added to the food (CDC, 1983).

Fortunately, the body has defense mechanisms against most potentially toxic substances. It can tolerate limited quantities even of cyanide – but the capacity of metabolic detoxification systems can be exceeded. Variety in the diets of the populations of industrial nations provides another measure of protection against this. Selection from among the large number of foods available tends to limit consumption of any one food-stuff. This makes it unlikely that deleterious substances present in certain foods will be consumed in amounts that are harmful.

Toxicity from foods occurs in many parts of the world, usually from naturally occurring toxicants and usually when the food containing the substance makes up a large part of the diet. In Central India, for example, where the seeds of a legume (*Lathyrus sativus*) related to the sweet pea are used as a staple, the disease neurolathyrism is endemic. The seeds contain a toxic amino acid (Roy, 1981) that causes weakness of the lower limbs. When the seeds make up a large part of the diet, paralysis and atrophy of the muscles can develop to the point where it becomes impos-sible to walk. Efforts are being made to breed varieties of *Lathyrus* that do not contain the toxicant (Swaminathan, 1974), but, in the meantime, the disease continues to be a serious health problem.

Failure to identify instances in which toxic reactions have resulted from chemical compounds added to foods, and the rarity of toxicity from accidental contamination with industrial chemicals and from naturally occurring toxicants in the U.S., is testimony in itself to the chemical safety of the food supply (Foster, 1982). It should not, however, lull us into complacency. It is important that the safety of substances added to foods be assured; that knowledge of potential toxicants occurring naturally in foods be expanded; that measures be taken to ensure that the food supply will not be contaminated with potentially toxic pesticides, heavy metals, and hazardous industrial chemicals. To maintain the impressive record of food safety of industrialized nations requires vigilance in identifying and eliminating potential hazards.

Coon (FNB, 1973, pp. 573–90) emphasizes in a discussion of this topic the importance of distinguishing between toxicity and hazard, the former being the potential to produce injury, the latter being the capacity to produce injury under the conditions of exposure. Oxalate is toxic but its presence in spinach is not a hazard. On a worldwide basis the naturally occurring toxicants have been the greatest hazards in foods. Man-made chemicals in foods "are not known to have been responsible for adverse effects on human health when such materials have been used in accordance with good agricultural and manufacturing practices" (FNB, 1973, p. 574). Foster (1982) has presented a comparison of deaths annually from various hazards in the United States, and notes that none occur from chemicals added to foods. He emphasizes that with reasonable care it is possible to prevent hazards. Food as a component of the environment is safer in industrialized than in non-industrialized nations and is safer now than in the past. With increased knowledge and application of that knowledge, as we have had in the past, we can look to a safer food supply for more of the world in the future. This is much the theme of a recent publication by the Food and Agriculture Organization of the U.N. (Ferrando, 1981a).

Nutritional inadequacy

During the first third of this century, pellagra was a serious medical problem in the U.S. The number of deaths from this disease ranged from 2,000 to as high as 6,000 per year (figure 18.2). The careful scientific research of Goldberger led to the recognition that pellagra was a nutritional deficiency disease. It was associated with a disproportionately high intake of corn and a low intake of animal products. It could be cured and prevented by consumption of foods containing high-quality protein. Subsequent research by Elvehjem and his associates led to the discovery of the vitamin niacin and to recognition that pellagra was a vitamin deficiency disease – niacin deficiency. The effectiveness of protein in curing the disease was later shown to be due to the ability of the body to convert the amino acid tryptophan to niacin. Soon thereafter, a program for fortification of cereal grains with niacin and other critical nutrients

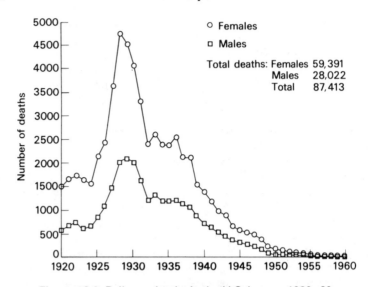

Figure 18.2 Pellagra deaths in the U.S. by sex, 1920–60.
Source: *Vital Statistics of the United States*, National Center for Health Statistics, Hyattsville, MD.
Note: the registration area included approximately 80 percent of the population in 1920 and the entire U.S. by 1933.
Source: Miller (1978).

was undertaken, and within a few years pellagra ceased to be a public health problem. This is an excellent example of the way serious health problems can be solved through basic nutritional, physiological and biochemical research (for references see Goldsmith, 1964; Miller, 1978). A similar pattern for the prevention of beri-beri, thiamin deficiency, has been documented in Japan; and for endemic goiter by fortification of salt with iodine, in Colombia and many other countries (DeMaeyer and Bengoa, 1971). Diseases attributable to deficiencies of specific nutrients do still occur, but much less frequently than heretofore, in many of the poorer nations. Vitamin A deficiency, for example, remains a major cause of blindness in southern Asia and parts of Latin America. The problem is recognized and widespread efforts are being undertaken to solve it (IVACG, 1977).

The nutritive value of the food supply in most industrialized countries has been improved in several ways in an effort to prevent other nutritional deficiency diseases: goiter – through iodization of salt; rickets – through vitamin D fortification of milk; anemia – through iron fortification of cereal grain products. When margarine became an inexpensive substitute for butter, it was fortified with Vitamin A to ensure that the nutritive value of the food supply would not deteriorate. Applications of information of this type to prevent and cure nutritional deficiency diseases

(DeMaeyer and Bengoa, 1971) throughout the world have resulted in such problems becoming far less severe in the world as a whole.

Comparison of the nutrient content of the food supply in the U.S. at intervals since 1910 has shown that the content of most essential nutrients has increased over the years (Gortner, 1975). The major changes that have occurred have been changes in gross composition. There has been a decrease equivalent to 10 percent of total calories in the starch content and an increase of 10 percent of total calories from fat, mainly from plant sources (table 18.2). The health significance of these changes has been the subject of much debate, as will be noted later. This pattern of change occurs, however, throughout the world, and even within countries, as the standard of living rises. It has been documented by FAO (Périssé *et al.*, 1969) and is the result of a shift in food use from plant to animal products (figure 18.3).

Recent health and nutrition surveys have found no evidence of nutritional deficiency diseases among the U.S. population (USDHEW, 1972). About 15 percent of those examined had mild, but non-debilitating, anemia, usually due to marginal iron nutriture. Between 1 and 5 percent appeared to have marginal intakes of one or more other nutrients. However, with 85 percent of the population surveyed showing no evidence of nutritional inadequacy, the U.S. food supply is obviously nutritionally adequate. Despite whatever changes may have occurred in the environment and in the food supply during the period of industrialization, there can be no doubt but that improved methods of processing, storage and transport have provided industrialized countries with a variety of foodstuffs that meet their nutritional needs fully, and ensure that health is not threatened from nutritional deficiencies.

Even with the ready availability of a nutritionally adequate food supply at reasonable cost, some people do not consume enough of all of the essential nutrients. Poverty, illness, alcoholism, ignorance, and neglect

TABLE 18.2   NUTRIENTS AVAILABLE FOR
CONSUMPTION PER DAY IN U.S.

	1909–13	1943–47	1970–74
Energy (kcal)	3,460	3,360	3,300
Protein (g)	100	100	101
Carbohydrate (g)	489	428	385
Fat (g)	125	142	155
Saturated (g)	50	54	56
Linoleic (g)	11	15	23
Cholesterol	509	577	556

After Gortner (1975).

A. E. Harper

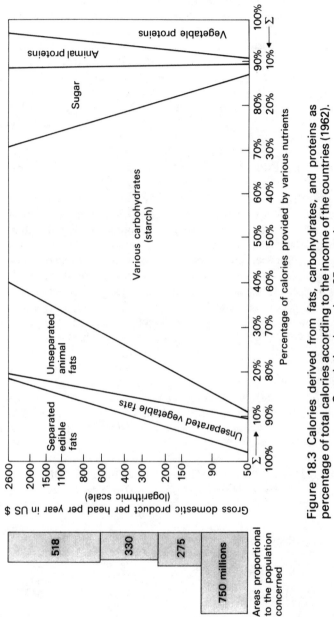

Figure 18.3 Calories derived from fats, carbohydrates, and proteins as percentage of total calories according to the income of the countries (1962). Correlation based on 85 countries.
Source: Périssé et al. (1969). p. 1.

can all lead to consumption of too little food or insufficient amounts of specific nutrients. Such problems do not result from nutritional inadequacy of the food supply. They occur most commonly, as was the case with pellagra, from consuming a limited number of foods, an inadequate amount of food, or, as with microbiological hazards, from inappropriate use of the food supply. These problems continue to pose threats to the health of many people in poor countries where certain important foods are available only seasonally, selection is limited, and income is low. Nonetheless, the situation has improved and, projecting on the basis of past progress, will continue to improve as development occurs.

Indicators of health status

Infant, childhood, and maternal mortality; other health indicators

At the turn of the century, childhood, and maternal mortality rates were high in the U.S. – they resembled those in many of the poor countries where malnutrition is prevalent today (figure 18.4). Unsanitary conditions leading to high rates of infection were widespread. Gastroenteritis and bronchial infections were major causes of death in the U.S. in 1900 (Omran, 1977). Death rates from these diseases are immensely higher among poorly nourished than among well-nourished populations. Although death rates from infectious diseases remain high in many of the poorer countries, they have been falling steadily for several decades in many. This is the result of application of medical advances throughout the world and efforts to improve sanitation. These trends are encouraging and, unless they are curtailed by disasters, natural or human in origin, can be expected to continue (DeMaeyer and Bengoa, 1971). It is noteworthy that infant mortality in many of the poor countries of the world in 1965 was considerably below that of either the United States or the United Kingdom in 1915 (table 18.3).

Throughout this century there have been steady and steep declines in infant, childhood, and maternal mortality in the U.S. (figure 18.4) and in other industrialized countries. In fact, death rates have declined impressively among all age groups but more slowly among those 45 years of age or older (figure 18.5). Life expectancy at birth in the U.S. has increased from 48 to 72 years (70 for men, 76 for women). These changes are indicative of major improvements in health. They have occurred in association with improvements in sanitation, housing, and nutrition (USDHEW, 1979). It is doubtful that they could have occurred without improvement of the food supply. There can be no question but that health has improved immensely in the industrialized nations during this century in association with whatever changes have occurred in the food supply. Infant mortality has declined (table 18.3), and life expectancy has

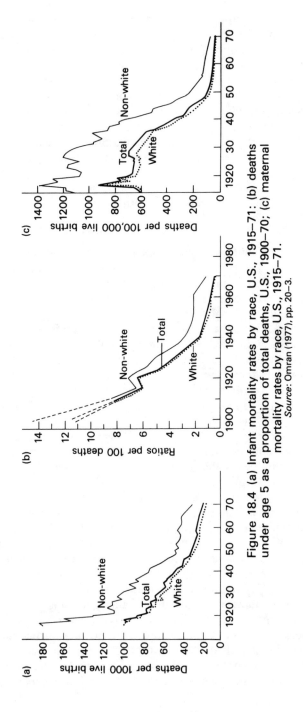

Figure 18.4 (a) Infant mortality rates by race, U.S., 1915–71: (b) deaths
under age 5 as a proportion of total deaths, U.S., 1900–70; (c) maternal
mortality rates by race, U.S., 1915–71.
Source: Omran (1977), pp. 20–3.

TABLE 18.3 INFANT MORTALITY:
DEATHS UNDER 1 YEAR PER 1000 LIVE BIRTHS

	U.S.	England and Wales	Japan	Chile	(Ceylon) Sri Lanka	Philippines
1915	100	110	160	254	171	–
1925	72	75	142	258	172	157
1935	56	57	107	251	263	153
1945	38	46	–	165	140	–
1955	26	25	40	119	72	84
1965	25	19	19	107	53	73
1974	17	16	11	71	45	–
1979	13	13	8	38	–	59

National Statistics collected by WHO, DeMaeyer and Bengoa (1971), and UN Demographic Yearbook 1981.

increased (table 18.4) steadily since the 1940s even in the poor, less industrialized countries (USDS, 1982).

Health status cannot be assessed solely from changes in life expectancy although it is probably the most widely used indicator. Another simple indicator of health status is days lost from work. Among those who are working in the United States, loss of time from work, according to the National Center for Health Statistics, is less than 6 days/year. This includes time lost by those who are in the older age groups and those who may lose months from work owing to serious accidents, which are the major cause of disability among people under 45 in the U.S. It is not possible in the face of such statistics to claim on any rational basis that health is unsatisfactory. As the Surgeon General stated in the quote at the beginning of this report, "The health of the American people has never been better." It is, of course, possible to envision that it could be better still. Health status in the U.S. is not as satisfactory as in some northern European countries and Japan, where infant death rates are lower. Nonetheless, the differences among the twenty countries in the world with the longest life expectancies at birth are small, and these countries have all undergone the types of environmental change associated with industrial development.

Obesity

The most common finding in the nutrition and health surveys done in the U.S. has been a high incidence of overweight and obesity. Obesity is not a disease but a condition that can lead, in its more severe forms, to disability. It is associated with increased incidence of diabetes, hypertension, and biliary disease, and through diabetes and hypertension, to

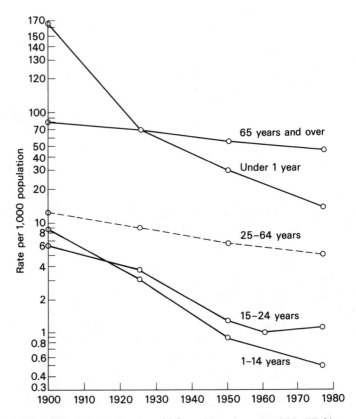

Figure 18.5 Death rates by age: U.S., selected years 1900–77. Note: 1977 data are provisional, data for all other years are final. Selected years are 1900, 1925, 1950, 1960 (for age group 15–24 years only) and 1977.
Source: USDHEW (1979), p. 5.

increased risk of heart disease. Quite apart from the increased risk of developing these diseases, the millions of dollars spent each year on advice and programs for weight reduction is evidence in itself of the undesirability of the condition. What is the relationship of this problem to changes that have occurred in the food supply?

One of the major guidelines of most public health organizations is "to maintain appropriate body weight." Here we have a dilemma. What is appropriate body weight? Bray (1978) noted that body weight about 20 percent above the so-called "ideal" weight was not associated with increased mortality. Keys (1981) found that if hypertension was removed from consideration, overweight was a risk factor for coronary heart disease only at the extremes of body weight. Andres (1980) noted that,

TABLE 18.4 LIFE EXPECTANCY AT BIRTH, IN YEARS

	1950/5	1955/60	1960/5	1965/70	1975
World	47	50	52	54	59
Industrialized nations	65	68	69	70	71
Less developed nations	42	45	48	50	54
Africa	36	38	41	43	46
Latin America	52	55	58	60	63
Asia	42	46	50	52	54

Cited from USDS (1982), p. 248.

among the elderly, the most desirable body weight for longevity was that currently considered as mildly obese. Thus, there is no justification for rigid views about weight control. Obvious obesity increases risk of developing several health problems but if moderate "overweight" is not accompanied by hypertension, it poses very little, if any, health hazard.

It is also important, even critical, to recognize that underweight is equally undesirable (Keys, 1981). This is particularly true in this age, in which women have been led to believe that they should resemble as closely as possible in body conformation the Parisian model or the marathon runner, and the health of many young women is in jeopardy from anorexia nervosa, a condition that results in emaciation from failure to eat enough to maintain appropriate body weight.

The question we are concerned with, however, is: "Can the high incidence of obesity in the U.S. be attributed to undesirable changes that have occurred in the nature of the food supply?" There is no evidence to support the idea that obesity is a function of diet composition (Van Italie, 1979). Obesity results from caloric intake in excess of expenditure regardless of the source of those calories. People differ in the efficiency with which they use calories and certainly it is easier to overeat a high-fat than a high-carbohydrate diet. It is no problem, however, to overeat a high carbohydrate diet. Many of the advocates of dietary guidelines for disease prevention have attributed the high incidence of overweight and obesity to nutrition education in which major emphasis is placed on eating a nutritionally adequate diet. This strange charge is worth examining.

The major recommendation for ensuring nutritional adequacy has been to consume the appropriate numbers of servings of foods from among the four major food groups in order to obtain the required quantities of essential nutrients from an amount of food that provides only 1200–1600 kilocalories; then, to make up the additional calories needed from among foods within or outside the major food groups

(USDA, 1957). This is scarcely a recommendation for over-consumption. It is a recommendation for moderation.

The temptation to overeat from an appetizing, nutritious, and affordable food supply is great whether the diet is high in fat or in carbohydrate, especially when physical activity is limited as it is in most highly industrialized societies. It is irrational to blame overeating to the point of obesity on the nature of the food supply. Overeating, or failing to balance food consumption and energy expenditure, may represent a problem for many people either in using the food supply appropriately or in maintaining an adequate level of physical activity but it certainly does not represent a hazard of the food supply itself.

Chronic and Degenerative Diseases

The most common indictment of the food supply today is the claim that the high incidence of, and death and disability from, chronic and degenerative diseases is associated with changes that have occurred in our food supply and diet during this century. This was the theme of 10 years of hearings of the U.S. Senate Select Committee on Nutrition and Human Needs (The McGovern Committee). It has been echoed by a number of consumer advocacy groups. A number of public health organizations have adopted similar views and claim that these diseases are epidemic. This hypothesis has been accepted widely. It is especially important, therefore, to evaluate critically information about relationships between the modern food supply and the incidence of chronic and degenerative disease. It is a subject that generates much more heat than light, especially in relation to public policy pronouncements.

It is instructive first to recall the major changes that have occurred in the U.S. food supply during this century. The proportion of carbohydrate in the diet has declined by about 10 percent of total calories, largely as the result of reduced consumption of potatoes and cereal grain products. The proportion of fat has increased by about 10 percent largely as the result of increased consumption of vegetable oils and substitution of animal products for cereal grains (table 18.2). This also results in some other changes. The quality of protein in the diet is improved; the amount of saturated fat in the diet would be expected to increase but in the U.S. vegetable oils have replaced much of the lard and butter formerly consumed, so saturated fat intake has changed only imperceptibly despite increased meat consumption and there has been a slow but gradual increase in consumption of polyunsaturated fat; the situation is similar with cholesterol, which would also have been expected to increase but has not, because of the substitution of plant for animal fats; minerals from animal products in the diet are probably better utilized than those from plant sources but overall the quantities of essential nutrients in the food supply have changed very little (Page and Friend, 1978; Gortner, 1975).

Interestingly, this type of pattern of change in diet (figure 18.3) is observed generally, according to FAO, as income increases (Périssé *et al.*, 1969). It is observed for countries in relation to national income and among income groups within countries. Substitution of animal products for plant products in diets as income rises would appear to be an almost universal phenomenon, except for groups who are vegetarians for a variety of reasons. In the past 20 years in Japan, e.g., consumption of meat and eggs has increased 2.5-fold; milk and dairy product consumption has more than tripled; consumption of cereal grains has fallen by 30 percent (Hosoya, 1982). It is changes of this type that are purported to be responsible for increased mortality from chronic and degenerative diseases. Such changes are represented as evidence of deterioration of the food supply (see Harper, 1980, 1981b; FNB, 1980; Levy *et al.*, 1979 for discussion and references).

Let us look now at changes in the major causes of death in the U.S. during this century. At the turn of the century, as has already been mentioned, most deaths resulted from infectious diseases (Omran, 1977). Nevertheless, the major single cause of death in the U.S. in the early 1900s was cardiovascular diseases (heart disease and stroke) (CVD), 14 percent. At present, infectious diseases are largely controlled; CVD account for close to 50 percent of all deaths. Cancer accounts for about 20 percent (figure 18.6) (Population Reference Bureau, 1977). Similar trends are observed in most western European countries but death rates from heart disease are usually lower than in the U.S. There is no question but that chronic and degenerative diseases are the major causes of death in the U.S. and in most of western Europe. This is a pattern of transition in the major causes of death that occurs in association with industrialization and a rising standard of living (Preston, 1976; USDS, 1982, pp. 249–50). Yet, while this shift in the causes of death has been occurring, death rates at all ages have fallen (figure 18.5) and life expectancy has lengthened. Rising life expectancy has also accompanied economic and social development throughout the world (table 18.4). It appears on the surface to be anomalous that a purported epidemic of chronic and degenerative diseases is accompanied by improved health and greater longevity. How is it explained?

Incidence of chronic and degenerative diseases

First, with the gradually decreasing death rates at all ages and a falling birth rate, the proportion of the population in the U.S. that is 65 years of age and older has increased from 4 percent to between 11 and 12 percent (figure 18.7) (Butler, 1977). In 1900 only 37 percent of infants born

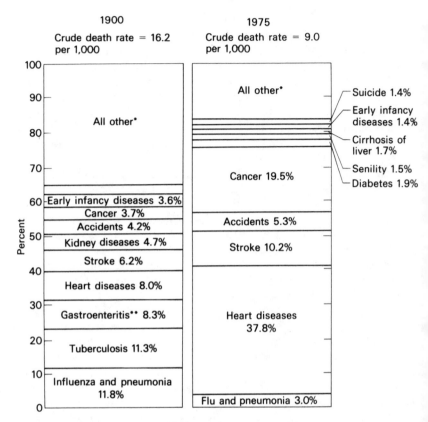

Figure 18.6 Major causes of death in the U.S., 1900–75 (as percentage of all deaths).
Source: Population Reference Bureau (1977).

*No disease in this category represents more than 2% of all deaths
**Inflammation of the stomach and intestines

reached 65 years of age, now over 75 percent of all infants born can expect to live for 65 years or more (figure 18.8) (Fries, 1980). A similar trend is evident in industrialized nations generally. Thus most people can now be expected to die of the chronic and degenerative diseases that are associated with aging. In most poor countries today the proportion of the population that is 65 years of age or over is as low as 2–3 percent (USDS, 1982, p. 18), and death rates generally are higher than in the industrialized countries. Thus a small proportion of deaths in such populations will be from diseases associated with aging. This was the situation in the U.S.

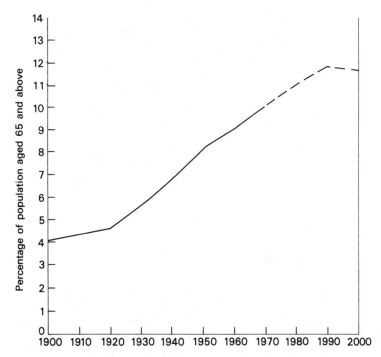

Figure 18.7 The percentage of population aged 65 and older has increased.
Source: National Center for Health Statistics, Butler (1977), p. 54.

early in this century; therefore, changes in death rates over time must be compared on some basis that takes into consideration the changing proportion of the population in different age groups especially as death rates from most diseases increase exponentially with increasing age (see Harper, 1982 for discussion).

The U.S. National Center for Health Statistics (NCHS) emphasized the importance of age-adjusted comparisons in the 1960s (Grove and Hetzel, 1968). It noted that between 1920 and 1960 the crude death rate from CVD had increased by 20 percent; but on an age-adjusted basis the death rate from CVD had decreased by 20 percent (figure 18.9). The age-adjusted death rate from CVD has continued to fall since between 1930 and 1940, so have death rates from heart disease (HD) and cerebro-vascular disease (stroke) (figure 18.10) (Harper, 1983a, b). Despite these continuous declines in CVD as a whole, the death rate from coronary heart disease (CHD) was reported to have risen between 1950 and 1968 (Ahrens *et al.*, 1979; NRC, 1982a). How does one account for this? Was there a valid basis for claiming, as most heart associations have, that we were suffering an "epidemic" of CHD?

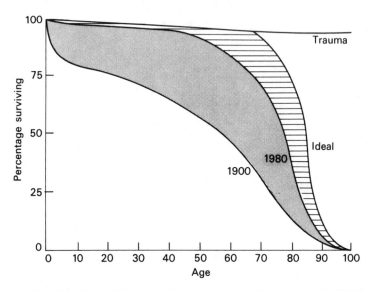

Figure 18.8 Survival of the American population. The curves for 1902 and 1980 depict, for persons born previously who would have been a particular age in 1900 and 1980, respectively, the percentage who were actually alive, e.g. of those who would have been 65 in 1900, 38 percent were alive; of those who would have been 65 in 1980, 78 percent were alive.
Source: Fries (1980), p. 131.

If we look carefully at U.S. health statistics we find that over the period between 1948 and 1968, while death rates from CHD were reported to be rising, death rates from several other important diseases of the heart were falling more rapidly than those from CHD were rising (figure 18.10) (Harper, 1983b). Recent charts of the NCHS (USDHHS, 1982) show this trend for the period between 1950 and 1979. I would therefore like to pose this question: "Why did mortality from CHD appear to be rising between 1950 and 1968 when mortality from diseases of the heart was falling? My answer is that, as the ability to diagnose various heart diseases improved, more and more deaths from diseases of the heart were attributed to CHD, and less and less to other categories of heart disease. How else can one account for the steady decline in the death rate from heart disease since 1940 and the decline in CHD mortality only since 1968, after the proportion of heart disease deaths attributed to CHD had risen from less than 30 percent in 1940 to 90 percent in 1968 (table 18.5).

I would submit that the so-called "epidemic" of heart disease in the U.S. has been a paper epidemic, particularly when the NCHS has shown conclusively that the overall age-adjusted death rates from CVD, HD

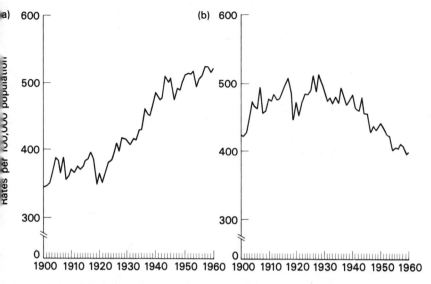

Figure 18.9 (a) Death rates for major cardiovascular–renal diseases: death-registration states, 1900–32, and U.S., 1933–60. (b) Age-adjusted death rates for major cardiovascular–renal diseases. Death-registration states, 1900–32, and U.S., 1933–60 (rates per 100,000 population.)
Source: Grove and Hetzel (1968) pp. 90–1.

and stroke have decreased steadily for over 40 years (figures 18.9 and 18.10) in association with whatever changes have occurred in the food supply (Harper, 1983a, b). It is noteworthy that these declines began in a population that had been consuming a diet in which the fat content and composition, and the cholesterol content, had changed little during the preceding 40 years – whatever slight trend there was, tended to be upward (figure 18.11, table 18.2) (Olson, 1981; Harper, 1983a).

Cancer death rates as a whole have not declined in the U.S. during this century. Nevertheless, they have not increased either (American Cancer Society, 1979). When the American Cancer Society tabulated age-adjusted death rates for a variety of cancers, it found that only bronchial cancer, attributed in large measure to excessive cigarette smoking, had increased significantly (figure 18.12). Gastric and uterine cancer mortality had decreased steadily since the 1930s and age-adjusted mortality rates from most other cancers had remained essentially unchanged; at least the Society concluded that it could not detect significant trends. The most recent report of the NCHS (USHHS, 1982) indicates that among adults under 65, mortality from cancers other than lung cancer has been declining slowly for about 20 years.

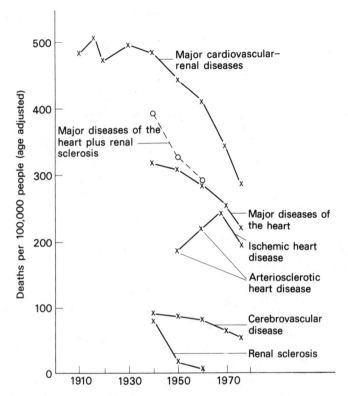

Figure 18.10 Changes in age-adjusted death rates from major cardio-vascular disease (based on Grove and Hetzel, 1968 and NCHS (HRA) 74–1853, 1974 and (PHS) 79 1222, 1978.
Source: Harper (1982).

Despite the evidence that age-adjusted death rates from chronic and degenerative diseases have either declined or remained constant in association with changes that have occurred in our diet, general diet modifications which include decreases in fat and cholesterol and increases in starch and polyunsaturated fat have been advocated ardently to control this group of diseases (Harper, 1981a, b). It is rarely noted that the decline in heart disease began in a population that had been consuming a diet that contained a high proportion of animal products and constant proportions of saturated fatty acids and cholesterol for the preceding 40 years.

After it was observed that coronary heart disease was associated with the formation of deposits in the arteries that were rich in cholesterol; that

TABLE 18.5 AGE-ADJUSTED DEATH RATES FROM TOTAL CARDIOVASCULAR (CVD) AND HEART DISEASES, AND PROPORTION OF HEART DISEASE DEATHS FROM CORONARY HEART DISEASE (CHD)

	Age-adjusted Death Rates per 1,000 population[a]			Proportion of Heart Disease Deaths (%)	
Year	CVD	Heart	CHD[b]	Non-coronary	Coronary
1940	486	315	69	78	22
1950	440	308	184	40	60
1960	399	286	215	25	75
1965	384	276	228	21	79
1968	368	270	243	10	90
1976	284	217	192	12	88

[a] Based on NCHS Publications No. 1677, 1978; and (HRA) 74-1853, 1974 and DHEW Publication No. (PHS) 79-1222, 1978.
[b] CHD = diseases of coronary arteries (1940);
     = arteriosclerotic heart disease (1950, 1960);
     = ischemic heart disease (1965, 1968, 1976).

the formation of such deposits was associated with high concentrations of cholesterol in the blood; and that the blood concentration of cholesterol tended to increase when the diet was rich in saturated fat, and in some species in cholesterol, and tended to decrease if saturated fat and cholesterol intake were reduced; the hypothesis that diets rich in animal fat were responsible for high mortality from coronary heart disease was widely accepted (Ernst and Levy, 1980). Proposals for controlling heart disease through modifying the national diet (by reducing the content of total fat, especially from animal sources, and increasing the content of fat from plant sources) were equally widely accepted. These were recommendations for returning to the diet of pre-industrial times.

How consistent is the evidence that the proposed changes in diet will improve the situation? In Norway and Sweden – where active campaigns to reduce fat, saturated fat and cholesterol intakes have been underway for several years – CHD mortality has increased as it has in many other countries (figure 18.13). In the U.S., Canada, and Australia, three countries with typical Western-type diets, it has decreased (Olson, 1981; Junge and Hoffmeister, 1982). Death rates in Israel, Chile, and Mexico – three countries with diets resembling closely those advocated for control of heart disease – differ by a factor of three (table 18.6). CHD mortality in Israel is higher than in the Scandinavian countries where diets resemble in composition that of the U.S.

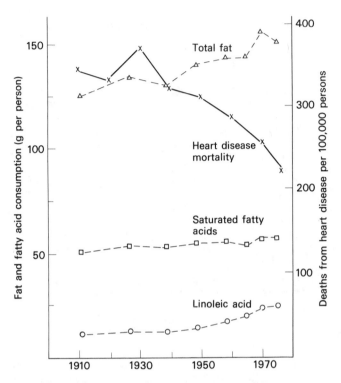

Figure 18.11 Age-adjusted death rate from heart disease and per capita
consumption of total fat and fatty acids.
Source: Harper (1982), see Harper (1983a), p. 677.

Intervention trials, in which either diet modification or drug treatment
has been used in an effort to reduce CHD mortality, mainly among men
who were considered to be at risk, have been disappointing (Ahrens,
1979; Ahrens *et al.*, 1979; Oliver, 1981; FNB, 1980; Olson, 1981). They
have provided evidence that such treatments will reduce serum cholesterol concentration between 8 and 15 percent. In some, the incidence of
non-fatal heart attacks has been reduced slightly, but taken altogether the
results of intervention trials have not provided convincing evidence that
overall death rates are reduced significantly by diet modification
(MRFIT, 1982; Oliver, 1983).

In evaluating the results of intervention trials, it is important to realize
that diet modification is often used in the treatment of patients with
diseases that are not caused by consumption of inadequate or inappropriate diets. Some metabolic impairments that result from non-nutritional
diseases, such as diabetes and renal disease, can be relieved by altering

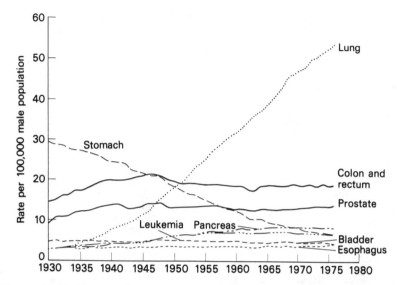

Figure 18.12 Male cancer death rates by site, U.S., 1930–76. Rate for the male population standardized for age on the 1940 U.S., population.
Sources: National Vital Statistics Division and Bureau of the Census, United States, and American Cancer Society (1979), p. 8.

the proportions of certain major dietary constituents. Diet modification to lower serum cholesterol concentration is recommended widely as therapy for individuals with impairment of lipid metabolism as a means of reducing their risk of developing severe atherosclerosis. Hence, evidence that there are individuals who respond favorably in dietary intervention trials does not prove that diet is a cause of the disease. All that the limited benefits observed in some of these trials prove, is that some individuals do respond to treatments designed to lower serum cholesterol concentration. It is not possible to establish accurately the incidence of genetic defects of lipid metabolism (Scriver, 1982). One would expect, nonetheless, that the proportion of subjects responding to dietary modifications would be much greater than is observed when estimates of the proportion of the population with some impairment of lipoprotein metabolism range as high as 5 percent (Blackburn, 1979).

The results of the Western Electric study (Shekelle *et al.*, 1981 and Commentary), which was acclaimed as having demonstrated for the first time the effectiveness of diet modification in reducing the incidence of CHD were inconsistent and, on critical evaluation, did not provide convincing evidence that dietary modification was an effective preventive measure for CHD. In fact, from the authors' own statistical analysis, diet accounted for less than 4 percent of the limited beneficial effects that were

Deaths per 100,000

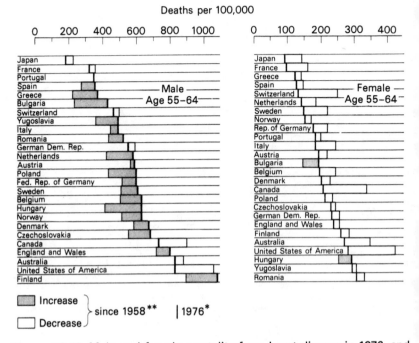

Figure 18.13 Male and female mortality from heart disease in 1976, and changes since 1958.
Source: Junge and Hoffmeister (1982), p. 119.

observed. When the number of risk factors for CHD is reported to be as high as 37 (Ernst and Levy, 1980), it should be clear that heart disease is a disease for which we know neither the cause nor the cure, nor how to prevent it.

More recently, information about diet and cancer has been reviewed in some detail (NRC, 1982b) and recommendations have been made for diet modifications as a measure for reducing cancer incidence. The major recommendation is to reduce fat consumption but, in contrast to the American Heart Association recommendations, it is to lower intake of polyunsaturated as well as saturated fat. The implication is that consumption of a diet resembling more closely that of the less developed countries will be an effective measure for controlling this disease. The report issued by the NRC has been criticized on several grounds, among them: that the associations between diet and cancer incidence detected through epidemiological studies, on which the report depends heavily, have not been consistent; that environmental variables associated with a high incidence of one type of cancer may be associated with a low incidence of

TABLE 18.6 SOME EXCEPTIONS TO THE RELATIONSHIP
BETWEEN DIET COMPOSITION AND AGE-ADJUSTED DEATH
RATES FROM HEART DISEASE IN MALES

Country	Death Rate per 100,000 (age 40–74)	Nutrients in food supply (%)		
		Fat		Carbohydrate
		Total	Animal	
Finland	755	30	25	58
United States	729	39	28	49
Denmark	373	39	29	50
Sweden	370	39	33	50
Norway	275	38	29	51
Chile	668	20	13	68
Israel	462	23	6	64
Mexico	244	23	9	66

After Kritchevsky, p. 281 in Levy *et al.*, 1979.

another; that the only cancer to have increased significantly in incidence
in the past 50 years in industrialized nations is bronchial cancer, which is
associated with heavy cigarette smoking; that steady declines have been
noted in the incidence of gastric and uterine cancers over many years;
that, not only is evidence of cause and effect relationships between diet
and cancer incidence lacking, it is not possible to predict effects of diet
modifications on the occurrence of cancers (CAST, 1982; Higginson,
1983). As with the controversy over dietary recommendations for
controlling heart disease, the question seems to be one of faith, i.e. how
much faith does one put in suggestive evidence. The Committee that has
advocated dietary modification (NRC, 1982b) stated clearly in its report:
"Unfortunately, it is not yet possible to make firm scientific pronouncements about the association between diet and cancer." This view is
reiterated by many cancer experts (Doll and Peto, 1981; Higginson, 1983;
Jensen, 1983) (see Peto, ch. 19 this volume).

It is difficult, indeed, to find convincing evidence that the food supply
of industrialized countries is responsible for high death rates from chronic
and degenerative diseases unless one accepts the view that improved diet
results in increased life expectancy and, therefore, in a high proportion of
the population living to old age. Among people between the age of 45 and
64 the death rate from chronic and degenerative diseases in the U.S. is
about 8 per 1000 individuals annually, about 4 per 1000 from CVD and 3
per 1000 from cancer. The high mortality from such diseases, 33 per 1000,

occurs among those over 65 years of age (USDHEW, 1978, 1979). It is associated with increased life expectancy and a high proportion of elderly people in the population whose physiological functions are known to deteriorate with increasing age (Harper, 1982, for references). This is borne out in an analysis by Preston (1976) of the effects of various causes of death on expected years of productive life, i.e. years before age 65. He notes that elimination of both cancer and cardiovascular diseases as causes of death would give an expected gain of less than 1.5 years in the average length of productive life in the U.S.

There is a population, however, between 35 and 60, mainly male, who are at high risk for CHD. Where we need to focus attention, and it is being done now, is on what is different about those who develop CHD at an early age and how to identify them. They require much more intensive and comprehensive medical care than recommendations for diet modification for the entire population. Cancer, unlike heart disease, is the cause of a relatively constant proportion of total deaths at all ages. These two diseases obviously have different bases. Until those who assume that the modern diet of industrialized nations is responsible for high death rates from chronic and degenerative diseases can make accurate predictions of the effects of diet modification on the susceptibility of a very high proportion of individuals to these diseases, a healthy skepticism of proposals for national diet modification is fully justified.

Diet and Life Expectancy

"The life expectancy of a population is perhaps the most all-inclusive and widely measured indicator of a nation's environmental health" (USDS, 1982). Life expectancies of the populations of six of the twenty countries with the highest life expectancies in the world are shown in table 18.7. These populations were selected because they differ greatly in mortality from heart disease. Japan, France, and Italy have low rates of heart disease; Sweden, the Netherlands, and the U.S. have much higher rates. Whatever may be the reasons, the major causes of death in these countries are distinctly different, yet life expectancies at birth of the three with high rates of heart disease are the same as those of the three with low rates of heart disease. They all have the same life expectancy at age 65 and the same 5–6 year difference in life expectancy between males and females.

It is obvious that, if longevity is used as the criterion of a desirable diet, the Japanese, the Scandinavian, the American, the Dutch, the French, and the Italian diets are equally satisfactory. It is unjustifiable and highly misleading to fault the diets of the industrialized nations on the grounds that they are associated with high mortality from chronic and degenerative diseases when populations consuming diets that are condemned for

TABLE 18.7 COMPARISON OF LIFE EXPECTANCY AT
BIRTH WITH MORTALITY OF MALES (35–74) FROM
HEART DISEASE

| | Life expectancy (year) (1975) | | | Age-adjusted mortality from heart disease[a] per 100,000 people |
| | At birth | | At age 65 | |
	Male	Female	Male	
Norway	72	77	14	581
Netherlands	71	77	14	502
United States	69	76	14	793
Japan	71	76	13	115
France	69	77	13	205
Italy[b]	69	75	13	309

After Stamler, p. 39, in Levy *et al.* 1979.
 [a] For 1973.
 [b] For 1972.

their high fat content have the same life expectancy as the populations of countries consuming diets resembling those advocated to prevent such diseases.

In relation to criticisms that the food supplies of the U.S., the Scandinavian countries, and the Netherlands are overloaded with sugar and fat, it is instructive to compare figures for consumption of fat and sugar with those for life expectancy in European countries (Roussos, 1978) (figure 18.14). Iceland, with the longest life expectancy in the world, has close to the highest sugar and fat consumption; countries such as Sweden and the Netherlands, just behind Iceland in their enviable health status, also consume high fat, high sugar diets. These observations are not put forward as the basis for advocating high fat and high sugar intakes, particularly for people whose energy expenditure is low, but obviously, if such diets are otherwise nutritionally adequate, they would not appear to present any unique hazard to the population as a whole even though they may not be appropriate for a portion of it. The populations of Sweden and Japan, whose health records are among the best in the world, consume distinctly different proportions of carbohydrate and fat. It is difficult, then, to find some basis, other than moral righteousness, for advocating some unique diet composition for assurance of health and longevity except for individuals who have impaired metabolic systems.

Despite the similarities in life expectancy between countries with distinctly different diets, mortality from major diseases differs greatly in different countries. If we accept that the genetic variability among people is similar from country to country – and observations that the offspring of

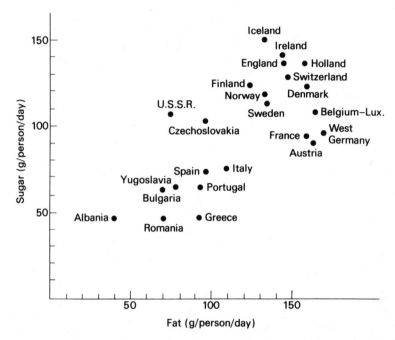

Figure 18.14 Interrelation between sugar (sucrose) and fat consumption in some European countries.
Source: Roussos, (1978), p. 174.

migrants tend to develop the disease pattern of their adopted country support this view (Blackburn, 1979) – then there seems to be little doubt that environment influences the pattern of diseases that are major causes of death. To assume that there is some uniform diet that will ensure unique health and longevity, and freedom from chronic and degenerative diseases, one must assume uniformity of the genetic make-up and adaptability of the entire population. Evidence that individuals differ greatly in their susceptibility to diseases and their tolerance of dietary constituents is well documented (Scriver, 1982). A proportion of the population is known to be uniquely genetically susceptible to diabetes, ischemic heart disease, hypertension, and some forms of cancer. The extent of this genetic variability, and its significance for treatment and prevention of disease, is only now beginning to be appreciated. It is a major area for future investigation. There are genetic defects that limit the tolerance of individuals for sugar, for fats, for salt, and for amino acids. Individuals with such defects would appear to represent a small, but significant, part of the population. They must also follow rigid, but different, dietary patterns from the norm and from each other to avoid complications from their genetic limitation.

On the other hand the majority of the population adapts readily to a wide variety of diets. This is borne out by the similar long life expectancies of populations in countries with widely different diets. To assume that their health will be improved by substituting the conjectured healthful diet of previous centuries for the current diet has no foundation in fact. To assume further that some diet modifications can be devised which will be equally effective in preventing all of the diseases associated with aging is not rational (Higginson, 1983). Mortality from heart disease differs greatly between countries with similar diets, as also does cancer mortality. It is also presumptuous to assume that these different groups, whether they need to or not, and whether it will be beneficial or not, should conform to a uniform set of dietary guidelines.

Finally, almost without exception, those who claim that diet has deteriorated as the result of industrial development and that they have a simple set of guidelines to remedy the problem, state unequivocally that even if the proposed diet is not beneficial, it will not cause any harm. This is a gratuitous argument. There is no way of knowing how such guidelines will be used by the public generally. We do know that in most of the populations cited as having low incidences of cancer and heart disease life expectancy is low, infant and child mortality are high, and the proportion of elderly people in the population is low. We also know that in countries that have had rapid industrial development accompanied by a shift toward the typical western diet, health has improved and life expectancy has increased (DeMaeyer and Bengoa, 1971; Hosoya, 1982). We know further that in Japan, where the diet is intermediate between that of the less developed and highly developed countries, life expectancy does not exceed that of Sweden and the Netherlands where diets are similar to those of other western industrialized countries.

The assumptions that underlie claims that the diets of industrialized nations have deteriorated, and proposals for prevention of chronic and degenerative diseases by simple diet modification, do not have a sound scientific basis. They are based on the assumption that when an association between the incidence of chronic and degenerative diseases and a particular dietary pattern has been demonstrated, public health policy should be developed around areas of consensus (Palmer, 1983). As has been reiterated frequently (FNB, 1980; Rosch, 1983) association does not prove causation. Also, consensus is the antithesis of science. The late Phillip Handler, past president of the U.S. National Academy of Sciences, was troubled by observations that public policy may be based on superficial and misleading interpretations of scientific evidence. He emphasized forcefully the over-riding necessity for scientific rigor in evaluating information being offered as the basis for formulation of public policy (see Harper, 1981c for references).

Perceptions and Realities

The subject of nutrition and health is not dealt with in detail in *Global 2000* (USDS, 1980). In fact, the terms "nutrition" and "health" are not included in the index. There is, nevertheless, a section on population in which mortality and life expectancy are discussed and a section on environment in which food and health are discussed briefly. These sections are among the most optimistic in the report. The fact that life expectancy of the population is perhaps the most all-inclusive indicator of a nation's environmental health (p. 88) is noted. An analysis is given of changes in life expectancies in both industrialized and less-developed countries (table 18.4). The striking increases in life expectancy, mentioned earlier, that have occurred in industrialized nations, are cited. Life expectancies in the less developed countries are shown to have increased by an average of 12 years in the past 25 years. The trends for increasing life expectancy are projected to continue for the next 25 years at very close to the same rate, and the conclusion is drawn that: "In no country is life expectancy expected to decline" (p. 248). These trends, that must be taken as evidence of an anticipated improvement in "environmental health" throughout the world, seem to be at variance with the pessimistic view of the outlook for the environment in the overall report that *Science* characterized as "gloomy"; *Time* as "extremely bleak"; and *Newsweek* as "grim." It would appear that, despite the bleakness and grimness of the outlook, health is expected to improve.

Following this optimistic outlook for continuing increases in life expectancy throughout the world – and a realistic acknowledgement that life expectancy in the industrialized nations, which now exceeds 70 years for males and 76 for females, can be expected to rise only slowly in the future – is a brief discussion implying that the current diet of the industri- alized nations is the major obstacle preventing even greater longevity. Diet is purported to be responsible for the high incidence of chronic and degenerative diseases which are resistant to treatment. What seems to have been overlooked is that the diets of the populations with the greatest longevity vary immensely.

It is not inconceivable that, as we learn more about the process of aging, about degenerative diseases, and particularly about genetic engin- eering, it may become possible to lengthen the human life span. It is notable that up to now, with increases of close to 30 years in life expect- ancy being documented during this century in industrialized countries, there is no evidence that human life span (longest documented individual lifetime) has been lengthened. We are learning that biological systems do seem to be born with the seeds of their own destruction built into their genetic codes. We also know that age at death is a biological variable that follows an essentially normal distribution such that, without unique medical intervention, the range of ages of death of the individuals in a population with a life expectancy of, say, 80, will be between 50 and 110. Perhaps we should concentrate our efforts more on why a small proportion of the population develops chronic and degenerative diseases at an early age and on how to improve life for the many who survive beyond 70 rather than divert our efforts and resources into immense studies directed toward proving that there is a simple solution for chronic and degenerative diseases – studies that one after another have failed to do so (MRFIT, 1982).

Somehow, since the discovery of antibiotics and the ability of modern medicine to prevent most deaths from infections, the fact of death seems to have become unacceptable to the public, to politicians, and even to much of the medical profession. This, together with acceptance of myths about the curative properties of foods and nutrients (Harper, 1980b), has perhaps led to the "public preoccupation with disease that is assuming the dimension of a national obsession" (Thomas, 1977); to the assumption that there are simple diet-related solutions for highly complex medical problems (Harper, 1981b); and to the acceptance of this assumption by politicians and government administrators who would adopt programs based on these assumed solutions as national policy. Wilson (1976) admonished social scientists about their role in the establishment of social policy ". . . many scholars who should have known better acquiesced in the process of allowing eager politicians to convert bad ideas into dubious policy – either by participating very much on the periphery of the process, or by failing to say, loudly and frequently enough, that the emperor had no clothes."

There are many problems of diet and disease, environment and health, that require attention now, and there will undoubtedly be new ones into the twenty-first century. It is important, as Foster (1982) has noted about food safety problems, that we "get our priorities straight [and] put our efforts on the real hazards." When health is better than it has been in the industrialized nations, and life expectancy is high, and rising throughout the world, we should not dissipate our energies on hypothetical and imaginary dangers. We should direct them into the scientific efforts needed to solve the real ones.

References

Ahrens, E. H., Jr. (1979) Dietary fats and coronary heart disease: unfinished business. *Lancet* 2, 1345–8.

Ahrens, E. J., Jr., Connor, W. E., Bierman, E. L. *et al.* (1979) The evidence relating six dietary factors to the nation's health. *Am. J. Clin. Nutr.* 32, 2621–748.

524   *A. E. Harper*

American Cancer Society (1979) *Cancer Facts and Figures*.

AMA (1979) *AMA Concepts of Nutrition and Health*. Chicago: AMA.

Ames, B. N. (1983) Dietary carcinogens and anticarcinogens. *Science* 221, 1256–64.

Andres, R. (1980) Effect of obesity on total mortality. *Int. J. Obesity* 4, 381–6.

Benarde, M. A. (1981) *The Food Additives Dictionary*, p. 92. New York: Simon & Schuster.

Blackburn, H. (1979) Diet and mass hyperlipidemia: public health considerations – a point of view. In: Levy, R. I. *et al.* (eds.), *Nutrition, Lipids and Coronary Heart Disease*, p. 328. New York: Raven Press.

Bray, G. A. (1978) To treat or not to treat – that is the question? In: Bray, G. A. (ed.), *Recent Advances in Obesity Research*, vol. 2, pp. 248–65. London: Newman Publishing Co.

Butler, R. N. (1977) Presentation in Diet Related to Killer Diseases: VII. Hearing before the Senate Select Committee on Nutrition and Human Needs, 23 September. Washington, D.C.: U.S. Govt. Printing Office.

Center for Disease Control (CDC) (1981) *Reported Morbidity and Mortality, Annual Summary, 1981*. Atlanta, GA: USDHHS CDC.

——, (1983) *Foodborne Disease Surveillance, Annual Summary, 1980*, p. 27. Atlanta, GA: USDHHS CDC.

Chou, M. (1979) The preoccupation with food safety. In: Chou, H. and Harmon, D. P., Jr. (eds.), *Critical Food Issues of the Eighties*. pp. 18–41. New York: Pergamon Press.

Council for Agricultural Science and Technology (CAST) (1982) *Diet, Nutrition and Cancer: A Critique*. Ames, Iowa: CAST.

DeMaeyer, E. M. and Bengoa, J. M. (1971) Mortality and morbidity in nutritional disorders. In: Scrimshaw, N. S. and Altschul, A. M. (eds.), *Amino Acid Fortification of Protein Foods*, pp. 376–94. Cambridge, MA: MIT Press.

Doll, R. and Peto, R. (1981) The causes of cancer: quantitative estimates of avoidable risks of cancer in the United States today. *J. Nat. Cancer Inst.* 66, 1191–308.

Ernst, N. and Levy, R. I. (1980) Diet, hyperlipidemia and atherosclerosis. In: Goodhart, R. S. and Shils, M. E. (eds.), *Modern Nutrition in Health and Disease*, Philadelphia: Lea & Fehiger.

Ferrando, R. (1981a) *Traditional and Non-Traditional Foods*. Rome: Food and Agriculture Organization.

——, (1981b) Residues of meats and additives. Studies and perspectives. In: Franklin, K. R. and Davis, P. N. (eds.), *Meat in Nutrition and Health*, pp. 151–81. Danville, IL: Interstate Publishers.

Food and Nutrition Board (FNB), Committee on Food Protection (1973) *Toxicants Occurring Naturally in Foods*, 2nd edn., Washington, D.C.: National Research Council/National Academy of Sciences.

——, (1980) *Toward Healthful Diets*. Washington, D.C.: National Research Council/National Academy of Sciences.

Foster, E. M. (1982) Is there a food safety crisis? *Nutrition Today* 17 (6), 6–13.

Fries, J. F. (1980) Aging, natural death and the compression of morbidity. *New Engl. J. Med.* 303, 130–35.

Goldsmith, G. A. (1964) The B vitamins: thiamine, riboflavin, niacin. In: Beaton, G. H. and McHenry, E. W. (eds.), *Nutrition – A Comprehensive Treatise*, vol. 2, New York: Academic Press.

Gortner, W. A. (1975) Nutrition in the United States, 1900 to 1974. *Cancer Res.* 35, 3246–53.

Grove, R. D. and Hetzel, A. M. (1968) *Vital Statistics Rates in the United States 1940 to 1960*. Washington, D.C.: National Center for Health Statistics, USDHEW.

Hall, R. L. (1973) Food additives. *Nutrition Today* 8 (4), 20–8.

Harper, A. E. (1980) Dietary goals – for what and for whom? In: Garry, P. J. (ed.), *Human Nutrition: Clinical and Biochemical Aspects*, pp. 81–98. Washington, D.C.: Am. Assoc. Clin. Chem.

——, (1981a) Dietary guidelines. National Live Stock and Meat Board, *Food & Nutrition News* 52 (4).

——, (1981b) Dietary goals. In: Ellenbogen, L. (ed.), *Controversies in Nutrition*, pp. 63–84. New York: Churchill Livingstone.

——, (1981c) Human nutrition: its scientific basis. In: Selvey, N. and White, P. L. (eds.), *Nutrition in the 1980s: Constraints on our Knowledge*, pp. 15–28. New York: Allan R. Liss.

——, (1982) Nutrition and longevity. *Am. J. Clin. Nutr.* 36, 737–49.

——, (1983a) Coronary heart disease – an epidemic related to diet? *Am. J. Clin. Nutr.* 37, 669–81.

——, (1983b) Diet and heart disease – a critical evaluation. *Dietary Fats and Health*, pp. 496–511. Champaign, IL: Am. Oil Chem. Soc.

Higginson, J. (1983) Summary: nutrition and cancer. *Cancer Res.* (Suppl.) 43, 2515s–18s.

Hosoya, N. (1982) Nutritional status in Japan. *Proc. Int. Symp. on Advanced Nutrition*, pp. 22–32. Dept. of Health, Taipei, Republic of China.

International Vitamin A Consultative Group (1977) *Guidelines for the Eradication of Vitamin A Deficiency and Xerophthalmia*. New York: The Nutrition Foundation, Inc.

Jensen, O. M. (1983) Epidemiological evidence associating lipids with cancer causation. In: Perkins, E. G. and Visek, W. J. (eds.), *Dietary Fats, and Health*, pp. 698–709. Champaign, IL: Am. Oil Chem. Soc.

Junge, B. and Hoffmeister, H. (1982) "Civilization-associated" diseases in Europe and industrial countries outside of Europe: regional differences and trends in mortality. *Preventive Med.* 11, 117–30.

Keys, A. (1981) Overweight, obesity, coronary heart disease and mortality. In: Selvey, N. and White, P. L. (eds.), *Nutrition in the 1980s: Constraints on our Knowledge*, pp. 31–48. New York: Alan R. Liss.

Levy, R. I., Rifkind, B. M., Dennis, B. H., and Ernst, N. D. (1979) *Nutrition in Health and Disease*, vol. I, *Nutrition, Lipids and Coronary Heart Disease*. New York: Raven Press.

Miller, D. F. (1978) Pellagra deaths in the United States. *Am. J. Clin. Nutr.* 31, 558.

Multiple Risk Factor Intervention Trial (1982) Risk factor changes and mortality results. *J. Am. Med. Assoc.* 248, 1465–77.

National Research Council (1982a) On some major human diseases. In: *Outlook for Science and Technology*, pp. 71–132. San Francisco: W. H. Freeman and Co.

——, (1982b) *Diet, Nutrition and Cancer*. Washington, D.C.: National Academy of Sciences.

Oliver, M. F. (1981) Serum cholesterol – the knave of hearts and the joker. *Lancet* 2, 1090–5.

Oliver, M. F. (1983) Should we not forget about mass control of coronary risk factors? *Lancet* 2, 37–8.

Olson, R. E. (1981) New horizons for meat and nutrition policy. In: *Meat in Nutrition and Health*, pp. 183–97. Chicago: National Live Stock and Meat Board.

Omran, A. R. (1977) Epidemiologic Transition in the US: The Health Factor in Population Change. *Popul. Bull.* 32 (2), Washington D.C.: Population Reference Bureau, Inc.

Page, L. and Friend, B. (1978) The changing United States diet. *Bioscience* 28, 192–7.

Palmer, S. (1983) Diet, nutrition, and cancer: the future of dietary policy. *Cancer Res.* (Suppl.) 43, 2509s–14s.

Périssé, J., Sizaret, F., and François, P. (1969) The effect of income on the structure of the diet. *FAO Nutrition Newsletter* 7, 1–9.

Population Reference Bureau (1977) *Major Causes of Death in the United States 1900 to 1975*, Washington, D.C.

Preston, S. H. (1976) *Mortality Patterns in Nation Populations*, pp. 48–62. New York: Academic Press.

Pyke, M. (1970) *Man and Food*. World University Library, pp. 168–226. New York: McGraw-Hill.

Rosch, P. V. (1983) Stress and cardiovascular disease. *Comprehensive Therapy* 9, 6–13.

Roussos, G. G. (1978) Health implications of changing sources of dietary sugars. In: White, P. L. and Selvey, N. (eds.), *Nutrition in Transition. Proc. West. Hemis. Nutr. Congress V*, pp. 171–86. Chicago: Am. Med. Assoc.

Roy, D. N. (1981) Toxic amino acids and proteins from Lathyrus plants and other leguminous species. *Nutr. Abst. Rev.* 51, 691–707.

Scriver, C. R. (1982) Window panes of eternity. Health, disease, and inherited risk. *Yale J. Biol. Med.* 55, 487–513.

Shekelle, R. B., *et al.* (1981) Diet, serum cholesterol and death from coronary heart disease. The Western Electric Study. *New Engl. J. Med.* 304, 65–70, and *Commentary*, pp. 1168–9.

Swaminathan, M. (1974) *Essentials of Food and Nutrition*, vol. 1, pp. 398–404; vol. 2, pp. 117–32. Madras: Ganesh & Co.

Thomas, L. (1977) On the science and technology of medicine, *Daedalus*, Winter 1977, pp. 35–46.

U.S. Dept. of Agriculture (USDA), Agricultural Research Service (1957) *Essentials of an Adequate Diet*. Home Economics Research Report No. 3. Washington, D.C.: USDA.

US Department of Health, Education and Welfare (USDHEW) (1972) *Ten-State Nutrition Survey, 1968 to 1970*. Pub (HSM) 72-8130-8134. DHEW, Washington, D.C.

——, (1978) *Facts of Life and Death*. Washington, D.C.: DHEW Publication No. (HRA) 74-1222, Washington, D.C.

——, (1979) *Healthy People – The Surgeon General's Report on Health Promotion and Disease Prevention*. DHEW Publication No. 79-55071, U.S. Govt. Printing Office.

U.S. Dept. of State (USDS) (1982) *The Global 2000 Report to the President*. Washington, D.C.: Government Printing Office. New York, N.Y.: Penguin Books.

Van Italie, T. B. (1979) Obesity: the American disease. *Food Technol.* December, 43–7.

Wilson, J. Q. (1976) The public disenchantment. *Am. Scholar* 45, 356–9.

19

Why Cancer?

RICHARD PETO

Editors' Note

Cancer as such was not discussed in *Global 2000*; and this authoritative recent review is an abstract of a much longer report that was specially prepared for the U.S. Congress's Office of Technology Assessment rather than for this volume (so royalties for its republication are assigned to OXFAM). This review of cancer's chief causes is nevertheless included here for three reasons: (1) cancer is one of the main ill effects that are popularly supposed to flow from environmental pollution, and one of the main reasons given for efforts to abate pollution; (2) there is a great deal of misinformation about the relationship between the environment and cancer; (3) only recently has it become possible to obtain such a well-balanced assessment of cancer's chief causes. Details of the arguments on which this review is based may be found in "The Causes of Cancer", by Richard Doll and Richard Peto (Oxford University Press, 1981; also available in the *Journal of the National Cancer Institute* 66, 1191–308), and in the chapter by Doll and Peto in the 1983 *Oxford Textbook of Medicine*.

Another authoritative recent review, by Bruce Ames, surveyed the wide variety of carcinogens and anti-carcinogens in our diet, and concluded that the human dietary intake of "Nature's pesticides" is likely to be several grams per day. This level is likely to be at least 10,000 times higher than the dietary intake of man-made pesticides.[1]

What is "Cancer"?

The various human cancers are diseases in which one of the many cells of which the normal body is composed gets altered in such a way that it inappropriately replicates itself again and again, producing millions of similarly affected self-replicating descendant cells, some of which may spread to distant parts of the body and eventually overwhelm it.

For perhaps a century or more, medicine has considered cancers arising from different organs of the body as being in many respects completely different diseases, and over the past few decades it has become clear that not only their clinical manifestations and prognoses but also their causes may differ enormously. So, it makes as little sense to lump together cancers of the lung, stomach, and intestine when considering the causes of cancer as to lump together cholera, tuberculosis, and syphilis when considering infective diseases. In particular, it is *not* true that how one lives makes no difference to whether or not one gets cancer but "merely determines where in the body the disease will be found". On the contrary, there is no general reason to expect that prevention of one type of cancer will cause any kind of compensatory increase in the onset rate of any unrelated type of cancer among people of a given age.

Although there are dozens of types and hundred of sub-types of cancer, a few types predominate in each country – but the particular types that predominate in different countries may differ. In both the United States and Britain cancer of the lung predominates, due chiefly to cigarettes, followed by cancers of the breast, large intestine, and (in Britain) stomach, none of which are much affected by tobacco. Together, these four types account for more than half of all cancer deaths. So, one chief aim of cancer research should be to devise practical methods for reducing the incidence of one or more of these particular four diseases, because even large reductions in minor types of cancer can have only minor effects on the total impact of cancer.

International Differences: Cancers Must Have Causes

Of these four diseases (of the lung, breast, large intestine, and stomach) only for lung cancer has an important cause been reliably identified. Despite this, each is known to be largely preventable. The evidence for their preventability is first that the onset rates of some of them are changing rapidly; among Americans of a given age there have been only minor fluctuations in disease onset rates for cancers of the breast and of the large intestine over the past few decades, but in almost all developed countries there have been vast increases in lung cancer – at least among smokers – and vast decreases in stomach cancer among both smokers and non-smokers. Every 20 or 30 years lung cancer mortality has doubled and stomach cancer mortality halved in many countries, so – since there has been little change in the curability of these two diseases – large causes must exist.

Second, for these four and for many other types of cancer there are huge differences in the onset rates recorded in different countries. The international differences in lung and stomach cancer are not likely to be chiefly of genetic origin, and nor are those in the other two diseases. For, among people of a given age in different countries, strong correlations exist between certain dietary factors and the onset rates for cancers of the breast and large intestine (figures 19.1 and 19.2). These striking correlations do not necessarily mean that the particular dietary factors used in figures 19.1 and 19.2 (fat or meat) must be among the important causes of these diseases: they *may* be causative, but reasonably good correlations can also be found with things like the number of telephones per head! But, what one *can* conclude from the existence of such strong correlations is that some important non-genetic cause or causes must exist for these two diseases, even though – unlike the other two diseases – their onset rates have been fairly steady for the past half-century in many countries.

In figures 19.1 and 19.2, each point represents one country and the cancer rates per 100,000 women relate to women of similar age, so they are not materially affected by the greater risks of premature death from other causes in poor countries. The (generally prosperous) countries where meat or fat consumption is highest are those where women of a given age are at greatest risk of developing cancer of the colon or breast. But, although the explanation of this remains obscure, this is *not* strong

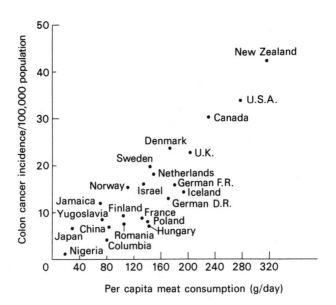

Figure 19.1 Relationship between meat consumption in various countries, and the risk, in those countries, of developing cancer of the colon. (The colon is the part of the large intestine where most cancers arise.)

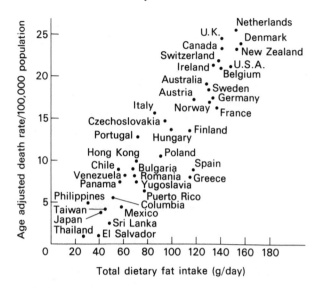

Figure 19.2 Relationship between fat consumption in various countries and the risk, in those countries, of death from breast cancer.

evidence that either fat or meat are important causes of these cancers; merely strong evidence that these cancers have causes.

Third, where migrants have been studied they generally develop internal cancer onset rates that are more similar to those of the population they have joined than to those of the genetically similar population in their country of origin. Comparisons of the cancer rates among blacks in the United States and blacks in West Africa, and comparisons of cancer rates among Japanese Americans and Japanese in Japan, show huge differences. This has been particularly true for cancers of the breast and large intestine, which again confirms that these two are both largely avoidable diseases. For example, at any given age cancer of the large intestine is approximately equally common among American whites and blacks, yet it is only about one-tenth as common among West African blacks.

Arguments based on such international comparisons suggest that about 90 percent of lung cancer and about 80–90 percent of breast cancer and large intestine cancer in Britain and American might be avoidable, and similar arguments for each other type of cancer suggest that in total at least 75 percent of all cases of internal cancer could be avoided by means that some populations have already adopted. Since there are presumably preventive strategies that no population happens yet to have tried, perhaps over 75 percent of cancer deaths in developed countries are in principle avoidable, although, apart from avoidance of tobacco, the important means of achieving this are far from being properly understood. The proportion of cancer deaths that will be found to be avoidable by practicable means is another question, since there are many aspects of the lifestyle in impoverished countries that people in affluent ones will not willingly adopt. For example, it has proved difficult enought to control the effects of tobacco, and it may prove even more difficult to control any dietary factors that turn out to be important determinants of cancer – except, perhaps, if the change involves prescription of a healthy foodstuff rather than proscription of an unhealthy one.

Ancient or Modern Causes?

So, most cancers have causes; but what may they be? Are they chiefly new, or old, aspects of our lifestyle or environment? Cancer is certainly much more talked about nowadays than in previous decades, but this is not of itself evidence that cancer rates among non-smokers of a given age are rising. Public awareness is influenced by the extensive media coverage of the growing body of cancer research; by the increasing willingness of cancer patients and their friends to discuss the disease openly rather than hush it up; by the substantial effects of tobacco on health and the publicity they receive; by the increasing numbers of people who live on into old age nowadays (cancer rates have always been far higher among the old than the young, so the more old people there are the more cancer deaths there will be, even if among people of a given age cancer onset rates were unchanged); and by the decrease in the toll taken by most other fatal diseases (as the percentage of deaths due to other diseases falls, even if the cancer rates do not change the percentage of deaths that are due to cancer must rise, and this will be noticed). For these and various other reasons, the increased public awareness of cancer and carcinogens cannot be taken as evidence for increasing cancer onset rates among people of a given age. More objective data must be sought.

Unfortunately, none of the available data are entirely satisfactory for the assessment of trends in cancer onset rates. Changes in the numbers of new cases (fatal or non-fatal) of cancer that are *recorded* are affected not only by changes in cancer onset rates but also by the changing degree of care with which non-fatal cancers are sought and their discovery recorded centrally. Likewise, changes in the numbers of deaths from cancer that are *recorded* are affected not only by changes in cancer onset rates and in the proportion of cancers that are cured, but also by the changing degree of care with which the causes of death – particularly of old people – are certified. Perhaps the best of the available data that bear on cancer onset rates are those relating to trends in *death* from various types of cancer during *middle* age, because although many cases of cancer are curable by surgery and radiotherapy, these treatments have both been widely available to middle-aged people for decades, and only for a few rather rare types of cancer have there been any large improvements demonstrated in curative treatment. For the common types of cancer, the likelihood of cure did not greatly improve between the 1950s and the early 1970s, and so in general the trends in mortality in figure 19.3 provide a fair indication of the corresponding real trends in disease onset rates.

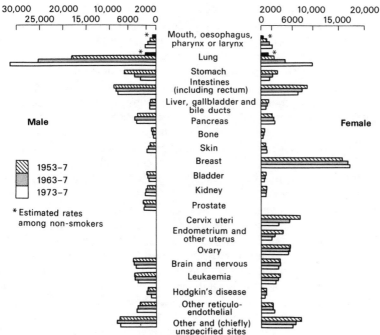

Annual deaths per 100 million Americans aged under 65

Figure 19.3 Trends during the past quarter-century in mortality from various types of cancer in the United States. Note the large increases in lung cancer mortality. Most of these trends (except for leukaemia and Hodgkin's disease) are not much affected by changes in treatment, for treatments for the common cancers were about as likely to effect cure in the 1950s as in the 1970s. All these death certification rates are "age-standardized", that is, they are adjusted for any effects of changes in the age structure of the U.S. population. The cited rates are per 100 million people under 65; since there are at present about 100 million Americans of each sex aged under 65, the cited rates are similar to the actual numbers of middle-aged Americans that die of these diseases each year.

No Generalized Increase in Cancer Among Non-smokers

Among American males the picture is dominated by the enormous and still increasing mortality from lung cancer, and there are also some smaller absolute increases in death from cancers of the mouth, throat, and larynx which, for obvious reasons, are the other parts of the body where tobacco greatly increases the risk of cancer. Apart from this, however, there is no indication of any generalized increase in non--respiratory-tract cancer, and indeed at one site – the stomach – a steady decrease has continued for at least half a century.

Among American females a similar picture emerges, except that the absolute increases in lung cancer will not be as clearly evident as among males for another decade or two, and that mortality from cancer of the uterus is also decreasing. This latter decrease chiefly involves mortality from cancer of the cervix (the neck of the uterus) rather than of the endometrium (the body of the uterus), but the former often gets confused with the latter on death certificates, causing what may be a largely artefactual decrease in endometrial cancer death certification rates.

It is known that the delayed effects of the adoption of cigarette smoking, which greatly increased during World War II in America, are the principal cause of the large current increases in lung cancer in that country. It is likely that improvements in genital hygiene, due to improved sanitation, have contributed to the decrease in cancer of the cervix, although in recent years cervical smears and prior hysterectomy have also helped. It is likely that some aspect of the modern American diet, possibly involving better food preservation, is chiefly responsible for the decrease in stomach cancer. However, apart from these changes there is, contrary to what many people imagine, no evidence of any generalized increase in cancer rates in the United States or Britain. Indeed, in Britain even the large increase in male lung cancer due to the delayed effects of the switch to cigarettes is virtually complete, so total UK cancer rates (including lung) are now slowly decreasing.

The fact that present-day cancer rates do not exhibit any generalized increase (apart from the effects of smoking) does not, of course, guarantee that all, or nearly all, of the recently introduced new chemicals, pesticides, pollutants, and habits are harmless. For, it may be decades before any cancer-causing effects they may have become clearly evident. Yet, it does guarantee that to concentrate on the scrutiny only of new environmental agents, to the exclusion of the investigation of long-established aspects of our way of life, is to ignore the possibility of preventing the continued occurrence of that mass of present-day cancers that are due to avoidable factors that must have characterized the lifestyle of much of the developed world at least throughout this century. Before discussing how we might set about investigating such factors, a review of what is already known about certain causes may be useful.

Common Misapprehensions: Infective and Genetic Factors

Although a few infective diseases may predispose to cancer, and the debility of advanced cancer may in turn predispose to some infection or other, cancer is not in general an infectious disease, and there is no reason to fear close contact with a cancer patient.

Also, although a few rare genetic conditions may strongly predispose to cancer, and some more common genetic conditions may less strongly predispose to cancer, there is no such thing as genetic immunity from cancer – although a remarkable number of smokers seem, at least in conversation, to believe they have it! In general, don't let the fact that a few of your relatives have died of cancer cause you undue fears about your own safety. Conversely, don't let the fact that your father or grandfather smoked forty cigarettes a day until the age of 90 lull you into a false sense of security. Cancer arises from three things: nature, nurture, and luck. In large populations the effect on internal cancer onset rates of nature and luck seem generally to average out and only nurture remain. So, study of cancer rates in relation to nurture tells us about the role of external factors, which is, both for government policy and for individual choices, the only thing of practical importance.

Tobacco

Observation of a few hundred thousand lifelong non-smokers for several years in the United States has revealed very low lung cancer rates. In contrast, in the United States as a whole some 95,000 people died of lung cancer in 1978. If the low lung cancer death rates among lifelong non-smokers had applied to the United States as a whole, only 12,000 would have died of the disease. Of course, people who are lifelong non-smokers may also differ in other ways from the lifestyle of the rest of the nation, but no such ways are known that are enormously relevant to lung cancer risks. So, it is reasonable to infer that, but for the effects of tobacco, only 10,000–15,000 Americans would have died of lung cancer in 1978. Consequently, tobacco must have caused about 80,000–85,000 American lung cancer deaths in 1978 – a figure which can be regarded as quite reliably known.[2] Similar arguments applied to other types of cancer that are affected by tobacco suggest that an additional 40,000 or so American cancer deaths were caused by tobacco. The 1978 total of 120,000–125,000 American cancer deaths due to tobacco is extremely large, and this annual total is still increasing by about 4,000 each year as the population ages and the delayed effects of past increases in cigarette use show up. Consequently, about 140-odd thousand cancer deaths will be caused by tobacco in 1984 – that is, about *one-third* of all American cancer deaths. For most people, this number is so large as to be literally incomprehensible. When it is remembered that in addition tobacco probably kills even more people by respiratory and heart disease than it does by cancer, it becomes clear how urgent it is that some means be sought of reducing the enormous number of premature deaths due to tobacco – about 300,000 per year, or 15 percent of all American deaths.

One possibility that bypasses many political difficulties is to encourage, perhaps by prevention of the advertising of cigarettes with more than 10 milligrams of tar, the continuing switch to lower-tar cigarettes, because there is accumulative evidence that these are indeed somewhat less carcinogenic (though there is no good evidence that they are less hazardous for respiratory and heart disease).

In Britain, where tobacco causes at least 100,000 out of our annual total of 600-odd thousand deaths, an alternative strategy that was, perhaps inadvertently, used to great effect in 1981 is to increase the real cost of cigarettes. It has been estimated that recent price increases, due chiefly to the 1981 budget, have caused between one and two million people in Britain to stop smoking. This may well save some hundreds of thousands of lives in the long run, because:

(1)	about a quarter of all regular cigarette smokers are killed before their time by tobacco;

(2)	some of those killed would have died soon anyway; but others would have lived on for another 5, 10, 20, 30 or more years, the average being 10–15 years;

(3)	those who stop smoking before they have got cancer or serious heart or lung disease avoid nearly all the risk of dying from tobacco.

A final course of action that may help a little is to try to make ordinary people appeciate these three facts. However, so far it is chiefly the more educated groups in Britain that have undergone a substantial change in their smoking habits since reliable evidence of the health hazard became available. (In Britain in 1980, 21 percent of professional people reported using cigarettes, compared with 57 percent of manual workers.) In America too, cigarette smoking is coming to show the same inverse social gradient as in Britain, with heavy smoking by unskilled workers.

However, in marked contrast with recent decreases in Britain, the

American cigarette industry had a record year in 1980/81 with the largest increase (2 percent) in cigarette sales for some years. Commenting on this, the chairman of the largest American cigarette manufacturer was reported as saying that he thought the "cancer problem" was no longer hitting sales as hard as before because "so many things have been linked to cancer" that people are getting sceptical. He may well be right, because only a remarkably perceptive citizen would guess, from a typical year's media coverage, that tobacco caused one-third of all cancer deaths, a total ten times greater than the next most important reliably known cause – and, indeed considerably greater than the number of deaths due to the total known effects of all other reliably known causes of cancer put together.

Alcohol

Alcohol too can cause cancer and probably accounts for about 12,000 cancer deaths every year in America. As an absolute number of people dying this too is large, but in comparison with the effect of tobacco it is much less significant. Expressed as a percentage, alcohol accounts for only 3 percent of all cancer deaths – chiefly cancers of the mouth, throat, and larynx. Alcohol appears to act chiefly by augmenting the effects of tobacco on these diseases. So, one person's cancer may have had more than one cause, and most of the cancers caused by alcohol could also have been avoided by avoidance of tobacco. Alcohol also causes many accidental and violent deaths, plus some deaths from liver disease, yet *moderate* use of alcohol may well prevent some deaths from heart disease. The net effects of alcohol on mortality are therefore substantially less – especially in view of the possible effect on heart disease – than those of tobacco.

Occupation

Dozens of occupations involve an excess risk of cancer, and probably many more occupational hazards still await discovery. As far as is known the worst such hazard is that due to asbestos dust which, because of its wide distribution, currently causes 1–2 percent of all cancer deaths. A tentative estimate may be made – by estimating for each sex the percent of each type of cancer that is due to occupation – that occupational factors account for about 4 percent of all American cancer deaths. Until more systematic evidence is sought, however, there is a two-fold uncertainty in this figure.

A growing source of difficulty in its estimation is the problem of making due allowance for the effects of tobacco. For example, single-handed general practitioners in Britain smoke more than hospital consultants, and get more lung cancer. Similarly, 10 years ago miners and quarrymen smoked nearly twice as much as administrators and managers, so the observation that they get nearly twice as much lung cancer is not evidence for any occupational hazard (except that of tobacco use). These contrasts will presumably be even greater in the future, because as public awareness of the hazards of tobacco has grown in Britain the professional classes have considerably reduced their cigarette consumption while unskilled workers have not. So, in the past decade the ratio of the percentage of cigarette smokers among unskilled manual workers to that among professional workers has increased from two-fold to three-fold. (Moreover, at least in America, manual workers tend to smoke cigarettes with higher tar contents.)

Despite various such uncertainties, however, there is no foundation for recent suggestions that 20–40 percent of all cancers are due to occupational factors. All these estimates appear to derive, directly or indirectly, from one unpublished American study which suffered from gross methodological defects that inflated the risk estimates by an order of magnitude. For example, its assumptions imply that, for two particular types of cancer, about 10 times as many cases should in theory be being caused by occupational factors in America than are actually observed in the whole United States from all cancers – occupational and other – of these two diseases! But, now that such rumours have begun to circulate they may continue to do so, because they are the sort of thing that many people would rather like to believe of the modern world, and in addition they are useful ammunition for people who wish, perhaps for good reasons, to emphasize the need for stronger unions or stronger legislative controls.

Returning to the more reasonable estimate that "only" a few percent of cancer deaths are due to occupational factors, the queston of what to do politically about such factors is still a difficult one. For, to control all occupational exposures to all chemicals is virtually impossible, while always to refuse to implement any controls until many workers have died, and many more have had the seeds of future cancers implanted in them, is barbarous. Laboratory tests must, despite the near-total qualitative uncertainty with which they predict human risk, somehow be used to help set priorities for the control of recent or future occupational exposure, but no wholly satisfactory way of utilitizing them has yet evolved. In the meantime, we could adopt a more systematic way of linking records of various occupational circumstances with cancer occurrence some decades later. Ths would probably bring forward substantially the time of recognition (and hence reduction) of at least a few occupational hazards, either of cancer or of some other disease.

Although both in America and Britain the proportion of all cancer deaths due to occupational factors may be "only" about 4 percent, the detection of occupational hazards should have a greater priority in any programme of cancer research than their proportional importance might suggest. For, once identified, it is usually practicable greatly to reduce such hazards.

Environmental Pollutants

The most important environmental pollutant has probably been urban air pollution by smoke, which may account – or have accounted – for as much as 1 percent of all cancer deaths, chiefly by enhancing the effects of tobacco on lung cancer. Tobacco smoking also complicated estimation of the effects of urban pollution, because there is little absolute difference between the lung cancer risks of urban and rural non-smokers, while the difference in risk between urban and rural smokers is in some instances as great for unpolluted as for polluted cities. This is perhaps because urban smokers have been exposed to cigarette smoke more intensively, or for a greater proportion of their adult lives, than rural smokers have. Fortunately, the great reduction in smoke levels over the past 25 years in many of the more heavily polluted cities means that the future effects of present levels of air pollution by smoke will probably be smaller than the present estimate of 1 percent, and on present evidence no other pollutants of air, food, or water seem likely to have any greater effects on current cancer rates. There is, however, too much uncertainty to justify complacency, especially about the hypothetical future effects of agents such as pesticides, herbicides, and food preservatives and sterilizants that must, of necessity, be used in biologically significant amounts.

Sexual Activity

Cancer of the uterine cervix is far commoner among prostitutes than nuns, because it appears chiefly to be caused by some sexually-transmitted infective agent – probably a virus (although perhaps not the herpes virus about which there have recently been such fears). Conversely, cancer of the breast is far commoner among nuns than prostitutes, since the earlier a woman becomes pregnant the lower her breast cancer risks will be in middle and old age. Risks for this and many other types of cancer appear to be influenced, either favourably or otherwise, by hormonal factors and deliberate favourable manipulation of these, or of some analogues of these, may ultimately be possible. Conversely, of course, inadvertent unfavourable manipulation of hormonal factors may occur. (Both of these possibilities are exemplified by recent studies on the oral contraceptive pill which suggest, with varying degrees of probability, that it can cause liver cancer, prevent ovarian cancer, cause cervical cancer, prevent endometrial cancer, cause breast cancer and prevent benign breast disease!)

Radiation

The three chief sources of radiation to which humans are exposed are sunlight; natural background radiation from minerals and cosmic rays; and the medical use of X-rays and radiotherapy. Assuming most skin cancer deaths are due to sunlight, and using current international estimates of radiation hazards, these three, together with the much smaller amounts from all other sources, probably account for about 3 percent of all cancer deaths. Only about 1 percent could reasonably be described as "avoidable", however – those due to unneccessary medical procedures or to excessive exposure to sunlight. (Since radiation from the military and civil nuclear industry amounts to less than 1 percent of background radiation, prolonged exposure to such levels would presumably account for only about 0.01 percent of future cancer deaths.)

Last But Not Least

Nutritional and other dietary factors are a chronic source of both frustration and excitement to epidemiologists. For many years there has been strong but indirect evidence that most of the types of cancer that are currently common could be substantially reduced by "suitable" modification of national eating habits. This remains extremely plausible, but there is still no precise and reliable evidence to show exactly what dietary changes would be of major importance. The chief need is therefore simply for continued research rather than prophylactic action. However, on present evidence a switch in developed countries towards a diet lower in animal products, particularly fat, and higher in plant products, particularly fibre, might be prudent.

Various particular types of fat, various particular types of dietary fibre or other carbohydrates, and various vitamins, trace elements and other micronutrients have been suspected of increasing or decreasing human cancer risks. Many of them can certainly have a profound effect on "spontaneous" cancer risks among experimental animals, as well as on the response of such animals to cancer-causing agents. However, in humans the role of such nutrients remains uncertain, though this may perhaps simply be because nobody has yet looked at the human evidence in the right way.

For example, consider the micronutrient beta-carotene, a yellow substance found in carrots and in certain dark green leafy vegetables. Of twenty epidemiological studies in various parts of the world, eighteen have indicated that people who eat more carotene than average have below-average cancer risks. Why? Is beta-carotene itself truly protective, is some other aspect of a vegetable-rich diet truly protective, or is such a diet merely an indicator of avoidance of some other truly harmful dietary factors? In general, how can we make progress from such suggestive but inconclusive observations towards reliable knowledge? Fortunately, human beings are a wild species, and no matter what habit it is that you want to study, you may find some group of humans somewhere in the world who are already doing it, and Alex Kalache, working in Oxford for the Imperial Cancer Research Fund, has investigated (with rather disappointing results) a remarkable natural experiment in Brazil, where one particular type of cooking oil that some but not all people use habitually is enormously rich in beta-carotene. In Boston, Charlie Hennekens is testing the effects of deliberately adding beta-carotene to the diets of apparently healthy people, and in America, Finland and elsewhere various agencies are collaborating to discover whether blood carotene levels are inversely predictive of future cancer risks.

If even half the difference in cancer risk between people with differing blood-carotene intake were indeed due to a protective effect of beta-carotene then this would be one of the more important findings in cancer research since the effects of tobacco were discovered – relevant perhaps to 10 or 20 percent of all cancer deaths. So, even though a successful outcome may not be probable, the fact that it is at least possible justifies these investigations. Also, even if carotene itself is not protective, some other dietary factors may well exist that really do cause the differences in cancer risk that are associated with carotene intake. Identification of these could similarly be relevant to 10 or 20 percent of all cancers.

Many dietary hypotheses await evaluation; some – such as the possible protective role of pentose-rich fibres – seeming already somewhat more promising than carotene. If the top ten or twenty are evaluated as carefully as carotene is now being evaluated, at least one or two ought to be confirmed. Consequently, it is reasonable to expect that dietary factors will eventually be found to have a major role in the avoidability of cancer, especially in view of the evidence summarised by Ames (1983).[1]

TABLE 19.1 FUTURE PERFECT. ESTIMATE OF THE PROPORTIONS OF CANCER DEATHS THAT WILL BE FOUND TO BE ATTRIBUTABLE TO VARIOUS FACTORS

	Percentage of all U.S. cancer deaths	
	Best estimate	Range of acceptable estimates
Tobacco	30	25–40
Alcohol	3	2–4
Diet	35	10–70
Food additives	<1	−5[b]–2
Sexual behaviour	1	1
Yet-to-be-discovered hormonal analogues of reproductive factors	−6	−12–0
Occupation	4	2–8
Pollution	2	1–5
Industrial products	<1	<1–2
Medicine and medical procedures	1	0.5–3
Geophysical factors (mostly natural background radiation and sunlight)	3	2–4
Infective processes	10?	1–?
Unknown	?[a]	?
Total	200% or more?[a]	

[a] Since one cancer may have two or more causes, the grand total in such a table will probably, when more knowledge is available, greatly exceed 200%. (It is merely a coincidence that the suggested figures in the present table happen to add up to nearly 100%.)
[b] The net effects of food additives may be protective, e.g. against stomach cancer.

Current and Developing Knowledge of Causes

Reasonable estimates and guesstimates of the likely roles of various factors discussed in this article are drawn together in table 19.1. This table is, however, not a summary of firm knowledge, but merely a prediction of what future research may reveal. If instead we were to tabulate what is reliably known (table 19.2) the resulting picture would be very different and far less promising. If the perspective on the causes of cancer suggested by these two tables is at least approximately correct, then the chief need is to do something about smoking, and to get reliable information about the effects of dietary, hormonal, and infective factors on human cancer – and, of course, on other human diseases. Towards this end, two rather opposite strategies may be envisaged, the *mechanistic* and the *black box* strategies.

TABLE 19.2 PRESENT IMPERFECT. RELIABLY ESTABLISHED (AS OF 1984), PRACTICABLE* WAYS OF AVOIDING THE ONSET OF LIFE-THREATENING CANCER

	Percentage of U.S. cancer deaths known to be thus avoidable
Avoidance of tobacco smoke	30
Avoidance of alcoholic drinks or mouthwashes	3
Avoidance of obesity	2
Regular cervical screening and genital hygiene	1
Avoidance of inessential medical use of hormones or radiology	<1
Avoidance of unusual exposure to sunlight	<1
Avoidance of known effects of current levels of exposure to carcinogens (for which there is good epidemiological evidence of human hazard) in	
(i) occupational context	<1
(ii) food, water, or urban air	<1

*Excluding ways such as prostatectomy, mastectomy, hysterectomy, oophorectomy, artificial menopause, or pregnancy.

Research Strategies: Progress from Ignorance?

The laboratory-based *mechanistic* strategy tries to discover how normal cells turn into cancer cells, and what agents cause this, inhibit it, or prevent the growth of cancer. The trouble is, of course, that there may be many qualitatively different ways of turning normal cells into cancer cells, with the ones that matter being those that underlie the common cancers; and, there is no guarantee whatever that the mechanisms of cancerous change that are currently being investigated in the laboratory do not differ so greatly from those that importantly affect people as to make the related laboratory findings of no direct human relevance. To underline these difficulties, laboratory studies have thus far failed to identify reliably which are the important carcinogens and co-carcinogens in tobacco smoke, and have consistently failed to reproduce in animals the carcinogenic effects in humans of alcohol.

By contrast, the epidemiologically based *black box* strategy tries to identify as many correlates, or inverse correlates, of human cancer risk as possible, without understanding exactly how cancer arises. Not all correlates point to true causes, of course; indeed, most of them do not. But, having identified many correlates or inverse correlates, it is reasonable to hope that further investigation of them, probably in collaboration with laboratory scientists, will lead to identification of a few truly causative or truly protective factors with respect to which humans already differ.

Thus far the *black box* approach has yielded by far the most important findings, including both the role of tobacco (which was discovered before even the structure of DNA was known, let alone the agents or mechanisms by which DNA is damaged) and also the reasons for expecting that a few more large causes still await discovery. However, although epidemiology continues to yield a stream of discoveries of minor causes of human cancer, it seems to be rather bogged down in its search for major discoveries. Indeed, in the quarter of a century since the discovery of the role of tobacco no other really major causes of cancer in developed countries have been *reliably* identified, although a major role of quid-chewing in Asian oral cancer and of hepatitis B and, probably, aflatoxin in tropical liver cancer, have been demonstrated. If dietary factors are as important as has been suggested, then perhaps the search for dietary correlates of cancer should progress from studies based, as in the past, chiefly on questionnaires, to studies based chiefly on biochemical analyses of biological materials such as blood. Most dietary factors have measurable efffects on the blood, and it would be interesting to discover which biochemical factors in apparently healthy people are correlated or inversely correlated with future cancer risks.

Somewhere there are undoubtedly major causes of cancer, and of many other diseases, awaiting discovery. All we need to do is ask the right questions in the right way in order to discover practicable ways of preventing the majority of the many deaths in middle age that still occur in developed countries. A search for biochemical correlates of disease is just one way of approaching such questions. Different scientists working in this area might have quite different views about the likely nature of future discoveries, and therefore about which research activities should receive the greatest priority. This fissiparous range of divergent opinions should not be used as evidence that the scientific method is faltering. On the contrary, too great a consensus about where we should go would be dangerous. The sometime acrimonious spectrum of opinions is one of the most valuable scientific assets when, as in the study of diet and chronic disease, all we know for certain is that we don't know very much for certain.

Notes

1   Bruce Ames, "Dietary carcinogens and anti-carcinogens"; *Science*, 23 September 1983, **221**, 1256–1264.
2   It does not, however, include the 5,000–10,000 Americans who, although actually dying of cigarette-induced lung cancer, were certified as having died of cancer of an "unspecified" site of primary origin. These will be counted eventually among the other types of cancer affected by tobacco.

20

The Hazards of
Nuclear Power

BERNARD L. COHEN

How well does the American public understand the hazards of nuclear power?

In a recent study in Oregon, groups of college students and members of the League of Women Voters were asked to rank 30 technologies and activities according to the "present risk of death" they pose to the average American.[1] Both groups ranked nuclear power No. 1, well ahead of motor vehicles which kill about 50,000 Americans each year, cigarette smoking which kills 150,000, and eleven others that kill over 1,000. How many can be expected to die annually from generation of nuclear power including the risk of accidents, radioactive waste, and all of the other dangers we hear so much about? According to estimates developed by government-sponsored research programs, about *ten* per year.[2] If you don't trust "the establishment", you might trust the leading anti-nuclear activist organization in the United States, the Union of Concerned Scientists (UCS), which estimates an average of 120 deaths per year[3] from nuclear power. In either case, it is obvious that nuclear power is perceived to be thousands of times more dangerous than it actually is, even by college students and League of Women Voters members who are well above average intelligence, education, and awareness of public issues.

A poll by the Opinion Research Corp.[4] found that about 80 percent of the American public believes that it is more dangerous to generate electricity from nuclear power than by burning coal. The relative danger of nuclear and coal-burning electricity generation is basically a scientific question; it has been dealt with by many scientific studies. All of them agree that, contrary to public opinion, coal is the more dangerous.[5] This includes studies sponsored by the U.S. National Academy of Sciences, the American Medical Association, the United Kingdom Health and Safety Executive, the Norwegian Ministry of Oil and Energy, the State Legislatures of Maryland and of Michigan, and many others. It has been conceded by the anti-nuclear activist UCS, by its Director Henry

Kendall,[6] and privately even by Mr. Anti-Nuke, Ralph Nader.[7] I know of no study that has reached the opposite conclusion, that nuclear is more dangerous than coal. In a 1981 magazine article,[8] I offered a $50 reward for information leading to my discovery of such a study, but in all this time no-one has tried to claim that reward. Clearly the 80 percent of the American public that believes coal burning to be safer than nuclear energy is *grossly misinformed.*

A recent poll[9] shows that 56 percent of the American public is opposed to having a nuclear power plant in their own community, whereas another[10] shows that this opinion is shared by only 31 percent of all scientists, by only 20 percent of scientists specializing in fields related to energy, and by only 2 percent of scientists specializing in radiation or nuclear science. This poll also shows that 89 percent of all scientists, and 95 percent of all scientists involved in energy-related fields, favor proceeding with the development of nuclear power, while among the public there is only a slight majority in favor.

Clearly, there is an enormous amount of public misunderstanding about nuclear power. I attribute this largely to four basic problems:

(1)   wildly exaggerated fear of radiation;
(2)   a highly distorted picture of reactor accidents;
(3)   grossly unjustified fears about disposal of radioactive waste;
(4)   failure to understand and quantify risk.

These problems are the subject of the remainder of this chapter.

Radiation

How dangerous is radiation?

Radiation consists of subatomic particles travelling at speeds 100,000 times faster than bullets fired from a rifle. They can readily penetrate deep inside the human body where a typical particle of radiation drastically alters 100,000 of the molecules of which our bodies are composed. Any one of these molecular alterations can develop into a cancer, or can cause genetic disease in later generations.

From this description it sounds as though being struck by a particle of radiation is a terrible tragedy. However, this cannot be so because every person on earth, and every person who has ever lived, has been struck by about a million particles of radiation every minute of his life from natural sources – cosmic rays coming down from outer space, and emissions from naturally radioactive materials in the ground, in our bodies, in the air we breathe, in the food we eat, and in various materials around us.

This radiation we are exposed to from natural sources is hundreds of times larger than the well-publicized radiation we may someday receive from the nuclear power industry. Moreover, natural radiation exposure varies considerably with geography and other factors. In Colorado, where the high altitude reduces the thickness of air that shields us from radiation coming from outer space and where the amount of uranium and thorium in the ground is abnormally large, the average exposure from natural sources is more than 50 percent *larger* than the national average; in Florida, it is 20 percent *below* average. Choice of building materials can have a substantial effect on radiation exposure. Living in a brick or stone house typically results in 20 percent higher exposure than living in a wood house, and some particular building materials, like the granite used in New York's Grand Central Station and in the Congressional office buildings in Washington, DC, can more than double exposure of those working in them.

Besides natural radiation, to which mankind has always been exposed, there is an important new source of radiation introduced in this century: medical X-rays. A typical X-ray exposes us to 100 billion particles of radiation, or about one fourth as much radiation exposure as the average American receives annually from natural sources. This is hundreds of times more radiation than we can ever expect to receive from the nuclear industry. Many X-rays are not made for medical purposes, but to protect hospitals and physicians against libel suits.

If we are all being struck by a million particles of radiation every minute, why don't we all develop cancer at an early age? The reason we don't is not because this level of radiation is "safe." Even a single particle of radiation can cause cancer, but the probability for it to do so is very small, about one chance in 40 quadrillion (i.e., 40 million billion). Hence, the million particles that strike us each minute have only one chance in 40 billion of causing a cancer. A human lifespan is about 40 million minutes; thus, all of the natural radiation to which we are exposed has one chance in 1000 (40 million/40 billion) of causing a cancer. Statistics show that our overall chance of dying from cancer is one in five, so only one in 200 of all cancers may be due to natural radiation.

The average exposure from a nuclear power plant to those who live closest to it is about 1 percent of their exposure to natural radiation; hence, if they live there for a lifetime, there is one chance in 100,000 that they will die of cancer as a result of exposure to radiation from the nuclear plant.

Scientific basis for risk estimates

How do we know these risks so quantitatively? Few fields of science have been investigated as thoroughly as the health effects of radiation. The

U.S. government has spent over $2 billion on this research since World War II, which has helped to produce over 40,000 scientific papers. Radiation-measuring techniques are well developed, highly accurate, extremely sensitive, and relatively cheap. Even student laboratories have instruments capable of detecting radiation levels millions of times lower than those normally associated with harm to health. By contrast, many air pollutants are quite difficult to measure even at 10 percent harmful levels.

Several prestigious scientific groups, notably the U.S. National Academy of Sciences Committee on Biological Effects of Ionizing Radiation (BEIR), the United Nations Scientific Committee on Effects of Atomic Radiation (UNSCEAR), the International Commission on Radiological Protection (ICRP), and the U.S. National Council on Radiation Protection and Measurements (NCRP), provide frequent summaries and evaluations of available data and recommend future research directions. Since 1977, BEIR,[11] UNSCEAR,[12] and ICRP[13] have all issued reports assessing the cancer risk from low-level radiation. We shall now review their methodology.

Radiation doses are expressed in millirem (mr), with each mr roughly equivalent to 5 billion particles of radiation. The average dose from natural radiation is about 100 mr per year, and medical X-rays give the average American an additional 40 mr per year. The above-mentioned studies by BEIR, UNSCEAR, and ICRP estimated that there should be one extra cancer for every 8 million mr of exposure to humans; or equivalently, every mr of exposure produces a 1-in-8-million chance of developing a fatal cancer.

The health effects of high-level radiation are rather well known.[11,12] Among the survivors of the atomic bomb attacks on Japan, there were 24,000 people who received an average exposure of 130,000 mr; about 120 extra cancers developed among them up to 1974. There were 15,000 British patients treated with X-rays for ankylosing spondylitis (arthritis of the spine) with doses averaging 370,000 mr; they had about 115 extra cancers. More than 900 Germans were treated for that same disease and for bone tuberculosis with injections of radium giving them an average of 4.4 million mr to the bone; 45 developed bone cancer (vs. 0.1 normally expected). About 1,700 American women employed during the 1920s painting radium on watch dial numerals used their tongues to put a fine tip on the brush, thereby allowing radium to enter their bodies; their average bone dose was 17 million mr, and 48 of them died of bone cancer (vs. 0.4 normally expected). Among 4,100 U.S. uranium miners exposed to excess levels of naturally radioactive radon gas due to poor mine ventilation, the average exposure to bronchial surfaces was 4.7 million mr, and up to 1972 there were 135 lung cancer deaths among them (vs. 16 normally expected). There have been several other miner groups that have experienced excess lung cancers, such as the group of 800 Canadian fluorspar miners whose average bronchial exposure was 2.8 million mr, resulting in 51 lung cancer deaths (vs. 2.8 expected). Finally, there have been a number of situations where high exposures have resulted in approximately 10 extra cancers: women in a Nova Scotia tuberculosis sanitarium exposed to excessive X-rays in the course of fluoroscopic examinations; U.S. women treated with X-rays for inflammation of the breasts following childbirth; American children treated with X-rays for enlargement of the thymus gland; patients in several countries fed a thorium compound to aid in X-ray contrast studies; and Marshall Islands natives exposed to fallout from a nuclear bomb test.

If one wants to find similar information on low-level radiation, however, statistical problems become severe. For example, suppose one found a group of 10,000 white males who had received an extra 10,000 mr of whole-body radiation. The easiest evidence to find would be excess leukemias because that disease develops earliest and is among the most sensitive to radiation. As a first approximation, we might use the results of high-level radiation studies, which show that leukemias are induced at a rate of about 1.0×10^{-9}/year per mr of exposure. We would then expect $(10,000 \times 10,000 \times 10^{-9}) = 0.1$ extra leukemias per year among this group. In the absence of radiation, one would expect 0.88 leukemias if we take statistics for the entire U.S. In the 25 years over which radiation is effective in causing leukemias, we then expect 22 ± 4.7 cases from natural causes versus 2.5 from the 10,000 mr radiation exposures. (The $\pm$ indicates the range of variations expected due to statistical fluctuations. If studies were made on a large number of groups, two-thirds of the results should lie between $(22 - 4.7) = 17.3$ and $(22 + 4.7) = 26.7$.) Obviously, the statistics here are marginal at best. However, the problem goes much deeper, since the total U.S. population is not a suitable control group. Cancer is largely caused by environmental factors and hence is subject to wide variations in incidence rates. For instance, the 0.88 leukemias expected for the U.S. in the absence of radiation varies from 1.0 in Minnesota and District of Columbia to 0.77 in Maine and New Mexico. This could vary the number of expected cases from 19 to 25, making it still more difficult to ascertain that there are two or three extra. Moreover, a group of people with 10,000 mr of extra radiation would typically have more environmental factors in common than merely living in the same state.

Therefore, any experimental study of effects of low-level radiation would need large populations and there would be considerable difficulty in selecting a control group. One way to achieve large numbers of subjects would be to use variations in natural radiation. For example, we could select citizens of Colorado, Wyoming, and New Mexico, who are exposed to about 5,000 mr more than the U.S. average over their lifetimes. However, the leukemia rates in these states are considerably below the U.S. average: 8.11 versus 8.81×10^{-5}/year for white males and 5.13 versus 5.74 for white females. The same is true for all cancers. The high natural radiation states have annual rates of 140×10^{-5} for white males and 114×10^{-5} for white females, while the U.S. average is 174 and 130 respectively. The fact that states with high natural radiation have considerably lower cancer rates than average is generally dismissed as indicating only that radiation is very far from being the principal cause of cancer. (This point is logically correct. Nevertheless, I am highly skeptical about whether that attitude would be accepted if states with high natural radiation happened to have somewhat higher than average cancer rates.)

Since there is little direct evidence on effects of low-level radiation, the simplest option is to obtain estimates from our abundant data on effects of high-level radiation, by assuming a linear dose–effect relationship. For example, if high-level dose D causes a cancer risk R, we assume that a dose $0.1\,D$ will cause a risk $0.1\,R$, and so on down to extremely low doses.

This linear risk vs dose relationship is nearly always used, with relatively minor variations, to estimate effects of low-level radiation. Moreover, when its use is recommended by the above-mentioned groups, it is accompanied by a statement that this is more likely to overestimate than to underestimate the effects of low-level radiation, and the minor variations from linear behavior often used[11] are such as to reduce, moderately, the effects at low levels. This may be described graphically by stating that the curve of cancer risk vs radiation dose is concave upward, i.e. it curves upward at high dose from a simple straight line.

The evidence supporting this viewpoint is as follows:[14]

(1) *Mechanism for radiation-induced cancer.* While there are many gaps and uncertainties in our understanding of the process by which radiation induces cancer, the general outline is reasonably clear, well supported by auxiliary experimental evidence, and widely accepted; it predicts a risk vs dose curve which is concave upward.

(2) *Chromosome damage.* Radiation induces cancer by damaging molecules of which chromosomes are composed. It sometimes does types of damage to these chromosomes that can be observed under a microscope. The curve of chromosome damage vs dose is concave upward.

(3) *Transformation to malignancy in mouse embryo cells.* Radiation can induce transformation to malignancy in mouse embryo cells grown in culture on laboratory dishes. The curve of frequency of transformation to malignancy vs dose is concave upward.

(4) *Radiation-induced cancer in laboratory animals.* Accurate data are available on radiation-induced cancer in laboratory animals.

In these studies the curve of cancer incidence vs dose is generally concave upward.

(5) *Leukemia among A-bomb survivors.* Leukemia is a type of cancer which is especially sensitive to radiation and tends to occur relatively soon after the exposure. Among the Japanese A-bomb survivors there were numerous cases among those exposed to high radiation doses but far less than expected from a linear risk vs dose relationship at lower doses, indicating a cancer risk vs radiation dose that is concave upward.

(6) *Bone cancer among radium dial painters.* Among the American women who ingested radium while painting radium on watch dials, there were fewer cases in the low-dose category than would be expected from a linear extrapolation from higher-dose data. The probability that this deficiency is due to statistical fluctuation is only a few percent.

(7) *Environmental radon exposure.* If the data on lung cancer among miners exposed to radon gas are extrapolated linearly to the doses received by the general population from environmental radon, they predict higher rates of lung cancer among non-cigarette smokers than are actually observed. Moreover, 50 percent of the extra lung cancers among the miners were of one particular type (small cell undifferentiated), whereas only 5 percent of lung cancers among non-smokers are of this type. When allowance is made for other causes of lung cancer among non-smokers, the discrepancy is even larger. This is strong evidence that a linear risk vs dose relationship overestimates effects at low doses.

(8) *Latent period increase with decreasing dose.* The time delay between exposure to radiation and development of the resulting cancer, called the "latent period," seems to increase as doses decrease. There is evidence for this among the radium dial painters and in several animal studies. For example, beagle dogs whose bones were exposed to 100 million mr developed bone cancer in an average of 2–3 years, whereas those exposed to 5 million mr developed bone cancer only after about 10 years, which is nearly a full life expctancy. From this trend we would expect cancer from low doses not to develop until long after the would-be victim has died from other causes. If this is true, low-level radiation becomes essentially harmless.

There have been a few papers purporting to give evidence that the cancer risk vs dose curve is concave downward, which would indicate that the linear assumption *under*-estimates the risk of low-level radiation. Each of these papers, however, has been severely criticized in the scientific literature, and none of them has received any degree of acceptance. They have been rejected by all groups charged with responsibilities in radiation protection.

Routine emissions from the nuclear industry

When a nuclear power plant is operating normally there are small quantities of radioactive gases and contaminants in water routinely released into the environment. More importantly, when the reactor fuel is chemically reprocessed, more radioactive gases are released at the reprocessing plant.

These routine releases have been studied in extensive detail[12] and great effort and expense have been applied to keep them as small as possible. Currently, the average American receives a radiation exposure less than 0.05 mr per year from these releases, but if all of our electricity were derived from nuclear power the average exposure would be about 0.2 mr per year. If this is multiplied by the U.S. population (2.3×10^8 people) and the cancer risk $1/(8 \times 10^6)$, we find that this might cause about six extra cancers each year in the United States, or about 0.02 for each year of operation of a large power plant. (We take a large power plant to be 1 million kilowatts, which is capable of powering a city of about 750,000 and refer to the effects of 1 year of its operation as effects/plant-year). Some of the radioactive gases released drift around the world exposing people in other countries. This raises the fatality toll to 0.1/plant-year over the next 500 years. If we add up effects into the infinite future, the result is 0.3 eventual fatalities per plant-year. These numbers are far below typical estimates of effects of air pollution from coal burning, which are about 25 fatalities per plant-year.[15]

Reactor Accidents

Many people are under the impression that a nuclear reactor can explode like an atomic bomb. It is very easy to prove with technical arguments that this is absolutely impossible, and this point is always conceded by anti-nuclear activists such as Ralph Nader. A story about nuclear power illustrated with a picture of a mushroom cloud is pure propaganda.

The fuel in a nuclear reactor is highly radioactive, but under normal circumstances this presents little danger because it is always surrounded by thick shielding material which stops the radiation. However, if there should be an accident in which the reactor fuel is melted, the more volatile components of the radioactivity could possibly escape from the plant and come in contact with the public, causing serious health consequences. This is the widely publicized reactor meltdown accident.

A nuclear power plant includes many levels of protection against such an eventuality, based on a "defense in depth" design philosophy. For example, such an accident could be initiated by a sudden rupture in the system allowing the cooling water to escape. The levels of protection against this are:

(1) The highest quality standards on materials and equipment in which such a rupture might occur.

(2) Elaborate inspection programs to detect flaws in the system using X-ray, ultrasonic, and visual techniques.

(3) Leak-detection systems of several types. Normally a rupture starts out as a small crack, allowing water to leak out slowly. Such leaks would be detected by these systems and repaired before a rupture could occur.

(4) Emergency cooling systems, which would rapidly replace the water lost in such a rupture accident, thereby restoring cooling to the reactor fuel. In this type of accident there are several different pumping systems, any one of which would provide sufficient water to avert a meltdown if all the others were somehow disabled.

(5) The containment, a powerful building in which the reactor is housed, which would normally hold the released radioactivity inside even if there were a meltdown.

Occasionally there is a failure at some power plant in one of these lines of defense – e.g. a valve that should be open is found to be closed – and this is often reported by the media as a near miss on a disaster. They just don't seem to understand the "defense in depth" concept. Of course it is possible that each line of defense will fail, one after the other, leading to a bad accident, but the probability of such a sequence of failures is very low. Moreover, the same reasoning applies to almost any other technology; in supplying gasoline to fuel our motor vehicles, for example, a sequence of highly improbable events can easily lead to a disaster such as burning down a large city, killing most of the inhabitants.

When all is said and done, how large is the risk to the public from a reactor meltdown accident? We give two estimates, one by a large study group sponsored by the U.S. Nuclear Regulatory Commission (NRC),[16] and the other by the Union of Concerned Scientists (UCS),[3] the most prominent anti-nuclear activist organization.

For the frequency of reactor meltdowns, NRC estimates one per 20,000 plant-years, whereas the UCS estimate is one per 2,000 plant-years. After more than 1,000 plant-years of commercial operation around the world and over 2,000 equivalent plant-years of naval reactor operation, all without a meltdown, the UCS estimate implies that we are lucky we haven't had one yet.

There is a widespread misunderstanding of the consequences of a meltdown. We often hear that it would kill tens of thousands of people and contaminate a whole state, but such statements are grossly misleading. The "containment" building would ordinarily contain the radioactive dust inside long enough (about 1 day) to clean it out of the air. For example, investigators of the Three Mile Island accident[17] all agree that even if there had been a meltdown, there would have been little harm to the public, because there is no reason to believe that the integrity of the containment would have been compromised. In most meltdowns no fatalities are expected.

There are events that could break open the containment, releasing radioactive dust into the environment, and if this happens the consequences depend on the timing and on weather conditions. In the most unfavorable conditions with a large containment break early in the accident, NRC estimates 48,000 fatalities, but this unusual combination is expected only once in 100,000 meltdowns.

According to NRC the average number of fatalities in a reactor meltdown is 400; according to UCS it is 5,000. A median estimate of the fatality rate due to air pollution from coal-burning is about 10,000 each year.[15] For reactor meltdowns to be as harmful as coal-burning, we would therefore need a meltdown every 2 weeks according to NRC, or every 6 months according to UCS. No-one has suggested that meltdowns will occur anywhere near that frequently.

When the frequency and consequence estimates are combined, NRC concludes that we may expect an average of 0.02 fatalities per plant-year; UCS predicts 2.4. Note that even the latter figure given by the leading anti-nuclear activist organization is still far less than the 25 fatalities per plant-year due to air pollution from coal-burning electricity generation.[15]

Of course these fatalities from air pollution are not detectable in the U.S. population in which 2 million people die every year. But the same is true of 98 percent of the fatalities from reactor meltdown accidents. For example, in the worst such accident considered by NRC, there would be 45,000 extra cancer deaths in a population of 10 million over 50 years. For each of these 10 million, the risk of dying from cancer would be increased from the normal risk of 20 percent to 20.5 percent. The present risk in different states varies between 16 percent and 24 percent, so the cancer risk in moving from one state to another is often many times larger than the risk from being involved in the worst nuclear accident.

Detectable fatalities occurring shortly after the accident and clearly attributable to it are rather rare. According to NRC, 98 percent of all meltdowns would cause no detectable fatalities, the average number for all meltdowns is 10, and the worst meltdown in the NRC analysis (a one in

100,000 occurrence) would cause 3,500. The largest coal-related incident to date was an air pollution episode in London in 1952 that caused 3,500 fatalities within a few days. Thus, as far as detectable fatalities are concerned, the worst nuclear accident in 100,000 meltdowns has already been equalled by coal burning.

The extent of land contamination in a reactor meltdown accident depends on one's definition of "contamination." The whole earth can be said to be contaminated because there is naturally occurring radioactivity everywhere. Many areas like Colorado can be considered contaminated because they have larger than normal natural radiation levels.

But if we use the internationally accepted definition of the level of contamination that calls for remedial action, the worst meltdown (one in 10,000) considered by NRC would contaminate an area equal to a circle of 30-mile radius. About 90 percent of this could be easily de-contaminated by use of fire hoses and plowing open fields, so the area where relocation of people is necessary would be equal to that of a 10-mile radius circle.

Forced relocation of people is not an unusual circumstance. It occurs in building dams where large areas are permanently flooded, in highway construction, in urban development, etc. In such situations the major consideration is the cost of relocating the people. Therefore, it seems reasonable to consider land contamination by a nuclear accident on the basis of its monetary cost.

According to NRC, the cost in the worst 0.01 percent of accidents can exceed $15 billion, but the average cost for all meltdowns is $100 million. Air pollution from coal burning also does property damage by soiling clothes, disintegrating building materials, inhibiting vegetation growth, etc. Estimates of the annual costs of this damage are in the range of $600 million per year.[18] At an average of $100 million per meltdown, we would need a reactor meltdown every 2 months to be as costly as the property damage from coal burning.

Radioactive Waste

There are several types of radioactive waste generated by the nuclear industry, but we will confine our attention to the two most important and potentially dangerous of these, the "high-level waste" and radon problems.

High-level waste[19]

When the fuel from a nuclear reactor has been mostly burned up, it is removed from the reactor. Currently, the plan is to ship it to a re-processing plant where it would be put through chemical procedures to remove the valuable components. The residual material, which contains nearly all of the radioactivity produced in the reactor, is called high-level waste. Concern has been raised about its disposal.

One important aspect of the high-level waste disposal question is the quantities involved: the waste generated by one large nuclear power plant in 1 year is about 6 cubic yards. This waste is 2 million times smaller by weight, and billions of times smaller by volume, than wastes from a coal-burning plant. The electricity generated by a nuclear plant in a year sells for more than $400 million, so if only 1 percent of the sales price were diverted to waste disposal, $4 million might be spent to bury this waste. Obviously, some very elaborate protective measures can be afforded.

Once the radioactive waste is buried, the principal concern is that it will be contacted by groundwater, dissolved into solution, and moved with the groundwater to the surface where it can get into food and drinking water supplies. How dangerous is this material to eat or drink? To explain this, we will take the quantity that would have to be ingested to give a person a 50 percent chance of death. When the waste is first buried it is highly toxic and a fatal dose is only 0.01 ounce. However, the radio-activity decays with time, so that after 600 years a fatal dose is about 1 ounce, making it no more toxic than some things kept in homes. After 10,000 years a lethal dose is 10 ounces.

When some people hear that nuclear waste must be carefully isolated for a few hundred years, they react with alarm. They point out that very few man-made structures, and few of our political, economic, and social institutions can be expected to last for hundreds of years. Such worries stem from our experience on the surface of the earth, where most things are short-lived. However, 2,000 feet below the surface the environment is quite different. Things remain essentially unchanged for millions of years.

In order to understand the very long-term (millions of years) hazard, the natural radioactivity in the ground is a good comparison. The ground is full of naturally radioactive materials, so that by adding nuclear waste to it the total radioactivity in the top 2,000 feet of U.S. soil would increase by only one part in 10 million per plant-year. Moreover, the radioactivity in the ground (except that very near the surface) does virtually no harm.

Waste burial plans would delay the release of the waste to the environment for a very long time, thus giving near-perfect protection from the short-term problem. Under these plans the rock formation chosen for burial will be well isolated from groundwater and expected to remain isolated for at least 1,000 years. If water did enter that rock formation it would have to dissolve a reasonable fraction of the surrounding rock before reaching the waste. The least favorable situation for this factor would be if the waste were buried in a salt formation, because salt is readily dissolved in water. However, in the New Mexico area being considered for an experimental repository, if all the water now flowing through the ground were diverted through the salt formation, the quantities of salt are so vast and the amount of water so meager that it would take 100,000 years to dissolve the salt around the buried waste from 1 year of all nuclear electricity in the U.S.

A third protection is the specific backfill material surrounding the waste package. Clays selected for this purpose swell up to seal very tightly when wet, thereby keeping out any appreciable amount of water. These materials are also highly efficient filters; if groundwater did get to the waste and dissolve some of it, these clays would filter the radioactive material out of solution before it could escape with the water.

Another safeguard is that the waste will be sealed in a corrosion-resistant casing. Casing materials are available that would not be dissolved even if soaked in groundwater for many thousands of years. Also the waste itself will be a rock-like material that would require thousands of years of soaking in water before dissolving. Groundwater is more like a "dampness" than a "soaking," thus dissolving things hundreds of times more slowly.

There is also a time delay. Groundwater moves quite slowly, usually only inches per day, and ordinarily must travel many miles before reaching the surface from 2,000 feet underground. Hence, even if the dissolved radioactive material moved with the groundwater, it would take about 1,000 years to reach the surface. But there are processes by which the rock constantly filters the radioactive materials out of the groundwater, causing it to migrate about a thousand times slower than the water itself. It would therefore take most of the radioactive materials a million years to reach the surface even if they were already dissolved in groundwater. Most of the radioactive materials are highly insoluble under geological conditions; thus, if they were in solution when the water encountered these conditions (chemically reducing, alkaline), they would precipitate out and form new rock material.

Finally, if radioactivity did reach surface waters, it would be detected easily – one millionth of the amounts that can be harmful are readily detected – and measures could be taken to prevent it from getting into drinking water or food.

With all these safeguards it seems almost impossible for much harm to result during the first few hundred years while the waste is highly toxic, and there is substantial protection over the long term.

One way of estimating the distant effects is to assume that an atom of buried waste has the same chance of escaping and of getting into a person as an atom of average rock. It can be shown that an atom of average rock submerged in flowing groundwater has about a one in 100 million chance per year of escaping into surface waters. Once in surface waters its chance of getting into a human body is about one in 10,000. If these probabilities are combined and applied to buried radioactive waste, the result indicates that the waste would eventually cause 0.018 fatalities per plant-year. Note that this is still 1,000 times less than the health effects of air pollution from coal burning.

If there is a problem in the above arguments, it would be in how buried radioactive waste differs from average rock. There are basically three differences. First, a shaft must be dug to bury the waste, giving a connection to the surface not usually present for rock; second, the radioactive waste emits heat, which is not a normal property of rock; and third, the waste is a foreign material, not in chemical equilibrium with the rock–groundwater regime. Solving the first problem depends on our ability to seal the shaft, and the technical community seems highly confident that this can be done to make the area as secure as if the shaft had never been dug.

The heat radiated from buried waste is enough to raise the temperature of the surrounding rock by about 200 degrees Farenheit. There has been concern that this might crack the rock, producing new pathways by which groundwater can reach the buried waste and through which the dissolved waste might escape. This problem has been studied intensively for over a decade, and the conclusion seems to be that there are no serious problems of this type. These studies are continuing, however.

If it is decided that the temperature must not be allowed to rise so high, there are two easy remedies: the waste can be distributed over a wider area to dilute the heating effect, or burial can be delayed to allow some of the radioactivity to decay. The latter option is especially effective since the rate of heat emission is decreased 10-fold after 100 years and 100-fold after 200 years. Also, the protective casings in which the waste will be enclosed are highly resistant to high-temperature groundwater.

The chemical equilibrium between rock and groundwater is a surface phenomenon. If a foreign rock, such as radioactive waste converted to a rock-like material, is introduced, the groundwater begins to dissolve it, but in the process precipitates out a highly insoluble material on its surface. Further dissolution of the foreign material can then only take place by diffusion through this surface layer, and that process thickens the latter which slows down the diffusion process. After a short time, chemical equillibrium is reached, with only a tiny quantity of the waste having been dissolved.

Since we have mentioned the ways in which buried waste is less secure than most rock, the ways in which it is more secure should be pointed out. The geological environment for the waste will be carefully selected and will be much more favorable than for average rock. The waste will be buried in a region with little or no groundwater, whereas our average rock is submerged in groundwater. Finally, the buried waste will be sealed in a leach-resistant casing that provides a complete and independent safety system which should avert danger even if all other protections fail.

Since most of the health impact of radioactive waste is expected to occur millions of years in the future, it is instructive to compare this with the cancer-causing solid wastes released in coal burning. Some of these, like arsenic, beryllium, cadmium, chromium, and nickel, are very long-lasting and their effects can therefore be calculated in a similar way as for radioactive wastes. When this is done they can be expected to cause about 70 eventual fatalities per plant-year, an effect thousands of times larger than the effects of nuclear waste. Also, solar electricity technologies require vast amounts of materials, and deriving these requires the burning of larger quantities of coal – about 3 percent as much coal as would be used to produce the same amount of energy by direct coal burning. Consequently, the wastes from solar technologies are hundreds of times more harmful than nuclear wastes. In addition, some solar technologies use large quantities of cadmium, which increases the health consequences considerably.

Radon problems[20]

There is one other aspect of nuclear power that involves important health impacts; namely the release of radon. Radon is a radioactive gas that naturally evolves from uranium. There has been some concern over increased releases of radon due to uranium mining and milling operations. These problems have now been substantially reduced by cleaning up those operations and covering the residues with several feet of soil. The health effects of this radon are several times larger than those from other

TABLE 20.1

Source	Deaths/plant-year over:	
	Next 500 years	Millions of years
Nuclear		
high-level waste	0.0001	0.018
radon emissions	− 0.065	− 450
low-level waste	0.0001	0.0004
Coal		
air pollution	25	25
radon emissions	0.11	30
cancer-causing chemicals	0.5	70
Solar photovoltaics[a]		
coal for materials	0.8	3.7
cadmium sulfide (if used)	0.8	80

[a] Results are those from producing the same amount of electricity as is generated by a large nuclear or coal plant in 1 year.

Bernard L. Cohen

nuclear wastes such as the high-level waste discussed above, but they are still a hundred times smaller than the effects of coal burning.

However, by far the most important impact of the nuclear industry on the radon problem is that by mining uranium out of the ground, we avert future radon emissions and thus avoid future health impacts. Most of the uranium is mined from deep underground, so one might think the radon could not escape. However, the ground is constantly eroding away, so eventually the uranium that is mined would have come to the surface where its radon emissions could cause lung cancers. When these effects are calculated, the result is an eventual *saving* of 450 lives per plant-year of operation. This saving is thousands of times larger than the lives calculated to be lost from radioactive waste.

The influence of coal burning on the radon problem is not inconsequential. Coal contains small amounts of uranium which are released into the environment when coal is burned. Calculations of this effect indicate that coal-burning electric power production will eventually cause 30 fatalities per plant-year through its radon releases.

Summary on waste

The number of deaths per plant-year generated in the preceding discussion (plus a few others) is summarized in table 20.1. Since many people (including myself) feel that it is meaningless to consider effects over many millions of years, a column has also been included summarizing effects realized over the next 500 years. It should be understood that the minus signs on the numbers for radon from nuclear power indicate lives *saved* rather than lost.

Risks in Perspective[21]

Risks are commonly stated in terms of probabilities of death at various ages, but in order to make them more understandable we express them as loss of life expectancy (LLE). (If our LLE from a particular risk is 1 day, that does *not* mean that each person will live a 1 day shorter life as a result of that risk. It means, rather, that the *average* shortening of each life is 1 day; for example, this would be true if one person in a thousand died 1000 days earlier as a result of that risk, and 999 in a thousand were unaffected.) The LLE for nuclear power, if all U.S. electricity were nuclear, is about 40 minutes (0.03 days) according to most scientific estimates, a little less than half from routine emissions of radioactivity, a similar amount from reactor accidents, and the rest from waste and miscellaneous sources. If we accept the anti-nuclear activist Union of Concerned Scientists estimates, the LLE from nuclear power is still only 1.5 days.

From coal burning air pollution, our LLE is something like 13 days. Oil burning kills people with air pollution and by causing fires, giving it an LLE of 4.5 days. Our use of natural gas causes death by explosions, asphyxiation, and fires, giving it an LLE of 2.5 days.

To put these numbers in perspective, we list in table 20.2 the number of days LLE from some other common risks we face.[21] It is clear from this list that the risks from nuclear power, or even from burning coal, oil, or gas, are among the least important risks we face.

There is a widespread impression that conservation, reducing our use of energy, is the safest energy strategy. Nothing could be further from the truth. One action driven by conservation is tightening up homes to reduce air leakage. This traps radon inside and thereby gives us an LLE of about 25 days. This makes conservation much more dangerous than nuclear power even from the standpoint of radiation alone. Another goal of our energy conservation efforts is to reduce sizes of motor vehicles. Table 20.2 shows that changing from large to small care gives us an LLE of 100 days, but if everyone changed, the effects would not be nearly that serious. However, most fatal accidents are due to collisions with fixed objects like poles, trees, or earth; thus the move to smaller cars will give us an LLE of perhaps 30 days.

Another consequence of energy conservation efforts is to reduce lighting. This could easily increase our risk of being murdered by 10 percent, giving us an LLE of 9 days. It might also increase our risk of falling by 10 percent, which would give us an LLE of 4 days. Since most motor vehicle accidents occur at night, we can expect reduced street and highway lighting to increase the frequency of motor vehicle accidents;

TABLE 20.2

Cigarette smoking (one pack/day)	1600 days
Being poor vs well-to-do	1400
Working as a miner	1000
Being overweight by 30 lb	900
Motor vehicle accidents	200
Small cars vs large cars	100
Being murdered	90
Falls	40
Drowning	40
Speed limit 55 mph → 65 mph	40
Poison + suffocation + asphyxiation	37
Fire, burns	27
Firearms	11
Nuclear power (UCS)	1.5
Nuclear power (NRC)	0.03

even if this increase is by only 3 percent, this gives us an LLE of 6 days. Any one of the items mentioned here makes energy conservation much more risky than nuclear power.

But far more important than any of these items is the danger that over-zealous conservation of energy may reduce our wealth. Modern production technologies require a lot of energy; it is frequently said that the historically high level of U.S. industrial production was due largely to plentiful cheap energy. Energy brings wealth, and employment of wealth uses energy.

How does wealth relate to health? In the United States, well-to-do people live about 4 years longer than poor people. Death rates from diseases such as tuberculosis, influenza, and pneumonia, and from accidents and suicide, are several times higher among the poor, and they are at least 10–30 percent higher from nearly every disease. Life expectancy in poor nations is typically 20 years less than in rich nations; it would be difficult to defend a position that the differences are racial, since American blacks live 20 years longer than African blacks and Japanese live 11 years longer than other East Asians. Clearly, wealth adds years to life expectancy. Therefore, if conserving energy reduces wealth, the ultimate health risks in conservation can be extremely large. This reasoning also applies to solar energy, which is expected to cost five times more than nuclear electricity.

Another approach to putting the risks of nuclear energy into proper perspective is to show what other risks they are equivalent to. In order to make this non-controversial, we use both the NRC and UCS estimates for risks of nuclear power, with the latter in parentheses.

The risks of having all electricity in the United States generated by nuclear power are equivalent to the following risks:

(1)   a regular smoker smoking one extra cigarette every 15 years (3 months);
(2)   an overweight person increasing his weight by 0.012 ounces (0.8 ounces);
(3)   raising the U.S. highway speed limit from 55 miles per hour (mph) to 55.006 mph (55.6 mph).

Why the Public Misunderstanding?

It must be clear to the reader by now that the risks of nuclear power are grossly exaggerated in the public mind. What is the reason for this gross misunderstanding?

The public gets most of its information from the news media, so if the public is misinformed the media must be held responsible. There is a serious problem here: the media, especially television, are primarily in the entertainment business. With a one-point increase in the Nielsen rating for network evening news worth $11 million per year in advertising revenue, every effort must be made to attract and maintain the interest of the audience. Stories about dangers of radiation excite the public and are therefore given wide coverage. Actually, there has not been a single fatal accident involving radiation for over 15 years, whereas there have been 2 million fatalities from other types of accidents in this country during this time period. Clearly, the media attention given to radiation is far out of proportion to its actual dangers. As a result, the public has been instilled with a fear of radiation completely out of proportion with reality.

Members of the media generally do not read the scientific literature. Their contact with science is often through a handful of publicity-seeking scientists who tell them what they want to hear. Any scientist who reports the slightest evidence that makes radiation seem dangerous gets tremendous coverage, while contrary evidence is generally ignored. As a result, we often hear reports that recent evidence indicates that radiation is more dangerous than it was believed to be 5 or 10 years ago, although there is no such accepted opinion in the scientific community.

As a consequence of this public misunderstanding, all new power plants ordered for the past several years have been coal-burners. Every time a coal-burning plant is built instead of a nuclear plant, many hundreds of people are condemned to premature death.

Notes and References

This chapter is based on the book by this author, *Before It's Too Late: A Scientist's Case for Nuclear Power*. Plenum Publ. Co., New York (1983).
1   P. Slovic, B. Fischoff, and S. Lichtenstein. Rating the risks, *Environment*, 21, 14 (April 1979).
2   This number will be justified later in this chapter.
3   Union of Concerned Scientists. *The Risks of Nuclear Power Reactors*, Cambridge, MA, 1977. They give 2.4 deaths/GWe-year, which, multiplied by 50 GWe, the total amount generated in the U.S., given 120 deaths/year.
4   Opinion Research Corp. "Public attitudes towards nuclear power vs other energy sources," *ORC Public Opinion Index*, 38 (17) (September 1980).
5   National Academy of Sciences Committee on Nuclear and Alternative Energy Systems. *Energy in Transition, 1985–2010*. W. H. Freeman and Co. San Francisco (1980). American Medical Association Council on Scientific Affairs. "Health evaluation of energy generating sources," *J. Amer. Med. Assoc*, 240 (1978), 2193. Nuclear Energy Policy Study Group. *Nuclear Power*

- *Issues and Choices.* Ballinger, Cambridge, MA (1977). Union of Concerned Scientists. *The Risks of Nuclear Power Reactors.* H. Kendall (Director) (1977). United Kingdom Health and Safety Executive. *Comparative Risks of Electricity Production Systems,* (1980). Norwegian Ministry of Oil and Energy. *Nuclear Power and Safety* (1978). Science Advisory Office, State of Maryland. *Coal and Nuclear Power* (1980). Legislative Office of Science Advisor, State of Michigan. *Coal and Nuclear Power* (1980).

6   H. Kendall, Physics Colloquium, at Carnegie–Mellon University (1980).

7   In answer to my question, Nader replied, "Maybe we can clean up coal, or maybe we shouldn't burn coal either."

8   B. L. Cohen, "How dangerous is radiation?", *Ascent Mag.* 2 (4), 9 (1981).

9   R. Kasperson, G. Berk, A. Sharaf, D. Pijawka and J. Wood. "Public opinion and nuclear energy: retrospect and prospect," *Sci. Technol., Hum. Values,* (Spring 1980), p. 11.

10 S. Rothman and S. R. Lichter. "The nuclear energy debate: scientists, the media, and the public" *Public Opinion* (August/September 1982).

11 National Academy of Sciences Committee on Biological Effects of Ionizing Radiation (BEIR), *The Effects on Populations of Exposure to Low Levels of Ionizing Radiation.* Washington, DC (1980). A very large number of references is given.

12 United Nations Scientific Committee on Affects of Atomic Radiation (UNSCEAR), *Sources and Effects of Ionizing Radiation.* United Nations (New York) (1977). A large number of references is given.

13 International Commission on Radiological Protection (ICRP). *Recommendations of the International Commission on Radiological Protection.* ICRP Publication No. 26. Pergamon Press, Oxford (1977).

14 B. L. Cohen. "The cancer risk from low level radiation," *Health Phys.* **39**, 659 (1980). Many references are given therein.

15 U.S. Senate Committee on Public Works. *Air Quality and Stationary Source Emission Control* (1975). R. Wilson, S. D. Colome, J. D. Spengler, and D. G. Wilson. *Health Effect of Fossil Fuel Burning.* Ballinger Publ. Co., Cambridge, MA (1980).

16 Reactor Safety Study, Nuclear Regulatory Com. Document WASH-1400, NUREG 75/014 (1975).

17 Report of the President's Commission on The Accident at Three Mile Island; J. B. Kemeny (Chairman). Washington, DC, October 1979. M. Rogovin (Director), Three Mile Island, A Report to the Commissioners and to the Public, Washington, DC (January 1980).

18 W. Ramsay, *The Unpaid Costs of Electrical Energy.* Johns Hopkins University Press, Baltimore (1979).

19 This discussion is based on a group of papers reviewed in B. L. Cohen, *Long Term Waste Problems from Electricity Production, Nuclear and Chemical Waste Management* (in print).

20 B. L. Cohen. "The role of radon in comparisons of environmental effects of nuclear energy, coal burning, and phosphate mining," *Health Phys.,* **40**, 19 (1981); "Health effects of radon from coal burning," *Health Phys.,* **42**, 725 (1982).

21   B. L. Cohen and I. S. Lee. "A catalog of risks," *Health Phys.*, **36**, 707 (1979). B. L. Cohen. "Perspective on occupational mortality risks," *Health Phys.*, **40**, 703 (1981).

21

Statement of Dissent

BERNARD L. COHEN

As a scientist I see no barriers to a bright future for America and for mankind. Irrespective of present trends, many minerals will eventually become more scarce and expensive, but we can develop substitutes for them. Food supply and environmental difficulties may well develop, but they can be solved. The only thing we need to handle these problems is an abundant and everlasting supply of cheap energy, and it is readily available in nuclear reactors, including the breeder. Given a rational and supportive public policy, science and technology can provide not only for the twenty-first century, but for ever.

However, in the past 10 years science has come under irrational attack from the forces of ignorance, and is losing public support. This process has essentially destroyed the key ingredient needed to provide our bright future – nuclear power, and is already zeroing in on other targets vital to our future. Our government's science and technology policy is now guided by uninformed and emotion-driven public opinion rather than by sound scientific advice. Unfortunately, this public opinion is controlled by the media, a group of scientific illiterates drunk with power, heavily influenced by irrelevant political ideologies, and so misguided as to believe that they are more capable than the scientific community of making scientific decisions. As a result our resources are being poured down rat-holes, and scientific endeavors vital to our future are being blocked. As an example of their accomplishments, by the year 2,000 electricity in the U.S.A. will be several times more expensive than necessary, and twice as expensive as in France and Japan.

Unless solutions can be found to this problem, I believe that the United States will enter the twenty-first century declining in wealth, power, and influence, and within the next century will become an impoverished nation. I therefore find it difficult to share in the optimism that characterizes this report. That does not mean that I sympathize with *Global 2000*; indeed, some of those who were most influential in its preparation have been among the leading perpetrators of the policies that are ruining us. The coming debacle I foresee is not due to the problems they describe, but to the policies they advocate.

Contributors *all male*

Harold J. Barnett is Professor of Economics Emeritus at Washington University, St Louis. His field is industrial organization, primarily natural resources, technology, and industry studies. His publications include *Atomic Energy in the U.S. Economy* (1979), *Study of Steel Prices* (1975), *Scarcity and Growth* (1963), and *Energy Uses and Supplies* (1950).

William J. Baumol holds a joint appointment in Economics at Princeton and New York Universities, and is a past President of the American Economics Association, and of the Association of Environmental and Resource Economists. He is the author of numerous books, including two written jointly with William Oates: *Theory of Environmental Policy* and *Economics, Environmental Policy, and the Quality of Life*.

Petr Beckmann was at the Institute of Radio Engineering and Electronics at the Czechoslovak Academy of Sciences until 1963. Invited as Visiting Professor to the University of Colorado in that year, he decided to remain in the West and became a full Professor of Electrical Engineering. He went into early retirement in 1981 to devote himself fully to the defense of science, technology and free enterprise through his monthly journal, *Access to Energy*. In addition to technical works on communications engineering, he is author of *The Health Hazards of Not Going Nuclear* (1976).

William M. Brown is Director of Energy and Technological Studies at the Hudson Institute. As an analyst, he has devoted most of his attention to energy policy, natural resources, technological forecasting, and national defense issues. He was on the professional staff of Hudson Institute from 1961 to 1967, and rejoined the Institute in 1975. Since then, he has played a major role in the Institute's *Prospects for Mankind* program, and in that capacity is co-author (with Herman Kahn and Leon Martel) of the Institute's book *The Next 200 Years* (1976). He has also been the project leader or principal investigator in several major studies of U.S. energy policy.

Marion Clawson is an agricultural economist with long experience in research into and administration of natural resource economics and development. For the past 28 years he has been at Resources for the Future, a private nonprofit research organization. His books include *Land for the Future, Economics of Outdoor Recreation, Suburban Land Conversion, Forests for Whom and for What?* and *New Deal Planning: the NRPB Experience*.

Bernard L. Cohen has since 1958 been a Professor of Physics at the University of Pittsburgh where he was Director of the Nuclear Laboratory from 1965 to 1978. Over the past decade his research has shifted from nuclear physics to problems of energy and the environment. The author of four books and numerous articles in scientific journals, he was elected Chairman of the American Nuclear Society Division of Environmental Sciences (1980–81).

Karl Cohen, retired Chief Scientist, Nuclear Energy Group, General Electric Company, began work on uranium isotope separation in 1940, and his book *Isotope Separation* (1945) is still the standard reference work in the field. He was a Director of the U.S. Committee for the World Energy Conference (1972–8), and an adviser to the Energy Project of IIASA (Vienna). He serves on the National Research Council panel reviewing the Waste Isolation Pilot Plant in New Mexico.

Steve H. Hanke is a Senior Fellow at the Heritage Foundation and a Professor of Applied Economics at the Johns Hopkins University. He is an Associate Editor of *The Water Resources Bulletin*. During 1981 and 1982 he served as a Senior Economist on the President's Council of Economic Advisers, where he designed the President's privatization programs.

A. E. Harper is Professor and Chairman of the Department of Nutritional Sciences at the University of Wisconsin-Madison, and serves as N.I.H. Fellow at INCAP in Guatemala City and at the London School of Hygiene and Tropical Medicine. He was vice-chairman of the White House Conference on Food, Nutrition and Health, 1969–70. His published works include over 300 essays on food, nutrition and health.

John Fraser Hart has been Professor of Geography at the University of Minnesota since 1967. He has served the Association of American Geographers as Executive Officer (1965–66), Editor of the *Annals* (1970–75), and President (1979–80). His principal research interest is in the geography of rural areas in the eastern United States, and he has published on subjects as diverse as population redistribution, landscape appreciation, and manure.

Earl O. Heady is Professor of Economics at Iowa State University, where he also serves as Charles F. Curtiss Distinguished Professor of Agriculture and Director of the Center for Agricultural and Rural Development. He has been Vice-President of the American Association of Agricultural Economists and of the Canadian Agricultural Economics Association, and permanent chairman of the East–West Seminars for Agricultural Economists. The author of 22 books, he has acted as consultant for numerous clients, including the governments of India, Ethiopia, Saudi Arabia, Romania, Mexico, Austria, Thailand, and the United Nations.

D. Gale Johnson is a Professor and Chairman of the Department of Economics at the University of Chicago. He was a member of the National Commission on Population Growth and the American Future (1970–72); consultant to the U.S. Council on International Economic Policy (1972–75), and the Steering Committee for the President's Food and Nutrition Study, National Research Council (1975–77). His most recent publications are *The Politics of Food* (edited, 1980), *Food and Agricultural Policy for the 1980s* (edited, 1981), *Progress of Economic*

Reform in the People's Republic of China (1982), and *Prospects for Soviet Agriculture in the 1980s* (with Karen Brooks, 1983).

H. E. Landsberg is Professor Emeritus at the Institute for Fluid Dynamics and Applied Mathematics, University of Maryland. He has served as President of the American Geophysical Union, and Vice-President of the American Meteorological Society, and as editor of *Advances in Geophysics* and of the *World Survey of Climatology*. He is the author of several hundred publications on climate.

Wallace E. Oates is a Professor of Economics at the University of Maryland, specializing in public finance and environmental economics. He is author of *Fiscal Federalism* and editor of *Financing the New Federalism*; with William Baumol, he is the author of two books: *The Theory of Environmental Policy* and *Economics, Environmental Policy, and the Quality of Life*.

Mark Perlman is University Professor of Economics, History, and Public Health at the University of Pittsburgh. The author of numerous works on economics and public health, he has also served as co-chairman for the International Economics Association Conference on the Economics of Health in Industrialized Nations and as co-editor for the International Congress on Health Economics at Leyden.

Richard Peto is Imperial Cancer Research Fund Reader in Cancer Studies, University of Oxford.

Roger Revelle is Professor of Science and Public Policy at the University of San Diego. Formerly Director of Harvard University's Center for Population Studies, he has been awarded the Bowie medal of the American Geophysical Union and the Aggasiz medal of the National Academy of Sciences.

Roger A. Sedjo has since 1977 been a Senior Fellow and Director of the Forest Economics and Policy Program of Resources for the Future. Before that, he had worked for a number of academic, consulting and government organizations, including the U.S. Agency for International Development (AID). His research areas have included international economics, economic development and natural resources. His books include *Policy Alternatives for Nonindustrial Private Forestlands, Government Interventions, Social Needs and the Management of U.S. Forests*, and *The Comparative Economics of Plantation Forestry: A Global Assessment*.

Julian L. Simon is a senior fellow at the Heritage Foundation and teaches at the University of Maryland. His most recent books are *The Ultimate Resource* and *The Economics of Population Growth*, both published by Princeton University Press. His other books include: *How to Start and Operate a Mail Order Business, Basic Research Methods in Social Science, Issues in the Economics of Advertising, The Management of Advertising, Applied Managerial Economics*, and *Patterns of Use of Books in Large Research Libraries* (with H. H. Fussler).

S. Fred Singer, a geophysicist, is Professor of Environmental Sciences at the University of Virginia. He has published extensively on global resource and environmental problems and has written or edited the following books: *Is There an Optimum Level of Population* (1971), *Global Effects of Environmental Pollution* (1970), *The Changing Global Environment* (1975), *Arid Zone Development* (1977), *Energy* (1979).

Earl R. Swanson became Professor of Agricultural Economics at the University of Illinois in 1958. He has been a leader in developing and applying the principles of production economics to farm management, soil and water conservation, and public policy alternatives in the complex area of environmental quality. In addition to his research contributions, he has been an influential editor of the *American Journal of Agricultural Economics*.

Gilbert F. White is Director of the Natural Hazards Applications and Information Center. He was previously Director of the Institute of Behavioral Sciences at the University of Colorado, and Professor of Geography at the University of Chicago. He has chaired the committees on Water, on Environmental Studies, and on Natural Resources for the National Research Council. He is joint editor of *The World Environment, 1972–82: A Report by the UN Environment Programme.*

Aaron Wildavsky is Professor of Political Science at the University of California, Berkeley, where he has been department chairman and Dean of the Graduate School of Public Policy. He has been President of the Russell Sage Foundation, Vice-President of the American Political Science Association, and member of the executive committee of the National Resources Council. He has written several books about the politics of government budget processes.

John P. Wise has spent most of his professional career with the National Marine Fisheries Service at its Woods Hole and Miami laboratories, and in Washington. He has also worked for the Food and Agriculture Organization of the United Nations in Argentina, Brazil, Tunisia and Uruguay. He is the author of numerous articles on assessment of living marine resources, marine biology and oceanography.

Index

Note: The page numbers in italic refer to figures

impact of alternative energy sources
on 416
impact of fossil fuel combustion on
290–2, 300, 301, 432–3, 443–4,
450–3, 472, 477, 552, 554, 555,
559, 560, 561
impact of higher incomes on 47
protection: effectiveness of policies
for 448–50, 451–4, 480;
government role in 47, 439n, 459;
mineral exploitation and 332–4
quality of: data on 439–40, 476–7;
deterioration in 442–4, 454–8;
impact of soil erosion on 211;
improvements in 444–54;
monitoring of 476–7; natural
causes of deterioration in 440–2;
see also pollution
environmental stress, *Global 2000*'s
prediction of 12–13, 45
equality, international mineral cartels'
attempt to achieve 327–9
errors, self-perpetuating, government
predictions characterized by 36
Europe
coal use 431
farm input prices 98

FAO
Agriculture, Toward 2000 70–3, 100,
106–7
fish catch predictions 119
food supply predictions 186–91
malnutrition estimates 76–7
fallowing 185, 187, 189
famine, decline in 77
farmers, government exploitation of
99–100, 110
farming *see* agriculture; food supply
farmland, *see* agricultural land
fat consumption, chronic and
degenerative diseases and 512–17,
519, 530–1, 540
fertility 26, 56–7, 58–61, *65*
fertilizer
groundwater pollution 487
increased atmospheric CO_2 as 198

prices 28, 97–9, 105, 218
fish
aquaculture 120–2, 123–5
prices 123, 124
resources: overexploitation 115;
predictions of 119
fish catch
possibilities of increasing 122–3
predictions 113, 119, 123–7
species composition 115, 119, 123
trends 2, 27, *28*, 113–15, 116–17
fish meal 122
fisheries
geographical distribution 115, 118
management 115
pollution 120, 125–6
floods 260
fog
caused by coal burning 450–1
control of 296
photochemical 479–80
food
access to related to income 67, 68,
69–70, 108–9
consumption: predictions 107;
trends 108
prices: energy prices and 27–8, 34,
97–101, 104–5; government
intervention in 88–9, 94–5,
99–100; predictions 69–70, 78, 93,
109, 219; trends 16, *18*, 68–9,
78–93
production: growth in 16–19, 73–4,
95–7, 101–3, 107; land resources
for *see* agricultural land;
predictions of 103–9; proportion
of resources devoted to 105–7, 109
trade 68, 69–70, 71, 85–7, 90–2, 94,
237–8
Food and Agriculture Organization *see*
FAO
food supply
additives to 492, 495–7
chronic and degenerative diseases in
relation to 506–21, 522, 530–1,
540–2, 544
fears of scarcity in 67, 70, 77–8,
103–4